AMERICAN PHILOSOPHY

A Historical Anthology

Due

AMERICAN PHILOSOPHY

A Historical Anthology

edited
with commentary by

Barbara MacKinnon

STATE UNIVERSITY OF NEW YORK PRESS
Albany

Published by
State University of New York Press, Albany

© 1985 State University of New York

For information, address State University of New York
Press, State University Plaza, Albany, N.Y., 12246

Library of Congress Cataloging in Publication Data
Main entry under title:

American Philosophy.

  (SUNY series in philosophy)
  Bibliography: p. xv
  1. Philosophy, American—Addresses, essays, lectures.
2. Philosophy—Addresses, essays, lectures.
I. MacKinnon, Barbara, 1937- . II. Series.
B851.A46 1984   191   84–2458
ISBN 0–87395–922–1
ISBN 0–87395–923–X (pbk.)
10 9 8 7 6 5 4 3 2 1

For E, J, and K

Contents

Preface

Philosophy, it has been said, begins in wonder, and one would like to believe that this is still its moving force. Philosophers have wondered about what was most real and most valuable, and even about their very ability to know anything about such matters. They have asked fundamental questions about the nature of language, society, art, history, politics, and science. Philosophers, however, do not limit themselves merely to asking questions. They attempt to give answers, to explain, to enlighten. Differing philosophical traditions employ different, often opposed, methods of developing answers. Yet there are some shared elements. Philosophy can be thought of as some form of rational, foundational, analytic or systematic examination of basic assumptions in the aforementioned fields.

This book is basically an anthology. It is a collection of writings of major American philosophies and philosophers—their best thoughts on philosophical issues.[1] While it may be argued that in many ways philosophy is transcultural, it has also been suggested that "Philosophy is its own time apprehended in thought." [2] Each age and culture, for example, has its own particular problems and its own modes of understanding. If this is so, this collection might provide a means for better understanding something of the spirit and history of the American people.

Nevertheless, it is difficult to overcome the belief that philosophy in this country was but the reworking of philosophies imported from elsewhere. It is true that the Puritans were occupied with reconciling their Calvinistic religious-philosophical beliefs with the empiricism of John Locke. John Locke, and in some way the English deists and the Scottish common sense philosophers, influenced the writings of some of our founding fathers, especially Franklin and Jefferson, on the topics of human rights and the nature of the human good. The influence of Kantian ideas on the transcendentalists, of utilitarianism, Darwinism, and Hegelianism on the pragmatists, and in this century the importation of positivism, Thomism, phenomenology, and analytic philosophy may also be cited in support of the belief that there is nothing original in American philosophy. However, when one examines the development of these philosophies in this country, one finds many examples of radical changes of direction that were taken, and even new and original developments within the movements. The early settlers of this country came to a new land ripe with possibilities, a land with an open future and little past, a land where the future would be determined by the settlers own decisions and actions. Thus it is not unlikely that when they came to think about the meaning of it all, their philosophies would be more future and action oriented, active, and pluralistic. Nevertheless, philosophers have disagreed with one another not only concerning whether there is any uniquely American philosophy, but also of what that uniqueness may consist.[3] This question is one that the reader of the book will do well to bring to the study of its contents. The epilogue, "Is There An American Philosophy," addresses the question in more detail.

This anthology reflects several years of teaching courses on the history of American philosophy to undergraduate students and the difficulty of finding an appropriate collection of readings to use as a text. Although a number of anthologies were available, none seemed to include the range of material for which I was looking.[4] It seemed important not only to familiarize students with that typically American version of philosophy—pragmatism—but also with the earlier thinkers and periods and likewise with something of twentieth-century philosophy in America. Introductions that would fill in the gaps, place points of view in historical perspective, and relate philosophical positions also seemed desirable. Bibliographies and study-guide questions could be useful for teaching and research purposes. Although this book was originally intended as a text for an American philosophy course, it may also serve as a companion to courses in other disciplines such as American history, literature, or government, since the philosophies are set within and related to particular developments of the time. Finally, the collection itself should be a valuable resource for those who would like to have in one volume a broad-ranging selection of key writings from classical and contemporary American philosophers.

Some aspects of the anthology require explanation. Part 1 is entitled "Early American Philosophy" because the philosophy included there is in many ways a prephilosophy. It is for the most part nontechnical (Jonathan Edwards is an exception) and written by persons whose main interests were other than philosophy itself. The Puritan writers were primarily theologians, the Enlightenment thinkers first of all statesmen, and the Transcendentalists mostly poets and social and literary critics. Nevertheless, there is much in their writings that is of strictly philosophical interest: the discussion of the nature of freedom by Edwards, the nature and basis of human rights and the good life in Franklin and Jefferson, and the nature and place of the individual in society by Emerson and Thoreau. Thus any anthology in American philosophy must surely include them. This section covers the period from approximately 1750 to 1850.

Part 2 is entitled "Classical American Philosophy." [5] A particular unity and dialogue can be found among the philosophers of the last half of the nineteenth century in this country. They knew each other, read each other's writings, and argued disputed points. This was the period of the pragmatists Charles Sanders Peirce, William James, and John Dewey. The Darwinian theory of evolution and the scientific method left indelible marks on the philosophy of this period. However, metaphysical issues and idealistic philosophies (Josiah Royce, for example) were also well and ably represented. We can date this period from approximately 1850 to 1910 (with the exception of John Dewey who died in 1952 and is also included in Part 3).

Part 3 poses particularly difficult problems concerning selection as well as organization. The types of philosophy that have been espoused in this country during the twentieth century are much more diverse and difficult to organize. [6] Moreover, it is less clear that there is anything particularly American about the philosophizing of this century. It may well be that when we have attained more distance from this period, the lines of development of each type of philosophy will become clearer. Some movements may fade into insignificance. However, we cannot know now which movements and philosophers will have lasting significance. For this reason I have, with some reluctance, opted for completeness, rather than brevity, for some account of every major trend. This decision leads to inclusion of more material than any course can reasonably cover. But it provides ample basis for readers to make their own selection of philosophers and methods of doing philosophy. In some cases the writers and selections were chosen because they exemplified a type of philosophizing or a particular problem. The bibliographies have also been necessarily selective and usually include only books rather than journal articles, even though in some cases the major writings of an author or philosophy may not be collected in book form.

Finally, I wish to thank those who have read or otherwise made helpful comments on particular chapters: Desmond FitzGerald for the chapter on Thomism and William Langan for the chapter on phenomenology. The University of San Francisco has graciously provided financial support to cover part of the fees for reprinting some of the selections. Finally, Edward MacKinnon read many of the chapters and provided helpful suggestions, particularly for the chapters on the new empiricism and language philosophy. Without his continued encouragement this book would never have been completed. To him and our two children, Jennifer and Kathleen, this volume is affectionately dedicated.

Notes

[1] With the exception of two Canadians (chapter XIV), the philosophers included lived and wrote in the United States. Primarily because of the limitations of the author, no attempt has been made to include Latin American philosophers or philosophies, nor has there been any attempt to include whatever written record might exist of native American philosophy.

[2] G. W. F. Hegel, *Hegel's Philosophy of Right,* trans. T. M. Knox (Oxford: Clarendon Press, 1942), p. 11. A similar interpretation may be made of a comment by Francis Bacon: "Rightly is truth called the daughter of time, not of authority" (*Novum Organum,* i, 84). And we find in Faust: "My worthy friend, grey are all theories, And green alone life's golden tree" trans. Bayard Taylor, I, iv, 509–14.

[3] See, for example, John E. Smith, *The Spirit of American Philosophy* (New York: Oxford University Press, 1963), pp. 187ff; idem, *Themes in American Philosophy* (New York: Harper and Row, 1970); Roy Wood Sellars, *Reflections on American Philosophy from Within* (Notre Dame, Ind.: Notre Dame University Press, 1969), pp. 26ff; Morton White, *Science and Sentiment in America* (New York: Oxford University Press, 1972), pp. 290–310.

[4] Other useful but differing anthologies include: Paul R. Anderson and Max H. Fisch, *Philosophy in America from the Puritans to James, with Representative Selections* (New York: Appleton-Century Co., 1939), Jos. Blau, *American Philosophic Addresses, 1700–1900* (New York: Columbia University Press, 1946), Milton R. Konvitz and Gail Kennedy, eds., *The American Pragmatists* (New York: Meridian Books, 1960); Walter Muelder, Laurence Sears and Anne Schlabach, *The Development of American Philosophy,* 2d ed. (Boston: Houghton Mifflin, 1960), Morton White, *Documents in the History of American Philosophy* (New York: Oxford University Press, 1972).

[5] The title and idea are derived from Max Fisch, *Classic American Philosophers* (New York: Appleton-Century-Crofts, 1951).

[6] Questions may be raised, for example, about a chapter that combines Realism and Naturalism and includes Santayana, about the placing of Wilfrid Sellars in the chapter on metaphysics rather than in the one about language philosophy, and about the titles of the chapters on language philosophy and the new empiricism. Some explanations of these and other perhaps puzzling choices can be found in the chapters themselves.

Bibliography

General Studies on American Philosophy

Blau, Joseph L. *Men and Movements in American Philosophy.* New York: Prentice-Hall, 1952.

Cohen, Morris R., *American Thought: A Critical Sketch.* Glencoe, Ill.: The Free Press, 1954.

Commager, Henry Steele, *The American Mind: An Interpretation of American Thought and Character since the 1880s.* New Haven: Yale University Press, 1950.

Curti, Merle, *The Growth of American Thought.* New York: Harper and Brothers, 1943. 2nd ed., 1951.

Flower, Elizabeth and Murray G. Murphy, *A History of Philosophy in America.* 2 vols. New York: Capricorn Books, 1977.

Kuklick, Bruce, *The Rise of American Philosophy: Cambridge, Massachusetts, 1860–1930.* New Haven: Yale University Press, 1977.

McDermott, John J., "The Renascence of Classical American Philosophy," *American Studies International* 16 (1978): pp. 5–17.

Novak, Michael, ed. *American Philosophy and the Future.* New York: Charles Scribner's, 1968.

Passmore, John, *A Hundred Years of Philosophy.* London: Gerald Duckworth and Co., 1957.

Schneider, Herbert W. *A History of American Philosophy.* New York: Columbia University Press, 1946. Rev. ed., 1963.

Shahan, Robt. W. and Kenneth R. Merrill, eds., *American Philosophy: From Edwards to Quine.* Norman, Okla.: The University of Oklahoma Press, 1977.

Smith, John, *Themes in American Philosophy.* New York: Harper and Row, Harper Torchbooks, 1970.

Townsend, Harvey G. *Philosophical Ideas in the United States.* Cincinnati: American Book Co., 1934.

Werkmeister, W. H. *A History of Philosophical Ideas in America.* New York: Ronald Press, 1949.

White, Morton, *Science and Sentiment in America: Philosophical Thought from Jonathan Edwards to John Dewey.* New York: Oxford University Press, 1972.

————. *Social Thought in America.* New York: Viking Press, 1949.

Part 1

Early American Philosophy

Chapter 1

Puritan Thought

When the term "puritan" is mentioned today, it most probably conjures up images of black hats, buckled shoes, long white aprons, and Thanksgiving dinners or of stark and strict morality. However the Puritans were not only that group of early New England settlers with whom these images are associated. Puritanism was primarily a religious movement that originated in England in the middle of the sixteenth century and spread throughout northern Europe. The name came from the fact that the Puritans were a group of English Protestants who desired to further purify the Church of England from ceremonial and authoritative elements and other Roman Catholic influences. Because some of them became dissatisfied with the progress of reform in England, they decided to separate themselves from the English church; first they moved to Holland, and from there to Plymouth in 1620. Another group of Puritans who wished to remain united with the English church emigrated to Massachusetts Bay in 1630. By 1634 there were some 10,000 who had followed, and they formed the various Puritan colonies in the New World. Those remaining in England finally seized power in 1649 and executed King Charles I.

The Puritans in this country had a mission. They wanted to set up an ideal "city of God" in the wilderness to make apostolic living a reality for all the world to see.[1] Their religious ideals stemmed from the Calvinism they espoused, including beliefs in the weakness and depravity of man and in a God who saves those whom he will by freely bestowing on them a saving, irresistable, and unearned grace that predestines those who receive it to eternal happiness. This doctrine was modified, however, by the inclusion of a covenantal or congregationalist theology. According to this theology, God's decrees are not completely arbitrary. God had made a covenant with man, according to which the elect then have a right by contract to receive grace. Church government was to a certain extent democratic. The members elected their church officials, even though the officials' power to govern was thought to come from God. One main source of this doctrine was Peter Ramus (1515–1586), a French Platonist converted to Calvinism who was murdered during a religious uprising. His sytem of logic used a method of analysis, of making distinctions and discriminations. Since laymen as well as scholars could use this logic, rationality ceased to be the prerogative of theologians and religious authorities. Nature was conceived of as the art work of God, created after the pattern of ideas in God's mind. Inquiry into the natural sciences was for the purpose of knowing the Divine ways in nature. Both in the social and in the natural order, Puritanism thus moved away from the arbitrary and irrational towards principles of general order and reason. "Thus the Puritans were well prepared to interpret natural law as divine order and social obligations as divine law." [2] The *Essay Concerning Human Understanding* of John Locke, the British empiricist (1632–1704), was introduced as a text at Yale College in 1717, and about the same time the *Opticks* and *Principia* of Isaac Newton, the father of modern science (1642–1727), were brought to Yale library in the Dummer collection — personal copies from the shelves of Newton himself. Locke's empiricism in theory of knowledge, Newton's experimental method in the study of physical nature, and the covenantal theology of the Puritans were major influences on the thought of the first genuine American philosopher, Jonathan Edwards.

JONATHAN EDWARDS (1703–1758)

The nineteenth-century historian, George Bancroft, has said of Jonathan Edwards, "He that would know the workings of the New England mind in the middle of the last century, and the throbbings of its heart must give his days and nights to the study of Jonathan Edwards." [3] The selections here included from this most famous of the Puritan divines will not occupy too many days and nights of study. Yet they can provide a good introduction to the major philosophical issues debated by the Puritans and give some idea of Edwards's own manner and stature as a philosopher. America had to wait some one-hundred-twenty years until a comparable systematic philosopher appeared.

Jonathan Edwards was born in 1703 in East Windsor, Connecticut. From 1716 until 1722 he studied at what was to be Yale College, completing four years of undergraduate study and two of theology. After graduation he served for one year as pastor of a Presbyterian church in New York City, tutored at Yale from 1724 to 1726, and then went to Northampton, Massachusetts where he was assistant minister to his grandfather, Solomon Stoddard. After Stoddard's death in 1727, Edwards continued there as pastor for twenty-five years until he was removed because of differences with his congregation on theological and practical religious matters. In 1757 he was invited to become president of what is now Princeton University. The following year he died from aftereffects of a small pox vaccination at the age of fifty-five.

Edwards is perhaps best known for his fiery sermons and his leadership in the religious revival in Northampton in the 1720s and 1730s. Less well known, though more significant in the present context, is the fact that he was an original and powerful thinker who accepted the challenge put to him and to Calvinism by eighteenth-century rationalism. For Edwards, religion, philosophy, and science were in harmony, not in conflict. While he used the modern thought and science of his day to defend Calvinist theology, much of his work is also of independent philosophic interest.[4]

As a student at Yale he read John Locke's *Essay* and said of it that he found more pleasure there "than the most greedy miser finds, when gathering up handfuls of silver and gold, from some newly discovered treasure."[5] A series of notes of philosophical reflections written during his senior year at Yale (when he was seventeen) shows his critical and creative response to his reading of Locke. Locke had said that all knowledge comes from sense experience. From this we derive simple ideas that can be built up into more complex ideas. However, our ideas are of the qualities of things, not the underlying substance which we know only by inference from the qualities. Locke distinguished primary qualities (extension, figure, rest, motion, solidity) from secondary (sounds, tastes, smells) and tertiary qualities (beauty, pain). Locke not only accepted the common doctrine that tertiary qualities are subjective, he went beyond it in his claim that secondary qualities are subjective as well. They are not in bodies as we experience them, although there is a power in the bodies to cause such sensations in us. However, primary qualities do exist in bodies as they are perceived by us.

In his early philosophical essay Edwards argued that colors are no more in things "than pain is in the needle."[6] We know a body for the most part by its color and figure (which is but the shape of the color, where it ends), as well as by some capacities it has to move and resist us. But these latter are all modes of resistance—it resists us in certain ways (figure) and resists us from space to space (motion). What is that that resists us so? Resistance itself is not what is resisted, for it is but a certain kind of experience or idea and is thus as much in the mind as the idea of color. What exists beyond that idea is simply the power of resistance. Since we experience no such thing as substance, which is the supposed source of this power, it is superfluous to believe it exists. Rather the power of resistance as well as the power to cause other ideas in us is the power of God being exercised in us in an orderly way. This orderly way in which ideas proceed is the regularity of nature and is but the series of ideas in God's mind. There is no other realm of substance with which to compare our ideas to see if they correspond to these things and thus are true. Truth is simply the certain, consistent order of relations among ideas or the agreement of our ideas with the ideas in God's mind.

God is eternal, active, and omnipresent. But space has these same qualities, and thus space itself must be God (see "Notes on Natural Science"). Newton had conceived of space as an absolute container of things (as time is of events). While for Newton space was God's sensorium (sense box), for Edwards space was identical with God. All exists in space, i.e. in God. Through his creative power, God holds everything in existence. The previous moment's existence of a being cannot be the cause of its present existence, for a being cannot operate where it is not existing and the past is not existent in the present. "Therefore the existence of created substances in each successive moment, must be the effect of the immediate agency, will, and power of God."[7] Natural causes are operating, but causality consists merely of antecedent and consequent and some mysterious power connecting them that is but God's creative power. This was also the God of religion, according to Edwards, the God on whom he rejoiced to be dependent. True religion consisted in having religious affections that were possible because of a grace that moved the heart as well as enlightened the mind.[8]

Freedom of the Will, published in 1754 when Edwards was fifty-one years old, is perhaps his greatest literary and sustained philosophical achievement.[9] The issue of freedom versus determinism was of central importance to Edwards because of the rise of Arminianism in his time. Jacob Arminius was a Dutch theologian who lived from 1560 to 1609. The movement named after him became a revolt against the Calvinist doctrine of irresistible grace. If grace was irresistible, the Arminians asked, how then could those who did good because of it be truly worthy of praise or those without it of blame, especially if nothing could be done to merit it? In other words, how could a person be morally responsible if his doing good works or ill were determined by his receipt of unearned, irresistible grace. Edwards's account is directed to answering this question.

As the selection included in this volume shows, his argument proceeds in this manner: The will is that power by which the person or the mind chooses anything. Why does a person choose one thing rather than another? Because a certain choice (of an action, object, etc.) is more agreeble to or pleases one better. Whatever moves or excites the mind in this way is called the motive for the choice, and thus the strongest motive determines the will to choose one thing rather than another. Or, more accurately, "the will always is as the greatest apparent good is."[10] Must one necessarily choose that which is most appealing? Is the will so moved necessarily? Is such a choice irresistible? Edwards responded that liberty is inconsistent only with certain kinds of necessity. Thus he distinguished natural and moral necessity. Natural necessity is that which occurs through the force of natural causes as the force of gravity; moral necessity occurs when persons are moved by certain habits, dispositions, or motives — as by love or virtue. And since freedom means doing as one wills or pleases, the only hindrances to it are those forces that make a person act contrary to his will. No one is responsible for acting under such contraints and thus can neither be praised nor blamed for the resulting action. However if a person does wrong when he does what he pleases, for this action he is responsible and blameworthy. He then acts as he pleases, and, if by certain dispositions or habits, also acts out of moral necessity.

Part of the consequence of grace is to make the good appealing to a person. Grace not only enlightens the mind but also moves the heart (see "On Religious Affections"). Good preaching used words that prepared the person for (if not actually causing) a kind of sensible experience of God and godly things. One problem with this account, according to the Arminians, was that if the motive for acting were determined by grace, and if we then act according to this motive, are we then not determined to do good and thus neither free, responsible, nor praiseworthy? Edwards, however, contended that if there be no more than a moral necessity of doing good or evil, i.e., if no other inability, constraint, or force were operating, then these good or evil acts are done freely and one is responsible for them. We are doing as we please or will and freedom means only this. Furthermore, he argued, the theories proposed by his opponents which made freedom consist of either indifference of will or self-determination of the will were contradictory. How could a will that was indifferent with regard to two choices be moved by either of them? On the other hand, if the will determines itself to move and the directing volition or choice is also free, it too must be determined by another choice; and if that choice is free, it must be determined by another and so on until either we come to a first choice that was not free or we go on indefinitely. And if the first is not free none of the rest are. Edwards sought to avoid these problems by his concept of freedom: We can do as we please (which is what is meant by freedom), but we cannot please as we please.

The issue of freedom of the will continued to be debated during and immediately after the time of Edwards, but the Arminians controlled the day. New England Puritanism had already moved Calvinism toward a more rational view of the action of God and nature. Arminianism moved it toward individualism. Edwards had tried to combine emphasis on the affections with a belief in the importance of reason and objective fact. After Edwards the head lost control of the heart, and the pietism of the Great Awakening and religious revivalism went off on its own. Those of a more rational persuasion moved in the direction of the Enlightenment thought, and the union of heart and head in the philsophy of Jonathan Edwards was submerged for a time.

Notes

[1] According to Perry Miller, this account is not quite accurate. The group who came to Plymouth in 1620 did so primarily to escape persecution, while the Massachusetts Bay

Company did intend to work out church reform in America and to be a guide to their slower brethren back home in England. However, the English brethren soom became embarrassed by the group in America, in particular by their intolerance, and the New England Puritans found themselves attempting to be a model to which none were looking for imitation. (See Perry Miller, *Errand into the Wilderness* [New York: Harper and Row, 1956], pp. 1-15.

[2] Herbert W. Schneider, *A History of American Philosophy,* 2d. ed. (New York: Columbia University Press, 1963), p. 12.

[3] Jonathan Edwards, in C. H. Faust and T. Johnson, eds., *Jonathan Edwards: Representative Selections* (New York: American Book Company, 1935), pp. xiv-xv.

[4] While many interpreters of Jonathan Edwards emphasize that he was primarily a theologian and a strong Calvinist, Perry Miller believed him to have already begun a naturalization of religion. Grace for Edwards, according to Miller, was not a supernatural addition to the natural powers of the person, but simply man's own power of perception and will. This power could be brought to the idea and experience of good and of God through effective preaching, and it also had perfectly natural effects in a good life. (See Perry Miller, *Jonathan Edwards* [New York: William Sloan Associates, 1949].)

[5] "The Life of President Edwards," in Jonathan Edwards, *The Works of President Edwards, with a Memoir of His Life,* ed. Sereno E. Dwight, 10 vols. (New York: S. Converse, 1830), p. 30.

[6] Jonathan Edwards, "Notes on the Mind," in *Puritan Sage: Collected Writings of Jonathan Edwards,* ed. Vergilius Ferm (New York: Library Publishers, 1953), p. 23.

[7] Jonathan Edwards, "On the Great Doctrine of Original Sin Defended," in Ferm, *Puritan Sage,* p. 529.

[8] Jonathan Edwards, "A Treatise Concerning Religious Affections," in Ferm, *Puritan Sage,* pp. 436-37.

[9] Jonathan Edwards, "A Careful and Strict Enquiry into the Modern Prevailing Notions of that Freedom of Will, Which is Supposed to be Essential to Moral Agency, Virtue and Vice, Reward and Punishment, Praise and Blame," in Ferm, *Puritan Sage,* pp. 480-515. See also the new edition with commentary by Paul Ramsey (New Haven: Yale University Press, 1957).

[10] "A Careful and Strict Enquiry . . . ," Ferm, *Puritan Sage,* p. 142.

JONATHAN EDWARDS

NOTES ON THE MIND (Ca. 1720) *

Truth is *The perception of the relations there are between ideas.* Falsehood is *The supposition of relations between ideas that are inconsistent with those ideas themselves;* not *their disagreement with things without.* All truth is in the mind, and only there. It is ideas, or what is in the mind, alone, that can be the object of the mind; and what we call Truth, is a consistent supposition of relations, between what is the object of the mind. Falsehood is an inconsistent supposition of relations. The Truth, that is in a mind, must be in that mind as to its object, and every thing pertaining to it. The only foundation of Error is inadequateness and imperfection of ideas; for, if the idea were perfect, it would be impossible but that all its relations should be perfectly perceived.

TRUTH, in the general, may be defined, after the most strict and metaphysical manner, *The consistency and agreement of our ideas, with the ideas of God.* I confess this, in ordinary conversation, would not half so much tend to enlighten one in the meaning of the word, as to say, *The agreement of our ideas with the things as they are,* But it should be enquired, What is it for our ideas to agree with things as they are? seeing

---

* Sereno E. Dwight, ed., *The Works of President Edwards, with a Memoir of His Life,* 10 vols. (New York: S. Converse, 1830).

9

that corporeal things exist no otherwise than mentally; and as for most other things, they are only abstract ideas. Truth, as to external things, is the consistency of our ideas with those ideas, or that train and series of ideas, that are raised in our minds, according to God's stated order and law.

TRUTH, as to abstract ideas, is the consistency of our ideas with themselves. As when our idea of a circle, or a triangle, or any of their parts, is agreeable to the idea we have stated and agreed to call by the name of a circle, or a triangle. And it may still be said, that Truth is, *the consistency of our ideas with themselves.* Those ideas are false, that are not consistent with the series of ideas, that are raised in our minds, by according to the order of nature.

Coroll. 1. Hence we see, in how strict a sence it may be said, that God is Truth itself.

Coroll. 2. Hence it appears, that Truth consists in having perfect and adequate ideas of things: For instance, if I judge truly how far distant the Moon is from the Earth, we need not say, that this Truth consists, in the perception of the relation, between the two ideas of the Moon and the Earth, but in the adequateness.

Coroll. 3. Hence Certainty is the clear perception of this perfection. Therefore, if we had perfect ideas of all things at once, that is, could have all in one view, we should know all truth at the same moment, and there would be no such thing at Ratiocination, or finding out Truth. And Reasoning is only of use to us, in consequence of the puacity of our ideas, and because we can have but very few in view at once.—Hence it is evident, that all things are *self-evident* to God.

EXISTENCE. If we had only the sense of Seeing, we should not be as ready to conclude the visible world to have been an existence independent of perception, as we do; because the ideas we have by the sense of Feeling, are as much mere ideas, as those we have by the sense of Seeing. But we know, that the things are objects of this sense, all that the mind views by Seeing, are merely mental Existences; because all these things, with all their modes, do exist in a looking-glass, where all will acknowledge, they exist only mentally.

It is now agreed upon by every knowing philosopher, that Colours are not really in the things, no more than Pain is in a needle; but strictly no where else but in the mind. But yet I think that Colour may have an existence out of the mind, with equal reason as any thing in Body has any existence out of the mind, beside the very substance of the body itself, which is nothing but the Divine power, or rather the Constant Exertion of it. For what idea is that, which we call by the name of Body? I find Colour has the chief share in it. 'Tis nothing but Colour, and Figure, which is the termination of this Colour, together with some powers, such as the power of resisting, and motion, &c. that wholly makes up what we call Body. And if that, which we principally mean by the thing itself, cannot be said to be in the thing itself, I think nothing can be. If Colour exists not out of the mind, then nothing belonging to Body, exists out of the mind but Resistance, which is Solidity, and the termination of this Resistance, with its relations, which is Figure, and the communication of this Resistance, from space to space, which is Motion; though the latter are nothing but modes of the former. Therefore, there is nothing out of the mind but Resistance. And not that neither, when nothing is actually resisted. Then, there is nothing but the Power of Resistance. And as Resistance is nothing else but the actual exertion of God's power, so the Power can be nothing else, but the constant Law or Method of that actual exertion. And how is there any Resistance, except it be in some mind, in idea? What is it that is resisted? It is not Colour. And what else is it? It is ridiculous to say, that Resistance is resisted. That, does not tell us at all what is to be resisted. There must be something resisted before there can be Resistance: but to say Resistance is resisted, is ridiculously to suppose Resistance, before there is any thing to be resisted. Let us suppose two globes only existing, and no mind. There is nothing there, *ex confesso,* but Resistance. That is, there is such a Law, that the space within the limits of a globular figure shall resist. Therefore, there is nothing there but a power, or an establishment. And if there be any Resistance really out of the mind, one power and establishment must resist another establishment and law of Resistance, which is exceedingly ridiculous. But yet it cannot be otherwise, if any way out of the mind. But now it is easy to conceive of Resistance, as a mode of an idea. It is easy to conceive of such a power, or constant manner of stopping or resisting a colour. The idea may be resisted, it may move, and stop and rebound; but how a mere power, which is nothing real, can move and stop, is inconceivable, and it is impossible to say a word about it without contradiction. The world is therefore an ideal one; and the Law of creating, and the succession, of these ideas is constant and regular.

Coroll. 1. How impossible is it, that the world should exist from Eternity, without a Mind.

Coroll. 2. Since it is so, and that absolute Nothing is such a dreadful contradiction; hence we learn the necessity of the Eternal Existence of an All-comprehending Mind; and that it is the complication of all contradictions to deny such a mind.

SUBSTANCE. It is intuitively certain, that, if Solidity be removed from Body, nothing is left but empty space. Now, in all things whatsoever, that, which cannot be removed without removing the whole thing, that thing which is removed is the thing itself, except it be mere circumstance and manner of existence, such as Time and Place; which are in the general necessary, because it implies a contradiction to existence itself, to suppose that it exists at no time and in no place, and therefore in order to remove time and place in the general, we must remove the thing itself: So if we remove Figure and Bulk and Texture, in the general; which may be reduced to that necessary circumstance of Place.

If, therefore, it implies a contradiction to suppose that Body, or any thing appertaining to Body, beside Space, exists, when Solidity is removed; it must be, either because Body is nothing but Solidity and Space, or else, that Solidity is such a mere circumstance and relation of existence, which the thing cannot be without, because whatever exists must exist in some circumstances or other, as at some time or some place. But we know, and every one perceives, it to be a contradiction to suppose, that Body or Matter exists without Solidity, for all the notion we have of Empty Space, is Space without Solidity, and all the notion we have of Full Space, is Space Resisting.

The reason is plain; for if it implies a contradiction to suppose Solidity absent, and the thing existing, it must be because Solidity is that thing, and so it is a contradiction to say the thing is absent from itself; or because it is such a mode, or circumstance, or relation, of the existence, as it is a contradiction to suppose existence at all without it, such as Time and Place, to which both Figure and Texture are reduced. For nothing can be conceived of, so necessarily in an existence, that it is a contradiction to suppose it without it, but the Existence itself, and those general Circumstances or Relations of existence, which the very supposition of existence itself implies.

Again, Solidity or Impenetrability is as much Action, or the immediate result of Action, as Gravity. Gravity by all will be confessed to be immediately from some active influence. Being a continual tendency in bodies to move, and being that, which will set them in motion though before at perfect rest, it must be the effect of something acting on that body. And it is as clear and evident, that action is as requisite to stop a body, that is already in motion, as in order to set bodies a moving, that are at perfect rest. Now we see continually, that there is a stopping of all motion, at the limits of such and such parts of Space, only this stoppage is modified and diversified according to certain Laws; for we get the idea and apprehension of Solidity, only and entirely, from the observation we make of that ceasing of motion, at the limits of some parts of Space, that already is, and that beginning of motion, that till now was not, according to a certain constant manner.

And why is it not every whit as reasonable, that we should attribute this action or effect, to the influence of some Agent, as that other action or effect which we call Gravity; which is likewise derived from our observation of the beginning and ceasing of motion, according to a certain method? In either case, there is nothing observed, but the beginning, increasing, directing, diminishing and ceasing of motion. And why is it not as reasonable to seek a reason, beside that general one, that it is something; which is no reason at all? I say, Why is it not as reasonable to seek a reason or cause of these actions, as well in one as in the other case? We do not think it sufficient to say, It is the nature of the unknown substance, in the one case; and why should we think is a sufficient explanation of the same actions or effects, in the other. By Substance, I suppose it is confessed, we mean only Something; because of Abstract Substance we have no idea, that is more particular than only existence in general. Now why is it not as reasonable, when we see something suspended in the air, set to move with violence towards the Earth, to rest in attributing of it to the nature of the something that is there; as when we see that motion, when it comes to such limits, all on a sudden cease, for this is all that we observe in falling bodies. Their falling is the action we call Gravity: their stopping upon the surface of the Earth, the action whence we gain the idea of Solidity. It was before agreed on all hands, that there is something there, that supports that resistance. It must be granted now, that that Something is a Being, that acts there, as much as that Being, that causes bodies to descend towards the centre. Here is something in these parts of space, that of itself produces effects, without previously being acted upon; for that Being that lays an arrest on bodies in motion, and immediately stops them when they come to such limits and bounds, certainly does as much, as that Being that sets a body in motion, that before was at rest. Now this Being, acting altogether of itself, producing new effects, that are perfectly arbitrary, and that are no way necessary of themselves; must be Intelligent and Voluntary. There is no reason, in the nature of the thing itself, why a body, when set in motion, should stop at such limits, more than at any other. It must therefore be some arbitrary, active and voluntary, Being, that determines it. If there were but one body in the Universe, that always in time past had been at rest, and should now, without any alteration, be set in motion; we might certainly conclude, that some voluntary Being set it in motion; because it can certainly be demonstrated, that it can be for no other reason. So with just the same reason, in the same manner, we may conclude, if the body had hitherto been in motion, and is at a certain point of space now stopped. And would it not be every whit as reasonable to conclude, it must be from such an Agent, as if, in certain portions of space, we observed bodies to be attracted a certain way, and so at once to be set into motion, or accelerated in motion. And it is not at all the less remarkable, because we receive the ideas of light and colours from those spaces; for we know that light and colours are not there, and are made entirely by such a resistance, together with attraction, that is antecedent to these qualities, and would be a necessary effect of a mere resistance of space without other substance.

The whole of what we any way observe, whereby we get the idea of Solidity, or Solid Body, are certain parts of Space, from whence we receive the ideas of light and colours; and certain sensations by the sense of feeling; and we observe that the places, whence we receive these sensations, are not constantly the same, but are successively different, and this light and colours are communicated from one part of space to another. And we observe that these parts of Space, from whence we receive these sensations, resist and stop other bodies, which we observe communicated successively through the parts of Space adjacent; and that those that there were before at rest, or existing constantly in one and the same part of Space, after this exist successively in different parts of Space, and these observations are according to certain stated rules. I appeal to any one that takes notice and asks himself; whether this be not all, that ever he experienced in the world, whereby he got these ideas; and that this is all that we have or can have any idea of, in relation to bodies. All that we observe of Solidity is, that certain parts of Space, from whence we receive the ideas of light and colours, and a few other sensations, do likewise resist any thing coming within them. It therefore follows, that if we suppose there be any thing else, than what we thus observe, it is but only by way of Inference.

I know that it is nothing but the Imagination will oppose me in this: I will therefore endeavour to help the Imagination thus. Suppose that we received none of the sensible qualities of light, colours, etc. from the resisting parts of Space, (we will suppose it possible for resistance to be without them,) and they were, to appearance, clear and pure; and all that we could possibly observe, was only and merely Resistance; we simply observed that Motion was resisted and stopped, here and there, in particular parts of Infinite Space. Should we not then think it less unreasonable to suppose, that such effects should be produced by some Agent, present in those parts of Space, though Invisible. If we, when walking upon the face of the Earth, were stopped at certain limits, and could not possibly enter into such a part of Space, nor make any body enter into it; and we could observe no other difference, no way, nor at any time, between that and other parts of clear space; should we not be ready to say, What is it stops us; What is it hinders all entrance into that place?

The reason, why it is so exceedingly natural to men, to suppose that there is some Latent *Substance,* or Something that is altogether hid, that upholds the properties of bodies, is, because all see at first sight, that the properties of bodies are such as need some Cause, that shall every moment have influence to their continuance, as well as a Cause of their first existence. All therefore agree, that there is Something that is there, and upholds these properties. And it is most true, there undoubtedly is; but men are wont to content themselves in saying merely, that it is Something; but that Something is He, "by whom all things consist."

NOTES ON NATURAL SCIENCE*

OF BEING

That there should absolutely be Nothing at all, is utterly impossible. The mind, let it stretch its conceptions ever so far, can never so much as bring itself to conceive of a state of perfect Nothing. It puts the mind into mere convulsion and confusion, to think of such a state: and it contradicts the very nature of the soul, to think that such a state should be. It is the greatest of contradictions, and the aggregate of all contradictions, to say that thing should not be. It is true, we cannot so distinctly show the contradiction in words; because we cannot talk about it, without speaking stark nonsense, and contradicting ourselves at every word: and because Nothing is that, whereby we distinctly show other particular contradictions. But here we are run up to our first principle, and have no other to explain the nothingness, or not being of Nothing by. Indeed we can mean nothing else by Nothing, but a state of absolute contradiction; and if any man thinks, that he can conceive well enough how there should be Nothing. I will engage, that what he means by Nothing, is as much Something, as any thing that he ever thought of in his life; and I believe, that if he knew what Nothing was, it would be intuitively evident to him that it could not be.—Thus we see it is necessary that some being should eternally be. And it is a more palpable contradiction still to say, that there must be Being somewhere, and not otherwhere, for the words *Absolute Nothing,* and *Where,* contradict each other. And, besides, it gives as great a shock to the mind, to think of pure Nothing being in any one place, as it does to think of it in all places: and it is self-evident, that there can be Nothing in one place, as well as in another; and if there can be in one, there can be all. So that we see that this Necessary, Eternal Being must be Infinite and Omnipresent.

This Infinite and Omnipresent being cannot be solid. Let us see how contradictory it is, to say that an Infinite being is solid; for solidity surely is nothing, but resistance to other solidities.—Space is this necessary, eternal, infinite, and omnipresent being. We find that we can, with ease, conceive how all other beings should not be. We can remove them out of our minds, and place some other in the room of them: but Space is the very thing, that we can never remove, and conceive of its not being. If a man would imagine Space any where to be divided, so as there should be nothing between the divided parts, there remains Space between, notwithstanding, and so the man contradicts himself. And it is self-evident I believe to every man, that Space is necessary, eternal, infinite and omnipresent. But I had as good speak plain: I have already said as much

---

* Ibid.

as, that Space is God. And it is indeed clear to me, that all the Space there is, not proper to body, all the Space there is without the bounds of Creation, all the Space there was before the Creation, is God himself; and no body would in the least pick at it, if it were not because of the gross conceptions, that we have of Space.

ON A DIVINE AND SUPERNATURAL LIGHT (1734) *

There is a twofold knowledge of good of which God has made the mind of man capable. The first, that which is merely notional; as when a person only speculatively judges that any thing is, which, by the agreement of mankind, is called good or excellent, *viz.* that which is most to general advantage, and between which and a reward there is a suitableness,—and the like. And the other is, that which consists in the sense of the heart, as when the heart is sensible of pleasure and delight in the presence of an idea of it. In the former is exercised merely the speculative faculty, or mind understanding, in distinction from the will or disposition of the soul. In the latter, the will, or inclination, or heart, are mainly concerned.

Thus there is a difference between having an *opinion,* that God is holy and gracious, and having a *sense* of the loveliness and beauty of that holiness and grace. There is a difference between having a rational judgment that honey is sweet, and having a sense of its sweetness. A man may have the former, that knows not how honey tastes; but a man cannot have the latter unless he has an idea of the taste of honey in his mind. So there is a difference between believing that a person if beautiful, and having a sense of his beauty. The former may be obtained by hearsay, but the latter only by seeing the countenance. When the heart is sensible of the beauty and amiableness of a thing, it necessarily feels pleasure in the apprehension. It is implied in a person's being heartily sensible of the loveliness of a thing, that the idea of it is pleasant to his soul; which is a far different thing from having a rational opinion that it is excellent.

ON RELIGIOUS AFFECTIONS (1746) *

Such is man's nature, that he is very inactive, any otherwise than he is influenced by either *love* or *hatred, desire, hope, fear,* or some other affection. These affections we see to be the moving springs in all the affairs of life, which engage men in all their pursuits; and especially in all affairs wherein they are earnestly engaged, and which they pursue with vigour. We see the world of mankind exceedingly busy and active; and their affections are the springs of motion; take away all *love* and *hatred,* all *hope* and *fear,* all *anger, zeal,* and affectionate *desire,* and the world

---

* Ibid.

would be, in a great measure, motionless and dead: there would be no such thing as activity amongst mankind, or any earnest pursuit whatsoever. It is affection that engages the covetous man, and him that is greedy of worldly profits; it is by the affections that the ambitious man is put forward in his pursuit of worldly glory; and the affections also actuate the voluptuous man, in his pleasure and sensual delights. The world continues, from age to age, in a continual commotion and agitation, in pursuit of these things; but take away affection, and the *spring* of all this motion would be gone; the motion itself would cease. And as in worldly things, worldly affections are very much the spring of men's motion and action; so in religious matters, the spring of their actions are very much religious affections: he that has doctrinal knowledge and speculation only, without affection, never is *engaged* in the business of religion.

From hence it follows, that in those gracious exercises and affections which are wrought in the saints, through the saving influences of the Spirit of God, there is a new inward *perception* or *sensation* of their minds, entirely different in its nature and kind, from any thing that ever their minds were the subjects of before they were sanctified. For, if God by his mighty power produces something that is new, not only in degree and circumstances, but in its whole nature—all that which could be produced by no exalting, varying, or compounding of what was there before, or by adding any thing of the like kind—then, doubtless, something entirely new is felt, or perceived. There is what some metaphysicians call a new *simple idea*. If grace be, in the sense above described, an entirely new kind of principle; then the *exercises* of it are also new. And if there be in the soul a new sort of conscious exercises, which the soul knew nothing of before, and which no improvement, composition, or management of what it was before could produce; then it follows that the mind has an entirely new kind of perception or sensation. Here is, as it were, a new *spiritual sense,* or a principle of new kind of perception or spiritual sensation, which is in its whole nature different from any former kinds of sensation of the mind, as tasting is diverse from any of the other senses. And something is perceived by a true saint, in the exercise of this new sense of mind, in spiritual and divine things, as entirely diverse from any thing that is perceived in them, by natural men, as the sweet taste of honey is diverse from the ideas men get of honey by only looking on and feeling it. So that the spiritual perceptions which a sanctified and spiritual person has, are not only diverse from all that natural men have as the perceptions of the same sense may differ one from another, but rather as the ideas and sensations of different senses differ. Hence the work of the Spirit of God in regeneration is often in scripture compared to the giving of a new sense, eyes to see, ears to hear, unstopping the ears of the deaf, opening the eyes of them that were born blind, and turning from darkness unto light. And because this spiritual sense is immensely the most noble and excellent, and that without which all other principles of perception, and all our faculties are useless and vain; therefore the giving of this new sense, with the blessed fruits and effects of it in the soul, is compared to raising the dead, and to a new creation.

This new spiritual sense, and the new dispositions that attend it, are no *new faculties,* but new *principles* of nature, I use the word *principles,* for want of a word of a more determined signification. By a *principle of nature* in this place, I mean that foundation which is laid in nature, either old or new, for any particular manner or kind of exercise of the faculties of the soul; or a natural habit, or foundation for action, giving a person ability and disposition to exert the faculties in exercises of such a certain kind; so that to exert the faculties in that kind of exercises, may be said to be his nature. So this new spiritual sense is not a new faculty of understanding, but it is a new foundation laid in the nature of the soul, for a new kind of exercises of the same faculty of understanding. So that the new holy disposition of heart that attends this new sense, is not a new faculty of will, but a foundation laid in the nature of the soul, for a new kind of exercises of the same faculty of will.

ON THE GREAT DOCTRINE OF ORIGINAL SIN DEFENDED (1758) *

That God does, by his immediate power, *uphold* every created substance in being, will be manifest, if we consider that their present existance is a *dependent* existence, and therefore is an *effect* and must have some *casue;* and the cause must be one of these two; either the *antecedent existence* of the same substance, or else the *power* of the *Creator.* But it cannot be *antecedent existence* of the same substance. For instance, the existence of the body of the *moon,* at this present moment cannot be the *effect* of its existence at the last foregoing moment. For not only was what existed the last moment, no active cause, but wholly a passive thing; but this also is to be considered, that no cause can produce effects in a *time and place* in which itself is *not.* It is plain, nothing can exert itself, or operate, *when* and *where* it is not existing. But the moon's past existence was neither *where* nor *when* its present existence is. In point of *time,* what is *past* entirely ceases when *present* existence begins; otherwise it would not be *past.* The past moment has ceased, and is gone when the present moment takes place; and no more *co-exists* with it, than any other moment that had ceased twenty years ago. Nor could the past existence of the particles of this *moving body* produce effects in any *other place,* than where it then was. But its existence at the present moment, in every point of it, is in a different *place* from where its existence was at the last preceding moment. From these things I suppose it will certainly

---

* Ibid.

follow, that the present existence, either of this, or any other created substance, cannot be an effect of its past existence. The existences (so to speak) of an effect, or thing dependent, in different parts of space or duration, though ever so near one to another, do not at all *co-exist* one with the other; and therefore are as truly different effects, as if those parts of space and duration were ever so far asunder. And the prior existence can no more be the proper cause of the new existence, in the next moment, or next part of space, than if it had been in an age before, or at a thousand miles distance, without any existence to fill up the intermediate time or space. Therefore the existence of created substances, in each successive moment, must be the effect of the *immediate* agency, will, and power of God.

FREEDOM OF THE WILL—PART I *

SECTION 1. CONCERNING THE NATURE OF THE WILL

It may possibly be thought, that there is no great need of going about to define or describe the "will"; this word being generally as well understood as any other words we can use to explain it: and so perhaps it would be, had not philosophers, metaphysicians and polemic divines brought the matter into obscurity by the things they have said of it. But since it is so, I think it may be of some use, and will tend to the greater clearness in the following discourse, to say a few things concerning it.

And therefore I observe, that the will (without any metaphysical refining) is plainly, that by which the mind chooses anything. The faculty of the will is that faculty or power or principle of mind by which it is capable of choosing: an act of the will is the same as an act of choosing or choice.

Thus an act of the will is commonly expressed by its pleasing a man to do thus or thus; and a man's doing as he wills, and doing as he pleases, are the same thing in common speech.

SECTION 2. CONCERNING THE DETERMINATION OF THE WILL

By "determining the will," if the phrase be used with any meaning, must be intended, causing that the act of the will or choice should be thus, and not otherwise: and the will is said to be determined, when, in consequence of some action, or influence, its choice is directed to, and fixed upon a particular object. As when we speak of the determination

---

* Jonathan Edwards, *Freedom of the Will* (1754; reprint, New York: Gould, Newman and Saxton, 1840), pp. 2, 16, 18–20, 23–30, 32–35, 40–41, 45–46, 49, 51, 56–57, 66–68, 81, 87–88, 125, 290–91, 299–300.

of motion, we mean causing the motion of the body to be such a way, or in such a direction, rather than another.

To talk of the determination of the will, supposes an effect, which must have a cause. If the will be determined, there is a determiner. This must be supposed to be intended even by them that say, the will determines itself. If it be so, the will is both determiner and determined; it is a cause that acts and produces effects upon itself, and is the object of its own influence and action.

With respect to that grand inquiry, what determines the will? It would be very tedious and unnecessary at present to enumerate and examine all the various opinions, which have been advanced concerning this matter; nor is it needful that I should enter into a particular disquisition of all points debated in disputes on that question, "Whether the will always follows the last dictate of the understanding." It is sufficient to my present purpose to say, "It is that motive, which, as it stands in the view of the mind, is the strongest, that determines the will;" but it may be necessary that I should a little explain my meaning in this.

By "motive," I mean the whole of that which moves, excites or invites the mind to volition, whether that be one thing singly, or many things conjunctly. Many particular things may concur and unite their strength to induce the mind; and when it is so, all together are as it were one complex motive. And when I speak of the "strongest motive," I have respect to the strength of the whole that operates to induce to a particular act of volition, whether that be the strength of one thing alone, or of many together.

And I think it must also be allowed by all, that everything that is properly called a motive, excitement or inducement to a perceiving willing agent, has some sort and degree of tendency, or advantage to move or excite the will, previous to the effect, or to the act of the will excited. This previous tendency of the motive is what I call the "strength of the motive."

I have rather chosen to express myself thus, that the will always *is* as the greatest apparent good, or "as what appears most agreeable, is," than to say that the will is "*determined* by" the greatest apparent good, or by what seems most agreeable; because an appearing most agreeable or pleasing to the mind, and the mind's preferring and choosing, seem hardly to be properly and perfectly distinct.

However, I think so much is certain, that volition, in no one instance that can be mentioned, is otherwise than the greatest apparent good is, in the manner which has been explained. The choice of the mind never departs from that which, at that time, and with respect to the direct and immediate objects of that decision of the mind, appears most agreeable and pleasing, all things considered. If the immediate objects of the will are a man's own actions, then those actions which appear most agreeable to him he wills. If it be now most agreeable to him, all things considered, to walk, then he now wills to walk. If it be now, upon the whole of what at present appears to him, most agreeable to speak, then he chooses to speak; if it suits him best to keep silence, then he chooses to keep silence. There is scarcely a plainer and more universal dictate of the sense and experience of mankind, than that, when men act voluntarily, and do what they please, then they do what suits them best, or what is most agreeable to them.

SECTION 3. CONCERNING THE MEANING OF THE TERMS NECESSITY, IMPOSSIBILITY, INABILITY, ETC.; AND OF CONTINGENCE

The words "necessary," "impossible," etc. are abundantly used in controversies about free will and moral agency; and therefore the sense in which they are used, should be clearly understood.

It follows from what has been observed, that when these terms "necessary," "impossible," "irresistible," "unable," etc. are used in cases wherein no opposition, or insufficient will or endeavor, is supposed, or can be supposed, but the very nature of the supposed case itself excludes and denies any such opposition, will or endeavor; these terms are then not used in their proper signification, but quite beside their use in common speech. . . .

. . . It appears from what has been said, that these terms "necessary," "impossible," etc. are often used by philosophers and metaphysicians in a sense quite diverse from their common use and original signification: for they apply them to many cases in which no opposition is supposed or supposable.

Philosophical necessity is really nothing else than the full and fixed connection between the things signified by the subject and predicate of a proposition, which affirms something to be true. When there is such a connection, then the thing affirmed in the proposition is necessary, in a philosophical sense; whether any opposition, or contrary effort be supposed, or supposable in the case, or no.

. . . And in this sense I use the word "necessity," in the following discourse, when I endeavor to prove "that necessity is not inconsistent with liberty."

SECTION 4. OF THE DISTINCTION OF NATURAL AND MORAL NECESSITY, AND INABILITY

That necessity which has been explained, consisting in an infallible connection of the things signified by the subject and predicate of a proposition, as intelligent beings are the subjects of it, is distinguished into moral and natural necessity.

. . . "moral necessity" signifies much the same as that high degree of probability, which is ordinarily sufficient to satisfy, and be relied upon by mankind, in their conduct and behavior in the world, as they would consult their own safety and interest, and treat others properly as members of society. And sometimes by "moral necessity" is meant that necessity of connection and consequence, which arises from such *moral causes,* as the strength of inclination, or motives, and the connection which there is in many cases between these, and such certain volitions and actions. And it is in this sense, that I use the phrase "moral necessity" in the following discourse.

By "natural necessity," as applied to men, I mean such necessity as men are under through the force of natural causes; as distinguished from what is called moral causes, such as habits and dispositions of the heart, and moral motives and inducements. Thus men placed in certain circumstances, are the subjects of particular sensations by necessity: they feel pain when their bodies are wounded; they see the objects presented before them in a clear light, when their eyes are opened: so they assent to the truth of certain propositions, as soon as the terms are understood; as that two and two make four, that black is not white, that two parallel lines can never cross one another: so by a natural necessity men's bodies move downwards, when there is nothing to support them.

What has been said of natural and moral necessity, may serve to explain what is intended by natural and moral *inability.* We are said to be *naturally* unable to do a thing, when we can't do it if we will, because what is most commonly called nature don't allow of it, or because of some impeding defect or obstacle that is extrinsic to the will; either in the faculty of understanding, constitution or body, or external objects. *Moral* inability consists not in any of these things; but either in the want of inclination; or the strength of a contrary inclination; or the want of sufficient motives in view, to induce and excite the act of the will, or the strength of apparent motives to the contrary.

To give some instances of this moral inability: A woman of great honor and chastity may have a moral inability to prostitute herself to her slave. A child of great love and duty to his parents, may be unable to be willing to kill his father. A very lascivious man, in case of certain opportunities and temptations, and in the absence of such and such restraints, may be unable to forbear gratifying his lust. A drunkard, under such and such circumstances, may be unable to forbear taking of strong drink.

A very malicious man may be unable to exert benevolent acts to an enemy, or to desire his prosperity: yea, some may be so under the power of a vile disposition, that they may be unable to love those who are most worthy of their esteem and affection. A strong habit of virtue and great degree of holiness may cause a moral inability to love wickedness in general, may render a man unable to take complacence in wicked persons or things; or to choose a wicked life, and prefer it to a virtuous life. And on the other hand, a great degree of habitual wickedness may lay a man under an inability to love and choose holiness; and render him utterly unable to love an infinitely holy Being, or to choose and cleave to him as his chief good.

SECTION 5. CONCERNING THE NOTION OF LIBERTY, AND OF MORAL AGENCY

The plain and obvious meaning of the words "freedom" and "liberty," in common speech, is power, opportunity, or advantage, that anyone has, to do as he pleases. Or in other words, his being free from hindrance or impediment in the way of doing, or conducting in any respect, as he wills. And the contrary to liberty, whatever name we call that by, is a person's being hindered or unable to conduct as he will, or being necessitated to do otherwise.

There are two things that are contrary to this which is called liberty in common speech. One is *constraint;* the same is otherwise called force, compulsion, and coaction; which is a person's being necessitated to do a thing *contrary* to his will. The other is *restraint;* which is his being hindered, and not having power to do *according* to his will.

But one thing more I would observe concerning what is vulgarly called liberty; namely, that power and opportunity for one to do and conduct as he will, or according to his choice, is all that is meant by it: without taking into the meaning of the word, anything of the cause or original of that choice; or at all considering how the person came to have such a volition; whether it was caused by some external motive, or internal habitual bias; whether it was determined by some internal antecedent volition, or whether it happened without a cause: whether it was necessarily connected with something foregoing, or not connected. Let the person come by his volition or choice how he will, yet, if he is able, and there is nothing in the way to hinder his pursuing and executing his will, the man is fully and perfectly free, according to the primary and common notion of freedom.

FREEDOM OF THE WILL—PART II*

SECTION 1. SHEWING THE MANIFEST INCONSISTENCE OF THE ARMINIAN NOTION OF LIBERTY OF WILL, CONSISTING IN THE WILL'S SELF-DETERMINING POWER

I shall suppose that the Arminians, when they speak of the will's determining itself, do by the will mean "the soul willing." I shall take it for granted, that when they speak of the will, as the determiner, they mean the soul in the exercise of a power of willing, or acting voluntarily.

Therefore, if the will determines all its own free acts, the soul determines all the free acts of the will in the exercise of a power of willing and choosing; or, which is the same thing, it determines them of choice; it determines its own acts by choosing its own acts. If the will determines the will, then choice orders and determines the choice: and acts of choice are subject to the decision, and follow the conduct of other acts of choice. And therefore if the will determines all its own free acts, then every free act of choice is determined by a preceding act of choice, choosing that act. And if that preceding act of the will or choice be also a free act, then by these principles, in this act too, the will is self-determined; that is, this, in like manner, is an act that the soul voluntarily chooses; or which is the same thing, it is an act determined still be a preceding act of the will, choosing that. And the like may again be observed of the last mentioned act. Which brings us directly to a contradiction: for it supposes an act of the will preceding the first act in the whole train, directing and determining the rest; or a free act of the will, before the first free act of the will. Or else we must come at last to an act of the will, determining the consequent acts, wherein the will is not self-determined, and so is not a free act, in this notion of freedom; but if the first act in the train, determining and fixing the rest, be not free, none of them all can be free; as is manifest at first view, but shall be demonstrated presently.

. . . There is a great noise made about self-determining power, as the source of all free acts of the will: but when the matter comes to be explained, the meaning is, that no power at all is the source of these acts, neither self-determining power, nor any other, but they arise from nothing; no cause, no power, no influence, being at all concerned in the matter.

However, this very thing, even that the free acts of the will are events which come to pass without a cause, is certainly implied in the Arminian notion of liberty of will; though it be very inconsistent with many other things in their scheme, and repugnant to some things implied in their notion of liberty. Their opinion implies, that the particular determination of volition is without any cause; because they hold the free acts of the will to be *contingent* events.

---

* Ibid.

SECTION 3. WHETHER ANY EVENT WHATSOEVER, AND VOLITION IN PARTICULAR, CAN COME TO PASS WITHOUT A CAUSE OF ITS EXISTENCE

Therefore I sometimes use the word "cause," in this inquiry, to signify any antecedent, either natural or moral, positive or negative, on which an event, either a thing, or the manner and circumstance of a thing, so depends, that it is the ground and reason, either in whole, or in part, why it is, rather than not; or why it is as it is, rather than otherwise; or, in other words, any antecedent with which a consequent event is so connected, that it truly belongs to the reason why the proposition which affirms that event, is true. . . .

I can conceive of nothing else that can be meant by the soul's having power to cause and determine its own volitions, as a being to whom God has given a power of action, but this; that God has given power to the soul, sometimes at least, to excite volitions at its pleasure, or according as it chooses. And this certainly supposes, in all such cases, a choice preceding all volitions which are thus caused, even the very first of them. Which runs into the forementioned great absurdity.

Therefore the activity of the nature of the soul affords no relief from the difficulties which the notion of a self-determining power in the will is attended with, nor will it help, in the least, its absurdities and inconsistencies.

SECTION 5. SHOWING, THAT IF THE THINGS ASSERTED IN THESE EVASIONS SHOULD BE SUPPOSED TO BE TRUE, THEY ARE ALTOGETHER IMPERTINENT AND CANNOT HELP THE CAUSE OF ARMINIAN LIBERTY; AND HOW (THIS BEING THE STATE OF THE CASE) ARINIAN WRITERS ARE OBLIGED TO TALK INCONSISTENTLY

If the will don't cause and determine the act by choice, it don't cause or determine it at all; for that which is not determined by choice, is not determined voluntarily or willingly: and to say, that the will determines something which the soul don't determine willingly, is as much as to say, that something is done by the will, which the soul don't do with its will.

So that if Arminian liberty of will, consisting in the will's determining its own acts, be maintained, the old absurdity and contradiction must be maintained, that every free act of will is caused and determined by a foregoing free act of will. Which don't consist with the free act's arising without any cause, and being so contingent, as not be fixed by anything foregoing. So that this evasion must be given up, as not at all relieving, and as that which, instead of supporting this sort of liberty, directly destroys it.

SECTION 6. CONCERNING THE WILL'S DETERMINING THINGS
WHICH ARE PERFECTLY INDIFFERENT IN THE VIEW OF THE
MIND

A great argument for self-determining power, is the supposed experience
we universally have of an ability to determine our wills, in cases wherein
no prevailing motive is presented: the will (as is supposed) has its choice
to make between two or more things, that are perfectly equal in the view
of the mind; and the will is apparently altogether indifferent; and yet we
find no difficulty in coming to a choice: the will can instantly determine
itself to one, by a sovereign power which it has over itself, without being
moved by any preponderating inducement.

. . . The very supposition which is here made, directly contradicts and
overthrows itself. For the thing supposed, wherein this grand argument
consists, is, that among several things the will actually chooses one before
another, at the same time that it is perfectly indifferent; which is the very
same thing as to say, the mind has a preference, at the same time that
it has no preference.

SECTION 10. OF THE CONSIDERATION OF THE ACTS OF THE WILL
WITH THE DICTATES OF THE UNDERSTANDING

It is manifest, that the acts of the will are none of them contingent in
such a sense as to be without all necessity, or so as not to be necessary
with a necessity of consequences and connection; because every act of
the will is some way connected with the understanding, and is as the
greatest apparent good is, in the manner which has already been explained;
namely, that the soul always wills or chooses that which, in the present
view of the mind, considered in the whole of that view, and all that
belongs to it, appears most agreeable.

FREEDOM OF THE WILL—PART IV*

SECTION 3. THE REASONS WHY SOME PEOPLE THINK IT
CONTRARY TO COMMON SENSE TO SUPPOSE THOSE THINGS
WHICH ARE NECESSARY TO BE WORTHY OF EITHER PRAISE OR
BLAME

IT IS abundantly affirmed and urged by Arminian writers, that it is
contrary to common sense, and the natural notions and apprehensions
of mankind, to suppose otherwise than that necessity (making no distinction between natural and moral necessity) is inconsistent with virtue
and vice, praise and blame, reward and punishment. And, their arguments

* Ibid

from hence have been greatly triumphed in; and have been not a little perplexing to many who have been friendly to the truth, as clearly revealed in the holy Scriptures: it has seemed to them indeed difficult, to reconcile Calvinistic doctrines with the notions men commonly have of justice and equity. And the true reasons of it seem to be these that follow.

'Tis indeed a very plain dictate of common sense, that natural necessity is wholly inconsistent with just praise or blame. If men do things which in themselves are very good, fit to be brought to pass, and very happy effects, properly against their wills, and can't help it; or do them from a necessity that is without their wills, or with which their wills have no concern or connection; then 'tis a plain dictate of common sense, that it's none of their virtue, nor any moral good in them; and that they are not worthy to be rewarded or praised; or at all esteemed, honored or loved on that account. . . .

But 'tis apparent, that the reverse of these things is true. If there be an approach to a moral necessity in a man's exertion of good acts of will, they being the exercise of a strong propensity to good, and a very powerful love to virtue; 'tis so far from being the dictate of common sense, that he is less virtuous, and the less to be esteemed, loved and praised; that 'tis agreeable to the natural notions of all mankind that he is so much the better man, worthy of greater respect, and higher commendation. And the stronger the inclination is, and the nearer it approaches to necessity in that respect, or to impossibility of neglecting the virtuous act, or of doing a vicious one; still the more virtuous, and worthy of higher commendation. And on the other hand, if a man exerts evil acts of mind; as for instance, acts of pride or malice, from a rooted and strong habit or principle of haughtiness and maliciousness, and a violent propensity of heart to such acts; according to the natural sense of all men, he is so far from being the less hateful and blamable on that account, that he is so much the more worthy to be detested and condemned by all that observe him.

SECTION 4. IT IS AGREEABLE TO COMMON SENSE AND THE NATURAL NOTIONS OF MANKIND, TO SUPPOSE MORAL NECESSITY TO BE CONSISTENT WITH PRAISE AND BLAME, REWARD AND PUNISHMENT

This will appear if we consider what the vulgar notion of blameworthiness is. The idea which the common people through all ages and nations have of faultiness, I suppose to be plainly this; "a person's being or doing wrong, with his own will and pleasure"; containing these two things: 1. His doing wrong, when he does as he pleases. 2. His pleasure's being wrong. Or in other words, perhaps more intelligibly expressing their notions, "a person's having his heart wrong, and doing wrong from his heart." And this is the sum total of the matter.

The things which have been said obviate some of the chief objections of Arminians against the Calvinistic doctrine of the *total depravity and corruption of man's nature,* whereby his heart is wholly under the power of sin, and he is utterly unable, without the interposition of sovereign grace, savingly to love God, believe in Christ, or do anything that is truly good and acceptable in God's sight. For the main objection against this doctrine is, that it is inconsistent with the freedom of man's will, consisting in indifference and self-determining power; because it supposes man to be under a necessity of sinning, and that God requires things of him, in order to his avoiding eternal damnation, which he is unable to do; and that this doctrine is wholly inconsistent with the sincerity of counsels, invitations, etc. Now this doctrine supposes *no other necessity* of sinning, than a moral necessity; which, as has been shewn, don't at all excuse sin; and supposes *no other inability* to obey any command, or perform any duty, even the most spiritual and exalted, but a moral inability, which, as has been proved, don't excuse persons in the nonperformance of any good thing, or make 'em not to be proper objects of commands, counsels and invitations. And moreover, it has beenshewn, that there is not, and never can be, either in existence, or so much as in idea, any such freedom of will, consisting in indifference and self-determination, for the sake of which, this doctrine of original sin is cast out; and that no such freedom is necessary, in order to the nature of sin, and a just desert of punishment.

The things which have been observed, do also take off the main objections of Arminians against the docrtine of *efficacious grace;* and at the same time, prove the grace of God in a sinner's conversion (if there be any grace or divine influence in the affair) to be efficacious, yea, and *irresistible* too, if by irresistible is meant, that which is attended with a moral necessity, which it is impossible should ever be violated by any resistance. The main objection of Arminians against this doctrine is, that it is inconsistent with their self-determining freedom of will; and that it is repugnant to the nature of virtue, that it should be wrought in the heart by the determining efficacy and power of another, instead of its being owing to a self-moving power; that in that case, the good which is wrought, would not be *our* virtue, but rather *God's* virtue; because it is not the person in whom it is wrought, that is the determining author of it, but God that wrought it in him. But the things which are the foundation of these objections, have been considered; and it has been demonstrated, that the liberty of moral agents does not consist in self-determining power; and that there is no need of any such liberty, in order to the nature of virtue; nor does it at all hinder, but that the state or act of the will may be the virtue of the subject, though it be not from self-determination, but the determination of an extrinsic cause; even so as to cause the event to be morally necessary to the subject of it. And as it has been proved, that nothing in the state or acts of the will of man is contingent; but that on the contrary, every event of this kind is necessary, by a moral necessity; and has also been now demonstrated, that the doctrine of an universal determining providence, follows from that doctrine of necessity, which was proved before; and so, that God does decisively, in his providence, order all the volitions of moral agents, either by positive influence or permission: and it being allowed on all hands, that what God does in the affair of man's virtuous volitions, whether it be more or less, is by some positive influence, and not by mere permission, as in the affair of a sinful volition: if we put these things together, it will follow, that God's assistance or influence, must be determining and decisive, or must be attended with a moral necessity of the event; and so, that God gives virtue, holiness and conversion to sinners, by an influence which determines the effect, in such a manner, that the effect will infallibly follow by a moral necessity; which is what Calvinists mean by efficacious and irresistible grace.

STUDY QUESTIONS

Review

1. Who were the Puritans, historically? Mention some of their religious beliefs that may have had some bearing on their philosophy.
2. Describe briefly the three major influences upon the thought of Jonathan Edwards mentioned in this chapter.
3. How did Edwards use Locke's theory of primary and secondary qualities to support his idealistic theory of knowledge?
4. How did the problem of grace figure in Edwards's discussion of the freedom of the will?
5. What kind of freedom do we have, according to Edwards? Are we then responsible for our actions?
6. What happened to the notion of freedom in the period immediately following Edwards?

For Further Thought

7. Do you think that so-called secondary qualities are subjective? In what sense, if at all, are they in the bodies of which they are qualities?
8. Are the so-called primary qualities in bodies? Do you agree with Edwards that they are all forms of resistance? Is resistance subjective? Is reality, then, ideas?
9. When one chooses something for some reason, is one choosing freely? Explain your answer.
10. Do you think that we at least sometimes make free choices? What do you mean by "free choice" ?

BIBLIOGRAPHY

General

Bercovitch, Sacvan. *The Puritan Origins of the American Self.* New Haven: Yale University Press, 1975.

Blau, Joseph L. *Men and Movements in American Philosophy,* pp. 1–35. Englewood Cliffs, N.J.: Prentice-Hall, 1952.

Carroll, Peter N. *Pritanism and the Wilderness: The Intellectual Significance of the New England Frontier, 1629–1700.* New York: Columbia University Press, 1969.

Conkin, Paul K. *Puritans and Pragmatists,* pp. 1–72. New York: Dodd, Mead and Co., 1968.

Emerson, Everett. *Puritanism in America.* Boston: G. K. Hall, 1977.

Flower, Elizabeth, and Murray G. Murphy. "Early American Philosophy: The Puritans." Chap. 10 in *A History of Philosophy in America.* Vol. 1. NY: Capricorn Books, 1977.

Kuklick, Bruce. *The Rise of American Philosophy.* New Haven: Yale University Press, 1977.

Miller, Perry. *Errand into the Wilderness.* New York: Harper and Row, 1956.

– – – *The New England Mind: From Colony to Province.* Cambridge: Harvard University Press, 1953.

– – –. *The New England Mind: The Seventeenth Century.* New York: Macmillan, 1939.

Morrison, Samuel Eliot. *The Oxford History of the American People.* Vol. I. New York: New American Library, 1965.

– – –. *Intellectual Life of Colonial New England.* Ithaca, N.Y.: Cornell University Press, 1960.

Ong, Walter J., S.J. *Ramus, Method, and the Decay of Dialogue.* Cambridge: Harvard University Press, 1958.

Perry, Ralph B. *Puritanism and Democracy.* New York: Vanguard Press, 1944.

Schneider, Herbert W. *A History of American Philosophy.* New York: Columbia University Press, 1946; rev. ed., 1963.

– – –. *The Puritan Mind.* New York: Henry Holt, 1930.

Shahan, Robt. W., and Kenneth R. Merrill., eds. *American Philosophy: from Edwards to Quine.* Norman: University of Oklahoma Press, 1977.

Stroh, Guy W. *American Philosophy from Edwards to Dewey.* Princeton: D. Van Nostrand, 1968.

Waller, Geo M., ed., *Puritanism in Early America.* Boston: D. C. Heath, 1950.

White, Morton. *Science and Sentiment in America: Philosophical Thought from Jonathan Edwards to John Dewey.* New York: Oxford University Press, 1972.

Ziff, Larzer. *Puritanism in America: New Cultures in a New World.* New York: Viking Press, 1973.

Jonathan Edwards

Edwards, Jonathan. *The Works of Jonathan Edwards.* Gen. ed. John E. Smith, Vol. 1, *Freedom of the Will,* Paul Ramsey (1957); vol. 2, *Religious Affections,* ed. John Smith (1959); vol. 3, *Original Sin,* ed. Clyde Holbrook (1970); vol. 4, *The Great Awakening,* ed. C. C. Goen (1972); vol. 5, *Apocalyptic Writings,* ed. Stephen

J. Stein (1977); vol. 6, *Scientific and Philosophical Writings,* ed. Wallace E. Anderson (1980). New Haven: Yale University Press.

— — —. *The Philosophy of Jonathan Edwards from His Private Notebooks.* Ed. H. G. Townsend. Eugene: University of Oregon Press, 1955.

— — —. *Puritan Sage: Collected Writings of Jonathan Edwards.* Ed. Vergilius Ferm. New York: Library Publishers, 1953.

— — —. *Images or Shadows of Divine Things.* Ed. Perry Miller. New Haven: Yale University Press, 1948. Reprint. Westport, Conn.: Greenwood, 1977.

— — —. *Jonathan Edwards: Representative Selections.* Ed. C. H. Faust and T. H. Johnson. New York: American Book Co., 1935; rev. ed., 1962.

— — —. *The Works of President Edwards, with a Memoir of His Life.* Ed. Sereno E. Dwight. 10 vols. New York: S. Converse, 1830.

Carpenter, Frederick. "The Radicalism of Jonathan Edwards." *New England Quarterly,* 4 (1931): pp. 629–44.

Cherry, Conrad, et al. *Jonathan Edwards: His Life and Influence,* E. Brunswick, N.J.: Fairleigh Dickinson University Press, 1975.

Erdt, Terrence. *Jonathan Edwards: Art and the Sense of the Heart.* Amherst: University of Massachusetts Press, 1980.

Faust, Clarence H., and Thomas T. Johnson. *Jonathan Edwards.* 1935. Reprint. Norwood, Pa.: Telegraph Books, 1981.

Fiering, Norman. *Jonathan Edwards' Moral Thought and Its British Context.* Chapel Hill: University of North Carolina Press, 1981.

Fisher, G. P. "The Philosophy of Jonathan Edwards." *North American Review* 138 (March 1879): pp. 284–303.

Flower, Elizabeth, and Murray G. Murphy. "Jonathan Edwards." In vol. 1, chap. 3 of *A History of Philosophy in America.* New York: Capricorn Books, 1977.

Gardiner, Harry N., ed. *Jonathan Edwards: A Retrospect.* New York: AMS Press, 1980.

— — —. "The Early Idealism of Jonathan Edwards." *Philosophical Review* 9 (1900): pp. 573–96.

Griffin, Edward M. *Jonathan Edwards.* Minneapolis: University of Minnesota Press, 1971.

Holbrook, C. A. "Jonathan Edwards and His Detractors." *Theology Today* 10 (October 1963): pp. 384–96.

— — —. "Edwards Re-examined." *Review of Metaphysics* 13 (June 1960): pp. 623–41.

Johnson, Thomas H. *Printed Writings of Jonathan Edwards, 1703–1758: A Bibliography.* New York: Benjamin Franklin, 1970.

Jones, Adam L. *Early American Philosophers,* New York: Ungar, 1958.

Lesser, M. X. *Jonathan Edwards: A Reference Guide.* Boston: G. K. Hall, 1981.

MacCracken, John H. "The Sources of Jonathan Edwards' Idealism." *Philosophical Review* 12 (1902): pp. 26–42.

Miller, Perry, *Jonathan Edwards.* New York: William Sloan Associates, 1949. Reprint. Amherst: University of Massachusetts Press, 1981.

Murphy, A. E. "Jonathan Edwards on Free Will and Moral Agency." *Philosophical Review* 68 (May 1959): pp. 181–202.

Rhoades, Donald H. "Jonathan Edwards: America's First Philosopher." *Personalist* 31 (Summer 1952): pp. 135–47.

Scheich, William J. *Critical Essays on American Literature.* Boston: G. K. Hall, 1980.

Smyth, E. G. "Jonathan Edwards' Idealism." *American Journal of Theology* 1 (October 1897): pp. 950–64.

Suter, R. "Note on Platonism in the Philosophy of Jonathan Edwards." *Harvard The-*
      ological Review 52 (October 1959): pp. 283–84.
Tufts, J. H. "Edwards and Newton." *Philosophical Review* 49 (Nov. 1940): pp. 609–22.
Winslow, Ola E. *Jonathan Edwards.* New York: Octagon Press, 1972.
Wright, Conrad. "Edwards and the Arminians on Freedom of the Will." *Harvard
      Theological Review* 35 (Oct 1942): pp. 241–61.

Chapter 2

The American Enlightenment

During the years just preceding and following the American Revolution (1750–1800) a certain climate of thought prevailed, one similar in spirit to its European counterpart. Those who best reflected this climate of thought were primarily men of action. Political life in those days was perfused with philosophical claims and arguments. In fact, according to Herbert Schneider, "there was no period in our history when the public interests of the people were so intimately linked to philosophic issues." [1] Nevertheless, statesmen were so busy fomenting a revolution and establishing a nation that they did not think through their philosophical viewpoints in much detail or depth. What philosophical arguments they developed must be gleaned from their speeches, tracts, pamphlets, letters, and sermons.

Thinkers of the European Enlightenment had stressed the value of man and the power of human reason. Although Jonathan Edwards was primarily a religious leader and a theologian, he had fashioned the most notable fusion of piety and reason in early America. However, in the transition from Puritanism to the American Enlightenment we witness the movement of Puritan piety and affection into the evangelical churches. The rational core of Puritanism was transformed into the enlightened worship of reason, nature, and man. For the Puritans, God was an absolute sovereign power. However, since He created nature according to rational laws, God was to a certain extent subject to these laws. Thus the successors of the Puritans concluded that divine intervention with nature was contrary to its laws (e.g. miracles) and must not be possible.

The rational religion of this period is known as deism, and it variously influenced the philosophical and religious views of the leaders of the American Enlightenment. From the word *deus,* deism implied a belief in God, but also supported a kind of religious unorthodoxy. Primarily a European movement, deists included such thinkers as Herbert of Cherbury (1585–1648), Voltaire (1694–1778), and Rousseau (1712–78).[2] In America Benjamin Franklin, Thomas Jefferson, Tom Paine, and Ethan Allen followed the deist creed. This creed included belief in one supreme God who is the first cause of the universe and its unalterable laws. Nature exemplified order and purposefulness, and God was its great engineer or watchmaker who could be known by human reason through a study of His handiwork. True piety consisted of leading a good life and attaining it for others. No special divine election was required; all could attain the rewards promised by divine goodness through their own efforts. Man was viewed as a free moral agent, and it was believed that the rewards of happiness were attained in this life as well as the next. Thus the deist tended to oppose religious authority and any aspects of Christianity that could not be known by reason alone — aspects such as sacraments, priesthood, and faith, all essential to traditional Christianity.

As God was bound by the lawfulness of nature, so also the king could rule only by the consent of the governed. Puritan theology also provided a basis for the social-contract doctrine of the Enlightenment period. According to the Puritan theory of church covenants, God agreed to do certain things for the elect, and the elect covenanted together with leaders of their own choosing. While for the Puritans all authority came from God, for the social-contract theorists it came from the consent of the governed. This notion was part of the social-contract theory of writers such as John Locke.[3] In a state of nature, according to Locke, men would overreach their neighbors and gather unreasonable amounts of power, honor, and property. Thus to avoid the resulting conflicts, men willingly surrender some of their freedom to the community, according to the will of the majority, for the sake of their own and the common good. When any ruler worked in opposition to this purpose of government, the governed had a right to overthrow him. Men have certain basic natural rights. Tom Paine gained a wide following for his pamphlets addressing the colonies' causes for grievance against the English crown and for his support generally of the basic rights of man.[4] Thomas Jefferson summarized these arguments in the Declaration of Independence.

Overall, this period exemplified a shift from metaphysical and moral dependence to independence, and from otherworldly to this-worldly concerns. Natural happiness replaced concern for divine salvation, confidence and reliance on human reason replaced dependence on divine enlightenment, and human freedom and the basic goodness and perfectibility of man replaced notions of divine predestination and human depravity. Of all the American Enlightenment thinkers, two who most exemplified this new spirit were Benjamin Franklin and Thomas Jefferson.

BENJAMIN FRANKLIN (1706–90)

Benjamin Franklin was born in Boston in 1706, the fifteenth of seventeen children. By age twelve he was apprenticed as a printer and ten years later was on his own as a printer and publisher. For a time he was deputy postmaster and justice of the peace in Philadelphia; later he became U.S. postmaster. Popular writings and political activities, well-publicized scientific experiments and innovative theory, all bore the stamp of Franklin's distinctive personality and made him one of the most widely known men of his era. In 1757 he was sent to London as colonial agent of the province of Philadelphia, he lived for sometime in France, but in 1775 he returned to aid the colonies and help draft the Declaration of Independence. The following year he returned to France to plead for aid to the colonies and was instrumental in obtaining French recognition of the colonies' independence. In 1785 he returned to the new nation where, in April 1790, he died at the age of eighty-four.

Benjamin Franklin was a self-made man and, perhaps because of this, was impatient with those who seemed not to make use of the opportunities provided them to improve and succeed. He was witty, free from provincial customs and prejudice, a practical moralist, an experimenter in natural phenomena, and an able and charming ambassador who was nevertheless quite independent and detached. He exemplifed the secular humanitarianism of his day and taught by his life as well as his pen the economic value of the traditional Puritan virtues.

As many deists did, Franklin held that God is the all-wise maker and governor of the universe.[5] In an early essay he argued that this belief implied that nothing in the world can be wrong and that there is no virtue or vice. Later he found this early bit of speculation to be in error. Even as a teenager he wrote a series of letters ridiculing the wealthy, wellborn, and pretentious (the "Do Good Papers"), and in 1729 began publishing a series called "Busybody Papers" that included his own ideas for self- and group improvement. Seventeen thirty-two saw the beginning of a project that was to continue for twenty-five years, his *Poor Richard's Almanack*[6] – perhaps the most widely read and best known of his writings. Popular and loosely organized, these regular publications included weather forecasts, times of tides, household recipes, holidays, medical advice, gossip, jokes, poetry, and proverbs. In his *Autobiography*, which is the only complete book written by Franklin, he said that he grew up convinced that "truth, sincerity, and integrity . . . were of the utmost importance to the felicity of life." Some actions were divinely or socially forbidden because they were bad in themselves, which was to say, because they did not promote happiness. Happiness was to be achieved through the practice of the traditional Puritan virtues of temperance, modesty, silence, order, frugality, industry, sincerity, and justice. Franklin, however, gave these virtues a new utilitarian function. The small section of the *Autobiography* written in 1784 details his scheme for moral perfection.[7]

A more philosophically reflective work modeled on the Dialogues of Plato, "A Dialogue Between Philocles and Horatio . . . Concerning Virtue and Pleasure" (1730), gave somewhat more detail on the nature of the goal to be achieved. Franklin opposed self-denial as such. Pleasure was the sole good, but one needed to be wise in one's pleasures, looking to the end and regarding the consequences. Thus a present pleasure may have to be sacrificed for the sake of a more enduring good. Are there any such enduring goods? Franklin's answer was that man's chief good consists in reasonable action, and that prudence and morality differ only in intention. The goal, happiness, is the same. In the final analysis, Franklin's argument is somewhat circular: true happiness and enduring goods are those that are reasonable, and those that are reasonable are those that lead to happiness. We never are told which kinds of happiness or what enduring goods are the goals of reasonable action. We do know, however, that education is helpful in procuring happiness, and that the attainment of it for its citizens is the sole purpose of government. Franklin remained skeptical to a certain extent. We never know, except perhaps by trying them out, whether certain means will actually bring about happiness. For example, he recommended the Constitution of 1787 only because it seemed to him that it was the best so far conceived, and that even so, wisdom and benevolence would be necessary for the successful practice of it.[8]

In his day Franklin was noted for his scientific work. Often he is viewed as a dabbler and as one whose only real concern was with devising practical inventions. This charge does have some truth. Franklin was concerned with the practical consequences of science. Even when he founded the American Philosophical Association in 1743, he did not stress speculative knowledge. His plan was entitled "A Proposal for Promoting Useful Knowledge Among the British Plantations in America." [9] This association was to bring together, chiefly through correspondence, "ingenious men" to share their useful knowledge and new discoveries in medicine, agriculture, mining, mathematics, and philosophy. It was established for the sake of letting light "into the nature of things," increasing the "power of man over matter," and multiplying "the conveniences or pleasures of life."

In spite of this practical orientation, Franklin must be accounted a theorist concerned with the proper interpretation of nature.[10] He was the first to suggest that electricity consists of one fluid (rather than two) that is dispersed throughout the substance of things. He guessed that electricity has a negative charge when the body that contains it has less than its "natural quantity" of the fluid. This state produces lightning — clouds contain less than their due amount of the electrical fluid and thus draw some from the earth. One can prevent the electricity from setting fire to houses by conducting it to the ground from whence it can obtain the missing fluid, thus bypassing the house (Franklin's famous lightning rods were for this purpose). The famed British physicist, J. J. Thomson, a century later wrote of the vision of Franklin: "We shall, I am sure, be struck by the similarity between some of the views which we are led to take by the results of the most recent researches [on electrons and electricity] with those enunciated by Franklin in the very infancy of the subject." [11]

One can foresee in Benjamin Franklin some of the tendencies of pragmatism.[12] If something did not work, it was, according to Franklin, frivolous and a waste of time. Thus he opposed much of philosophical speculation. He would agree that whatever worked for the production of happiness was good and true. It was thus that the Divine Creator had arranged all things, for He was a benevolent God, and those who found the right means would succeed even as Franklin himself had done.

THOMAS JEFFERSON (1743–1826)

Thomas Jefferson was born on 13 April 1743 in Shadwell, Virginia on an estate of several thousand acres, most of which he later inherited. After a classical education, Jefferson studied law at William and Mary College in Williamsburg. Law led him into politics, and in 1769 he was elected to the House of Burgesses. He learned architecture from books and designed his own house in Monticello. In 1775 he was elected as delegate to the Continental Congress; the following year he did the majority of the writing of the Declaration of Independence. In 1779 he was elected governor of Virginia and in the same year introduced a Bill for Religious Freedom in the Virginia Assembly. He was elected in 1783 to the U.S. Congress, but spent the following five years as minister to France. In 1789 he was appointed secretary of state, and was elected vice-president in 1796 and president of the United States four years later. After serving two terms he refused renomination and returned to Monticello where he died 4 July 1826, fifty years after the signing of the Declaration of Independence.

While lauding the common man, Jefferson was himself anything but common. Jefferson's contemporaries recognized him as a lawyer, amateur scientist, architect, inventor, farmer, and statesman. Yet as he indicated on his own tombstone, he himself wanted to be remembered for three achievements: his authorship of the Declaration of Independence, his responsibility for the adoption of a Bill of Rights establishing religious freedom in Virginia, and his founding of the University of Virginia.[13] These achievements exemplified the three major causes in which he believed and for which he never ceased to work: political democracy, religious liberty, and universal education.

Basic to all of these causes was a firmly held belief in the innate goodness and rationality of every person. Each person is endowed by nature (or creator, or birth) with a sense of right and wrong, a kind of sixth sense that is usually called conscience. Although not everyone has the same degree of conscience, Jefferson thought that it could be perfected through exercise. But there are no rules of morality that can be learned and made into a science, according to Jefferson. In fact if one compared the moral judgments of the ploughman with those of the professor, the former would probably fare better, since the latter might be confused by artificial rules. Why, then, do people differ so much as to what is right or wrong? Jefferson's answer was that because acts vary in their usefulness in different countries and for different persons, these acts must also vary in their moral value, for utility is the moral standard.

We have certain natural wants and from these come our natural rights. Because these rights are from nature, they are inalienable. His list included not only the three mentioned in the Declaration of Independence (life, liberty, and the pursuit of happiness), but also the rights of freedom of thought and speech, freedom of conscience, personal freedom, and a right to property. These rights can be exercised freely so long as they do not harm others. Moreover, some of these rights need society's guarantee since our power to exercise them is insufficient of itself. Government is based on the will of the people and must remain responsive to them. They are its best censors. For a time the people may go astray, and the will of the majority may be wrong, yet this situation will eventually right itself. The more the people can do for themselves the better, and thus the less government the better. To keep government alive and responsive, a little rebellion now and then is advisable, perhaps as often as every twenty years!

Universal education through college, Jefferson believed, would be the best safeguard of the nation's freedom and happiness. He had confidence in the natural intelligence and goodness of man and thus believed that if someone knew the right he would follow it. For this reason there should be no restrictions put on man's mind, not even that of religious authority. No one should be forced to believe any particular religious creed nor worship in any particular manner. Rational persuasion should be used instead. By his own standards Jefferson was a religious person. Yet, like many deists of his day, he opposed the Christian tradition that revelation is necessary for a knowledge of God. Reason can know the existence of an intelligent and powerful creator. No one, he felt, can advance the cause of religion while dispensing with such basic religious truth.

Thomas Jefferson was fundamentally a humanist who had a vision of free minds in a free society. Given sufficient room, support, and education, people would know the right and govern themselves for the best. Not all have agreed with Jefferson's optimistic view of man, but part of his view is written into one of the most basic political documents of this country, the Declaration of Independence.

REACTION TO THE ENLIGHTENMENT

"The Enlightenment began in complacency and ended in fear."[1] While perhaps a bit strong, this description of the reaction to the Enlightenment captures some of the withdrawal from the Enlightenment spirit that took place in the first half of the nineteenth century. Overall this period is best described as a movement away from espousal of values of change and novelty toward those of stability and permanence, from optimism, confidence, openness, and the freedom of speculation to suspicion and reliance on authority. In the political arena, the framers of the Constitution introduced certain elements of structure and a strong central government. The Declaration of Independence's affirmation of man's right to happiness was succeeded by the Constitution's concern with the rights of property owners. After the French Revolution and the anarchy that followed, many began to doubt the ability of ordinary people to govern themselves in a reasonable way. A growing belief in a natural aristocracy tended to overshadow the Enlightenment belief in the innate intelligence and goodness of all men. In the debate over slavery one can witness the extent to which many did not support a belief in equality of basic human rights.

In the sphere of religion, there is further evidence of a withdrawal fror the Enlightenment creed. On the frontier the revivalist movement continuec, but religious orthodoxy replaced natural religion and denominations began to be organized. Any scientific theories that were not reconcilable with Christian orthodox beliefs became suspect. In place of philosophy as a search for wisdom, philosophy as a technical discipline was substituted. A concern for the instruction and teaching of philosophy developed in American colleges; philosophy came to be viewed as a body of truths that could be systematized and learned. Textbooks that embodied these truths were produced, often by minister–college presidents. Thus Francis Wayland, president of Brown University, in the introduction to his *Elements of Moral Science* (1835), wrote: "I have attempted to present and illustrate the important truths in intellectual philosophy rather than the inferences which may be drawn from them. . . . I have rarely gone into extended moral discussions but contented myself with the attempt to state the moral law and the reason of it in as few and as comprehensive terms as possible." [15] Philosophy courses were divided into natural philosophy (natural science), mental philosophy (including what is now covered by psychology, epistemology, logic, and metaphysics), and moral philosophy (including politics and economics). Each of these areas relied upon the basic tenets of a Scottish philosophy developed chiefly by Thomas Reid called commonsense realism. Realism seemed less open to speculation than idealism. Moreover, it was used to justify and support traditional beliefs in God and the immateriality and immortality of the soul. Philosophy became isolated from the business of life and from other disciplines, which were left without the benefit of philosophical argument and support. This reaction to the optimism, freedom, and rationalism of the Enlightenment persisted into the latter half of the nineteenth century, even while transcendentalism and pragmatism became dominant philosophies.

Notes

[1] Schneider, *History of American Philosophy,* p. 29.

[2] The titles of some deist works are symbolic of their beliefs: William Wollaston's *The Religion of Nature Delineated* (1724), Immanuel Kant's *Religion within the Limits of Reason Alone* (1792–94), and Ethan Allen's *Reason the Only Oracle of Man* (1784).

[3] See John Locke's *Two Treatises of Government* (1690).

[4] Thomas Paine was the fiery publicist who lived from 1737 to 1809 and is noted for *Common Sense,* a pamphlet that was the first public appeal for American independence; *The Rights of Man,* an argument for democracy against aristocracy; and *The Age of Reason,* a defense of deism and a critique of Christianity.

[5] See the selections here included from Franklin's essay "A Dissertation on Liberty and Necessity, Pleasure and Pain," 1725.

[6] See selections here included from *Poor Richard's Almanac.*

[7] See the selection here included from the *Autobiography.*

[8] See the selection here included from Franklin's "Speech in the Philadelphia Convention at its Final Session," 17 September, 1787.

[9] See the selection here included from "Proposal."

[10] See the selections here included from his scientific writings.

[11] Quoted in Nathan G. Goodman, ed., *A Benjamin Franklin Reader* (New York: Thomas Y. Crowell, 1945), p. 360. Franklin's science was limited to the extent that he lacked the mathematics necessary even to read Newton's *Principia,* and while he worked out an explanatory hypothesis for electricity, he did not work out quantitative concepts to aid in control and prediction.

[12] Pragmatism will be discussed in chapters 5–8.

[13] See selections here included from the Bill of Rights and the Declaration of Independence.

[14] Schneider, *History of American Philosophy,* p. 31.

[15] Quoted in Blau, *American Philosophic Addresses,* p. 81.

BENJAMIN FRANKLIN

A Dialogue Between Philocles and Horatio, Meeting Accidentally in the Fields, Concerning Virtue and Pleasure (1730) *

[*The Pennsylvania Gazette,* 23 June 1730]

PHILOCLES. My friend Horatio! I am very glad to see you; prithee, how came such a man alone? And musing too? What misfortune in your pleasures has sent you to philosophy for relief.

HORATIO. You guess very right, my dear Philocles! We pleasure-hunters are never without them; and yet, so enchanting is the game, we can't quit the chase! How calm and undisturbed is your life! How free from present embarrassments and future cares! I know you love me, and look with compassion upon my conduct; show me then the path which leads up to that constant and invariable good, which I have heard you so beautifully describe, and which you seem so fully to possess.

PHIL. There are few men in the world I value more than you, Horatio! for, amidst all your foibles and painful pursuits of pleasure, I have oft observed in you an honest heart, and a mind strongly bent toward virtue. I wish, from my soul, I could assist you in acting steadily the part of a reasonable creature; for, if you would not think it a paradox, I should tell you I love you better than you do yourself.

---
* Albert H. Smyth, ed., *The Writings of Benjamin Franklin,* 10 vols. (New York: Macmillan, 1905–7), vol. 2, pp. 157–60.

HOR. A paradox indeed! Better than I do myself! When I love my dear self so well that I love everything else for my own sake.

PHIL. He only loves himself well, who rightly and judiciously loves himself.

HOR. What do you mean by that, Philocles! You men of reason and virtue are always dealing in mysteries, though you laugh at them when the church makes them. I think he loves himself very well and very judiciously too, as you call it, who allows himself to do whatever he pleases.

PHIL. What, though it be to the ruin and destruction of that very self which he loves so well! That man alone loves himself rightly, who procures the greatest possible good to himself through the whole of his existence; and so pursues pleasure as not to give for it more than 'tis worth.

PHIL. Suppose, Horatio, that a friend of yours entered into the world, about two-and-twenty, with a healthful vigorous body, and a fair plentiful estate of about five hundred pounds a year: and yet, before he had reached thirty, should, by following his pleasures, and not, as you say, duly regarding consequences, have run out of his estate, and disabled his body to that degree that he had neither the means nor capacity of enjoyment left, nor anything else to do but wisely shoot himself through the head to be at rest; what would you say to this unfortunate man's conduct? Is it wrong by opinion or fancy only? Or is there really a right and wrong in the case? Is not one opinion of life and action juster than another? Or, one sort of conduct preferable to another? Or, does that miserable son of pleasure appear as reasonable and lovely a being in your eyes, as a man who, by prudently and rightly gratifying his natural passions, had preserved his body in full health, and his estate entire, and enjoyed both to a good old age, and then died with a thankful heart for the good things he had received, and with an entire submission to the will of him who first called him into being? Say, Horatio: are these men equally wise and happy? And is everything to be measured by a mere fancy and opinion, without considering whether that fancy or opinion be right?

HOR. Hardly so neither, I think; yet sure the wise and good author of nature could never make us to plague us. He could never give us passions, on purpose to subdue and conquer them; nor produce this self of mine, or any other self, only that it may be denied; for that is denying the works of the great Creator himself.

A SECOND DIALOGUE (1730) *

[*The Pennsylvania Gazette,* 9 July 1730]

PHILOCLES. Dear Horatio! where hast thou been these three or four months? What new adventures have you fallen upon since I met you in

---

* Ibid., pp. 163–70.

these delightful, all-inspiring fields, and wondered how such a pleasure-hunter as you could bear being alone?

HORATIO. O Philocles, thou best of friends, because a friend to reason and virtue, I am very glad to see you. Don't you remember, I told you then that some misfortunes in my pleasures had sent me to philosophy for relief? But now I do assure you, I can, without a sigh, leave other pleasures for those of philosophy; I can hear the word *Reason* mentioned, and virtue praised, without laughing. Don't I bid fair for conversion, think you?

PHIL. Very fair, Horatio! for I remember the time when reason, virtue, and pleasure, were the same thing with you: when you counted nothing good but what pleased, nor any thing reasonable but what you got by; when you made a jest of a mind, and the pleasures of reflection, and elegantly placed your sole happiness, like the rest of the animal creation, in the gratifications of sense.

HOR. I did so. But in our last conversation, when walking upon the brow of this hill, and looking down on that broad, rapid river, and yon widely extended beautifully varied plain, you taught me another doctrine. You showed me that self-denial, which above all things I abhorred, was really the greatest good, and the highest self-gratification, and absolutely necessary to produce even my own darling sole good, pleasure.

PHIL. True, I told you that self-denial was never a duty but when it was a natural means of procuring more pleasure than we could taste without it; that as we all strongly desire to live, and to live only to enjoy, we should take as much care about our future as our present happiness, and not build one upon the ruins of the other: that we should look to the end, and regard consequences: and if, through want of attention, we had erred, and exceeded the bounds which nature had set us, we were then obliged, for our own sakes, to refrain or deny ourselves a present momentary pleasure for a future, constant, and durable good.

HOR. You have shown, Philocles, that self-denial, which weak or interested men have rendered the most forbidding, is really the most delightful and amiable, the most reasonable and pleasant thing in the world. In a word, if I understand you aright, self-denial is in truth, self-recognising, self-acknowledging, or self-owning. But now, my friend! you are to perform another promise, and show me the path which leads up to that constant, durable, and invariable good, which I have heard you so beautifully describe, and which you seem so fully to possess: Is not this good of yours a mere chimera? Can anything be constant in a world which is eternally changing and which appears to exist by an everlasting revolution of one thing into another, and where everything without us, and everything within us, is in perpetual motion? What is this constant, durable good then, of yours? Prithee, satisfy my soul, for I'm all on fire and impatient to enjoy her. Produce this eternal blooming Goddess with never-fading charms, and see whether I won't embrace her with as much eagerness and rapture as you.

PHIL. You seem enthusiastically warm, Horatio; I will wait till you are cool enough to attend to the sober, dispassionate voice of reason.

HOR. You mistake me, my dear Philocles! my warmth is not so great as to run away with my reason; it is only just raised enough to open my faculties and fit them to receive those eternal truths, and that durable good, which you so triumphantly boasted of. Begin, then; I'm prepared.

PHIL. I will. I believe, Horatio, with all your skepticism about you, you will allow that good to be constant which is never absent from you, and that to be durable, which never ends but with your being.

HOR. Yes, go on.

PHIL. That can never be the good of a creature, which, when present, the creature may be miserable, and when absent, is certainly so.

HOR. I think not; but pray explain what you mean; for I am not much used to this abstract way of reasoning.

PHIL. I mean all the pleasures of sense. The good of man cannot consist in the mere pleasures of sense; because, when any one of those objects which you love is absent, or can't be come at, you are certainly miserable; and if the faculty be impaired, though the object be present, you can't enjoy it. So that this sensual good depends upon a thousand things without and within you, and all out of your power. Can this then be the good of man? Say, Horatio! what think you, Is not this a chequered, fleeting, fantastical good? Can that, in any propriety of speech, be called the good of man which even, while he is tasting, he may be miserable, and which, when he cannot taste, he is necessarily so? Can that be our good, which costs us a great deal of pains to obtain; which cloys in possessing; for which we must wait the return of appetite before we can enjoy again? Or, is that our good which we can come at without difficulty; which is heightened by possession; which never ends in weariness and disappointment; and which, the more we enjoy, the better qualified we are to enjoy on?

HOR. The latter, I think; but why do you torment me thus? Philocles! show me this good immediately.

PHIL. I have showed you what it is not; it is not sensual, but it is rational and moral good. It is doing all the good we can to others, by acts of humanity, friendship, generosity, and benevolence. This is that constant and durable good, which will afford contentment and satisfaction always alike, without variation or diminution. I speak to your experience now, Horatio! Did you ever find yourself weary of relieving the miserable, or of raising the distressed into life or happiness? Or rather, don't you find the pleasure grow upon you by repetition, and that it is greater in the reflection than in the act itself? Is there a pleasure upon earth to be compared with that which arises from the sense of making others happy? Can this pleasure ever be absent, or ever end but with your being? Does it not always accompany you? Doth not it lie down and rise with you, live as long as you live, give you consolation in the article of death, and remain with you in that gloomy hour when all other things are going to forsake you, or you them?

HOR. How glowingly you paint, Philocles! Methinks Horatio is amongst the enthusiasts. I feel the passion: I am enchantingly convinced, but I don't know why; overborn by something stronger than reason. Sure some Divinity speaks within me; but prithee, Philocles, give me cooly the cause, why this rational and moral good so infinitely excels the mere natural or sensual.

PHIL. I think, Horatio, that I have clearly shown you the difference between merely natural or sensual good, and rational or moral good. Natural or sensual pleasure continues no longer than the action itself; but this divine or moral pleasure continues when the action is over, and swells and grows upon your hand by reflection. The one is inconstant, unsatisfying, of short duration, and attended with numberless ills; the other is constant, yields full satisfaction, is durable, and no evils preceding, accompanying, or following it. But, if you enquire further into the cause of this difference, and would know why the moral pleasures are greater than the sensual, perhaps the reason is the same as in all other creatures, that their happiness or chief good consists in acting up to their chief faculty, or that faculty which distinguishes them from all creatures of a different species. The chief faculty in a man is his reason; ad consequently his chief good, or that which may be justly called his good, consists not merely in action, but in reasonable action. By reasonable actions, we understand those actions which are preservative of the human kind, and naturally tend to produce real and unmixed happiness; and these actions, by way of distinction, we call actions morally good.

HOR. You speak very clearly, Philocles; but, that no difficulty may remain upon my mind, pray tell me what is the real difference between natural good and ill, and moral good and ill, for I know several people who use the terms without ideas.

PHIL. That may be. The difference lies only in this: that natural good and ill is pleasure and pain; moral good and ill is pleasure or pain produced with intention and design; for it is the intention only that makes the agent morally good or bad.

HOR. But may not a man, with a very good intention, do an ill action?

PHIL. Yes, but, then he errs in his judgment, though his design be good. If his error is inevitable, or such as, all things considered, he could not help, he is inculpable; but if it arose through want of diligence in forming his judgment about the nature of human actions, he is immoral and culpable.

HOR. I find, then, that in order to please ourselves rightly, or to do good to others morally, we should take great care of our opinions.

PHIL.　Nothing concerns you more; for, as the happiness or real good of men consists in right action, and right action cannot be produced without right opinion, it behoves us, above all things in this world, to take care that our opinions of things be according to the nature of things. The foundation of all virtue and happiness is thinking rightly. He who sees an action is right, that is, naturally tending to good, and does it because of that tendency, he only is a moral man; and he alone is capable of that constant, durable, and invariable good, which has been the subject of this conversation.

HOR.　How, my dear philosophical guide, shall I be able to know, and determine certainly, what is right and wrong in life?

PHIL.　As easily as you distinguish a circle from a square, or light from darkness. Look, Horatio, into the sacred book of nature; read your own nature, and view the relation which other men stand in to you, and you to them; and you'll immediately see what constitutes human happiness, and consequently what is right.

HOR.　We are just coming into town, and can say no more at present. You are my good genius, Philocles. You have shown me what is good. You have redeemed me from the slavery and misery of folly and vice, and made me a free and happy being.

PHIL.　Then I am the happiest man in the world. Be steady, Horatio! Never depart from reason and virtue.

HOR.　Sooner will I lose my existence. Good night, Philocles.

PHIL.　Adieu! dear Horatio!

POOR RICHARD'S ALMANAC (1733–58) *

Though modesty is a virtue, bashfulness is a vice.

Content is the philosopher's stone that turns all it touches into gold.

Many have quarrelled about religion that never practised it.

A lie stands on one leg, truth on two.

All mankind are beholden to him that is kind to the good.

Half the truth is often a great lie.

Observe all men: thyself most.

Trust thyself, and another shall not betray thee.

Pain wastes the body; pleasures, the understanding.

Eat to live, and not live to eat.

There are three things extremely hard, steel, a diamond, and to know one's self.

Death takes no bribes.

---

* Philadelphia: B. Franklin and D. Hall, 1757.

None preaches better than the ant, and she says nothing.

Diligence overcomes difficulties, sloth makes them.

The busy man has few idle visitors; to the boiling pot the flies come not.

Lost time is never found again.

Idleness is the greatest prodigality.

All things are cheap to the saving, dear to the wasteful.

Spare and have is better than spend and crave.

Keep thy shop, and thy shop will keep thee.

Death takes no bribes.

No gains without pains.

Well done is twice done.

Little strokes fell big oaks.

Early to bed and early to rise, Makes a man healthy, wealthy, and wise.

God helps them that helps themselves.

Happy's the wooing that's not long a doing.

Marry your son when you will, but your daughter when you can.

Haste makes waste.

He that has not got a wife, is not yet a complete man.

A penny saved is two pence clear.

To err is human, to repent divine; to persist devilish.

Well done is better than well said.

Love your neighbor; yet don't pull down your hedge.

Sin is not hurtful because it is forbidden, but it is forbidden because it is hurtful.

Friendship cannot live with ceremony, nor without civility.

AUTOBIOGRAPHY (1771–?)*

It was about this time I conceiv'd the bold and arduous project of arriving at moral perfection. I wish'd to live without committing any fault at any time; I would conquer all that either natural inclination, custom, or company might lead me into. As I knew, or thought I knew, what was right and wrong, I did not see why I might not always do the one and avoid the other. But I soon found I had undertaken a task of more difficulty than I had imagined. While my care was employ'd in guarding against one fault, I was often surprised by another; habit took the advantage of inattention; inclination was sometimes too strong for reason. I concluded, at length, that the mere speculative conviction that it was our

* Smyth, *Writings of Benjamin Franklin,* vol. 1, pp. 326–30.

interest to be completely virtuous, was not sufficient to prevent our slipping; and that the contrary habits must be broken, and good ones acquired and established, before we can have any dependence on a steady, uniform rectitude of conduct. For this purpose I therefore contrived the following method.

In the various enumerations of the moral virtues I had met with in my reading, I found the catalogue more or less numerous, as different writers included more or fewer ideas under the same name. Temperance, for example, was by some confined to eating and drinking, while by others it was extended to mean the moderating every other pleasure, appetite, inclination, or passion, bodily or mental, even to our avarice and ambition. I propos'd to myself, for the sake of clearness, to use rather more names, with fewer ideas annex'd to each, than a few names with more ideas; and I included under thirteen names of virtues all that at that time occurr'd to me as necessary or desirable, and annexed to each a short precept, which fully express'd the extent I gave to its meaning.

These names of virtues, with their precepts, were:

1. TEMPERANCE
Eat not to dullness; drink not to elevation.

2. SILENCE
Speak not but what may benefit others or yourself; avoid trifling conversation.

3. ORDER
Let all your things have their places; let each part of your business have its time.

4. RESOLUTION
Resolve to perform what you ought; perform without fail what you resolve.

5. FRUGALITY
Make no expense but to do good to others or yourself: i.e., waste nothing.

6. INDUSTRY
Lose no time; be always employ'd in something useful; cut off all unnecessary actions.

7. SINCERITY
Use no hurtful deceit; think innocently and justly, and, if you speak, speak accordingly.

8. JUSTICE
Wrong none by doing injuries, or omitting the benefits that are your duty.

9. MODERATION
Avoid extreams: forbear resenting injuries so much as you think they deserve.

10. CLEANLINESS

Tolerate no uncleanliness in body, cloaths, or habitation.

11. TRANQUILITY

Be not disturbed at trifles, or at accidents common or unavoidable.

12. CHASTITY

Rarely use venery but for health or offspring, never to dullness, weakness, or the injury of your own or another's peace or reputation.

13. HUMILITY

Imitate Jesus and Socrates.

My intention being to acquire the habitude of all these virtues, I judg'd it would be well not to distract my attention by attempting the whole at once, but to fix it on one of them at a time; and, when I should be master of that, then to proceed to another, and so on, till I should have gone thro' the thirteen; and, as the previous acquisition of some might facilitate the acquisition of certain others, I arrang'd them with that view, as they stand above. Temperance first, as it tends to procure that coolness and clearness of head, which is so necessary where constant vigilance was to be kept up, and guard maintained against the unremitting attraction of ancient habits, and the force of perpetual temptations. This being acquir'd and establish'd, Silence would be more easy; and my desire being to gain knowledge at the same time that I improv'd in virtue, and considering that in conversation it was obtain'd rather by the use of the ears than of the tongue, and therefore wishing to break a habit I was getting into of prattling, punning, and joking, which only made me acceptable to trifling company, I gave *Silence* the second place. This and the next, *Order,* I expected would allow me more time for attending to my project and my studies. *Resolution,* once become habitual, would keep me firm in my endeavors to obtain all the subsequent virtues: *Frugality* and Industry freeing me from my remaining debt, and producing affluence and independence, would make more easy the practice of Sincerity and Justice, etc., etc. Conceiving then, that, agreeably to the advice of Pythagoras in his Golden Verses, daily examination would be necessary, I contrived the following method for conducting that examination.

I made a little book, in which I allotted a page for each of the virtues. I rul'd each page with red ink, so as to have seven columns, one for each day of the week, marking each column with a letter for the day. I cross'd these columns with thirteen red lines, marking the beginning of each line with the first letter of one of the virtues, on which line, and in its proper column, I might mark, by a little black spot, every fault I found upon examination to have been committed respecting that virtue upon that day.

PROPOSALS RELATING TO THE EDUCATION OF YOUTH IN PENNSYLVANIA (1749)*

The good education of youth has been esteemed by wise men in all ages as the surest foundation of the happiness both of private families and of commonwealths. Almost all governments have therefore made it a principal object of their attention to establish and endow with proper revenues such seminaries of learning, as might supply the succeeding age with men qualified to serve the public with honor to themselves and to their country.

SPEECH IN THE PHILADELPHIA CONVENTION AT ITS FINAL SESSION (17 SEPTEMBER 1787)*

Thus I consent, Sir, to this constitution, because I expect no better, and because I am not sure that it is not the best. The opinions I have had of its errors I sacrifice to the public good . . .

. . . Much of the strength and efficiency of any government, in procuring and securing happiness to the people depends on *opinion,* on the general opinion of the goodness of that government, as well as of the wisdom and integrity of its governors. I hope, therefore, for our own sakes, as a part of the people, and for the sake of our posterity, that we shall all heartily and unanimously in recommending this constitution wherever our influence may extend, and turn our future thoughts and endeavors to the means of having it *well administered.*

PLAN FOR THE AMERICAN PHILOSOPHICAL ASSOCIATION: "A PROPOSAL FOR PROMOTING USEFUL KNOWLEDGE AMONG THE BRITISH PLANTATIONS IN AMERICA" (1743)*

The English are possessed of a long tract of continent, from Nova Scotia to Georgia, extending north and south through different climates, having different soils, producing different plants, mines, and minerals, and capable of different improvements, manufactures, etc.

The first drudgery of settling new colonies, which confines the attention of people to mere necessaries, is now pretty well over; and there are many in every province in circumstances that set them at ease, and afford leisure to cultivate the finer arts and improve the common stock of knowledge. To such of these who are men of speculation, many hints must from time to time arise, many observations occur, which, if well examined, pursued, and improved, might produce discoveries to the

---

* Ibid., vol. 2, p. 388.
* Ibid., vol. 9, pp. 608–9.
* Ibid., vol. 2, pp. 228–30.

advantage of some or all of the British plantations, or to the benefit of mankind in general.

But as from the extent of the country such persons are widely separated, and seldom can see and converse or be acquainted with each other, so that many useful particulars remain uncommunicated, die with the discoverers, and are lost to mankind; it is, to remedy this inconvenience for the future, proposed,

That one society be formed of *virtuosi* or ingenious men, residing in the several colonies, to be called *The American Philosophical Society,* who are to maintain a constant correspondence.

That Philadelphia, being the city nearest the center of the continent colonies, communicating with all of them northward and southward by post, and with all the islands by sea, and having the advantage of a good growing library, be the center of the society.

That at Philadelphia there be always at least seven members viz., a physician, a botanist, a mathematician, a chemist, a mechanician, a geographer, and a general natural philosopher besides a president, treasurer, and secretary.

That these members meet once a month, or oftener, at their own expense, to communicate to each other their observations and experiments, to receive, read, and consider such letters, communications, or queries as shall be sent from distant members; to direct the dispersing of copies of such communications as are valuable, to other distant members, in order to procure their sentiments thereupon.

That the subjects of the correspondence be: all new-discovered plants, herbs, trees, roots, their virtues, uses, etc.; methods of propagating them, and making such as are useful, but particular to some plantations, more general; improvements on vegetable juices, as ciders, wines, etc.; new methods of curing or preventing diseases; all new-discovered fossils in different countries, as mines, minerals, and quarries; new and useful improvements in any branch of mathematics; new discoveries in chemistry, such as improvements in distillation, brewing and assaying of ores: new mechanical inventions for saving labour, as mills and carriages, and for raising and conveying water, draining of meadows, etc.; all new arts trades, and manufactures, that may be proposed or thought of; surveys, maps and charts of particular parts of the seacoasts or inland countries; course and junction of rivers and great roads, situation of lakes and mountains, nature of the soil and produce many new methods of improving the breed of useful animals introducing other sorts from foreign countries; new improvements in planting, gardening, and clearing land; and all philsophical experiments that let light into the nature of things, tend to increase the power of man over matter, and multiply the conveniences or pleasures of life.

TO PETER COLLINSON, ON EXPERIMENTS AND THEORIES ON THE ELEMENTAL NATURE OF CLOUDS (SEPTEMBER 1753)*

I cannot forbear venturing some few conjectures on this occasion: They are what occur to me at present, and, though future discoveries should prove them not wholly right, yet they may in the meantime be of some use, by stirring up the curious to make more experiments, and occasion more exact disquisitions.

I conceive, then, that this globe of earth and water, with its plants, animals, and buildings, have diffused throughout their substance, a quantity of the electric fluid, just as much as they can contain, which I call the *natural quantity.*

That this natural quantity is not the same in all kinds of common matter under the same dimensions, nor in the same kind of common matter in all circumstances; but a solid foot for instance, of one kind of common matter may contain more of the electric fluid than a solid foot of some other kind of common matter; and a pound weight of the same kind of common matter may, when in a rarer state, contain more of the electric fluid than when in a denser state.

For the electric fluid, being attracted by any portion of common matter, the parts of that fluid (which have among themselves a mutual repulsion) are brought so near to each other by the attraction of the common matter that absorbs them, as that their repulsion is equal to the condensing power of attraction in common matter; and then such portion of common matter will absorb no more.

Bodies of different kinds, having thus attracted and absorbed what I call their *natural quantity,* i.e., just as much of the electric fluid as is suited to their circumstances of density, rarity, and power of attracting, do not then show any signs of electricity among each other.

And if more electric fluid be added to one of these bodies, it does not enter, but spreads on the surface, forming an atmosphere; and then such body shows signs of electricity.

I have in a former paper compared common matter to a sponge, and the electric fluid to water: I beg leave once more to make use of the same comparison, to illustrate further my meaning in this particular.

When a sponge is somewhat condensed by being squeezed between the fingers, it will not receive and retain so much water as when in its more loose and open state.

If *more* squeezed and condensed, some of the water will come out of its inner parts and flow on the surface.

If the pressure of the fingers be entirely removed, the sponge will not only resume what was lately forced out, but attract an additional quantity.

---

* Ibid., vol. 3, pp. 154–56.

As the sponge in its rarer state will *naturally* attract and absorb *more* water, and in its denser state will *naturally* attract and absorb *less* water, we may call the quantity it attracts and absorbs in either state its *natural quantity,* the state being considered.

Now what the sponge is to water, the same is water to the electric fluid.

When a portion of water is in its common dense state, it can hold no more electric fluid than it has; if any be added it spreads on the surface.

When the same portion of water is rarefied into vapor, and forms a cloud, it is then capable of receiving and absorbing a much greater quantity; there is room for each particle to have an electric atmosphere.

Thus water, in its rarefied state, or in the form of a cloud, will be in a negative state of electricity; it will have less than its *natural quantity;* that is, less than it is naturally capable of attracting and absorbing in that state.

Such a cloud, then, coming so near the earth as to be within striking distance, will receive from the earth a flash of the electric fluid; which flash, to supply a great extent of cloud, must sometimes contain a very great quantity of that fluid.

Or such a cloud, passing over woods of tall trees, may, from the points and sharp edges of their moist top leaves, receive silently some supply.

A cloud, being by any means supplied from the earth, may strike into other clouds that have not been supplied, or not so much supplied; and those to others, till an equilibrium is produced among all the clouds that are within striking distance of each other.

The cloud thus supplied, having parted with much of what it first received, may require and receive a fresh supply from the earth, or from some other cloud, which, by the wind, is brought into such a situation as to receive it more readily from the earth.

Hence repeated and continual strokes and flashes till the clouds have all got nearly their natural quantity as clouds, or till they have descended in showers, and are united again with this terraqueous globe, their original.

Thus thunderclouds are generally in a negative state of electricity compared with the earth, agreeable to most of our experiments.

THOMAS JEFFERSON

FIRST INAUGURAL (1891)*

THE ESSENTIAL PRINCIPLES OF THE AMERICAN GOVERNMENT

It is proper you should understand what I deem the essential principles of this government and consequently those which ought to shape its administration.

I will compress them in the narrowest compass they will bear, stating the general principle, but not all it's limitations.

Equal and exact justice to all men, of whatever state or persuasion, religious or political:

Peace, commerce, and honest friendship with all nations, entangling alliances with none:

The support of the State governments in all their rights, as the most competent administrations for our domestic concerns, and the surest bulwarks against anti republican tendencies:

The preservation of the General government, in it's whole constitutional vigor, as the sheet anchor of our peace at home, and safety abroad.

A jealous care of the right of election by the people, a mild and sage corrective of abuses, which are lopped by the sword of revolution, where peaceable remedies are unprovided.

---

* Paul L. Ford, ed., *Jefferson's Writings,* 10 vols. (New York: G. P. Putnam's, 1892), vol. 8, pp. 4–5.

LETTER TO P. S. DuPONT de NEMOURS (24 APRIL 1816)*

ON MAJORITIES AND MORALITY

I believe with you that morality, compassion, generosity, are innate elements of the human constitution; that there exists a right independent of force; that a right to property is founded in our natural wants, in the means with which we are endowed to satisfy these wants, and the right to what we acquire by those means without violating the similar rights of other sensible beings; that no one has a right to obstruct another, exercising his faculties innocently for the relief of sensibilities made a part of his nature; that justice is the fundamental law of society; that the majority, oppressing an individual, is guilty of a crime, abuses its strength, and by acting on the law of the strongest breaks up the foundations of society; that action by the citizens in person, in affairs within their reach and competence, and in all others by representatives, chosen immediately, and removable by themselves, constitutes the essence of a republic.

LETTER TO DAVID HUMPHREYS (18 MARCH 1789)*

ON CERTAIN RIGHTS

There are rights which it is useless to surrender to the government, and which governments have yet always been fond to invade. These are the rights of thinking, and publishing our thoughts by speaking or writing; the right of free commerce; the right of personal freedom.

LETTER TO GEORGE WYTHE (13 AUGUST 1786)*

ON PUBLIC EDUCATION

I think by far the most important bill in our whole code is that for the diffusion of knowledge among the people. No other sure foundation can be devised, for the reservation of freedom and happiness. . . . Preach, my dear Sir, a crusade against ignorance; establish & improve the law for educating the common people. Let our countrymen know that the people alone can protect us against these evils,[1] and that the tax which will be paid for this purpose is not more than the thousandth part of

---

* Ibid., vol. 10, p. 24.
* Ibid., vol. 5, pp. 89–90.
* Ibid., vol. 4, pp. 268–69.
* [1] The miseries of the common people of France at that time.

what will be paid to kings, priests & nobles who will rise up among us if we leave the people in ignorance.

FROM THE BILL ESTABLISHING RELIGIOUS FREEDOM INTRODUCED BY JEFFERSON IN THE VIRGINIA LEGISLATURE (13 JUNE 1779)*

SECTION I. Well aware that the opinions and belief of men depend on their own will, but follow involuntarily the evidence proposed to their minds; that Almighty God hath created the mind free, and manifested his supreme will that free it shall remain by making it altogether insusceptible of restraint; that all attempts to influence it by temporal punishments, or burthens, or by civil incapacitations, tend only to beget habits of hypocrisy and meanness and are a departure from the plan of the holy author of our religion, who being lord both of body and mind, yet choose not to propagate it by coercions on either, as was in his Almighty power to do, but to exalt it by its influence on reason alone.

SECTION II. We the General Assembly of Virginia do enact that no man shall be compelled to frequent or support any religious worship, place, or ministry whatsoever, nor shall be enforced, restrained, molested, or burthened in his body or goods, or shall otherwise suffer, on account of his religious opinions or belief; but that all men shall be free to profess, and by argument to maintain, their opinions in matters of religion, and that the same shall in no wise diminish, enlarge, or affect their civil capacities.

LETTER TO EDWARD CARRINGTON (16 JANUARY 1787)*

. . . The tumults in America, I expected would have produced in Europe an unfavorable opinion of our political state. But it has not. On the contrary, the small effect of those tumults seems to have given more confidence in the firmness of our governments. The interposition of the people themselves on the side of government has had a great effect on the opinion here. I am persuaded myself that the good sense of the people will always be found to be the best army. They may be led astray for a moment, but will soon correct themselves. The people are the only censors

* Ibid., vol. 2, pp. 238–39.
* P. S. Foner, ed., *The Basic Writings of Thomas Jefferson* (New York: Wiley Book Co., 1944), pp. 549–50.

of their governors: and even their errors will tend to keep these to the true principles of their institution. To punish these errors too severely would be to suppress the only safeguard of the public liberty. The way to prevent these irregular interpositions of the people is to give them full information of their affairs thro' the channel of the public papers, and to contrive that those papers should penetrate the whole mass of the people. The basis of our governments being the opinion of the people, the very first object should be to keep that right; and were it left to me to decide whether we should have a government without newspapers, or newspapers without a government, I should not hesitate a moment to prefer the latter. But I should mean that every man should receive those papers and be capable of reading them. I am convinced that those societies (as the Indians) which live without government enjoy in their general mass an infinitely greater degree of happiness than those who live under European governments. Among the former, public opinion is in the place of law, and restrains morals as powerfully as laws ever did any where. Among the latter, under pretence of governing they have divided their nations into two classes, wolves and sheep. I do not exaggerate. This is a true picture of Europe. Cherish therefore the spirit of our people, and keep alive their attention. Do not be too severe upon their errors, but reclaim them by enlightening them. If once they become inattentive to the public affairs, you and I, and Congress, and Assemblies, judges and governors shall all become wolves. It seems to be the law of our general nature, in spite of individual exceptions; and experience declares that man is the only animal which devours his own kind, for I can apply no milder term to the governments of Europe, and to the general prey of the rich on the poor.

LETTER TO PETER CARR (10 AUGUST 1787)*

Moral philosophy. I think it lost time to attend lectures in this branch. He who made us would have been a pitiful bungler if he had made the rules of our moral conduct a matter of science. For one man of science, there are thousands who are not. What would have become of them? Man was destined for society. His morality therefore was to be formed to this object. He was endowed with a sense of right and wrong merely relative to this. This sense is as much a part of his nature as the sense of hearing, seeing, feeling; it is the true foundation of morality, and not the το χαλον truth, &c., as fanciful writers have imagined. The moral sense, or conscience, is as much a part of man as is leg or arm. It is given to all human beings in a stronger or weaker degree, as force of members is given them in a greater or less degree. It may be strengthened by exercise, as may any particular limb of the body. This sense is submitted

---

* Ibid., pp. 549–50.

indeed in some degree to the guidance of reason; but it is a small stock which is required for this: even a less one than what we call Common sense. State a moral case to a ploughman and a professor. The former will decide it as well, and often better than the latter, because he has not been led astray by artificial rules.

LETTER TO THOMAS LAW (13 JUNE 1814)*

The want or imperfection of the moral sense in some men, like the want or imperfection of the senses of sight and hearing in others, is not proof that it is a general characteristic of the species. When it is wanting, we endeavor to supply the defect by education, by appeals to reason and calculation, by presenting to the being so unhappily conformed, other motives to do good and to eschew evil, such as the love, or the hatred, or rejection of those among whom he lives, and whose society is necessary to his happiness and even existence; demonstrations by sound calculation that honesty promotes interest in the long run; the rewards and penalties established by the laws; and ultimately the prospects of a future state of retribution for the evil as well as the good done while here. These are the correctives which are supplied by education, and which exercise the functions of the moralist, the preacher, and legislator; and they lead into a course of correct action all those whose disparity is not too profound to be eradicated. Some have argued against the existence of a moral sense, by saying that if nature had given us such a sense, impelling us to virtuous actions, and warning us against those which are vicious, then nature would also have designated, by some particular ear-marks, the two sets of actions which are, in themselves, the one virtuous and the other vicious. Whereas, we find, in fact, that the same actions are deemed virtuous in one country and vicious in another. The answer is, that nature has constituted *utility* to man, the standard and test of virtue. Men living in different countries, under different circumstances, different habits and regiments, may have different utilities; the same act, therefore, may be useful, and consequently virtuous in one country which is injurious and vicious in another differently circumstanced. I sincerly, then, believe with you in the general existence of a moral instinct. I think it the brightest gem with which the human character is studded, and the want of it as more degrading than the most hideous of the bodily deformities.

---

* A. E. Bergh, ed., *The Writings of Thomas Jefferson,* 20 vols. (Washington, D.C.: Thomas Jefferson Memorial Assoc., 1904), vol. 14, pp. 142–43.

LETTER TO JAMES MADISON
(30 JANUARY 1787)*

Societies exist under three forms sufficiently distinguishable. 1. Without government, as among our Indians. 2. Under governments wherein the will of every one has a just influence, as is the case in England in a slight degree, and in our states in a great one. 3. Under governments of force: as is the case in all other monarchies and in most of the other republics. To have an idea of the curse of existence under these last, they must be seen. It is a government of wolves over sheep. It is a problem, not clear in my mind, that the 1st. condition is not the best. But I believe it to be inconsistent with any great degree of population. The second state has a great deal of good in it. The mass of mankind under that enjoys a precious degree of liberty and happiness. It has it's evils too: the principal of which is the turbulence to which it is subject. But weigh this against the oppressions of monarchy, and it becomes nothing. *Malo periculosam, libertatem quam quietam servitutem.* Even this evil is productive of good. It prevents the degeneracy of government, and nourishes a general attention to the public affairs. I hold it that a little rebellion now and then is a good thing, and as necessary in the political world as storms in the physical.

THE DECLARATION OF INDEPENDENCE
(4 JULY 1776)*

When in the course of human events it becomes necessary for one people to dissolve the political bands which have connected them with another, and to assume among the powers of the earth, the separate and equal station to which the laws of Nature and of Nature's God entitle them, a decent respect to the opinions of mankind requires that they should declare the causes which impel them to the separation. We hold these truths to be self-evident, that all men are created equal, that they are endowed by their Creator with certain inalienable Rights, that among these are life, liberty and the pursuit of happiness. That to secure these rights, governments are instituted among men, deriving their just powers from the consent of the governed, that whenever any form of government becomes destructive of these ends, it is the right of the people to alter or to abolish it, and to institute new government, laying its foundation on such principles and organizing its powers in such form, as to them shall seem most likely to effect their safety and happiness. Prudence, indeed, will dictate that governments long established should not be changed for light and transient causes; and accordingly all experience hath shown that mankind are more disposed to suffer, while evils are sufferable,

* Foner, *Basic Writings,* p. 551.

than to right themselves by abolishing the forms to which they are accustomed. But when a long train of abuses and usurpations, pursuing invariably the same object evinces a design to reduce them under absolute despotism, it is their right, it is their duty, to throw off such government, and to provide new guards for their future security.

REFLECTIONS ON THE ARTICLES OF CONFEDERATION.*

ON THE DISTINCTION BETWEEN NATURAL AND CIVIL RIGHTS

Suppose twenty persons, strangers to each other, to meet in a country not before inhabited. Each would be a sovereign in his own natural right. His will would be his law, but his power, in many cases, inadequate to his right, and the consequence would be that each might be exposed, not only to each other but to the other nineteen.

It would then occur to them that their condition would be much improved, if a way could be devised to exchange that quantity of danger into so much protection, so that each individual should possess the strength of the whole number. As all their rights, in the first case are natural rights, and the exercise of those rights supported only by their own natural individual power, they would begin by distinguishing between those rights they could individually exercise fully and perfectly and those they could not.

Of the first kind are the rights of thinking, speaking, forming and giving opinions, and perhaps all those which can be fully exercised by the individual without the aid of exterior assistance—or in other words, rights of personal competency. Of the second kind are those of personal protection, of acquiring and possessing property, in the exercise of which the individual natural power is less than the natural right.

Having drawn this line they agree to retain individually the first class of rights or those of personal competency; and to detach from their personal possession the second class, or those of defective power and to accept in lieu thereof a right to the whole power produced by a condensation of all the parts. These I conceive to be civil rights or rights of compact, and are distinguishable from natural rights, because in the one we act wholly in our own person, in the other we agree not to do so, but act under the guarantee of society.

. . . God forbid we should ever be twenty years without such a rebellion. The people cannot be all, and always, well-informed. The part which is wrong will be discontented in proportion to the importance of the facts they misconceive. If they remain quiet under such misconceptions it is a lethargy, the forerunner of death to the public liberty. We have

* G. Chinard, *Thomas Jefferson* (Boston: Little, Brown, 1929), pp. 80–81.

had 13 states independent 11 years. There has been one rebellion. That comes to one rebellion in a century and a half for each state. What country before ever existed a century and a half without a rebellion? and what country can preserve its liberties if their rulers are not warned from time to time that their people preserve the spirit of resistance?

LETTER TO JOHN ADAMS (11 APRIL 1823)*

Indeed, I think that every Christian sect gives a great handle to atheism by their general dogma, that, without a revelation, there would not be sufficient proof of the being of a God. Now one-sixth of mankind only are supposed to be Christians: the other five-sixths then, who do not believe in the Jewish and Christian revelation, are without a knowledge of the existence of a God! This gives completely a *gain de cause* to the disciples of Ocellus, Timaeus, Spinoza, Diderot, and D'Holbach. The argument which they rest on as triumphant and unanswerable is, that in every hypothesis of cosmogony, you must admit an eternal pre-existence of something; and according to the rule of sound philosophy you are never to employ two principles to solve a difficulty when one will suffice. They say then, that it is more simple to believe at once in the eternal pre-existence of the world, as it is now going on, and may forever go on by the principle of reproduction which we see and witness, than to believe in the eternal pre-existence of an ulterior cause, or creator of the world, a being whom we see not and know not, of whose form, substance and mode, or place of existence, or of action, no sense informs us, no power of the mind enables us to delineate or comprehend. On the contrary, I hold (without appeal to revelation) that when we take a view of the universe, in its parts, general or particular, it is impossible for the human mind not to perceive and feel a conviction of design, consummate skill, and indefinite power in every atom of its composition. . . .

. . . We see, too, evident proofs of the necessity of a superintending power, to maintain the universe in its course and order. Stars, well known, have disappeared, new ones have come into view; comets, in their incalculable courses, may run foul of suns and planets, and require renovation under other laws, certain races of animals are become extinct; and were there no restoring power, all existences might extinguish successively, one by one, until all should be reduced to a shapeless chaos. So irresistible are these evidences of an intelligent and powerful agent, that, of the infinite numbers of men who have existed through all time, they have believed, in the proportion of a million at least to unit, in the hypothesis of an external pre-existence of a creator, rather than in that of a self-existent universe.

---

* Bergh, *Writings,* vol. 15, pp. 425–27.

STUDY QUESTIONS

Review

1. What is deism? How did it influence the Enlightenment thinkers?
2. Compare the Puritan theory of church covenant with the social-contract theory of government.
3. Compare the Puritan view of nature and of the good with that of the Enlightenment thinkers. Give an example from Benjamin Franklin's works.
4. How did Jefferson's belief in the innate goodness and rationality of men influence his social philosophy?
5. Describe the reaction to the Enlightenment.

For Further Thought

6. If you believe that God exists, how would your views differ (if they would) from those of the deists with regard to the relation of God to nature and men.
7. What do you think of ''happiness'' as a moral standard?
8. Do you think there are such things as ''natural rights''? How would you argue that there are? In other words, how would you try to convince a disbeliever that we do have certain rights such as the rights to life, liberty, or the pursuit of happiness?

BIBLIOGRAPHY

General

Becker, Carl L. *The Heavenly City of Eighteenth Century Philosophers.* New York: Harcourt, Brace, 1922.

Blau, Joseph L. *Men and Movements in American Philosophy,* pp. 36–109. Englewood Cliffs, N. J.: Prentice-Hall, Inc., 1952.

Coleman, F. M. *Hobbes and America: Exploring the Constitutional Foundations.* Toronto: University of Toronot Press, 1977.

Hibben, John G. *The Philosophy of the Enlightenment.* New York: Charles Scribner's, 1910.

Hindle, Brooke. *The Pursuit of Science in Revolutionary America.* Chapel Hill: University of North Carolina Press, 1927.

Koch, Adrienne. *Power, Morals, and the Founding Fathers: Essays in Interpretation of the American Enlightenment.* Ithaca, N. Y. Cornell University Press, 1961.

– – –. ''Pragmatic Wisdom and the American Enlightenment,'' *William and Mary Quarterly* 18 (October 1961): pp. 313–29.

Koch, G. Adolf. *Republican Religion: The American Revolution and the Cult of Reason.* New York: Henry Holt, 1933.

Konvitz, Milton. *The Constitution and Civil Rights.* New York: Columbia University Press, 1947.

Lokken, Roy N. ''The Concept of Democracy in Colonial Political Thought'' *William and Mary Quarterly* (October 1959): pp.

MacIver, R. M. "The Philosophical Background of the Constitution." *Journal of Social Philosophy* 3 (1937-38): pp. 201-9.

Madison, Charles A. "Anarchism in the United States." *Journal of the History of Ideas* 6 (January 1945): pp. 46-66.

Moras, Herbert M. *Deism in Eighteenth Century America.* New York: Columbia University Press, 1934.

Padover, Saul K., ed. *The World of the Founding Fathers: Their Basic Ideas on Freedom and Self-Government.* New York: 1960.

Rossiter, Clinton. *Seedtime of the Republic: The Origin of the American Tradition of Political Liberty.* New York: 1953.

Schneider, Herbert W. *A History of American Philosophy.* Harcourt, Brace, 2d ed. New York: Columbia University Press, 1963.

Benjamin Franklin

Franklin, Benjamin. *The Autobiography of Benjamin Franklin.* Ed. J. A. May et al. Norton Critical Editions series. New York: Norton, 1983.

— — —. *Benjamin Franklin: The Autobiography and Other Writings.* Ed. Peter Shaw. New York: Bantam Press, 1982.

— — —. *The Autobiography of Benjamin Franklin.* Ed. R. Jackson Wilson. New York: Random House, 1981.

— — —. *Benjamin Franklin: Autobiography and Selected Writings.* New York: Modern Library, 1981.

— — —. *The Papers of Benjamin Franklin.* Ed. Leonard W. Labaree et al. 7 vols., 1706-58. New Haven: Yale University Press, 1959-

— — —. *A Benjamin Franklin Reader.* Ed. Nathan G. Goodman. New York: Thomas Y. Crowell, 1945.

— — —. *Benjamin Franklin: Representative Selections, with Introduction, Bibliography, and Notes.* Ed. Frank L. Mott and Chester E. Jorgenson. New York: American, 1936.

— — —. *The Writings of Benjamin Franklin.* Ed. Albert H. Smyth. 10 vols. New York: Macmillan, 1905-7.

Aldridge, Alfred O. *Benjamin Franklin and Nature's God.* Durham, N. C.: Duke University Press, 1967.

Amacher, Richard E. *Benjamin Franklin,* New Haven: New College University Press, 1962.

Becker, Carl L. Benjamin Franklin. Ithaca, N. Y.: Cornell University Press, 1946.

Clark, Ronald W. *Benjamin Franklin: A Biography.* New York: Random House, 1983.

Cohen, I. Bernard. *Benjamin Franklin: Scientist and Statesman.* New York: Scribner's, 1975.

— — —. *Franklin and Newton: An Inquiry into Speculative Newtonian Experimental Science and Franklin's Work in Electricity as an Example Thereof.* Philadelphia: American Philosophical Society, 1956.

— — —. *Benjamin Franklin: His Contributions to the American Tradition.* Indianapolis: Bobbs Merrill Co., 1953.

Heilbron, John L. *Electricity in the Seventeenth and Eighteenth Centuries: A Study of Early Modern Physics.* Berkeley: University of California Press, 1979.

Jacobs, Wilbur R. *Benjamin Franklin: Statesman, Philosopher, or Materialist?*Melbourne, Fla.: Krieger Press, 1976.

Koch, Adrienne. "Franklin and Pragmatic Wisdom." In *Power, Morals, and the Founding Fathers*. Ithaca, N. Y.: Cornell University Press, 1961.

Parton, James. *Life and Times of Benjamin Franklin*. 2 vols. New York, 1865.

Rossiter, Clinton. "The Political Theory of Benjamin Franklin." *Pennsylvania Magazine of History and Biography,* July 1952.

Schneider, H. W. "The Significance of Benjamin Franklin's Moral Philosophy." In *Studies in the History of Ideas*. Vol. 2, pp. 293-312. New York: Columbia University Press, 1925.

Stourzh, G. "Reason and Power in Benjamin Franklin's Political Thought." *American Political Science Review* 47 (December 1953): pp. 1092-115.

Van Doren, Carl. *Benjamin Franklin*. New York: Viking Press, 1938. Reprint. Westport, Conn.: Greenwood, 1973.

Thomas Jefferson

Jefferson, Thomas. *The Portable Thomas Jefferson*. Ed. Merrill D. Peterson. New York: Viking Press, 1975.

– – –. *Basic Writings of Thomas Jefferson*. Ed. Philip S. Foner. New York: Wiley Book Co., 1944.

– – –. *The Complete Jefferson*. Ed. Saul K. Padover. New York: Duell, Sloan, and Pearce, 1943.

– – –. *Jeffersonian Principles: Extracts from the Writings of Thomas Jefferson*. Ed. James T. Adams. Boston: Little, Brown, 1928.

– – –. *The Writings of Thomas Jefferson*. Ed. A. Bergh. 20 vols. Washington, D. C.: Thomas Jefferson Memorial Assn., 1903.

– – –. *The Writings of Thomas Jefferson*. Ed. Paul L. Ford. 10 vols. New York: G. P. Putnam, 1892-99.

Admas, W. Howard. *The Eye of Thomas Jefferson*. 1976. Reprint. Charlottesville: University Press of Virginia, 1981.

Banning, Lance. *The Jefferson Persuasion: Evolution of a Party Ideology*. Ithaca, N. Y.: Cornell University Press, 1978.

Becker, Carl L. *Declaration of Independence: A Study in the History of Political Ideas*. New York: Random House, 1958.

Boltorff, Wm. K. *Thomas Jefferson*. Boston: G. K. Hall, 1979.

Boorstein, Daniel J. *The Lost World of Thomas Jefferson*. Chicago: University of Chicago Press, 1981.

Chinard, Gilbert. *Thomas Jefferson: The Apostle of Americanism*. University of Michigan Press, 1939; rev. ed., 1957.

Cohen, I. Bernard, ed. *Thomas Jefferson and the Sciences: An Original Anthology*. Salem, N. Y.: Ayer Publishing Co., 1980.

Commager, Henry S. *Jefferson, Nature, and the Enlightenment: Spread of the Enlightenment from Old World to New*. New York: Braziller, 1975.

Dewey, John. *The Living Thoughts of Thomas Jefferson*. 1941. Reprint. Century Press, 1982.

Koch, Adrienne. *The Philosophy of Thomas Jefferson*. New York: Columbia University Press, 1943.

Lehmann-Hartleben, Karl. *Thomas Jefferson: American Humanist.* New York: Macmillan, 1947.

Malone, Dumas. *Jefferson and the Ordeal of Liberty.* Boston: Little, Brown, 1962.

— — —. *Jefferson and the Rights of Man.* Boston: Little, Brown, 1951.

Mansfield, Harvey C., Jr., ed. *Thomas Jefferson: Selected Writings.* Arlington Heights, Ill.: Harlan Davidson Press, 1979.

Padover, Saul K. *Jefferson.* Rev. and abr. ed. New York: New American Library, 1952.

Peterson, Merrill D. *The Jefferson Image in the American Mind.* New York: Oxford University Press, 1960.

Randall, H. S. *Life of Thomas Jefferson.* New York: Derby and Jackson, 1958.

Schachner, Nathan. *Thomas Jefferson.* New York: Appleton-Century-Crofts, 1951.

Chapter 3

Transcendentalism

For some Americans the Enlightenment had been a liberating influence because of its emphasis on the benevolence of God and the natural goodness and rights of man. For others, however, the Enlightenment appeared theologically dangerous and philosophically irresponsible. Meanwhile, yet another reaction to the Enlightenment was surfacing, but one with a different spirit — transcendentalism. Transcendentalism first appeared as a development within the Unitarian or liberal left wing of the Protestant Congregationalist church. The ministers who initiated the movement had a mixed reaction to the heritage of the Enlightenment. On the one hand they were inspired by the secular morality, the natural religion, and the aura of disciplined rationality that characterized the Enlightenment at its best. On the other hand these ministers generally found Enlightened religion too cold and impersonal, Enlightened ethics and politics too materialistic, and the prevailing scientific view of nature too confining. However, these liberal ministers also opposed the dogmatism and system building that characterized the orthodox ecclesiastical reaction to the Enlightenment. In its place they substituted an idealistic romanticism of an individualistic and naturalistic variety.

To the degree that one can date the origin of any movement, one can pinpoint the beginning of the transcendentalist movement on the date of the first meeting of the so-called Transcendental or Hedge Club in the Boston study of George Ripley on 19 September 1836. Disappointed at the dullness of a Harvard bicentennial address, Ripley, Henry Hedge, and Ralph Waldo Emerson decided to meet by themselves. Their discussions continued for seven or eight years, every time Hedge came to town. They wanted, as they said, to "see how far it would be possible for earnest minds to meet." If their minds were earnest they were also diverse, as were their ideas on the new views in philosophy, theology, and literature. At times their group also included William Ellery Channing, Theodore Parker, Henry David Thoreau, Bronson Alcott, Orestes Brownson, and Margaret Fuller. They worked together editing a critical journal, the *Dial*, which collapsed because of financial problems after four years, and they established Brook Farm — a commune to promote human culture, wisdom, justice, and love. Brook Farm failed, some said, because their free spirits would not easily be organized in the way required to run the farm. Some of the minister participants of the group remained within Unitarianism, others became secular preachers. Orestes Brownson founded a school for creative education. Margaret Fuller foreshadowed contemporary women's views by her belief that a woman's best friends were to be found among other women and that man would not find his fulfillment until woman found hers. Many in the group were also strong abolitionists.

The transcendentalists fashioned a new, distinctively American, stream of thought with ideas flowing from such diverse sources as Platonism, the English Romantic poets, and German idealism. According to the Platonic tradition, the universe is the expression of mind and is ruled by moral laws. True reality, identified with the good and the one, is known by a type of mystical vision or insight. The transcendentalists also found inspiration in the English Romantic poets Wordsworth and Coleridge, especially in the latter's *Aids to Reflection* which was published in the United States in 1829. In his introduction to this edition, Adam Marsh noted that knowledge was to be found through reflection on the "inward consciousness," and that what each found within his own self would be identical with the intuition of others. Coleridge had been influenced by the German idealist, Schelling, who wrote that we possess an active, creative kind of immediate knowledge — esthetic intuition — that coincides with the active principle within nature. Because of this immediate relation to the active principle within nature, Schelling held that each individual consciousness could possess the truth directly. Nature known through sense experience was indirect and often deceptive. Coleridge believed himself to be following Kant when he made his distinction between scientific knowledge (understanding) and feeling knowledge (reason), the latter being primary; the transcendentalists agreed with Coleridge's view. The word "transcendental" itself and the transcendental method was derived from Kant, but with a sense that was not Kant's. For Kant the transcendental method was the search for the conditions of knowledge, elements of the mind itself that we bring to experience. Kant, in fact, argued that any attempt to extend human reason beyond the limits of possible experience leads only to error and delusion. The transcendentalists, on the other hand, applied the term to all nonexperiential thought or "whatever belongs to the class of intuitive thought." [1]

What then is transcendentalism? It is a philosophical method, mood, and temper. The transcendentalists were not technical philosophers. Their writings are short on argument and long on poetry and sentiment. Nevertheless, three basic themes run through their writings — the divinity of nature, the worth of the individual person, and the capacity of each person to know the truth directly. The nature they worshipped was not the machine world of Newtonian quantitative physics, dark, cold, and impersonal. It was a qualitatively alive world, full of novelty, growth, and surprises. Like man, it too possessed soul; in fact nature was the symbol and expression of the one divine spirit that pervades all things. This spirit is within man as an immanent principle of both being and knowledge. Each person, they believed, has within him and is a spark of the divine. This was the basis for their doctrine of self-trust. However, no attempt was made to explain how all could be one while, at the same time, individuals could remain truly distinct from one another and from the one. Each person possessed divine intuitive powers. Through the exercise of these powers the individual was thought to be able to know nature, not as a collection of facts fragmented by sensation and then reassembled by science, but through a poetic, creative knowledge of nature's underlying conformity to the powers of the mind. Such knowledge transcends sense experience.

The transcendentalists sought to transcend anything that would restrict free, intuitive, individual thought — institutions, tradition, and conventional morality. They were antislavery, anti-imperialist, antibureaucratic, and anticultural, but they were also cultivated persons with cultured tastes. While they lauded the abilities of the common people, they associated mostly with their own type and wrote critically of the crowd mentality. Society may promote individual development, but whenever society proves to be a barrier, then it must be shunned. In spite of their advice to each man to read the spirit within himself and nature as he saw it, the transcendentalists did read the classics. A critical retrospective can readily highlight the philosophical limitations and sentimental excesses of this movement. Nevertheless, transcendentalism represents a unique and influential movement in the history of American philosophy. In the selections from Emerson and Thoreau here included, one can glimpse something of the spirit animating the movement they led.

RALPH WALDO EMERSON (1803–82)

Ralph Waldo Emerson was born in Boston on 25 May 1803 into a respected upper-class family of several generations of Protestant clergymen. His father died when he was young, leaving the family with good name but poor finances. Nevertheless, young Emerson attended Boston Latin School and then graduated from Harvard in 1821, after a rather undistinguished academic career. He attended some classes at Harvard Divinity School and, though he never completed the course of studies, was invited to be minister of Old North Church in Boston in 1829. In the same year he married a young woman who died two years later, leaving him much depressed but with a small inheritance from her family. Though the church to which he ministered was on the liberal side of Congregationalism —

a Unitarian church — Emerson was too unorthodox for even this parish and resigned after only one year. This personal loss and professional failure precipitated a crisis from which he sought relief by traveling to Europe where he hoped to meet some of his idols such as Wordsworth, Coleridge, and Carlyle. The ocean trip itself proved more important than any travel or meetings in England. At sea Emerson found the solitude and serenity for philosophical reflection. He pondered the belief that God is to be found in the depth of the soul, an inner presence conferring on the individual an inestimable dignity, worth, and power.

On his return to the United States, he remarried, settled in Concord, and became a lecturer popular not only in New England but also in the mid-Atlantic states and the Middle West. He was associated with the *Dial* and the Transcendental Club, but refused to join the experimental Brook Farm commune. When the proslavery Fugitive Slave Law began to be enforced in Massachusetts, Emerson actively associated himself with the cause of abolition. He entertained John Brown in his home and spoke out strongly in his defense after Harper's Ferry. When Emersom died at the age of seventy-nine in 1882, the townspeople of Concord held a funeral for him where he was eulogized as a poet and seer.

Emerson never extolled logical consistency; he wrote that one must not hold to doctrines held yesterday simply because one held them yesterday. In spite of this evaluation, his own thought exhibits an underlying unity and consistency. His first essay or pamphlet, "Nature," published anonymously in 1836, was not well received. In it Emerson wrote that nature is known best not by the passive observer, but by the person who goes out to meet it as a lover. We can feel a sympathy with nature because we have moods similar to its moods. Emerson himself experienced a mystic oneness with nature, an experience in which he felt himself "part and parcel of God." [2] However, he believed that nature serves a variety of functions — commodity, beauty, language, and discipline — each function more spiritual than the former one. As commodity, nature provides us with food, clothing, and shelter. It also serves to delight us by its natural forms, as well as by the intelligible order and creativity it manifests. Furthermore, we use natural terms or words to express moral and intellectual facts. Natural facts themselves symbolize spiritual facts; we speak of firmness of character as the firmness of rocks, for example. Finally, Emerson believed that nature is a discipline for our minds and souls. It teaches us such intellectual truths as likeness and difference, as well as moral laws. As common sense views it, nature is concrete and material. But our senses are not accurate and cannot be trusted: there is as much or more of a basis for seeing the world as ideal, as the projection of a world mind, than as seeing it as concrete and material. However, the appearances remain the same regardless of which interpretation is taken. Amidst the variety, there is a hidden unity, for the variety is a manifold projection of one spirit. This vision of an underlying unity was presented as something to be seen with the eyes of the mind — the transcendental faculty.

Emerson did not rely on technical formulations or sustained arguments to elaborate and support this vision.

Much the same thesis is presented in Emerson's essay "The Transcendentalist." [3] In it he defines transcendentalism as idealism — a way of regarding will, thought, inspiration, and miracle as the real — in opposition to what the materialist takes as real, namely, fact, history, animal wants, and force of circumstances. If mind and will are basic, then people are not slaves of circumstances but can recreate them. In his essay "The Oversoul," Emerson writes in much the same vein. "Man is a stream whose source is hidden." The universe is at base a *uni*-verse, one, an expression or projection of one soul that works itself out in time and shows itself in the variety of natural, social, and cultural phenomena.

These metaphysical doctrines were also the basis for Emerson's ethical views. His "American Scholar" address delivered at Harvard in 1837 was well received, unlike his book of the previous year. In the address he spoke of the functionalism he saw about him.[4] There are, he contended, no whole men, but only amputated parts strutting about. The scholar is the amputated head, a mere thinker, or worse, a parrot of the thinking of others. A true scholar needs to live and experience as well as to think. Why go to books and authors who are dead, for they present but one point of view of the universal mind and are not sufficient food for all time. Emerson advised his hearers each to rely on his own experience and to walk with his own feet. This advice was also given in his essay "Self-Reliance," published in 1841.[5] Believe in yourself, have confidence in your own thoughts; to imitate others is to commit suicide. Since you share the life by which all natural things exist, why do you now act as if you did not know the meaning of nature, he asks. This essay probably contains the most recognizable Emerson quotations, among them: "Whoso would be a man must be a non-conformist," and "A foolish consistency is the hobgoblin of little minds." [6]

In 1838 Emerson delivered an address before the senior graduating class of Harvard Divinity School. The clergymen and officers of the school found this lecture so objectionable that Emerson was not invited back to lecture at Harvard for thirty years. In this provocative lecture, he criticized the ministry and even disputed the thesis that Christianity is unique. The essence of religion, he claimed, is the moral sentiment that manifests itself in love, temperance, and justice and that was preached and revealed in India, Egypt, and China, as well as in Palestine. Emerson, eschewing authorities, advised the young ministerial students to preach out of their own hearts rather than rely on tradition. This spirit is the basis for his opposition to any institution on which men would rely in place of their own intuition and initiative. The state, for example, is but the work of man and thus imperfect. If men were true individuals and wise, a state would not be needed. In fact, in preview of Thoreau's "Civil Disobedience," Emerson wrote that the less government the better. "The appearance of character makes the state unnecessary." [7]

Emerson lived through the slavery debate, the Mexican War, and the Civil War and its aftermath. It is reported that he often took long walks in the woods around Walden Pond to regain his faith in the goodness of the universe. In this he is also reminiscent of Thoreau.

HENRY DAVID THOREAU (1817–72)

Henry David Thoreau was born in Concord, Massachusetts in 1817 to a middle class working family. He attended Harvard College where he was a classics major, read widely, and was interested in Eastern thought as is evidenced by his collection of oriental scriptures. For a short time he taught at Concord's town school and then, with his brother, in a private academy. In 1841, he took up residence at Emerson's home. He had been attracted to Emerson in spirit and by hearing his ''American Scholar'' address. He worked as a handyman for Emerson and also did some surveying and pencil making. By 1842, some of Thoreau's essays were published in the transcendentalist journal, the *Dial*. However, in 1845 he retreated to Walden Pond in the hope of eventually establishing himself as a writer and poet. There, on a plot of ground belonging to Emerson, Thoreau built a house and lived alone until 1847. His first purpose in going to Walden, he wrote, was to get in touch with nature, with the basic facts of life, with life's essence, so that when he died he might not find out that he had not lived.[8] While there he wrote his reflections on a river trip made with his brother, *A Week on the Concord and Merrimack Rivers;* but the work was so filled with scholarly allusions that it was not well received. Also while at the pond Thoreau scrawled out the first draft of his book *Walden*.[9] His life at the pond was not that of a complete recluse, for he had visitors and also made a number of trips away from Walden. Nevertheless, the sojourn in the wilderness symbolizes something of the temperament of the man. Thoreau never developed any close or enduring friendships even though many respected him for his integrity and genius. While he never married, he did develop a close relationship with Emerson's second wife while he was living at their home. Thoreau was forthright and brusque and is believed to have felt more at home with nature than with other humans. He was more anarchistic and less conforming than Emerson; he was also less idealistic. Nature, for Thoreau, was less a deity than a setting for bringing out the best in man. He went his own way because, as he explains in *Walden,* ''If a man does not keep pace with his companions, perhaps it is because he hears a different drummer. Let him step to the music which he hears, however measured or far away.'' [10]

Thoreau's essay ''Civil Disobedience'' was published in 1849. Some of its ideas were provoked by the incident of Thoreau's being jailed for refusing to pay his taxes.[11] Thoreau would have no part of the injustice of the state, nor would he contribute money that would be used to fight the unjust Mexican War or pay for the enforcement of the Fugitive Slave Law. His friends bailed him out of jail and thereafter paid his taxes so he would not be jailed again.

This brief incarceration is the setting for the famous, though perhaps fictional, anecdote of Emerson's visit to the jail. To Emerson's question, "What are you doing in there? " Thoreau replied: "What are you doing out there? " When a state is unjust, the best place for a just man is in prison, he wrote in "Civil Disobedience." One must not wait until a majority vote can correct an injustice, rather one must fight back with one's whole self. To be right is of itself to be a majority, a majority of one. Government, in Thoreau's opinion, had helped the people but little in the country's history. Not only was the less government the better, but the government that governs best governs not at all. In spite of this ideal, Thoreau believed that contemporary circumstances necessitated a more just government and that the business of pursuing justice should not be left to individuals. In 1907 while in South Africa, Mahatma Gandhi read Thoreau's "Civil Disobedience" and was deeply impressed by the work and its author. This essay of Thoreau's seems to have influenced Gandhi's development of his own doctrine of passive resistance.

Thoreau met John Brown and was much moved by this antislavery leader; subsequent lectures and writings by Thoreau present an impassioned defense of Brown's position. In his essay "Slavery in Massachusetts," Thoreau argued that we are all slaves if we submit to the governance of our lives by money, fame, and busywork. In "Life Without Principle" he wrote that to free oneself from political tyranny is not sufficient; there are also moral and economic tyrannies from which man must be freed.[12] In this regard Thoreau is a forerunner of Karl Marx and Sören Kierkegaard and their critique of mass society and the alienation of man. However, unlike Marx, Thoreau believed that man is basically a slave to himself and thus that he, not the economic structure of the society, is responsible for his condition. Society, he wrote, is often cheap and superficial, and too much culture stagnates. One needs to be turned out of doors where all good things are wild and free.

Thoreau died of tuberculosis in 1872 at the age of forty-five. He was less well received by the people of his day than was Emerson. He could not quite turn a phrase as Emerson could, nor was he as affable. But his writings show the same spark of genius or of the divine, as Emerson would put it. And Emerson would add that there is but one truth to which each could be attuned if he would but turn within and become self-reliant.

Notes

[1] "The Transcendentalist," in *The Selected Writings of Ralph Waldo Emerson,* ed. Brooks Atkinson (New York: Modern Library, 1940), p. 93.

[2] Ralph Waldo Emerson, "Nature," in *Selected Writings,* p. 6. See included selections.

[3] See the selections from "The Transcendentalist" and "The Oversoul" here included.

[4] Emerson, *Selected Writings,* pp. 45ff. See selections here included.

[5] Ibid., pp. 145ff. See selections here included.

[6] Ibid., pp. 148, 152.

[7] Emerson, "Politics," in *Selected Writings,* pp. 422ff.

[8] *Walden,* in *The Portable Thoreau,* ed. Carl Bode, rev. ed. (New York: Viking Press, 1962), p. 343.

[9] First published in 1854.

[10] *Walden.*

[11] Thoreau, "Civil Disobedience," in *Portable Thoreau,* pp. 109ff. See selections here included.

[12] Thoreau, "Life Without Principle," in *Portable Thoreau,* pp. 631f. See selections here included.

RALPH WALDO EMERSON

NATURE (1836)*

OUR age is retrospective. It builds the sepulchres of the fathers. It writes biographies, histories, and criticism. The foregoing generations beheld God and nature face to face; we, through their eyes. Why should not we also enjoy an *original relation to the universe?* Why should not we have a poetry and philosophy of insight and not of tradition, and a religion by revelation to us, and not the history of theirs? Embosomed for a season in nature, whose floods of life stream around and through us, and invite us, by the powers they supply, to action proportioned to nature, why should we grope among the dry bones of the past, or put the living generation into masquerade out of its faded wardrobe? The sun shines to-day also. There is more wool and flax in the fields. There are new lands, new men, new thoughts. Let us demand our own works and laws and worship. . . .

When we speak of nature in this manner, we have a distinct but most poetical sense in the mind. We mean the integrity of impression made by manifold natural objects. It is this which distinguishes the stick of timber of the wood-cutter from the tree of the poet. The charming landscape which I saw this morning is indubitably made up of some

---

* *The Complete Works of Ralph Waldo Emerson*, 14 vols. (Boston: Houghton Mifflin, 1903–4), vol. 1, pp. 3, 8–10, 12–13, 15, 19–20, 22–24, 25–27, 29–30, 33–34, 36–37, 40–43, 47–49, 56, 61, 63–64, 66–69.

twenty or thirty farms. Miller owns this field, Locke that, and Manning the woodland beyond. But none of them owns the landscape. There is a property in the horizon which no man has but he whose eye can integrate all the parts, that is, the poet. This is the best part of these men's farms, yet to this their warranty-deeds give no title.

To speak truly, few adult persons can see nature. Most persons do not see the sun. At least they have a very superficial seeing. The sun illuminates only the eye of the man, but shines into the eye and the heart of the child. The lover of nature is he whose inward and outward senses are still truly adjusted to each other; who has retained the spirit of infancy even into the era of manhood. His intercourse with heaven and earth becomes part of his daily food. In the presence of nature a wild delight runs through the man, in spite of real sorrows. Nature says—he is my creature, and maugre all his impertinent griefs, he shall be glad with me. Not the sun or the summer alone, but every hour and season yields its tribute of delight; for every hour and change corresponds to and authorizes a different state of the mind, from breathless noon to grimmest midnight. Nature is a setting that fits equally well a comic or a mourning piece. In good health, the air is a cordial of incredible virtue. Crossing a bare common, in snow puddles, at twilight, under a clouded sky, without having in my thoughts any occurrence of special good fortune, I have enjoyed a perfect exhilaration. I am glad to the brink of fear. In the woods, too, a man casts off his years, as the snake his slough, and at what period soever of life is always a child. In the woods is perpetual youth. Within these plantations of God, a decorum and sanctity reign, a perennial festival is dressed, and the guest sees not how he should tire of them in a thousand years. In the woods, we return to reason and faith. There I feel that nothing can befall me in life—no disgrace, no calamity (leaving me my eyes), which nature cannot repair. Standing on the bare ground—my head bathed by the blithe air and uplifted into infinite space— all mean egotism vanishes. I become a transparent eyeball; I am nothing; I see all; the currents of the Universal Being circulate through me; I am part or parcel of God. The name of the nearest friend sounds then foreign and accidental: to be brothers, to be acquaintances, master or servant, is then a trifle and a disturbance. I am the lover of uncontained and immortal beauty. In the wilderness I find something more dear and connate than in streets or villages. In the tranquil landscape, and especially in the distant line of the horizon, man beholds somewhat as beautiful as his own nature.

COMMODITY

WHOEVER considers the final cause of the world will discern a multitude of uses that enter as parts into that result. They all admit of being thrown into one of the following classes: Commodity; Beauty; Language; and Discipline.

Under the general name of commodity, I rank all those advantages which our senses owe to nature. This, of course, is a benefit which is temporary and mediate, not ultimate, like its service to the soul. Yet although low, it is perfect in its kind, and is the only use of nature which all men apprehend . . . . Beasts, fire, water, stones, and corn serve him. The field is at once his floor, his work-yard, his play-ground, his garden, and his bed.

> More servants wait on man
> Than he'll take notice of.

Nature, in its ministry to man, is not only the material, but is also the process and the result. All the parts incessantly work into each other's hands for the profit of man. The wind sows the seed; the sun evaporates the sea; the wind blows the vapor to the field; the ice, on the other side of the planet, condenses rain on this; the rain feeds the plant; the plant feeds the animal; and thus the endless circulations of the divine charity nourish man.

BEAUTY

A NOBLER want of man is served by nature, namely, the love of Beauty.

The ancient Greeks called the world χόσμοζ, beauty. Such is the constitution of all things, or such the plastic power of the human eye, that the primary forms, as the sky, the mountain, the tree, the animal, give us a delight *in and for themselves;* a pleasure arising from outline, color, motion, and grouping. This seems partly owing to the eye itself. The eye is the best of artists.

But this beauty of Nature which is seen and felt as beauty, is the least part. The shows of day, the dewy morning, the rainbow, mountains, orchards in blossom, stars, moonlight, shadows in still water, and the like, if too eagerly hunted, become shows merely, and mock us with their unreality

The presence of a higher, namely, of the spiritual element is essential to its perfection. The high and divine beauty which can be loved without effeminacy, is that which is found in combination with the human will. Beauty is the mark God sets upon virtue. Every natural action is graceful. Every heroic act is also decent, and causes the place and the bystanders to shine

There is still another aspect under which the beauty of the world may be viewed, namely, as it becomes an object of the intellect. Beside the relation of things to virtue, they have a relation to thought. The intellect searches out the absolute order of things as they stand in the mind of God. . . . Nothing divine dies. All good is eternally reproductive. The beauty of nature re-forms itself in the mind, and not for barren contemplation, but for new creation. . . .

The world thus exists to the soul to satisfy the desire of beauty. This element I call an ultimate end. No reason can be asked or given why the soul seeks beauty. Beauty, in its largest and profoundest sense, is one expression for the universe. God is the all-fair. Truth, and goodness, and beauty, are but different faces of the same All.

LANGUAGE

LANGUAGE is a third use which Nature subserves to man. Nature is the vehicle of thought, and in a simple, double, and three-fold degree.

1. Words are signs of natural facts.
2. Particular natural facts are symbols of particular spiritual facts.
3. Nature is the symbol of spirit.

1. Words are signs of natural facts. The use of natural history is to give us aid in supernatural history; the use of the outer creation, to give us language for the beings and changes of the inward creation. Every word which is used to express a moral or intellectual fact, if traced to its root, is found to be borrowed from some material appearance. *Right* means *straight; wrong* means *twisted; Spirit* primarily means *wind; transgression,* the crossing of a *line; supercilious,* the *raising of the eyebrow.*

2. But this origin of all words that convey a spiritual import—so conspicuous a fact in the history of language—is our least debt to nature. It is not words only that are emblematic; it is things which are emblematic. Every natural fact is a symbol of some spiritual fact. Every appearance in nature corresponds to some state of the mind, and that state of the mind can only be described by presenting that natural appearance as its picture. An enraged man is a lion, a cunning man is a fox, a firm man is a rock, a learned man is a torch. A lamb is innocence; a snake is subtle spite; flowers express to us the delicate affections. Light and darkness are our familiar expression for knowledge and ignorance; and heat for love. Visible distance behind and before us, is respectively our image of memory and hope.

Who looks upon a river in a meditative hour and is not reminded of the flux of all things? Throw a stone into the stream, and the circles that propagate themselves are the beautiful type of all influence. Man is conscious of a universal soul within or behind his individual life, wherein, as in a firmament, the natures of Justice, Truth, Love, Freedom, arise and shine. This universal soul he calls Reason: it is not mine, or thine, or his, but we are its: we are its property and men. . . .

. . . When simplicity of character and the sovereignty of ideas is broken up by the prevalence of secondary desires—the desire of riches, of pleasure, of power, and of praise—and duplicity and falsehood take place of simplicity and truth, the power over nature as an interpreter of the will is in a degree lost; new imagery ceases to be created, and old words are perverted to stand for things which are not; a paper currency is employed, when there is no bullion in the vaults. In due time the fraud is manifest, and words lose all power to stimulate the understanding or the affections. . . .

In like manner, the memorable words of history and the proverbs of nations consist usually of a natural fact, selected as a picture or parable of a moral truth. Thus: A rolling stone gathers no moss; A bird in the hand is worth two in the bush; A cripple in the right way will beat a racer in the wrong; Make hay while the sun shines. . . .

. . . There sits the Sphinx at the road-side, and from age to age, as each prophet comes by, he tries his fortune at reading her riddle. There seems to be a necessity in spirit to manifest itself in material forms; and day and night, river and storm, beast and bird, acid and alkali, preëxist in necessary Ideas in the mind of God, and are what they are by virtue of preceding affections in the world of spirit. A Fact is the end or last issue of spirit. The visible creation is the terminus or the circumference of the invisible world.

DISCIPLINE

IN VIEW of the significance of nature, we arrive at once at a new fact, that nature is a discipline. This use of the world includes the preceding uses, as parts of itself.

Space, time, society, labor, climate, food, locomotion, the animals, the mechanical forces, give us sincerest lessons, day by day, whose meaning is unlimited. They educate both the Understanding and the Reason.

. . . nature is a discipline of the understanding in intellectual truths. Our dealing with sensible objects is a constant exercise in the necessary lessons of difference, of likeness, of order, of being and seeming, of progressive arrangement; of ascent from particular to general; of combination to one end of manifold forces.

Sensible objects conform to the premonitions of Reason and reflect the conscience. All things are moral; and in their boundless changes have an unceasing reference to spiritual nature. Therefore is nature glorious with form, color, and motion; that every globe in the remotest heaven, every chemical change from the rudest crystal up to the laws of life, every change of vegetation from the first principle of growth in the eye of a leaf, to the tropical forest and antediluvian coal-mine, every animal function from the sponge up to Hercules, shall hint or thunder to man the laws of right and wrong, and echo the Ten Commandments. . . .

. . . Nothing in nature is exhausted in its first use. When a thing has served an end to the uttermost, it is wholly new for an ulterior service. In God, every end is converted into a new means. Thus the use of commodity, regarded by itself, is mean and squalid. But it is to the mind an education in the doctrine of Use, namely, that a thing is good only so far as it serves; that a conspiring of parts and efforts to the production of an end is essential to any being. The first and gross manifestation of this truth is our inevitable and hated training in values and wants, in corn and meat.

. . . The moral influence of nature upon every individual is that amount of truth which it illustrates to him. Who can estimate this? Who can guess how much firmness the sea-beaten rock has taught the fisherman? How much tranquillity has been reflected to man from the azure sky, over whose unspotted deeps the winds forevermore drive flocks of stormy clouds, and leave no wrinkle or stain? How much industry and providence and affection we have caught from the pantomime of brutes? What a searching preacher of self-command is the varying phenomenon of Health!

IDEALISM

THUS is the unspeakable but intelligible and practicable meaning of the world conveyed to man, the immortal pupil, in every object of sense. To this one end of Discipline, all parts of nature conspire.

A noble doubt perpetually suggests itself—whether this end be not the Final Cause of the Universe; and whether nature outwardly exists. It is a sufficient account of that Appearance we call the World, that God will teach a human mind, and so makes it the receiver of a certain number of congruent sensations, which we call sun and moon, man and woman, house and trade. In my utter impotence to test the authenticity of the report of my senses, to know whether the impressions they make on me correspond with outlying objects, what difference does it make whether Orion is up there in heaven, or some god paints the image in the firmament of the soul? . . .

. . . Whether nature enjoy a substantial existence without, or is only in the apocalypse of the mind, it is alike useful and alike venerable to me. Be it what it may, it is ideal to me so long as I cannot try the accuracy of my senses. . . .

But whilst we acquiesce entirely in the permanence of natural laws, the question of the absolute existence of nature still remains open. It is the uniform effect of culture on the human mind, not to shake our faith in the stability of particular phenomena, as of heat, water, azote; but to lead us to regard nature as phenomenon, not a substance; to attribute necessary existence to spirit; to esteem nature as an accident and an effect. . . .

Thus even in physics, the material is degraded before the spiritual. The astronomer, the geometer, rely on their irrefragable analysis, and disdain the results of observation. The sublime remark of Euler on his law of arches, "This will be found contrary to all experience, yet is true;"

had already transferred nature into the mind, and left matter like an
outcast corpse.

SPIRIT

And all the uses of nature admit of being summed in one, which yields
the activity of man an infinite scope. Through all its kingdoms, to the
suburbs and outskirts of things, it is faithful to the cause whence it had
its origin. It always speaks of Spirit. It suggests the absolute. It is a
perpetual effect. It is a great shadow pointing always to the sun behind
us.

But when, following the invisible steps of thoughts, we come to inquire,
Whence is matter? and Whereto? many truths arise to us out of the
recesses of consciousness. We learn that the highest is present to the soul
of man; that the dread universal essence, which is not wisdom, or love,
or beauty, or power, but all in one, and each entirely, is that for which
all things exist, and tht by which they are; that spirit creates; that behind
nature, throughout nature, spirit is present; one and not compound it
does not act upon us from without, that is, in space and time, but
spiritually, or through ourselves: therefore, that spirit, that is, the Supreme
Being, does not build up nature around us, but puts it forth through us,
as the life of the tree puts forth new branches and leaves through the
pores of the old. As a plant upon the earth, so a man rests upon the
bosom of God; he is nourished by unfailing fountains, and draws at his
need inexhaustible power. Who can set bounds to the possibilities of
man?

PROSPECTS

IN INQUIRIES respecting the laws of the world and the frame of things,
the highest reason is always the truest. That which seems faintly possible,
it is so refined, is often faint and dim because it is deepest seated in the
mind among the eternal verities, Empirical science is apt to cloud the
sight and by the very knowledge of functions and processes to bereave
the student of the manly contemplation of the whole. The savant becomes
unpoetic. But the best read naturalist who lends an entire and devout
attention to truth, will see that there remains much to learn of his relation
to the world, and that it is not to be learned by any addition or subtraction
or other comparison of known quantities, but is arrived at by untaught
sallies of the spirit, by a continual self-recovery, and by entire humility.
He will perceive that there are far more excellent qualities in the student
than preciseness and infallibility; that a guess is often more fruitful than
an indisputable affirmation, and that a dream may let us deeper into the
secret of nature than a hundred concerted experiments.

THE AMERICAN SCHOLAR (1837)*

Mr. President and Gentlemen:

In this hope I accept the topic which not only usage but the nature of our association seem to prescribe to this day—the AMERICAN SCHOLAR. Year by year we come up hither to read one more chapter of his biography. Let us inquire what light new days and events have thrown on his character and his hopes.

It is one of those fables which out of an unknown antiquity convey an unlooked-for wisdom, that the gods, in the beginning, divided Man into men, that he might be more helpful to himself; just as the hand was divided into fingers, the better to answer its end.

The old fable covers a doctrine ever new and sublime; that there is One Man—present to all particular men only partially, or through one faculty; and that you must take the whole society to find the whole man. Man is not a farmer, or a professor, or an engineer, but he is all. Man is priest, and scholar, and statesman, and producer, and soldier. In the *divided* or social state these functions are parcelled out to individuals, each of whom aims to do his stint of the joint work, whilst each other performs his. The fable implies that the individual, to possess himself, must sometimes return from his own labor to embrace all the other laborers. But, unfortunately, this original unit, this fountain of power, has been so distributed to multitudes, has been so minutely subdivided and peddled out, that it is spilled into drops, and cannot be gathered. The state of society is one in which the members have suffered amputation from the trunk, and strut about so many walking monsters—a good finger, a neck, a stomach, an elbow, but never a man.

In this distribution of functions the scholar is the delegated intellect. In the right state he is *Man Thinking*. In the degenerate state, when the victim of society, he tends to become a mere thinker, or still worse, the parrot of other men's thinking.

Hence, instead of Man Thinking, we have the bookworm. Hence the book-learned class who value books, as such; not as related to nature and the human constitution, but as making a sort of Third Estate with the world and the soul. Hence the restorers of readings, the emendators, the bibliomaniacs of all degrees.

Books are the best of things, well used; abused, among the worst. What is the right use? What is the one end which all means go to effect? They are for nothing but to inspire. I had better never see a book than to be warped by its attraction clean out of my own orbit, and made a satellite instead of a system. The one thing in the world, of value, is the active soul. This every man is entitled to; this every man contains within

---

* Ibid., vol. 2, pp. 82–84, 89–90, 94–95, 107–8, 111, 115.

him, although in almost all men obstructed and as yet unborn. The soul active sees absolute truth and utters truth, or creates. In this action it is genius; not the privilege of here and there a favorite, but the sound estate of every man. In its essence it is progressive. The book, the college, the school of art, the institution of any kind, stop with some past utterance of genius. This is good, say they,—let us hold by this. They pin me down. They look backward and not forward. But genius looks forward: the eyes of man are set in his forehead, not in his hindhead: man hopes: genius creates. . . .

There goes in the world a notion that the scholar should be a recluse, a valetudinarian,—as unfit for any handiwork or public labor as a penknife for an axe. The so-called "practical men" sneer at speculative men, as if, because they speculate or *see,* they could do nothing.

. . . Action is with the scholar subordinate, but it is essential. Without it he is not yet man. Without it thought can never ripen into truth. Whilst the world hangs before the eye as a cloud of beauty, we cannot even see its beauty. Inaction is cowardice, but there can be no scholar without the heroic mind. The preamble of thought, the transition through which it passes from the unconscious to the conscious, is action. Only so much do I know, as I have lived. Instantly we know whose words are loaded with life, and whose not.

. . . For a man, rightly viewed, comprehendeth the particular natures of all men. Each philosopher, each bard, each actor has only done for me, as by a delegate, what one day I can do for myself. The books which once we valued more than the apple of the eye, we have quite exhausted. What is that but saying that we have come up with the point of view which the universal mind took through the eyes of one scribe; we have been that man, and have passed on. First, one, then another, we drain all cisterns, and waxing greater by all these supplies, we crave a better and more abundant food. The man has never lived that can feed us ever. The human mind cannot be enshrined in a person who shall set a barrier on any one side to this unbounded, unboundable empire. It is one central fire, which, flaming now out of the lips of Etna, lightens the capes of Sicily, and now out of the throat of Vesuvius, illuminates the towers and vineyards of Naples. It is one light which beams out of a thousand stars. It is one soul which animates all men.

. . . ask not for the great, the remote, the romantic; what is going in Italy or Arabia; what is Greek art, or Provençal minstrelsy; I embrace the common, I explore and sit at the feet of the familiar, the low. Give me insight into to-day, and you may have the antique and future worlds.

. . . We will walk on our own feet; we will work with our own hands; we will speak our own minds. The study of letters shall be no longer a name for pity, for doubt, and for sensual indulgence. The dread of man and the love of man shall be a wall of defence and a wreath of joy around all. A nation of men will for the first time exist, because each believes himself inspired by the Divine Soul which also inspires all men.

DIVINITY SCHOOL ADDRESS (1838)*

The sentiment of virtue is a reverence and delight in the presence of certain divine laws. . . . Yet, as this sentiment is the essence of all religion, let me guide your eye to the precise objects of the sentiment, by an enumeration of some of those classes of facts in which this element is conspicuous.

The intuition of the moral sentiment is an insight of the perfection of the laws of the soul. These laws execute themselves. They are out of time, out of space, and not subject to circumstance. Thus in the soul of man there is a justice whose retributions are instant and entire. He who does a good deed is instantly ennobled. He who does a mean deed is by the action itself contracted. He who puts off impurity, thereby puts on purity. If a man is at heart just, then in so far is he God; the safety of God, the immortality of God, the majesty of God do enter into that man with justice. If a man dissemble, deceive, he deceives himself, and goes out of acquaintance with his own being. . . .

These facts have always suggested to man the sublime creed that the world is not the product of manifold power, but of one will, of one mind; and that one mind is everywhere active, in each ray of the star, in each wavelet of the pool; and whatever opposes that will is everywhere balked and baffled, because things are made so, and not otherwise. Good is positive. Evil is merely privative, not absolute: it is like cold, which is the privation of heat. All evil is so much death of nonentity. Benevolence is absolute and real. So much benevolence as a man hath, so much life hath he. For all things proceed out of this same spirit, which is differently named love, justice, temperance, in its different applications, just as the ocean receives different names on the several shores which it washes. All things proceed out of the same spirit. . . .

This sentiment lies at the foundation of society, and successively creates all forms of worship. The principle of veneration never dies out. Man fallen into superstition, into sensuality, is never quite without the visions of the moral sentiment. In like manner, all the expressions of this sentiment are sacred and permanent in proportion to their purity. The expressions of this sentiment affect us more than all other compositions. The sentences of the oldest time, which ejaculate this piety, are still fresh and fragrant. This thought dwelled always deepest in the minds of men in the devout and contemplative East; not alone in Palestine, where it reached its purest expression, but in Egypt, in Persia, in India, in China. . . .

---

* Ibid., pp. 121–24, 126, 145–46, 149–51.

Let me admonish you, first of all, to go alone; to refuse the good models, even those which are sacred in the imagination of men, and dare to love God without mediator or veil. Friends enough you shall find who will hold up to your emulation Wesleys and Oberlins, Saints and Prophets. Thank God for these good men, but say, "I also am a man." Imitation cannot go above its model. The imitator dooms himself to hopeless mediocrity. The inventor did it because it was natural to him, and so in him it has a charm. In the imitator something else is natural, and he bereaves himself of his own beauty, to come short of another man's.

Yourself a newborn bard of the Holy Ghost, cast behind you all conformity, and acquaint men at first hand with Deity. Look to it first and only, that fashion, custom, authority, pleasure, and money, are nothing to you—are not bandages over your eyes, that you cannot see—but live with the privilege of the immeasurable mind. . . .

And now let us do what we can to rekindle the smouldering, nigh quenched fire on the altar. The evils of the church that now is are manifest. The question returns, What shall we do? I confess, all attempts to project and establish a Cultus with new rites and forms, seem to me vain. Faith makes us, and not we it, and faith makes its own forms. All attempts to contrive a system are as cold as the new worship introduced by the French to the goddess of Reason—to-day, pasteboard and filigree, and ending to-morrow in madness and murder. Rather let the breath of new life be breathed by you through the forms already existing. For if once you are alive, you shall find they shall become plastic and new. The remedy to their deformity is first, soul, and second, soul, and evermore, soul. . . .

I look for the hour when that supreme Beauty which ravished the souls of those Eastern men, and chiefly of those Hebrews, and through their lips spoke oracles to all time, shall speak in the West also. The Hebrew and Greek Scriptures contain immortal sentences, that have been bread of life to millions. But they have no epical integrity; are fragmentary; are not shown in their order to the intellect. I look for the new Teacher that shall follow so far those shining laws that he shall see them come full circle; shall see their rounding complete grace; shall see the world to be the mirror of the soul; shall see the identity of the law of gravitation with purity of heart; and shall show that the Ought, that Duty, is one thing with Science, with Beauty, and with Joy.

THE TRANSCENDENTALIST (1842)*

What is popularly called Transcendentalism among us, is Idealism; Idealism as it appears in 1842. As thinkers, mankind have ever divided into two sects, Materialists and Idealists; the first class founding on

---

* Ibid., pp. 329–31, 334, 339–40, 359.

experience, the second on consciousness; the first class beginning to think from the data of the senses, the second class perceive that the senses are not final, and say, The senses give us representations of things, but what are the things themselves, they cannot tell. The materialist insists on facts, on history, on the force of circumstances and the animal wants of man; the idealist on the power of Thought and of Will, on inspiration, on miracle, on individual culture. These two modes of thinking are both natural, but the idealist contends that his way of thinking is in higher nature. . . .

The idealist, in speaking of events, sees them as spirits. He does not deny the sensuous fact: by no means; but he will not see that alone. He does not deny the presence of this table, this chair, and the walls of this room, but he looks at these things as the reverse side of the tapestry, as the *other end,* each being a sequel or completion of a spiritual fact which nearly concerns him. This manner of looking at things transfers every object in nature from an independent and anomalous position without there, into the consciousness. . . .

From this transfer of the world into the consciousness, this beholding of all things in the mind, follow easily his whole ethics. It is simpler to be self-dependent. The height, the deity of man is to be self-sustained, to need no gift, no foreign force. Society is good when it does not violate me, but best when it is likest to solitude. Everything real is self-existent. Everything divine shares the self-existence of Deity. All that you call the world is the shadow of that substance which you are, the perpetual creation of the powers of thought, of those that are dependent and of those that are independent of your will. Do not cumber yourself with fruitless pains to mend and remedy remote effects; let the soul be erect, and all things will go well. You think me the child of my circumstances: I make my circumstance. . . .

It is well known to most of my audience that the Idealism of the present day acquired the name of Transcendental from the use of that term by Immanuel Kant, of Königsberg, who replied to the skeptical philosophy of Locke, which insisted that there was nothing in the intellect which was not previously in the experience of the senses, by showing that there was a very important class of ideas or imperative forms, which did not come by experience, but through which experience was acquired; that these were intuitions of the mind itself; and he denominated them *Transcendental* forms. The extraordinary profoundness and precision of that man's thinking have given vogue to his nomenclature, in Europe and America, to that extent that whatever belongs to the class of intuitive thought is popularly called at the present day *Transcendental.*

Although, as we have said, there is no pure Transcendentalist, yet the tendency to respect the intuitions and to give them, at least in our creed, all authority over our experience, has deeply colored the conversation and poetry of the present day; and the history of genius and of religion in these times, though impure, and as yet not incarnated in any powerful individual, will be the history of this tendency. . . .

Amidst the downward tendency and proneness of things, when every voice is raised for a new road or another statute or a subscription of stock; for an improvement in dress, or in dentistry; for a new house or a larger business; for a political party, or the division of an estate; will you not tolerate one or two solitary voices in the land, speaking for thoughts and principles not marketable or perishable? Soon these improvements and mechanical inventions will be superseded; these modes of living lost out of memory; these cities rotted, ruined by war, by new inventions, by new seats of trade, or the geologic changes: all gone, like the shells which sprinkle the sea-beach with a white colony to-day, forever renewed to be forever destroyed. But the thoughts which these few hermits strove to proclaim by silence as well as by speech, not only by what they did, but by what they forbore to do, shall abide in beauty and strength, to reorganize themselves in nature, to invest themselves anew in other, perhaps higher endowed and happier mixed clay than ours, in fuller union with the surrounding system.

SELF-RELIANCE (1841)*

To believe your own thought, to believe that what is true for you in your private heart is true for all men—that is genius. Speak your latent conviction, and it shall be the universal sense; for the inmost in due time becomes the outmost, and our first thought is rendered back to us by the trumpets of Last Judgment. Familiar as the voice of the mind is to each, the highest merit we ascribe to Moses, Plato and Milton is that they set at naught books and traditions, and spoke not what men, but what *they* thought. A man should learn to detect and watch that gleam of light which flashes across his mind from within, more than the lustre of the firmament of bards and sages. Yet he dismisses without notice his thought, because it is his. in every work of genius we recognize our own rejected thoughts; they come back to us with a certain alienated majesty. Great works of art have no more affecting lesson for us than this. They teach us to abide by our spontaneous impression with good-humored inflexibility then most when the whole cry of voices is on the other side. Else tomorrow a stranger will say with masterly good sense precisely what we have thought and felt all the time, and we shall be forced to take with shame our own opinion from another.

There is a time in every man's education when he arrives at the conviction that envy is ignorance; that imitation is suicide; that he must take himself for better for worse as his portion; that though the wide universe is full of good, no kernel of nourishing corn can come to him

* Ibid., vol. 2, pp. 45–46, 50, 53–54, 57, 63–64.

but through his toil bestowed on that plot of ground which is given to him to till.

Whoso would be a man, must be a nonconformist. He who would gather immortal palms must not be hindered by the name of goodness, but must explore if it be goodness. Nothing is at last sacred but the integrity of your own mind. Absolve you to yourself, and you shall have the suffrage of the world. I remember an answer which when quite young I was prompted to make to a valued adviser who was wont to importune me with the dear old doctrines of the church. On my saying, "What have I to do with the sacredness of traditions, if I live wholly from within?" my friend suggested—"But these impulses may be from below, not from above." I replied, "They do not seem to me to be such; but if I am the Devil's child, I will live then from the Devil." No law can be sacred to me but that of my nature. Good and bad are but names very readily transferable to that or this; the only right is what is after my constitution; the only wrong what is against it. . . .

. . . It is easy in the world to live after the world's opinion; it is easy in solitude to live after our own; but the great man is he who in the midst of the crowd keeps with perfect sweetness the independence of solitude.

A foolish consistency is the hobgoblin of little minds, adored by little statesmen and philosophers and divines. With consistency a great soul has simply nothing to do. He may as well concern himself with his shadow on the wall. Speak what you think now in hard words and to-morrow speak what to-morrow thinks in hard words again, though it contradict every thing you said to-day.—"Ah, so you shall be sure to be misunderstood." . . .

The magnetism which all original action exerts is explained when we inquire the reason of self-trust. Who is the Trustee? What is the aboriginal Self, on which a universal reliance may be grounded? What is the nature and power of that science-baffling star, without parallax, without calculable elements, which shoots a ray of beauty even into trivial and impure actions, if the least mark of independence appear? The inquiry leads us to that source, at once the essence of genius, of virtue, and of life, which we call Spontaneity or Instinct. We denote this primary wisdom as Intuition, whilst all later teachings are tuitions. In that deep force, the last fact behind which analysis cannot go, all things find their common origin. For the sense of being which in calm hours rises, we know not how, in the soul, is not diverse from things, from space, from light, from time, from man, but one with them and proceeds obviously from the same source whence their life and being also proceed. We first share the life by which things exist and afterwards see them as appearances in nature and forget that we have shared their cause.

THE OVERSOUL (1841)*

There is a difference between one and another hour of life in their authority and subsequent effect. Our faith comes in moments; our vice is habitual. Yet there is a depth in those brief moments which constrains us to ascribe more reality to them than to all other experiences. For this reason the argument which is always forthcoming to silence those who conceive extraordinary hopes of man, namely the appeal to experience, is for ever invalid and vain. We give up the past to the objector, and yet we hope. He must explain this hope. We grant that human life is mean, but how did we find out that it was mean? What is the ground of this uneasiness of ours; of this old discontent? What is the universal sense of want and ignorance, but the fine innuendo by which the soul makes its enormous claim? Why do men feel that the natural history of man has never been written, but he is always leaving behind what you have said of him, and it becomes old, and books of metaphysics worthless? The philosophy of six thousand years has not searched the chambers and magazines of the soul. In its experiments there has always remained, in the last analysis, a residuum it could not resolve. Man is a stream whose source is hidden. Our being is descending into use from we know not whence. The most exact calculator has no prescience that somewhat incalculable may not balk the very nex moment. I am constrained every moment to acknowledge a higher origin for events than the will I call mine.

As with events, so is it with thoughts. When I watch that flowing river, which, out of regions I see not, pours for a season its streams into me, I see that I am a pensioner; not a cause but a surprised spectator of this ethereal water; that I desire and look up and put myself in the attitude of reception, but from some alien energy the visions come.

The Supreme Critic on the errors of the past and the present, and the only prophet of that which must be, is that great nature in which we rest as the earth lies in the soft arms of the atmosphere; that Unity, that Over-Soul, within which every man's particular being is contained and made one with all other; that common heart of which all sincere conversation is the worship, to which all right action is submission; that overpowering reality which confutes our tricks and talents, and constrains every one to pass for what he is, and to speak from his character and not from his tongue, and which evermore tends to pass into our thought and hand and become wisdom and virtue and power and beauty. We live in succession, in division, in parts, in particles. Meantime within man is the soul of the whole; the wise silence; the universal beauty, to which every part and particle is equally related; the eternal ONE. And this deep power in which we exist and whose beatitude is all accessible to us, is not only self-sufficing and perfect in every hour, but the act of

---

* Ibid., pp. 265–69, 271, 280–81.

seeing and the thing seen, the seer and the spectacle, the subject and the object, are one. We see the world piece by piece, as the sun, the moon, the animal, the tree; but the whole, of which these are the shining parts, is the soul. Only by the vision of that Wisdom can the horoscope of the ages be read, and by falling back on our better thoughts, by yielding to the spirit of prophecy which is innate in every man. . . .

. . . What we commonly call man, the eating, drinking, planting, counting man, does not, as we know him, represent himself, but misrepresents himself. Him we do not respect, but the soul, whose organ he is, would he let it appear through his action, would make our knees bend. When it breathes through his intellect, it is genius; when it breathes through his will, it is virtue; when it flows through his affection, it is love. . . .

. . . We are wiser than we know. If we will not interfere with our thought, but will act entirely, or see how the thing stands in God, we know the particular thing, and every thing, and every man. For the Maker of all things and all persons stands behind us and casts his dread omniscience through us over things. . . .

. . . A thrill passes through all men at the reception of new truth, or at the performance of a great action, which comes out of the heart of nature. In these communications the power to see is not separated from the will to do, but the insight proceeds from obedience, and the obedience proceeds from a joyful perception. Every moment when the individual feels himself invaded by it is memorable. By the necessity of our constitution a certain enthusiasm attends the individual's consciousness of that divine presence. The character and duration of this enthusiasm vary with the state of the individual, from an ecstasy and trance and prophetic inspiration—which is its rarer appearance—to the faintest glow of virtuous emotion, in which form it warms, like our household fires, all the families and associations of men, and makes society possible.

POLITICS (1844)*

In dealing with the State we ought to remember that its institutions are not aboriginal, though they existed before we were born; that they are not superior to the citizen; that every one of them was once the act of a single man; every law and usage was a man's expedient to meet a particular case; that they all are imitable, all alterable; we may make as good, we may make better. . . .

. . . politics rest on necessary foundations, and cannot be treated with levity. Republics abound in young civilians who believe that the laws make the city, that grave modifications of the policy and modes of living and employments of the population, that commerce, education and religion

---

* Ibid., vol. 3, pp. 199–200, 215–16.

may be voted in or out; and that any measure, though it were absurd, may be imposed on a people if only you can get sufficient voices to make it a law. But the wise know that foolish legislation is a rope of sand which perishes in the twisting; that the State must follow and not lead the character and progress of the citizen; the strongest usurper is quickly got rid of; and they only who build on Ideas, build for eternity; and that the form of government which prevails is the expression of what civilization exists in the population which permits it. The law is only a memorandum. We are superstitious, and esteem the statute somewhat: so much life as it has in the character of living men is its force. The statute stands there to say, Yesterday we agreed so and so, but how feel ye this article to-day?

Hence the less government we have the better—the fewer laws, and the less confided power. The antidote to this abuse of formal government is the influence of private character, the growth of the Individual; the appearance of the principal to supersede the proxy; the appearance of the wise man; of whom the existing government is, it must be owned, but a shabby imitation. That which all things tend to educe; which freedom, cultivation, intercourse, revolutions, go to form and deliver, is character; that is the end of Nature, to reach unto this coronation of her king. To educate the wise man the State exists, and with the appearance of the wise man the State expires. The appearance of character makes the State unnecessary.

HENRY DAVID THOREAU

WALDEN, OR, LIFE IN THE WOODS (1854)*

I went to the woods because I wished to live deliberately, to front only the essential facts of life, and see if I could not learn what it had to teach, and not, when I came to die, discover that I had not lived. I did not wish to live what was not life, living is so dear; nor did I wish to practice resignation, unless it was quite necessary. I wanted to live deep and suck out all the marrow of life, to live so sturdily and Spartan-like as to put to rout all that was not life, to cut a broad swath and shave close, to drive life into a corner, and reduce it to its lowest terms, and, if it proved to be mean, why then to get the whole and genuine meanness of it, and publish its meanness to the world; or if it were sublime, to know it by experience, and be able to give a true account of it in my next excursion. For most men, it appears to me, are in a strange uncertainty about it, whether it is of the devil or of God, and have *somewhat hastily* concluded that it is the chief end of man here to "glorify God and enjoy him forever."

Still we live meanly, like ants; though the fable tells us that we were long ago changed into men; like pygmies we fight with cranes; it is error upon error, and clout upon clout, and our best virtue has for its occasion a superfluous and evitable wretchedness. Our life is frittered away by

* *The Writings of Henry David Thoreau* (Boston: Houghton Mifflin, 1893), vol. 2, pp. 143–44, 146, 151–55.

detail. An honest man has hardly need to count more than his ten fingers, or in extreme cases he may add his ten toes, and lump the rest. Simplicity, simplicity, simplicity! . . .

Why should we live with such hurry and waste of life? We are determined to be starved before we are hungry. Men say that a stitch in time saves nine, and so they take a thousand stitches today to save nine tomorrow. As for *work*, we haven't any of any consequence.

Shams and delusions are esteemed for soundest truths, while reality is fabulous. If men would steadily observe realities only, and not allow themselves to be deluded, life, to compare it with such things as we know, would be like a fairy tale and the Arabian Nights' Entertainments. If we respected only what is inevitable and has a right to be, music and poetry would resound along the streets. When we are unhurried and wise, we perceive that only great and worthy things have any permanent and absolute existence—that petty fears and petty pleasures are but the shadow of the reality. This is always exhilarating and sublime. By closing the eyes and slumbering, and consenting to be deceived by shows, men establish and confirm their daily life of routine and habit everywhere, which still is built on purely illusory foundations. Children, who play life, discern its true law and relations more clearly than men, who fail to live it worthily, but who think that they are wiser by experience, that is, by failure. I have read in a Hindu book that "there was a king's son, who, being expelled in infancy from his native city, was brought up by a forester, and, growing up to maturity in that state, imagined himself to belong to the barbarous race with which he lived. One of his father's ministers, having discovered him, revealed to him what he was, and the misconception of his character was removed, and he knew himself to be a prince. So soul," continues the Hindu philosopher, "from the circumstances in which it is placed, mistakes its own character, until the truth is revealed to it by some holy teacher, and then it knows itself to be *Brahme.*" I perceive that we inhabitants of New England live this mean life that we do because our vision does not penetrate the surface of things. We think that that *is* which *appears* to be. If a man should walk through this town and see only the reality, where, think you, would the "Mill-dam" go to? If he should give us an account of the realities he beheld there, we should not recognize the place in his description. Look at a meeting-house, or a courthouse, or a jail, or a shop, or a dwelling-house, and say what that thing really is before a true gaze, and they would all go to pieces in your account of them. Men esteem truth remote, in the outskirts of the system, behind the farthest star, before Adam and after the last man. In eternity there is indeed something true and sublime. But all these times and places and occasions are now and here. God himself culminates in the present moment, and will never be more divine in the lapse of all the ages. And we are enabled to apprehend at all what is sublime and noble only by the perpetual instilling and drenching of the reality that surrounds us. The universe constantly and obediently answers to our conceptions; whether we travel fast or slow, the track is laid for us. Let us spend our lives in conceiving then. The poet or the artist never yet had so fair and noble a design but some of his posterity at least could accomplish it.

Time is but the stream I go a-fishing in. I drink at it; but while I drink I see the sandy bottom and detect how shallow it is. Its thin current slides away, but eternity remains. I would drink deeper; fish in the sky, whose bottom is pebbly with stars. I cannot count one. I know not the first letter of the alphabet. I have always been regretting that I was not as wise as the day I was born. The intellect is a cleaver; it discerns and rifts its way into the secret of things. I do not wish to be any more busy with my hands than is necessary. My head is hands and feet. I feel all my best faculties concentrated in it. My instinct tells me that my head is an organ for burrowing, as some creatures use their snout and forepaws, and with it I would mine and burrow my way through these hills. I think that the richest vein is somewhere hereabouts; so by the divining rod and thin rising vapors I judge; and here I will begin to mine.

CIVIL DISOBEDIENCE (1849)*

I heartily accept the motto, "That government is best which governs least"; and I should like to see it acted up to more rapidly and systematically. Carried out, it finally amounts to this, which also I believe— "That government is best which governs not at all"; and when men are prepared for it, that will be the kind of government which they will have. Government is at best but an expedient; but most governments are usually, and all governments are sometimes, inexpedient. The objections which have been brought against a standing army, and they are many and weighty, and deserve to prevail, may also at last be brought against a standing government. The standing army is only an arm of the standing government. The government itself, which is only the mode which the people have chosen to execute their will, is equally liable to be abused and perverted before the people can act through it. Witness the present Mexican war, the work of comparatively a few individuals using the standing government as their tool; for, in the outset, the people would not have consented to this measure.

But to speak practically and as a citizen, unlike those who call themselves no-government men, I ask for, not at once no government, but *at once* a better government. Let every man make known what kind

---

* Henry David Thoreau, *Miscellanies* (Boston: Houghton Mifflin, 1893), pp. 131–34, 136–37, 140, 144–47, 149–50, 169–70. "Civil Disobedience" was first published in 1849 under the title "Resistance to Civil Government" in *Aesthetic Papers,* ed. Elizabeth Peabody.

of government would command his respect, and that will be one step toward obtaining it.

After all, the practical reason why, when the power is once in the hands of the people, a majority are permitted, and for a long period continue, to rule is not because they are most likely to be in the right, nor because this seems fairest to the minority, but because they are physically the strongest. But a government in which the majority rule in all cases cannot be based on justice, even as far as men understand it. Can there not be a government in which majorities do not virtually decide right and wrong, but conscience?—in which majorities decide only those questions to which the rule of expediency is applicable? Must the citizen ever for a moment, or in the least degree, resign his conscience to the legislator? Why has every man a conscience, then? I think that we should be men first, and subjects afterward. It is not desirable to cultivate a respect for the law, so much as for the right. The only obligation which I have a right to assume is to do at any time what I think right. It is truly enough said that a corporation has no conscience; but a corporation of conscientious men is a corporation *with* a conscience. Law never made men a whit more just; and, by means of their respect for it, even the well-disposed are daily made the agents of injustice.

How does it become a man to behave toward this American government today? I answer, that he cannot without disgrace be associated with it. I cannot for an instant recognize that political organization as *my* government which is the *slave's* government also.

All men recognize the right of revolution; that is, the right to refuse allegiance to, and to resist, the government, when its tyranny or its inefficiency are great and unendurable. But almost all say that such is not the case now. But such was the case, they think, in the Revolution of '75. If one were to tell me that this was a bad government because it taxed certain foreign commodities brought to its ports, it is most probable that I should not make an ado about it, for I can do without them. All machines have their friction; and possibly this does enough good to counterbalance the evil. At any rate, it is a great evil to make a stir about it. But when the friction comes to have its machine, and oppression and robbery are organized, I say, let us not have such a machine any longer. In other words, when a sixth of the population of a nation which has undertaken to be the refuge of liberty are slaves, and a whole country is unjustly overrun and conquered by a foreign army, and subjected to military law, I think that it is not too soon for honest men to rebel and revolutionize. What makes this duty the more urgent is the fact that the country so overrun is not our own, but ours is the invading army.

All voting is a sort of gaming, like checkers or backgammon, with a slight moral tinge to it, a playing with right and wrong, with moral questions; and betting naturally accompanies it. The character of the voters is not staked. I cast my vote, perchance, as I think right; but I am not vitally concerned that that right should prevail. I am willing to leave it to the majority. Its obligation, therefore, never exceeds that of expediency. Even voting *for the right* is *doing* nothing for it. It is only expressing to men feebly your desire that it should prevail. A wise man will not leave the right to the mercy of chance, nor wish it to prevail through the power of the majority. There is but little virtue in the action of masses of men. When the majority shall at length vote for the abolition of slavery, it will be because they are indifferent to slavery, or because there is but little slavery left to be abolished by their vote. *They* will then be the only slaves. Only *his* vote can hasten the abolition of slavery who asserts his own freedom by his vote.

Unjust laws exist: shall we be content to obey them, or shall we endeavor to amend them, and obey them until we have succeeded, or shall we transgress them at once? Men generally, under such a government as this, think that they ought to wait until they have persuaded the majority to alter them. They think that, if they should resist, the remedy would be worse than the evil. But it is the fault of the government itself that the remedy *is* worse than the evil. *It* makes it worse. Why is it not more apt to anticipate and provide for reform? Why does it not cherish its wise minority? Why does it cry and resist before it is hurt? Why does it not encourage its citizens to be on the alert to point out its faults, and *do* better than it would have them? Why does it always crucify Christ, and excommunicate Copernicus and Luther, and pronounces Washington and Franklin rebels?

One would think, that a deliberate and practical denial of its authority was the only offence never contemplated by government; else, why has it not assigned its definite, its suitable and proportionate, penalty? If a man who has no property refuses but once to earn nine shillings for the State, he is put in prison for a period unlimited by any law that I know, and determined only by the discretion of those who placed him there; but if he should steal ninety times nine shillings from the State, he is soon permitted to go at large again.

If the injustice is part of the necessary friction of the machine of government, let it go, let it go: perchance it will wear smooth—certainly the machine will wear out. If the injustice has a spring, or a pulley, or a rope, or a crank, exclusively for itself, then perhaps you may consider whether the remedy will not be worse than the evil; but if it is of such a nature that it requires you to be the agent of injustice to another, then, I say , break the law. Let your life be a counter-friction to stop the machine. What I have to do is to see, at any rate, that I do not lend myself to the wrong which I condemn.

As for adopting the way which the State has provided for remedying the evil, I know not of such ways. They take too much time, and a man's life will be gone. I have other affairs to attend to. I came into this world, not chiefly to make this a good place to live in, but to live in it, be it good or bad. A man has not everything to do, but something; and because he cannot do *everything,* it is not necessary that he should do *something* wrong. . . .

. . . Moreover, any man more right than his neighbors constitutes a majority of one already.

Under a government which imprisons any unjustly, the true place for a just man is also a prison. The proper place today, the only place which Massachusetts has provided for her freer and less desponding spirits, is in her prisons, to be put out and locked out of the State by her own act, as they have already put themselves out by their principles. It is there that the fugitive slave, and the Mexican prisoner on parole, and the Indian come to plead the wrongs of his race should find them; on that separate, but more free and honorable, ground, where the State places those who are not *with* her, but *against* her—the only house in a slave State in which a free man can abide with honor. If any think that their influence would be lost there, and their voices no longer afflict the ear of the State, that they would not be as an enemy within its walls, they do not know by how much truth is stronger than error, nor how much more eloquently and effectively he can combat injustice who has experienced a little in his own person. Cast your whole vote, not a strip of paper merely, but your whole influence. A minority is powerless while it conforms to the majority; it is not even a minority then; but it is irresistible when it clogs by its whole weight. If the alternative is to keep all just men in prison, or give up war and slavery, the State will not hesitate which to choose. If a thousand men were not to pay their tax-bills this year, that would not be a violent and bloody measure, as it would be to pay them, and enable the State to commit violence and shed innocent blood. This is, in fact, the definition of a peaceable revolution, if any such is possible. If the tax-gatherer, or any other public officer, asks me, as one has done, "But what shall I do? " my answer is, "If you really wish to do anything, resign your office." When the subject has refused allegiance, and the officer has resigned his office, then the revolution is accomplished. But even suppose blood should flow. Is there not a sort of blood shed when the conscience is wounded? Through this wound a man's real manhood and immortality flow out, and he bleeds to an everlasting death. I see this blood flowing now.

I have paid no poll-tax for six years. I was put into a jail once on this account, for one night; and, as I stood considering the walls of solid stone, two or three feet thick, the door of wood and iron, a foot thick, and the iron grating which strained the light, I could not help being struck with the foolishness of that institution which treated me as if I were mere flesh and blood and bones, to be locked up. I wondered that it should have concluded at length that this was the best use it could put me to, and had never thought to avail itself of my services in some way. I saw that, if there was a wall of stone between me and my townsmen, there was a still more difficult one to climb or break through before they could get to be as free as I was.

The authority of government, even such as I am willing to submit to—for I will cheerfully obey those who know and can do better than I, and in many things even those who neither know nor can do so well—is still an impure one: to be strictly just, it must have the sanction and consent of the governed. It can have no pure right over my person and property but what I concede to it. The progress from an absolute to a limited monarchy, from a limited monarchy to a democracy, is a progress toward a true respect for the individual. Even the Chinese philosopher was wise enough to regard the individual as the basis of the empire. Is a democracy, such as we know it, the last improvement possible in government? Is it not possible to take a step further towards recognizing and organizing the rights of man? There will never be a really free and enlightened State until the State comes to recognize the individual as a higher and independent power, from which all its own power and authority are derived, and treats him accordingly. I please myself with imagining a State at last which can afford to be just to all men, and to treat the individual with respect as a neighbor; which even would not think it inconsistent with its own repose if a few were to live aloof from it, not meddling with it, nor embraced by it, who fulfilled all the duties of neighbors and fellow men. A State which bore this kind of fruit, and suffered it to drop off as fast as it ripened, would prepare the way for a still more perfect and glorious State, which also I have imagined, but not yet anywhere seen.

LIFE WITHOUT PRINCIPLE (1863)*

Let us consider the way in which we spend our lives.

This world is a place of business. What an infinite bustle! I am awaked almost every night by the panting of the locomotive. It interrupts my dreams. There is no sabbath. It would be glorious to see mankind at leisure for once. It is nothing but work, work, work. I cannot easily buy a blankbook to write thoughts in; they are commonly ruled for dollars and cents. An Irishman, seeing me making a minute in the fields, took it for granted that I was calculating my wages. If a man was tossed out of a window when an infant, and so made a cripple for life, or scared out of his wits by the Indians, it is regretted chiefly because he was thus incapacitated for—business! I think that there is nothing, not even crime,

---

* Ibid., pp. 254–55, 258–59, 272, 279–80. "Life Without Principle" was first published posthumously in the October 1863 *Atlantic Monthly*.

more opposed to poetry, to philosophy, ay, to life itself, than this incessant business. . . .

The aim of the laborer should be, not to get his living, to get "a good job," but to perform well a certain work; and, even in a pecuniary sense, it would be economy for a town to pay its laborers so well that they would not feel that they were working for low ends, as for a livelihood merely, but for scientific, or even moral ends. Do not hire a man who does your work for money, but him who does it for love of it.

To speak impartially, the best men that I know are not serene, a world in themselves. For the most part, they dwell in forms, and flatter and study effect only more finely than the rest. We select granite for the underpinning of our houses and barns; we build fences of stone; but we do not ourselves rest on an underpinning of granitic truth, the lowest primitive rock. Our sills are rotten. What stuff is the man made of who is not coexistent in our thought with the purest and subtilest truth? I often accused my finest acquaintances of an immense frivolity; for, while there are manners and compliments we do not meet, we do not teach one another the lessons of honesty and sincerity that the brutes do, or of steadiness and solidity that the rocks do. The fault is commonly mutual, however; for we do not habitually demand any more of each other. . . .

. . . Knowledge does not come to us by details, but in flashes of light from heaven. Yes, every thought that passes through the mind helps to wear and tear it, and to deepen the ruts, which, as in the streets of Pompeii, evince how much it has been used. How many things there are concerning which we might well deliberate whether we had better know them—had better let their peddling-carts be driven, even at the slowest trot or walk, over that bridge of glorious span by which we trust to pass at last from the farthest brink of time in the nearest shore of eternity! Have we no culture, no refinement—but skill only to live coarsely and serve the Devil?—to acquire a little worldly wealth, or fame, or liberty, and make a false show with it, as if we were all husk and shell, with no tender and living kernel to us? Shall our institutions be like those chestnut burs which contain abortive nuts, perfect only to prick the fingers?

STUDY QUESTIONS

Review

1. Who were the transcendentalists and when did the movement originate? What were some of the views they held in common?
2. What is Emerson's view of nature? Compare it with that of the Enlightment.
3. What were the basic ideas that Emerson conveyed in "The Oversoul," "The American Scholar," "Self-Reliance," and the "Divinity School Address"?

4. What was Thoreau's idea of nature? Did it differ any from that of Emerson? From the Puritans?
5. Explain Thoreau's position on the justification of civil disobedience.

For Further Thought

6. What do you think of nature? Do you think of it as something alien or very different from man? As something akin to you? As something spirited or god filled? As one whole or a multitude? Anything else?
7. What do you think about learning? Is knowledge for the sake of knowledge a worthwhile ideal? Can one "know" only what he or she has lived? Should schools be separated from the business of life? Why or why not?
8. Do you think that civil disobedience is ever justified? When and why?

BIBLIOGRAPHY

General

Barbour, Brian M., ed. *American Transcendentalism.* Notre Dame, Ind.: University of Notre Dame Press, 1973.

Blau, Joseph L. "New England's Wild Oats." Chap. 4 in *Men and Movements in American Philosophy.* Englewood Cliffs, N.J.: Prentice-Hall, 1952.

— — —. "Kant in America." *Journal of Philosophy* 5 (23 December 1954): pp. 874-78.

Boas, George, ed. *Romanticism in America.* Baltimore: Johns Hopkins University Press, 1940.

Brooks, Van Wyck. *The Flowering of New England.* Boston: Houghton Mifflin, 1938.

Christy, Arthur. *The Orient in American Transcendentalism.* New York: Columbia University Press, 1932.

Frothingham, Octavius. *Transcendentalism in New England.* New York: G. P. Putnam's, 1880. Reprint. New York: Harper, 1959.

Goddard, H. C. *Studies in New England Transcendentalism.* New York: Columbia University Press, 1908.

Kaplan, N., and T. Katsanos. *Origins of American Transcendentalism.* New Haven: New College University Press, 1975.

Koster, Donald N. *Transcendentalism in America.* Boston: G. K. Hall, 1975.

Matthiessen, F. O. *American Renaissance.* New York: Oxford University Press, 1941.

Miller, Perry. *The Transcendentalists: An Anthology.* Cambridge: Harvard University Press, 1950.

Schneider, Herbert. "The Transcendental Temper." Chap. 5 in *A History of American Philosophy.* New York: Columbia University Press, 1963.

Emerson

Emerson, Ralph Waldo. *The Portable Emerson.* Rev. ed. by Carl Bode in collaboration with Malcolm Cowley. New York: Penguin Books, 1981.

— — —. *Selected Essays, Lectures, and Poems of Ralph Waldo Emerson.* Ed. R. E. Spiller. New York: Washington Square Press, Pocket Books, 1965.

— — —. *Selected Writings of Ralph Waldo Emerson.* Ed. Wm. H. Gilman. New York: New American Library, Signet Classics, 1965.

— — —. *The Early Lectures of Ralph Waldo Emerson.* Ed. S. E. Whicher and R. E. Spiller. 3 vols. Cambridge: Harvard University Press, 1959.

— — —. *The Selected Writings of Ralph Waldo Emerson.* Ed. Brooks Atkinson. New York: Modern Library, 1940.

— — —. *The Works of Ralph Waldo Emerson.* 14 vols. Boston: Houghton Mifflin, 1903–04.

Allen, Gay W. *Waldo Emerson: A Biography.* New York: Viking Press, 1981.

Bolton, Sarah K. *Ralph Waldo Emerson.* Folcroft, Pa.: Folcroft Press, 1977.

Brown, Stewart G. "Emerson's Platonism." *New England Quarterly* 18 (1945): pp. 325–45.

Brukholder, Robert E., and Joel Myerson, eds. *Critical Essays on Ralph Waldo Emerson.* Boston: G. K. Hall, 1983.

Cabot, James Elliot. *A Memoir of Ralph Waldo Emerson.* 2 vols. Boston: Houghton Mifflin, 1887.

Cameron, Kenneth W. *Emerson, the Essayist: An Outline of His Philosophical Development Through 1836.* 2 vols. Raleigh, N. C.: Thistle Press, 1945.

Carpenter, F. I. *Emerson and Asia.* Cambridge: Harvard University Press, 1930.

Christy, Arthur. *Orient in American Transcendentalism: A Study of Emerson, Thoreau, and Alcott.* New York: Octagon Press, 1963.

Dewey, John. "Emerson — The Philosopher of Democracy." *International Journal of Ethics* 13 (1902–3): pp. 405–13.

Duncan, Jeffrey L. *The Power and Form of Emerson's Thought.* Charlottesville: University Press of Virginia, 1974.

Gray, Henry David. *Emerson: A Statement of New England Transcendentalism as Expressed in the Philosophy of its Chief Exponent.* Stanford: Stanford University Press, 1917.

James, William. "Addresses at the Emerson Centenary in Concord." In *Memories and Studies.* New York: Longmans, Green, and Co., 1911.

Konvitz, M., and S. Whicher, eds. *Emerson: A Collection of Critical Essays.* Englewood Cliffs, N.J.: Prentice-Hall, 1962.

Padover, Saul K. "Ralph Waldo Emerson: The Moral Voice in Politics." *Political Science Quarterly* 74 no. 3 (September 1959): pp. 334–50.

Porte, Joel. *Prospect and Retrospect.* Cambridge: Harvard University Press, 1982.

— — —. *Emerson and Thoreau: Transcendentalists in Conflict.* Middletown, Conn.: Wesleyan University Press, 1966.

Rusk, Ralph L. *The Life of Ralph Waldo Emerson.* New York: Charles Scribner's, 1949.

Santayana, George. "Emerson." Chap. 8 in *Interpretation of Poetry and Religion.* New York: Charles Scribner's, 1900.

Welleck, René. "Emerson and German Philosophy." *New England Quarterly* 16 (1943): pp. 41–62.

Thoreau

Thoreau, Henry David. *The Portable Thoreau.* Ed. Carl Bode. New York: Viking Press, 1947; rev. ed., 1964.

— — —. *Henry David Thoreau: Representative Selections.* Ed. B. V. Crawford. New York: American Book Co., 1934.

— — —. *The Works of Henry D. Thoreau.* Concord edition. 5 vols. Boston: Houghton Mifflin, 1929.

— — —. *The Writings of Henry David Thoreau.* Walden edition. 20 vols. 1906. Reprint. Boston: Houghton Mifflin, 1949.

Borst, Raymond R. *Henry David Thoreau: A Descriptive Bibliography.* Pittsburgh: University of Pittsburgh Press, 1981.

Bridgman, Richard. *Dark Thoreau.* Lincoln: University of Nebraska Press, 1982.

Canby, Henry S. *Thoreau.* Boston: Houghton Mifflin, 1939.

Cavell, Stanley. *The Senses of Walden.* Berkeley: Calif.: North Point Press, 1981.

Channing, William E. *Thoreau: Poet-Naturalist.* Cheshire, Conn.: Biblo Press, 1902.

Daugherty, James. *Henry David Thoreau: A Man for Our Time.* New York: Viking Press, 1967.

Deshmukh, D. G. *Thoreau and Indian Thought.* New York: AMS Press, 1974.

Edel, Leon. *Henry David Thoreau.* Minneapolis: University of Minnesota Press, 1970.

Harding, Walter. *The Days of Henry Thoreau.* New York: Alfred A. Knopf, 1965.

— — —, ed. *Thoureau Centennial.* Albany: State University of New York Press, 1964.

— — —, ed. *Thoreau: A Century of Criticism.* Dallas: Southern Methodist University Press, 1954.

Harding, Walter, et. al., eds. *Henry David Thoreau: Studies and Commentaries.* E. Brunswick, N.J.: Fairleigh Dickinson, 1972.

Kwiat, Joseph J. "Thoreau's Philosophical Apprenticeship." *New England Quarterly* 18 (1945): pp. 51–69.

Krutch, Joseph Wood. *Henry David Thoreau.* New York: W. Sloane Assoc., 1948.

Mackaye, James, ed. *Thoreau: Philosopher of Freedom: Writings on Liberty.* New York: Vanguard Press, 1930.

Madison, Charles A. "Henry David Thoreau: Transcendental Individualist." *Ethics* 54 (1943–44): pp. 110–23.

Paul, Sherman. *The Shores of America: Thoreau's Inward Exploration.* Urbana: University of Illinois Press, 1958.

Sanborn, Franklin B. *Henry D. Thoreau.* Boston: Houghton Mifflin, 1889.

Stoller, Leo. *After Walden: Thoreau's Changing Views on Economic Man.* Stanford: Stanford University Press, 1957.

Van Doren, Mark. *Henry David Thoreau: A Critical Study.* Boston: Houghton Mifflin, 1916.

Part 2

Classical American Philosophy

Chapter 4

Evolutionary Thought

While philosophy and philosophers have often been influenced by the scientific thought of their day, the new theories in science in the mid-nineteenth century were especially significant for philosophers of that period, this fact also helps to account for the development of a type of philosophy significantly different from transcendentalism. Of particular interest for an understanding of the development of American philosophy in the latter half of the nineteenth century are the new ideas put forward concerning the age and development of man, life, and the cosmos — new evolutionary theories. One might think of the publication in 1859 of Darwin's *Origin of Species* as the beginning of new thinking in this area, but there were actually several significant developments in evolutionary thinking during the previous century. Even in the United States debate concerning evolution had begun so that by the time Darwin's amazing work was published, the groundwork for its acceptance, or at least the basis for a discussion of it, had already been laid. Because of the relevance of these theories to the philosophy of this and later periods, a summary of evolutionary thought is provided here.

EIGHTEENTH- AND NINETEENTH-CENTURY EVOLUTIONARY THOUGHT

The major developments and speculations that occurred during this period took place not only in biology but also in the areas of paleontology, geology, cosmology, and philosophy.[1] In biology, Linnaeus (1707–78) had established a means of classification of animals, dividing them according to their characteristics into various more or less general and inclusive classes. In the middle of the eighteenth century, however, the French naturalist Buffon (1707–88) had written that species were not fixed as Linneaus's classification system suggested, but varied in their external form according to the influence of factors within their physical environments. Part of this debate concerning the fixity of species centered around the manner or mechanism by which such changes could occur. According to another French naturalist, Lamarck (1744–1829), the term "species" was more difficult to define than had been hitherto thought. Evolutionary changes, moreover, were gradual, he held, and may take place through the inheritance of acquired characteristics, for example through the passing on to offspring of organs that have been developed through use. These variations, nevertheless, were often still thought to take place chiefly within a species.

Reaction to such ideas in this country among those who were aware of them were generally favorable. For example, the American professor of philosophy and later president of what is now Princeton University, Samuel Stanhope Smith, in a lecture entitled "The Causes of the Variety of Complexion and Figure in the Human Species," delivered in 1787 before the American Philosophical Society at Philadelphia suggested that all human beings were descended from a single pair of ancestors and that present differences between various groups today were due to modifications within the environment such as effect of climate or even the "state of society."[2] This view was opposed by others such as Louis Agassiz, leading American geologist, paleontologist, and zoologist, who held that there were probably different original varieties of men — different races from the beginning.[3]

Several interesting and influential organized developments in the areas of paleontology and geology occurred during the first half of the nineteenth century. New discoveries of fossil remains in Europe and America enabled those who studied them to arrange the fossils in such a way as to show a development in anatomical structure of various animals. Some theorists pointed out that such development would have required a much longer period of time than the six thousand years thought to be the age of the earth. Through the geological discoveries of James Hutton (1726–97) and the extremely influential popularization of Hutton's views in Sir Charles Lyell's *Principles of Geology,* published and republished from 1830 to 1875, the uniformitarian theory won acceptance over earlier catastrophe theories. The uniformitarian theory, attributing geological changes to forces such as erosion still operative in nature, postulated immense periods of time for significant geological changes. Many of these ideas were made available in America through the writings of Edward Hitchcock of Amherst College whose *Elementary Geology* (1841) ran to thirty editions in twenty years.[4]

In addition to such scientific discoveries and debates, evolutionary ideas also had sources in several philosophical theories. Of particular influence were the German Romantic thinkers of the late eighteenth and early nineteenth centuries, especially Hegel (1770-1831) and Schelling (1775-1854). We have already seen some of the influence of their idealism on the thought of the transcendentalists. The cosmos is not static, according to these thinkers, but moving, progressive, and organic. For Hegel the cosmos is the continuos development and manifestation of an Absolute Spirit. The doctrines of these philosophers were made known in America through the work of Johann Bernard Stallo, a German immigrant, in his *General Principles of the Philosophy of Nature* (1848).[5]

The historical evolutionary theory of the French positivist Auguste Comte (1798-1857) was both influential and the source of much controversy. According to Comte, the human mind as manifested in the sciences of man progresses through three separate, irreversible, and inevitable stages of development: the theological, metaphysical, and scientific. In the first stage, the theological, everything in nature is animated with a will and life similar to man's, the method of explanation here is chiefly myth. In the second stage, the metaphysical, things and events are explained by their causes, forms and powers. In the third stage, the scientific or positive stage, such explanations are replaced by a study of laws "of relations of succession and resemblance," the method of modern science. The ethics that paralleled the third stage was a new religion of humanism. Debate in the United States centered on the basis and evidence of Comte's thesis, the inevitability and discontinuity of the stages, and the implications of his theory for religion and society. Much of the writing of John Fiske was meant to counter Comte's particular interpretation of what it means to be scientific, while the ideas of Chauncy Wright are in many ways continuous with those of Comte (see the explanation and selections from Fiske and Wright included in this chapter).

The two thinkers who caused the most controversy and discussion during this period, however, were Herbert Spencer (1820-1903) and Charles Darwin (1809-82). The distinction between them can be likened to that between a supporter of evolution and a supporter of evolutionism — evolution being "a scientific theory within a specific field" while evolutionism is "a generalization invading every field of study from biology and cosmology to sociology and philosophy of history." [6] Spencer was an evolutionist while Darwin is known for his particular theory of evolution. Darwin gave an empirical basis for notions within a restricted field, and Spencer turned this notion into a key idea in a synoptic vision that included the cosmos, life, man, and human conduct. Although Herbert Spencer was writing along this line nine years before the 1859 publication of Darwin's *Origin of Species,* he was influenced by Darwin's writings. John Fiske was among the many who were influenced by Spencer's synoptic evolutionary vision; he is Spencer's most ardent summarizer. (The details of Spencer's theory can be found in this chapter in the summary of Fiske's own thought.)

The basic form that Spencer believed evolution takes can be described as follows: The law of progress is the same everywhere. All evolutionary development takes the form of a movement from the simple to the complex, from the homogeneous to the heterogeneous, from the undifferentiated to the differentiated. The process of dissolution is also at work in the universe, but evolution, the opposite process, is a movement of integration, a movement to more stable, defined, and heterogeneous forms. This movement occurs in cosmic development in the formation of solar systems from an original nebular mass, in the evolution of life forms from primitive organisms to complex living bodies, and in human life in the growth and development of language and social organization. Spencer was not a great philosopher, but he had a great influence on American philosophy. His *Principles of philosophy* (1862) is probably his best known work. Although British, he did spend seven weeks in this country in 1882.[7]

Charles Darwin, however, caused, and still causes, the most controversy.[8] Darwin's *Origin of Species* is a thoroughly documented elaboration and defense of the doctrine of descent through natural selection (although he also believed in what he called sexual selection and in the inheritance to some degree of acquired characteristics). This defense was partially based on observations he made during the voyage of the Beagle (1831–36), especially those made on the islands of the Galápagos Archipelago off the west coast of South America. Here he observed the variations of differently situated animals of the same species. He argued that, in the struggle for existence, favorable variations tend to be preserved and unfavorable variations destroyed. The difference between variations within a species and variations between species tended to be erased. All variations were differences of degree rather than of kind. The causes of the variations — the laws governing inheritance — were, he admitted, unknown. (Mendel made certain discoveries in genetics between 1858 and 1865, but his work was not generally known until it was rediscovered after 1900.) The first edition of some 1350 copies of *Origin of Species* was sold the same day it was released, so well recognized and respected was Darwin's work even before this publication. What was new in *Origin of Species* was not so much Darwin's thesis but the detail and thoroughness of the documentation that he provided for it, even though this documentation supplied only indirect evidence for the theory. It did not take long for others to apply this theory to the evolution of man, so that by the time Darwin's *Descent of Man* was published in 1871 the controversy over this issue was well under way. The reception of Darwin's work in the United States varied. There was no widespread acceptance for some twenty-five years. Already in 1860 Asa Gray, a most-respected American scientist and professor of botany at Harvard, gave *Origin of Species* a full, critical, and favorable review. However, Louis Agassiz, also at Harvard, disagreed with Gray on the mechanism of natural selection. And Charles Hodge, professor of systematic theology at Princeton, responded in 1870 in a lecture entitled "What is Darwinism?" that the theory was but atheism.[9]

PHILOSOPHICAL ISSUES RAISED BY THESE EVOLUTIONARY THEORIES

The issues with philosophical relevance that were raised and the controversies that surrounded the Darwinian and other theories of evolution occurred not only in theology and cosmology, but in psychology and social theory as well. To the theologians, evolution seemed to demand changes in man's way of thinking about God and God's relation to the universe or creation, as well as man's idea about himself and his place in the universe. How could the idea of a personal God who created and cared for his creation be reconciled with the blind and often brutal ways of evolution by natural selection? Was God to be thought of, as the deists argued, as nothing but a remote first cause who set the universe in motion and then left it to blind forces of its own? Was man, who had been thought to be little less than the angels, only a little higher than the brutes?

Answers to these questions varied. Some attempted to reconcile evolution with former theological ideas. Thus Alexander Winchell, professor of geology and zoology at Syracuse University, held that natural selection itself required a planner and designer. That history would be so unified as to culminate in man some theologians took as an argument for the existence of a plan and a planner. Evolution, some held, is the orderly method by which God created or creates the universe. There were other, more speculative views like that of Joseph LeConte who made notable geological and other scientific contributions and taught at the University of California at Berkeley from 1874 to 1901. Evolution, he wrote, is "a process of continuous creation by an immanent will in nature." [10] This will is but one of many forms of a basic energy that is able to be changed from gross matter, to life, to mind, and to self-consciousness. Was there some basic life urge or force within the evolutionary process? How else, some wondered, could one get more from less, the higher from the lower?

Less speculative were the theological concerns of those who sought to compare the evolutionary account of geological epochs with the biblical account of creation. How could the Bible be authoritative, as it was generally held to be, if it disagreed with the results of commonly accepted science? One positive approach to this problem was that of Edward Hitchcock; in his *The Religion of Geology* (1851) he sought to distinguish the biblical from the scientific manner or form of language. The Bible was never meant to be a scientific text, he argued. Biblical language is imprecise, metaphorical, and the language of common life and common sense, while scientific language is technical and literal. Thus there is no conflict between their accounts, for they have different purposes and a different significance. [11]

Related to the issue of whether or not there was plan in the universe, in particular a divine plan behind or within the development of nature, was another central philosophical question raised by the thinkers of this period: Are the changes that take place in the process of evolution due to chance or are they a matter of certain determining and determinable causes? Absolute chance would be difficult to reconcile with the notion of a divine plan. However, according to James McCosh of Princeton, the chance variations were simply the special interventions of God; the spontaneous variations that were naturally selected for were God's special providences or interventions into the otherwise lawful workings of nature. Thus natural selection is but divine election. The Calvinists tended to support and emphasize the ideas of struggle and supernatural selection while the more Unitarian or liberal-oriented theologians stressed the notion of immanent design.[12]

The issue of causality, or chance versus determinism, was central to the thought of one of the most noteworthy philosophers of this period, Chauncey Wright, and later to C. S. Peirce. According to Wright, Darwin himself did not mean to suggest that the variations were not caused. Rather Darwin only meant that the causal forces were very complicated and difficult to determine and thus used the words "chance" or "accidental" to mean only this. (See the later discussion of Wright's ideas and the selections included from his writings on this issue.) But is this what is meant by chance in ordinary usage? Or does chance imply some uncaused and spontaneous happening that is not the result of prior forces or causes, knowable or unknowable?

In addition to these problems in the areas of theology and cosmic speculation, there were also philosophically related problems concerning man and his individual and socio-cultural development that evolutionary theories raised in the minds of American philosophers of this period. For many religious people, man's position according to evolutionary theory had been drastically changed. Was his existence as well to be thought of as an accident and not the result of a special divine plan? More generally, thinkers were concerned about the properties of intelligence, self-consciousness, free choice, and sociality that were supposed to be unique to man. Were these too brought about by gradual and accidental adaptations? Was the difference between animal sentience and human intelligence, between instinct and reason, but a matter of degree rather than of kind? What did it matter? Darwin's *Descent of Man* provoked much discussion over the issue of man. And Darwin himself was somewhat perplexed about how to explain the transition from instinct to reason. So concerned was he that he asked his American disciple Chauncey Wright to help him clarify these matters: "As your mind is so clear, and as you consider so carefully the meaning of words, I wish you would take some incidental occasion to consider when a thing may be properly said to be effected by the mind of man."[13] Wright responded with an eighty-page essay entitled "The Evolution of Self-Consciousness" in which he proposed that the new human faculties were simply the old faculties put to new uses (see more detail in the discussion on Wright). According to others, mind developed under the play of social and natural forces as a tool that better enabled the organism to live successfully in the environment, to foresee the future, and so better be able to change the environment to meet its own needs.[14] Evolution was said to be able to explain not only the development of reason but also the development of language, customs, and law. These were but other instances of adaptation on the part of man to the changing conditions and to his own social environment. According to James Mark Baldwin of Princeton and Johns Hopkins, groups that are dominant fashion their members to social cooperation, thus making man more social by overcoming his natural individualism and aggressiveness.[15] Spencer became a symbol of this attempt to explain social development in evolutionary terms by his comparison of the forms of organisms with the forms of societies. John Fiske developed a particular explanation of how the formation of societies and the lengthened infancy of humans contributed to human development.

At this time, and influenced by some aspects of the Darwinian theory of evolution, a theory was proposed that has come to be known as "Social Darwinism." According to William Graham Sumner (1840–1910), one of Social Darwinism's foremost representatives, and others, the processes of natural selection and survival of the fittest became the means of explaining the social development of man. Society is the result of a social struggle in which each man must pursue his own good at the expense of others less capable than he. Some people succeed over others, and it is right that they do so. Better the survival of the fittest than of the unfit! [16] Self-made millionaires were supposed to be good examples of the fittest who survived very well. It was also hoped, however, that allowing the fit rather than the unfit to survive would be to the economic good of the whole society, and that the struggle of each for his own good would contribute to the good of each and to the evolution of the species as a whole.

Another viewpoint was that of Lester Ward who in *The Psychic Factors of Civilization* (1893) and *Dynamic Sociology* (1883) argued that society was not the result of natural but artificial selection, that society was not the unthinking working of nature but the thoughtful and planned work of human intelligence. Thus humanity was not required to follow the harsh laws of natural selection but could rise to respect human beings and to protect the weak among them.[17] Social evolution, according to one's interpretation, thus could be used to support either the status quo and the position of the wealthy or the position that all social structures were changeable and temporary—that they could be molded and changed by man to suit his own needs and ideals.

On the whole evolutionary thought worked to increase men's awareness of time, history, and change, with regard to nature, man, and his own institutions, while it also raised serious philosophical questions. Although it is fairly safe to say that there were no outstanding philosophers in America during this period, two thinkers do stand out above the rest — John Fiske for his breadth of thought if not for his originality, and Chauncey Wright for his originality if not for his breadth and completeness. Thus we shall give more detail here of their thought and writings, which were influenced by evolutionary thought in different ways. John Dewey's essay, "The Influence of Darwin on Philosophy" is also included in this chapter rather than in the later chapter on Dewey because of its obvious relevance to the topic.

JOHN FISKE (1842–1901)

John Fiske was born in 1842 in Hartford, Connecticut of parents who were English, upper-middle-class descendents of Puritans.[18] He eventually went to study at Harvard which better accorded with his unorthodox tendencies than the more orthodox Yale. At Harvard he studied geology, Greek literature, comparative linguistics, and history. At age eighteen he published a review of Buckle's *History of the Civilization of England* in which the influence of process views of the universe and of Herbert Spencer's views in particular could be found. Spencer's writings had suggested to Fiske that not only were there laws to which natural development conformed, but that social changes also developed in an orderly fashion and in fact conformed to the same laws as nature. Fiske had also read Comte while a student at Harvard, and had even been punished for reading him during church services. While he admired Comte's attempt to frame laws for social development, in Fiske's view it was Spencer, not Comte, who had the correct form of the laws.

While Fiske's mature philosophy is chiefly a version of Spencer's, Fiske's interest lay mainly in history and humanistic studies; thus he was more interested in human development than Spencer, who had a better scientific background than Fiske. Fiske had always desired a teaching career in which he could use and share his philosophical ideas. Yet because of his unorthodoxy he found it difficult to gain a teaching position at Harvard. However, he was appointed assistant librarian there, and this position gave him a base from which to lecture and write. His *Outlines of Cosmic Philosophy* was developed from a series of lectures he gave at Harvard and in London in 1869 and 1871, and was the work that Fiske himself considered his greatest philosophical contribution and of which most of his later writings were an extension. His use of the term "cosmic" he believed was significant since it differentiated his work from several other types of philosophy.[19] By his use of this term he wanted to suggest that philosophy should show forth the orderly succession of phenomena known as natural development and thus be distinguished from those theological systems that rely on miracles and special creations. The term signifies that the true philosophy should deal with the totality of phenomena and holds that everything with which philosophy can deal lies within this system, that there should be no metaphysics of what transcends nature, and finally that his account is a synthetic or unified account of the cosmos and thus to be distinguished from that positivistic philosophy that denies such an account is possible. It is "a system which, without making appeal to data that are ontological or to agencies that are extra-cosmic, brings all known truths concerning the coexistence and succession of phenomena into relation with one another as the corollaries of a single primordial truth, which is alleged of the omnipresent Existence (ignored by Positivism), whereof the phenomenal world is the multiform manifestation."[20]

In the selection from Fiske included in this chapter we find a more explicit statement of some of the ideas contained within his cosmic philosophy. For example, he held a rather Kantian form of the view that all knowledge is relative. All we know is what our own way of perceiving allows us to know. Thus we can never know how things in themselves are apart from our way of viewing them, and the stormy history of metaphysics shows us what happens when people try to say otherwise. However, the fact that we do not know the true causes of the universe does not mean that they do not exist. There could be a realm that we cannot understand, and possibly a being that could know them as they are. Nevertheless we should be concerned with what we can know rather than with what we cannot know. Our criterion for deciding what is true of things physical that we do experience is their persistent continuance as appearances. Any consistently confirmed and coherent system developed to explain the facts must correspond with them.

One of the thorniest problems of modern philosophy was the nature of causation and our reasons for believing that every event had a cause. This notion was important for certain views of science and knowledge as well as for believing things about what was beyond experience yet supposed to be the "cause" of what we experienced. Fiske believed that the law of causation is a necessary truth in the sense that we have never found a case where there was an effect without a cause and because we continue to believe that evidence will continue to support this law. However Fiske also held that we have no experience of any hidden powers and to us causation seems to be but invariable sequence. Nevertheless, we can suppose that there may be such a thing as a universal force equivalent in some way to the force we feel in muscular resistance. "Unknowable Absolute," "Force," and "Power" are different symbols for this same fact. It is this same reality of which Comte had said there were three different explanations, paralleled by three different stages of social development. According to Fiske, in each case society was symbolizing, in however different ways, the same eternal fact.

While Fiske followed Spencer's explanation of the law of evolution, he went beyond Spencer in emphasizing notions of intellectual and social development. The chief problem people had with the theory of evolution as applied to the development of humans from animals was the difference they saw between intellect in man and instinct in animals. According to Fiske, if one looks at the extremes of intellect and instinct, the difference becomes a problem, but if one avoids the extremes and considers the small differences between some primitive men and some animals, the problem is reduced. When men formed communities, a new order of evolution was inaugurated. Not only were there gradual changes in human anatomy, but old nerve channels were given new functions by the changing environment, natural and social. Fiske does not present, as does Chauncey Wright, a detailed explanation of how the development of intelligence occurs. He does, however, develop a somewhat unique theory of the evolution of man's sense of morality. As in the rest of his theory of evolution, Fiske looks to antecedents, here emotional antecedents, that he finds in the experience of pleasure and pain. An animal feels pleasure at the presence of what is beneficial to it and pain at what is harmful. Thus it begins to associate good with pleasure and bad with pain and to seek the one and avoid the other. So far, however, this notion would explain only egoism and hedonism, not man's moral sense which extends to a concern for the well-being of others.

Fiske attempts to explain how this sense came about by noting the peculiarity of the prolonged infancy of the human being. The complexity of intellectual action requires a developed nervous system for its base. Fiske believed that the nervous system continues to develop after birth and that the prolonged infancy of humans gives them a chance to develop the potential for a higher form of intelligence. The prolonged infancy also provides a basis for a greater parental affection and group cohesiveness, and from this flows the sympathy humans have for others, first those closest to themselves and then those farther away. This sympathy, he believes, is the source of their moral sense.

In 1884 and 1885 Fiske was invited to deliver lectures before the transcendentalist and idealist gathering known as the Concord Summer School of Philosophy. His first lecture was entitled "The Destiny of Man" and the second "The Idea of God as Affected by Modern Knowledge." [21] Fiske had always been concerned about the relation between philosophy and theology or religion, and in these lectures (as well as in the final chapters of the *Outlines of Cosmic Philosophy*) he concentrates his attention on these problems. God is defined in the second lecture as "the Infinite and Eternal Energy from which all things proceed." [22] How he reconciled statements such as this with his views on the relativity of knowledge is not clear. Nature, he said, is but God's orderly action and in fact a manifestation in different ways of the life energy that is God. In place of the concept of providence, which consisted of arbitrary divine interventions, Fiske spoke of the laws of nature as the work of God. There is no conflict between science and religion, yet religious knowledge or belief is of no help to science. Science must still explore particular phenomena and their interrelations.

Fiske resigned his position as librarian at Harvard in 1879 in order to have more time to devote to his lectures and writing. He died at Gloucester, Massachusetts on 7 July 1901.

CHAUNCEY WRIGHT (1830–75)

Only in the last few decades has the significance of Chauncey Wright's work been taken seriously. He was born in 1830 in Northampton, Massachusetts, lead a relatively uneventful life, wrote only a few essays and several articles, and died at the age of forty-five. Yet these limited writings manifested an uncommon analytic philosophical ability. When reading these rather difficult works, one finds oneself at a level of thinking new in the history of American philosophy.[23]

Wright entered Harvard College in 1848 and there studied chiefly mathematics and philosophy. From 1852 to 1870 he worked as a mathematician making computations for the *Nautical Almanac*. He became interested in the writings of Darwin, John Stuart Mill, Spencer, and Sir William Hamilton, and in response to their works began a series of philosophical articles published beginning in 1864 in the *North American Review*. In 1870 and 1874 he lectured at Harvard, first in psychology and then in physics, and in 1874 he was appointed an instructor at Harvard in mathematical physics. These positions were but briefly held, due chiefly to the difficulties he had communicating with students (a problem that did not seem to be present in his individual contacts or tutoring, however). His main source of living was his articles and some tutoring. He regularly met in Cambridge in the 1870s with the group of pragmatists whose gatherings were later to be called the Metaphysical Club. Here he was an acknowledged leader and exchanged ideas with the other members, including Charles Sanders Peirce, William James, Oliver W. Holmes, Jr., occasionally John Fiske, and others. In 1872 Wright went to Europe where he visited with Charles Darwin. His irregular habits and his periods of melancholy probably contributed to his early death which occurred while he was writing at his desk on 11 September 1875.

Wright may be said to be the first technical philosopher of science in America and many of the philosophical problems with which he dealt were in this area. The meaning and significance of the theory of evolution by natural selection, the nature of scientific explanation and its method and concepts, and the meaning of causality are among the problems treated in the selections from Wright's work that are included in this volume.

Unlike John Fiske, Chauncey Wright did not consider Herbert Spencer to be a great thinker or philosopher. Wright thought that Spencer inordinately generalized from only a few scientific instances, using the results of science but not contributing anything new to knowledge. Wright believed that the value of any theory was in its "capacity to enlarge our experience" by helping us notice what we had not before noticed and otherwise might continue to overlook. Scientific theories in particular provide us with "working ideas" and are "finders, not merely summaries of truth." [24] Some have pointed out the similarity between this view of Wright's and John Dewey's later form of pragmatism which holds that all ideas are experimental — working hypotheses or instruments for our various purposes. Wright's view, however, was more limited in its application than that of Dewey.

Wright was most impressed with the method of science and the strides made in contemporary science. To what was this progress due, he asked in his essay on Spencer. It was not that modern science possessed a new method, that it used induction rather than deduction, that it stressed facts rather than theories or ideas. Rather progress was due to the difference between what he called the objective and the subjective method. The objective method consisted of verification by empirical tests — either by direct appeal to facts or by indirect verification whereby contact is made with facts only in conjunction with other ideas or concepts. The subjective method consisted of appeals to internal-evidence tests such as "reasonableness," or the "data of self-consciousness," or perhaps the inability to believe otherwise. Whether the origin of a theory was imagination or experience, what counted was the mode of verification.[25]

In 1859 Wright read *Origin of Species* and became an ardent disciple of Charles Darwin. The respect was mutual, and, when in 1871 Wright sent Darwin a copy of his paper entitled "The Genesis of Species," Darwin replied, "I have hardly ever in my life received an article which has given me so much satisfaction as the review which you have been so kind as to send me. Will you provisionally give me permission to reprint your article as a pamphlet?" [26] Wright agreed and thus became a participant in the English controversy over Darwin. One of the problems that was part of this Darwinian controversy at the time was the issue of "accidental variation." Did Darwin mean to infer that the whole of the arrangement of nature and species as we find them today was the result of accident, of chance? One of Darwin's opponents, St. George Mivart, supposed that Darwin implied this notion. But Wright argued that by the term "accident" Darwin did not mean to point to exceptions to the law of causation. Rather he simply meant that the causality involved was complex and unknown to us. If we had been able to know all of the complex of causes and their interrelations, we would have been able to know the result of their conjunction. To explain an event, moreover, would be to show that it has or will result, according to fixed laws or principles, from other occurrences. Thus even man's origin can be so explained.

Many have no problem with the theory of evolution by natural selection until they come to the issue of man. In 1870 Wright wrote an extended essay entitled "The Evolution of Self-Consciousness" that explains his own position on the question of how man and reflective intelligence could have evolved. Evolution does not imply, he insisted, that a continuity or similarity in kind exists between the faculties of men and animals. What is actually involved is a case of new and different uses of old powers. That certain faculties such as the hand or voice can have many uses is obvious. One can say that, as in the case of the evolution of intelligence and self-consciousness, the new uses were potentially, but only potentially, present in the older powers. What is distinctive about self-consciousness, and how could it develop from former powers? According to Wright, self-consciousness has evolved as man has become better able to form and focus on images. Instead of being totally involved in what the image represents, man is able to focus on the image itself as a sign of something else. There is both an external and an internal sign; when one can think about the internal sign, in other words, think about thoughts as well as things, then one has the ability to be self-conscious, according to Wright. It is an old power, the ability to form images, which differs only in degree in men and animals, but one that gives rise to a difference in kind in powers or uses.

The final section of Wright's comments discusses the supposed general conflict between science and theology or religion. According to Wright, there need be no real conflict between science and religion. Where seeming conflicts between religious belief and scientific truth arise, Wright suggests that the beliefs may not be true religious beliefs but superstition. Thus he seems to infer that science, not religious belief, is the basic criterion of truth. Nevertheless, while there need be no conflict between the two fields, Wright believed that scientific facts should not be used to support religious beliefs. That the universe exists for some purpose cannot be proved by science, even though such a belief may have another source. Wright's influence on and similarity to Peirce, James, Dewey, and some contemporary philosophers of science, have been often pointed out,[27] but the merits of his writings must be evaluated on their own account.

JOHN DEWEY AND THE INFLUENCE OF DARWIN ON PHILOSOPHY

While a separate chapter is devoted to John Dewey, one of the major and most well-known American philosophers, there are many ways in which evolutionary theories have influenced or are compatible with the philosophical views of Dewey. Here we concentrate on the significance his own views of evolution have for philosophy. In his essay, "Darwin's Influence on Philosophy" (1909), Dewey suggests that Darwin's *Origin of Species* had wide-ranging influence, sparking new ideas not only in biology but in logic, morals, politics, and religion. In fact, the book contributed to "a new intellectual temper"; it changed conceptions strong in philosophy for 2000 years. According to Dewey, philosophy inherited the belief of Plato and Aristotle that all things that change do so in the direction or under the form of some final purpose that is built into the organism or being, directing its growth and contributing to a constancy in the midst of its changing. True knowledge or science grasps this permanence in change; it goes beyond the flux to a vision of permanency that endures.

The Darwinian theory of natural selection, constant chance (accidental) variations, and survival of the fittest, according to Dewey, resstored chance and change to their rightful positions. They were no longer to be thought of as incomplete, unreal, and unworthy of study and interest. Science itself was given a new goal. Instead of concentrating on the whole, the final, and the stable, it was directed to the study of specific changes and consequences and to the present conditions rather than to some ultimate end. At the level of social concern, men were then able to concentrate on changing conditions and piecemeal progress.

In reading this chapter on the influence of evolutionary thought on American philosophy, it might be well to set the period in perspective. American philosophy had not yet come of age, so to speak, something that happened only with the pragmatic philosophies described in the following chapter. Nevertheless, in the problems and issues raised by evolution and in the attempt to deal with these issues by the variety of lesser thinkers of this period, we find the beginning of something new in American philosophy. Moreover, the movement from transcendentalism to pragmatism cannot be adequately understood without some examination of what occurred in this transitional period.

Notes

[1] An excellent sourcebook on the scientific developments of this period is *Science in the Nineteenth Century,* ed. René Taton (New York: Basic Books, 1961).

[2] Schneider, *History of American Philosophy,* pp. 299–300.

[3] Ibid., pp. 300–302, Agassiz's "Essay on Classification" (1857) as well as other nineteenth-century views on the "fixity of species" and other evolutionary issues may be found in *Darwin,* ed. Philip Appleman (W. W. Norton, New York, 1970).

[4] Schneider, *History of American Philosophy,* p. 322; Jos. Blau, *Men and Movements in American Philosophy* (Englewood Cliffs, N.J.: Prentice-Hall, 1952), p. 153. Another book that summarized many of the new scientific discoveries for American thinkers was *Kosmos* published by F. A. vonHumboldt between 1845 and 1851.

[5] Some of these more idealistic theories will be discussed in chapter 9.

[6] Philip P. Wiener, *Evolution and the Founders of Pragmatism* (Cambridge: Harvard University Press, 1949), p. 6.

[7] For a discussion of Spencer see *First Principles,* 6th ed. (1862; London, 1937) and B. P. Bowne, *The Philosophy of Herbert Spencer* (New York, 1874).

[8] For more information on Darwin see *Darwin,* ed. Philip Appleman, which contains selections from Darwin's writings as well as essays showing Darwin's influence on science and on theological and philosophical thought.

[9] Schneider, *History of American Philosophy,* p. 324.

[10] Ibid., p. 313.

[11] Schneider, *History of American Philosophy,* pp. 322, 325.

[12] Ibid, pp. 330–31.

[13] See Philip P. Wiener, "Chauncey Wright, Darwin, and Scientific Neutrality," *Journal of the History of Ideas,* (1945); p. 34. Quoted in Schneider *History of American Philosophy,* p. 304.

[14] This type of view can be found in the writings of the group of philosophers at the University of Chicago during the early twentieth century, a group that included John Dewey and George H. Mead.

[15] Schneider, *History of American Philosophy,* p.340. Also see Schneider's discussion of the socio-economic theories of Thorstein Veblen on pp. 349ff.

[16] Schneider, *History of American Philosophy,* p. 338; William Graham Sumner, *Essays,* ed. A. G. Keller and M. R. Davie, vol. 2 (New Haven; Yale University Press, 1934), p. 56. An essay by Andrew Carnegie, "The Gospel of Wealth" (1900), and another by John Louis O'Sullivan, "Manifest Destiny" (1885), are among those included in the cited work on *Darwin,* ed. P. Appleman.

[17] Schneider, *History of American Philosophy,* pp. 341–43.

[18] See George P. Winston, *John Fiske* (New York: Twayne Publishers, 1972) for a general description of Fiske's life and writings.

[19] "Preface," *Outlines of Cosmic Philosophy,* in *The Miscellaneous Writings of John Fiske* (1874; reprint, Boston: Houghton Mifflin, 1902), vol. 1, pp. x–xv.

[20] Ibid., p. xii.

[21] The Concord Summer School of philosophy was originated by Bronson Alcott, himself associated with Emerson and the transcendentalist movement, in order to make known the work being done by a certain group of Hegelians in St. Louis (see chapter 6 on the St. Louis Hegelians). Fiske's second lecture was published as *The Idea of God as Affected by Modern Knowledge* (Boston: Houghton Mifflin, 1887).

[22] Ibid., p. xxv.

[23] Wright's major writings are published in *Philosophical Discussions,* ed. Charles Eliot Norton (1877; reprint, New York: Burt Franklin, 1971). Also see Edward H. Madden, *Chauncey Wright* (New York: Twayne Publishers, 1964); idem, *Chauncey Wright and the Foundations of Pragmatism* (Seattle: University of Washington Press, 1963).

[24] *Wright, Philosophical Discussions,* pp. 55–56. See selections appended.

[25] See selections appended.

[26] Quoted in Madden, *Chauncey Wright,* p. 19; see *Letters of Chauncey Wright,* ed. J. B. Thayer (Cambridge, Mass.: John Wilson and Son, 1878), pp. 230–31.

[27] Madden, *Chauncey Wright and the Foundations of Pragmatism.*

JOHN FISKE

THE RELATIVITY OF KNOWLEDGE*

The history of metaphysical speculation—if we leave out of the account all psychological inquiry, which is a very different matter—is little else than the history of a series of persistent attempts to frame tenable hypotheses concerning the origin of the universe, the nature of its First Cause, and the ultimate constitution of the matter which it contains. History teaches us that all such attempts have failed; and furnishes us with ample inductive or empirical evidence that the human mind is incapable of attaining satisfactory conclusions concerning the First Cause, the Infinite, the Absolute, or the intimate nature of things. We accordingly say for brevity's sake that we cannot know the Absolute, but only the Relative; and in saying so, we implicitly assert two practical conclusions:

First, we cannot know things as they exist independently of our intelligence, but only as they exist in relation to our inteligence.

Secondly, the possibilities of thought are not identical or coextensive with the possibilities of things. A proposition is not necessarily true because we can clearly conceive its terms; nor is a proposition necessarily untrue because it contains terms which are to us inconceivable. . . .

. . . By no power of conception or subtilty of reasoning can we break down or undermine the eternal wall which divides us from the knowledge

---

* *John Fiske's Miscellanious Writings* vol. 1, Boston: Houghton Mifflin, 1902–04, *Outlines of Cosmic Philosophy,* vol. 1, pp. 14, 21, 22.

of things in themselves. If we attempt to frame any hypothesis concerning their nature, origin, or modes of action, we find ourselves speedily check-mated by alternative impossibilities. And if, resting in despair after all our efforts have proved fruitless, we inquire why this is so, we find that from the very organization of our minds, we can frame no cognition into which there do not enter the elements of *likeness, difference,* and *relation;* so that the Absolute, which presents none of these elements, is utterly and forever unknowable.

What is the meaning of this conclusion, when translated from the metaphysical language in which I have expressed it into language that is somewhat more familiar? It means not only that the Deity, in so far as absolute and infinite, is inscrutable by us, and that every hypothesis of ours concerning its nature and attributes can severe only to illustrate our mental impotence; but it also means much more than this. It means that the Universe in itself is likewise inscrutable; that the vast synthesis of forces without us, which in manifold contact with us is from infancy till the close of life continually arousing us to perceptive activity, can never be known by us as it exists objectively, but only as it affects our con-sciousness.

THE TEST OF TRUTH*

At the outset of our inquiry, Truth was provisionally defined as the correspondence between the subjective order of our conceptions and the objective order of the relations among things. But this is the definition of that Absolute Truth, which implies an experience of the objective order in itself, and of such truth we can have no criterion. It was this which Mr. Mill must have had in mind, when he let fall the much criticised suggestion that in some distant planet the sum of two and two might be five. But such a statement is inadequate; for when we speak of planets and numbers, we are tarrying within the region of things accessible to intelligence, and within this region we cannot admit the possibility of two and two making five. It is nevertheless imaginable that somewhere there may be a mode of existence, different from intelligence, and inconceivable by us because wholly alien from our experience, upon which numerical limitations like ours would not be binding. The utter blankness of un-certainty in which such a suggestion leaves us may serve as an illustration of the theorem that we can have no criterion of Absolute Truth, or of truth that is not correlated with the conditions of our intelligence.

But the lack of any such criterion in no way concerns us as intelligent beings. The only truth with which we have any concern is Relative Truth,— the truth that is implicated with whatever can in any way come within our cognizance. For relative truth our inquiry has established this criterion.

---

* Ibid., pp. 102–4.

When any given order among our conceptions is so coherent that it cannot be sundered except by the temporary annihilation of some one of its terms, there must be a corresponding order among phenomena. And this, as we have seen, is because the order of our conceptions is the expression of our experience of the order of phenomena. I will only add that what we mean by *reality* is "inexpugnable persistence in consciousness;" so that when the unknown objective order of things produces in us a subjective order of conceptions which persists in spite of every effort to change it, the subjective order is in every respect as real to us as the objective order would be if we could know it. And this is all the assurance we need, as a warrant for science, and as a safeguard against scepticism.

CAUSATION*

In the course of our examination of the Kantian doctrine of Necessary Truths, the origin and justification of our belief in the necessity of causation was incidentally discussed. We found that this belief can be explained and defended only as the product of a mental limitation due to absolute uniformity of experience. We believe that, under the requisite conditions, fire burned before we were born, that it now burns in regions to which we have never had access, and that it will continue to burn as long as the world lasts, simply because we are incapable of forming conceptions of which the materials are not supplied by experience, and because experience has never presented to our consciousness an instance of fire which, under the requisite conditions for burning, did not burn. Or, in other words, we believe that in the absence of preventive conditions, fire must always and everywhere burn, because our concept of fire is the concept of a thing which burns, and this concept has been formed exclusively by our experience of fire.

Causation may therefore be defined as the unconditional invariable sequence of one event, or concurrence of events, upon another; and this is all that is given in the phenomenon. But metaphysics is not content with this conception of Cause. It prefers to regard causation as a kind of constraint by which the antecedent event obliges the consequent event to follow it. It postulates a hidden power, an *occulta vis,* in the cause, which operates as an invincible nexus between it and the effect. That matter as objectively existing may exert upon matter some constraining power which, as forever unknowable by us, may be called an *occulta vis,* I readily grant. Thought is not the measure of things, and it was therefore unphilosophical in Hume to deny the existence of any such unknown power. Things may exist, in heaven and on earth, which are neither dreamt of in our philosophy nor conceivable by our intelligence. Respecting the external reality we say nothing: we only affirm that no such *occulta vis* is given in the

---

* Ibid., pp. 215–16, 227, 229.

phenomenon of causation. Any hypothesis which postulates such an unknown element as a means of explaining the phenomenon is unverifiable, and, as such, science cannot admit it, nor can our Cosmic Philosophy admit it.

ANTHROPOMORPHISM AND COSMISM*

According to Comte, philosophy began in fetishism; as science progressively arranged phenomena in groups of wider and wider generality, philosophy passed through polytheism into monotheism; and as with its increasing generality, the primitive anthropomorphic conception of cause faded away, becoming replaced by the conception of an unknowable Cause manifested in phenomena, philosophy became metaphysical: finally, when the unknowable Cause is wholly ignored, and no account is taken of anything beyond the immediate content of observed facts, philosophy becomes positive.

. . . Now in the scientific explanation, we omit also the conception of a specific *nisus* or effort, and regard the falling of the tree as an event invariably consequent upon the blowing of the wind with a given momentum. Here, perhaps, it may seem that we quite get rid of every subjective or anthropomorphic element. But this is a mistake. The use of the word "momentum" shows how we are compelled to conceive the event as a manifestation of force. We may abolish the figment of a specific *occulta vis;* but strive as we will, we cannot mentally represent the event otherwise than as a differential result of the excess of one quantum of force over another quantum of force. And what do we mean by force? Our conception of force is nothing but a generalized abstraction from our sensations of muscular resistance. That such a conception is merely symbolic, that it does not truly represent the real force objectively existing, I have already shown. Nevertheless from the relativity of our thought, such is the only conception which we can frame. Therefore, I repeat, from first to last, whether we give a theological, a metaphysical, or a scientific explanation of any phenomenon, we alike interpret it in terms of consciousness. Whether we frame the crude conception of an arbitray volition, or the refined conception of a uniformly conditioned force, we must equally admit that our subjective feelings are the only materials with which the conception can be framed. The consciousness of force remains dominant from first to last, and can be abolished only by abolishing consciousness itself.

But now, in the second place, this final scientific conception of a uniformly conditioned force cannot even be framed save by postulating an unconditioned Power existing independently of consciousness, to which no limit is conceivable in time or space, and of which all phenomena,

---

* Ibid., pp. 253–55.

as known to us, are the manifestations. It was demonstrated above, in the fourth chapter, that without postulating such an Absolute Existence, we can frame no theory whatever, either of external or of internal phenomena, even our proof of the relativity of knowledge immediately becoming nonsense in such case. It was shown that the existence of such a Power independent of us is an element involved in our consciousness of our own existence—is, in short, the "obverse of our self-consciousness." Thus the three stages disappear entirely, and the three terminal conceptions which are allaged as distinctively characteristic of the stages are seen to be identical. The God of the monotheist, the Nature of the metaphysician, and the Absolute Being which science is compelled to postulate, differ only as symbols differ which stand for the same eternal fact.

ORGANIZATION OF THE SCIENCE*

The results obtained in the course of the preceding inquiry have added depth and precision to our conception of the Scope of Philosophy. In coming to look upon all phenomena as manifestations of a Power unknowable in itself, yet knowable in the order of its phenomenal manifestations, we have virtually come to declare that the true business of philosophy is the determination of the order of the phenomena in which this omnipresent Power is manifested. And thus we arrive by another road at the very same definition of Philosophy which was previously given; and we see that the progress of deanthropomorphization, while leaving the religious attitude of philosophy entirely unchanged, has at the same time precisely limited its scope in making it the Synthesis of the general truths of science into a system of universal truth.

EVOLUTION AND DISSOLUTION*

It is necessary for us therefore, having finished our analysis, to begin the work of synthesis. In the course of our search for the widest generalizations of Physics, we discovered, as the most concrete result of analysis, that there is going on throughout the known universe *a continuous redistribution of matter and motion.* Let us now, following out the hint of our imaginary interlocutor, endeavour to ascertain the extent, character, and direction of this continuous redistribution. Have the infinitude of changes in the aspect of things, which the rhythm of motion necessitates, any common character, and if they have, what is that character? Are the redistributions of matter and motion, which are going on all around us, aimless and unrelated, or do they tend in common toward some definable

---

* Ibid., vol. 2, p. 3.
* Ibid., pp. 189–90, 199–201.

result? Can any formula be found which will express some dynamic principle, true of the whole endless metamorphosis?

As finally amended then, our formula asserts that the career of any composite body is a series of more or less complicated rhythms, of which the differential result is, *at first,* the integration of its constituent matter and the dissipation of part of its contained motion, and, *at last,* the diffusion of its constituent matter accompanied by reabsorption of the lost motion, or its equivalent.

It is now the time to apply to these antagonist processes some more convenient and accurate names than the half-dozen pairs of correlative synonyms by which we have thus far described them. The names selected by Mr. Spencer will be practically justified by the entire exposition contained in the following chapters; but even the cases already fragmentarily studied enable us partly to realize the significance of the terms Evolution and Dissolution, by which he has designated these processes. In Mr. Spencer's terminology, the integration of matter and concomitant dissipation of motion is Evolution—while the abosrption of motion and concomitant disintegration of matter is Dissolution.

THE LAW OF EVOLUTION*

The exposition will be rendered clearer by the preliminary explanation of four technical terms, which will continually recur, and which must be thoroughly understood before any further step can be taken toward comprehending the Law of Evolution. These terms are neither obscure in themselves, nor newly coined, but because we shall henceforth employ them in a strict and special sense, they require careful definition.

I. An object is said to be *homogeneous* when each of its parts is like every other part. An illustration is not easy to find, since perfect homogeneity is not known to exist. But there is such a thing as relative homogeneity; and we say that a piece of gold is homogeneous as compared with a piece of wood; or that a wooden ball is homogeneous as compared with an orange.

II. An object is said to be *heterogenous* when its parts do not all resemble one another. All known objects are more or less heterogeneous. But, relatively speaking, a tree is said to be heterogeneous as compared with the seed from which it has sprung; and an orange is heterogeneous as compared with a wooden ball.

III. *Differentiation* is the arising of an unlikeness between any two of the units which go to make up an aggregate. It is the process through which objects increase in heterogeneity. A piece of cast-iron before it is exposed to the air is relatively homongeneous. But when, by exposure to

* Ibid., pp. 218–21.

the air, it has acquired a coating of ferric oxide, or iron-rust, it is relatively heterogeneous. The units composing its outside are unlike the units composing its inside; or, in other words, its outside is differentiated from its inside.

IV. The term *integration* we have already partly defined as the concentration of the material units which go to make up any aggregate. But a complete definition must recognize the fact, that, along with the integration of wholes, there goes on (in all cases in which structural complexity is attained) an integration of parts. This secondary integration may be defined as the segregation, or grouping together, of those units of a heterogeneous aggregate which resemble one another. A good example is afforded by crystallization. The particles of the crystalizing substance, which resemble each other, and which do not resemble the particles of the solvent fluid, gradually unite to form the crystal, which is thus said to be *integrated* from the solution. Integration is also seen in the rising of cream upon the surface of a dish of milk, and in the frothy collection of carbonic acid bubbles covering a newly filled glass of ale.

Obviously as it is through differentiation that an aggregate increases in *heterogeneity,* so it is through integration that an aggregate increases in *definiteness,* of structure and function. But there is still another way in which integration is expemplified. Along with increasing heterogeneity and definiteness of structure and function, the evolution of an aggregate is marked by the increasing subordination of the various functions, with their structures, to the requirements of the general functional activity of the aggregate. In other words, along with growing specialization of parts, there is a growing cooperation of parts, and an ever-increasing mutual dependence among parts. An illustration is furnished by the contrasted facts, that a slightly evolved animal, like a common earthworm, may be cut in two without destroying the life of either part; while a highly evolved animal, like a dog, is destroyed if a single artery is severed, or if any one of the viscera is prevented from discharging its peculiar functions. This third kind of integration is the process through which an evolving aggregate increases in *coherence.* And with this, our definition of the factors which concur in the process of evolution is complete.

We are now prepared to show inductively that wherever, as in organic aggregates, the conditions permit, *the integration of matter and concomitant dissipation of motion, which primarily constitutes Evolution, is attended by a continuous change from indefinite, incoherent homogeneity to definite, coherent heterogeneity of structure and function, through successive differentiations and integrations.* In illustration of this statement, let us describe first some of the differentiations, and secondly some of the integrations, which successively occur during the development of an individual organism.

GENESIS OF MAN, INTELLECTUALLY*

The chief difficulty which most persons find in accepting the Doctrine of Evolution as applied to the origin of the human race is the difficulty of realizing in imagination the kinship between the higher and the lower forms of intelligence and emotion. And this difficulty is enhanced by a tendency of which our daily associations make it hard to rid ourselves. There is a tendency to exaggerate the contrasts which really exist, by leaving out of mind the intermediate phenomena and considering only the extremes. Many critics, both among those who are hostile to the development theory and among those who regard it with favour, habitually argue as if the intelligence and morality of the human race might be fairly represented by the intelligence and morality of a minority of highly organized and highly educated people in the most civilized communities. When speaking of mankind they are speaking of that which is represented to their imagination by the small number of upright, cultivated, and well-bred people with whom they are directly acquainted, and also to some extent by a few of those quite exceptional men and women who have left names recorded in history. Though other elements are admitted into the conception, these are nevertheless the ones which chiefly give to it its character. Employing then this conception of mankind, abstracted from these inadeqaute instances, our critics ask us how it is possible to imagine that a race possessed of such a godlike intellect, such a keen aesthetic sense, and such a lofty soul, should ever have descended from a race of mere brutes.

Social evolution therefore, regarded as a complicated series of intellectual and emotional changes determined by the aggregation of men into communities, is a new order of evolution, more highly compounded than any that had gone before it. When, in the course of the struggle for existence, men began to unite in family groups of comparatively permanent organization, a new era was begun in the progress of things upon the earth's surface. A new set of structural and functional changes began, which for a long while proceeding with the slowness characteristic of the early stages of every order of evolution, are at last proceeding with a rapidity only to be slackened when some penultimate stage of equilibrium is approached. Hence it is in the highest degree unphilosophical to attempt to explain the present position of civilized man solely by reference to the laws of organic and psychical evolution as obtained by the study of life in general. It is for biology to explain the differences between the human hand and foot and the hands and feet of the other primates; but the chief differences between civilized man and the other members of the order to which he belongs are psychological differences, and the immense series

---

* Ibid., vol. 4, pp. 46–47, 58–59.

of psychical changes to which they are due has been all along determined by social conditions.

GENESIS OF MAN, MORALLY*

There are two things, said Kant, which fill me with awe because of their sublimity,—the starry heavens above us, and the moral law within us. From the modern point of view there is interest as well as instruction to be found in the implied antithesis. While in the study of the steller universe we contemplate the process of evolution on a scale so vast that reason and imagination are alike baffled in the effort to trace out its real significance, and we are overpowered by the sense of the infinity that surrounds us; on the other hand, in the study of the moral sense we contemplate the last and noblest product of evolution which we can ever know,—the attribute latest to be unfolded in the development of psychical life, and by the possession of which we have indeed become as gods, knowing the good and the evil.

. . . Admitting the truth of the Kantian position, that there exists in us a moral sense for analyzing which our individual experience does not afford the requisite data, and which must therefore be regarded as ultimate for each individual, it is nevertheless open to us to inquire into the emotional antecedents of this organized moral sense as exhibited in ancestral types of psychical life. The inquiry will result in the conviction that the moral sense is not ultimate, but derivative, and that it has been built up out of slowly organized experiences of pleasures and pains.

If the tentacles of a polyp are rudely struck by some passing or approaching body, the whole polyp contracts violently in such a manner as to throw itself slightly out of the way; but if a fragment of assimilable food, floating by, happens to touch one of the tentacles gently, the tentcale grasps it and draws it slowly down to the polyp's digestive sac. Now between these contrasted actions there is no such psychical difference as accompanies the similarly contrasted human actions of taking food and ducking the head to avoid a blow; for the polyp's contractions, being simply reflex actions of the lowest sort, are unattended by states of consciousness, either agreeable or disagreeable. Nevertheless there is one respect in which the two cases perfectly agree. In both cases there is a seeking of that which is beneficial to the organism, and a shunning of that which, is injurious. And while, in the case of the polyp, there is no conscious pleasure or pain, we may fairly surmise that, as soon as any animal's psychical life becomes sufficiently complex to be attended by distinct states of consciousness, the presence of that which is beneficial is accompanied by a pleasurable feeling which leads to the seeking of it,

---

* Ibid., pp. 104, 108, 111–12, 124–5, 130–33, 136–37.

while the pressence of that which is injurious is accompanied by a painful feeling which leads to the shunning of it.

In our theory of pleasure and pain, which if taken as ultimate would be hedonism, the well-being of the community has been as far as possible omitted from the account. Wherever I have introduced references to social phenomena, I have considered them only in their effects upon the fulness of life of the individual. In dealing with the incentives to action in a race of brute animals, the foregoing considerations would be sufficient. But in the so-called utilitarian theory as it is now to be expounded, the well-being of the community, even when incompatible with that of the individual, is the all-important consideration.

It will be remembered that, in treating of the parallel evolution of the mind and the nervous system, it was shown that the increase of intelligence in complexity and speciality involves a lengthening of the period during which the nervous connections involved in ordinary adjustments are becoming organized. Even if the physical interpretation there given should turn out to be inadequate, the fact remains undeniable, that while the nervous connections accompanying a simple intelligence are already organized at birth, the nervous connections accompanying a complex intelligence are chiefly organized after birth. Thus there arise the phenomena of infancy, which are non-existent among those animals whose physical actions are purely reflex and instinctive. Infancy, psychologically considered, is the period during which the nerve connections and correlative ideal associations necessary for self-maintenance are becoming permanently established. Now this period, which only begins to exist when the intelligence is considerably complex, becomes longer and longer as the intelligence increases in complexity. In the human race it is much longer than in any race of mammals, and it is much longer in the civilized man than in the savage. Indeed among the educated classes of civilized society, its average duration may be said to be rather more than a quarter of a century, since during all this time those who are to live by brain work are simply acquiring the capacity to do so, and are usually supported upon the products of parental labour.

It need not be said that, on the general theory of evolution, the passage from the short infancy of other primates to the relatively long infancy witnessed among the lowest contemporary savages cannot have been a sudden one.

ANTHROPOMORPHIC THEISM*

Though the mediaeval conception of an arbitrary providence, overruling natural laws and occasionally setting them aside, influenced by human

---

* Ibid., 186–87.

petitions to bring about special results by extraordinary means, and singling out nations or individuals as the objects of its favour or displeasure, has been partially abandoned for a more refined conception of theism, in which the Deity is represented as working through natural laws; yet the survival of the doctrine of final causes shows that a strong element of anthropomorphism is retained even in the latter conception. The doctrine of final causes ultimately reposes on the assumption that God entertains intentions and purposes closly resembling in kind, though greatly excelling in degree of sagacity, the purposes and intentions of man. In accordance with this view, we are told that it will not do to content ourselves with the discovery of Law, but that we must also look about for indications of Purpose; since Law is not, relatively to our human understanding, an ultimate fact, but may be recognized by us as the expression of the will of a Lawgiver. Everything that exists—it is said—has been created to subserve some design, and is a means to the accomplishment of some end; and the detection of this end, the penetration of this design, must assist us greatly in the scientific study of the universe.

DARWINISM VERIFIED*

From an obverse point of view it might be argued that since a philosophical theism must regard Divine power as the immediate source of all phenomena alike, therefore science cannot properly explain any particular group of phenomena by a direct reference to the action of Deity. Such a reference is not an explanation, since it adds nothing to our previous knowledge either of the phenomena or of the manner of Divine action. The business of science is simply to ascertain in what manner phenomena co-exist with each other or follow each other, and the only kind of explanation with which it can properly deal is that which refers one set of phenomena to another set. In pursuing this its legitimate business, science does not trench on the province of theology in any way, and there is no conceivable occasion for any conflict between the two. From this and the previous considerations, taken together, it follows not only that such explanations as are contained in the Newtonian and Darwinian theories are entirely consistent with theism, but also that they are the only kind of explanations with which science can properly concern itself at all. To say that complex organisms were directly created by the Deity is to make an assertion which, however true in a theistic sense, is utterly barren. It is of no profit to theism, which must be taken for granted before the assertion can be made; and it is of no profit to science, which must still ask its question, "How? " But a special reason may be assigned why Nature, which never makes long jumps, must have been incapable of making this particular jump. Throughout the animal kingdom the

---

* Ibid., *Darwinism and Other Essays,* vol. 8, pp. 7–8.

period of infancy is correlated with feelings of parental affection, sometimes confined to the mother, but often shared by the father, as in the case of animals which mate. Where, as among the lower animals, there is no infancy, there is no parental affection. Where the infancy is very short, the parental feeling, though intense while it lasts, presently disappears, and the offspring cease to be distinguished from strangers of the same species. And in general the duration of the feelings which ensure the protection of the offspring is determined by the duration of the infancy. The agency of natural selection in maintaining this balance is too obvious to need illustration. Hence, if long infancies could have suddenly come into existence among a primitive race of ape-like men, the race would have quickly perished from inadequate persistence of the parental affections. The prolongation must therefore have been gradual, and the same increase of intelligence to which it was due must also have prolonged the correlative parental feelings, by associating them more and more with anticipations and memories. The concluding phases of this long change may be witnessed in the course of civilization. Our parental affections now endure through life—and while their fundamental instinct is perhaps no stronger than in savages, they are, nevertheless, far more effectively powerful, owing to our far greater power of remembering the past and anticipating the future.

Thus we cross the chasm which divides animality from humanity, gregariousness from sociality, hedonism from morality, the sense of pleasure and pain from the sense of right and wrong. For note that by the time integration has resulted in the establishment of a permanent family group with definite relationships between the members, the incentives to action in each member of the group have become quite different from what they were in state of mere gregariousness. Sympathy, or the power of ideally reproducing in one's self the pleasures and pains of another person, is manifested in a rudimentary form by all gregarious animals of moderate intelligence. Not unfrequently, as Mr. Darwin shows, a baboon has been known to risk his life to save that of a comrade; and the higher apes habitually take under their care young orphans of their own species. It is eveident that this power of sympathy must be strenthened and further developed when a number of individuals are brought into closer and more enduring relationships, even though these come far short of what, from our modern ethical standard, would be termed loving.

CHAUNCEY WRIGHT

THE PHILOSOPHY OF HERBERT SPENCER*

Why the inductive and mathematical sciences, after their first rapid development at the culmination of Greek civilization, advanced so slowly for two thousand years,—and why in the following two hundred years a knowledge of natural and mathematical science has accumulated, which so vastly exceeds all that was previously known that these sciences may be justly regarded as the products of our own times,—are questions which have interested the modern philosopher not less than the objects with which these sciences are more immediately conversant. Was it in the employment of a new method of research, or in the exercise of greater virtue in the use of old methods, that this singular modern phenomenon had its origin? Was the long period one of arrested development, and is the modern era one of a normal growth: or should we ascribe the characteristics of both periods to so-called historical accidents,—to the influence of conjunctions in circumstances of which no explanation is possible, save in the omnipotence and wisdom of a guiding Providence?

The explanation which has become commonplace, that the ancients employed deduction chiefly in their scientific inquiries, while the moderns employ induction, proves to be too narrow, and fails upon close examination to point with sufficient distinctness the contrast that is evident

* Chauncey Wright, "The Philosophy of Herbert Spencer," *North American Review*, 100 (April, 1865), pp. 423–476.

between ancient and modern scientific doctrines and inquiries. For all knowledge is founded on observation, and proceeds from this by analysis and synthesis, by synthesis and analysis, by induction and deduction, and if possible by verification, or by new appeals to observation under the guidance of deduction,—by steps which are indeed correlative parts of one method; and the ancient sciences afford examples of every one of these methods, or parts of the one complete method, which have been generalized from the examples of science.

The attempt to discover the explanation of this phenomenon is the antithesis of "facts" and "theories" or "facts" and "ideas,"—in the neglect among the ancients of the former, and their too exclusive attention to the latter,—proves also to be too narrow, as well as open to the charge of vagueness. For, in the first place, the antithesis is not complete. Facts and theories are not co-ordinate species. Theories, if true, are facts,—a particular class of facts indeed, generally complex ones, but still facts. Facts, on the other hand, even in the narrowest signification of the word, if they be at all complex, and if a logical connection subsists between their constituents, have all the positive attributes of theories.

Nevertheless, this distinction, however inadequate it may be to explain the source of true method in science, is well founded, and connotes an important character in true method. A fact is a proposition of which the verification by an appeal to the primary sources of our knowledge or to experience is direct and simple. A theory, on the other hand, if true, has all the characteristics of a fact, except that its verification is possible only by indirect, remote, and difficult means. To convert theories into facts is to add *simple verification,* and the theory thus acquires the full characteristics of a fact.

Modern science deals then no less with theories than with facts, but always as much as possible with the verification of theories,—if not to make them facts by simple verification through experiment and observation, at least to prove their truth by indirect verification.

The difference, then, between ancient and modern science is not truly characterized by any of the several explanations which have been proposed. The explanation, however, which, in our opinion, comes nearest to the true solution, and yet fails to designate the real point of difference, is that which the positivists find in the distinction between "objective method" and "subjective method." The objective method is verification by sensuous tests, tests of sensible experience,—a deduction from theory of consequences, of which we may have sensible experiences if they be true. The subjective method, on the other hand, appeals to the tests of internal evidence, tests of reason, and the data of self-consciousness. But whatever be the origin of the theories of science, whether from a systematic examination of empirical facts by conscious induction, or from the natural biases of the mind, the so-called intuitions of reason, in other words what seems probable without a distinct survey of our experiences,—whatever the origin, real or ideal, the *value* of these theories can only be tested, say the positivists, by an appeal to sensible experience, by deductions from them of consequences which we can confirm by the undoubted testimony of the senses. Thus, while ideal or transcendental elements are admitted into scientific researches, though in themselves insusceptible of simple verification, they must still show credentials from the senses, either by affording from themselves consequences capable of sensuous verification, or by yielding such consequences in conjunction with ideas which by themselves are verifiable.

It is through the past labors of an author that we must judge of his qualifications for future work, and the completeness of his preparation. Mr. Spencer's writings evince an extensive knowledge of facts political and scientific, but extensive rather than profound, and mainly at second hand. It is not, of course, to be expected that a philosopher will be an original investigator in all the departments of knowledge with which he is obliged to have dealings. He must take much at second hand. But original investigations in some department of empirical science are a discipline which best tests and develops even a philosopher's powers. He has in this at least an experience of what is requisite to an adequate comprehension of facts. He learns how to make knowledge profitable to the ascertainment of new truths,—an art in which the modern natural philosopher excels. By new truths must be understood such as are not implied in what we already know, or educible from what is patent to common observation. However skillfully the philosopher may apply his analytical processes to the abstraction of the truths involved in patent facts, the utility of his results will depend not so much on their value and extent as mere abstractions, as on their capacity to enlarge our experience by bringing to notice residual phenomena, and making us observe what we have entirely overlooked, or search out what has eluded our observation. Such is the character of the principles of modern natural philosophy, both mathematical and physical. They are rather the eyes with which nature is seen, than the elements and constituents of the objects discovered. It was in a clear apprehension of this value in the principles of mathematical and experimental science, that the excellence of Newton's genius consisted; and it is this value which the Positive Philosophy most prizes. But this is not the value which we find in Mr. Spencer's speculations.

Mr. Spencer is not a positivist, though that was not a very culpable mistake which confounded his speculations with the writings of this school. For however much he differs from the positivists in his methods and opinions, he is actuated by the same confidence in the capacities of a scientific method, and by the same disrespect for the older philosophies. Mr. Spencer applies a method for the ascertainment of ultimate truths, which a positivist would regard as correct only on the supposition that the materials of truth have all been collected, and that the research of science is no longer for the enlargement of our experience or for the informing of the mind. Until these conditions be realized, the positivist regards such attempts as Mr. Spencer's as not only faulty, but positively pernicious and misleading. Nothing justifies the development of abstract principles in science but their utility in enlarging our concrete knowledge of nature. The ideas on which mathematical Mechanics and the Calculus are founded, the morphological ideas of Natural History, and the theories of Chemistry are such working ideas,—finders, not merely summaries of truth.

But Mr. Spencer thinks he has established his "Law of Evolution" by induction. The examples from which he has analyzed his law, the examples of progress in the development of the several elements of civilization, such as languages, laws, fashions, and ideas,—the hypothetical examples of the Nebular Hypothesis and the Development Hypothesis, and the example of embryological development (the only one our conceptions of which are not liable to be tainted by teleological biases),— are examples which, according to Mr. Spencer's philosophy, afford both the definition and its justification. In other words, his definitions are only carefully elaborated general descriptions in abstract terms; or statements of facts which are observed in numerous instances or classes of instances, in terms detached from all objects, in abstract terms, of which the intension is fully known, but of which the extension is unknown except through the descriptions they embody. This, though a useful, is a precarious kind of induction, and is apt to lead to premature and false generalizations, or extensions of descriptions to what is hypothetical or unknown.

THE GENESIS OF SPECIES*

Mr. Darwin . . . has not in his works repeated with sufficient frequency his faith in the universality of the law of causation, in the phenomena of general physiology or theoretical biology, as well as in all the rest of physical nature. He has not said often enough, it would appear, that in referring any effect to "accident," he only means that its causes are like particular phases of the weather, or like innumerable phenomena in the concrete course of nature generally, which are quite beyond the power of finite minds to anticipate or to account for in detail, though none the less really determinate or due to regular causes. That he has committed this error appears from the fact that his critic, Mr. Mivart, has made the mistake, which nullifies nearly the whole of his criticism, of supposing that "the theory of Natural Selection may (though it need not) be taken in such a way as to lead men to regard the present organic world as formed, so to speak, *accidentally,* beautiful and wonderful as is confessedly the hap-hazard result" (p. 33). Mr. Mivart, like many another writer,

---

* *North American Review,* July 1871, pp. 68ff.

seems to forget the age of the world in which he lives and for which he writes,—the age of "experimental philosophy," the very standpoint of which, its fundamental assumption, is the universality of physical causation. This is so familiar to minds bred in physical studies, that they rarely imagine that they may be mistaken for disciples of Democritus, or for believers in "the fortuitous concourse of atoms," in the sense, at least, which theology has attached to this phrase. If they assent to the truth that may have been meant by the phrase, they would not for a moment suppose that the atoms move fortuitously, but only that their conjunctions, constitating the actual concrete orders of events, could not be anticipated except by a knowledge of the natures and regular histories of each and all of them,—such knowledge as belongs only to omniscience.

EVOLUTION BY NATURAL SELECTION*

Accidents in the ordinary every-day sense are causes in every concrete course of events,—in the weather, in history, in politics, in the market,— and no theory of these events can leave them out. Explanation of the events consists in showing how they will result, or have resulted, through certain fixed principles or laws of action from the occasions or opportunities, which such accidents present. Given the state of the atmosphere over a large district in respect to temperature, moisture, pressure, and motion,—none of which could have been anticipated without similar data for a short time before, all in fact being accidents,—and the physical principles of meteorology might enable us to explain the weather that immediately follows. So with the events of history, etc. In no other sense are accidents supposed as causes in the theory of natural selection. Accidental variations and surrounding conditions of existence, and the previous condition of the organic world, (none of which could have been anticipated from anything we actually know, all in fact being "accidents")—these are the causes which present the occasions or opportunities through which principles of utility and advantage are brought to bear in changing structures and habits and improving their adaptations.

EVOLUTION OF SELF-CONSCIOUSNESS*

It has come to be understood, and very generally allowed, that the conception of the origin of man as an animal race, as well as the origin of individual men within it, in accordance with the continuity of organic development maintained in the theory of evolution, does not involve any very serious difficulties, or difficulties so great as are presented by any other hypothesis of this origin, not excepting that of "special creation";—

* *North American Review,* July 1872, pp. 6–7.
* *North American Review,* April 1873, pp. 245–47, 255–58, 263.

if that can be properly called a hypothesis, when it is, in fact, a resumption of all the difficulties of natural explanation, assuming them to be insuperable and summarizing them under a single positive name. Yet in this evolution, the birth of self-consciousness is still thought by many to be a step not following from antecedent conditions in "nature," except in an incidental manner, or in so far only as "natural" antecedents have prepared the way for the "supernatural" advent of the self-conscious soul.

Independently of the form of expression, and of the false sentiment which is the motive of the antithesis in this familiar conception, or independently of its mystical interest, which has given to the words "natural" and "supernatural" their commonly accepted meanings, there is a foundation of scientific truth in the conception. For the word "evolution" conveys a false impression to the imagination, not really intended in the scientific use of it. It misleads by suggesting a continuity in the *kinds* of powers and functions in living beings, that is, by suggesting transition by insensible steps from one *kind* to another, as well as in the *degrees* of their importance and exercise at different stages of development. The truth is on the contrary, that according to the theory of evolution, new uses of old powers arise discontinuously both in the bodily and mental natures of the animal, and in its individual developments, as well as in the development of its race, although, at their rise, these uses are small and of the smallest importance to life. They seem merged in the powers to which they are incident, and seem also merged in the special purposes or functions in which, however, they really have no part, and which are no parts of them. Their services or functions in life, though realized only incidentally at first, and in the feeblest degree, are just as distinct as they afterwards come to appear in their fullest development. The new uses are related to older powers only as *accidents,* so far as the special services of the older powers are concerned, although, from the more general point of view of natural law, their relations to older uses have not the character of accidents, since these relations are, for the most part, determined by universal properties and laws, which are not specially related to the needs and conditions of living beings. Thus the uses of limbs for swimming, crawling, walking, leaping, climbing, and flying are distinct uses, and are related to each other only through the general mechanical principles of locomotion, through which some one use, in its first exercise, may be incident to some other, though, in its full exercise and perfection of special service, it is independent of the other, or has only a common dependence with the other or more general conditions.

Many mental as well as bodily powers thus have mixed natures, or independent uses; as, for example, the powers of the voice to call and allure, to warn and repeal, and its uses in music and language; or the numerous uses of the human hand in services of strength and dexterity. And, on the contrary, the same uses are, in some cases, realized by independent organs as, for example, respiration in water and in the air by gills and lungs, or flight by means of fins, feathers, and webs. The appearance of a really new power in *nature* (using this word in the wide meaning attached to it in science), the power of flight in the first birds, for example, is only involved potentially in previous phenomena. In the same way, no act of self-consciousness, however elementary, may have been realized before man's first self-conscious act in the animal world; yet the act may have been involved potentially in pre-existing powers or causes.

So far as images act in governing trains of thought and reasoning, they act as signs; but, with reference to the more vivid outward signs, they are, in the animal mind merged in the things signified, like stars in the light of the sun. Hence, language in its narrower sense, as the instrument of reflective thought, appears to depend directly on the intensity of significant, or representative, images; since the power to attend to these and intensify them still further, at the same time that an equivalent outward sign is an object of attention, would appear to depend solely on the relative intensities of the two states, or on the relations of intensity in perception and imagination, or in original and revived impressions. The direct power of attention to intensify a revived impression in imagination does not appear to be different in kind from the power of attention in perception, or in outward impressions generally. But this direct power would be obviously aided by the indirect action of attention when fixed by an outward sign, provided attention could be directed to both at the same time; as a single glance may comprehend in one field of view the moon or the brighter planets and the sun, since the moon or planet is not hidden like the stars, by the glare of day.

As soon, then, as the progress of animal intelligence through an extension of the range in its powers of memory, or in revived impressions, together with a corresponding increase in the vividness of these impressions, has reached a certain point (a progress in itself useful, and therefore likely to be secured in some part of nature, as one among its numerous grounds of selection, or lines of advantage), it becomes possible for such an intelligence to fix its attention on a vivid outward sign, without losing sight of, or dropping out of distinct attention, an image or revived impression; which latter would only serve, in case of its spontaneous revival in imagination, as a sign of the same thing, or the same event. Whether the vivid outward sign be a real object or event, of which the revived image is the counterpart, or whether it be a sign in a stricter meaning of the term,—that is, some action, figure, or utterance, associated either naturally or artificially with all similar objects or events, and, consequently, with the revived and representative image of them,—whatever the character of this outward sign may be, provided the representative image, or inward sign, still retains, in distinct consciousness, its power as such, then the outward sign may be consciously recognized as a substitute for the inward one, and a consciousness of simultaneous internal and external suggestion, or significance, might be realized; and the contrast of thoughts and things, at least in their power of suggesting that of which they may be coincident signs, could, for the first time, be perceptible. This would plant the germ of the distinctively human form of self-consciousness.

. . . Thought, hence forward, may be an object to thought in its distinct contrast, as an inward sign, with the outward and more vivid sign of that which they both suggest, or revive from memory. This contrast is heightened if the outward one is more strictly a sign; that is, is not the perception of an object or event, of which the inward and representative image is a counterpart, but is of a different nature, for instance some movement or gesture or vocal utterance, or some graphic sign, associated by contiguity with the object or event, or, more properly, with its representative image. The "concept" so formed is not a thing complete in itself, but is essentially a cause, or step, in mental trains. The outward sign, the image, or inward sign, and the suggested thought, or image, form a train, like a train which might be wholly within the imagination. This train is present, in all its three constituents, to the first, or immediate, consciousness, in all degrees of intelligence; but in the revival of it, in the inferior degrees of intelligence, the middle term is obliterated, as in the trains of thought above considered. The animal has in mind only an image of the sign, previously present in perception, followed now immediately by an image of what was suggested through the obliterated mental image. But the latter, in the higher degrees of intelligence, is distinctly recalled as a middle term. In the revival of past trains, which were first produced through outward signs, the dumb animal has no consciousness of there having been present more than one of the two successive signs, which, together with the suggested image, formed the actual train in its first occurrence. The remembered outward sign is now a thought, or image, immediately suggesting or recalling that which was originally suggested by a feebler intermediate step.

. . . Reflection would thus be, not what most metaphysicians appear to regard it, a fundamentally new faculty in man, as elementary and primordial as memory itself, or the power of abstractive attention, or the function of signs and representative images in generalization; but it would be determined in its contrasts with other mental faculties by the nature of its objects. On its subjective side it would be composed of the same mental faculties—namely, memory, attention, abstraction—as those which are employed in the primary use of the senses. It would be engaged upon what these senses have furnished to memory; but would act as independently of any orders of grouping and succession presented by them, as the several senses themselves do of one another. To this extent, reflection is a distinct faculty, and though, perhaps, not peculiar to man, is in him so prominent and marked in its effects on the development of the individual mind, that it may be regarded as his most essential and elementary mental distinction in kind. For differences of degrees in causes may make differences of kinds in effects.

NATURAL THEOLOGY AS A POSITIVE SCIENCE*

Cultural history and anatomy have hitherto furnished the principal grounds to the theologian for the speculation of final causes, since these sciences exhibit many instances of a complex combination of causes in the structures and habits of organic bodies, and at the same time a distinct and peculiar class of effects, namely, those which constitute the well-being and perfection of organic life; and from these causes and effects, regarded as means and ends in the order of nature, the arguments and illustrations of natural theology have been chiefly drawn.

But the facts of these sciences are not merely the most useful to the theologian; they are indeed indispensable, and occupy a peculiar position in his argument, since they alone afford the class of effects on which, assumed as ends, the speculation of final causes ultimately rests.

Only by assuming human welfare, or with this the welfare also of other sentient beings, to the end for which the universe exists, that the doctrine of final causes has hitherto found any support in natural sciences.

Though it is still maintained by theologians that the arguments for design are properly inductive arguments, yet the physical proofs of natural theology are not regarded by many modern writers as having any independent weight; and it is in mental and moral science that the facts are sought which will warrant the induction of design from the general phenomena of nature. It is hardly considered logical, even by the theological writers of our day, to conclude, with Paley, "that the works of nature proceed from intelligence and design; because, in the properties of relation to a purpose, subserviency to a use, they resemble what intelligence and design are constantly producing, and what nothing [which we know] except intelligence and design ever produce at all." For it is denied by the physical philosopher that causes and effects in natural phenomena can be interpreted into the terms of natural theology by any key which science itself affords. By what criterion, he would ask, can we distinguish among the numberless effects, that are also causes, and among the causes that may, for aught we can know, be also effects,—how can we distinguish which are the means and which are the ends? What effects are we warranted by observation in calling final, or final causes, or the ends for which the others exist? The belief on other grounds that there *are* final causes, that the universe exists for some purpose, is one thing; but the belief that science discloses, or even that science can disclose, what this purpose is, is quite a different thing.

---

* *North American Review*, January 1865, pp. 177, 179–80, 183–85.

. . . It is from the illegitimate pretensions of natural theology that the figment of a conflict between science and religion has arisen; and the efforts of religious thinkers to counteract the supposed atheistical tendencies of science, and to give a religious interpretation to its facts, have only served to deepen the false impression that such a conflict actually exists, so that revolutions in scientific theories have been made to appear in the character of refutations of religious doctrines.

. . . When a proof of special design is invalidated by the discovery that a particular effect in the operations of nature, which previously appeared to result from a special constitution and adjustment of certain forces, is really a consequent of the general properties of matter,—which, for example, the laws of planetary motion were shown to result from the law of universal gravitation, and the mathematical plan of the solar system was seen to be a consequent of a single universal principle,—the harm, if there be any, results from the theologian's mistakes, and not from the corrections of science. He should refrain from attributing any special plan or purpose to the creation, if he would find in science a constant support to religious truth. But this abstinence does not involve a withdrawal of the mind from the proper religious interests of natural science, nor weaken a legitimate faith in final causes. Even the Newtonian mechanism of the heavens, simple, primordial, and necessary as it seems, still discloses to the devout mind evidence of a wisdom unfathomable, and of a design which transcends interpretation; and when, in the more complicated order of organic life, surprising and beautiful adaptations inspire in the naturalist the conviction that purpose and intelligence are manifested in them,— that they spring from a nature akin to the devising power of his own mind,—there is nothing in science or philosophy which can legitimately rebuke his enthusiasm,—nothing, unless it be the dogmatism which would presumptuously interpret as science what is only manifest to faith, or would require of faith that it shall justify itself by proofs.

JOHN DEWEY

DARWIN'S INFLUENCE UPON PHILOSOPHY*

I

That the publication of the *Origin of Species* marked an epoch in the development of the natural sciences is well known to the layman. That the combination of the very words origin and species embodied an intellectual revolt and introduced a new intellectual temper is easily overlooked by the expert. The conceptions that had reigned in the philosophy of nature and knowledge for two thousand years, the conceptions that had become the familiar furniture of the mind, rested on the assumption of the superiority of the fixed and final; they rested upon treating change and origin as signs of defect and unreality. In laying hands upon the sacred ark of absolute permanency, in treating the forms that had been regarded as types of fixity and perfection as originating and passing away, the *Origin of Species* introduced a mode of thinking that in the end was bound to transform the logic of knowledge, and hence the treatment of morals, politics and religion.

No wonder then that the publication of Darwin's book, a half century ago, precipitated a crisis. The true nature of the controversy is easily

One of a course of lectures entitled "Charles Darwin and His Influence on Science" given at Columbia University in 1909, this essay was first published in *Popular Science Monthly* 75 (July 1909): pp. 90–98. Reprinted from *Popular Science* with permission of Times Mirror Magazines, Inc.

concealed from us, however, by the theological clamor that attended it. The vivid and popular features of the anti-Darwinian row tended to leave the impression that the issue was between science on one side and theology on the other. Such was not the case—the issue lay primarily within science itself, as Darwin himself early recognized. The theological outcry he discounted from the start, hardly noticing it save as it bore upon the "feelings of his female relatives." But for two decades before final publication he contemplated the possibility of being put down by his scientific peers as a fool or as crazy; and he set, as the measure of his success, the degree in which he should affect three men of science: Lyell in geology, Hooker in botany and Huxley in zoology.

Religious considerations lent fervor to the controversy, but they did not provoke it. Intellectually, religious emotions are not creative but conservative. They attach themselves readily to the current view of the world and consecrate it. They steep and dye intellectual fabrics in the seething vat of emotions; they do not form their warp and woof. There is not, I think, an instance of any large idea about the world being independently generated by religion. However much the ideas that rose up like armed men against Darwinism owed their intensity to religious associations, their origin and meaning are to be sought elsewhere.

II

Few words in our language foreshorten intellectual history as does the word species. The Greeks in initiating the intellectual life of Europe, were impressed by characteristic traits of the life of plants and animals; so impressed indeed that they made these traits the key to defining nature and to explaining mind and society. And truly, life is so wonderful that a seemingly successful reading of its mystery might well lead men to believe that the key to the secrets of heaven and earth was in their hands. The Greek rendering of this mystery, the Greek formulation of the aim and standard of knowledge, was in the course of time embodied in the word species and controlled philosophy for two thousand years. To understand the intellectual face-about expressed in the phrase "Origin of species," we must, then, understand the long dominant idea against which it was a protest.

Consider how men were impressed by the facts of life. Their eyes fell upon certain things slight in bulk, and frail in structure. To every appearance, these perceived things were inert and passive. Suddenly, under certain circumstances, these things—henceforth known as seeds or eggs or germs—begin to change, to change rapidly in size, form and qualities. Rapid and extensive changes occur, however, in many things—as when wood is touched by fire. But the changes in the living thing are orderly; they are cumulative; they tend constantly in one direction; they do not, like other changes, destroy or consume, or pass fruitless into wandering

flux; they realize and fulfill. Each successive stage, no matter how unlike
its predecessor, preserves its net effect and also prepares the way for a
fuller activity on the part of its successor. In living beings changes do
not happen as they seem to elsewhere, any which way; the earlier changes
are regulated in view of later results. This progressive organization does
not cease till there is achieved a true final term, a τελòs, a complete,
perfected end. This final form exercises in turn a plenitude of functions,
not the least noteworthy of which is production of germs like those from
which it took its own origin, germs capable of the same cycle of self-
fulfilling activity.

But the whole miraculous tale is not yet told. The same drama is
enacted to the same destiny in countless myriads of individuals so sundered
in time, so severed in place, that they have no opportunity for mutual
consultation and no means of interaction. As an old writer quaintly said,
"things of the same kind go through the same formalities"—celebrates,
as it were, the same ceremonial rites.

This formal activity which operates throughout a series of changes
and holds them to a single course; that subordinates their aimless flux
to its own perfect manifestation; which, leaping the boundaries of space
and time, keeps individuals in spite of their being distant in space and
remote in time to a uniform type of structure and function: this principle
seemed to give insight into the very nature of reality itself. To it Aristotle
gave the name ειδος. This term the scholastics translated as *species*.

The force of this term was deepened by its application to everything
in the universe that observes order in flux and manifests constancy through
change. From the casual drift of daily weather, through the uneven
recurrence of seasons and unequal return of seed time and harvest, up
to the majestic sweep of the heavens—the image of eternity in time—
and from this to the unchanging pure and contemplative intelligence
beyond nature lies one unbroken fulfillment of ends. Nature as a whole,
is a progressive realization of purpose strictly comparable to the realization
of purpose in any single plant or animal.

The conception of ειδος, species, the fixed form and final cause, was
the central principle of knowledge as well as of nature. Upon it rested
the logic of science. Change as change is mere flux and lapse; it insults
intelligence. Genuinely to know is to grasp a permanent end that realizes
itself through changes, holding them thereby within the metes and bounds
of fixed truth. Completely to know is to relate all special forms to their
one single end and good: pure contemplative intelligence. Since, however,
the scene of nature which directly confronts us is in change, nature as
directly and practically experienced cannot satisfy the conditions of knowledge. Human experience is also in flux, and hence the instrumentalities
of sense perception and of inference based upon observation are condemned in advance. Science is compelled to aim at realities lying behind
and beyond the processes of nature, and to carry on its search for those

realities by means of rational forms transcending ordinary modes of perception and inference.

There are, indeed, but two alternative courses. We must either find the appropriate objects and organs of knowledge in the mutual interactions of changing things; or else, to escape the infection of change, we must seek them in some transcendent and supernal region. The human mind, deliberately as it were, exhausted the logic of the changeless, the final and the transcendent, before it essayed adventure on the pathless wastes of generation and transformation. We dispose all too easily of the efforts of the schoolmen to interpret nature and mind in terms of real essences, hidden forms and occult faculties, forgetful of the seriousness and dignity of the ideas that lay behind. We dispose of them by laughing at the famous gentleman who accounted for the fact that opium put people to sleep on the ground it had a dormitive faculty. But the doctrine, held in our own day, that knowledge of the plant that yields the poppy consists in referring the peculiarities of an individual to a type, to a universal form, a doctrine so firmly established that any other method of knowing was conceived to be unphilosophical and unscientific, was a survival of precisely the same logic. This identity of conception in the scholastic and anti-Darwinian theory may well suggest greater sympathy for what has become unfamiliar and greater humility regarding the further unfamiliarities that history has in store.

Darwin was not, of course, the first to question the classic philosophy of nature and of knowledge. The beginnings of the revolution are in the physical science of the sixteenth and seventeenth centuries. When Galileo said: "It is my opinion that the earth is very noble and admirable by reason of so many and so different alterations and generations which are incessantly made therein," he expressed the changed temper that was coming over the world; the transfer of interest from the permanent to the changing. When Descartes said: "The nature of physical things is much more easily conceived when they are beheld coming gradually into existence, than when they are only considered as produced at once in a finished and perfect state," the modern world became self-conscious of the logic that was henceforth to control it, the logic of which Darwin's *Origin of Species* is the latest scientific achievement. Without the methods of Copernicus, Kepler, Galileo and their successors in astronomy, physics and chemistry, Darwin would have been helpless in the organic sciences. But prior to Darwin the impact of the new scientific method upon life, mind and politics, had been arrested for the most part, because between these ideal or moral interests and the inorganic world there intervened the kingdom of plants and animals. The gates of the garden of life were barred to the new ideas while only through this garden was there access to mind and politics. The influence of Darwin upon philosophy resides in his having freed the new logic for application to mind and morals by conquering the phenomena of life. When he said of species what Galileo had said of the earth, *e pur se muove,* he emancipated once for all genetic and experimental ideas as an organon of asking questions and looking for explanations in philosophy.

III

The exact bearings upon philosophy of the new logical outlook are, of course, as yet, uncertain and inchoate. We live in the twilight of intellectual transition. One must add the rashness of the prophet to the stubbornness of the partisan to venture a systematic exposition of the influence upon philosophy of the Darwinian method. At best, we can but inquire as to its general bearing—the effect upon mental temper and complexion, upon that body of half-conscious, half-instinctive intellectual aversions and preferences which determine, after all, our more deliberate intellectual enterprises. In this vaguer inquiry there happens to exist as a kind of touchstone one problem of great historic significance that has also been much discussed in Darwinian literature. I refer to the old problem of design versus chance, mind versus matter, as the causal explanation, first and final, of things.

As we have already seen, the classic notion of species carried with it the idea of purpose. In all living forms, a specific type is present directing the earlier stages of growth to the realization of its own perfection. Since this purposive regulative principle is not visible to the senses, it follows that it must be an ideal or rational force. Since, however, the perfect form is gradually approximated through the sensible changes, it also follows that in and through a sensible realm a rational ideal force is working out its own ultimate manifestation. These two inferences were extended to nature: (a) She does nothing in vain; but all for an ulterior purpose. (b) Within natural sensible events there is therefore contained a spiritual causal force, which as spiritual escapes perception, but is apprehended by an enlightened reason. (c) The manifestation of this principle brings about a subordination of matter and sense to its own realization, and this ultimate fulfillment is the goal of nature and man. The design argument thus operated in two directions. Purposefulness accounted for the intelligibility of nature and the possibility of science, while the absolute or cosmic character of this purposefulness gave sanction and worth to the moral and religious endeavors of man. Science was underpinned and morals authorized by one and the same principle, and their mutual agreement was eternally guaranteed.

This philosophy remained, in spite of sceptical and polemic outbursts, the official and the regnant philosophy of Europe for over two thousand years. The expulsion of fixed first and final causes from astronomy, physics, and chemistry had indeed given the doctrine something of a shock. But, on the other hand, increased acquaintance with the details of plant and animal life operated as a counterbalance and perhaps even strengthened the argument from design. The marvelous adaptations of organisms to their environment, of organs to the organism, of unlike parts of a complex organ—like the eye—to the organ itself; the foreshadowing by lower forms of the higher; the preparation in earlier stages of growth for organs that only later had their functioning—these things were increasingly recognized with the progress of botany, zoology, paleontology, and embryology. Together, they added such prestige to the design argument that by the late eighteenth century it was, as approved by the sciences of organic life, the central point of theistic and idealistic philosophy.

The Darwinian principle of natural selection cut straight under this philosophy. If all organic adaptations are due simply to constant variation and the elimination of those variations which are harmful in the struggle for existence that is brought about by excessive reproduction, there is no call for a prior intelligent causal force to plan and preordain them. Hostile critics charged Darwin with materialism and with making chance the cause of the universe.

Some naturalists, like Asa Gray, favored the Darwinian principle and attempted to reconcile it with design. Gray held to what may be called design on the installment plan. If we conceive the "stream of variations" to be itself intended, we may suppose that each successive variation was designed from the first to be selected. In that case, variation, struggle and selection simply define the mechanism of "secondary causes" through which the "first cause" acts; and the doctrine of design is none the worse off because we know more of its *modus operandi*.

Darwin could not accept this mediating proposal. He admits or rather he asserts that it is "impossible to conceive this immense and wonderful universe including man with his capacity of looking far backward and far into futurity as the result of blind chance or necessity." [1] But nevertheless he holds that since variations are in useless as well as useful directions, and since the latter are shifted out simply by the stress of the conditions of struggle for existence, the design argument as applied to living beings is unjustifiable; and its lack of support there deprives it of scientific value as applied to nature in general. If the variations of the pigeon, which under artificial selection give the pouter pigeon, are not preordained for the sake of the breeder, by what logic do we argue that variations resulting in natural species are predesigned? [2]

IV

So much for some of the more obvious facts of the discussion of design versus chance as causal principles of nature and of life as a whole. We

---

[1] *Life and Letters,* vol. 1, p. 282; cf. 285.—D.
[2] *Life and Letters,* vol. 2, pp. 146, 170, 245; vol. 1, 283–84. See also the closing portion of his "Variations of Animals and Plants under Domestication."—D.

brought up this discussion, you recall, as a crucial instance. What does our touchstone indicate as to the bearing of Darwinian ideas upon philosophy? In the first place, the new logic outlaws, flanks, dismisses—what you will—one type of problem and substitutes for it another type. Philosophy forswears inquiry after absolute origins and absolute finalities in order to explore specific values and the specific conditions that generate them.

Darwin concluded that the impossibility of assigning the world to chance as a whole and to design in its parts indicated the insolubility of the question. Two radically different reasons, however, may be given as to why a problem is insoluble. One reason is that the problem is too high for intelligence; the other is that the question in its very asking makes assumptions that render the question meaningless. The latter alternative is unerringly pointed to in the celebrated case of design versus chance. Once admit that the sole verifiable or fruitful object of knowledge is the particular set of changes that generate the object of study, together with the consequences that further flow from it, and no intelligible question can be asked about what, by assumption, lies outside. To assert—as is often asserted—that specific values of particular truths, social bonds and forms of beauty, if they can be shown to be generated by concretely knowable conditions, are meaningless and in vain; to assert that they are justified only when they and their particular causes and effects have all at once been gathered up into some inclusive first cause and some exhaustive final goal, is intellectual atavism. Such argumentation is reversion to the logic that explained the extinction of fire by water through the formal essence of aqueousness and the quenching of thirst by water through the final cause of aqueousness. Whether used in the case of the special event or in that of life as a whole, such logic only abstracts some aspect of the existing course of events in order to reduplicate it as a petrified eternal principle by which to explain the very changes of which it is the formalization.

When Henry Sidgwick casually remarked in a letter that as he grew older his interest in what or who made the world was altered into interest in what kind of a world it is anyway, his voicing of a common experience of our own day illustrates also the nature of that intellectual transformation effected by the Darwinian logic. Interest shifts from the wholesale essence back of special changes to the question of how these special changes serve and defeat concrete purposes; shifts from an intelligence that shaped things once for all, to the particular intelligences which things are even now shaping; shifts from an ultimate goal of good to the direct increments of justice and happiness that intelligent administration of existent conditions may beget and that present carelessness or stupidity will destroy or forego.

In the second place, the classic type of logic inevitably set philosophy upon proving that life *must* really have certain qualities and values—no matter how experience presents the matter—because of some remote cause and eventual goal, while the logic of the new science frees philosophy from this apologetic habit and temper. The duty of wholesale justification inevitably accompanies all thinking that makes the meaning of special occurrences depend upon something that lies once and for all behind them. The habit of derogating from present meanings and uses prevents our looking the facts of experience in the face; it prevents serious acknowledgment of the evils they present and serious concern with the goods they promise but do not yet fulfill. It turns thought to the business of finding a wholesale transcendent remedy for the one and guarantee for the other. One is reminded of the way many moralists and theologians greeted Herbert Spencer's recognition of an unknowable energy from which welled up the phenomenal physical processes without and the conscious operations without. Merely because Spencer labeled his unknowable energy "God," this faded piece of metaphysical goods was greeted as an important and grateful concession to the reality of the spiritual realm. Were it not for the deep hold of the habit of seeking justification for ideal values in the remote and transcendent, surely this reference of them to an unknowable absolute would be despised in behalf of the daily demonstrations of experience that knowable energies are daily generating about us precious values.

The displacing of this wholesale type of philosophy will doubtless not arrive by sheer logical disproof, but rather by growing recognition of its futility. Were it a thousand times true that opium produces sleep because of its dormitive energy, the inducing of sleep in the tired and the recovery to waking life of the poisoned, would not be thereby one least step forwarded. And were it a thousand times dialectically demonstrated that life as a whole is regulated by a transcendent principle to a final inclusive goal, truth and error, health and disease, good and evil, hope and fear in the concrete would remain none the less just what and where they now are. To improve our education, to ameliorate our manners, to advance our politics, we must have recourse to specific conditions of generation.

Finally, the new logic introduces responsibility into the intellectual life. To idealize and rationalize the universe at large is after all a confession of inability to master the courses of things that specifically concern us. As long as mankind suffered from this impotency, naturally it shifted a burden of responsibility which it could not carry over to the more competent shoulders of the transcendent cause. But if insight into specific conditions of value and into specific consequences of ideas is possible, philosophy must in time become a method of locating and interpreting the more serious of the conflicts that occur in life, and a method of projecting ways for dealing with them: a method of moral and political diagnosis and prognosis.

The claim to formulate a priori the legislative constitution of the universe is by its nature a claim that may lead into elaborate dialectic developments. But it is also one which removes these very conclusions from subjection to experimental test, for, by definition, these results make no differences in the detailed course of events. But a philosophy that humbles its pretensions to the work of projecting hypotheses for the education and conduct of mind, individual and social, is thereby subjected to test by the way in which the ideas it propounds work out in practice. In having modesty forced upon it, philosophy also acquires responsibility.

Doubtless I may seem to have violated the implied promise of my earlier remarks and to have turned both prophet and partisan. But in anticipating the direction of the transformations in philosophy to be wrought by the Darwinian genetic and experimental logic, I do not profess to speak for any changes save those wrought in those who yield themselves consciously or unconsciously to this logic. No one can fairly deny that at present there are evident two effects of the Darwinian mode of thinking. On the one hand, there are making many sincere and vital efforts to revise our traditional philosophic conceptions in accordance with its demands. On the other hand, there is as definitely a reerudescence of absolutistic philosophies; an assertion of a type of philosophic knowing distinct from that of the sciences, which opens to us another kind of reality from that to which the sciences give access; an appeal through experience to something that radically transcends experiences. This re-action affects popular creeds and religious movements as well as technical philosophies. In other words, the very conquest of the biological sciences by the new ideas has led many to effect a more explicit and rigid separation of philosophy from science.

Old ideas give way slowly, for they are more than abstract logical forms and categories. They are habits, predispositions, deeply engrained attitudes of aversion and preference. Moreover, the conviction persists—though history shows it to be a hallucination—that all the questions that the human mind has asked are questions that can be answered in terms of the alternatives that the questions themselves present. But, in fact, intellectual progress usually occurs through sheer abandonment of such questions, together with both of the alternatives they assume. . . .

. . . We do not solve them: we get over them. Old questions are solved by disappearing, evaporating, while new questions corresponding to the changed attitude of endeavor and preference take their place. Doubtless the greatest dissolvent of old questions, the greatest precipitant of new methods, new intentions, new problems, is the one effected by the scientific revolution completed in the *Origin of Species*.

STUDY QUESTIONS

Review

1. Describe some of the evolutionary developments that influenced the thinking of the philosophers of the latter half of the nineteenth century.

2. Explain three philosophical problems that were raised by the various evolutionary theories.
3. Compare the theories of evolution of Herbert Spencer and Charles Darwin.
4. What is Social Darwinism? What aspects of Darwin's theory of evolution does it build on?
5. In what ways does the cosmic philosophy of John Fiske mirror the philosophy of Herbert Spencer? In what ways does it differ from or add to it?
6. What are some of the issues concerning the nature of science and scientific theories with which Chauncey Wright dealt in his writings? Elaborate on his position on one of them.

For Further Thought

7. One of the issues that was debated during this period was whether or not nature gives evidence of a design and a designer. Use the arguments of any of the philosophers discussed in this chapter, or your own, to answer this question.
8. Summarize the position of Wright on the issue of chance versus determinism. Do you think this is a defensible position? Why or why not?
9. The theory of the evolution of man gives rise to particular problems, for example those concerning the nature and genesis of human intelligence and self-consciousness. In what way do you think these abilities differ from animal instinct and sentience? Could the former have evolved from these animal abilities? Is Wright's explanation of how they evolved satisfactory? Why or why not?
10. Is there necessary conflict between science and religion? How would you explain those cases in which they seem to hold different views on the same subject? Is Fiske's or Wright's position on this issue satisfactory?

BIBLIOGRAPHY

Evolutionary Thought

Appleman, Philip, ed. *Darwin: Texts, Backgrounds, Contemporary Opinion, and Critical Essays.* New York: W. W. Norton, 1970.
Barnett, S. A., ed. *A Century of Darwin.* London: Heinemann, 1958.
Blau, Joseph. "The Biologizing of Philosophy." Chap. 5 in *Men and Movements in American Philosophy.* Englewood Cliffs, N.J.: Prentice-Hall, 1952.
Darwin, Charles. *Descent of Man.* New York: Appleton, 1871-72.
— — —. *On the Origin of Species.* London: John Murray, 1859.
Eiseley, L. *Darwin's Century.* New York: Doubleday, 1958.
Gillispie, Charles C. *Genesis and Geology: The Impact of Scientific Discoveries upon Religious Beliefs in the Decades before Darwin.* New York: Harper and Brothers, 1951.
Hofstadter, Richard. *Social Darwinism in American Thought, 1860-1915.* Philadelphia: University of Pennsylvania Press, 1944.
Lovejoy, Arthur O. "Some Eighteenth Century Evolutionists." *Popular Science Monthly* 65 (1904): pp. 238-51; 323-40.

Lyell, Sir Charles. *Principles of Geology.* London: John Murray, 1875.

— — —. "The Argument for Organic Evolution before 'The Origin of Species.' " *Popular Science Monthly* 75 (1909): pp. 499–514, 537–49.

Murray, R. H. *Science and Scientists in the Nineteenth Century.* London: The Sheldon Press, 1925.

Osborn, H. F. *From the Greeks to Darwin.* 2d. ed. New York: C. Scribner's Sons, 1929.

Persons, Stow, ed. *Evolutionary Thought in America.* New Haven: Yale University Press, 1950.

Schmidt, E. O. *The Doctrine of Descent and Darwinism.* New York: Appleton, 1876.

Schneider, H. "Evolution and Human Progress." Chap. 6 in *A History of American Philosophy.* New York: Columbia University Press, 1963.

Simpson, George G. *The Meaning of Evolution.* New Haven: Yale University Press, 1949.

Singer, C. *A History of Biology.* 3d ed. London: Abelard-Schuman, 1959.

Taton, René, ed. *Science in the Nineteenth Century.* New York: Basic Books, 1961.

Wiener, Philip P. *Evolution and the Founders of Pragmatism.* Cambridge: Harvard University Press, 1949.

John Fiske

Fiske, John. *Historical Writings of John Fiske.* 12 vols. Norward, Pa.: Norwood Press, 1902.

— — —. *The Miscellaneous Writings of John Fiske.* 12 vols. Boston: Houghton Mifflin, 1902–04.

Berman, Milton. *John Fiske: The Evolution of a Popularizer.* Cambridge: Harvard University Press, 1961.

Clark, John Spencer. *John Fiske: The Life and Letters.* Boston: Houghton Mifflin, 1917.

Winston, George P. *John Fiske.* New York: Twayne Publishers, 1972.

Chauncey Wright

Wright, Chauncey. *Philosophical Writings: Representative Selections.* Ed. Edward H. Madden. New York: Liberal Arts Press, 1958.

— — —. *Letters.* Ed. J. B. Thayer. Cambridge: John Wilson and Son, 1878.

— — —. *Philosophical Discussions.* Ed. C. E. Norton. New York: Henry Holt, 1877.

Blau, Joseph L. "Chauncey Wright: Radical Empiricist." *New England Quarterly* 19 (1946): pp. 495–517.

Madden, Edward H. *Chauncey Wright.* New York: Twayne Publishers, 1964.

— — —. *Chauncey Wright and the Foundations of Pragmatism.* Seattle: University of Washington Press, 1963.

— — —. "Wright, James, and Radical Empiricism." *Journal of Philosophy* 51 (1954): pp. 868–74.

— — —. "Pragmatism, Positivism, and Chauncey Wright." *Philosophy and Phenomenological Research* 14 (1953): pp. 62–71.

———. "Chauncey Wright: Forgotten American Philosopher." *American Quarterly* 4 (1952): pp. 24–34.

White, Morton. "Chauncey Wright: Empiricist Philosopher of Evolutionary Science." in *Science and Sentiment in America,* pp. 120–43. New York: Oxford University Press, 1972.

Chapter 5

Pragmatism

It has often been suggested that pragmatism is a distinctly American philosophy because not only was pragmatism the only philosophy produced in America that was not an adaptation or variation of European or British philosophies, but it was also a natural product of the American spirit and way of life.[1] This viewpoint, together with various commonsense notions associated with the term "pragmatic," has contributed to some misunderstanding of pragmatism as a philosophy. This is not to deny the uniquely American character or origin of pragmatism nor to assert that the many meanings of the term "pragmatic" have nothing in common with its philosophical usage. There may be some truth to the position that pragmatism is a natural outgrowth of the situation in which the early settlers of this country found themselves. Because of the all-consuming practical demands of pioneering life in a new land that was a wilderness, a philosophy that originated here might naturally be predisposed to oppose irrelevant thinking and to favor practical intelligence.[2] Moreover, during the latter part of the nineteenth century when pragmatism as a philosophy was developing, America was rapidly becoming an industrialized nation. Capitalism and market competition were becoming part of the so-called American way of life. During this period it was appropriate that ideas were thought of as having a "cash value."[3] The early settlers had left homelands rich in traditions and history to come to a new country rich in possibilities. This collective experience may have contributed to pragmatism's emphasis on the future rather than on the past. Beliefs, ideas, and theories were understood in terms of their practical consequences, their setting of certain expectations or habits of acting. They were tools for understanding and civlizing the world.

The peculiar situation of the early Americans may also partly account for their belief in the contingency and plasticity of nature — that what each person does makes a difference and that the world can be changed for the better. That the early settlers had to endure physical hardships and mold nature to meet their needs may have contributed to a particular philosophical conception of the nature of experience. Experience could be no passive matter of the intellect alone, but must be thought of as an active living through, suffering, enjoying, and making. However, to suppose that these elements of early American life actually caused a philosophy such as pragmatism to develop in this country supposes some sort of materialistic determinism. It is sufficient to believe that the unusual American situation might have predisposed its thinkers to certain philosophical beliefs or that it might have had some less-than-predetermining influence.

The term "pragmatic" is closely allied in meaning with the term "practical." That the philosophy was called "pragmatism" rather than "practicalism" was not meant to deny the importance of practice or action to the American pragmatist philosophers. Ideas have value in terms of their usefulness, and our practical needs may in some cases influence what we may rightly believe. But it was the Kantian distinction between *practisch* and *pragmatisch* that grounded the choice of terms.[4] The Kantian term meaning practical referred to rules of art or skill of whatever sort, while the term meaning pragmatic referred to the use of human reason or intelligence as a guide for the attainment of human happiness or the realization of human purposes. Thus pragmatism is more aptly designated by a term less liable to association with pure expediency and more likely to stress the connection of thought with the fulfillment of human purpose.

Darwinism, utilitarianism, and empiricism have also been linked to the development of American pragmatism. In publishing *Origin of Species* in 1859, Darwin shook the world's faith in the existence of stable, fixed forms of being and turned its attention to the developing, changing world and to the struggle and adaptation to environmental demands that it embodied. For the pragmatist, human life and knowledge are contingent; what we believe or hold as true is tentative; and those ideas that remain after continued testing (their struggle for existence) are the final truth. Utilitarianism had stressed the belief that the worth of any action was determined by its utility — its productiveness of human happiness. In pragmatism, ideas are useful and truth is a species of good, i.e., what is good for us to believe. Empiricism directed philosophers to seek substantive knowledge in sense experience rather than in what might seem reasonable to believe. Each pragmatist in his own way stressed the importance of experience as the touchstone of knowledge that provides the concrete meaning of ideas and is the source of continued growth in understanding. However, each pragmatist also held that the human knower was not a passive observer but an active inquirer who sought to make sense out of experience or solve problems it presented. Experience was rich and filled with possibility. While pragmatism may have been influenced by other philosophies, it was not just a conjunction of these various influences or beliefs, but a unique creative blend.

Pragmatism can be said to have originated in the philosophical discussions of members of the so-called Metaphysical Club which met in Cambridge, Massachusetts in the 1870s. As Peirce later recalls:

> It was in the earliest seventies that a knot of us young men in Old Cambridge, calling ourselves, half-ironically, half-defiantly, "The Metaphysical Club," — for agnosticism was then riding its high horse, and was frowning superbly upon all metaphysics — used to meet, sometimes in my study, sometimes in that of William James.[5]

Elsewhere he notes, "It was there that the name and doctrine of pragmatism saw the light."[6] Among those who participated in the group's meetings were Charles Sanders Peirce and William James, whom Peirce himself labeled "men of science"; Chauncey Wright, who, Peirce said, had "a most penetrating intellect"; John Fiske and Francis Ellingwood Abbot, who did not always agree with the others; Nicholas St. John Green, who impressed them all with the doctrine of Alexander Bain that a belief "is that upon which a man is prepared to act"; and Oliver Wendell Holmes, who later embodied pragmatic elements in his legal philosophy.[7] It was Peirce, however, who placed so much emphasis on this club and its discussions as instrumental to the formulation of pragmatism. According to his recollection, Peirce was also the one who presented there the first paper outlining ideas that are basic to the movement.

However, the paper in which Peirce outlined these ideas was never published, though the ideas were probably those embedded in two articles entitled "The Fixation of Belief" and "How To Make Our Ideas Clear" that Peirce did publish in 1877 and 1878 in the *Popular Science Monthly*.[8] These two articles, however, remained largely unnoticed until William James gave an address entitled "Philosophical Conceptions and Practical Results" in 1898 to the Philosophical Club at the University of California at Berkeley.[9] In this address and again in 1907 James gives Peirce credit for first formulating the doctrine of pragmatism. However, as James's interpretation of pragmatism developed in ways that made Peirce want to disassociate himself from it, Peirce coined the term "pragmaticism" for his own views — a term, as he said, "which is ugly enough to be safe from kidnappers."[10]

To list the defining characteristics of pragmatism is a much more difficult task, one reason being that as the ideas took shape in the writings of particular philosophers who have been called pragmatists (primarily Charles Sanders Peirce, William James, and John Dewey), their versions differed in significant ways. Nevertheless pragmatism may not unreasonably be defined as a philosophy that holds that there is a close interrelation and an interdependence between theory and practice, between knowledge and action. For Peirce pragmatism was primarily a theory of the meaning of terms and a theory of belief. The best way to clarify the meaning of a belief or concept was to delineate the expected practical consequences that would result from believing it. For James it was a tool for clarifying ideas or solving metaphysical puzzles by giving them concrete exper-iential meaning and a theory of truth or what we are justified in believing. According to James, we are justified in holding as true those ideas that "work" for us in certain specified ways. For Dewey pragmatism was a theory about the nature and purpose of human knowledge, according to which knowledge is experimentally produced and ideas are instruments or tools for understanding and civilizing the world. Moreover, in the writings of Peirce and James in particular, but also in Dewey's work in some ways, we see the influence of their views on a wide range of philosophical issues — not only on moral and religious issues but on cosmological and metaphysical ones as well.[11]

The extent to which pragmatism continued to influence twentieth-century philosophy is of some interest. It has been argued, for example, that later developments in positivism and empiricism show signs of pragmatism's influence and have certain pragmatic characteristics.[12] Conceptual schemes are no longer thought to be verified piece by piece, but as a whole and on the basis of their "efficacy in communication and prediction."[13] Moreover, the ideal that philosophy contributes to the solution of *human* problems rather than just to the problems of philosophers has been resurrected in the later half of the twentieth century. The pragmatists would be pleased. Moreover, Peirce, James, and Dewey also contributed to the ongoing philosophical discussion of the nature of man and the universe.

Notes

[1] Roy Wood Sellars, *Reflections on American Philosophy,* p. 26.

[2] See Perry Miller, "Errand into the Wilderness," *William and Mary Quarterly* 10 (1953): pp. 3–32; idem, *Errand into the Wilderness.* The title is from a sermon by Rev. Samuel Danforth in 1670. Rather than Frederick Jackson Turner's thesis that democracy came out of the forest, Miller supports the idea that it was the form, the errand, the situation of the early Americans, that controlled the matter. The errand was to establish a biblical polity, a city upon the hill for all to see.

[3] William James, "The Meaning of Pragmatism," chap. 2 in *Pragmatism* (New York: Longmans Green, 1907).

[4] Charles S. Peirce, "What Pragmatism Is," *The Monist* (1905).

[5] *Collected Papers of Charles Sanders Peirce,* ed. Charles Hartshorne and Paul Weiss (Cambridge: Harvard University Press, 1931–35), vol. 5, p. 12. Also see the more complete reference and description of Peirce's comments about the Metaphysical Club in Wiener, *Founders of Pragmatism,* pp. 18ff.

[6] Wiener, *Founders of Pragmatism,* p. 20.

[7] Ibid.

[8] Charles Sanders Peirce, "The Fixation of Belief," *Popular Science Monthly* 12 (1877): pp. 1–15: idem, "How to Make Our Ideas Clear," *Popular Science Monthly* 12 (1878): pp. 286–302.

[9] William James, "Philosophical Conceptions and Practical Results," *University of California Chronicle,* 1898, p. 24.

[10] Peirce, "What Pragmatism Is," *The Monist* (1905).

[11] See James's *A Pluralistic Universe* and Peirce's later work on the categories necessity, and cosmology as noted in the following chapters.

[12] Richard Rorty, *Philosophy and the Mirror of Nature* (Princeton: Princeton University Press, 1979). See also his *Consequences of Pragmatism* (Minneapolis: University of Minnesota Press, 1982).

[13] Ernest Gellner, "The Last Pragmatist: The Philosophy of W. V. O. Quine," *Times Literary Supplement,* 25 July 1975, p. 848.

CHARLES SANDERS PEIRCE

WHAT PRAGMATISM IS*

The writer of this article has been led by much experience to believe that every physicist, and every chemist, and, in short, every master in any department of experimental science, has had his mind molded by his life in the laboratory to a degree that is little suspected. The experimentalist himself can hardly be fully aware of it, for the reason that the men whose intellects he really knows about are much like himself in this respect. With intellects of widely different training from his own, whose education has largely been a thing learned out of books, he will never become inwardly intimate, be he on ever so familiar terms with them; for he and they are as oil and water, and though they be shaken up together, it remarkable how quickly they will go their several mental ways, without having gained more than a faint flavor from the association. Were those other men only to take skillful soundings of the experimentalist's mind— which is just what they are unqualified to do, for the most part—they would soon discover that, excepting perhaps upon topics where his mind is trammeled by personal feeling or by his bringing up, his disposition is to think of everything just as everything is thought of in the laboratory, that is, as a question of experimentation. Of course, no living man possesses in their fullness all the attributes characteristic of his type: it is not the typical doctor whom you will see every day driven in buggy or coupe,

---

* *The Monist* (1905), pp. 161ff.

not is it the typical pedagogue that will be met with in the first schoolroom you enter. But when you have found, or ideally constructed upon a basis of observation, the typical experimentalist, you will find that whatever assertion you may make to him, he will either understand as meaning that if a given prescription for an experiment ever can be and ever is carried out in act, an experience of a given description will result, or else he will see no sense at all in what you say. If you talk to him as Mr. Balfour talked not long ago to the British Association saying that "the physicist . . . seeks for something deeper than the laws connecting possible objects of experience," that "his object is a physical reality" unrevealed in experiments, and that the existence of such nonexperiential reality "is the unalterable faith of science," to all such ontological meaning, you will find the experimentalist mind to be color-blind. What adds to that confidence in this, which the writer owes to his conversations with experimentalists, is that he himself may almost be said to have inhabited a laboratory from the age of six until long past maturity; and having all his life associated mostly with experimentalists, it has always been with a confident sense of understanding them and of being understood by them.

That laboratory life did not prevent the writer (who here and in what follows simply exemplifies the experimentalist type) from becoming interested in methods of thinking; and when he came to read metaphysics, although much of it seemed to him loosely reasoned and determined by accidental prepossessions, yet in the writings of some philosophers, especially Kant, Berkeley, and Spinoza, he sometimes came upon strains of thought that recalled the ways of thinking of the laboratory, so that he felt he might trust to them; all of which has been true of other laboratory men.

Endeavoring, as a man of that type naturally would, to formulate what he so approved, he framed the theory that a *conception,* that is, the rational purport of a word or other expression, lies exclusively in its conceivable bearing upon the conduct of life; so that, since obviously nothing that might not result from experiment can have any direct bearing upon conduct, if one can define accurately all the conceivable experimental phenomena which the affirmation or denial of a concept could imply, one will have therein a complete definition of the concept, and *there is absolutely nothing more in it.* For this doctrine he invented the name *pragmatism.* Some of his friends wished him to call it *practicism* or *praticalism* (perhaps on the ground that *prakitkós* is better Greek than *pragmatikós*). But for one who had learned philosophy out of Kant, as the writer, along with nineteen out of every twenty experimentalists who have turned to philosophy, had done, and who still thought in Kantian terms most readily, *praktisch* and *pragmatisch* were as far apart as the two poles, the former belonging in a region of thought where no mind of the experimentalist type can ever make sure of solid ground under his feet, the latter expressing relation to some definite human purpose. Now quite the most striking feature of the new theory was its recognition of an inseparable connection between rational cognition and rational purpose; and that consideration it was which determined the preference for the name *pragmatism*.

Concerning the matter of philosophical nomenclature, there are a few plain considerations which the writer has for many years longed to submit to the deliberate judgment of those few fellow students of philosophy who deplore the present state of that study, and who are intent upon rescuing it therefrom and bringing it to a condition like that of the natural sciences, where investigators, instead of condemning each the work of most of the others as misdirected from beginning to end, cooperate, stand upon one another's shoulders, and multiply incontestable results; where every observation is repeated, and isolated observations go for little; where every hypothesis that merits attention is subjected to severe but fair examination, and only after the predictions to which it leads have been remarkably borne out by experience is trusted at all, and even then only provisionally; where a radically false step is rarely taken, even the most faulty of those theories which gain wide credence being true in their main experimental predictions. To those students, it is submitted that no study can become scientific in the sense described until it provides itself with a suitable technical nomenclature, whose every term has a single definite meaning universally accepted among students of the subject, and whose vocables have no such sweetness or charms as might tempt loose writers to abuse them—which is a virtue of scientific nomenclature too little appreciated. It is submitted that the experience of those sciences which have conquered the greatest difficulties of terminology, which are unquestionably the taxonomic sciences, chemistry, mineralogy, botany, zoology, has conclusively shown that the only way in which the requisite unanimity and requisite ruptures with individual habits and preferences can be brought about is so to shape the canons of terminology that they shall gain the support of *moral principle* and of every man's sense of decency; and that, in particular (under defined restrictions), the general feeling shall be that he who introduces a new conception into philosophy is under an obligation to invent acceptable terms to express it, and that when he has done so, the duty of his fellow students is to accept those terms, and to resent any wresting of them from their original meanings, as not only a gross discourtesy to him to whom philosophy was indebted for each conception, but also as an injury to philosophy itself; and furthermore, that once a conception has been supplied with suitable and sufficient words for its expression, no other *technical* terms denoting the same things, considered in the same relations, should be countenanced. Should this suggestion find favor, it might be deemed needful that the philosophians in congress assembled should adopt, after due deliberation, convenient canons to limit the application of the principle. Thus, just as is done in chemistry, it might be wise to assign fixed meanings to certain prefixes and suffixes. For example, it might be agreed, perhaps, that the prefix *prope-* should mark a broad and rather indefinite extension of the meaning of the term to which it was prefixed; the name of a doctrine would naturally end in *-ism*, while *-icism* might mark a more strictly defined acception of that doctrine, etc. Then again, just as in biology no account is taken of terms antedating LinnYus, so in philosophy it might be found best not to go back of the scholastic terminology. To illustrate another sort of limitation, it has probably never happened that any philosopher has attempted to give a general name to his own doctrine without that name's soon acquiring in common philosophical usage a signification much broader than was originally intended. Thus, special systems go by the names Kantianism, Benthamism, Comteanism, Spencerianism, etc., while transcendentalism, utilitarianism, positivism, evolutionism, synthetic philosophy, etc., have irrevocably and very conveniently been elevated to broader governments.

After awaiting in vain, for a good many years, some particularly opportune conjuncture of circumstances that might serve to recommend his notions of the ethics of terminology, the writer has now, at last, dragged them in over head and shoulders, on an occasion when he has no specific proposal to offer nor any feeling but satisfaction at the course usage has run without any canons or resolutions of a congress. His word "pragmatism" has gained general recognition in a generalized sense that seems to argue power of growth and vitality. The famed psychologist, James, first took it up, seeing that his "radical empiricism" substantially answered to the writer's definition of pragmatism, albeit with a certain difference in the point of view. Next, the admirably clear and brilliant thinker, Mr. Ferdinand C. S. Schiller, casting about for a more attractive name for the "anthropomorphism" of his *Riddle of the Sphinx,* lit, in that most remarkable paper of his on "Axioms as Postulates," upon the same designation "pragmatism," which in its original sense was in generic agreement with his own doctrine, for which he has since found the more appropriate specification "humanism," while he still retains "pragmatism" in a somewhat wider sense. So far all went happily. But at present, the word begins to be met with occasionally in the literary journals, where it gets abused in the merciless way that words have to expect when they fall into literary clutches. Sometimes the manners of the British had effloresced in scolding at the word as ill-chosen—ill chosen, that is, to express some meaning that it was rather designed to exclude. So then, the writer, finding his bantling "pragmatism" so promoted, feels that it is time to kiss his child good-bye and relinquish it to its higher destiny; while to serve the precise purpose of expressing the original definition, he begs to announce the birth of the word "pragmaticism," which is ugly enought to be safe from kidnappers.*

Much as the writer has gained from the perusal of what other pragmatists have written, he still thinks there is a decisive advantage in his original conception of the doctrine. From this original form every truth that follows from any of the other forms can be deduced, while some errors can be avoided into which other pragmatists have fallen. The original view appears, too, to be more compact and unitary conception than the others. But its capital merit, in the writer's eyes, is that it more readily connects itself with a critical proof of its truth. Quite in accord with the logical order of investigation, it usually happens that one first forms an hypothesis that seems more and more reasonable the further one examines into it, but that only a good deal later gets crowned with an adequate proof. The present writer, having had the pragmatist theory under consideration for many years longer than most of its adherents, would naturally have given more attention to the proof to it. At any rate, in endeavoring to explain pragmatism, he may be excused for confining himself to that form of it that he knows best. In the present article there will be space only to explain just what this doctrine (which, in such hands as it has now fallen into, may probably play a pretty prominent part in the philosophical discussions of the next coming years) really consists in. Should the exposition be found to interest readers of *The Monist,* they would certainly be much more interested in a second article which would give some samples of the manifold applications of pragmaticism (assuming it to be true) to the solution of problems of different kinds. After that, readers might be prepared to take an interest in a proof that the doctrine is true—a proof which seems to the writer to leave no reasonable doubt on the subject, and to be the one contribution of value that he has to make to philosophy. For it would essentially involve the establishment of the truth of synechism.

The bare definition of pragmatism could convey no satisfactory comprehension of it to the most apprehensive of minds, but requires the commentary to be given below. Moreover, this definition takes no notice of one or two other doctrines without the previous acceptance (or virtual acceptance) of which pragmaticism itself would be a nullity. They are included as a part of the pragmatism of Schiller, but the present writer prefers not to mingle different propositions. The preliminary propositions had better be stated forthwith.

---

* To show how recent the general use of the word "pragmatism" is, the writer may mention that, to the best of his belief, he never used it in copy for the press before today, except by particular request, in *Baldwin's Dictionary.* Toward the end of 1890, when this part of the *Century Dictionary* appeared, he did not deem that the word had sufficient status to appear in that work. But he has used it continually in philosophical conversation since, perhaps, the midseventies.

The difficulty in doing this is that no formal list of them has ever been made. They might all be included under the vague, maxim, "Dismiss make-believes." Philosophers of very diverse stripes propose that philosophy shall take its start from one or another state of mind in which no man, least of all a beginner in philosophy, actually is. One proposes that you shall begin by doubting everything, and says that there is only one thing that you cannot doubt, as if doubting were "as easy as lying." Another proposes that we should begin by observing "the first impressions of sense," forgetting that our very percepts are the results of cognitive elaboration. But in truth, there is but one state of mind from which you can "set out," namely, the very state of mind in which you actually find yourself at the time you do "set out"—a state in which you are laden with an immense mass of cognition already formed, of which you cannot divest yourself if you would; and who knows whether, if you could, you would not have made all knowledge impossible to yourself? Do you call it *doubting* to write down on a piece of paper that you doubt? If so, doubt has nothing to do with any serious business. But do not make believe; if pedantry has not eaten all the reality out of you, recognize, as you must, that there is much that you do not doubt, in the least. Now that which you do not at all doubt, you must and do regard as infallible, absolute truth. Here breaks in Mr. Make-Believe: "What! Do you mean to say that one is to believe what is not true, or that what a man does not doubt is *ipso facto* true? " No, but unless he can make a thing white and black at one, *he* has to regard what he does not doubt as absolutely true. Now you, *per hypothesiu*, are that man. "But you tell me there are scores of things I do not doubt. I really cannot persuade myself that there is not some one of them about which I am mistaken." You are adducing one of your make-believe facts, even if it were established, would only go to show that doubt had a *limen,* that is, is only called into being by a certain finite stimulus. You only puzzle yourself by talking of this metaphysical "truth"and metaphysical "falsity," that you know nothing about. All you have any dealings with are your doubts and beliefs,* with the course of life that forces new beliefs upon you and gives you power to doubt old beliefs. If your terms "truth" and "falsity" are taken in such senses as to be definable in terms of doubt and belief and the course of experience (as for example they would be if you were to define the "truth" as that to a belief in which belief would tend it if were to tend indefinitely toward absolute fixity), well and good; in that case, you are only talking about doubt and belief. But if by truth and falsity you mean something not definable in terms of doubt and belief in any way, then you are talking of entities of whose existence you can know nothing, and which

---

* It is necessary to say that "belief" is throughout used merely as the name of the contrary to doubt, without regard to grades of certainty or to the nature of the proposition held for true, i.e., "believed."

Ockham's razor would clean shave off. Your problems would be greatly simplified if, instead of saying that you want to know the "Truth," you were simply to say that you want to attain a state of belief unassailable by doubt.

Belief is not a momentary mode of consciousness; it is a habit of mind essentially enduring for some time, and mostly (at least) unconscious; and like other habits, it is (until it meets with some surprise that begins its dissolution) perfectly self-satisfied. Doubt is of an altogether contrary genus. It is not a habit, but the privation of a habit. Now a privation of a habit, in order to be anything at all, must be a condition of erratic activity that in some way must get superseded by a habit.

Among the things which the reader, as a rational person, does not doubt is that he not merely has habits, but also can exert a measure of self-control over his future actions; which means, however, *not* that he can impart to them any arbitarily assignable character, but, on the contrary, that a process of self-preparation will tend to impart to action (when the occasion for it shall arise) one fixed character, which is indicated and perhaps roughly measured by the absence (or slightness) of the feeling of self-reproach, which subsequent reflection will induce. Now, this subsequent reflection is part of the self-preparation for action on the next occasion. Consequently, there is a tendency, as action is repeated again and again, for the action to approximate indefinitely toward the perfection of that fixed character, which would be marked by entire absence of self-reproach. The more closely this is approached, the less room for self-control there will be; and where no self-control is possible there will be no self-reproach.

These phenomena seem to be the fundamental characteristics which distinguish a rational being. Blame, in every case, appears to be a modification, often accomplished by a transference, or "projection," of the primary feeling of self-reproach. Accordingly, we never blame anybody for what had been beyond his power of previous self-control . Now, thinking is a species of conduct which is largely subject to self-control. In all their features (which there is no room to describe here), logical self-control is a perfect mirror of ethical self-control—unless it be rather a species under that genus. In accordance with this, what you cannot in the least help believing is not, justly speaking, wrong belief. In other words, for you it is the absolute truth. True, it is conceivable that what you cannot help believing today, you might find you thoroughly disbelieve tomorrow. But then there is a certain distinction between things you "cannot" do, merely in the sense that nothing stimulates you to the great effort and endeavors that would be required, and things you cannot do because in their own nature they are insusceptible of being put into practice. In every stage of your excogitations, there is something of which you can only say, "I cannot think otherwise," and your experientially based hypothesis is that the impossibility is of the second kind.

There is no reason why "thought," in what has just been said, should be taken in that narrow sense in which silence and darkness are favorable to thought. It should rather be understood as covering all rational life, so that an experiment shall be an operation of thought. Of course, that ultimate state of habit to which the action of self-control ultimately tends, where no room is left for further self-control, is, in the case of thought, the state of fixed belief, or perfect knowledge.

Two things here are all-important to assure oneself of and to remember. The first is that a person is not absolutely an individual. His thoughts are what he is "saying to himself," that is, is saying to that other self that is just coming into life in the flow of time. When one reasons, it is that critical self that one is trying to persuade; and all thought whatsoever is a sign, and is mostly of the nature of language. The second thing to remember is that the man's circle of society (however widely or narrowly this phrase may be understood) is a sort of loosely compacted person, in some respects of higher rank than the person of an individual organism. It is these two things alone that render it possible for you—but only in the abstract, and in a Pickwickian sense—to distinguish between absolute truth and what you do not doubt.

STUDY QUESTIONS

Review

1. What are some of the ways in which the American experience may have influenced the pragmatists?
2. What is pragmatism?
3. Where and when and with whom did it originate?
4. Where did the term "pragmatism" come from and what does it mean?
5. In what ways are Darwinism, utilitarianism, and empiricism similar to pragmatism?

For Further Thought

6. What do you usually associate with the phrase "Yankee pragmatism" or the term "pragmatic"? From what you know of the philosophy called pragmatism, do you believe there is any basis for these commonly made associations?
7. What are some different ways in which you think ideas or theories are related to action or practice?

BIBLIOGRAPHY

Ayer, A. J. *The Origins of Pragmatism.* San Francisco: Freeman, Cooper and Co., 1968.
Bawden, H. Heath. *The Principles of Pragmatism.* Boston: Houghton Mifflin, 1910.

Blau, Joseph. "Pragmatic Perspectives." Chap. 7 in *Men and Movements in American Philosophy*. Englewood Cliffs, N. J.: Prentice-Hall, 1952.

Childs, John Lawrence. *American Pragmatism and Education: An Interpretation and Criticism*. New York: Henry Holt, 1956.

Dewey, John. "The Development of American Pragmatism." In *Studies in the History of Ideas*. New York: Columbia University Press, 1925.

Eames, S. Morris. *Pragmatic Naturalism*. Carbondale: Southern Illinois University Press, 1977.

Fisch, Max. *Classic American Philosophers*. New York: Appleton-Century-Crofts, 1951.

— — —. "A Chronicle of Pragmaticism, 1865-1879." *The Monist* 48 (1964): pp. 441-66.

— — —. "Alexander Bain and the Genealogy of Pragmatism." *Journal of the History of Ideas* 15 (June 1954): pp. 413-44.

Hartshorne, Charles. *Creativity in American Philosophy*. Albany: State University of New York Press, 1984.

Hook, Sidney. *Pragmatism and the Tragic Sense of Life*. New York: Basic Books, 1974.

Kennedy, Gail, ed. *Pragmatism and American Culture*. Boston: Heath, 1950.

Kennedy, Gail, and Milton Konvitz, eds. *The American Pragmatists: Selected Writings*. New York: Meridian Books, 1960.

Kurtz, Paul. *American Philosophy in the Twentieth Century*. Vol. 2, *From Pragmatism to Philosophical Analysis*. New York: Macmillan, 1966.

Lovejoy, Arthur O. "The Thirteen Pragmatisms." *Journal of Philosophy, Psychology, and Scientific Methods* 5 (1908): pp. 6-12, 29-39.

McDermott, John J. *The Culture of Experience: Philosophical Essays in the American Grain*. New York: New York University Press, 1976.

— — —. *The American Angle of Vision*. New York: Cross Currents Paperback, 1966.

Madden, E. H. *Chauncey Wright and the Foundations of Pragmatism*. Seattle: University of Washington Press, 1963.

Mills, C. W. *Sociology and Pragmatism*. Ed. Irving L. Horowitz. New York: Oxford University Press, 1969.

Moore, Addison. *Pragmatism and Its Critics*. Chicago: University of Chicago Press, 1910.

Moore, E. C. *American Pragmatism: Peirce, James, and Dewey*. New York: Columbia University Press, 1961.

Morris, Charles W. *The Pragmatic Movement in American Philosophy*. New York: Braziller, 1970.

— — —. *Logical Positivism, Pragmatism, and Scientific Empiricism*. Paris: Herman, 1937.

Pratt, James B. *What Is Pragmatism?* New York: Macmillan, 1909.

Rorty, Amelie. *Pragmatic Philosophy: An Anthology*. New York: Doubleday, 1966.

Rorty, Richard. *Consequences of Pragmatism*. Minneapolis: University of Minnesota Press, 1982.

— — —. *Philosophy and the Mirror of Nature*. Princeton: Princeton University Press, 1979.

Rosenthal, Sandra B. "Recent Perspectives in American Pragmatism." *Transactions of the Charles S. Peirce Society* 10 (1974): pp. 76-93, 166-184.

Rucker, Darnell. *The Chicago Pragmatists*. Minneapolis: University of Minnesota Press, 1969.

Scheffler, Israel. *Four Pragmatists: A Critical Introduction to Peirce, James, Mead, and Dewey*. New York: Humanities Press, 1974.

Smith, John. *Purpose and Thought: The Meaning of Pragmatism*. New Haven: Yale University Press, 1978.

– – –. *The Spirit of American Philosophy.* New York: Oxford University Press, 1966.

Thayer, H. S., ed. *Pragmatism: The Classic Writings.* Indianapolis: Hackett Publishing Co., 1982.

– – –. *Meaning and Action: A Critical History of Pragmatism.* Indianapolis: Hackett Publishing Co., 1981.

White, Morton G. *Pragmatism and the American Mind.* New York: Oxford University Press, 1973.

Wiener, Philip P. *Evolution and the Founders of Pragmatism.* Cambridge: Harvard University Press, 1949.

Chapter 6

The Pragmaticism and Metaphysics of Charles Sanders Peirce

Charles S. Peirce was born in Cambridge, Massachusetts in 1839, the son of Benjamin Peirce, a noted Harvard mathematician-astronomer. Charles's exceptional intellect was early recognized by his family and he was trained accordingly, receiving his B.A. and M.A. at Harvard in 1858 and 1862 respectively. In 1863 he was awarded summa cum laude the first advanced degree in chemistry at Harvard. This degree as well as his first work experience gives evidence of his strong interest in science. He was assistant at the Harvard observatory from 1869 to 1872 where he carried out astronomical observations and measurements of the light of the stars. The only book he ever published, *Photometric Researches* (1878), was based on these scientific observations. For the next thirty years he worked intermittently as an experimental scientist for the U.S. Coast and Geodetic Survey where he did some significant work in determining the intensity of gravity by means of the pendulum. While he never retained a permanent academic position, he lectured at Johns Hopkins from 1879 to 1884 and occasionally at Harvard. He inherited a house in Milford, Pennsylvania, where he retired, remaining rather poor and supporting himself and his ailing wife with stipends from published articles and reviews. However he was unable to bring his philosophical work to completion in any lengthy form. Peirce died after a battle with cancer in 1914.

During his own lifetime Peirce was not generally well known, despite the recognition given him by James and his position in the so-called Metaphysical Club. Because of the sparse and scattered character of his writings, they did not become well known until they were collected and published from 1931 to 1936. However, since that time he has come to be regarded by some as the founder of pragmatism, and one respected philosopher has written of him: "There is a fair concensus among historians of ideas that C. S. Peirce remains the most original, versatile and comprehensive philosophic mind this country has yet produced." [1] While Peirce is best known as the initiator of pragmatism, he had a broad range of philosophical interests which he was attempting to synthesize. [2] The summary of and selections from his works which follow will attempt to give some further idea of the nature and range of his thought.

While Peirce is best known for his particular formulations of pragmatism, his philosophy includes original ideas on the theory of signs and on issues in metaphysics and logic. To understand his pragmatism it is best to place it in perspective by summarizing some of his other views. He was interested, for example, in the problem of universals: what the relation is between the universal or general concepts of which we can conceive (for example, "red") and existents in the external world (red things). According to some medieval philosophers called extreme realists, general concepts stand for something real outside the mind, something mental like themselves. We think about redness and there also exists outside our mind the quality of redness as a nonphysical entity. Other medieval philosophers held just the opposite view, nominalism. According to this view universals exist neither outside our minds nor within them. Concepts are individual, simply names used to stand for the many individual things that exist. The solution to this problem was important for Peirce because, if there were no universals or general concepts, then science with its universal terms and general laws was open to question. Peirce himself held a moderate realist view. He believed in the existence of universals or generals; he held that they stood for real general qualities not existing apart from but only within the many individual entities of our experience. Another way to put it is that for Peirce the referent of a concept was to be found in the experience of specific objects. [3]

Peirce was also interested in the metaphysical question of whether there are a specific number of distinct kinds of beings. This too was an age-old problem going back as far as Aristotle. These basic kinds of being Aristotle, and Peirce after him, called categories. According to Peirce all beings can be divided into three irreducible and independent categories: firstness, secondness, and thirdness. Everything that exists is either a firstness (for example a possibility, an idea, an unactualized essence such as redness), a secondness (for example, an actually existing redness in some red object), or a thirdness (the relating of these two in a general concept, meaning, or law, such as the idea that traffic lights are sometimes red). Moreover in whatever field it occurs — psychology, biology, etc. — firstness is simple immediacy, secondness is reaction of one thing or quality with another, and thirdness is the idea of the relation of these two.[4] Peirce used his theory of the three categories of being to explain the nature of thought and signs. All thought is of the nature of a sign and as such involves a triadic relation. It relates one thing to another by means of a third. His theory of universals also played a role here; according to this theory there were real meanings or capacities in things which were the referents of our thoughts. This capacity or quality was related to the thing by means of the intepretation of the thinker.

As his pragmatism developed, these metaphysical and language theories also took on a new shape for Peirce. The meaning of a general term came to be thought of as a way of listing the firstness and secondness involved in a thirdness, the concept or term. So the idea of an automobile, (thirdness) could be explained in terms of turning the key in the ignition (acting, or secondness) and the resulting hearing of the motor start (sensation, or firstness). The idea of a car thus consists of all those experiences that result from the ways we act toward the car.

This is the essence also of Peirce's pragmatism viewed as a theory of meaning. In his article "How To Make Our Ideas Clear" Peirce disagreed with Descartes' view that we can clarify the meaning of ideas by being able to mentally recognize them (clarity) and distinguish them from other ideas (distinctness). Clarity of meaning, he said, can only be had by seeing the relation of our concept to events in the world. In order to clarify the meaning of an idea for ourselves we should ask, "What practical bearings does this concept have or what practical effects does it suggest? " The conception of these practical effects is the idea's meaning. Peirce puts it this way:

> It appears, then, that the rule for attaining . . . clearness of apprehension is as follows: consider what effects, which might conceivably have practical bearings, we conceive the object of our conception to have. Then, our conception of these effects is the whole of our conception of the object.[5]

Now, the phrase "practical effects" is not itself very clear. But it appears that it includes not only the ways in which the object will respond to our particular tests or behavior with regard to it, but also how we ourselves will practically behave concerning this object if we believe this or that about it. We expect "hard" things to react in particular ways, and we ourselves will react toward hard things according to our beliefs about "hardness." The meaning of other terms can be clarified in this same way. "True" thus pragmatically means the opinion that is fated to be agreed to by all who investigate it, according to Peirce. In other words, it is defined by telling what will result if certain persons (the community of investigators) do a certain thing (search, investigate, experiment). Truth is something to be known, not just by any knower but by all knowers. It is reached only in the long run, perhaps an ideal to strive for but one that will never actually be attained. If truth is as Peirce says "fated" to be attained, then there must be something in the nature of things that gives a direction to the investigation, and thus some ways to proceed are better than others.

Peirce's theory of belief accounts not only for the nature and genesis of belief, but also explains better and worse ways of developing and "fixing" beliefs. Beliefs originate in doubt and their sole purpose is to satisfy that doubt. We only think when we have a reason to, and for Peirce that reason is dissatisfaction that accompanies doubt. We are unsure what to believe or do, so we try out various possibilities in imagination. Peirce calls this process of thinking "inquiry." When we finally settle (if only temporarily) on a particular new belief, it is because this belief satisfies our doubt. Our new belief, moreover, does not render us in a state of passive satisfaction, but rather establishes in us a habit of response, a particular mode of reacting. If we have certain beliefs about hard heavy things, for example, we will not attempt to walk through them, and we will expect and be ready to exert energy if we attempt to lift them. Different beliefs, according to Peirce, are distinguished by the different habits to which they give rise. If there is no practical difference between two beliefs in this respect, then there is no difference worth mentioning.

There are also better and worse ways for developing and holding on to or "fixing" our beliefs. The worse ways are the methods of tenacity, authority, and the a priori method. The better way is the method of modern science. Some people hold on to their beliefs with such tenacity that they will not even consider any opposing views. This method may give a certain peace of mind, but it is also bound to fail. A slightly better method is that in which one relies not on oneself but on an authority in some matter. Here again, this method works well only in closed societies where there are no other conflicting opinions or authorities allowed. A more rational method is one that appeals to what seems agreeable or conformable to reason. However, while seemingly objective, this method, according to Peirce, is really very subjective. What seems rational to any one person is really a matter of taste and fashion. A better way of arriving at and fixing beliefs is the method of science. It is based on realism, on an interest in apprehending facts. It is public (open to all, tests can be done by more than one person), self-correcting (contains within its own method a way of weeding out or correcting false or unverifiable hypotheses), and relies on a community effort (where no one limited individual but the efforts of many are put together to reach the goal). Peirce's statement that the sole function of a belief is to satisfy one's doubt has to be complemented by these other comments about the better and worse ways of being satisfied.

Some interpretations of Peirce distinguish various periods in his thought; a later period, after 1890, seems more devoted than earlier ones to the development of a philosophical system, an overall view of things according to which everything can be interpreted. His categories were meant to do this, as were several theses of the later period that were named by him *tychism, synechism,* and *agapism.*[6] These terms embody a theory of cosmic evolution in which chance, continuity, and love play key roles. According to Peirce, the cosmos is developing gradually toward an ideal state, directed by a cosmic purpose. However, the achievement of the goal must not be inevitable. Peirce opposed a purely deterministic theory of evolution and believed that variety could have occurred only if chance or spontaneity were present in the universe. There are no purely mechanical responses. Rather, matter and mind are two extremes or limits in a continuity of intermediates, and matter is simply mind that has become totally habit-bound or frozen. Only that that contains elements of mind can evolve or develop, according to Peirce. Moreover, selfish competition and destruction never bring about growth. Growth is achieved only by an action that includes, supports, and perfects others, i.e. through the movement of agapistic love. However suggestive they may be, these views were never completely developed by Peirce. Moreover, while Peirce was an original and unusually gifted thinker, even the originator of perhaps the most unique philosophy America has had to offer, it remained for William James to develop and make known many of those views.

Notes

[1] Ernest Nagel *Scientific American* 200 (1959): p. 185, as quoted in *Charles S. Peirce: The Essential Writings*, ed. E. C. Moore (New York: Harper and Row, 1972), p. 1.

[2] As to whether or not Peirce's work presents a coherent philosophical synthesis, see the disagreements among interpreters summarized in Vincent G. Potter, *Charles S. Peirce: On Norms and Ideals* (Worcester, Mass.: University of Massachusetts Press, 1967), pp. ix–x.

[3] See *Collected Papers of Charles Sanders Peirce*, 5.503, 5.77n1, and 8.12; also the discussion in Moore, *Charles S. Peirce*, pp. 4–10.

[4] Peirce, *Collected Papers*; vol. 4, pp. 435n1; vol. 5, p. 9; Moore, *Charles S. Peirce*, pp. 16–21; Potter, Charles S. Peirce: on Norms and Ideals (Worcester: University of Massachusetts Press, 1967), pp. 8–25.

[5] Peirce, "How to Make Our Ideas Clear". Selection is included in this chapter.

[6] See Potter; and Smith, *Spirit of American Philosophy*, pp. 31–37. Also see Peirce's essay "Evolutionary Love" and other essays in his *Monist* series of 1891-93, in Moore, *Charles S. Peirce*, pp. 158-260, and his contributions to James Baldwin's *Dictionary of Philosophy and Psychology*, published in 1902 and also included in Moore.

CHARLES SANDERS PEIRCE

THE FIXATION OF BELIEF*

III

We generally know when we wish to ask a question and when we wish to pronounce a judgment, for there is a dissimilarity between the sensation of doubting and that of believing.

But this is not all which distinguishes doubt from belief. There is a practical difference. Our beliefs guide our desires and shape our actions. The Assassins, or followers of the Old Man of the Mountain, used to rush into death at his least command, because they believed that obedience to him would insure everlasting felicity. Had they doubted this, they would not have acted as they did. So it is with every belief, according to its degree. The feeling of believing is a more or less sure indication of there being established in our nature some habit which will determine our actions. Doubt never has such an effect.

Nor must we overlook a third point of difference. Doubt is an uneasy and dissatisfied state from which we struggle to free ourselves and pass into the state of belief: while the latter is a calm and satisfactory state which we do not wish to avoid, or to change to a belief in anything else.†

---

* Charles S. Peirce, "The Fixation of Belief," *Popular Science Monthly* 12 (1877): pp. 1–15.
† I am not speaking of secondary effects occasionally produced by the interference of other impulses.

On the contrary, we cling tenaciously, not merely to believing, but to believing just what we do believe.

Thus, both doubt and belief have positive effects upon us, though very different ones. Belief does not make us act at once, but puts us into such a condition that we shall behave in a certain way, when the occasion arises. Doubt has not the least effect of this sort, but stimulates us to action until it is destroyed. This reminds us of the irritation of a nerve and the reflex action produced thereby; while for the analogue of belief, in the nervous system, we must look to what are called nervous associations—for example, to that habit of the nerves in consequence of which the smell of a peach will make the mouth water.

The irritation of doubt causes a struggle to attain a state of belief. I shall term this struggle *inquiry,* though it must be admitted that this is sometimes not a very apt designation.

The irritation of doubt is the only immediate motive for the struggle to attain belief. It is certainly best for us that our beliefs should be such as may truly guide our actions so as to satisfy our desires; and this reflection will make us reject any belief which does not seem to have been so formed as to insure this result. But it will only do so by creating a doubt in the place of that belief. With the doubt, therefore, the struggle begins, and with the cessation of doubt it ends. Hence, the sole object of inquiry is the settlement of opinion. We may fancy that this is not enough for us, and that we seek not merely an opinion, but a true opinion. But put this fancy to the test, and it proves groundless; for as soon as a firm belief is reached we are entirely satisfied, whether the belief be false or true. And it is clear that nothing out of the sphere of our knowledge can be our object, for nothing which does not affect the mind can be a motive for a mental effort. The most that can be maintained is that we seek for a belief that we shall *think* to be true. But we think each one of our beliefs to be true, and, indeed, it is mere tautology to say so.

That the settlement of opinion is the sole end of inquiry is a very important proposition. It sweeps away, at once, various vague and erroneous conceptions of proof. A few of these may be noticed here.

1. Some philosophers have imagined that to start an inquiry it was only necessary to utter or question or set it down on paper, and have even recommended us to begin our studies with questioning everything! But the mere putting of a proposition into the interrogative form does not stimulate the mind to any struggle after belief. There must be a real and living doubt, and without all this, discussion is idle.

2. It is a very common idea that a demonstration must rest on some ultimate and absolutely indubitable propositions. These, according to one school, are first principles of a general nature; according to another, are first sensations. But, in point of fact, an inquiry, to have that completely satisfactory result called demonstration, has only to start with propositions

perfectly free from all actual doubt. If the premises are not in fact doubted at all, they cannot be more satisfactory than they are.

3. Some people seem to love to argue a point after all the world is fully convinced of it. But no further advance can be made. When doubt ceases, mental action on the subject comes to an end; and, if it did go on, it would be without a purpose, except that of self-criticism.

V.

If the settlement of opinion is the sole object of inquiry, and if belief is of the nature of a habit, why should we not attain the desired end, by taking any answer to a question, which we may fancy, and constantly reiterating it to ourselves, dwelling on all which may conduce to that belief, and learning to turn with contempt and hatred from anything which might disturb it? This simple and direct method is really pursued by many men. I remember once being entreated not to read a certain newspaper lest it might change my opinion upon free-trade. "Lest I might be entrapped by its fallacies and misstatements" was the form of expression. "You are not," my friend said, "a special student of political economy. You might, therefore, easily be deceived by fallacious arguments upon the subject. You might, then, if you read this paper, be led to believe in protection. But you admit that free-trade is the true doctrine; and you do not wish to believe what is not true." I have often known this system to be deliberately adopted. Still oftener, the instinctive dislike of an undecided state of mind, exaggerated into a vague dread of doubt, makes men cling spasmodically to the views they already take. The man feels that if he only holds to his belief without wavering, it will be entirely satisfactory. Nor can it be denied that a steady and immovable faith yields great peace of mind. It may, indeed, give rise to inconveniences, as if a man should resolutely continue to believe that fire would not burn him, or that he would be eternally damned if he received his *ingesta* otherwise than through a stomach-pump. But then the man who adopts this method will not allow that its inconveniences are greater than its advantages. He will say, "I hold steadfastly to the truth and the truth is always wholesome." And in many cases it may very well be that the pleasure he derives from his calm faith overbalances any inconveniences resulting from its deceptive character. Thus, if it be true that death is annihilation, then the man who believes that he will certainly go straight to heaven when he dies, provided he have fulfilled certain simple observances in this life, has a cheap pleasure which will not be followed by the least disappointment. A similar consideration seems to have weight with many persons in religious topics, for we frequently hear it said, "Oh, I could not believe so-and-so, because I should be wretched if I did." When an ostrich buries its head in the sand as danger approaches, it very likely takes the happiest course. It hides the danger, and then calmly says there is no danger; and, if it feels perfectly sure there is none, why should it raise its head to see? A man may go through life, systematically keeping out of view all that might cause a change in his opinions, and if he only succeeds—basing his method, as he does, on two fundamental psychological laws—I do not see what can be said against his doing so. It would be an egotistical impertinence to object that his procedure is irrational, for that only amounts to saying that his method of settling belief is not ours. He does not propose to himself to be rational, and indeed, will often talk with scorn of man's weak and illusive reason. So let him think as he pleases.

But this method of fixing belief, which may be called the method of tenacity, will be unable to hold its ground in practice. The social impulse is against it. The man who adopts it will find that other men think differently from him, and it will be apt to occur to him in some saner moment that their opinions are quite as good as his own, and this will shake his confidence in his belief. This conception, that another man's thought or sentiment may be equivalent to one's own, is a distinctly new step, and a highly important one. It arises from an impulse too strong in man to be suppressed, without danger of destroying the human species. Unless we make ourselves hermits, we shall necessarily influence each other's opinions; so that the problem becomes how to fix belief, not in the individual merely, but in the community.

Let the will of the state act, then, instead of that of the individual. Let an institution be created which shall have for its object to keep correct doctrines before the attention of the people, to reiterate them perpetually, and to teach them to the young; having at the same time power to prevent contrary doctrines from being taught, advocated, or expressed. Let all possible causes of a change of mind be removed from men's apprehensions. Let them be kept ignorant, lest they should learn of some reason to think otherwise than they do. Let their passions be enlisted, so that they may regard private and unusual opinions with hatred and horror. Then, let all men who reject the established belief be terrified into silence. Let the people turn out and tar-and-feather such men, or let inquisitions be made into the manner of thinking of suspected persons, and, when they are found guilty of forbidden beliefs, let them be subjected to some signal punishment. When complete agreement could not otherwise be reached, a general massacre of all who have not thought in a certain way has proved a very effective means of settling opinion in a country. If the power to do this be wanting, let a list of opinions be drawn up, to which no man of the least independence of thought can assent, and let the faithful be required to accept all these propositions, in order to segregate them as radically as possible from the influence of the rest of the world.

This method has, from the earliest times, been one of the chief means of upholding correct theological and political doctrines, and of preserving their universal or catholic character. In Rome, especially, it has been practiced from the days of Numa Pompilius, to those of Pius Nonus. This is the most perfect example in history; but wherever there is a priesthood—and no religion has been without one—this method has been more or less made use of. Wherever there is an aristocracy, or a guild, or any association of a class of men whose interests depend or are supposed to depend on certain propositions, there will be inevitably found some traces of this natural product of social feeling. Cruelties always accompany this system; and when it is consistenly carried out, they become atrocities of the most horrible kind in the eyes of any rational man. Nor should this occasion surprise, for the officer of a society does not feel justified in surrendering the interests of that society for the sake of mercy, as he might his own private interests. It is natural, therefore, that sympathy and fellowship should thus produce a most ruthless power.

In judging this method of fixing belief, which may be called the method of authority, we must, in the first place, allow its immeasurable mental and moral superiority to the method of tenacity. Its success is proportionally greater; and in fact it has over and over again worked the most majestic results. The mere structures of stone which it has caused to be put together—in Siam, for example, in Egypt, and in Europe—have many of them a sublimity hardly more than rivaled by the greatest works of nature. And, except the geological epochs, there are no periods of time so vast as those which are measured by some of these organized faiths. If we scrutinize the matter closely, we shall find that there has not been one of their creeds which has remained always the same; yet the change is so slow as to be imperceptible during one person's life, so that individual belief remains sensibly fixed. For the mass of mankind, then, there is perhaps no better method than this. If it is their highest impulse to be intellectual slaves, then slaves they ought to remain.

But no institution can undertake to regulate opinions upon every subject. Only the most important ones can be attended to, and on the rest men's minds must be left to the action of natural causes. This imperfection will be no source of weakness so long as men are in such a state of culture that one opinion does not influence another—that is, so long as they cannot put two and two together. But in the most priest-ridden states some individuals will be found who are raised above that condition. These men possess a wider sort of social feeling; they see that men in other countries and in other ages have held to very different doctrines from those which they themselves have been brought up to believe; and they cannot help seeing that it is the mere accident of their having been taught as they have, and of their having been surrounded with the manners and associations they have, that has caused them to believe as they do and not far differently. And their candor cannot resist the reflection that there is no reason to rate their own views at a higher value than those of other nations and other centuries; and this gives rise to doubts in their minds.

They will further perceive that such doubts as these must exist in their minds with reference to every belief which seems to be determined by the caprice either of themselves or of those who originated the popular opinions. The willful adherence to a belief, and the arbitrary forcing of it upon others, must, therefore, both be given up and a new method of settling opinions must be adopted, which shall not only produce an impulse to believe, but shall also decide what proposition it is which is to be believed. Let the action of natural preferences be unimpeded, then, and under their influence let men conversing together and regarding matters in different lights, gradually develop beliefs in harmony with natural casues. This method resembles that by which conceptions of art have been brought to maturity. The most perfect example of it is to be found in the history of metaphysical philosophy. Systems of this sort have not usually rested upon observed facts, at least not in any great degree. They have been chiefly adopted because their fundamental propositions seemed "agreeable to reason." This is an apt expression; it does not mean that which agrees with experience, but that which we find ourselves inclined to believe. Plato, for example, finds it agreeable to reason that the distances of the celestial spheres from one another should be proportional to the different lengths of strings which produce harmonious chords. Many philosophers have been led to their main conclusions by considerations like this; but this is the lowest and least developed form which the method takes, for it is clear that another man might find Kepler's [earlier] theory, that the celestial spheres are proportional to the inscribed and circumscribed spheres of the different regular solids, more agreeable to *his* reason. But the shock of opinions will soon lead men to rest on preference of a far more universal nature. Take, for example, the doctrine that man only acts selfishly—that is, from the consideration that acting in one way will afford him more pleasure than acting in another. This rests on no fact in the world, but it has had a wide acceptance as being the only reasonable theory.

This method is far more intellectual and respectable from the point of view of reason than either of the others which we have noticed. But its failure has been the most manifest. It makes of inquiry something similar to the development of taste; but taste, unfortunately, is always more or less a matter of fashion, and accordingly, metaphysicians have never come to any fixed agreement, but the pendulum has swung backward and forward between a more material and a more spiritual philosophy, from the earliest times to the latest. And so from this, which has been called the *a priori* method, we are driven, in Lord Bacon's phrase, to a true induction. We have examined into this *a priori* method as something which promised to deliver our opinions from their accidental and capricious element. But development, while it is a process which climinates the effect of some casual circumstances, only magnifies that of others. This method, therefore, does not differ in a very essential way from that of authority. The government may not have lifted its finger to influence my convictions; I may have been left outwardly quite free to choose, we will say, between monogamy and polygamy, and appealing to my conscience only, I may have concluded that the latter practice is in itself licentious. But when I come to see that the chief obstacle to the spread of Christianity among a people of as high culture as the Hindoos has been a conviction of the immorality of our way of treating women, I cannot help seeing that, though governments do not interfere, sentiments in their development will be very greatly determined by accidental causes. Now, there are some people, among whom I must suppose that my reader is to be found, who, when they see that any belief of theirs is determined by any circumstance extraneous to the facts, will from that moment not merely admit in words that that belief is doubtful, but will experience a real doubt of it, so that it ceases in some degree at least to be a belief.

To satisfy our doubts, therefore, it is necessary that a method should be found by which our beliefs may be caused by nothing human, but by some external permanency—by something upon which our thinking has no effect. Some mystics imagine that they have such a method in a private inspiration from on high. But that is only a form of the method of tenacity, in which the conception of truth as something public is not yet developed. Our external permanency would not be external, in our sense, if it was restricted in its influence to one individual. It must be something which affects, or might affect, every man. And, though these affections are necessarily as various as are individual conditions, yet the method must be such that the ultimate conclusion of every man shall be the same, or would be the same if inquiry were sufficiently persisted in. Such is the method of science. Its fundamental hypothesis, restated in more familiar language, is this: There are real things, whose characters are entirely independent of our opinions about them; those realities affect our senses according to regular laws, and, though our sensations are as different as our relations to the objects, yet, by taking advantage of the laws of perception, we can ascertain by reasoning how things really are, and any man, if he have sufficient experience and reason enough about it, will be led to the one true conclusion. The new conception here involved is that of reality. It may be asked how I know that there are any realities. If this hypothesis is the sole support of my method of inquiry, my method of inquiry must not be used to support my hypothesis. The reply is this: 1, If investigation cannot be regarded as proving that there are real things, it at least does not lead to a contrary conclusion; but the method and the conception on which it is based remain ever in harmony. No doubts of the method, therefore, necessarily arise from its practice, as is the case with all the others. 2, The feeling which gives rise to any method of fixing belief is a dissatisfaction at two repugnant propositions. But here already is a vague concession that there is some *one* thing to which a proposition should conform. Nobody, therefore, can really doubt that there are realities, or, if he did, doubt would not be a source of dissatisfaction. The hypothesis, therefore, is one which every mind admits. So that the social impulse does not cause men to doubt it. 3, Everybody uses the scientific method about a great many things, and only ceases to use it when he does not know how to apply it. 4, Experience of the method has not led us to doubt it, but, on the contrary, scientific investigation has had the most wonderful triumphs in the way of settling opinion. These afford the explanation of my not doubting the method or the hypothesis which it supposes; and not having any doubt, nor believing that anybody else whom I could influence has, it would be the merest babble for me to say more about it. If there be anybody with a living doubt upon the subject, let him consider it.

To describe the method of scientific investigation is the object of this series of papers. At present I have only room to notice some points of contrast between it and other methods of fixing belief.

This is the only one of the four methods which presents any distinction of a right and a wrong way. If I adopt the method of tenacity and shut myself out from all influences, whatever I think necessary to doing this is necessary according to that method. So with the method of authority: the state may try to put down heresy by means which, from a scientific point of view, seem very ill-calculated to accomplish its purpose; but the only test *on that method* is what the state thinks, so that it cannot pursue the method wrongly. So with the *a priori* method. The very essence of it is to think as one is inclined to think. All metaphysicians will be sure to do that, however they may be inclined to judge each other to be perversely wrong. The Hegelian system recognizes every natural tendency of thought as logical, although it is certain to be abolished by counter-tendencies. Hegel thinks there is a regular system in the succession of these tendencies, in consequence of which, after drifting one way and the other for a long time, opinion will at last go right. And it is true that metaphysicians get the right ideas at last; Hegel's system of Nature represents tolerably the science of his day; and one may be sure that whatever scientific investigation has put out of doubt will presently receive *a priori* demonstration on the part of the metaphysicians. But with the scientific method the case is different. I may start with known and observed facts to proceed to the unknown; and yet the rules which I follow in doing so may not be such as investigation would approve. The test of whether I am truly following the method is not an immediate appeal to my feelings and purposes, but, on the contrary, itself involves the application of the method. Hence, it is that bad reasoning as well as good reasoning is possible; and this fact is the foundation of the practical side of logic.

It is not to be supposed that the first three methods of settling opinion present no advantage whatever over the scientific method. On the contrary, each has some peculiar convenience of its own. The *a priori* method is

distinguished for its comfortable conclusions. It is the nature of the process
to adopt whatever belief we are inclined to, and there are certain flatteries
to one's vanities which we all believe by nature, until we are awakened
from our pleasing dream by rough facts. The method of authority will
always govern the mass of mankind; and those who wield the various
forms of organized force in the state will never be convinced that dangerous
reasoning ought not to be suppressed in some way. If liberty of speech
is to be untrammeled from the grosser forms of constraint, then uniformity
of opinion will be secured by a moral terrorism to which the respectability
of society will give its thorough approval. Following the method of
authority is the path of peace. Certain non-conformities are permitted;
certain others (considered unsafe) are forbidden. These are different in
different countries and in different ages; but, wherever you are let it be
known that you seriously hold a tabooed belief, and you may be perfectly
sure of being treated with a cruelty no less brutal but more refined than
hunting you like a wolf. Thus, the greatest intellectual benefactors of
mankind have never dared, and dare not now, to utter the whole of their
thought; and thus a shade of *prima facie* doubt is cast upon every
proposition which is considered essential to the security of society. Singularly enough, the persecution does not all come from without; but a
man torments himself and is oftentimes most distressed at finding himself
believing propositions which he has been brought up to regard with
aversion. The peaceful and sympathetic man will, therefore, find it hard
to resist the temptation to submit his opinions to authority. But most of
all I admire the method of tenacity for its strength, simplicity, and
directness. Men who pursue it are distinguished for their decision of
character, which becomes very easy with such a mental rule. They do
not waste time in trying to make up their minds to what they want, but,
fastening like lightning upon whatever alternative comes first, they hold
to it to the end, whatever happens, without an instant's irresolution. This
is one of the splendid qualities which generally accompany brilliant,
unlasting success. It is impossible not to envy the man who can dismiss
reason, although we know how it must turn out at last.

Such are the advantages which the other methods of settling opinions
have over scientific investigation. A man should consider well of them;
and then he should consider that, after all, he wishes his opinions to
coincide with the fact, and that there is no reason why the results of
those first three methods should do so. To bring about this effect is the
prerogative of the method of science. Upon such considerations he has
to make his choice—a choice which is far more than the adoption of any
intellectual opinion, which is one of the ruling decisions of his life, to
which when once made he is bound to adhere. The force of habit will
sometimes cause a man to hold on to old beliefs after he is in a condition
to see that they have no sound basis. But reflection upon the state of the
case will overcome these habits, and he ought to allow reflection full

weight. People sometimes shrink from doing this, having an idea that beliefs are wholesome which they cannot help feeling rest on nothing. But let such persons suppose an analogous though different case from their own. Let them ask themselves what they would say to a reformed Mussulman who should hesitate to give up his old notions in regard to the relations of the sexes; or to a reformed Catholic who should still shrink from the Bible. Would they not say that these persons ought to consider the matter fully, and clearly understand the new doctrine, and then ought to embrace it in its entirety? But, above all, let it be considered that what is more wholesome than any particular belief is integrity of belief; and that to avoid looking into the support of any belief from a fear that it may turn out rotten is quite as immoral as it is disadvantageous. The person who confesses that there is such a thing as truth, which is distinguished from falsehood simply by this, that if acted on it should, on full consideration, carry us to the point we aim at and not astray, and then, though convinced of this, dares not know the truth and seeks to avoid it, is in a sorry state of mind, indeed.

Yes, the other methods do have their merits: a clear logical conscience does cost something—just as any virtue, just as all that we cherish, costs us dear. But, we should not desire it to be otherwise. The genius of a man's logical method should be loved and reverenced as his bride, whom he has chosen from all the world. He need not condemn the others; on the contrary, he may honor them deeply, and in doing so he only honors her the more. But she is the one that he has chosen, and he knows that he was right in making that choice. And having made it, he will work and fight for her, and will not complain that there are blows to take, hoping that there may be as many and as hard to give, and will strive to be the worthy knight and champion of her from the blaze of whose splendors he draws his inspiration and his courage.

HOW TO MAKE OUR IDEAS CLEAR*

I

Whoever has looked into a modern treatise on logic of the common sort, will doubtless remember the two distinctions between *clear* and *obscure* conceptions, and between *distinct* and *confused* conceptions. They have lain in the books now for nigh two centuries, unimproved and unmodified, and are generally reckoned by logicians as among the gems of their doctrine.

---

* Charles S. Peirce, "How To Make Our Ideas Clear," *Popular Science Monthly* 12 (1878): pp. 286–302.

A clear idea is defined as one which is so apprehended that it will be recognized wherever it is met with, and so that no other will be mistaken for it. If it fails of this clearness, it is said to be obscure.

This is rather a neat bit of philosophical terminology; yet, since it is clearness that they were defining, I wish the logicians had made their definition a little more plain. Never to fail to recognize an idea, and under no circumstances to mistake another for it, let it come in how recondite a form it may, would indeed imply such prodigious force and clearness of intellect as is seldom met with in this world. On the other hand, merely to have such an acquaintance with the idea as to have become familiar with it, and to have lost all hesitancy in recognizing it in ordinary cases, hardly seems to deserve the name of clearness of apprehension, since after all it only amounts to a subjective feeling of mastery which may be entirely mistaken. I take it, however, that when the logicians speak of "clearness," they mean nothing more than such a familiarity with an idea, since they regard the quality as but a small merit, which needs to be supplemented by another, which they call *distinctness.*

A distinct idea is defined as one which contains nothing which is not clear. This is technical language; by the *contents* of an idea logicians understand whatever is contained in its definition. So that an idea is *distinctly* apprehended, according to them, when we can give a precise definition of it, in abstract terms. Here the professional logicians leave the subject; and I would not have troubled the reader with what they have to say if it were not such a striking example of how they have been slumbering through ages of intellectual activity, listlessly disregarding the enginery of modern thought, and never dreaming of applying its lessons to the improvement of logic. It is easy to show that the doctrine that familiar use and abstract distinctness make the perfection of apprehension, has its only true place in philosophies which have long been extinct; and it is now time to formulate the method of attaining to a more perfect clearness of thought, such as we see and admire in the thinkers of our own time.

When Descartes set about the reconstruction of philosophy, his first step was to (theoretically) permit skepticism and to discard the practice of the schoolmen of looking to authority as the ultimate source of truth. That done, he sought a more natural fountain of true principles, and professed to find it in the human mind; thus passing, in the directest way, from the method of authority to that of apriority, as described in my first paper ["The Fixation of Belief"]. Self-consciousness was to furnish us with our fundamental truths, and to decide what was agreeable to reason. But since, evidently, not all ideas are true, he was led to note, as the first condition of infallibility, that they must be clear. The distinction between an idea *seeming* clear and really being so, never occurred to him. Trusting to introspection, as he did, even for a knowledge of external things, why should he question its testimony in respect to the contents of our own minds? But then, I suppose, seeing men, who seemed to be quite clear and positive, holding opposite opinions upon fundamental principles, he was further led to say that clearness of ideas is not sufficient, but that they need also to be distinct, i.e., to have nothing unclear about them. What he probably meant by this (for he did not explain himself with precision) was that they must sustain the test of dialectical examination; that they must not only seem clear at the outset, but that discussion must never be able to bring to light points of obscurity connected with them.

Such was the distinction of Descartes, and one sees that it was precisely on the level of his philosophy. It was somewhat developed by Leibniz. This great and singular genius was as remarkable for what he failed to see as for what he saw. That a piece of mechanism could not do work perpetually without being fed with power in some form, was a thing perfectly apparent to him; yet he did not understand that the machinery of the mind can only transform knowledge, but never originate it, unless it be fed with facts of observation. He thus missed the most essential point of the Cartesian, philosophy, which is, that to accept propositions which seem perfectly evident to us is a thing which, whether it be logical or illogical, we cannot help doing. Instead of regarding the matter in this way, he sought to reduce the first principles of science to formulas which cannot be denied without self-contradiction, and was apparently unaware of the great difference between his position and that of Descartes. So he reverted to the old formalities of logic and above all, abstract definitions played a great part in his philosophy. It was quite natural therefore, that on observing that the method of Descartes labored under the difficulty that we may seem to ourselves to have clear apprehensions of ideas which in truth are very hazy, no better remedy occurred to him than to require an abstract definition of every important term. Accordingly, in adopting the distinction of *clear* and *distinct* notions, he described the latter quality as the clear apprehension of everything contained in the definition; and the books have ever since copied his words. There is no danger that his chimerical scheme will ever again be overvalued. Nothing new can ever be learned by analyzing definitions. Nevertheless, our existing beliefs can be set in order by this process, and order is an essential element of intellectual economy, as of every other. It may be acknowledged, therefore, that the books are right in making familiarity with a notion the first step toward clearness of apprehension, and the defining of it the second. But in omitting all mention of any higher perspicuity of thought, they simply mirror a philosophy which was exploded a hundred years ago. That much-admired "ornament of logic"—the doctrine of clearness and distinctness—may be pretty enough, but it is high time to relegate to our cabinet of curiosities the antique *bijou,* and to wear about us something better adapted to modern uses.

The very first lesson that we have a right to demand that logic shall teach us is how to make our ideas clear; and a most important one it is, depreciated only by minds who stand in need of it. To know what we think, to be masters of our own meaning, will make a solid foundation for great and weighty thought. . . .

II

The principles set forth in the first of these papers lead, at once, to a method of reaching a clearness of thought of a far higher grade than the "distinctness" of the logicians. We have there found that the action of thought is excited by the irritation of doubt, and ceases when belief is attained; so that the production of belief is the sole function of thought. All these words, however, are too strong for my purpose. It is as if I had described the phenomena as they appear under a mental microscope. Doubt and Belief, as the words are commonly employed, relate to religious or other grave discussions. But here I use them to designate the starting of any question, no matter how small or how great, and the resolution of it. If, for instance, in a horsecar, I pull out my purse and find a five-cent nickel and five coppers, I decide, while my hand is going to the purse, in which way I will pay my fare. To call such a question Doubt, and my decision Belief, is certainly to use words very disproportionate to the occasion. To speak of such a doubt as causing an irritation which needs to be appeased, suggests a temper which is uncomfortable to the verge of insanity. Yet, looking at the matter minutely, it must be admitted that, if there is the least hesitation as to whether I shall pay the five coppers or the nickel (as there will be sure to be, unless I act from some previously contracted habit in the matter), though irritation is too strong a word, yet I am excited to such small mental activity as may be necessary to deciding how I shall act. Most frequently doubts arise from some indecision, however momentary, in our action. Sometimes it is not so. I have, for example, to wait in a railway station, and to pass the time I read the advertisements on the walls. I compare the advantages of different trains and different routes which I never expect to take, merely fancying myself to be in a state of hesitancy, because I am bored with having nothing to trouble me. Feigned hesitancy, whether feigned for mere amusement or with a lofty purpose, plays a great part in the production of scientific inquiry. However the doubt may originate, it stimulates the mind to an activity which may be slight or energetic, calm or turbulent. Images pass rapidly through consciousness, one incessantly melting into another, until at last, when all is over—it may be in a fraction of a second, in an hour, or after long years—we find ourselves decided as to how we should act under such circumstances as those which occasioned our hesitation. In other words, we have attained belief.

In this process we observe two sorts of elements of consciousness, the distinction between which may best be made clear by means of an illustration. In a piece of music there are the separate notes, and there is the air. A single tone may be prolonged for an hour or a day, and it exists as perfectly in each second of that time as in the whole taken together; so that, as long as it is sounding, it might be present to a sense from which everything in the past was as completely absent as the future itself. But it is different with the air, the performance of which occupies a certain time, during the portions of which only portions of it are played. It consists in an orderliness in the succession of sounds which strike the ear at different times; and to perceive it there must be some continuity of consciousness which makes the events of a lapse of time present to us. We cannot be said to directly hear it, for we hear only what is present at the instant, and an orderliness of succession cannot exist in an instant. These two sorts of objects, what we are *immediately* conscious of and what we are *mediately* conscious of, are found in all consciousness. Some elements (the sensations) are completely present at every instant so long as they last, while others (like thought) are actions having beginning, middle, and end, and consist in a congruence in the succession of sensations which flow through the mind. They cannot be immediately present to us, but must cover some portion of the past or future. Thought is a thread of melody running through the succession of our sensations.

We may add that just as a piece of music may be written in parts, each part having its own air, so various systems of relationship of succession subsist together between the same sensations. These different systems are distinguished by having different motives, ideas, or functions. Thought is only one such system; for its sole motive, idea, and function is to produce belief, and whatever does not concern that purpose belongs to some other system of relations. The action of thinking may incidentally have other results. It may serve to amuse us, for example, and among *dilettanti* it is not rare to find those who have so perverted thought to the purposes of pleasure that it seems to vex them to think that the questions upon which they delight to exercise it may ever get finally settled; and a positive discovery which takes a favorite subject out of the arena of literary debate is met with ill-concealed dislike. This disposition is the very debauchery of thought. But the soul and meaning of thought, abstracted from the other elements which accompany it, though it may be voluntarily thwarted, can never be made to direct itself toward anything but the production of belief. Thought in action has for its only possible motive the attainment of thought at rest; and whatever does not refer to belief is no part of the thought itself.

And what, then, is belief? It is the demi-cadence which closes a musical phrase in the symphony of our intellectual life. We have seen that it has just three properties: first, it is something that we are aware of; second, it appeases the irritation of doubt; and, third, it involves the establishment in our nature of a rule of action, or, say for short, a *habit*. As it appeases the irritation of doubt, which is the motive for thinking, thought relaxes, and comes to rest for a moment when belief is reached. But, since belief is a rule for action, the application of which involves further doubt and further thought, at the same time that it is a stopping-place, it is also a new starting-place for thought. That is why I have permitted myself to call it thought at rest, although thought is essentially an action. The *final* upshot of thinking is the exercise of volition, and of this thought no longer forms a part; but belief is only a stadium of mental action, an effect upon our nature due to thought, which will influence future thinking.

The essence of belief is the establishment of a habit, and different beliefs are distinguished by the different modes of action to which they give rise. If beliefs do not differ in this respect, if they appease the same doubt by producing the same rule of action, then no mere differences in the manner of consciousness of them can make them different beliefs, any more than playing a tune in different keys is playing different tunes.

From all these sophisms we shall be perfectly safe so long as we reflect that the whole function of thought is to produce habits of action; and that whatever there is connected with a thought, but irrelevant to its purpose, is an accretion to it; but no part of it. If there be a unity among our sensations which has no reference to how we shall act on a given occasion, as when we listen to a piece of music, why we do not call that thinking. To develop its meaning, we have, therefore, simply to determine what habits it produces, for what a thing means is simply what habits it involves. Now, the identity of a habit depends on how it might lead us to act, not merely under such circumstances as are likely to arise, but under such as might possibly occur, no matter how improbable they may be. What the habit is depends on *when* and *how* is causes us to act. As for the *when,* every stimulus to action is derived from perception; as for the *how,* every purpose of action is to produce some sensible result. Thus, we come down to what is tangible and practical as the root of every real distinction of thought, no matter how subtle it may be; and there is no distinction of meaning so fine as to consist in anything but a possible difference of practice.

It appears, then, that the rule of attaining the third grade of clearness of apprehension is as follows: consider what effects, which might conceivably have practical bearings, we conceive the object of our conception to have. Then, our conception of these effects is the whole of our conception of the object.

III

Let us illustrate this rule by some examples; and, to begin with the simplest one possible, let us ask what we mean by calling a thing *hard*. Evidently that it will not be scratched by many other substances. The whole conception of this quality, as of every other, lies in its conceived effects. There is absolutely no difference between a hard thing and a soft thing so long as they are not brought to the test. Suppose, then, that a diamond could be crystallized in the midst of a cushion of soft cotton, and should remain there until it was finally burned up. Would it be false to say that that diamond was soft? This seems a foolish question, and would be so, in fact, except in the realm of logic. There such questions are often of the greatest utility as serving to bring logical principles into sharper relief than real discussions ever could. In studying logic we must not put them aside with hasty answers, but must consider them with attentive care, in order to make out the principles involved. We may, in the present case, modify our question, and ask what prevents us from saying that all hard bodies remain perfectly soft until they are touched, when their hardness increases with the pressure until they are scratched. Reflection will show that the reply is this: there would be no *falsity* in such modes of speech. They would involve a modification of our present usage of speech with regard to the words "hard" and "soft," but not of their meanings. For they represent no fact to be different from what it is; only they involve arrangements of facts which would be exceedingly maladroit. This leads us to remark that the question of what would occur under circumstances which do not actually arise is not a question of fact, but only of the most perspicuous arrangement of them. For example, the question of free-will and fate in its simplest form, stripped of verbiage, is something like this: I have done something of which I am ashamed; could I, by an effort of the will, have resisted the temptation, and done otherwise? The philosophical reply is that this is not a question of fact, but only of the [possible] arrangement of facts. Arranging them so as to exhibit what is particularly pertinent to my question—namely, that I ought to blame myself for having done wrong—it is perfectly true to say that, if I had willed to do otherwise than I did, I should have done otherwise. On the other hand, arranging the facts so as to exhibit another important consideration, it is equally true that when a temptation has once been allowed to work, it will, if it has a certain force, produce its effect, let me struggle how I may. There is no objection to a contradiction in what would result from a false supposition. The *reductio ad absurdum* consists in showing that contradictory results would follow from a hypothesis which is consequently judged to be false. Many questions are involved in the free-will discussion, and I am far from desiring to say that both sides are equally right. On the contrary, I am of opinion that one side [determinism] denies important facts, and that the other does not. But what I do say is that the above single question was the origin of the whole doubt; that, had it not been for this question, the controversy would never have arisen; and that this question is perfectly solved in the manner which I have indicated.

Let us next seek a clear idea of Weight. This is another very easy case. To say that a body is heavy means simply that, in the absence of opposing force, it will fall. This (neglecting certain specifications of how it will fall, etc., which exist in the mind of the physicist who uses the word) is evidently the whole conception of weight. It is a fair question whether some particular facts may not *account* for gravity; but what we mean by the force itself is completely involved in its effects.

IV

Let us approach the subject of logic, and consider a conception which particularly concerns it, that of *reality*. Taking clearness in the sense of familiarity, no idea could be clearer than this. Every child uses it with perfect confidence, never dreaming that he does not understand it. As for clearness in its second grade, however, it would probably puzzle most men, even among those of a reflective turn of mind, to give an astract definition of the real. Yet such a definition may perhaps be reached by considering the points of difference between reality and its opposite, fiction. A figment is a product of somebody's imagination; it has such characters as his thought impresses upon it. That those characters are independent of how you or I think is an external reality. There are, however, phenomena within our own minds, dependent upon our thought, which are at the same time real in the sense that we really think them. But though their characters depend on how we think, they do not depend on what we think those characters to be. Thus, a dream has a real existence as a mental phenomenon, if somebody has really dreamt it; that he dreamt so and so, does not depend on what anybody thinks was dreamt, but is completely independent of all opinion on the subject. On the other hand, considering, not the fact of dreaming, but the thing dreamt, it retains its peculiarities by virtue of no other fact than that it was dreamt to possess them. Thus we may define the real as that whose characters are independent of what anybody may think them to be.

But, however satisfactory such a definition may be found, it would be a great mistake to suppose that it makes the idea of reality perfectly clear. Here, then, let us apply our rules. According to them, reality, like every other quality, consists in the peculiar, sensible effects which things partaking of it produce. The only effect which real things have is to cause belief, for all the sensations which they excite emerge into consciousness in the form of beliefs. The question, therefore, is, how is true belief (or belief in the real) distinguished from false belief (or belief in fiction). Now, as we have seen in the former paper, the ideas of truth and falsehood, in their full development, appertain exclusively to the scientific method of settling opinion. A person who arbitrarily chooses the propositions which he will adopt can use the word truth only to emphasize the expression of his determination to hold on to his choice. Of course, the method of tenacity never prevailed exclusively; reason is too natural to men for that. But in the literature of the Dark Ages we find some fine examples of it. When Scotus Erigena is commenting upon a poetical passage in which hellebore is spoken of as having caused the death of Socrates, he does not hesitate to inform the inquiring reader that Helleborus and Socrates were two eminent Greek philosophers, and that the latter having been overcome in argument by the former took the matter to heart and died of it! What sort of an idea of truth could a man have who could adopt and teach, without the qualification of a "perhaps," an opinion taken so entirely at random? The real spirit of Socrates, who I hope would have been delighted to have been "overcome in argument," because he would have learned something by it, is in curious contrast with the naïve idea of the glossist, for whom (as for the "born missionary" of today) discussion would seem to have been simply a struggle. When philosophy began to awake from its long slumber, and before theology completely dominated it, the practice seems to have been for each professor to seize upon any philosophical position he found unoccupied and which seemed a strong one, to intrench himself in it, and to sally forth from time to time to give battle to the others. Thus, even the scanty records we possess of those disputes enable us to make out a dozen or more opinions held by different teachers at one time concerning the question of nominalism and realism. Read the opening part of the *Historia Calamitatum* of Abélard, who was certainly as philosophical as any of his contemporaries, and see the spirit of combat which it breathes. For him, the truth is simply his particular stronghold. When the method of authority prevailed, the truth meant little more than the Catholic faith. All the efforts of the scholastic doctors are directed toward harmonizing their faith in Aristotle and their faith in the Church, and one may search their ponderous folios through without finding an argument which goes any further. It is noticeable that where different faiths flourish side by side, renegades are looked upon with contempt even by the party whose belief they adopt; so completely has the idea of loyalty replaced that of truth-seeking. Since the time of Descartes, the defect in the conception of truth has been less apparent. Still, it will sometimes strike a scientific man that the philosophers have been less intent on finding out what the facts are than on inquiring what belief is most in harmony with their system. It is hard to convince a follower of the *a priori* method by adducing facts; but show him that an opinion he is defending is inconsistent with what he has laid down elsewhere, and he will be very apt to retract it. These minds do not seem to believe that disputation is ever to cease; they seem to think that the opinion which is natural for one man is not so for another, and that belief will, consequently, never be settled. In contenting themselves with fixing their own opinions by a method which would lead another man to a different result, they betray their feeble hold of the conception of what truth is.

On the other hand, all the followers of science are fully persuaded that the processes of invetigation, if only pushed far enough, will give one certain solution to each question to which they can be applied. One man may investigate the velocity of light by studying the transits of Venus and the aberration of the stars; another by the oppositions of Mars and the eclipses of Jupiter's satellites; a third by the method of Fizeau; a fourth by that of Foucault; a fifth by a motions of the curves of Lissajoux; a sixth, a seventh, an eighth, and a ninth, may follow the different methods of comparing the measures of statical and dynamical electricity. They may at first obtain different results, but, as each perfects his method and his processes, the results will move steadily together toward a destined center. So with all scientific research. Different minds may set out with the most antagonistic views, but the progress of investigation carries them by a force outside of themselves to one and the same conclusion. This activity of thought by which we are carried, not where we wish, but to a foreordained goal, is like the operation of destiny. No modification of the point of view taken, no selection of other facts for study, no natural bent of mind even, can enable a man to escape the predestinate opinion. This great law is embodied in the conception of truth and reality. The opinion which is fated† to be ultimately agreed to by all who investigate is what we mean by the truth, and the object represented in this opinion is the real. That is the way I would explain reality.

THE ARCHITECTURE OF THEORIES*

Of the fifty or hundred systems of philosophy that have been advanced at different times of the world's history, perhaps the larger number have been not so much results of historical evolution as happy thoughts that have accidently occurred to their authors. An idea that has been found interesting and fruitful has been adopted, developed, and forced to yield explanations of all sorts of phenomena. The English have been particularly given to this way of philosophising; witness, Hobbes, Hartley, Berkeley, James, Mill. Nor has it been by any means useless labor; it shows us what the true nature and value of the ideas developed are, and in that way affords serviceable materials for philosophy. Just as if a man, being

---

† Fate means merely that which is sure to come true, and can nohow be avoided. It is a superstition to suppose that a certain sort of events are ever fated, and it is another to suppose that the word "fate" can never be freed from its superstitious taint. We are all fated to die.

* Charles S. Peirce, "The Architecture of Theories," *The Monist,* January 1891.

seized with the conviction that paper was a good material to make things of, were to go to work to build a *papier mâché* house, with roof of roofing-paper, foundations of pasteboard, windows of paraffined paper, chimneys, bath tubs, locks, etc., all of different forms of paper, his experiment would probably afford valuable lessons to builders, while it would certainly make a detestable house, so those one-idea'd philosophies are exceedingly interesting and instructive, and yet are quite unsound.

The remaining systems of philosophy have been of the nature of reforms, sometimes amounting to radical revolutions, suggested by certain difficulties that have been found to beset systems previously in vogue; and such ought certainly to be in large part the motive of any new theory. This is like partially rebuilding a house. The faults that have been committed are, first, that the dilapidations have generally not been sufficiently thoroughgoing, and second, that not sufficient pain has been taken to bring the additions into deep harmony with the really sound parts of the old structure.

When a man is about to build a house, what a power of thinking he has to do before he can safely break ground! With what pains he has to excogitate the precise wants that are to be supplied. What a study to ascertain the most available and suitable materials, to determine the mode of construction to which those materials are best adapted, and to answer a hundred such questions! Now without riding the metaphor too far, I think we may safely say that the studies preliminary to the construction of a great theory should be at least as deliberate and thorough as those that are preliminary to the building of a dwelling-house.

That systems ought to be constructed architectonically has been preached since Kant, but I do not think the full import of the maxim has by any means been apprehended. What I would recommend is that every person who wishes to form an opinion concerning fundamental problems, should first of all make a complete survey of human knowledge, should take note of all the valuable ideas in each branch of science, should observe in just what respect each has been successful and where it has failed, in order that in the light of the thorough acquaintance so attained of the available materials for a philosophical theory and of the nature and strength of each, he may proceed to the study of what the problem of philosophy consists in, and of the proper way of solving it. I must not be understood as endeavoring to state fully all that these preparatory studies should embrace; on the contrary, I purposely slur over many points, in order to give emphasis to one special recommendation, namely, to make a systematic study of the conceptions out of which a philosophical theory may be built, in order to ascertain what place each conception may fully occupy in such a theory, and to what uses it is adapted.

The adequate treatment of this single point would fill a volume, but I shall endeavor to illustrate my meaning by glancing at several sciences and indicating conceptions in them serviceable for philosophy. As to the results to which long studies thus commenced have led me, I shall just give a hint at their nature.

We may begin with dynamics—field in our day of perhaps the grandest conquest human science has ever made—I mean the law of the conservation of energy. But let us revert to the first step taken by modern scientific thought—and a great stride it was—the inauguration of dynamics by Galileo. A modern physicist on examining Galileo's works is surprised to find how little experiment had to do with the establishment of the foundations of mechanics. His principal appeal is to common sense and *il lume naturale.* He always assumes that the true theory will be found to be a simple and natural one. And we can see why it should indeed be so in dynamics. For instance, a body left to its own inertia moves in a straight line, and a straight line appears to us the simplest of curves. In *itself,* no curve is simpler than another. A system of straight lines has intersections precisely corresponding to those of a system of like parabolas simply placed, or to those of any one of an infinity of systems of curves. But the straight line appears to us simple, because, as Euclid says, it lies evenly between its extremities; that is, because viewed endwise it appears as a point. That is, again, because light moves in straight lines. Now, light moves in straight lines because of the part that the straight line plays in the laws of dynamics. Thus it is that our minds having been formed under the influence of phenomena governed by the laws of mechanics, certain conceptions entering into those laws become implanted in our minds, so that we readily guess at what the laws are. Without such a natural prompting, having to search blindfold for a law that would suit the phenomena, our chance of finding it would be as one to infinity. The further physical studies depart from phenomena that have directly influenced the growth of the mind, the less we can expect to find the laws that govern them "simple" that is, composed of a few conceptions natural to our minds.

The researches of Galileo, followed up by Christiaan Huygens and others, led to those modern conceptions of Force and Law, which have revolutionized the intellectual world. The great attention given to mechanics in the seventeenth century soon so emphasized these conceptions as to give rise to the Mechanical Philosophy, or doctrine that all the phenomena of the physical universe are to be explained upon mechanical principles. Newton's great discovery imparted a new impetus to this tendency. The old notion that heat consists in an agitation of corpuscles was now applied to the explanation of the chief properties of gases. The first suggestion in this direction was that the pressure of gases is explained by the battering of the particles against the walls of the containing vessel, which explained Boyle's law of the compressibility of air. Later, the expansion of gases, Avogadro's chemical law, the diffusion and viscosity of gases, and the action of Sir William Crookes's radiometer were shown to be consequences of the same kinetical theory; but other phenomena, such as the ratio of the specific heat at constant volume to that at constant pressure require additional hypotheses, which we have little reason to suppose are simple, so that we find ourselves quite afloat. In like manner with regard to light, that it consists of vibrations was almost proved by the phenomena of diffraction, while those of polarization showed the excursions of the particles to be perpendicular to the line of propagation; but the phenomena of dispersion, etc., require additional hypotheses that may be very complicated. Thus, the further progress of molecular speculation appears quite uncertain. If hypotheses are to be tried haphazardly or simply because they will suit certain phenomena, it will occupy the mathematical physicists of the world say half a century on the average to bring each theory to the test, and since the number of possible theories may go up into the trillions, only one of which can be true, we have little prospect of making further solid additions to the subject in our time. When we come to atoms, the presumption in favor of a simple law seems very slender. There is room for serious doubt whether the fundamental laws of mechanics hold good for single atoms, and it seems quite likely that they are capable of motion in more than three dimensions.

To find out much more about molecules and atoms, we must search out a natural history of laws of nature, which may fulfill that function that the presumption in favor of simple laws fulfilled in the early days of dynamics, by showing us what kind of laws we have to expect and by answering such questions as this: Can we with reasonable prospect of not wasting time, try the supposition that atoms attract one another inversely as the seventh power of their distances, or can we not? To suppose univeral laws of nature capable of being apprehended by the mind and yet having no reason for their special forms, but standing inexplicable and irrational, is hardly a justifiable position. Uniformities are precisely the sort of facts that need to be accounted for. That a pitched coin should sometimes turn up heads and sometimes tails calls for no particular explanation; but if it shows heads every time, we wish to know how this result has been brought about. Law is *par excellence* the thing that wants a reason.

Now the only possible way of accounting for the laws of nature and for uniformity in general is to suppose them results of evolution. This supposes them not to be absolute, not to be obeyed precisely. It makes an element of indeterminacy, spontaneity, or absolute chance in nature. Just as, when we attempt to verify any physical law, we find our observations cannot be precisely satisfied by it, and rightly attribute the discrepancy to errors of observation, so we must suppose far more minute discrepancies to exist owing to the imperfect cogency of the law itself, to a certain swerving of the facts from any definite formula.

Herbert Spencer wishes to explain evolution upon mechanical principles. This is illogical, for four reasons. First, because the principle of evolution requires no extraneous cause; since the tendency to growth can be supposed itself to have grown from an infinitesimal germ accidentally started. Second, because law ought more than anything else to be supposed a result of evolution. Third, because exact law obviously never can produce heterogeneity out of homogeneity; and arbitrary heterogeneity is the feature of the universe the most manifest and characteristic. Fourth, because the law of the conservation of energy is equivalent to the proposition that all operations governed by mechanical laws are reversible; so that an immediate corollary from it is that growth is not explicable by those laws, even if they be not violated in the process of growth. In short, Spencer is not a philosophical evolutionist, but only a half-evolutionist—or, if you will, only a semi-Spencerian. Now philosophy requires thoroughgoing evolutionism or none.

The theory of Darwin was that evolution had been brought about by the action of two factors; first, heredity, as a principle making offspring nearly resemble their parents, while yet giving room for "sporting," or accidental variations—for very slight variations often, for wider ones rarely; and, second, the destruction of breeds or races that are unable to keep the birth rate up to the death rate. This Darwinian principle is plainly capable of great generalization. Wherever there are large numbers of objects, having a tendency to retain certain characters unaltered, this tendency, however, not being absolute but giving room for chance variations, then, if the amount of variation is absolutely limited in certain directions by the destruction of everything that reaches those limits, there will be a gradual tendency to change in directions of departure from them. Thus, if a million players sit down to bet at an even game, since one after another will get ruined, the average wealth of those who remain will perpetually increase. Here is indubitably a genuine formula of possible evolution, whether its operation accounts for much or little in the development of animal and vegetable species.

The Lamarckian theory also supposes that the development of species has taken place by a long series of insensible changes, but it supposes that those changes have taken place during the lives of the individuals, in consequence of effort and exercise, and that reproduction plays no part in the process except in preserving these modifications. Thus, the Lamarckian theory only explains the development of characters for which individuals strive, while the Darwinian theory only explains the production of characters really beneficial to the race, though these may be fatal to individuals.* But more broadly and philosophically conceived, Darwinian evolution is evolution by the operation of chance, and the destruction of bad results, while Lamarckian evolution is evolution by the effect of habit and effort.

---

* The neo-Darwinian, August Weismann, has shown that mortality would almost necessarily result from the action of the Darwinian principle.

A third theory of evolution is that of Clarence King. The testimony of monuments and of rocks is that species are unmodified or scarcely modified, under ordinary circumstances, but are rapidly altered after cataclysms or rapid geological changes. Under novel circumstances, we often see animals and plants sporting excessively in reproduction, and sometimes even undergoing transformations during individual life, phenomena no doubt due partly to the enfeeblement of vitality from the breaking up of habitual modes of life, partly to changed food, partly to direct specific influence of the element in which the organism is immersed. If evolution has been brought about in this way, not only have its single steps not been insensible, as both Darwinians and Lamarckians suppose, but they are furthermore neither haphazard on the one hand, nor yet determined by an inward striving on the other, but on the contrary are effects of the changed environment, and have a positive general tendency to adapt the organism to that environment, since variation will particularly affect organs at once enfeebled and stimulated. This mode of evolution, by external forces and the breaking up of habits, seems to be called for by some of the broadest and most important facts of biology and paleontology; while it certainly has been the chief factor in the historical evolution of institutions as in that of ideas; and cannot possibly be refused a very prominent place in the process of evolution of the universe in general.

Passing to psychology, we find the elementary phenomena of mind fall into three categories. First, we have feelings, comprising all that is immediately present, such as pain, blue, cheerfulness, the feeling that arises when we contemplate a consistent theory, etc. A feeling is a state of mind having its own living quality, independent of any other state of mind. Or, a feeling is an element of consciousness that might conceivably override every other state until it monopolized the mind, although such a rudimentary state cannot actually be realized, and would not properly be consciousness. Still, it is conceivable, or supposable, that the quality of blue should usurp the whole mind, to the exclusion of the ideas of shape, extension, contrast, commencement, and cessation, and all other ideas, whatsoever. A feeling is necessarily perfectly simple, *in itself,* for if it had parts these would also be in the mind, whenever the whole was present, and thus the whole could not monopolize the mind.*

Besides feelings, we have sensations of reaction; as when a person blindfolded suddenly runs against a post, when we make a muscular effort, or when any feeling gives way to a new feeling. Suppose I had nothing in my mind but a feeling of blue, which were suddenly to give place to a feeling of red; then, at the instant of transition there would be a shock, a sense of reaction, my blue life being transmuted into red life. If I were

---

* A feeling may certainly be compounded, but only in virtue of a perception that is not that feeling nor any feeling at all.

further endowed with a memory, that sense would continue for some time, and there would also be a peculiar feeling or sentiment connected with it. This last feeling might endure (conceivably, I mean) after the memory of the occurrence and the feelings of blue and red had passed away. But the *sensation* of reaction cannot exist except in the actual presence of the two feelings blue and red to which it relates. Wherever we have two feelings and pay attention to a relation between them of whatever kind, there is the sensation of which I am speaking. But the sense of action and reaction has two types: it may either be a perception of relation between feeling and something out of feeling. And this sense of external reaction again has two forms; for it is either a sense of something happening to us, by no act of ours, we being passive in the matter, or it is a sense of resistance, that is, of our expending feeling upon something without. The sense of reaction is thus a sense of connection or comparison between the feelings, either, *a,* between one feeling and another, or *b,* between feeling and its absence or lower degree; and under *b* we have, first, the sense of the access of feeling, and second, the sense of remission of feeling.

Very different both from feelings and from reaction-sensations or disturbances of feeling are general conceptions. When we think, we are conscious that a connection between feelings is determined by a general rule, we are aware of being governed by a habit. Intellectual power is nothing but facility in taking habits and in following them in cases essentially analogous to, but in nonessentials widely remote from, the normal cases of connections of feelings under which those labits were formed.

The one primary and fundamental law of mental action consists in a tendency to generalization. Feeling tends to spread, connections between feelings awaken feelings; neighboring feelings become assimilated; ideas are apt to reproduce themselves. These are so many formulations of the one law of the growth of mind. When a disturbance of feeling takes place, we have a consciousness of gain, the gain of experience; and a new disturbance will be apt to assimilate itself to the one that preceded it. Feelings, by being excited, become more easily excited, especially in the ways in which they have previously been excited. The consciousness of such a habit constitutes a general conception.

The cloudiness of psychological notions may be corrected by connecting them with physiological conceptions. Feeling may be supposed to exist, wherever a nerve cell is in an excited condition. The disturbance of feeling, or sense of reaction, accompanies the transmission of disturbance between nerve cells or from a nerve cell to a muscle cell or the external stimulation of a nerve cell. General conceptions arise upon the formation of habits in the nerve matter, which are molecular changes consequent upon its activity and probably connected with its nutrition.

The law of habit exhibits a striking contrast to all physical laws in the character of its commands. A physical law is absolute. What it requires is an exact relation. Thus, a physical force introduces into a motion a component motion to be combined with the rest by the parallelogram of forces; but the component motion must actually take place exactly as required by the law of force. On the other hand, no exact conformity is required by the mental law. Nay, exact conformity would be in downright conflict with the law; since it would instantly crystallize thought and prevent all further formation of habit. The law of mind only makes a given feeling *more likely* to arise. It thus resembles the "non-conservative" forces of physics, such as viscosity and the like, which are due to statistical uniformities in the chance encounters of trillions of molecules.

The old dualistic notion of mind and matter, so prominent in Cartesianism, as two radically different kinds of substance, will hardly find defenders today. Rejecting this, we are driven to some form of hylopathy, otherwise called monism. Then the question arises whether physical laws on the one hand, and the psychical law on the other are to be taken.

(A) as independent, a doctrine often called *monism,* but which I would name *neutralism;* or,

(B) the psychical law as derived and special, the physical law alone as primordial, which is *materialism;* or,

(C) the physical law as derived and special, the psychical law alone as primordial, which is *idealism.*

The materialistic doctrine seems to me quite as repugnant to scientific logic as to common sense; since it requires us to suppose that a certain kind of mechanism will feel, which would be a hypothesis absolutely irreducible to reason—an ultimate, inexplicable regularity; while the only possible justification of any theory is that it should make things clear and reasonable.

Neutralism is sufficiently condemned by the logical maxim known as Ockham's razor, i.e., that not more independent elements are to be supposed than necessary. By placing the inward and outward aspects of substance on a par, it seems to render both primordial.

The one intelligible theory of the universe is that of objective idealism, that matter is effete mind, inveterate habits becoming physical laws. But before this can be accepted it must show itself capable of explaining the tridimensionality of space, the laws of motion, and the general characteristics of the universe, with mathematical clearness and precision; for no less should be demanded of every philosophy.

Among the many principles of logic that find their application in philosophy, I can here only mention one. Three conceptions are perpetually turning up at every point in every theory of logic, and in the most rounded systems they occur in connection with one another. They are conceptions so very broad and consequently indefinite that they are hard to seize and may be easily overlooked. I call them the conceptions of First, Second, Third. First is the conception of being or existing independent of anything else. Second is the conception of being relative to, the conception of reaction with, something else. Third is the conception of mediation, whereby a first and second are brought into relation. To illustrate these ideas, I will show how they enter into those we have been considering. The origin of things, considered not as leading to anything, but in itself, contains the idea of First, the end of things that of Second, the process mediating between them that of Third. A philosophy that emphasizes the idea of the One, is generally a dualistic philosophy in which the conception of Second receives exaggerated attention; for this One (though of course involving the idea of First) is always the other of a manifold that is not one. The idea of the Many, because variety is arbitrariness and arbitrarines is repudiation of any Secondness, has for its principal component the conception of First. In psychology Feeling is First, Sesne of reaction Second, General conception Third, or mediation. In biology, the idea of arbitrary sporting is First, heredity is Second, the process whereby the accidental characters become fixed is Third. Chance is First, Law is Second, the tendency to take habits is Third. Mind is First, Matter is Second, Evolution is Third.

Such are the materials out of which chiefly a philosophical theory ought to be built, in order to represent the state of knowledge to which the nineteenth century has brought us. Without going into other important questions of philosophical architectonic, we can readily foresee what sort of metaphysics would appropriately be constructed from those conceptions. Like some of the most ancient and some of the most recent speculations it would be a Cosmogonic Philosophy. It would suppose that in the beginning—infinitely remote—there was a chaos of unpersonalized feeling, which being without connection or regularity would properly be without existence. This feeling, sporting here and there in pure arbitrariness, would have started the germ of a generalizing tendency. Its other sportings would be evanescent, but this would have a growing virtue. Thus, the tendency to habit would be started; and from this with the other principles of evolution all the regularities of the universe would be evolved. At any time, however, an element of pure chance survives and will remain until the world becomes an absolutely perfect, rational, and symmetrical system, in which mind is at last crystallized in the infinitely distant future.

That idea has been worked out by me with elaboration. It accounts for the main features of the universe as we know it—the characters of time, space, matter, force, gravitation, electricity, etc. It predicts many more things that new observations can alone bring to the test. May some future student go over this ground again, and have the leisure to give his results to the world.

UNIFORMITY*

(1) A fact consisting in this: that, of a certain genus of facts, a proportion approaching unity (the whole) belong, in the course of experience, to a certain species; so that, though of itself the knowledge of this uniformity gives no information concerning a certain thing or character, yet it will strengthen any inductive conclusion of a certain kind.

It is, therefore, a high objective probability concerning an objective probability. There are, in particular, four classes of uniformities, the knowledge of any of which, or of its falsity, may deductively strengthen or weaken an inductive conclusion. These four kinds of uniformity are as follows:

i. The members of a class may present an extraordinary resemblance to one another in regard to a certain line of characters. Thus, the Icelanders are said to resemble one another most strikingly in their opinions about general subjects. Knowing this, we should not need to question many Icelanders, if we found that the first few whom we met all shared a common superstition, in order to conclude with considerable confidence that nearly all Icelanders were of the same way of thinking. Philodemus insists strongly upon this kind of uniformity as support of induction.

ii. A character may be said that, in whatever genus it occurs at all, it almost always belongs to all the species of that genus; or this uniformity may be lacking. Thus, when only white swans were known, it would have been hazardous to assert that all swans were white, because whiteness is not usually a generic character. It is considerably more safe to assert that all crows are black, because blackness is oftener a generic character. This kind of uniformity is especially emphasized by Mill as important in inductive inquiries.

iii. A certain set of characters may be intimately connected so as to be usually all present or all absent from certain kinds of objects. Thus, the different chemical reactions of gold are so inseparable that a chemist need only to succeed in getting, say, the purple of Cassius, to be confident that the body under examination will show every reaction of gold.

iv. Of a certain object it may be known that its characteristic is that when it possesses one of a set of characters within a certain group of such sets, it possesses the rest. Thus, it may be known of a certain man that to whatever party he belongs, he is apt to embrace without reserve the entire creed of that party. We shall not, then, need to know many of his opinions, say in regard to politics, in order to infer with great confidence his position upon other political questions.

(2) The word "uniformity" plays such a singular and prominent *rôle* in the logic of Mill that it is proper to note it. He was apt to be greatly

---

* Charles S. Peirce, "Uniformity," in *Dictionary of Philosophy and Psychology,* ed. James Baldwin, 1902.

influenced by Ockham's razor in forming theories that he defended with
great logical acumen; but he differed from other men of that way of
thinking in that his natural candor led to his making many admissions
without perceiving how fatal they were to his negative theories. In addition
to that, perhaps more than other philosophers, in endeavoring to embrace
several ideas under a common term, he often leaves us at a loss to find
any other character common and peculiar to those notions except that
of their having received from him that common designation. In one
passage of his *System of Logic* (1842), he declares, in reference to the
difference in strength between two inductive conclusions, that whoever
shall discover the cause of that difference will have discovered the secret
of inductive reasoning. When, therefore, he shortly afterwards points out
that the distinction between those two inductions is that one of them is
supported by a uniformity of the second of the above four classes, while
the other is met by a distinct diversity of the same kind, and when he
himself gives to that uniformity this designation when he afterwards
declares that the validity of induction depends upon uniformity, his reader
naturally supposes he means uniformity in that sense. But we find that
he employs the word for quite another purpose. Namely, he does not like
the word *law,* as applied to an inductive generalization of natural facts—
such as the "law" of gravitation—because it implies an element in nature,
the reality of a general, which no nominalist can admit. He, therefore,
desires to call the reality to which a true universal proposition about
natural phenomena corresponds, a "uniformity." The implication of the
word, thus used, is that the facts are, in themselves, entirely disconnected,
and that it is the mind alone which unites them. One stone dropping to
the earth has no real connection with another stone dropping to the earth.
It is, surely, not difficult to see that this theory of uniformities, far from
helping to establish the validity of induction, would be, if consistently
admitted, an insuperable objection to such validity. For if two facts, *A*
and *B,* are entirely independent in their real nature, then the truth of *B*
cannot follow, either necessarily or probably, from the truth of *A.* If I
have tried the experiment with a million stones and have found that
every one of them fell when allowed to drop, it may be very natural for
me to believe that almost any stone will act in the same way. But if it
can be proved that there is no real connection between the behavior of
different stones, then there is nothing for it but to say that it was a chance
coincidence that those million stones all behaved in the same way; for
if there was any *reason* for it, and they *really* dropped, there was a *real
reason,* that is, a real general. Now, if it is mere chance that they all
dropped, that affords no more reason for supposing that the next will
drop, than my throwing three double-sixes successively with a pair of
dice is a reason for thinking that the next throw will be double-sixes.

(3) But now we find that Mill's good sense and candor will not allow
him to take the course that a Hobbes would have taken, and utterly deny

the validity of induction; and this leads to a new use of the word *uniformity,* in which he speaks of the "uniformity of nature." Before asking exactly what this phrase means, it may be noted that, whatever it means, the assertion of it is an assent to scholastic realism, except for a difference of emphasis. For to say that throughout the whole course of experience, events always, or even only usually, happen alike under the same conditions (what is usually called the "invariability" of nature), is to assert an agreement (complete or partial) that could not be ascribed to chance without self-contradiction. For chance is merely the possible discrepancy between the character of the limited experience to which it belongs and the whole course of experience. Hence, to say that of the *real,* objective facts some *general* character can be predicated, is to assert the reality of a general. It only differs from scholastic realism in that Mill and his followers treat this aspect of the matter lightly—that is to say, the objective reality of the general—while the Scholastics regarded it as a great and vital feature of the universe. Instead of "uniformity" now importing that what others call "laws" are fabrications of the human mind, this "uniformity of nature" is erected by Mill into the greatest of laws and absolutely objective and real.

Let us now inquire what the "uniformity of nature," with its synonymous expressions that "the future resembles the past," and so forth, can mean. Mill says that it means that if all the circumstances attending two phenomena are the same, they will be alike. But taken strictly this means absolutely nothing, since no two phenomena ever can happen in circumstances precisely alike, nor are two phenomena precisely alike. It is, therefore, necessary to modify the statement in order to give it any meaning at all; and it will be found that, however it may be so modified, the moment it begins to carry a definite meaning, one of three things results: it becomes either, first, grossly false, or, second, an assertion that there is really no good reason to believe even approximately true, or thirdly, it becomes a quasi-subjective truth, not lending any color of validity to induction proper. If, for example, we were to say that under any given species of circumstances presenting any similarity, phenomena of any given genus would be found to have a specific general resemblance in contrast with the specific character of phenomena of the same genus occurring under a different species of circumstances of the same genus, this would be monstrously false, whether intended as an absolutely universal proposition or merely as one approximately true. Let, for example, the genus of phenomena be the values of the throws of a pair of dice in a given series of successive throws indefinitely continued. Let the first species of circumstances be that the ordinal number of a throw in the series is *prime*. It is pretty certain that there would be no general character in the corresponding values of throws to distinguish them from those that would result when the ordinal number is divisible by 2, or by 3, or by any other prime. It thus appears that when we take *any* genus of circumstances, the law turns out false. Suppose, then, that we modify it by saying that, taking any genus of phenomena and separating this into two species, there will be found in the discoverable circumstances *some* general resemblance for all those attending phenomena of the same species in contrast to those attending phenomena of the other species. This is a proposition that there is not the slightest reason to believe. Take, for example, as the genus of phenomena, the many thousands of Latin descriptions of American species of plants by Asa Gray and his scholars. Now consider the species of this genus of phenomena that agree in this respect, that the two first words of the description have their first vowels the same. There is no reason to suppose that there was any general respect in which the circumstances of that species of the genus of phenomena agree with one another and differ from others, either universally or usually. It is a mere chance result. It is true that some persons will not be inclined to assent to this judgment; but they cannot prove it otherwise. It can afford no adequate basis for induction. We see, then, that when we consider *all* phenomena, there is no way of making the statement sufficiently definite and certain. Suppose, then, that we attempt still another modification of the law, that, of *interesting* resemblances and differences between phenomena, some considerable proportion are accompanied by corresponding resemblances and differences between those of the circumstances that appear to us to be *pertinent*. The proposition is now rather psychological than metaphysical. It would be impossible, with any evidentiary basis, to strengthen the expression "some considerable proportion"; and in other respects the statement is vague enough. Still, there is sufficient truth in it, perhaps, to warrant the presumptive adoption of hypotheses, provided this adoption merely means that they are taken as sufficiently reasonable to justify some expense in experimentation to test their truth by induction; but it gives no warrant at all to induction itself. For, in the first place, induction needs no such dubious support, since it is mathematically certain that the general character of a limited experience will, as that experience is prolonged, approximate to the character of what will be true in the long run, if anything is true in the long run. Now all that induction infers is what would be found true in the usual course of experience, if it were indefinitely prolonged. Since the method of induction must generally approximate to that truth, that is a sufficient justification for the use of that method, although no definite probability attaches to the inductive conclusion. In the second place, the law, as now formulated, neither helps nor hinders the validity of induction proper; for induction proper consists in judging of the relative frequency of a character among all the individuals of a class by the relative frequency of that character among the individuals of a random sample of that class. Now the law, as thus formulated, may tend to make our hypothesis approximately true; but that advantage has been gained before the operation of induction, which merely tests the hypothesis, begins. This inductive operation is just as valid when the hypothesis is bad as when it is good, when the character dealt with is trivial as when it is interesting. The ratio that induction ascertains may be nearer ½, and more remote from 1 or 0, when the characters are uninteresting; and in that case a large number of instances will usually be requisite for obtaining the ratio with any given degree of precision (for if the ratio is really 1 or 0, it will be almost a miracle if in the sample it is far from that ratio, although this will not be impossible, if the whole class is infinite), but the essential validity of the process of induction remains unaffected by that circumstance.

What is usually meant by the uniformity of nature probably is that in proportion as the circumstances are alike or unlike, so are any phenomena connected with them alike or unlike. It may be asked to what degree nature is uniform in that sense. The only tenable answer is that it is as little uniform as it possibly could be imagined to be; for were any considerable proportion of existing uniformities, or laws, of nature destroyed, others would necessarily thereby result.

In fact, the great characteristic of nature is its diversity. For every uniformity known, there would be no difficulty in pointing out thousands of nonuniformities; but the diversities are usually of small use to us, and attract the attention of poets mainly, while the uniformities are the very staff of life. Hence, the higher and wider are our desires, the greater will be the general impression of uniformity produced upon us by the contemplation of nature as it interests us.

(4) There are senses in which nature may not irrationally be held to be uniform; but opinions differ very widely as to the extent and nature of this uniformity. The chief of these are as follows:

(*a*) The majority of physicists, at least of the older generation, hold, with regard to the physical universe, that its elements are masses, their positions, and the variations of these positions with time. It is believed that every motion exactly obeys certain laws of attraction and repulsion; and there is no other kind of law, except that each atom or corpuscle is a center of energy arranged in equipotential surfaces about it, which follow a regular law; and that this is a permanency. But the equations of motion are differential equations of the second order, involving, therefore, two arbitrary constants for each moving atom or corpuscle, and there is no uniformity connected with these constants. At least, no such uniformity is, with the least probability, discoverable. As for the distribution of potential about an atom or corpuscle, it is regular; but there is no ulterior reason for that regularity, or, at least, none is probably discoverable. What is absolutely beyond discovery, whether direct and specific or indirect and general, may be considered to be nonexistent.

From this usual and in some sense standard opinion there are many divergences in both directions. First, in the direction of greater uniformity.

(*b*) Some hold that there is some exact uniformity in the arbitrary constants of the motion of the atoms, so that, for example, perhaps at some initial instant they all had some symmetrical or regular arrangement, like a pack of cards unshuffled; and that the velocities at that instance were regular also. But this regularity being of a purely aesthetic or formal kind, and the laws of motion equally formal and unrelated to any purpose, it follows that all kinds of arrangements will be produced, ungoverned by any uniformity, but mere effects of chance. Three stars may, for example, at some instant form an equilateral triangle, but there would be no particular reason for this: It would be merely a casual coincidence.

(c) Others go further and maintain that the constants of position and velocity are subject to a law not merely formal, but are governed by final causes in such a way that there is no arrangement or coincidence whatever that was not specially intended by the Creator. To this theory, such words as *pro*-vidence and *fore*-knowledge are ill adapted; because the two constants that each atom or corpuscle has, remain constant throughout all time, and ought not to be considered as having been fixed at any particular epoch. The very idea is that the arrangement is determined by what would be the result of different arrangements at each period of time. If, for example, a given prayer effects rain, it must be supposed that in view of that prayer, and as its consequence, the different atoms had the appropriate constants; but that these were not given to the atoms at any particular epoch, being permanent values. Any intentional action on the part of a free agent is to be explained in the same way. If an agent is to be supposed really free, it is difficult to see what other physical explanation is compatible with the exactitude of law. This seems to be substantially the notion of most of those who have supported free will.

On the other hand, many philosophers suppose a less degree of uniformity in nature than is supposed in opinion *(a)*. Of these the following have come to the present writer's notice as being actually defended.

(d) Some suppose that while law is absolute, yet there are constantly arising cases analogous to unstable equilibrium in which, owing to a passage of a velocity through infinity or otherwise, the law does not determine what the motion shall be. Thus if one Boscovichian point attracts another inversely as the square of the distance, and they move in one straight line, then when they come together they may move through one another, or move backwards on the same line, or may separate along any other line, without violating the differential equation. Such "singularities," as the mathematicians say, are theoretically possible; and may be supposed to occur very often. But to suppose that free action becomes possible in such a way is very illogical. In the first place it supposes a direct interaction between "mind" and matter, infinitesimal, no doubt, but none the less real. Why not better suppose a slight but finite action of this kind and so avoid the following objections? Namely, in the second place, this is to put faith, not scientific credence, in the inductive laws of matter infinitely beyond what induction can ever warrant. We know very well that mind, in some sense, acts on matter, and matter on mind:

the question is *how*. It is not in speculation of this fanciful kind that the true answer is likely to be found. In the third place, although this speculation wanders so far beyond all present knowledge, it nevertheless comes into conflict with a legitimate induction, namely, the supposition of any real "singularity" or breach of continuity in nature is in as distinct conflict with all our knowledge as is a miracle.

(e) Sundry far less tenable hypotheses of lacunae between inviolable laws have often been proposed. One opinion frequently met with is that the law of energy does not prescribe the direction of velocity; but only its amount; so that the mind can cause atoms to "swerve," in regular Lucretian fashion. This singular notion has even been embraced by mathematicians, who are thinking of a projectile shot into a curved tube, or other case of an equation of condition. Of course, if mind can construct absolute constraints, it can much easier exert force that is finite. Other writers suppose lacunae, without telling us of what particular description they are; they seem to think law is absolute as far as it goes, but that its jurisdiction is limited.

(f) Much more philosophical and less logically objectionable is the notion of St. Augustine and others (it is near to the opinion of Aristotle) that the only fundamental kind of causation is the action of final causes; and that efficient causation is, in all cases, secondary. Accordingly, when a miracle occurs there is no violation of the real *cursus naturae,* but only of the apparent course of things.

(g) The hypothesis suggested by the present writer is that all laws are results of evolution; that underlying all other laws is the only tendency that can grow by its own virtue, the tendency of all things to take habits. Now since this same tendency is the one sole fundamental law of mind, it follows that the physical evolution works towards ends in the same way that mental action works towards ends, and thus in one aspect of the matter it would be perfectly true to say that final causation is alone primary. Yet, on the other hand, the law of habit is a simple formal law, a law of efficient causation; so that either way of regarding the matter is equally true, although the former is more fully intelligent. Meantime, if law is a result of evolution, which is a process lasting through all time, it follows that no law is absolute. That is, we must suppose that the phenomena themselves involve departures from law analogous to errors of observation. But the writer has not supposed that this phenomenon had any connection with free will. In so far as evolution follows a law, the law of habit, instead of being a movement from homogeneity to heterogeneity, is growth from difformity to uniformity. But the chance divergences from law are perpetually acting to increase the variety of the world, and are checked by a sort of natural selection and otherwise (for the writer does not think the selective principle sufficient), so that the general result may be described as "organized heterogeneity," or better rationalized variety. In view of the principle of continuity, the supreme

guide in framing philosophical hypotheses, we must, under this theory, regard matter as mind whose habits have become fixed so as to lose the powers of forming them and losing them, while mind is to be regarded as a chemical genus of extreme complexity and instability. It has acquired in a remarkable degree a habit of taking and laying aside habits. The fundamental divergences from law must here be most extraordinarily high, although probably very far indeed from attaining any directly observable magnitude. But their effect is to cause the laws of mind to be themselves of so fluid a character as to simulate divergences from law. All this, according to the writer, constitutes a hypothesis capable of being tested by experiment.

EVOLUTIONARY LOVE*

Philosophy, when just escaping from its golden pupa-skin, mythology, proclaimed the great evolutionary agency of the universe to be Love. Or, since this pirate-lingo, English, is poor in such-like words, let us say Eros, the exuberance-love. Afterwards, Empedocles set up passionate-love and hate as the two coördinate powers of the universe. In some passages, kindness is the word. But certainly, in any sense in which it has an opposite, to be senior partner of that opposite, is the highest position that love can attain. Nevertheless, the ontological gospeller, in whose days those views were familiar topics, made the One Supreme Being, by whom all things have been made out of nothing, to be cherishing-love. What, then, can he say to hate? Never mind, at this time, what the scribe of the apocalypse, if he were John, stung at length by persecution into a rage unable to distinguish suggestions of evil from visions of heaven, and so become the Slanderer of God to men, may have dreamed. The question is rather what the sane John thought, or ought to have thought, in order to carry out his idea consistently. His statement that God is love seems aimed at that saying of Ecclesiastes that we cannot tell whether God bears us love or hatred. "Nay," says John, "we can tell, and very simply! We know and have trusted the love which God hath in us. God is love." There is no logic in this, unless it means that God loves all men. In the preceding paragraph, he had said, "God is light and in him is no darkness at all." We are to understand, then, that as darkness is merely the defect of light, so hatred and evil are mere imperfect stages of αγαπη and αγαθον, love and loveliness. This concords with that utterance reported in John's Gospel: "God sent not the Son into the world to judge the world; but that the world should through him be saved. He that believeth on him is not judged: he that believeth not hath been judged already. . . . And this is the judgment, that the light is come into the world, and that men loved darkness rather than the light." That is to say, God visits no

---

* Charles S. Peirce, "Evolutionary Love," *The Monist,* 1893.

punishment on them; they punish themselves, by their natural affinity for the defective. Thus, the love that God is, is not a love of which hatred is the contrary; otherwise Satan would be a coördinate power; but it is a love which embraces hatred as an imperfect stage of it, an Anteros— yea, even needs hatred and hatefulness as its object. For self-love is no love; so if God's self is love, that which he loves must be defect of love; just as a luminary can light up only that which otherwise would be dark. Henry James, the Swedenborgian, says: "It is no doubt very tolerable finite or creaturely love to love one's own in another, to love another for his conformity to one's self: but nothing can be in more flagrant cotrast with the creative Love, all whose tenderness *ex vi termini* must be reserved only for what intrinsically is most bitterly hostile and negative to itself." This is from *Substance and Shadow: an Essay on the Physics of Creation.* It is a pity he had not filled his pages with things like this, as he was able easily to do, instead of scolding at his reader and at people generally, until the physics of creation was wellnigh forgot. I must deduct, however, from what I just wrote: obviously no genius could make his every sentence as sublime as one which discloses for the problem of evil its everlasting solution.

The movement of love is circular, at one and the same impulse projecting creations into independency and drawing them into harmony. This seems complicated when stated so; but it is fully summed up in the simple formula we call the Golden Rule. This does not, of course, say, Do everything possible to gratify the egoistic impulses of others, but it says, Sacrifice your own perfection to the perfectionment of your neighbour. Nor must it for a moment be confounded with the Benthamite, or Helvetian, or Beccarian motto, Act for the greatest good of the greatest number. Love is not directed to abstractions but to persons; not to persons we do not know, nor to numbers of people, but to our own dear ones, our family and neighbours. "Our neighbour," we remember, is one whom we live near, not locally perhaps, but in life and feeling.

Everybody can see that the statement of St. John is the formula of an evolutionary philosophy, which teaches that growth comes only from love, from—I will not say self-*sacrifice,* but from the ardent impulse to fulfill another's highest impulse. Suppose, for example, that I have an idea that interests me. It is my creation. It is my creature . . . it is a little person. I love it; and I will sink myself in perfecting it. It is not by dealing out cold justice to the circle of my ideas that I can make them grow, but by cherishing and tending them as I would the flowers in my garden. The philosophy we draw from John's gospel is that this is the way mind develops; and as for the cosmos, only so far as it yet is mind, and so has life, is it capable of further evolution. Love, recognizing germs of loveliness in the hatful, gradually warms it into life, and makes it lovely. That is the sort of evolution which every careful student of my essay "The Law of Mind" must see that *synechism* calls for.

The nineteenth century is now fast sinking into the grave, and we all begin to review its doings and to think what character it is destined to bear as compared with other centuries in the minds of future historians. It will be called, I guess, the Economical Century; for political economy has more direct relations with all the branches of its activity than has any other science. Well, political economy has its formula of redemption, too. It is this: Intelligence in the service of greed ensures the justest prices, the fairest contracts, the most enlightened conduct of all the dealings between men, and leads to the *summum bonum,* food in plenty and perfect comfort. Food for whom? Why, for the greedy master of intelligence. I do not mean to say that this is one of the legitimate conclusions of political economy, the scientific character of which I fully acknowledge. But the study of doctrines, themselves true, will often temporarily encourage generalizations extremely false, as the study of physics has encouraged necessitarianism. What I say, then, is that the great attention paid to economical questions during our century has induced an exaggeration of the beneficial effects of greed and of the unfortunate results of sentiment, until there has resulted a philosophy which comes unwittingly to this, that greed is the great agent in the elevation of the human race and in the evolution of the universe.

The *Origin of Species* of Darwin merely extends politico-economical views of progress to the entire realm of animal and vegetable life. The vast majority of our contemporary naturalists hold the opinion that the true cause of those exquisite and marvellous adaptations of nature for which, when I was a boy, men used to extol the divine wisdom is that creatures are so crowded together that those of them that happen to have the slightest advantage force those less pushing into situations unfavourable to multiplication or even kill them before they reach the age of reproduction. Among the animals, the mere mechanical individualism is vastly reënforced as a power making for good by the animal's ruthless greed. As Darwin puts it on his title-page, it is the struggle for existence; and he should have added for his motto: Every individual for himself, and the Devil take the hindmost! Jesus, in his sermon on the Mount, expressed a different opinion.

Here, then, is the issue. The gospel of Christ says that progress comes from every individual merging his individuality in sympathy with his neighbours. On the other side, the conviction of the nineteenth century is that progress takes place by virtue of every individual's striving for himself with all his might and trampling his neighbour under foot whenever he gets a chance to do so. This may accurately be called the Gospel of Greed.

Much is to be said on both sides. I have not concealed, I could not conceal, my own passionate predilection. Such a confession will probably shock my scientific brethren. Yet the strong feeling is in itself, I think, an argument of some weight in favour of the agapastic theory of evolution,—so far as it may be presumed to bespeak the normal judgment of the Sensible Heart. Certainly, if it were possible to believe in agapasm without believing it warmly, that fact would be an argument against the truth of the doctrine. At any rate, since the warmth of feeling exists, it should on every account be candidly confessed; especially since it creates a liability to one-sidedness on my part against which it behooves my readers and me to be severally on our guard.

The modes of evolution have . . . been brought before us: evolution by fortuitous variation, evolution by mechanical necessity, and evolution by creative love. We may term them *tychastic* evolution, or *tychasm,* *anancastic* evolution, or *anancasm,* and *agapastic* evolution, or *agapasm.* The doctrines which represent these are severally of principal importance, we may term *tychasticism, anancasticism,* and *agapasticism.* On the other hand the mere propositions that absolute chance, mechanical necessity, and the law of love, are severally operative in the cosmos, may receive the names of *tychism, anancism,* and *agapism.*

All three modes of evolution are composed of the same general elements. Agapasm exhibits them the most clearly. The good result is here brought to pass, first, by the bestowal of spontaneous energy by the parent upon the offspring, and, second, by the disposition of the latter to catch the general idea of those about it and thus to subserve the general purpose. In order to express the relation that tychasm and anancasm bear to agapasm, let me borrow a word from geometry. An ellipse crossed by a straight line is a sort of cubic curve; for a cubic is a curve which is cut thrice by a straight line; now a straight line might cut the ellipse twice and its associated straight line a third time. Still the ellipse with the straight line across it would not have the characteristics of a cubic. It would have, for instance, no contrary flexure, which no true cubic wants; and it would have two nodes, which no true cubic has. The geometers say that it is a *degenerate* cubic. Just so, tychasm and anancasm are degenerate forms of agapasm.

Men who seek to reconcile the Darwinian idea with Christianity will remark that tychastic evolution, like the agapastic, depends upon a reproductive creation, the forms preserved being those that use the spontaneity conferred upon them in such wise as to be drawn into harmony with their original, quite after the Christian scheme. Very good! This only shows that just as love cannot have a contrary, but must embrace what is most opposed to it, as a degenerate case of it, so tychasm is a kind of agapasm. Only, in the tychastic evolution progress is solely owing to the distribution of the napkin-hidden talent of the rejected servant among those not rejected, just as ruined gamesters leave their money on the table to make those not yet ruined so much the richer. It makes the felicity of the lambs just the damnation of the goats, transposed to the other side of the equation. In genuine agapasm, on the other hand, advance takes place by virtue of a positive sympathy among the created springing from continuity of mind. This is the idea which tychasticism knows not how to manage.

The anancasticist might here interpose, claiming that the mode of evolution for which he contends agrees with agapasm at the point at which tychasm departs from it. For it makes development go through certain phases, having its inevitable ebbs and flows, yet tending on the whole to a foreordained perfection. Bare existence by this its destiny betrays an intrinsic affinity for the good. Herein, it must be admitted, anancasm shows itself to be in a broad acception a species of agapasm. Some forms of it might easily be mistaken for the genuine agapasm. The Hegelian philosophy is such an anancasticism. With its revelatory religion, with its synechism (however imperfectly set forth), with its "reflection," the whole idea of the theory is superb, almost sublime. Yet, after all, living freedom is practically omitted from its method. The whole movement is that of a vast engine, impelled by a *vis a tergo,* with a blind and mysterious fate of arriving at a lofty goal. I mean that such an engine *would* be, if it really worked; but in point of fact, it is a Keely motor. Grant that it really acts as it professes to act, and there is nothing to do but accept the philosophy. But never was there seen such an example of a long chain of reasoning,—shall I say with a flaw in every link?—no, with every link a handful of sand, squeezed into shape in a dream. Or say, it is a pasteboard model of a philosophy that in reality does not exist. If we use the one precious thing it contains, the idea of it, introducing the tychism which the arbitrariness of its every step suggests, and make that the support of a vital freedom which is the breadth of the spirit of love, we may be able to produce that genuine agapasticism, at which Hegel was aiming.

STUDY QUESTIONS

Review

1. What is Peirce's "pragmatic theory of meaning" ?
2. How are his metaphysical categories related to this theory?
3. What ways of fixing belief does Peirce find unacceptable, and what way does he believe is best?
4. Explain Peirce's views on chance and determinism, and matter and mind.

For Further Thought

5. Do you believe that the method of science, as described by Peirce, is the best way of finding the truth? What do you think of his definition of truth?
6. Is a belief a habit of action, i.e., always directed to behavior?

7. What do you think of the relation between doubt and belief? For example, is real doubt required to provoke us to question and change our beliefs? Is a belief satisfactory if it satisfies doubt?
8. What do you think of the attempt by philosophers to develop categories for explaining reality or types of things?
9. Do you think that Peirce's explanation of matter as habit-bound mind is reasonable?

BIBLIOGRAPHY

Peirce, Charles Sanders. *Writings of Charles S. Peirce: A Chronological Edition.* Ed. Edward C. Moore, Max H. Fisch, et al. Vol. 1, *1857–66.* Vol. 2, *1867–71.* 20 vols. Bloomington: Indiana University Press, 1982– .

— — —. *The New Elements of Mathematics.* Ed. Carolyn Eisele. 4 vols. Hawthorne, N. Y.: Mouton Publishing, 1976.

— — —. *Values in a Universe of Chance.* Ed. Philip P. Wiener. Stanford: Stanford University Press, 1958.

— — —. *Charles S. Peirce: Essays in the Philosophy of Science.* Ed. Vincent Tomas. New York: Liberal Arts Press, 1957.

— — —. *The Philosophy of Peirce: Selected Writings.* Ed. Justus Buchler. New York: Harcourt, Brace, 1940.

— — —. *Collected Papers of Charles Sanders Peirce.* Vols. 1–6, ed. Charles Hartshorne and Paul Weiss. Vols. 7 and 8, ed. A. W. Burks. Cambridge: Harvard University Press, 1931–58.

— — —. *Chance, Love, and Logic.* Ed. M. R. Cohen. New York: Harcourt, Brace, 1923. Reprint. New York: George Braziller, 1956.

— — —. *Journal of Philosophy, Psychology, and Scientific Methods* 12 (1916). Peirce commemorative issue.

Almeder, Robt. *The Philosophy of Charles Peirce.* New Jersey: Rowman and Littlefield, 1980.

Apel, K. O. *Charles S. Peirce: From Pragmatism to Pragmaticism.* Trans. John Michael Krois. Introduction by R. Bernstein. Amherst: University of Massachusetts Press, 1981.

Bernstein, R. J., ed. *Perspectives on Peirce: Critical Essays on Charles Sanders Peirce.* New Haven: Yale University Press, 1965.

Boler, J. F. *Charles Peirce and Scholastic Realism.* Seattle: University of Washington Press, 1963.

Buchler, Justus. *Charles Peirce's Empiricism.* New York: Harcourt, Brace, 1939.

Feibleman, James. *An Introduction to Perice's Philosophy.* New York: Harpers, 1946.

Fisch, Max H. "Peirce's Place in American Thought." *Ars Semeiotica* 1 (1977): pp. 21–37.

Fitzgerald, J. J. *Perice's Theory of Signs as Foundation for Pragmatism.* Studies in Philosophy, no. 11. The Hague: Mouton, 1966.

Freeman, Eugene. *The Relevance of Charles Peirce.* Monist Library of Philosophy. LaSalle, Ill.: Open Court Publishing, forthcoming.

— — —. *The Categories of Charles Peirce.* Chicago: University of Chicago Libraries, 1937.

Gallie, W. B. *Peirce and Pragmatism.* Harmondsworth-Middlesex: Penguin Books, 1952.

Goudge, Thomas Anderson. *The Thought of C. S. Peirce.* Toronto: University of Toronto Press, 1950.

Ketner, Kenneth L. Christian J. W. Kloesel, Joseph M. Ransdell, eds. *A Comprehensive Bibliography and Index of the Published Works of Charles S. Peirce with a Bibliography of Secondary Studies.* Microfiche edition. Lubbock: Texas Tech Press, 1977.

Ketner, Kenneth L., and James E. Cook, eds. *Charles Sanders Peirce: Contribution to "The Nation."* 3 vols. Lubbock: Texas Tech Press, 1975–79.

Moore, Edward C., and Richard S. Robin, eds. *Studies in the Philosophy of Charles Sanders Peirce.* Second series. Amherst: University of Massachusetts Press, 1964.

Murphey, M. G. *The Development of Peirce's Philosophhy.* Cambridge: Harvard University Press, 1961.

Potter, Vincent G. *Charles S. Peirce: On Norms and Ideals.* Worcester: University of Massachusetts Press, 1967.

Reilly, Francis E. *Charles Peirce's Theory of Scientific Method.* New York: Fordham University Press, 1970.

Rescher, Nicholas. *Peirce's Philosophy of Science.* Notre Dame, Ind.: University of Notre Dame Press, 1978.

Robin, Richard. *Annotated Catalogue of the Papers of Charles S. Peirce.* Amherst: University of Massachusetts Press, 1967.

Skagestad, Peter. *The Road to Inquiry: Charles Peirce's Pragmatic Realism.* New York: Columbia University Press, 1981.

Thompson, M. H. *The Pragmatic Philosophy of C. S. Perice.* Chicago: University of Chicago Press, 1953.

Wiener, Philip P., and Frederick H. Young, eds. *Studies in the Philosophy of Charles Sanders Peirce.* Cambridge: Harvard University Press, 1952.

Chapter 7

The Pragmatism and Radical Empiricism of William James

More than anyone else, William James stands in the eyes of the world as the representative American philosopher. His life marks the period in which American academic thought ceased to follow European philosophy and displayed a marked originality. James himself contributed greatly to this development. His philosophy was distinctively American in its formulation and phraseology. Although some European developments approximated it, the idea of pragmatism also was hailed as native American. His frequent travels in Europe, his command of languages, and his great personal charm, all contributed to the spread of his ideas. These factors together with the instrinsic importance of what he had to say, have resulted in the translation of his works into all major languages. James is probably the one American philosopher who has been read the world over.[1]

While not every interpreter of American philosophy would agree fully with this characterization of the significance of the person and philosophy of William James, all agree that he is a central figure in American philosophy. James was born in New York in 1842 (though he is actually counted a New Englander, which is where he later lived and wrote). His grandfather, an Irish immigrant, left a rather large estate to his children, thus providing the James family with the leisure and means to pursue learning and travel. William's father, Henry James, Sr., was a friend of Emerson, who used to visit the family household, and also a renowned man himself. James's brother, Henry James, Jr., the famous novelist whose works emphasized the psychological development of character, is considered one of the forerunners of the "stream of consciousness" novel. William himself was always concerned with the inner life of man.

William James was schooled partly in America and partly in Europe where he traveled frequently. In 1864 he entered Harvard Medical School and in 1869 obtained a doctorate of medicine. His program included a biological expedition up the Amazon River. As a young man he dabbled in painting and went through periods of bad health and depression. In 1872 he became an instructor of anatomy and physiology at Harvard and beginning in 1875 taught courses there in psychology. It was at Harvard that he opened the first experimental laboratory in psychology in this country. From psychology he developed an interest in philosophy and began teaching courses in that subject at Harvard in 1879. His work in psychology which led him to reflect on philosophical issues and which itself contains many philosophical reflections, led to his publication in 1890 of *The Principles of Psychology.*

James was much in demand as a lecturer. In 1904, for example, he received one hundred invitations to speak. At his first lecture, part of a series of lectures later published as *Pragmatism,* there were 1100 persons in attendance, and *Pragmatism* went through five printings in 1907 alone. James was a professional philosopher who managed to avoid professionalism. However, as has been pointed out, he paid a price for such relevance and popularity. His terminology was often loose, and he confused the similar with the identical.[2] Nevertheless, his philosophy is as rich as he believed the world itself to be.

In 1879 in an article entitled "The Sentiment of Rationality," James's belief in the significance of the feeling or passional side of man is already evident.[3] A philosophy, he said, is a conception of the world, a general frame of things. For a person to believe in any such view, it must pass the test of rationality. However, the rationality intended by James is as much a matter of feeling as of thought. Of two philosophies, that seem equally consistent with the facts, the one that satisfies our impulses and aesthetic demands will be taken as more rational. No philosophy will be accepted, that does not satisfy our needs. A philosophy must be congruent with our spontaneous powers, such as the impulse to "take life strivingly."[4] All philosophical theories as well as all conceptions are ways of handling things for certain purposes; they are teleological instruments. Thus we must ask of any proposed system what purpose it serves. James did not distinguish the criteria or conditions on which a philosophy or concept will be accepted by people from the conditions of its truth. True to his psychological bent, his emphasis is on the former, but he also tends not to be concerned with such distinctions.

The same theme is developed further in his more famous essay, "The Will to Believe," published in 1896.[5] Here again he makes the point that our passional or volitional nature lies at the root of all our convictions. The essay is a defense of our right to adopt a believing attitude in spite of the fact that our merely logical intellect may not have been coerced. There are certain times when not enough evidence is available for believing one hypothesis rather than another, and yet we *must* act or make an option (the hypothesis is forced); each hypothesis is equally appealing (is living rather than dead), and the decision is one that is important, vital to one's life, a unique opportunity (momentuous rather than trivial). In these cases of what James calls "genuine options" (those that are living, forced, and momentuous) "our passional nature not only lawfully may, but must decide." In such cases, as the saying goes, not to decide is also to decide. We can either take the stance that avoiding error is most important and then we will hestitate to decide on such grounds, or we will take the position that losing the truth is the worse consequence and that the chance of gaining the truth thus outweighs the risk of being duped.

Moral questions in particular are often such genuine options. The solution and consequent action cannot wait for proof. Shall we, for example, believe there really is something that we ought to do? Does it make any difference whether we believe either that there are such obligations or that everything simply is what it is and there is no better or worse? What difference does believing in freedom or determinism make to a person's actual living? This question James believed to be insoluble from a strictly theoretical point of view.[6] He himself suggests that belief in a deterministic world would make regret, for example, impossible, for one only regrets what one thinks might not have been. Or if one thinks that tragic events necessarily occur, then one must become either nihilistic or unconcerned, neither of which James believes lead to a very fulfilling life. Finally, in some cases the willingness to believe when one is uncertain can make a difference in the outcome. Only when one believes that one can succeed in a feat can one actually succeed; only when one believes that something is there, some quality of another person or of the world, can one actually be in a position to see it. Some religious beliefs are grounded in this way, as well as the simple belief that life is worth living.[7]

The basic point of view in these lectures provides a basis for understanding James's pragmatism. However, he graciously attributes its origin to Peirce. In his explanation of "What Pragmatism Means" James refers to Peirce's theory of meaning, illustrating it with his own interesting example of a dispute over whether or not a particular squirrel can properly be said to "go around" a tree.[8] James's suggestion is that to settle this as well as other metaphysical disputes, one needs only to inquire about what is "practically mean[t]" by the relevant terms in the discussion. Pragmatism, as James saw it, was thus a method of settling metaphysical disputes. It was a method characterized by looking away from first things such as closed theories or fixed principles of deduction and instead looking toward last things such as facts, action, and consequences. Theories are not primarily something of an end but provide rather a beginning; they are like tickets on which we can ride as we seek to understand and act.

James's pragmatic theory of truth simply put is this — the instrumental truth of an idea is its ability to carry or be of use to us. And how is it of use to us? First of all we consider true whatever will best handle (explain) new experience without too much disruption of old beliefs. Since we need to account for new experience, our old truths need continuously to be revised. Secondly James suggests that that theory is good and can be held true that will best predict future experience. Thirdly he says that that theory is true that best harmonizes with other experiences and beliefs. Finally, keeping in mind his "Will to Believe," he also argues that whatever belief leads to a better and more fulfilling life is, or can be held as true. At times he suggests that each person could hold as true whatever is helpful to him to believe, however different their beliefs. Then again he retracts this extreme, subjective view and claims that a theory must work for all and in the long run. Nevertheless, it is James's account of truth that comes closest to the identification of truth with "expedience." The true, he says, is whatever proves itself to be good in the way of belief, whatever it would be good for us to believe. Truth is thus a species of good. As can be seem, James's theory of truth lacks much in the way of clarification, distinction, and exactitude. Perhaps the fact that many of his writings were summaries of lectures given in a semipopular vein explains the absence of technical clarification.

A summary of the philosophy of William James would not be complete without a discussion, however brief, of his so-called radical empiricism.[9] He once said that he preferred this name over pragmatism for his philosophy, calling it a tough-minded position. The position is one that goes to the facts, as he says, and is pluralistic and skeptical. However, James also characterized this position as pessimistic, materialistic, irreligious, and fatalistic — none of which his philosophy was. In fact his philosophy contains many of the qualities he used to characterize the opposite position, a tender-minded position. The tender-minded philosophy, he said, was rationalistic, intellectualistic, and idealistic (which his position was not), and also religious and free willist (which his position was).

According to a radical empiricist, what is given to us is a world of pure experience, a world in which distinctions are not as yet made, a "booming buzzing confusion." We actively seek to emerge from this confusion. James's brand of empiricism does not picture the knower as a passive receiver of data, as did much of British empiricism, yet there is no active self in James's philosophy. In initial, unreflective experience both the self and the world are present. However, they are not present as two parts that can be distinguished as such, but rather as two different points of view, two different ways of looking at experience. My experience of a room, for example, can be viewed in relation to a series of past, present, and future experiences which is my "self," or in relation to the other events in the history of "the room." The self is thus simply a stream of interconnected experiences, a flow of consciousness. James's radical empiricism also includes the belief that relations as well as things are objects of experience and have a certain metaphysical independence. Things come and go and take on new relations. Thus no " block universe" exists in which everything is permanently and tightly connected. The universe, as James conceived it, is a pluralistic one and one in which it is possible for the human freedom within it to make a difference.

Finally, James's treatment of religion is also very empirical and individualistic. He approaches religion as a psychologist and asks about the variety of religious experiences that people have and the differences those experiences make or do not make in their individual lives.[10] Moreover since the world is loose and there is room for freedom, there can be no absolutely powerful God. James believed that God must grow with the world. He can be "no gentleman" out of touch with or unconcerned about the world. The readings exerpted here from James's work should give the reader worthwhile first hand experience of the philosophy of this best-known American pragmatist, perhaps the best-known American philosopher.

Notes

[1] In an introduction to the chapter on William James by Paul Henle, in Fisch, *Classic American Philosophers,* p. 115.

[2] William James, *The Principles of Psychology,* 2 vols. (New York: Henry Holt, 1890. For comments about the looseness of James's terminology see Smith, *Spirit of American Philosophy,* pp. 38ff.

[3] William James, "The Sentiment of Rationality," *Mind* (July 1879).

[4] In addition and in particular James contended that historically philosophies have taken basically two different forms — the tender- and tough-minded types. As a philosopher is temperamentally tender or tough minded he will espouse one or the other kind of philosophy, basically empiricist or rationalist.

[5] William James, "The Will to Believe," *New World* 5 (1896): pp. 327–47. Reprinted in *The Will to Believe and Other Essays in Popular Philosophy* (New York: Longmans, Green, 1907), pp. 197–236.

[6] William James, "The Dilemma of Determinism," *Unitarian Review,* September 1884; reprinted in *Essays in Pragmatism,* ed. Alburey Castell (New York: Hafner Publishing Co., 1948), pp. 37–64.

[7] See James's essay "Is Life Worth Living? " *International Journal of Ethics,* October 1895. Reprinted in *Essays on Faith and Morals,* ed. R. B. Perry (New York: Meridian Books, 1962), pp. 1–31.

[8] William James, "What Pragmatism Means," in *Pragmatism: A New Name for Some Old Ways of Thinking* (New York: Longmans, Green, 1907), pp. 43–66.

[9] See William James, *Essays in Radical Empiricism* (New York: Longmans, Green, 1920); idem, *A Pluralistic Universe* (New York: Longmans, Green, 1932). First published in 1909 as the Hibbert Lectures.

[10] *Varieties of Religious Experience* (New York: Mentor Books, 1961). First published in 1901-2 as *The Gifford Lectures.*

William James

WHAT PRAGMATISM MEANS*

Some years ago, being with a camping party in the mountains, returned from a solitary ramble to find every one engaged in a rocious metaphysical dispute. The *corpus* of the dispute was a squirrel—a live squirrel supposed to be clinging to one side of a tree-trunk; while over against the tree's opposite side a human being was imagined to stand. This human witness tries to get sight of the squirrel by moving rapidly round the tree, but no matter how fast he goes, the squirrel moves as fast in the opposite direction, and always keeps the tree between himself and the man, so that never a glimpse of him is caught. The resultant metaphysical problem now is this: *Does the man go round the squirrel or not?* He goes round the tree, sure enough, and the squirrel is on the tree; but does he go round the squirrel? In the unlimited leisure of the wilderness, discussion had been worn threadbare. Every one had taken sides, and was obstinate; and the numbers on both sides were even. Each side, when I appeared, therefore appealed to me to make it a majority. Mindful of the scholastic adage that whenever you meet a contradiction you must make a distinction, I immediately sought and found one, as follows: "Which party is right," I said, "depends on what you *practically mean* by 'going round' the squirrel. If you mean passing from the north of him to the east, then to

* William James, "What Pragmatism Means, Lecture 2 in *Pragmatism: A New Name for Some Old Ways of Thinking* (New York: Longmans, Green, 1907), pp. 43–66.

the south, then to the west, and then to the north of him again, obviously the man does go round him, for he occupies these successive positions. But if on the contrary you mean being first in front of him, then on the right of him, then behind him, then on his left, and finally in front again, it is quite as obvious that the man fails to go round him, for by the compensating movements the squirrel makes, he keeps his belly turned towards the man all the time, and his back turned away. Make the distinction, and there is no occasion for any further dispute. You are both right and both wrong according as you conceive the verb 'to go round' in one practical fashion or the other."

Although one or two of the hotter disputants called my speech a shuffling evasion, saying they wanted no quibbling or scholastic hair-splitting, but meant just plain honest English "round," the majority seemed to think that the distinction had assuaged the dispute.

I tell this trivial anecdote because it is a peculiarly simple example of what I wish now to speak of as *the pragmatic method.* The pragmatic method is primarily a method of settling metaphysical disputes, that otherwise might be interminable. Is the world one or many?—fated or free?—material or spiritual?—here are notions either of which may or may not hold good of the world; and disputes over such notions are unending. The pragmatic method in such cases is to try to interpret each notion by tracing its respective practical consequences. What difference would it practically make to any one if this notion rather than that notion were true? If no practical difference whatever can be traced, then the alternatives mean practically the same thing, and all dispute is idle. Whenever a dispute is serious, we ought to be able to show some practical difference that must follow from one side or the other's being right.

A glance at the history of the idea will show you still better what pragmatism means. The term is derived from the same Greek word πράγμα, meaning action, from which our words "practice" and "practical" come. It was first introduced into philosophy by Mr. Charles Peirce in 1878. In an article entitled "How to Make Our Ideas Clear," in the *Popular Science Monthly* for January of that year Mr. Peirce, after pointing out that our beliefs are really rules for action, said that, to develop a thought's meaning, we need only determine what conduct it is fitted to produce: that conduct is for us its sole significance. And the tangible fact at the root of all our thought-distinctions, however subtle, is that there is no one of them so fine as to consist in anything but a possible difference of practice. To attain perfect clearness in our thoughts of an object, then, we need only consider what conceivable effects of a practical kind the object may involve—what sensations we are to expect from it, and what reactions we must prepare. Our conception of these effects, whether immediate or remote, is then for us the whole of our conception of the object, so far as that conception has positive significance at all.

This is the principle of Peirce, the principle of pragmatism. It lay entirely unnoticed by any one for twenty years, until I, in an address before Professor Howison's Philosophical Union at the University of California, brought it forward again and made a special application of it to religion. By that date (1898) the times seemed ripe for its reception. The word "pragmatism" spread, and at present it fairly spots the pages of the philosophic journals. On all hands we find the "pragmatic movement" spoken of, sometimes with respect, sometimes with contumely, seldom with clear understanding. It is evident that the term applies itself conveniently to a number of tendencies that hitherto have lacked a collective name, and that it has "come to stay."

To take in the importance of Peirce's principle, one must get accustomed to applying it to concrete cases. I found a few years ago that Ostwald, the illustrious Leipzig chemist, had been making perfectly distinct use of the principle of pragmatism in his lectures on the philosophy of science, though he had not called it by that name.

"All realities influence our practice," he wrote me, "and that influence is their meaning for us. I am accustomed to put questions to my classes in this way: In what respects would the world be different if this alternative or that were true? If I can find nothing that would become different, then the alternative has no sense."

That is, the rival views mean practically the same thing, and meaning, other than practical, there is for us none. Ostwald in a published lecture gives this example of what he means. Chemists have long wrangled over the inner constitution of certain bodies called "tautomerous." Their properties seemed equally consistent with the notion that an instable hydrogen atom oscillates inside of them, or that they are instable mixtures of two bodies. Controversy raged, but never was decided. "It would never have begun," says Ostwald, "if the combatants had asked themselves what particular experimental fact could have been made different by one or the other view being correct. For it would then have appeared that no difference of fact could possibly ensue; and the quarrel was as unreal as if, theorizing in primitive times about the raising of dough by yeast, one party should have invoked a 'brownie,' while another insisted on an 'elf' as the true cause of the phenomenon." *

It is astonishing to see how many philosophical disputes collapse into insignificance the moment you subject them to this simple test of tracing a concrete consequence. There can *be* no difference anywhere that doesn't

---

* "Theorie und Praxis," *Zeitschrift des Oesterreichischen Ingenieur-u. Architecien-Vereins,* 1905, Nr. 4 u. 6. I find a still more radical pragmaticism than Ostwald's in an address by Professor W. S. Franklin: "I think that the sickliest notion of physics, even if a student gets it, is that it is 'the science of masses, molecules, and the ether.' And I think that the healthiest notion, even if a student does not wholly get it, is that physics is the science of the ways of taking hold of bodies and pushing them!" (*Science,* January 2, 1903).

make a difference elsewhere—no difference in abstract truth that doesn't express itself in a difference in concrete fact and in conduct consequent upon that fact, imposed on somebody, somehow, somewhere, and somewhen. The whole function of philosophy ought to be to find out what definite difference it will make to you and me, at definite instants of our life, if this world-formula or that world-formula be the true one.

There is absolutely nothing new in the pragmatic method. Socrates was an adept at it. Aristotle used it methodically. Locke, Berkeley, and Hume made momentous contributions to truth by its means. Shadworth Hodgson keeps insisting that realities are only what they are "known as." But these forerunners of pragmatism used it in fragments: they were preluders only. Not until in our time has it generalized itself, become conscious of a universal mission, pretended to a conquering destiny. I believe that in that destiny, and I hope I may end by inspiring you with my belief.

Pragmatism represents a perfectly familiar attitude in philosophy, the empiricist attitude, but it represents it, as it seems to me, both in a more radical and in a less objectionable form than it has ever yet assumed. A pragmatist turns his back resolutely and once for all upon a lot of inveterate habits dear to professional philosophers. He turns away from abstraction and insufficiency, from verbal solutions, from bad *a priori* reasons, from fixed principles, closed systems, and pretended absolutes and origins. He turns towards concreteness and adequacy, towards facts, towards action and towards power. That means the empiricist temper regnant and the rationalist temper sincerely given up. It means the open air and possibilities of nature, as against dogma, artificiality, and the pretence of finality in truth.

At the same time it does not stand for any special results. It is a method only. But the general triumph of that method would mean an enormous change in what I called in my last lecture the "temperament" of philosophy. Teachers of the ultra-rationalistic type would be frozen out, much as the courtier type is frozen out in republics, as the ultramontane type of priest is frozen out in protestant-lands. Science and metaphysics would come much nearer together, would in fact work absolutely hand in hand.

Metaphysics has usually followed a very primitive kind of quest. You know how men have always hankered after unlawful magic, and you know what a great part in magic *words* have always played. If you have his name, or the formula of incantation that binds him, you can control the spirit, afrite, or whatever the power may be. Solomon knew the names of all the spirits, and having their names, he held them subject to his will. So the universe has always appeared to the natural mind as a kind of enigma, of which the key must be sought in the shape of some illuminating or power-bringing word or name. That word names the universe's *principle,* and to possess it is after a fashion to possess the universe itself. "God," "Matter," "Reason," "the Absolute," "Energy," are so many solving names. You can rest when you have them. You are at the end of your metaphysical quest.

But if you follow the pragmatic method, you cannot look on any such word as closing your quest. You must bring out of each word its practical cash-value, set it at work within the stream of your experience. It appears less as a solution, then, than as a program for more work, and more particularly as an indication of the ways in which existing realities may be *changed.*

Theories thus become instruments, not answers to engimas, in which we can rest. We don't lie back upon them, we move forward, and, on occasion, make nature over again by their aid. Pragmatism unstiffens all our theories, limbers them up and sets each one at work. Being nothing essentially new, it harmonizes with many ancient philosophic tendencies. It agrees with nominalism, for instance, in always appealing to particulars; with utilitarianism in emphasizing practical aspects; with positivism in its disdain for verbal solutions, useless questions and metaphysical abstractions.

All these, you see, are *anti-intellectualist* tendencies. Against rationalism as a pretension and a method pragmatism is fully armed and militant. But, at the outset, at least, it stands for no particular results. It has no dogmas, and no doctrines save its method. As the young Italian pragmatist Papini has well said, it lies in the midst of our theories, like a corridor in a hotel. Innumerable chambers open out of it. In one you may find a man writing an atheistic volume; in the next some one on his knees praying for faith and strength; in a third a chemist investigating a body's properties. In a fourth a system of idealistic metaphysics is being excogitated; in a fifth the impossibility of metaphysics is being shown. But they all own the corridor, and all must pass through it if they want a practicable way of getting into or out of their respective rooms.

No particular results then, so far, but only an attitude of orientation, is what the pragmatic method means. *The attitude of looking away from first things, principles, "categories," supposed necessities; and of looking towards last things, fruits, consequences, facts.*

So much for the pragmatic method! You may say that I have been praising it rather than explaining it to you, but I shall presently explain it abundantly enough by showing how it works on some familiar problems. Meanwhile the word pragmatism has come to be used in a still wider sense, as meaning also a certain *theory of truth.* I mean to give a whole lecture to the statement of that theory, after first paving the way, so I can be very brief now. But brevity is hard to follow, so I ask for your redoubled attention for a quarter of an hour. If much remains obscure, I hope to make it clearer in the later lectures.

One of the most successfully cultivated branches of philosophy in our time is what is called inductive logic, the study of the conditions under which our sciences have evolved. Writers on this subject have begun to show a singular unanimity as to what the laws of nature and elements of fact mean, when formulated by mathematicians, physicists and chemists. When the first mathematical, logical, and natural uniformities, the first *laws,* were discovered, men were so carried away by the clearness, beauty and simplification that resulted, that they believed themselves to have diciphered authentically the eternal thoughts of the Almighty. His mind also thundered and reverberated in syllogisms. He also thought in conic sectins, squares and roots and ratios, and geometrized like Euclid. he made Kepler's laws for the planets to follow; he made velocity increase proportionally to the time in falling bodies; he made the law of the sines for light to obey when refracted; he established the classes, orders, families and genera of plants and animals, and fixed the distances between them. He thought the archetypes of all things, and devised their variations; and when we rediscover any one of these his wondrous institutions, we seize his mind in its very literal intention.

But as the sciences have developed further, the notion has gained ground that most, perhaps all, of our laws are only approximations. The laws themselves, moreover, have grown so numerous that there is no counting them; and so many rival formulations are proposed in all the branches of science that investigators have become accustomed to the notion that no theory is absolutely a transcript of reality, but that any one of them may from some point of view be useful. Their great use is to summarize old facts and to lead to new ones. They are only a man-made language, a conceptual shorthand, as some one calls them, in which we write our reports of nature; and languages, as is well known, tolerate much choice of expression and many dialects.

Thus human arbitrariness has driven divine necessity from scientific logic. If I mention the names of Sigwart, Mach, Ostwald, Pearson, Milhaud, Poincaré, Duhem, Ruyssen, those of you who are students will easily identify the tendency I speak of, and will think of additional names.

Riding now on the front of this wave of scientific logic Messrs. Schiller and Dewey appear with their pragmatistic account of what truth everywhere signifies. Everywhere, these teachers say, "truth" in our ideas and beliefs means the same thing that it means in science. It means, they say, nothing but this, *that ideas (which themselves are but parts of our experience) become true just in so far as they help us to get into satisfactory relation with other parts of our experience,* to summarize them and get about among them by conceptual short-cuts instead of following the interminable succession of particular phenomena. Any idea upon which we can ride, so to speak; any idea that will carry us prosperously from any one part of our experience to any other part, linking things satisfactorily, working securely, simplifying, saving labor; is true for just so much, true in so far forth, true *instrumentally.* This is the "instrumental" view of truth taught so successfully at Chicago, the view that truth in our ideas means their power to "work," promulgated so brilliantly at Oxford.

Messrs. Dewey, Schiller, and their allies, in reaching this general conception of all truth, have only followed the example of geologists, biologists and philologists. In the establishment of these other sciences, the successful stroke was always to take some simple process actually observable in operation—as denudation by weather, say, or variation from parental type, or change of dialect by incorporation of new words and pronunciations—and then to generalize it, making it apply to all times, and produce great results by summating its effects through the ages.

The observable process which Schiller and Dewey particularly singled out for generalization is the familiar one by which any individual settles into *new opinions*. The process here is always the same. The individual has a stock of old opinions already, but he meets a new experience that puts them to a strain. Somebody contradicts them; or in a reflective moment he discovers that they contradict each other; or he hears of facts with which they are incompatible; or desires arise in him which they cease to satisfy. The result is an inward trouble to which his mind till then had been a stranger, and from which he seeks to escape by modifying his previous mass of opinions. He saves as much of it as he can, for in this matter of belief we are all extreme conservatives. So he tries to change first this opinion, and then that (for they resist change very variously), until at last some new idea comes up which he can graft upon the ancient stock with a minimum of disturbance of the latter, some idea that mediates between the stock and the new experience and runs them into one another most felicitously and expediently.

This new idea is then adopted as the true one. It preserves the older stock of truths with a minimum of modification, stretching them just enough to make them admit the novelty, but conceiving that in ways as familiar as the case leaves possible. An *outrée* explanation, violating all our preconceptions, would never pass for a true account of a novelty. We should scratch round industriously till we found something less ex-centric. The most violent revolutions in an individual's beliefs leave most of his old order standing. Time and space, cause and effect, nature and history, and one's own biography remain untouched. New truth is always a go-between, a smoother-over of transitions. It marries old opinion to new fact so as ever to show a minimum of jolt, a maximum of continuity. We hold a theory true just in proportion to its success in solving this "problem of maxima and minima." But success in solving this problem is eminently a matter of approximation. We say this theory solves it on the whole more satisfactorily than that theory; but that means more satisfactorily to ourselves, and indivudals will emphasize their points of satisfaction differently. To a certain degree, therefore, everything here is plastic.

The point I now urge you to observe particularly is the part played by the older truths. Failure to take account of it is the source of much of the unjust criticism levelled against pragmatism. Their influence is absolutely controlling. Loyalty to them is the first principle—in most cases it is the only principle; for by far the most usual way of handling phenomena so novel that they would make for a serious rearrangement of our preconception is to ignore them altogether, or to abuse those who bear witness for them.

You doubtless wish examples of this process of truth's growth, and the only trouble is their superabundance. The simplest case of new truth is of course the mere numerical addition of new kinds of facts, or of new single facts of old kinds, to our experience—an addition that involves no alteration in the old beliefs. Day follows day, and its contents are simply added. The new contents themselves are not true, they simply *come* and *are*. Truth is *what we say about* them, and when we say that they have come, truth is satisfied by the plain additive formula.

But often the day's contents oblige a rearrangement. If I should now utter piercing shrieks and act like a maniac on this platform, it would make many of you revise your ideas as to the probable worth of my philosophy. "Radium" came the other day as part of the day's content, and seemed for a moment to contradict our ideas of the whole order of nature, that order having come to be identified with what is called the conservation of energy. The mere sight of radium paying heat away indefinitely out of its own pocket seemed to violate that conservation. What to think? If the radiations from it were nothing but an escape of unsuspected "potential" energy, pre-existent inside of the atoms, the principle of conservation would be saved. The discovery of "helium" as the radiation's outcome, opened a way to this belief. So Ramsay's view is generally held to be true, because, although it extends our old ideas of energy, it causes a minimum of alteration in their nature.

I need not multiply instances. A new opinion counts as "true" just in proportion as it gratifies the individual's desire to assimilate the novel in his experience to his beliefs in stock. It must both lean on old truth and grasp new fact; and its success (as I said a moment ago) in doing this, is a matter for the individual's appreciation. When old truth grows, then, by new truth's addition, it is for subjective reasons. We are in the process and obey the reasons. That new idea is truest which performs most felicitously its function of satisfying our double urgency. It makes itself true, gets itself classed as true, by the way it works; grafting itself then upon the ancient body of truth, which thus grows much as a tree grows by the activity of a new layer of cambium.

Now Dewey and Schiller proceed to generalize this observation and to apply it to the most ancient parts of truth. They also once were plastic. They also were called true for human reasons. They also mediated between still earlier truths and what in those days were novel observations. Purely objective truth, truth in whose establishment the function of giving human satisfaction in marrying previous parts of experience with newer parts played no rôle whatever, is nowhere to be found. The reasons why we call things true is the reason why they *are* true, for "to be true" *means* only to perform this marriage-function.

The trail of the human serpent is thus over everything. Truth independent; truth that we *find* merely; truth no longer malleable to human need; truth incorrigible, in a word; such truth exists indeed superabundantly—or is supposed to exist by rationalistically minded thinkers; but then it means only the dead heart of the living tree, and is being there means only that truth also has its paleontology, and its "prescription," and may grow stiff with years of veteran service and petrified in men's regard by sheer antiquity. But how plastic even the oldest truths nevertheless really are has been vividly shown in our day by the transformation of logical and mathematical ideas, a transformation which seems even to be invading physics. The ancient formulas are reinterpreted as special expressions of much wider principles, principles that our ancestors never got a glimpse of in their present shape and formulation.

Mr. Schiller still gives to all this view of truth the name of "Humanism," but, for this doctrine too, the name of pragmatism seems fairly to be in the ascendant, so I will treat it under the name of pragmatism in these lectures.

Such then would be the scope of pragmatism—first, a method; and second, a genetic theory of what is meant by truth. And these two things must be our future topics.

THE WILL TO BELIEVE*

In the recently published Life by Leslie Stephen of his brother, Fitz-James, there is an account of a school to which the latter went when he was a boy. The teacher, a certain Mr. Guest, used to converse with his pupils in this wise: "Gurney, what is the difference between justification and sanctification?—Stephen, prove the omnipotence of God! " etc. In the midst of our Harvard freethinking and indifference we are prone to imagine that here at your good old orthodox College conversation continues to be somewhat upon this order; and to show you that we at Harvard have not lost all interest in these vital subjects, I have brought with me tonight something like a sermon on justification by faith to read to you—I mean an essay in justification *of* faith, a defense of our right to adopt a believing attitude in religious matters, in spite of the fact that

---

* William James, "The Will to Believe," in *The Will to Believe and Other Essays in Popular Philosophy* (New York: Longmans, Green, 1896), pp. 1–4, 11, 22–29. Also published in *New World,* June 1896; this essay was given as an address to the Philosophical clubs of Yale and Brown universities.

our merely logical intellect may not have been coerced. "The Will to Believe," accordingly, is the title of my paper.

I have long defended to my own students the lawfulness of voluntarily adopted faith; but as soon as they have got well imbued with the logical spirit, they have as a rule to admit my contention to be lawful philo-sophically, even though in point of fact they were personally all the time chock-full of some faith or other themselves. I am all the while, however, so profoundly convinced that my own position is correct, that your invitation has seemed to me a good occasion to make my statements more clear. Perhaps your minds will be more open than those with which I have hitherto had to deal. I will be as little technical as I can, though I must begin by setting up some technical distinctions that will help us in the end.

I

Let us give the name of *hypothesis* to anything that may be proposed to our belief; and just as the electricians speak of live and dead wires, let us speak of any hypothesis as either *live* or *dead*. A live hypothesis is one which appeals as a real possibility to him to whom it is proposed. If I ask you to believe in the Mahdi, the notion makes no electric connection with your nature—it refuses to scintillate with any credibility at all. As an hypothesis it is completely dead. To an Arab, however (even if he be not one of the Mahdi's followers), the hypothesis is among the mind's possibilities: it is alive. This shows the deadness and liveness in an hypothesis are not intrinsic properties, but relations to the individual thinker. They are measured by his willingness to act. The maximum of liveness in an hypothesis means willingness to act irrevocably. Practically, that means belief; but there is some believing tendency wherever there is willingness to act at all.

Next, let us call the decision between two hypotheses an *option*. Options may be of several kinds. They may be—first, *living* or *dead;* secondly, *forced* or *avoidable;* thirdly, *momentous* or *trivial;* and for our purposes we may call an option a *genuine* option when it is of the forced, living, and momentous kind.

1. A living option is one in which both hypotheses are live ones. If I say to you: "Be a theosophist or be a Mohammedan," it is probably a dead option, because for you neither hypothesis is likely to be alive. But if I say: "Be an agnostic or be a Christian," it is otherwise: trained as you are, each hypothesis makes some appeal, however small, to your belief.

2. Next, if I say to you: "Choose between going out with your umbrella or without it," I do not offer you a genuine option, for it is not forced. You can easily avoid it by not going out at all. Similarly, if I say, "Either love me or hate me," "Either call my theory true or call it false," your

option is avoidable. You may remain indifferent to me, neither loving nor hating, and you may decline to offer any judgment as to my theory. But if I say, "Either accept this truth or go without it," I put on you a forced option, for there is no standing place outside of the alternative. Every dilemma based on a complete logical disjunction, with no possibility of not choosing, is an option of this forced kind.

3. Finally, if I were Dr. Nansen and proposed to you to join my North Pole expedition, your option would be momentous; for this would probably be your only similar opportunity, and your choice now would either exclude you from the North Pole sort of immortality altogether or put at least the chance of it into your hands. He who refuses to embrace a unique opportunity loses the prize as surely as if he tried and failed. *Per contra,* the option is trivial when the opportunity is not unique, when the stake is insignificant, or when the decision is reversible if it later prove unwise. Such trivial options abound in the scientific life. A chemist finds an hypothesis live enough to spend a year in its verification: he believes in it to that extent. But if his experiments prove inconclusive either way, he is quit for his loss of time, no vital harm being done.

It will facilitate our discussion if we keep all these distinctions well in mind.

. . . The thesis I defend is, briefly stated, this: *Our passional nature not only lawfully may, but must, decide on option between propositions, whenever it is a genuine option that cannot by its nature be decided on intellectual grounds; for to say, under such circumstances, "Do not decide, but leave the question open," is itself a passional decision—just like deciding yes or no—and is attended with the same risk of losing the truth.* The thesis thus abstractly expressed will, I trust, soon become quite clear.

Moral questions immediately present themselves as questions whose solution cannot wait for sensible proof. A moral question is a question not of what sensibly exists, but of what is good, or would be good if it did exist. Science can tell us what exists; but to compare the *worths,* both of what exists and of what does not exist, we must consult not science, but what Pascal calls our heart. Science herself consults her heart when she lays it down that the infinite ascertainment of fact and correction of false belief are the supreme goods for man. Challenge the statement, and science can only repeat it oracularly, or else prove it by showing that such ascertainment and correction bring man all sorts of other goods which man's heart in turn declares. The question of having moral beliefs at all or not having them is decided by our will. Are our moral preferences true or false, or are they only odd biological phenomena, making things good or bad for *us,* but in themselves indifferent? How can your pure intellect decide? If your heart does not *want* a world of moral reality, your head will assuredly never make you believe in one. Mephistophelian scepticism, indeed, will satisfy the head's play-instincts much better than any rigorous idealism can. Some men (even at the student age) are so naturally cool-hearted that the moralistic hypothesis never has for them any pungent life, and in their supercilious presence the hot young moralist always feels strangely ill at ease. The appearance of knowingness is on their side, of *naïveté* and gullibility on his. Yet, in the inarticulate heart of him, he clings to it that he is not a dupe, and that there is a realm in which (as Emerson says) all their wit and intellectual superiority is no better than the cunning of a fox. Moral scepticism can no more be refuted or proved by logic than intellectual scepticism can. When we stick to it that there *is* truth (be it of either kind), we do so with our whole nature, and resolve to stand or fall by the results. The sceptic with his whole nature adopts the doubting attitude; but which of us is the wiser, Omniscience only knows.

Turn now from these wide questions of good to a certain class of questions of fact, questions concerning personal relations, states of mind between one man and another. *Do you like me or not?*—for example. Whether you do or not depends, in countless instances, on whether I meet you half-way, am willing to assume that you must like me, and show you trust and expectation. The previous faith on my part in your liking's existence is in such cases what makes your liking come. But if I stand aloof, and refuse to budge an inch until I have objective evidence, until you shall have done something apt, as the absolutists say, *ad extorquendum assensum meum,* ten to one your liking never comes. How many women's hearts are vanquished by the mere sanguine insistence of some man that they *must* love him! he will not consent to the hypothesis that they cannot. The desire for a certain kind of truth here brings about that special truth's existence; and so it is in innumerable cases of othe sorts. Who gains promotions, boons, appointments, but the man in whose life they are seen to play the part of live hypotheses, who discounts them, sacrifices other things for their sake before they have come, and takes risks for them in advance? His faith acts on the powers above him as a claim, and creates its own verification.

A social organism of any sort whatever, large or small, is what it is because each member proceeds to his own duty with a trust that the other members will simultaneously do theirs. Wherever a desired result is achieved by the co-operation of many independent persons, its existence as a fact is a pure consequence of the precursive faith in one another of those immediately concerned. A government, an army, a commercial system, a ship, a college, an athletic team, all exist on this condition, without which not only is nothing achieved, but nothing is even attempted. A whole train of passengers (individually brave enough) will be looted by a few highwaymen, simply because the latter can count on one another, while each passenger fears that if he makes a movement of resistance, he will be shot before any one else backs him up. If we believed that the whole car-full would rise at once with us, we should each severally rise, and train-robbing would never even be attempted. There are, then, cases where a fact cannot come at all unless a preliminary faith exists in its coming. *And where faith in a fact can help create the fact,* that would be an insane logic which should say that faith running ahead of scientific evidence is the "lowest kind of immorality" into which a thinking being can fall. Yet such is the logic by which our scientific absolutists pretend to regulate our lives!

X

In truths dependent on our personal action, then, faith based on desire is certainly a lawful and possibly an indispensable thing.

But now, it will be said, these are all childish human cases, and have nothing to do with great cosmical matters, like the question of religious faith. Let us then pass on to that. Religions differ so much in their accidents that in discussing the religious question we must make it very generic and broad. What then do we now mean by the religious hypothesis? Science says things are; morality says some things are better than other things; and religion says essentially two things.

First, she says that the best things are the most eternal things, the overlapping things, the things in the universe that throw the last stone, so to speak, and say the final word. "Perfection is eternal"—this phrase of Charles Secrétan seems a good way of putting this first affirmation of religion, an affirmation which obviously cannot yet be verified scientifically at all.

The second affirmation of religion is that we are better off even now if we believe her first affirmation to be true.

Now, let us consider what the logical elements of this situation are *in case the religious hypothesis in both its branches be really true.* (Of course, we must admit that possibility at the outset. If we are to discuss the question at all, it must involve a living option. If for any of you religion be a hypothesis that cannot, by any living possibility, be true, then you need go no farther. I speak to the "saving remnant" alone.) So proceeding, we see, first, that religion offers itself as a *momentous* option. We are supposed to gain, even now, by our belief, and to lose by our non-belief, a certain vital good. Secondly, religion is a *forced* option, so far as that good goes. We cannot escape the issue by remaining sceptical and waiting for more light, because, although we do avoid error in that way *if religion be untrue,* we lose the good, *if it be true,* just as certainly as if we positively chose to disbelieve. It is as if a man should hesitate indefinitely to ask a certain woman to marry him because he was not perfectly sure that she would prove an angel after he brought her home. Would he not cut himself off from the particular angel-possibility as decisively as if he went and married some one else? Scepticism, then, is not avoidance of option; it is option of a certain particular kind of risk.

Better risk loss of truth than chance of error—that is your faith-vetoer's exact position. He is actively playing his stake as much as the believer is; he is backing the field against the religious hypothesis, just as the believer is backing the religious hypothesis against the field. To preach scepticism to us as a duty until "sufficient evidence" for religion be found, is tantamount therefore to telling us, when in presence of the religious hypotehesis, that to yield to our fear of its being error is wiser and better than to yield to our hope that it may be true. It is not intellect against all passions, then; it is ony intellect with one passion laying down its law. And by what, forsooth, is the supreme wisdom of this passion warranted? Dupery for dupery, what proof is there that dupery through hope is so much worse than dupery through fear? I, for one, can see no proof; and I simply refuse obedience to the scientist's command to imitate his kind of option, in a case where my own stake is important enough to give me the right to choose my own form of risk. If religion be true and the evidence for it be still insufficient, I do not wish, by putting your extinguisher upon my nature (which feels to me as if it had after all some business in this matter), to forfeit my sole chance in life of getting upon the winning side—that chance depending, of course, on my willingness to run the risk of acting as if my passional need of taking the world religiously might be prophetic and right.

All this is on the supposition that it really may be prophetic and right, and that, even to us who are discussing the matter, religion is a live hypothesis which may be true. Now, to most of us religion comes in a still further way that makes a veto on our active faith even more illogical. The more perfect and more eternal aspect of the universe is represented in our religions as having personal form. The universe is no longer a mere *It* to us, but a *Thou,* if we are religious; and any relation that may be possible from person to person might be possible here. For instance, although in one sense we are passive portions of the universe, in another we show a curious autonomy, as if we were small active centres on our own account. We feel, too, as if the appeal of religion to us were made to our own active good-will, as if evidence might be forever withheld from us unless we met the hypothesis half-way. To take a trivial illustration: just as a man who in a company of gentlemen made no advances, asked a warrant for every concession, and believed no one's word without proof, would cut himself off by such churlishness from all the social rewards that a more trusting spirit would earn—so here, one who should shut himself up in snarling logicality and try to make the gods extort his recognition willy-nilly, or not get it at all, might cut himself off forever from his only opportunity of making the gods' acquaintance. This feeling, forced on us we know not whence, that by obstinately believing that thee are gods (although not to do so would be so easy both for our logic and our life) we are doing the universe the deepest service we can, seems part of the living essence of the religious hypothesis. If the hypothesis *were* true in all its parts, including this one, then pure intellectualism, with its veto on our making willing advances, would be an absurdity; and some participation of our sympathetic nature would be logically required. I, therefore, for one, cannot see my way to accepting the agnostic rules for truth-seeking, or wilfully agree to keep my willing nature out of the game. I cannot do so for this plain reason, that *a rule of thinking which would absolutely prevent me from acknowledging certain kinds of truth if those kinds of truth were really there, would be an irrational rule.* That for me is the long and short of the formal logic of the situation, no matter what the kinds of truth might materially be.

THE DILEMMA OF DETERMINISM*

A common opinion prevails that the juice has ages ago been pressed out of the free-will controversy, and that no new champion can do more than warm up stale arguments which every one has heard. This is a radical mistake. I know of no subject less worn out, or in which inventive genius has a better chance of breaking open new ground—not, perhaps, of forcing a conclusion or of coercing assent, but of deepening our sense of what the issue between the two parties really is, of what the ideas of fate and of free will imply. At our very side almost, in the past few years, we have seen falling in rapid succession from the press works that present the alternative in entirely novel lights. Not to speak of the English disciples of Hegel, such as Green and Bradley; not to speak of Hinton and Hodgson, nor of Hazard here—we see in the writings of Renouvier, Fouillée, and Delboeuf† how completely changed and refreshed is the form of all the old disputes. I cannot pretend to vie in originality with any of the masters I have named, and my ambition limits itself to just one little point. If I can make two of the necessarily implied corollaries of determinism clearer to you than they have been made before, I shall have made it possible for you to decide for or against that doctrine with a better understanding of what you are about. And if you prefer not to decide at all, but to remain doubters, you will at least see more plainly what the subject of your hesitation is. I thus disclaim openly on the threshold all pretension to prove to you that the freedom of the will is true. The most I hope is to induce some of you to follow my own example in assuming it true,

---

* James, "The Dilemma of Determinism," in *Will to Believe*, pp. 145–51, 159–63, 175–79. This essay was given as an address to Harvard Divinity School students and was published in the *Unitarian Review*, September 1884.
† And I may now say Charles S. Peirce—see the *Monist*, for 1892–93.

and acting as if it were true. If it be true, it seems to me that this is involved in the strict logic of the case. Its truth ought not to be forced willy-nilly down our indifferent throats. It ought to be freely espoused by men who can equally well turn their backs upon it. In other words, our first act of freedom, if we are free, ought in all inward propriety to be to affirm that we are free. This should exclude, it seems to me, from the free-will side of the question all hope of a coercive demonstration—a demonstration which I, for one, am perfectly contented to go without.

With thus much understood at the outset, we can advance. But not without one more point understood as well. The arguments I am about to urge all proceed on two suppositions: first, when we make theories about the world and discuss them with one another, we do so in order to attain a conception of things which shall give us subjective satisfaction; and, second, if there be two conceptions, and the one seems to us, on the whole, more rational than the other, we are entitled to suppose that the more rational one is the truer of the two. I hope that you are all willing to make these suppositions with me; for I am afraid that if there be any of you here who are not, they will find little edification in the rest of what I have to say. I cannot stop to argue the point; but I myself believe that all the magnificent achievements of mathematical and physical science—our doctrines of evolution, of uniformity of law, and the rest— proceed from our indomitable desire to cast the world into a more rational shape in our minds than the shape into which it is thrown there by the crude order of our experience. The world has shown itself, to a great extent, plastic to this demand of ours for rationality. How much farther it will show itself plastic no one can say. Our only means of finding out is to try; and I, for one, feel as free to try conceptions of moral as of mechanical or of logical rationality. If a certain formula for expressing the nature of the world violates my moral demand, I shall feel as free to throw it overboard, or at least to doubt it, as if it disappointed my demand for uniformity of sequence, for example; the one demand being, so far as I can see, quite as subjective and emotional as the other is. The principle of causality, for example—what is it but a postulate, an empty name covering simply a demand that the sequence of events shall some day manifest a deeper kind of belonging of one thing with another than the mere arbitrary juxtaposition which now phenomenally appears? It is as much an altar to an unknown god as the one that Saint Paul found at Athens. All our scientific and philosophic ideals are altars to unknown gods. Uniformity is as much so as is free will. If this be admitted, we can debate on even terms. But if any one pretends that while freedom and variety are, in the first instance, subjective demands, necessity and uniformity are something altogether different, I do not see how we can debate at all.*

To begin, then, I must suppose you acquainted with all the usual arguments on the subject. I cannot stop to take up the old proofs from causation, from statistics, from the certainty with which we can foretell one another's conduct, from the fixity of character, and all the rest. But there are two *words* which usually encumber these classical arguments, and which we must immediately dispose of if we are to make any progress. One is the eulogistic word *freedom,* and the other is the opprobrious word *chance.* The word "chance" I wish to keep, but I wish to get rid of the word "freedom." Its eulogistic associations have so far overshadowed all the rest of its meaning that both parties claim the sole right to use it, and determinists today insist that they alone are freedom's champions. Old-fashioned determinism was what we may call *hard* determinism. It did not shrink from such words as fatality, bondage of the will, necessitation, and the like. Nowadays, we have a *soft* determinism which abhors harsh words, and, repudiating fatality, necessity, and even predetermination, says that its real name is freedom; for freedom is only necessity understood, and bondage to the highest is identical with true freedom. Even a writer as little used to making capital out of soft words as Mr. Hodgson hesitates not to call himself a "free-will determinist."

Now, all this is a quagmire of evasion under which the real issue of fact has been entirely smothered. Freedom in all these senses presents simply no problem at all. No matter what the soft determinist mean by

---

* The whole history of popular beliefs about Nature refutes the notion that the thought of a universal physical order can possibly have arisen from the purely passive reception and association of particular perceptions. Indubitable as it is that men infer from known cases to unknown, it is equally certain that this procedure, if restricted to the phenomenal materials that spontaneously offer themselves, would never have led to the belief in a general uniformity, but only to the belief that law and lawlessness rule the world in motley alternation. From the point of view of strict experience, nothing exists but the sum of particular perceptions, with their coincidences on the one hand, their contradictions on the other.

"That there is more order in the world than appears at first sight is not discovered *till the order is looked for.* The first impulse to look for it proceeds from practical needs: where ends must be attained, we must know trustworthy means which infallibly possess a property, or produce a result. But the practical need is only the first occasion for our reflection on the conditions of true knowledge; and even were there no such need, motives would still be present for carrying us beyond the stage of mere association. For not with an equal interest, or rather with an equal lack of interest, does man contemplate those natural processes in which a thing is linked with its former mate, and those in which it is linked to something else. *The former processes harmonize with the conditions of his own thinking:* the latter do not. In the former, his *concepts, general judgments,* and *inferences* apply to reality: in the latter, they have no such application. And thus the intellectual satisfaction which at first comes to him without reflection, at least excites in him the conscious wish to find realized throughout the entire phenomenal world those rational continuities, uniformities, and necessities which are the fundamental element and guiding principle of his own thought" (Sigwart, *Logik,* bd. 2, s. 382).

it—whether he mean the acting without external constraint; whether he mean the acting rightly, or whether he mean the acquiescing in the law of the whole—who cannot answer him that sometimes we are free and sometimes we are not? But there *is* a problem, an issue of fact and not of words, an issue of the most momentous importance, which is often decided without discussion in one sentence—nay, in one clause of a sentence—by those very writers who spin out whole chapters in their eforts to show what "true" freedom is; and that is the question of determinism, about which we are to talk tonight.

Fortunately, no ambiguities hang about this word or about its opposite, indeterminism. Both designate an outward way in which things may happen, and their cold and mathematical sound has no sentimental associations that can bribe our partiality either way in advance. Now, evidence of an external kind to decide between determinism and indeterminism is, as I intimated a while back, strictly impossible to find. Let us look at the difference between them and see for ourselves. What does determinism profess?

It professes that those parts of the universe already laid down absolutely appoint and decree what the other parts shall be. The future has no ambiguous possibilities hidden in its womb: the part we call the present is compatible with only one totality. Any other future complement than the one fixed from eternity is impossible. The whole is in each and every part, and welds it with the rest into an absolute unity, an iron block, in which there can be no equivocation or shadow of turning.

> With earth's first clay they did the last man knead,
> And there of the last harvest sowed the seed.
> And the first morning of creation wrote
> What the last dawn of reckoning shall read.

Indeterminism, on the contrary, says that the parts have a certain amount of loose play on one another, so that the laying down of one of them does not necessarily determine what the others shall be. It admits that possibilities may be in excess of actualities, and that things not yet revealed to our knowledge may really in themselves be ambiguous. Of two alternative futures which we conceive, both may now be really possible; and the one become impossible only at the very moment when the other excludes it by becoming real itself. Indeterminism thus denies the world to be one unbending unit of fact. It says there is a certain ultimate pluralism in it; and, so saying, it corroborates our ordinary unsophisticated view of things. To that view, actualities seem to float in a wider sea of possibilities from out of which they are chosen; and, *somewhere,* indeterminism says, such possibilities exist, and form a part of truth.

Determinism, on the contrary, says they exist *nowhere,* and that necessity on the one hand and impossibility on the other are the sole categories of the real. Possibilities that fail to get realized are, for determinism, pure illusions: they never were possibilities at all. There is nothing inchoate, it says, about this universe of ours, all that was or is or shall be actual in it having been from eternity virtually there. The cloud of alternatives our minds escort this mass of actuality withal is a cloud of sheer deceptions, to which "impossibilities" is the only name that rightfully belongs.

The issue, it will be seen, is a perfectly sharp one, which no eulogistic terminology can smear over or wipe out. The truth *must* lie with one side or the other, and its lying with one side makes the other false.

I wish first of all to show you just what the notion that this is a deterministic world implies. The implications I call your attention to are all bound up with the fact that it is a world in which we constantly have to make what I shall, with your permission, call judgments of regret. Hardly an hour passes in which we do not wish that something might be otherwise; and happy indeed are those of us whose hearts have never echoed the wish of Omar Khayam—

That we might clasp, ere closed, the book of fate,
And make the writer on a fairer leaf
Inscribe our names, or quite obliterate.

Ah! Love, could you and I with fate conspire
To mend this sorry scheme of things entire,
Would we not shatter it to bits, and then
Remould it nearer to the heart's desire?

Now, it is undeniable that most of these regrets are foolish, and quite on a par in point of philosophic value which the criticisms on the universe of that friend of our infancy, the hero of the fable "The Atheist and the Acorn"—

Fool! had that bough a pumpkin bore,
Thy whimsies would have worked no more, etc.

Even from the point of view of our own ends, we should probably make a botch of remodelling the universe. How much more then from the point of view of ends we cannot see! Wise men therefore regret as little as they can. But still some regrets are pretty obstinate and hard to stifle— regrets for acts of wanton cruelty or treachery, for example, whether performed by others or by ourselves. Hardly any one can remain *entirely* optimistic after reading the confession of the murderer at Brockton the other day: how, to get rid of the wife whose continued existence bored him, he inveigled her into a desert spot, shot her four times, and then, as she lay on the ground and said to him, "You didn't do it on purpose, did you, dear? " replied, "No, I didn't do it on purpose," as he raised a rock and smashed her skull. Such an occurrence, with the mild sentence and self-satisfaction of the prisoner, is a field for a crop of regrets, which one need not take up in detail. We feel that, although a perfect mechanical fit to the rest of the universe, it is a bad moral fit, and that something else would really have been better in its place.

But for the deterministic philosophy the murder, the sentence, and the prisoner's optimism were all necessary from eternity; and nothing else for a moment had a ghost of a chance of being put into their place. To admit such a chance, the determinists tell us, would be to make a suicide of reason; so we must steel our hearts against the thought. And here out plot thickens, for we see the first of those difficult implications of determinism and monism which it is my purpose to make you feel. If this Brockton murder was called for by the rest of the universe, if it had to come at its preappointed hour, and if nothing else would have been consistent with the sense of the whole, what are we to think of the universe? Are we stubbornly to stick to our judgment of regret, and say, though it *couldn't* be, yet it *would* have been a better universe with something different from this Brockton murder in it? That, of course, seems the natural and spontaneous thing for us to do; and yet it is nothing short of deliberately espousing a kind of pessimism. The judgment of regret calls the murder bad. Calling a thing bad means, if it mean anything at all, that the thing ought not to be, that something else ought to be in its stead. Determinism, in denying that anything else can be in its stead, virtually defines the universe as a place in which what ought to be is impossible—in other words, as an organism whose constitution is afflicted with an incurable taint, an irremediable flaw. The pessimism of a Schopenhauer says no more than this—that the murder is a symptom; and that it is a vicious symptom because it belongs to a vicious whole, which can express its nature no otherwise than by bringing forth just such a symptom as that at this particular spot. Regret for the murder must transform itself, if we are determinists and wise, into a larger regret. It is absurd to regret the murder alone. Other things being what they are, *it* could not be different. What we should regret is that whole frame of things of which the murder is one member. I see no escape whatever from this pessimistic conclusion if, being determinists, our judgment of regret is to be allowed to stand at all.

The only deterministic escape from pessimism is everywhere to abandon the judgment of regret. That this can be done, history shows to be not impossible. The devil, *quoad existentiam,* may be good. That is, although he be a *principle* of evil, yet the universe, with such a principle in it, may practically be a better universe than it could have been without. On every hand, in a small way, we find that a certain amount of evil is a condition by which a higher form of good is brought. There is nothing to prevent anybody from generalizing this view, and trusting that if we could but see things in the largest of all ways, even such matters as this Brockton murder would appear to be paid for by the uses that follow in their train. An optimism *quand même,* a systematic and infatuated optimism like that ridiculed by Voltaire in his *Candide,* is one of the possible ideal ways in which a man may train himself to look on life. Bereft of dogmatic hardness and lit up with the expression of a tender and pathetic hope, such an optimism has been the grace of some of the most religious characters that ever lived.

> Throb thine with Nature's throbbing breast,
> And all is clear from east to west.

Even curelty and treachery may be among the absolutely blessed fruits of time, and to quarrel with any of their details may be blasphemy. The only real blasphemy, in short, may be that pessimistic temper of the soul which lets it give way to such things as regrets, remorse, and grief.

Thus, our deterministic pessimism may become a deterministic optimism at the price of extinguishing our judgment of regret.

But does not this immediately bring us into a curious logical predicament? Our determinism leads us to call our judgments of regret wrong, because they are pessimistic in implying that what is impossible yet ought to be. But how then about the judgments of regret themselves? If they are wrong, other judgments, judgments of approval presumably, ought to be in their place. But as they are necessitated, nothing else *can* be in their place; and the universe is just what it was before—namely, a place in which what ought to be appears impossible. . . .

But this brings us right back, after such a long detour, to the question of indeterminism and to the conclusion of all I came here to say tonight. For the only cosistent way of representing a pluralism and a world whose parts may affect one another through their conduct being either good or bad is the indeterministic way. What interest, zest, or excitement can there be in achieving the right way, unless we are enabled to feel that the wrong way is also a possible and a natural way—nay, more, a menacing and an imminent way? And what sense can there be in condemning ourselves for taking the wrong way, unless we need have done nothing of the sort, unless the right way was open to us as well? I cannot understand the willingness to act, no matter how we feel, without the belief that acts are really good and bad. I cannot understand the belief that an act is bad, without regret at its happening. I cannot understand regret without the admission of real, genuine possibilities in the world. Only *then* is it other than a mockery to feel, after we have failed to do our best, that an irreparable opportunity is gone from the universe, the loss of which it must forever after mourn.

If you insist that this is all superstition, that possibility is in the eye of science and reason impossibility, and that if I act badly 'tis that the universe was foredoomed to suffer this defect, you fall right back into the dilemma, the labyrinth, of pessimism and subjectivism, from out of whose toils we have just wound our way.

Now, we are of course free to fall back, if we please. For my own part, though, whatever difficulties may beset the philosophy of objective right and wrong, and the indeterminism it seems to imply, determinism, with its alternative of pessimism or romanticism, contains difficulties that are greater still. But you will remember that I expressly repudiated awhile ago the pretension to offer any arguments which could be coercive in a so-called scientific fashion in this matter. And I consequently find myself, at the end of this long talk, obliged to state my conclusions in an altogether personal way. This personal method of appeal seems to be among the very conditions of the problem; and the most any one can do is to confess as candidly as he can the grounds for the faith that is in him, and leave his example to work on others as it may.

Let me, then, without circumlocution say just this. The world is enigmatical enough in all conscience, whatever theory we may take up toward it. The indeterminism I defend, the free-will theory of popular sense based on the judgment of regret, represents that world as vulnerable, and liable to be injured by certain of its parts if they act wrong. And it represents their acting wrong as a matter of possibility or accident, neither inevitable nor yet to be infallibly warded off. In all this, it is a theory devoid either of transparency or of stability. It gives us a pluralistic, restless universe, in which no single point of view can ever take in the whole scene; and to a mind possessed of the love of unity at any cost, it will, no doubt, remain forever inacceptable. A friend with such a mind once told me that the thought of my universe made him sick, like the sight of the horrible motion of a mass of maggots in their carrion bed.

But while I freely admit that the pluralism and the restlessness are repugnant and irrational in a certain way, I find that every alternative to them is irrational in a deeper way. The indeterminism with its maggots, if you please to speak so about it, offends only the native absolutism of my intellect—an absolutism which, after all, perhaps, deserves to be snubbed and kept in check. But the determinism with its necessary carrion, to continue the figure of speech, and with no possible maggots to eat the latter up, violates my sense of moral reality through and through. When, for example, I imagine such carrion as the Brockton murder, I cannot conceive it as an act by which the universe, as a whole, logically and necessarily expresses its nature without shrinking from complicity with such a whole. And I deliberately refuse to keep on terms of loyalty with the universe by saying blankly that the murder, since it does flow from the nature of the whole, is not carrion. There are *some* instinctive reactions which I, for one, will not tamper with. The only remaining alternative, the attitude of gnostical romanticism, wrenches my personal instincts in quite as violent a way. It falsifies the simple objectivity of their deliverance. It makes the goose-flesh the murder excites in me a sufficient reason for the perpetration of the crime. It transforms life from a tragic reality into an insincere melodramatic exhibition, as foul or as tawdry as any one's diseased curiosity pleases to carry it out. And with its consecration of the *roman naturaliste* state of mind, and its enthronement of the baser crew of Parisian *littérateurs* among the eternally indispensable organs by which the infinite spirit of things attains to that subjective illumination which is the task of life, it leaves me in presence of a sort of subjective carrion considerably more noisome than the objective carrion I called it in to take away.

No! better a thousand times, than such systematic corruption of our moral sanity, the plainest pessimism, so that it be straightforward; but better far then that the world of chance. Make as great an uproar about chance as you please, I know that chance means pluralism and nothing more. If some of the members of the pluralism are bad, the philosophy of pluralism, whatever broad views it may deny me, permits me, at least, to turn to the other members with a clean breast of affection and an unsophisticated moral sense. And if I still wish to think of the world as a totality, it lets me feel that a world with a *chance* in it of being altogether good, even if the chance never come to pass, is better than a world with no such chance at all. That "chance" whose very notion I am exhorted and conjured to banish from my view of the future as the suicide of reason concerning it, that "chance" is—what? Just this—the chance that in moral respects the future may be other and better than the past has been. This is the only chance we have any motive for supposing to exist. Shame, rather, on its repudiation and its denial! For its presence is the vital air which lets the world live, the salt which keeps it sweet.

DOES "CONSCIOUSNESS" EXIST? *

"Thoughts" and "things" are names for two sorts of object, which common sense will always find contrasted and will always practically oppose to each other. Philosophy, reflecting on the contrast, has varied in the past in her explanations of it, and may be expected to vary in the future. At first, "spirit and matter," "soul and body," stood for a pair of equipollent substances quite on a par in weight and interest. But one day Kant undermined the soul and brought in the transcendental ego, and ever since then the bipolar relation has been very much off its balance. The transcendental ego seems nowadays in rationalist quarters to stand for everything, in empiricist quarters for almost nothing. In the hands of such writers as Schuppe, Rehmke, Natorp, Münsterberg—at any rate in his earlier writings, Schubert-Soldern and others, the spiritual principle attenuates itself to a thoroughly ghostly condition, being only a name for the fact that the "content" of experience *is known*. It loses personal form

---

* William James, "Does 'Consciousness' Exist?" *Journal of Philosophy, Psychology, and Scientific Methods* 1, no. 18 (1 September 1904): pp. 477–91. Reprinted in William James, *Essays in Radical Empiricism* (New York: Longmans, Green, 1912), chap. 1.

and activity—these passing over to the content—and becomes a bare *Bewusstheit* or *Bewusstsein überhaupt,* of which in its own right absolutely nothing can be said.

I believe that "consciousness," when once it has evaporated to this estate of pure diaphaneity, is on the point of disappearing altogether. It is the name of a nonentity, and has no right to a place among first principles. Those who still cling to it are clinging to a mere echo, the faint rumor left behind by the disappearing "soul" upon the air of philosophy. During the past year, I have read a number of articles whose authors seemed just on the point of abandoning the notion of conscious- ness[1] and substituting for it that of an absolute experience not due to two factors. But they were not quite radical enough, not quite daring enough in their negations. For twenty years past I have mistrusted "con- sciousness" as an entity; for seven or eight years past I have suggested its non-existence to my students, and tried to give them its pragmatic equivalent in realities of experience. It seems to me that the hour is ripe for it to be openly and universally discarded.

To deny plumply that "consciousness" exists seems so absurd on the face of it—for undeniably "thoughts" do exist—that I fear some readers will follow me no farther. Let me then immediately explain that I mean only to deny that the word stands for an entity, but to insist most emphatically that it does stand for a function. There is, I mean, no aboriginal stuff or quality of being, contrasted with that of which material objects are made, out of which our thoughts of them are made; but there is a function in experience which thoughts perform, and for the perfor- mance of which this quality of being is invoked. That function is *knowing.* "Consciousness" is supposed necessary to explain the fact that things not only are, but get reported, are known. Whoever blots out the notion of consciousness from his list of first principles must still provide in some way for that function's being carried on.

I

My thesis is that if we start with the supposition that there is only one primal stuff or material in the world, a stuff of which everything is composed, and if we call that stuff "pure experience," then knowing can easily be explained as a particular sort of relation towards one another into which portions of pure experience may enter. The relation itself is a part of pure experience; one of its "terms" becomes the subject or

---

[1] Articles by Baldwin, Ward, Bawden, King, Alexander and others. Dr. Perry is frankly over the border.

bearer of the knowledge, the knower,[2] the other becomes the object known. This will need much explanation before it can be understood. The best way to get it understood is to contrast it with the alternative view; and for that we may take the recentest alternative, that in which the evaporation of the definite soul-substance has proceeded as far as it can go without being yet complete. If neo-Kantism has expelled earlier forms of dualism, we shall have expelled all forms if we are able to expel neo-Kantism in its turn.

For the thinkers I call neo-Kantian, the word consciousness today does no more than signalize the fact that experience is indefeasibly dualistic in structure. It means that not subject, not object, but object-plus-subject is the minimum that can actually be. The subject-object distinction meanwhile is entirely different from that between mind and matter, from that between body and soul. Souls were detachable, had separate destinies; things could happen to them. To consciousness as such nothing can happen, for, timeless itself, it is only a witness of happenings in time, in which it plays no part. It is, in a word, but the logical correlative of "content" in an Experience of which the peculiarity is that *fact comes to light* in it, that *awareness of content* takes place. Consciousness as such is entirely impersonal—"self" and its activities belong to the content. To say that I am self-conscious, or conscious of putting forth volition, means only that certain contents, for which "self" and "effort of will" are the names, are not without witness as they occur.

Thus, for these belated drinkers at the Kantian spring, we should have to admit consciousness as an "epistemological" necessity, even if we had no direct evidence of its being there.

But in addition to this, we are supposed by almost every one to have an immediate consciousness of consciousness itself. When the world of outer fact ceases to be materially present, and we merely recall it in memory, or fancy it, the consciousness is believed to stand out and to be felt as a kind of impalpable inner flowing, which, once known in this sort of experience, may equally be detached in presentations of the outer world. "The moment we try to fix our attention upon consciousness and to see *what,* distinctly, it is," says a recent writer, "it seems to vanish. It seems as if we had before us a mere emptiness. When we try to introspect the sensation of blue, all we can see is the blue; the other element is as if it were diaphanous. Yet it can be distinguished if we look attentively enough, and know that there is something to look for." [3] "Consciousness" *(Bewusstheit),* says another philosopher, "is in explicable and hardly describable, yet all conscious experiences have this in common that what we call their content has this peculiar reference to a center for

---

[2] In my *Psychology* I have tried to show that we need no knower other than the "passing thought."

[3] G. E. Moore: *Mind,* vol. 12, N. S., p. 450.

which 'self' is the name, in virtue of which reference alone the content is subjectively given, or appears. . . . While in this way consciousness, or reference to a self, is the only thing which distinguishes a conscious content from any sort of being that might be there with no one conscious of it, yet this only ground of the distinction defies all closer explanations. The existence of consciousness, although it is the fundamental fact of psychology, can indeed be laid down as certain, can be brought out by analysis, but can neither be defined nor deduced from anything but itself." [4]

"Can be brought out by analysis," this author says. This supposes that the consciousness is one element, moment, factor—call it what you like—of an experience of essentially dualistic inner constitution, from which, if you abstrct the content, the consciousness will remain revealed to its own eye. Experience, at this rate, would be much like a paint of which the world pictures were made. Paint has a dual constitution, involving, as it does, a menstruum[5] (oil, size or what not) and a mass of content in the form of pigment suspended therein. We can get the pure menstruum by letting the pigment settle, and the pure pigment by pouring off the size or oil. We operate here by physical subtraction; and the usual view is, that by mental subtraction we can separate the two factors of experience in an analogous way—not isolating them entirely, but distinguishing them enough to know that they are two.

II

Now my contention is exactly the reverse of this. *Experience, I believe, has no such inner duplicity; and the separation of it into consciousness and content comes, not by way of subtraction, but by way of addition—*the addition, to a given concrete piece of it, of other sets of experiences, in connection with which severally its use or function may be of two different kinds. The paint will also serve here as an illustration. In a pot in a paint-shop, along with other paints, it serves in its entirety as so much saleable matter. Spread on a canvas, with other paints around it, it represents, on the contrary, a feature in a picture and performs a spiritual function. Just so, I maintain, does a given undivided portion of experience, taken in one context of associates, play the part of a knower, of a state of mind, of "consciousness"; while in a different context the same undivided bit of experience plays the part of a thing known, of an

---

[4] Paul Natorp: *Einleitung in die Psychologie,* 1888, pp. 14, 112.
[5] "Figuratively speaking, consciousness may be said to be the one universal solvent or menstruum, in which the different kinds of psychic acts and facts are contained, whether in concealed or in obvious form" G. T. Ladd: *Psychology, Descriptive and Explanatory,* 1894, p. 30.

objective "content." In a word, in one group it figures as a thought, in another group as a thing. And, since it can figure in both groups simultaneously we have every right to speak of it as subjective and objective both at once. The dualism connoted by such double-barrelled terms as "experience," "phenomenon," "datum," *"Vorfindung"*—terms which, in philosophy at any rate, tend more and more to replace the single-barrelled terms of "thought" and "thing"—that dualism, I say, is still preserved in this account, but reinterpreted, so that, instead of being mysterious and elusive, it becomes verifiable and concrete. It is an affair of relations, it falls outside, not inside, the single experience considered, and can always be particularized and defined.

The entering wedge for this more concrete way of understanding the dualism was fashioned by Locke when he made the word "idea" stand indifferently for thing and thought, and by Berkeley when he said that what common sense means by realities is exactly what the philosopher means by ideas. Neither Locke nor Berkeley thought his truth out into perfect clearness, but it seems to me that the conception I am defending does little more than consistently carry out the "pragmatic" method which they were the first to use.

If the reader will take his own experiences, he will see what I mean. Let him begin with a perceptual experience, the "presentation," so called, of a physical object, his actual field of vision, the room he sits in, with the book he is reading as its center; and let him for the present treat this complex object in the common-sense way as being "really" what it seems to be, namely, a collection of physical things cut out from an environing world of other physical things with which these physical things have actual or potential relations. Now at the same time it is just *those self-same things* which his mind, as we say, perceives; and the whole philosophy of perception from Democritus's time downwards has been just one long wrangle over the paradox that what is evidently one reality should be in two places at once, both in outer space and in a person's mind. "Representative" theories of perception avoid the logical paradox, but on the other hand they violate the reader's sense of life, which knows no intervening mental image but seems to see the room and the book immediately just as they physically exist.

The puzzle of how the one identical room can be in two places is at bottom just the puzzle of how one identical point can be on two lines. It can, if it be situated at their intersection; and similarly, if the "pure experience" of the room were a place of intersection of two processes, which connected it with different groups of associates respectively, it could be counted twice over, as belonging to either group, and spoken of loosely as existing in two places, although it would remain all the time a numerically single thing.

Well, the experience is a member of diverse processes that can be followed away from it along entirely different lines. The one self-identical thing has so many relations to the rest of experience that you can take it in disparate systems of association, and treat it as belonging with opposite contexts. In one of these contexts it is your "field of consciousness"; in another it is "the room in which you sit," and it enters both contexts in its wholeness, giving no pretext for being said to attach itself to consciousness by one of its parts or aspects, and to outer reality by another. What are the two processes, now, into which the room-experience simultaneously enters in this way?

One of them is the reader's personal biography, the other is the history of the house of which the room is part. The presentation, the experience, the *that* in short (for until we have decided *what* it is it must be a mere *that*) is the last term of a train of sensations, emotions, decisions, movements, classifications, expectations, etc., ending in the present, and the first term of a series of similar "inner" operations extending into the future, on the reader's part. On the other hand, the very same *that* is the *terminus ad quem* of a lot of previous physical operations, carpentering, papering, furnishing, warming, etc., and the *terminus a quo* of a lot of future ones, in which it will be concerned when undergoing the destiny of a physical room. The physical and the mental operations form curiously incompatible groups. As a room, the experience has occupied that spot and had that environment for thirty years. As your field of consciousness it may never have existed until now. As a room, attention will go on to discover endless new details in it. As your mental state merely, few new ones will emerge under attention's eye. As a room, it will take an earthquake, or a gang of men, and in any case a certain amount of time, to destroy it. As your subjective state, the closing of your eyes, or any instantaneous play of your fancy will suffice. In the real world, fire will consume it. In your mind, you can let fire play over it without effect. As an outer object, you must pay so much a month to inhabit it. As an inner content, you may occupy it for any length of time rent-free. If, in short, you follow it in the mental direction, taking it along with events of personal biography solely, all sorts of things are true of it which are false, and false of it which are true if you treat it as a real thing experienced, follow it in the physical direction, and relate it to associates in the outer world.

I think I may now claim to have made my thesis clear. Consciousness connotes a kind of external relation, and does not denote a special stuff or way of being. *The peculiarity of our experiences, that they not only are, but are known, which their "conscious" quality is invoked to explain, is better explained by their relations—these relations themselves being experiences—to one another.*

A WORLD OF PURE EXPERIENCE*

I. RADICAL EMPIRICISM

I give the name of 'radical empiricism' to my *Weltanschauung*. Empiricism is known as the opposite of rationalism. Rationalism tends to emphasize universals and to make wholes prior to parts in the order of logic as well as in that of being. Empiricism, on the contrary, lays the explanatory stress upon the part, the element, the individual, and treats the whole as a collection and the universal as an abstraction. My description of things, accordingly, starts with the parts and makes of the whole a being of the second order. It is essentially a mosaic philosophy, a philosophy of plural facts, like that of Hume and his descendants, who refer these facts neither to Substances in which they inhere nor to an Absolute Mind that creates them as its objects. But it differs from the Humian type of empiricism in one particular which makes me add the epithet radical.

To be radical, an empiricism must neither admit into its constructions any element that is not directly experienced, nor exclude from them any element that is directly experienced. For such a philosophy, *the relations that connect experiences must themselves be experienced relations, and any kind of relation experienced must be accounted as 'real' as anything else in the system.* Elements may indeed be redistributed, the original placing of things getting corrected, but a real place must be found for every kind of thing experienced, whether term or relation, in the final philosophic arrangement.

Now, ordinary empiricism, in spite of the fact that conjunctive and disjunctive relations present themselves as being fully co-ordinate parts of experience, has always shown a tendency to do away with the connections of things, and to insist most on the disjunctions. Berkeley's nominalism, Hume's statement that whatever things we distinguish are as 'loose and separate' as if they had 'no manner of connection,' James Mill's denial that similars have anything 'really' in common, the resolution of the causal tie into habitual sequence, John Mill's account of both physical things and selves as composed of discontinuous possibilities, and the general pulverization of all Experience by association and the mind-dust theory, are examples of what I mean.

The natural result of such a world-picture has been the efforts of rationalism to correct its incoherencies by the addition of trans-experiential agents of unification, substances, intellectual categories and powers, or Selves; whereas, if empiricism had only been radical and taken everything that comes without disfavor, conjunction as well as separation, each at

---

* William James, "A World of Pure Experience," *Journal of Philosophy, Psychology, and Scientific Methods* 1, no. 20 (29 September 1904); no. 21 (13 October 1904). Reprinted in James, *Radical Empiricism,* chap. 2.

its face value, the results would have called for no such artificial correction. *Radical empiricism,* as I understand it, *does full justice to conjunctive relations,* without, however, treating them as rationalism always tends to treat them, as being true in some supernal way, as if the unity of things and their variety belonged to different orders of truth and vitality altogether.

II. CONJUNCTIVE RELATIONS

Relations are of different degrees of intimacy. Merely to be 'with' one another in a universe of discourse is the most external relation that terms can have, and seems to involve nothing whatever as to farther consequences. Simultaneity and time-interval come next, and then space-adjacency and distance. After them, similarity and difference, carrying the possibility of many inferences. Then relations of activity, tying terms into series involving change, tendency, resistance, and the causal order generally. Finally, the relation experienced between terms that form states of mind, and are immediately conscious of continuing each other. The organization of the Self as a system of memories, purposes, strivings, fulfilments of disappointments, is incidental to this most intimate of all relations, the terms of which seem in many cases actually to compenetrate and suffuse each other's being.

Philosophy has always turned on grammatical particles. With, near, next, like, from, towards, against, because, for, through, my—these words designate types of conjunctive relation arranged in a roughly ascending order of intimacy and inclusiveness. *A priori,* we can imagine a universe of withness but no nextness; or one of nextness but no likeness, or of likeness with no activity, or of activity with no purpose, or of purpose with no ego. These would be universes, each with its own grade of unity. The universe of human experience is, by one or another of its parts, of each and all these grades. Whether or not it possibly enjoys some still more absolute grade of union does not appear upon the surface.

Taken as it does appear, our universe is to a large extent chaotic. No one single type of connection runs through all the experiences that compose it. If we take space-relations, they fail to connect minds into any regular system. Causes and purposes obtain only among special series of facts. The self-relation seems extremely limited and does not link two different selves together. *Prima facie,* if you should liken the universe of absolute idealism to an aquarium, a crystal globe in which goldfish are swimming, you would have to compare the empiricist universe to something more like one of those dried human heads with which the Dyaks of Borneo deck their lodges. The skull forms a solid nucleus; but innumerable feathers, leaves, strings, beads, and loose appendices of every description float and dangle from it, and, save that they terminate in it, seem to have nothing to do with one another. Even so my experiences and yours float and dangle, terminating, it is true, in a nucleus of common perception, but for the most part out of sight and irrelevant and unimaginable to one another. This imperfect intimacy, this bare relation of *withness* between some parts of the sum total of experience and other parts, is the fact that ordinary empiricism over-emphasizes against rationalism, the latter always tending to ignore it unduly. Radical empiricism, on the contrary, is fair to both the unity and the disconnection. It finds no reason for treating either as illusory. It allots to each its definite sphere of description, and agrees that there appear to be actual forces at work which tend, as time goes on, to make the unity greater.

The conjunctive relation that has given most trouble to philosophy is *the co-conscious transition,* so to call it, by which one experience passes into another when both belong to the same self. About the facts there is no question. My experiences and your experiences are 'with' each other in various external ways, but mine pass into mine, and yours pass into yours in a way in which yours and mine never pass into one another. Within each of our personal histories, subject, object, interest and purpose *are continuous or may be continuous.** Personal histories are processes of change in time, and *the change itself is one of the things immediately experienced.* 'Change' in this case means continuous as opposed to discontinuous transition. But continuous transition is one sort of a conjunctive relation; and to be a radical empiricist means to hold fast to this conjunctive relation of all others, for this is the strategic point, the position through which, if a hole be made, all the corruptions of dialectics and all the metaphysical fictions pour into our philosophy. The holding fast to this relation means taking it at its face value, neither less nor more; and to take it at its face value means first of all to take it just as we feel it, and not to confuse ourselves with abstract talk *about* it, involving words that drive us to invent secondary conceptions in order to neutralize their suggestions and to make our actual experience again seem rationally possible.

What I do feel simply when a later moment of my experience succeeds an earlier one is that though they are two moments, the transition from the one to the other is *continuous.* Continuity here is a definite sort of experience; just as definite as is the *discontinuity-experience* which I find it impossible to avoid when I seek to make the transition from an experience of my own to one of yours. In this latter case I have to get on and off again, to pass from a thing lived to another thing only conceived, and the break is positively experienced and noted. Though the functions exerted by my experience and by yours may be the same (*e.g.,* the same

---

* The psychology books have of late described the facts here with approximate adequacy. I may refer to the chapters on 'The Stream of Thought' and on the Self in my own *Principles of Psychology,* as well as to S. H. Hodgson's *Metaphysic of Experience,* vol. 1, ch. 7 and 8.

objects known and the same purposes followed), yet the sameness has in this case to be ascertained expressly (and often with difficulty and uncertainty) after the break has been felt; whereas in passing from one of my own moments to another the sameness of object and interest is unbroken, and both the earlier and the later experience are of things directly lived.

There is no other *nature,* no other whatness than this absence of break and this sense of continuity in that most intimate of all conjunctive relations, the passing of one experience into another when they belong to the same self.

A PLURALISTIC UNIVERSE*

In spite of rationalism's disdain for the particular, the personal, and the unwholesome, the drift of all the evidence we have seems to me to sweep us very strongly towards the belief in some form of superhuman life with which we may, unknown to ourselves, be co-conscious. We may be in the universe as dogs and cats are in our libraries, seeing the books and hearing the conversation, but having no inkling of the meaning of it all. The intellectualist objections to this fall away when the authority of intellectualist logic is undermined by criticism, and then the positive empirical evidence remains. . . .

. . . The outlines of the superhuman consciousness thus made probable must remain, however, very vague, and the number of functionally distinct 'selves' it comports and carries has to be left entirely problematic. It may be polytheistically or it may be monotheistically conceived of. Fechner, with his distinct earth-soul functioning as our guardian angel, seems to me clearly polytheistic; but the word 'polytheism' usually gives offence, so perhaps it is better not to use it. Only one thing is certain, and that is the result of our criticism of the absolute: the only way to escape from the paradoxes and perplexities that a consistently thought-out monistic universe suffers from as from a species of autointoxication— the mystery of the 'fall' namely, of reality lapsing into appearance, truth into error, perfection into imperfection; of evil, in short; the mystery of universal determinism, of the block-universe eternal and without a history, etc.;—the only way of escape, I say, from all this is to be frankly pluralistic and assume that the superhuman consciousness, however vast it may be, has itself an external environment, and consequently is finite. . . .

The line of least resistance, then, as it seems to me, both in theology and in philosophy, is to accept, along with the superhuman consciousness, the notion that it is not all-embracing, the notion, in other words, that

---

* William James, *A Pluralistic Universe* (New York: Longmans, Green, 1909), pp. 309–11, 319–24, 327–8. Lecture 8 from the Hibbert Lectures on the Current Situation in Philosophy, delivered at Manchester College, Oxford, 1909.

there is a God, but that he is finite, either in power or in knowledge, or in both at once. These, I need hardly tell you, are the terms in which common men have usually carried on their active commerce with God; and the monistic perfections that make the notion of him so paradoxical practically and morally are the colder addition of remote professional minds operating *in distans* upon conceptual substitutes for him alone. . . .

No matter what the content of the universe may be, if you only allow that it is *many* everywhere and always, that *nothing* real escapes from having an environment; so far from defeating rationality, as the absolutists so unanimously pretend, you leave it in possession of the maximum amount of rationality practically attainable by our minds. Your relations with it, intellectual, emotional, and active, remain fluent and congruous with your own nature's chief demands.

It would be a pity if the word 'rationality' were allowed to give us trouble here. It is one of those eulogistic words that both sides claim—for almost no one is willing to advertise his philosophy as a system of irrationality. But like most of the words which people used eulogistically, the word 'rational' carries too many meanings. The most objective one is that of the older logic—the connexion between two things is rational when you can infer one from the other, mortal from Socrates, *e.g.;* and you can do that only when they have a quality in common. But this kind of rationality is just that logic of identity which all disciples of Hegel find insufficient. They supersede it by the higher rationality of negation and contradiction and make the notion vague again. Then you get the aesthetic or teleologic kinds of rationality, saying that whatever fits in any way, whatever is beautiful or good, whatever is purposive or gratifies desire, is rational in so far forth. Then again, according to Hegel, whatever is 'real' is rational. I myself said awhile ago that whatever lets loose any action which we are fond of exerting seems rational. It would be better to give up the word 'rational' altogether than to get into a merely verbal fight about who has the best right to keep it.

Perhaps the words 'foreignness' and 'intimacy,' which I put forward in my first lecture, express the contrast I insist on better than the words 'rationality' and 'irrationality'—let us stick to them, then. I now say that the notion of the 'one' breeds foreignness and that of the 'many' intimacy, for reasons which I have urged at only too great length, and with which, whether they convince you or not, I may suppose that you are now well acquainted. But what at bottom is meant by calling the universe many or by calling it one?

Pragmatically interpreted, pluralism or the doctrine that it is many means only that the sundry parts of reality *may be externally related.* Everything you can think of, however vast or inclusive, has on the pluralistic view a genuinely 'external' environment of some sort or amount. Things are 'with' one another in many ways, but nothing includes everything, or dominates over everything. The word 'and' trails along after every sentence. Something always escapes. 'Ever not quite' has to be said of the best attempts made anywhere in the universe at attaining all-inclusiveness. The pluralistic world is thus more like a federal republic than like an empire or a kingdom. However much may be collected, however much may report itself as present at any effective centre of consciousness or action, something else is self-governed and absent and unreduced to unity.

Monism, on the other hand, insists that when you come down to reality as such, to the reality of realities, everything is present to *everything* else in one vast instantaneous co-implicated completeness—nothing can in *any* sense, functional or substantial, be really absent from anything else, all things interpenetate and telescope together in the great total conflux.

For pluralism, all that we are required to admit as the constitution of reality is what we ourselves find empirically realized in every minimum of finite life. Briefly it is this, that nothing real is absolutely simple, that every smallest bit of experience is a *multum in parvo* plurally related, that each relation is one aspect, character, or function, way of its being taken, or way of its taking something else; and that a bit of reality when actively engaged in one of these relations is not *by that very fact* engaged in all the other relations simultaneously. The relations are not *all* what the French call *solidaires* with one another. Without losing its identity a thing can either take up or drop another thing, like the log I spoke of, which by taking up new carriers and dropping old ones can travel anywhere with a light escort.

For monism, on the contrary, everything, whether we realize it or not, drags the whole universe along with itself and drops nothing. The log starts and arrives with all its carriers supporting it. If a thing were once disconnected, it could never be connected again, according to monism. The pragmatic difference between the two systems is thus a definite one. It is just thus, that if *a* is once out of sight of *b* or out of touch with it, or, more briefly, 'out' of it at all, then, according to monism, it must always remain so, they can never get together; whereas pluralism admits that on another occasion they may work together, or in some way be connected again. Monism allows for no such things as 'other occasions' in reality—in *real* or absolute reality, that is.

The difference I try to describe amounts, you see, to nothing more than the difference between what I formerly called the each-form and the all-form of reality. Pluralism lets things really exist in the each-form of distributively. Monism thinks that the all-form or collective-unit form is the only form that is rational. The all-form allows of no taking up and dropping of connexions, for in the all the parts are essentially and eternally co-implicated. In the each-form, on the contrary, a thing may be connected by intermediary things, with a thing with which it has no immediate or essential connexion. It is thus at all times in many possible connexions which are not necessarily actualized at the moment. They depend on which actual path of intermediation it may functionally strike into: the word 'or' names a genuine reality. Thus, as I speak here, I may look ahead *or* to the right *or* to the left, and in either case the intervening space and air and ether enable me to see the faces of a different portion of this audience. My being here is independent of any one set of these faces. . . .

One's general vision of the probable usually decides such alternatives. They illustrate what I once wrote of as the 'will to believe.' In some of my lectures at Harvard I have spoken of what I call the 'faith-ladder,' as something quite different from the *sorites* of the logic-books, yet seeming to have an analogous form. I think you will quickly recognize in yourselves, as I describe it, the mental process to which I give this name.

A conception of the world arises in you somehow, no matter how. Is it true or not? you ask.

It *might* be true somewhere, you say, for it is not self-contradictory.

It *may* be true, you continue, even here and now.

It is *fit* to be true, it would be *well if it were true,* it *ought* to be true, you presently feel.

It *must* be true, something persuasive in you whispers next; and then—as a final result—

It shall be *held for true,* you decide; it *shall be* as if true, for *you.*

And your acting thus may in certain special cases be a means of making it securely true in the end.

Not one step in this process is logical, yet it is the way in which monists and pluralists alike espouse and hold fast to their visions. It is life exceeding logic, it is the practical reason for which the theoretic reason finds arguments after the conclusion is once there. In just this way do some of us hold to the unfinished pluralistic universe; in just this way do others hold to the timeless universe eternally complete.

STUDY QUESTIONS

Review

1. What does James mean by the "sentiment of rationality" ? What is the difference between a "tough-minded" temperament and a "tender-minded" one?
2. In what different senses would James interpret the term "works" in the pragmatic maxim: "whatever works is true" ?
3. What are "genuine options" and how do they function as part of James theory of the "will" or "right" to believe?
4. What is meant by the term "radical" in James's "radical empiricism" ? How does his empiricism differ from traditional British empiricism?

For Further Thought

5. Do our desires and wishes ever determine what we believe? Can or would it be good to be able to transcend their influence so as to judge "objectively"?

6. Do any of the senses of "works" in James's pragmatic theory of truth seem to you more reasonable than the others? i.e., can his pragmatic theory of truth be saved?

7. What do you think of James's characterization of our immediate experience as a "booming-buzzing confusion"? Do you think that relations such as "next to," etc. are as real in our immediate experience as objects such as books?

8. Do you think that we can experience a "self" in our immediate experience? Or is it something that we reason to rather than experience? What kind of self is it?

BIBLIOGRAPHY

James, William. *The Works of William James.* Ed. Frederick Burkhardt. 7 vols. to date. Cambridge: Harvard University Press, 1975– .

— — —. *The Writings of William James.* Ed. John J. McDermott. Chicago: The University of Chicago Press, 1977.

— — —. *Selected Letters.* Ed. Elizabeth Hardwick. New York: Farrar, Straus, and Cudahy, 1961.

— — —. *Collected Essays and Reviews.* New York: Longmans, Green, 1920.

— — —. *The Letters of William James.* Ed. Henry James. 2 vols. New York: Longmans, Green, 1920.

— — —. *Essays in Radical Empiricism.* New York: Longmans, Green, 1912.

— — —. *Memories and Studies.* New York: Longmans, Green, 1911.

— — —. *Some Problems of Philosophy: A Beginning of an Introduction to Philosophy.* New York: Longmans, Green, 1911.

— — —. *The Meaning of Truth: A Sequel to "Pragmatism."* New York: Longmans, Green, 1909.

— — —. *A Pluralistic Universe.* New York: Longmans, Green, 1909.

— — —. *Pragmatism: A New Name for Some Old Ways of Thinking.* New York: Longmans, Green, 1907.

— — —. *The Varieties of Religious Experience: A Study in Human Nature.* New York: Longmans, Green, 1902.

— — —. *The Will to Believe and Other Essays in Popular Philosophy.* New York: Longmans, Green, 1896.

— — —. *The Principles of Psychology.* 2 vols. New York: Henry Holt, 1890.

Blanchard, Brand, and Herbert Schneider, eds. *In Commemoration of William James, 1842–1942.* New York: Columbia University Press, 1942.

Allen, Gay Wilson, ed. *A William James Reader.* Boston: Houghton Mifflin, 1971.

— — —. *William James: A Biography.* New York: Viking Press, 1967.

Blau, Joseph, ed. *Pragmatism and Other Essays.* New York: Washington Square Press, 1963.

Brennan, Bernard P. *The Ethics of William James.* New York: Bookman Associates, 1961.

Corti, Walter Robert, ed. *The Philosophy of William James.* Hamburg: Felix Meiner Verlag, 1976.

Dewey, John. "The Vanishing Subject in the Psychology of James." *Journal of Philosophy* 37 (1940): pp. 589–99.

Edie, James M. "William James and Phenomenology." *Review of Metaphysics* 23 (1970): pp. 481–526.

Flournoy, Theodore. *The Philosophy of William James.* Trans. E. B. Holt and Wm. James Jr. New York: Henry Holt, 1917.

Grattan, C. Hartley. *The Three Jameses: A Family of Minds, Henry James, Sr., William James, Henry James.* New York: Longmans, Green, 1932.

Kallen, Horace M. *William James and Henri Bergson.* Chicago: University of Chicago Press, 1914.

Levinson, H. S. *Science, Metaphysics, and the Chance of Salvation: An Interpretation of the Thought of William James.* Missoula, Mon.: Scholars Press, 1978.

McDermott, John J. Annotated bibliography. *The Writings of William James.* Chicago: University of Chicago Press, 1977.

Macleod, William J. "James' 'Will to Believe': Revisited." *Personalist* 38 (1967): pp. 149–66.

Madden, E. "Wright, James and Radical Empiricism." *Journal of Philosophy* 41 (1954): pp. 868–74.

Martland, T. R., Jr. *Metaphysics of William James and John Dewey.* New York: Philosophical Library, 1963.

Moore, E. C. *William James.* New York: Washington Square Press, 1965.

Morris, L. R. *William James: The Message of a Modern Mind.* New York: Charles Scribner's, 1950.

Perry, Ralph Barton. *In the Spirit of William James.* New Haven: Yale University Press, 1938.

— — —. *The Thought and Character of William James: Revealed in Unpublished Correspondence and Notes, Together with His Published Writings.* 2 vols. Boston: Little, Brown, 1935.

— — —. *Annotated Bibliography of the Writings of William James.* New York: Longmans, Green, 1920.

— — —. "The Philosophy of Henry James," Appendix in *Present Philosophical Tendencies.* New York: Longmans, Green, 1912.

Reck, Andrew J., ed. *Introduction to William James.* Bloomington: Indiana University Press, 1967.

Roth, John K. *Freedom and the Moral Life: The Ethics of William James.* Philadelphia: Westminster Press, 1969.

Royce, Josiah. *William James and Other Essays on the Philosophy of Life.* New York: Macmillan, 1911.

Sabin, Ethel E. *William James and Pragmatism.* Lancaster, Pa., 1916.

Santayana, George. Chap. 3 in *Character and Opinion in the United States, with Reminiscences of William James and Josiah Royce and Academic Life in America.* New York: Charles Scribner's, 1920.

Schiller, F. C. S. "William James and Empiricism." *Journal of Philosophy* 25 (1928): pp. 155–62.

— — —. "William James and the Making of Pragmatism." *Personalist* 8 (1927): pp. 81–93.

Seigfried, Charlene Haddock. *Chaos and Context: A Study of William James.* Athens: Ohio University Press, 1978.

Suckiel, Ellen K. *The Pragmatic Philosophy of William James.* Notre Dame, Ind.: University of Notre Dame Press, 1982.

Vanden Burgt, Robt. J. *The Religious Philosophy of William James.* Chicago: Nelson-Hall, 1981.

Wild, John. *The Radical Empiricism of William James.* New York: Doubleday, 1969.

Wilshire, Bruce. *William James and Phenomenology: A Study of the Principles of Psychology.* Bloomington: Indiana University Press, 1968.

— — —, ed. *William James: The Essential Writings.* New York: Harper Torchbooks, 1971.

Chapter 8

The Experimentalism
and Naturalism
of John Dewey

John Dewey was born in a rural town in Vermont in 1859. The date is symbolically significant for it was also the year of publication of Darwin's *Origin of Species*. As one interpreter of American philosophy has written of Dewey:

> The version of man as a changing and developing being in the midst of an environment which fosters and at the same time threatens his life was decisive for Dewey. Organism and environment, development and struggle, precariousness and stability — these are the basic ingredients of the cosmic mixture.[1]

Dewey attended the University of Vermont, a transcendentalist stronghold at the time, where not biological origins but transcendental beliefs in the primacy of spirit over matter would have been stressed. But Dewey refused to choose between matter and spirit. He believed that all such either-or dualisms are wrongheaded and set himself the task to show philosophically how they could be overcome.[2] After his graduation from the University of Vermont, Dewey spent a few years teaching high school, first in Oil City, Pennsylvania and then in Vermont. He once wrote in an autobiographical essay that persons and events influenced him more than books. The existential precariousness of life in the poor Pennsylvania mining town of Oil City might have been just such an influence.

During this time Dewey submitted some articles to the Hegelian-oriented *Speculative Journal of Philosophy* in St. Louis. He was encouraged by the editors, who advised him to do graduate work in philosophy. As a result Dewey attended Johns Hopkins University from 1882 to 1884. Although Peirce was teaching logic there at the time, Dewey was more impressed by the Hegelian speculations of George Morris, whose view of the whole universe as a developing organism impressed Dewey. Dewey, in turn, seems to have impressed Morris so that when Morris moved to the University of Michigan, he invited Dewey to follow him there, offering Dewey a position teaching philosophy. Dewey taught at Michigan from 1885 to 1894 except for one year (1888) spent at the University of Minnesota. It was at the University of Michigan that Dewey met and befriended George Herbert Mead. While there is insufficient space in a text of this kind for a detailed study of the philosophy of Mead, it is well to note briefly something of the unique character of his thought, if only because of his influence on Dewey.

Mead worked in those areas of philosophy that border on psychology and developed what has been called a "psychology of social behaviorism." [3] According to Mead, mind and self were developments within nature (something that Dewey also holds). In particular Mead sought to explain how human communication develops within this context. A self, he argued, can develop only in relation to other selves and in a social setting. The basic form of communication on which Mead based his theory of self-development was the gesture — language being but vocal gesture. A gesture communicates meanings and is not simply a means of self-expression. Mind and self develop when gestures can be internalized. Provided that an organism has the requisite biological equipment, it can participate in what Mead calls a social act, one in which the organism can use another's acts as guides to the completion of his own act. How a person reacts depends on what he sees another do. When the individual can interpret the meaning of his own gestures, then these gestures become significant. The individual must be able to call forth within himself the response that his gesture will produce in an other individual and to use this knowledge of how the other will respond to guide his own behavior. He must be able to take on the role of the other, a generalized other, and see himself, so to speak, from that perspective. Mead, like Peirce, never produced any complete works; thus it is difficult to piece together his philosophy from articles and transcriptions of student notes of his lectures. It is also difficult to say which way the line of influence between Dewey and Mead went, though probably it ran in both directions.

Both Dewey and Mead moved in 1894 to the newly opened University of Chicago — Dewey to chair the departments of philosophy, psychology, and education. It was at Chicago that Dewey developed his own philosophy and also continued his involvement with a variety of practical projects. While at

Michigan he had been actively involved in politics, and thus was no ivory-tower philosopher. In Chicago he was associated with the social work done at Jane Adams's Hull House and directed his own experimental elementary school, the Laboratory School. Here some of his particular theories about the nature and development of knowledge were put into practice.[4] Dewey sought to combine action or practice with theory, both in his philosophy and in his life. The title of his work, *Essays in Experimental Logic,* suggests that even logic must touch down in experience or experiment. If logic gives us rules for good thinking, we learn which kind of thinking works best from experience. In 1905 Dewey went to teach at Columbia University in New York where he remained teaching and writing until his retirement in 1930. During this time he traveled in Europe and the Orient and in 1918 lectured in China and Japan. (One of these series of lectures is published as *Reconstruction in Philosophy.*)[5] His other writings are too numerous to mention, covering as they did the fields of philosophy of art, religion, education, science, and politics, and numbering over eight hundred items. After his retirement from teaching he continued to write and lecture, leading an active life until his death in 1952 at the age of ninety-three.

One of the key terms in the philosophy of John Dewey is "experience," the term he used to denote all the active interchanges that go on within nature — interchanges that are chemical, biological, and human. Dewey was primarily interested in the human kind of experience. He defines man and his way of experiencing basically in biological terms, as an organism developing within an environment — nature — of which he is a part.

The various ways in which man interacts are simply different kinds of human experience. Basically the four modes of human experience are *instinctive, cognitive, emotive,* and *decisional.* Man, for Dewey, is neither primarily a soul nor matter but a creature of *habit and instinct.* At times, however, man's habitual ways of functioning are insufficient, he reaches an impasse and habit breaks down. He pauses in order to consider which way to turn. This is the root of the *cognitive* response. The cognitive response or interaction is called forth by a problematic situation. One is lost in the woods; there is a fork in the road. The process involved here is an organic one. Dewey, accordingly, objects to a mechanically conceived stimulus-response theory. According to Dewey the stimulus is a set of conditions to be met, a problem to be solved, and thus is already directed towards the response, which itself is a response to these conditions.[6] Since the problematic situation that provokes this response is an unresolved situation, like a state of doubt, Dewey defined thinking as "a response to the doubtful as such."[7] One resolved the doubt by a process of inquiry in which one formulated new ideas or new plans of action. One first located the nature of the problem; then formed ideas, hypotheses, or possible plans of action; and finally chose one plan to try out. If this plan did not work, one revised the old plan or tried a new one. This process is the heart of Dewey's form of pragmatism called instrumentalism. Mind or human intelligence develops from and is an instrument for problem solving.

Another side of Dewey's pragmatism and his discussion of cognitive experience begins with a criticism of what he calls the "spectator view of knowledge," which takes the object of knowledge to be unchanging Platonic ideas or ideals that must be sought through contemplation.[8] Dewey believed that this type of philosophy encouraged an inordinate quest for certainty and led to a denigration of action and a diminution of concern for the problems of this life. For Dewey the ideal of knowing is that method used by the experimental scientist. The scientist only achieves knowledge by means of action, by directing, questioning, and manipulating data. The process is piecemeal, its conclusions temporary, and its progress gradual. Inquiry and human knowledge are thus experimental as well as instrumental, Dewey contended.

Exclusive emphasis on this aspect of Dewey's thought has led some interpreters to suppose that he was concerned only with the active side of human life and experience. However, according to Dewey, cognitive experience is but one kind of experience. *Emotive or aesthetic experience* is also an important human response. Nor is it unusual or rare. Every experience in so far as it is final and complete is aesthetic. Dewey characterized this type of experience as immediate, individualized, and consummatory or final. It is immediate in that it rests on an enjoyment or appreciation of a present situation. One does not proceed to reflect on the situation as problematic (cognitive) or to change it (volitional), although these modes may precede or follow an aesthetic experience. Secondly, the experience is individualized in that it is concerned with elements of a particular discrete situation (object or event) rather than with some general or abstract aspect of it. Thus the poetic table is the unique table of perception with all its peculiar scratches and history, whereas the table of science is the table in so far as it is like other tables or objects of its type. Thirdly, aesthetic experience is consummatory or final. It is complete and valuable in itself and arouses no search for some other experience. Dewey's work *Art as Experience* contains his views on aesthetic experience as well as on other problems in aesthetics.[9]

For Dewey, *religious experience* is but an intense aesthetic experience. Dewey rejected the kind of religion based on a creed about some other world which, he thought, diverted men from a concern for the people and problems of this world.[10] Moreover, he "broadened" the concept of religion so that it included all of the forces that adjust men to life. By adjustment Dewey meant not simply accommodation (which was too passive an attitude) nor adaptation (which involved only partial self-involvement). Rather any cause that brings about an enduring modification of and harmonizes many aspects of one's self, he deemed religious. In particular, a religious attitude has three basic characteristics. The first is a sense of wholeness or continuity of the self with nature, a feeling that we are together in nature and sustained in our feebleness by a sense of this enveloping whole. Secondly, it must include a sense of the possibilities of existence or nature. Nature is an open and fertile source. Ideals should be realistic, not utopian. In other words, they should be grounded in the real possibilities present in nature. Faith in such ideals and devotion to their realization is religious when it is wholehearted, inclusive, and socially binding. Finally, while for Dewey religion is a wholly naturalistic enterprise, one may, if one realizes the correct meaning of the term, use the word "God" to stand for the active relationship between the ideals, their natural base, and humans who desire and seek to realize them. Dewey thought the term "God" appropriate because of his view that all notions of God somehow contain the union of ideal and actual. Traditional notions of God usually picture Him as already existent, whereas for Dewey, ideals, whether singly or in their conjunction, are to be made. While Dewey's description of the religious experience, an experience of oneness with a whole greater than oneself in which one is included, has much in common with traditions of mysticism in both East and West, and his notion of a god in process is not without precedent in contemporary philosophy of religion, his own naturalistic interpretation of God and religious belief is in many ways antagonistic to traditional religious beliefs and theories.

In addition to cognitive and aesthetic or religious experiences, Dewey held that there is a distinct kind of response, *decision-making,* in which we directly move to change the face of nature. Such an experience may occur at the conclusion of a cognitive, problem-solving experience, or an aesthetic experience, or may be governed by religious belief. Nevertheless in itself such an experience is distinct. Moral decisions were of particular interest to Dewey, and he wrote at various times on the nature and basis of morality.[11] His moral theory is consistent both with his beliefs on the nature of thinking and problem solving in general and his belief that man is one of the beings of nature. However, we reserve further discussion of these views for a later chapter on twentieth-century American moral philosophy.

While we have discussed John Dewey's philosophy in conjunction with the pragmatic movement in late-nineteenth-century America, Dewey lived long after the other founders of that movement died. (James died in 1910, Peirce in 1914, and Dewey in 1952.) Thus, while Dewey's pragmatism is best seen as related to and flowing out of that of Peirce and James, Dewey's philosophy also contains elements that move him beyond the nineteenth century. And one might ask whether pragmatism itself was simply a development of the nineteenth century, a development that did not live beyond that time. We shall postpone temporarily further reflection on this question. However, the idea that philosophical theories or concepts are motivated and evaluated by their utility in serving our various needs is not exclusively a nineteenth-century idea.

Notes

[1] Smith, *Spirit of American Philosophy,* p. 117.
[2] Some of the dualisms that Dewey sought to overcome in his philosophy are those of theory and practice, fact and value, mind and body, the stable and the contingent.

[3] For sources of Mead's works see the following collections and studies: *Mind, Self, and Society,* ed. C. W. Morris (Chicago: University of Chicago Press, 1934); *The Philosophy of the Act,* ed. C. W. Morris (Chicago: University of Chicago Press, 1938); David L. Miller, *George Herbert Mead* (Austin: University of Texas Press, 1973). The latter contains a very good bibliography of the works of Mead as well as a fine summary of his philosophy.

[4] The basic elements of Dewey's philosophy of education can be found in *The School and Society* (Chicago, 1900), *The Child and the Curriculum* (Chicago, 1902), and *Democracy and Education* (New York, 1916).

[5] John Dewey, *Reconstruction in Philosophy* (New York: Henry Holt, 1920; reprinted with new introduction, New York: Mentor Books, 1950).

[6] John Dewey, "The Reflex Arc Concept in Psychology," *The Psychological Review* 3 (1896): pp. 357–70. Reprinted with some revisions as "The Unit of Behavior," in *Philosophy and Civilization* (New York: Minton, Balch and Co., 1934), pp. 233–48.

[7] John Dewey, *The Quest for Certainty: A Study of the Relation of Knowledge and Action* (1929; reprint, New York: Capricorn Books, 1960).

[8] Ibid., chaps. 1 and 2.

[9] John Dewey, *Art as Experience* (1934; reprint, New York: Capricorn Books, 1958.

[10] John Dewey, *A Common Faith* (New Haven: Yale University Press, 1934; paperback edition, 1967).

[11] Some of the works of Dewey that contain the essentials of his moral philosophy are *Reconstruction in Philosophy, Ethics* (with J. H. Tufts), *Human Nature and Conduct, Authority and the Individual,* and *Theory of Valuation.* See the bibliography for complete references.

JOHN DEWEY

THE QUEST FOR CERTAINTY*

CHAPTER 1. ESCAPE FROM PERIL

Man who lives in a world of hazards is compelled to seek for security. He has sought to attain it in two ways. One of them began with an attempt to propitiate the powers which environ him and determine his destiny. It expressed itself in supplication, sacrifice, ceremonial rite and magical cult. In time these crude methods were largely displaced. The sacrifice of a contrite heart was esteemed more pleasing than that of bulls and oxen; the inner attitude of reverence and devotion more desirable than external ceremonies. If man could not conquer destiny he could willingly ally himself with it; putting his will, even in sore affliction, on the side of the powers which dispense fortune, he could escape defeat and might triumph in the midst of destruction.

The other course is to invent arts and by their means turn the powers of nature to account; man constructs a fortress out of the very conditions and forces which threaten him. He builds shelters, weaves garments, makes flame his friend instead of his enemy, and grows into the complicated arts of associated living. This is the method of changing the world

* John Dewey, *The Quest for Certainty* (New York: Minton, Balch, 1929; N.Y.: G. P. Putnam's Sons, 1960), pp. 3–8, 81–87, 98–100, 223–31, 234–35. Reprinted by permission of G. P. Putnam's Sons. Copyright 1929 by John Dewey; copyright renewed 1957.

through action, as the other is the method of changing the self in emotion and idea. It is a commentary on the slight control man has obtained over himself by means of control over nature, that the method of action has been felt to manifest dangerous pride, even defiance of the powers which be.

The depreciation of action, of doing and making, has been cultivated by philosophers. But while philosophers have perpetuated the derogation by formulating and justifying it, they did not originate it. They glorified their own office without doubt in placing theory so much above practice. But independently of their attitude, many things conspired to the same effect. Work has been onerous, toilsome, associated with a primeval curse. It has been done under compulsion and the pressure of necessity, while intellectual activity is associated with leisure. On account of the unpleasantness of practical activity, as much of it as possible has been put upon slaves and serfs. Thus the social dishonor in which this class was held was extended to the work they do. There is also the age-long association of knowing and thinking with immaterial and spiritual principles, and of the arts, of all practical activity in doing and making, with matter. For work is done with the body, by means of mechanical appliances and is directed upon material things. The disrepute which has attended the thought of material things in comparison with immaterial thought has been transferred to everything associated with practice.

One might continue in this strain. The natural history of conceptions about work and the arts if it were traced through a succession of peoples and cultures would be instructive. But all that is needed for our purpose is to raise the question: Why this invidious discrimination? A very little reflection shows that the suggestions which have been offered by way of explanation themselves need to be explained. Ideas derived from social castes and emotional revulsions are hardly reasons to be offered in justification of a belief, although they may have a bearing on its causation. Contempt for matter and bodies and glorification of the immaterial are affairs which are not self-explanatory. And, as we shall be at some pains to show later in the discussion, the idea which connects thinking and knowing with some principle or force that is wholly separate from connection with physical things will not stand examination, especially since the whole-hearted adoption of experimental method in the natural sciences.

Practical activity deals with individualized and unique situations which are never exactly duplicable and about which, accordingly, no complete assurance is possible. All activity, moreover, involves change. The intellect, however, according to the traditional doctrine, may grasp universal Being, and Being which is universal is fixed and immutable. Wherever there is practical activity we human beings are involved as partakers in the issue. All the fear, disesteem and lack of confidence which gather about the thought of ourselves, cluster also about the thought of the actions in which we are partners. Man's distrust of himself has caused him to desire to get beyond and above himself; in pure knowledge he has thought he could attain this self-transcendence.

There is no need to expatiate upon the risk which attends overt action. The burden of proverbs and wise saws is that the best laid plans of men as of mice gang agley. Fortune rather than our own intent and act determines eventual success and failure. The pathos of unfulfilled expectation, the tragedy of defeated purpose and ideals, the catastrophes of accident, are the commonplaces of all comment on the human scene. We survey conditions, make the wisest choice we can; we act, and we must trust the rest to fate, fortune or providence. Moralists tell us to look to the end when we act and then inform us that the end is always uncertain. Judging, planning, choice, no matter how thoroughly conducted, and action no matter how prudently executed, never are the sole determinants of any outcome. Alien and indifferent natural forces, unforeseeable conditions enter in and have a decisive voice. The more important the issue, the greater is their say as to the ulterior event.

. . . The quest for certainty is a quest for a peace which is assured, an object which is unqualified by risk and the shadow of fear which action casts. For it is not uncertainty *per se* which men dislike, but the fact that uncertainty involves us in peril of evils. Uncertainty that affected only the detail of consequences to be experienced provided they had a warrant of being enjoyable would have no sting. It would bring the zest of adventure and the spice of variety. Quest for complete certainty can be fulfilled in pure knowing alone. Such is the verdict of our most enduring philosophic tradition.

CHAPTER 4. ARTS OF ACCEPTANCE AND CONTROL

Before engaging in consideration of the significance of the method of science for formation of the theory of knowledge and of mind, we shall take up some general points. These are all connected, at bottom, with the contrast between the idea of experience framed when arts mainly routine, skills acquired by *mere* exercise and practice, and the idea of experience appropriate when arts have become experimental: or, put briefly, between experience as *empirical* and as *experimental.* "Experience" once meant the results accumulated in memory of a variety of past doings and undergoings that were had without control by insight, when the net accumulation was found to be practically available in dealing with present situations. Both the original perceptions and uses and the application of their outcome in present doings were accidental—that is, neither was determined by an understanding of the relations of cause and effect, of means and consequences, involved. In that sense they were non-rational, non-scientific. A typical illustration is a bridge builder who constructs simply on the basis of what has been done and what happened in the past, without reference to knowledge of strains and stresses, or in general of physical relationships actually involved; or the art of medicine, as far as it rests simply upon the accidents of remedial measures used in the past without knowledge of *why* some worked and others did not. A measure of skill results, but it is the fruit of cut and dried methods, of trial and error—in short it is "empirical."

The disparaging notion of experience framed under such conditions is an honest report of actual conditions; philosophers in setting experience down as inherently inferior to rational science were truthful. What they added was another matter. It was a statement that this inferiority was inherently connected with the body, with the senses, with material things, with the uncertainly changing as over against the certain because immutable. Unfortunately their theories in explanation of the defects of experience persisted and became classic after experience itself, in some of its forms, had become experimental in the sense of being directed by understanding of conditions and their consequences. Two points are especially significant with reference to the split thus produced between the traditional theory of experience and that which results from noting its experimental character.

In the traditional theory, which still is the prevailing one, there were alleged to exist inherent defects in perception and observation as means of knowledge, in reference to the subject-matter they furnish. This material, in the older notion, is inherently so particular, so contingent and variable, that by no possible means can it contribute to *knowledge;* it can result only in opinion, mere belief. But in modern science, there are only *practical* defects in the senses, certain limitations of vision, for example, that have to be corrected and supplemented by various devices, such as the use of the lens. Every insufficiency of observation is an instigation to invent some new instrument which will make good the defect, or it is a stimulus to devising indirect means, such as mathematical calculations, by which the limitations of sense will be circumvented. The counterpart of this change is one in the conception of thought and its relation to knowing. It was earlier assumed that higher knowledge must be supplied by pure thought; pure because apart from experience, since the latter involves the senses. Now it is taken for granted that thought, while indispensable to knowledge of natural existence, can never in itself provide that knowledge. Observation is indispensable both to provide authentic materials to work upon and to test and verify the conclusions reached by theoretical considerations. A specified kind of experience is indispensable to science instead of all experience setting a limit to the possibility of true science.

There is an objective counterpart of this shift. In the older theory, sense and experience were barriers to true science because they are implicated in natural change. Their appropriate and inevitable subject-matter was variable and changing things. Knowledge in its full and valid sense is possible only of the immutable, the fixed; that alone answers the quest for certainty. With regard to changing things, only surmise and opinion are possible, just as practically these are the source of peril. To a scientific man, in terms of what he does in inquiry, the notion of a natural science which should turn its back upon the changes of things, upon events, is simply incomprehensible. What he is interested in knowing, in understanding, are precisely the changes that go on; they set his problems, and problems are solved when changes are interconnected with one another. Constants and relative invariants figure, but they are relations between changes, not the constituents of a higher realm of Being. With this modification with respect to the object comes one in the structure and content of "experience." Instead of there being a fixed difference between it and something higher—rational thought—there is a difference between two kinds of experience; one which is occupied with uncontrolled change and one concerned with directed and regulated change. And this difference, while fundamentally important, does not mark a fixed division. Changes of the first type are something *to be brought under control* by means of action directed by understanding of relationships.

In the old scheme, knowledge, as science, signified precisely and exclusively turning away from change to the changeless. In the new experimental science, knowledge is obtained in exactly the opposite way, namely, through deliberate institution of a definite and specified course of change. The method of physical inquiry is to introduce some change in order to see what other change ensues; the correlation between these changes, when measured by a series of operations, constitutes the definite and desired object of knowledge. There are two degrees of control of change which differ practically but are alike in principle. In astronomy, for example, we cannot introduce variation into remote heavenly bodies. But we can deliberately alter the conditions under which we observe them, which is the same thing in principle of logical procedure. By special instruments, the use of lens and prism, by telescopes, spectroscopes, interferometers, etc., we modify observed data. Observations are taken fron widely different points in space and at successive times. By such means interconnected variations are observed. In physical and chemical matters closer at hand and capable of more direct manipulation, changes introduced affect the things under inquiry. Appliances and re-agents for bringing about variations in the things studied are employed. The progress of inquiry is identical with advance in the invention and construction of physical instrumentalities for producing, registering and measuring changes.

Moreover, there is no difference in logical principle between the method of science and the method pursued in technologies. The difference is practical; in the scale of operations conducted; in the lesser degree of control through isolation of conditions operative, and especially in the purpose for the sake of which regulated control of modifications of natural existences and energies is undertaken; especially, since the dominant motive of large scale regulation of the course of change is material comfort or pecuniary gain. But the technique of modern industry, in commerce, communication, transportation and all the appliances of light, heat and electricity, is the fruit of the modern application of science. And this so-called "application" signifies that the same kind of intentional introduction and management of changes which takes place in the laboratory is induced in the factory, the railway and the power house.

The central and outstanding fact is that the change in the method of knowing, due to the scientific revolution begun in the sixteenth and seventeenth centuries, has been accompanied by a revolution in the attitude of man toward natural occurrences and their interactions. This transformation means, as was intimated earlier, complete reversal in the traditional relationship of knowledge and action. Science advances by adopting the instruments and doings of directed practice, and the knowledge thus gained becomes a means of the development of arts which bring nature still further into actual and potential service of human purposes and valuations. The astonishing thing is that in the face of this change wrought in civilization, there still persist the notions about mind and its organs of knowing, together with the inferiority of practice to intellect, which developed in antiquity as the report of a totally different situation.

While the traits of experimental inquiry are familiar, so little use has been of them in formulating a theory of knowledge and of mind in relation to nature that a somewhat explicit statement of well known facts is excusable. They exhibit true outstanding characteristics. The first is the obvious one that all experimentation involves *overt* doing, the making of definite changes in the environment or in our relation to it. The second is that experiment is not a random activity but is directed by ideas which have to meet the conditions set by the need of the problem inducing the active inquiry. The third and concluding feature, in which the other two receive their full measure of meaning, is that the outcome of the directed activity is the construction of a new empirical situation in which objects are differently related to one another, and such that the *consequences* of directed operations form the objects that have the property of being *known*.

. . . Just what did the new experimental method do to the qualitative objects of ordinary experience? Forget the conclusions of Greek philosophy, put out of the mind all theories about knowledge and about reality. Take the simple direct facts: Here are the colored, resounding, fragrant, lovable, attractive, beautiful things of nature which we enjoy, and which we suffer when they are hateful, ugly, disgusting. Just what is the effect upon them wrought by physical science?

If we consent for the time being to denude the mind of philosophical and metaphysical presuppositions, and take the matter in the most simple and naïve way possible, I think our answer, stated in technical terms, will be that it *substitutes data for objects.* (It is not meant that the outcome is the whole effect of the experimental method; that as we saw at the outset is complex; but that the first effect as far as stripping away qualities is concerned is of this nature.) That Greek science operated with *objects* in the sense of the stars, rocks, trees, rain, warm and cold days of ordinary experience is evident enough. What is signified by saying that the first effect of experimentation was to reduce these things from the status of objects to that of data may not be so clear.* By data is signified subject-matter for *further* interpretation; something to be thought about. *Objects* are finalities; they are complete, finished; they call for thought only in the way of definition, classification, logical arrangement, subsumption in syllogisms, etc. But data signify "material to serve"; they are indications, evidence, signs, clues to and of something still to be reached; they are intermediate, not ultimate; means, not finalities.

In a less technical way the matter may be stated as follows: The subject-matter which had been taken as satisfying the demands of knowledge, as the material with which to frame solutions, became something which set *problems.* Hot and cold, wet and dry, light and heavy, instead of being self-evident matters with which to explain phenomena, were things to be investigated; they were "effects," not causal principles; they set question marks instead of supplying answers. The differences between the earth, the region of the planets, and the heavenly ether, instead of supplying ultimate principles which could be used to mark off and classify things, were something to be explained and to bring under identical principles. Greek and medieval science formed an art of accepting things as they are enjoyed and suffered. Modern experimental science is an art of control.

The remarkable difference between the attitude which accepts the objects of ordinary perception, use and enjoyment as final, as culminations of natural processes and that which takes them as starting points for reflection and investigation, is one which reaches far beyond the technicalities of science. It marks a revolution in the whole spirit of life, in the entire attitude taken toward whatever is found in existence. When the things which exist around us, which we touch, see, hear and taste are regarded as interrogations for which an answer must be sought (and must be sought by means of deliberate introduction of changes till they are reshaped into something different), nature as it already exists ceases to be something which must be accepted and submitted to, endured or enjoyed, just as it is. It is now something to be modified, to be intentionally controlled. It is material to act upon so as to transform it into new objects which better answer our needs. Nature as it exists at any particular time

---

* For this shift from objects to data see G. H. Mead's essay in the volume entitled *Creative Intelligence,* New York, 1917.

is a challenge, rather than a completion; it provides possible starting points and opportunities rather than final ends.

In short, there is a change from knowing as an esthetic enjoyment of the properties of nature regarded as a work of divine art, to knowing as a means of secular control—that is, a method of purposefully introducing changes which will alter the direction of the course of events.

CHAPTER 9. THE SUPREMACY OF METHOD

Uncertainty is primarily a practical matter. It signifies uncertainty of the *issue* of present experiences; these are fraught with future peril as well as inherently objectionable. Action to get rid of the objectionable has no warrant of success and is itself perilous. The intrinsic troublesome and uncertain quality of situations lies in the fact that they hold outcomes in suspense; they move to evil or to good fortune. The natural tendency of man is to do something at once; there is impatience with suspense, and lust for immediate action. When action lacks means of control of external conditions, it takes the form of acts which are the prototypes of rite and cult. Intelligence signifies that direct action has become indirect. It continues to be overt, but it is directed into channels of examination of conditions, and doings that are tentative and preparatory. Instead of rushing to "do something about it," action centers upon finding out something about obstacles and resources and upon projecting inchoate later modes of definite response. Thinking has been well called deferred action. But not all action is deferred; only that which is final and in so far productive of irretrievable consequences. Deferred action is present exploratory action.

The first and most obvious effect of this change is the quality of action is that the dubious or problematic situation becomes *a* problem. The risky character that pervades a situation as a whole is translated into an object of inquiry that locates what the trouble is, and hence facilitates projection of methods and means of dealing with it. Only after expertness has been gained in special fields of inquiry does the mind set out at once from problems: even then in novel cases, there is a preliminary period of groping through a situation which is characterized throughout by confusion, instead of presenting a clear-cut problem for investigation.

Many definitions of mind and thinking have been given. I know of but one that goes to the heart of the matter: response to the doubtful as such. No inanimate thing reacts to things *as* problematic. Its behavior to other things is capable of description in terms of what is determinately there. Under given conditions, it just reacts or does not react. Its reactions merely enstate a new set of conditions, in which reactions continue without regard to the nature of their outcome. It makes no difference, so to say, to a stone what are the results of its interactions with other things. It enjoys the advantage that it makes no difference how it reacts, even if

the effect is its own pulverization. It requires no argument to show that
the case is different with a living organism. To live signifies that a
connected continuity of acts is effected in which preceding ones prepare
the conditions under which later ones occur. There is a chain of cause
and effects, of course, in what happens with inanimate things. But for
living creatures, the chain has a particular cumulative continuity, or else
death ensues.

As organisms become more complex in structure and thus related to
a more complex environment, the importance of a particular act in
establishing conditions favorable to subsequent acts that sustain the continuity of the life process, becomes at once more difficult and more
imperative. A juncture may be so critical that the right or wrong present
move signifies life or death. Conditions of the environment become more
ambivalent: it is more uncertain what sort of action they call for in the
interests of living. Behavior is thus compelled to become more hesitant
and wary, more expectant and preparatory. In the degree that responses
take place to the doubtful *as* the doubtful, they acquire *mental* quality.
If they are such as to have a directed tendency to change to precarious
and problematic into the secure and resolved, they are *intellectual* as well
as mental. Acts are then relatively more instrumental and less consummatory or final; even the latter are haunted by a sense of what may issue
from them.

This conception of the mental brings to unity various modes of
response; emotional, volitional and intellectual. It is usual to say that
there is no fundamental difference among these activities—that they are
all different phases or aspects of a common action of mind. But I know
of but one way of making this assertion good: that in which they are
seen to be distinctive modes of response to the uncertain. The emotional
aspect of responsive behavior is its *immediate* quality. When we are
confronted with the precarious, an ebb and flow of emotion marks a
disturbance of the even tenor of existence. Emotions are conditioned by
the indeterminateness of present situations with respect to their issue.
Fear and hope, joy and sorrow, aversion and desire, as perturbations, are
qualities of a divided response. They involve concern, solicitude, for what
the present situation may *become*. "Care" signifies two quite different
things: fret, worry and anxiety, and cherishing attention to that in whose
potentialities we are interested. These two meanings represent different
poles of reactive behavior to a present having a future which is ambiguous.
Elation and depression, moreover, manifest themselves only under conditions wherein not everything from start to finish is completely determined and certain. They may occur at a final moment of triumph or
defeat, but this moment is one of victory or frustration in connection
with a previous course of affairs whose issue was in suspense. Love for
a Being so perfect and complete that our regard for it can make no
difference to it is not so much affection as (a fact which the scholastics

saw) it is concern for the destiny of our own souls. Hate that is sheer antagonism without any element of uncertainty is not an emotion, but is an energy devoted to ruthless destruction. Aversion is a state of affectivity only in connection with an obstruction offered by the disliked object or person to an end made uncertain by it.

The volitional phase of mental life is notoriously connected with the emotional. The only difference is that the latter, is the immediate, the cross-sectional, aspect of response to the uncertain and precarious, while the volitional phase is the tendency of the reaction to modify indeterminate, ambiguous conditions in the direction of a preferred and favored outcome; to actualize one of its possibilities rather than another. Emotion is a hindrance or an aid to resolute will according as it is overwhelming in its immediacy or as it marks a gathering together of energy to deal with the situation whose issue is in doubt. Desire, purpose, planning, choice, have no meaning save in conditions where something is at stake, and where action in one direction rather than another may eventuate in bringing into existence a new situation which fulfills a need.

The intellectual phase of mental action is identical with an *indirect* mode of response, one whose purpose is to locate the nature of the trouble and form an idea of how it may be dealt with—so that operations may be directed in view of an intended solution. Take any incident of experience you choose, seeing a color, reading a book, listening to conversation, manipulating apparatus, studying a lesson, and it has or has not intellectual, cognitive, quality according as there is deliberate endeavor to deal with the indeterminate so as to dispose of it, to settle it. Anything that may be called knowledge, or a known object, marks a question answered, a difficulty disposed of, a confusion cleared up, an inconsistency reduced to coherence, a perplexity mastered. Without reference to this mediating element, what is called knowledge is but direct and unswerving action or else a possessive enjoyment. Similarly, thinking is the actual transition from the problematic to the secure, as far as that is intentionally guided. There is no separate "mind" gifted in and of itself with a faculty of thought; such a conception of thought ends in postulating the mystery of a power outside of nature and yet able to intervene within it. Thinking is objectively discoverable as that mode of serial responsive behavior to a problematic situation in which transition to the relatively settled and clear is effected.

The concrete pathologies of belief, its failures and perversions, whether of defect or excess, spring from failure to observe and adhere to the principle that knowledge is the completed resolution of the inherently indeterminate or doubtful. The commonest fallacy is to suppose that since the state of doubt is accompanied by a feeling of uncertainty, knowledge arises when this feeling gives way to one of assurance. Thinking then ceases to be an effort to effect change in the objective situation and is replaced by various devices which generate a change in feeling or "consciousness." Tendency to premature judgment, jumping at conclusions, excessive love of simplicity, making over of evidence to suit desire, taking the familiar for the clear, etc., all spring from confusing the feeling of certitude with a certified situation. Thought hastens toward the settled and is only too likely to force the pace. The natural man dislikes the disease which accompanies the doubtful and is ready to take almost any means to end it. Uncertainty is got rid of by fair means or foul. Long exposure to danger breeds an overpowering love of security. Love for security, translated into a desire not to be disturbed and unsettled, leads to dogmatism, to acceptance of beliefs upon authority, to intolerance and fanaticism on one side and to irresponsible dependence and sloth on the other.

Here is where ordinary thinking and thinking that is scrupulous diverge from each other. The natural man is impatient with doubt and suspense; he impatiently hurries to be shut of it. A disciplined mind takes delight in the problematic, and cherishes it until a way out is found that approves itself upon examination. The questionable becomes an active questioning, a search; desire for the emotion of certitude gives place to quest for the objects by which the obscure and unsettled may be developed into the stable and clear. The scientific attitude may almost be defined as that which is capable of enjoying the doubtful; scientific method is, in one aspect, a technique for making a productive use of doubt by converting it into operations of definite inquiry. No one gets far intellectually who does not "love to think," and no one loves to think who does not have an interest in problems as such. Being on the alert for problems signifies that mere organic curiosity, the restless disposition to meddle and reach out, has become a truly intellectual curiosity, one that protects a person from hurrying to a conclusion and that induces him to undertake active search for new facts and ideas. Skepticism that is not such a search is as much a personal emotional indulgence as is dogmatism. Attainment of the relatively secure and settled takes place, however, only with respect to *specified* problematic situations; quest for certainty that is universal, applying to everything, is a compensatory perversion. One question is disposed of; another offers itself and thought is kept alive.

When we compare the theory of mind and its organs which develops from analysis of what takes place when precarious situations are translated into statement and resolution of problems, with other theories, the outstanding difference is that the first type of theory introduces no elements save such as are public, observable, and verifiable. In general, when there is discourse about the mental organs and processes of knowing we are told about sensations, mental images, consciousness and its various states, as if these were capable of identification in and of themselves. These mental organs having had meaning assigned to them in isolation from the operations of resolving a problematic situation, are then used to give an account of the actual operations of knowing. The more evident and observable is thus "explained" in terms of the obscure, the obscurity being hidden from view because of habits that have the weight of tradition behind them.

We do not need to repeat the results of the previous discussion. They are all connected with the theory that inquiry is a set of operations in which problematic situations are disposed of or settled. Theories which have been criticized all rest upon a different supposition; namely, that the properties of the states and acts of mind involved in knowing are capable of isolated determination—of description apart from overt acts that resolve indeterminate and ambiguous situations. The fundamental advantage of framing our account of the organs and processes of knowing on the pattern of what occurs in experimental inquiry is that nothing is introduced save what is objective and is accessible to examination and report. If it is objected that such an examination itself involves mind and its organs, the rejoinder is that the theory we have advanced is self-applying. Its only "assumption" is that something is done, done in the ordinary external sense of that word, and that this doing has consequences. We define mind and its organs in terms of this doing and its results, just as we define or frame ideas of stars, acids, and digestive tissues in terms of *their* behavior. If it be urged that we do not know whether the results of the directed operations are really knowledge or not, the answer is the objection assumes that we have some kind of advance intimation of what sort of a thing knowledge must be, and hence can use this conception as a standard for judging particular conclusions. The theory in question makes no such assumption. It asserts that by some operations conclusions emerge in which objects once uncertain and confused are rendered clear and stable. Alter names as much as you please; refuse to call one set of consequences knowledge and another error, or reverse the appellations, and these consequences remain just what they are. They present the difference between resolved and clarified situations and disordered and obscure ones. A rose by another name would smell as sweet; the gist of the theory advanced is to point to operations performed and to the consequences which issue from them.

Another point of difference is that traditional theories of mind and its organs of knowledge isolate them from continuity with the natural world. They are, in the literal sense of the word, super-natural or extra-natural. The problem of mind and body, of how it happens that bodily structures are involved in observing and thinking, is then unavoidable. When little was known about organic structures, one reason for looking down upon perception was that its connection with bodily organs, the eye and ear and hand, could not escape notice, while thought could be regarded as a purely spiritual act. But now we are aware that the exercise of thought bears the same relation to the brain that perception bears to sense organs, and that there is no separation, structural or functional, between the eye and ear and the central organs. Consequently it is impossible to think of sense as quasi-physical and thought as purely mental, as if the mental meant just the non-material. Yet we retain theories about the mental formed before we had this knowledge. Consequently, since those theories isolate knowing from doing, the dependence of knowing upon bodily organs becomes a mystery—a "problem."

But if knowing is one mode of doing, then it, as well as other modes of doing, properly involves bodily instruments. The metaphysical problem of the relation of mind and body is converted into a question, to be solved by observation of facts, of a differentiation of actions into those on a strictly physiological level, and those which, because of directed quality and distinctive consequences, are mental.

While traditional theories regard mind as an intruder from without into the natural development, or evolution, of organic structures, or else in the interest of natural continuity feel compelled to deny that mental behavior has any differential features, the theory that organic responses have mental quality in the degree in which they deal with the uncertain recognizes both continuity and difference. It can, in principle if not as yet in detail, give a genetic account of the development of mental and intellectual processes. There is neither a sudden jump from the merely organic to the intellectual, nor is there complete assimilation of the latter to primitive modes of the former.

The organism is a part of the natural world; its interactions with it are genuine additive phenomena. When, with the development of symbols, also a natural occurrence, these interactions are directed towards anticipated consequences, they gain the quality of intelligence, and knowledge accrues. Problematic situations when they are resolved then gain the meaning of all the relations which the operations of thought have defined. Things that were causally effective in producing experienced results became means to consequences; these consequences incorporate in themselves all the meanings found in the causes which *intentionally* produce them. The supposed grounds for opposing human experience to the reality of nature disappear. Situations have problematic and resolved characters in and through the actual interactions of the organism and the environment. To refuse to treat these qualities as characteristic of nature itself is due to an arbitrary refusal to ascribe to some modes of interaction the existential character which is assigned as a matter of course to others.

We have seen that situations are precarious and perilous because the persistence of life-activity depends upon the influence which present acts have upon future acts. The continuity of a life-process is secured only as acts performed render the environment favorable to subsequent organic acts. The formal generalized statement of this fact is as follows: The occurrence of problematic and unsettled situations is due to the *characteristic union of the discrete or individual and the continuous or relational.* All perceived objects are individualized. They are, as such, wholes complete in themselves. Everything directly experienced is qualitatively unique; it has its own focus about which subject-matter is arranged, and this focus never exactly recurs. While every such situation shades off indefinitely, or is not sharply marked off from others, yet the pattern of arrangement of content is never exactly twice alike.

If the interactions involved in having such an individualized situation in experience were wholly final or consummatory, there would be no such thing as a situation which is problematic. In being individual and complete in itself, just what it is and nothing else, it would be discrete in the sense in which discreteness signifies complete isolation. Obscurity, for example, would be a final quality, like any other quality and as good as any other— just as the dusk of twlight is enjoyed instead of being troublesome until we need to see something the dusk interferes with seeing. Every situation has vagueness attending it, as it shades off from a sharper focus into what is indefinite; for vagueness is added quality and not something objectionable except as it obstructs gaining an eventual object.

There are situations in which self-enclosed, discrete, individualized characters dominate. They constitute the subject-matter of esthetic experience; and every experience is esthetic in as far as it is final or arouses no search for some other experience. When this complete quality is conspicuous the experience is denominated esthetic. The fine arts have as their purpose the construction of objects of just such experiences; and under some conditions the completeness of the object enjoyed gives the experience a quality so intense that it is justly termed religious. Peace and harmony suffuse the entire universe gathered up into the situation having a particular focus and pattern. These qualities mark any experience in as far as its final character dominates; in so far a mystic experience is simply an accentuated intensification of a quality of experience repeatedly had in the rhythm of experiences.

RECONSTRUCTION IN MORAL CONCEPTIONS*

The impact of the alteration in methods of scientific thinking upon moral ideas is, in general, obvious. Goods, ends are multiplied. Rules are softened into principles, and principles are modified into methods of understanding. Ethical theory began among the Greeks as an attempt to find a regulation for the conduct of life which should have a rational basis and purpose instead of being derived from custom. But reason as a substitute for custom was under the obligation of supplying objects and laws as fixed as those of custom had been. Ethical theory ever since has been singularly hypnotized by the notion that its business is to discover some final end

---

* John Dewey, "Reconstruction in Moral Conceptions," chap. 7 in *Reconstruction in Philosophy* (New York: Henry Holt, 1920; Boston: Beacon Press, 1948), pp. 161–63, 174–75. Reprinted by permission of Beacon Press. Copyright © 1948 by Beacon Press.

or good or some ultimate and supreme law. This is the common element among the diversity of theories. Some have held that the end is loyalty or obedience to a higher power or authority; and they have variously found this higher principle in Divine Will, the will of the secular ruler, the maintenance of institutions in which the purpose of superiors is embodied, and the rational consciousness of duty. But they have differed from one another because there was one point in which they were agreed: a single and final source of law. Others have asserted that it is impossible to locate morality in conformity to law-giving power, and that it must be sought in ends that are goods. And some have sought the good in self-realization, some in holiness, some in happiness, some in the greatest possible aggregate of pleasures. And yet these schools have agreed in the assumption that there is a single, fixed and final good. They have been able to dispute with one another only because of their common premise.

The question arises whether the way out of the confusion and conflict is not to go to the root of the matter by questioning this common element. Is not the belief in the single, final and ultimate (whether conceived as good or as authoritative law) an intellectual product of that feudal organization which is disappearing historically and of that belief in a bounded, ordered cosmos, wherein rest is higher than motion, which has disappeared from natural science? It has been repeatedly suggested that the present limit of intellectual reconstruction lies in the fact that it has not as yet been seriously applied in the moral and social disciplines. Would not this further application demand precisely that we advance to a belief in a plurality of changing, moving, individualized goods and ends, and to a belief that principles, criteria, laws are intellectual instruments for analyzing individual or unique situations?

Inquiry, discovery take the same place in morals that they have come to occupy in sciences of nature. Validation, demonstration become experimental, a matter of consequences. Reason, always an honorific term in ethics, becomes actualized in the methods by which the needs and conditions, the obstacles and resources, of situations are scrutinized in detail, and intelligent plans of improvement are worked out. Remote and abstract generalities promote jumping at conclusions, "anticipations of nature." Bad consequences are then deplored as due to natural perversity and untoward fate. But shifting the issue to analysis of a specific situation makes inquiry obligatory and alert observation of consequences imperative. No past decision nor old principle can ever be wholly relied upon to justify a course of action. No amount of pains taken in forming a purpose in a definite case is final; the consequences of its adoption must be carefully noted, and a purpose held only as a working hypothesis until results confirm its rightness. Mistakes are no longer either mere unavoidable accidents to be mourned or moral sins to be expiated and forgiven. They are lessons in wrong methods of using intelligence and instructions as to a better course in the future. They are indications of the need of revision, development, readjustment. Ends grow, standards of judgment are improved. Man is under just as much obligation to develop his most advanced standards and ideals as to use conscientiously those which he already possesses. Moral life is protected from falling into formalism and rigid repetition.

The process of growth, of improvement and progress, rather than the static outcome and result, becomes the significant thing. Not health as an end fixed once and for all, but the needed improvement in health— a continual process—is the end and good. The end is no longer a terminus or limit to be reached. It is the active process of transforming the existent situation. Not perfection as a final goal, but the ever-enduring process of perfecting, maturing, refining is the aim in living. Honesty, industry, temperance, justice, like health, wealth and learning, are not goods to be possessed as they would be if the expressed fixed ends to be attained. They are directions of change in the quality of experience. Growth itself is the only moral "end."

A COMMON FAITH*

I do not suppose for many minds the dislocation of the religious from a religion is easy to effect. Tradition and custom, especially when emotionally charged, are a part of the habits that have become one with our very being. But the possibility of the transfer is demonstrated by its actuality. Let us then for the moment drop the term "religious," and ask what are the attitudes that lend deep and enduring support to the processes of living. I have, for example, used the words "adjustment" and "orientation." What do they signify?

While the words "accommodation," "adaptation," and "adjustment" are frequently employed as synonyms, attitudes exist that are so different that for the sake of clear thought they should be discriminated. There are conditions we meet that cannot be changed. If they are particular and limited, we modify our own particular attitudes in accordance with them. Thus we accommodate ourselves to changes in weather, to alterations in income when we have no other recourse. When the external conditions are lasting we become inured, habituated, or, as the process is now often called, conditioned. The two main traits of this attitude, which I should like to call accommodation, are that it affects *particular* modes of conduct, not the entire self, and that the process is mainly *passive*. It may, however, become general and then it becomes fatalistic resignation or submission. There are other attitudes toward the environment that are also particular but that are more active. We re-act against conditions and endeavor to change them to meet our wants and demands. Plays in a foreign language

---

* John Dewey, *A Common Faith* (New Haven: Yale University Press, 1934), pp. 15–17, 20–23, 42–43. Reprinted by permission of Yale University Press.

are "adapted" to meet the needs of an American audience. A house is rebuilt to suit changed conditions of the household; the telephone is invented to serve the demand for speedy communication at a distance; dry soils are irrigated so that they may bear abundant crops. Instead of accommodating ourselves to conditions, we modify conditions so that they will be accommodated to our wants and purposes. This process may be called adaptation.

Now both of these processes are often called by the more general name of adjustment. But there are also changes in ourselves in relation to the world in which we live that are much more inclusive and deep seated. They relate not to this and that want in relation to this and that condition of our surroundings, but pertain to our being in its entirety. Because of their scope, this modification of ourselves is enduring. It lasts through any amount of vicissitude of circumstances, internal and external. There is a composing and harmonizing of the various elements of our being such that, in spite of changes in the special conditions that surround us, these conditions are also arranged, settled, in relation to us. This attitude includes a note of submission. But it is voluntary, not externally imposed; and as voluntary it is something more than a mere Stoical resolution to endure unperturbed throughout the buffetings of fortune. It is more outgoing, more ready and glad, than the latter attitude, and it is more active than the former. And in calling it voluntary, it is not meant that it depends upon a particular resolve or volition. It is a change *of* will conceived as the organic plenitude of our being, rather than any special change *in* will.

It is the claim of religions that they effect this generic and enduring change in attitude. I should like to turn the statement around and say that whenever this change takes place there is a definitely religious attitude. It is not *a* religion that brings it about, but when it occurs, from whatever cause and by whatever means, there is a religious outlook and function.

. . . belief or faith has also a moral and practical import. Even devils, according to the older theologians, believe—and tremble. A distinction was made, therefore, between "speculative" or intellectual belief and an act called "justifying" faith. Apart from any theological context, there is a difference between belief that is a conviction that some end should be supreme over conduct, and belief that some object or being exists as a truth for the intellect. Conviction in the moral sense signifies being conquered, vanquished, in our active nature by an ideal end; it signifies acknowledgment of its rightful claim over our desires and purposes. Such acknowledgment is practical, not primarily intellectual. It goes beyond evidence that can be presented to *any* possible observer. Reflection, often long and arduous, may be involved in arriving at the conviction, but the import of thought is not exhausted in discovery of evidence that can justify intellectual assent. The authority of an ideal over choice and conduct is the authority of an ideal, not of a fact, of a truth guaranteed to intellect, not of the status of the one who propounds the truth.

• • • •

What has been said does not imply that all moral faith in ideal ends is by virtue of that fact religious in quality. The religious is "morality touched by emotion" only when the ends of moral conviction arouse emotions that are not only intense but are actuated and supported by ends so inclusive that they unify the self. The inclusiveness of the end in relation to both self and the "universe" to which an exclusive self is related is indispensable. According to the best authorities, "religion" comes from a root that means being bound or tied. Originally, it meant being bound by vows to a particular way of life—as *les religieux* were monks and nuns who had assumed certain vows. The religious attitude signifies something that is bound through imagination to a *general* attitude. This comprehensive attitude, moreover, is much broader than anything indicated by "moral" in its usual sense. The quality of attitude is displayed in art, science and good citizenship.

If we apply the conception set forth to the terms of the definition earlier quoted, these terms take on a new significance. An unseen power controlling our destiny becomes the power of an ideal. All possibilities, as possibilities, are ideal in character. The artist, scientist, citizen, parent, as far as they are actuated by the spirit of their callings, are controlled by the unseen. For all endeavor for the better is moved by faith in what is possible, not by adherence to the actual. Nor does this faith depend for its moving power upon intellectual assurance or belief that the things worked for must surely prevail and come into embodied existence. For the authority of the object to determine our attitude and conduct, the right that is given it to claim our allegiance and devotion is based on the intrinsic nature of the ideal. . . .

The import of the question extends far. It determines the meaning given to the word "God." On one score, the word can mean only a particular Being. On the other score, it denotes the unity of all ideal ends arousing us to desire and actions. Does the unification have a claim upon our attitude and conduct because it is already, apart from us, in realized existence, or because of its own inherent meaning and value? Suppose for the moment that the word "God" means the ideal ends that at a given time and place one acknowledges as having authority over his volition and emotion, the values to which one is supremely devoted, as far as these ends, through imagination, take on unity. If we make this supposition, the issue will stand out clearly in contrast with the doctrine of religions that "God" designates some kind of Being having prior and therefore non-ideal existence.

The word "non-ideal" is to be taken literally in regard to some religions that have historically existed, to all of them as far as they are neglectful of moral qualities in their divine beings. It does not apply in the same *literal* way to Judaism and Christianity. For they have asserted that the Supreme Being has moral and spiritual attributes. But it applies to them none the less in that these moral and spiritual characters are thought of as properties of a particular existence and are thought to be of religious value for us because of this embodiment in such an existence. Here, as far as I can see, is the ultimate issue as to the difference between *a* religion and the religious as a function of experience.

The idea that "God" represents a unification of ideal values that is essentially imaginative in origin when the imagination supervenes in conduct is attended with verbal difficulties owing to our frequent use of the word "imagination" to denote fantasy and doubtful reality. But the reality of ideal ends as ideals is vouched for by their undeniable power in action. An ideal is not an illusion because imagination is the organ through which it is apprehended. For *all* possibilities reach us through the imagination. In a definite sense the only meaning that can be assigned the term "imagination" is that things unrealized in fact come home to us and have power to stir us. The unification effected through imagination is not fanciful, for it is the reflex of the unification of practical and emotional attitudes. The unity signifies not a single Being, but the unity of loyalty and effort evoked by the fact that many ends are one in the power of their ideal, or imaginative, quality to stir and hold us.

We may well ask whether the power and significance in life of the traditional conceptions of God are not due to the ideal qualities referred to by them, the hypostatization of them into an existence being due to a conflux of tendencies in human nature that converts the object of desire into an antecedent reality (as was mentioned in the previous chapter).

STUDY QUESTIONS

Review

1. Why is Dewey's philosophy said to be biological in orientation?
2. Why is Dewey's pragmatism often called "instrumentalism"? Why "experimentalism"?
3. How does Dewey explain mind? How does he reconcile this concept with his overall naturalism?
4. Compare Dewey and Mead on the nature and origin of mind.
5. How does Dewey characterize aesthetic experience?
6. How is religious experience similar to and different from aesthetic experience, according to Dewey?
7. Summarize Dewey's views on democracy and education.

For Further Thought

1. Do you think Dewey's view of knowledge is too oriented to doing or making? What about knowledge for its own sake and the idea of a liberal education?
2. Is Dewey correct in his description of aesthetic experience?
3. What do you think of Dewey's "reinterpretation" of traditional terms of religion?
4. Are Dewey's and Mead's explanation of the origin of mind adequate? If such an explanation is not accepted, then are we not left with its opposite, i.e., a view of mind as alien to this world and of man as a soul stuck in a body?

BIBLIOGRAPHY

John Dewey. *The Collected Works of John Dewey; The Early Works,* 1882–1898 (5 vols.), *The Middle Works,* 1899–1924 (15 vols.), *The Later Works,* 1925–1953 (3 vols. to date; 16 vols. projected.) Ed. JoAnn Boydston. Carbondale: Southern Illinois University Press, 1969–   .

— — —. *The Philosophy of John Dewey.* Ed. John J. McDermott. 2 vols. New York: G. P. Putnam's, 1973.

— — —. *On Experience, Nature, and Freedom.* Ed. R. Bernstein. New York: Liberal Arts Press, 1960.

— — —. *Freedom and Culture.* New York: G. P. Putnam's, 1939.

— — —. *Theory of Valuation.* Chicago: University of Chicago Press, 1939.

— — —. *Logic: The Theory of Inquiry.* New York: Henry Holt, 1938.

— — —. *Liberalism and Social Action.* New York: G. P. Putnam's, 1935.

— — —. *Art as Experience.* New York: Minton, Balch, 1934.

— — —. *A Common Faith.* New Haven: Yale University Press, 1934.

— — —. *Philosophy and Civilization.* New York: Minton, Balch, 1931.

— — —. *Individualism, Old and New.* New York: Minton, Balch, 1930. Reprint. New York: Capricorn Books, 1962.

— — —. *The Quest for Certainty.* New York: Minton, Balch, 1929. Reprint. New York: Capricorn Books, 1960.

— — —. *The Public and Its Problems.* New York: Henry Holt, 1927.

— — —. *Experience and Nature.* Chicago: Open Court, 1925.

— — —. *Human Nature and Conduct: An Introduction to Social Psychology.* New York: Henry Holt, 1922.

— — —. *Reconstruction in Philosophy.* New York: Henry Holt, 1920.

— — —. *Democracy and Education.* New York: Macmillan, 1916.

— — —. *Essays in Experimental Logic.* Chicago: University of Chicago Press, 1916.

— — —. *The Influence of Darwin on Philosophy and Other Essays in Contemporary Thought.* New York: Henry Holt, 1910.

Dewey, John, and J. H. Tufts. *Ethics.* New York: Henry Holt, 1908. Dewey's portion of this book is published separately as *Theory of the Moral Life.* New York: Holt, Rinehart, and Winston, 1960.

Bernstein, R. *John Dewey.* New York: Washington Square Press, 1967. Reprint. Reseda, Calif.: Ridgeview, 1981.

Blewett, John, ed. *John Dewey: His Thought and Influence.* New York: Fordham University Press, 1960.

Boydston, JoAnn, and Kathleen Poulos. *Checklist of Writings about John Dewey.* Carbondale: Southern Illinois University Press, 1978.

Cahn, Steven M., ed. *New Studies in the Philosophy of John Dewey.* Hanover, N.H.: University Press of New England, 1977.

Couglan, Neil. *Young John Dewey.* Chicago: University of Chicago Press, 1975.

Dicker, George. *Dewey's Theory of Knowledge.* Philadelphia: Philosophical Monographs, 1976.

Dykhuizen, George. *The Life and Mind of John Dewey.* Carbondale: Southern Illinois University Press, 1973.

Edman, Irwin, ed. *John Dewey: His Contribution to the American Tradition.* Indianapolis: Bobbs-Merrill, 1955.

Essays in Honor of John Dewey, on the Occasion of His Seventieth Birthday. New York: Henry Holt, 1929.

Feldman, William Taft. *The Philosophy of John Dewey: A Critical Analysis.* Baltimore: Johns Hopkins University Press, 1934.

Geiger, George. *John Dewey in Perspective.* New York: Oxford University Press, 1958.

Gouinlock, James. *John Dewey's Philosophy of Value.* New York: Humanities Press, 1972.

Hook, Sidney, ed. *John Dewey: Philosopher of Science and Freedom.* New York: Dial Press, 1950.

— — —. *John Dewey: An Intellectual Portrait.* New York: John Day, 1939.

Howard, Delton T. *John Dewey's Logical Theory.* New York: Longmans, Green, 1918.

Kennedy, Gail. "The Process of Evaluation in a Democratic Community." *Journal of Philosophy* 56 (1959): pp. 253-63.

— — —. "The Hidden Link in Dewey's Theory of Evaluation. "*Journal of Philosophy*52 (1955): pp. 85–94.

— — —. "Science and the Transformation of Common Sense: The Basic Problem of Dewey's Philosophy." *Journal of Philosophy* 51 (1954): pp. 313–26.

Levitt, Morton. *Freud and Dewey on the Nature of Man.* New York: Philosophical Library, 1960.

Mead, G. H. "The Philosophy of John Dewey." *International Journal of Ethics* 46 (1935): pp. 64–81.

Morgnbesser, Sidney. *Dewey and His Critics: Essays from the Journal of Philosophy.* N.Y. Journal of Philosophy, Inc., 1977.

Nathanson, Jerome. *John Dewey: The Reconstruction of the Democratic Life.* New York: Charles Scribner's, 1951.

Peters, R. S., ed. *John Dewey Reconsidered.* London: Routledge and Kegan Paul, 1977.

Santayana, G. "Dewey's Naturalistic Metaphysics." In *Obiter Scripta.* New York: Charles Scribner's, 1936.

Schilpp, Paul A., ed. *The Philosophy of John Dewey.* Evanston, Ill.: Northwestern University Press, 1939.

Thayer, H. S. *The Logic of Pragmatism: An Examination of John Dewey's Logic.* New York: Humanities Press, 1952.

Thomas, Milton H., ed. *John Dewey: A Centennial Bibliography.* Chicago: University of Chicago Press, 1962.

White, Morton G. *The Origin of Dewey's Instrumentalism.* New York: Columbia University Press, 1943.

Chapter 9

The Idealism and Absolute Pragmatism of Josiah Royce

Metaphysical idealism is the view that fundamental reality is of the nature of mind or ideas. By the end of the nineteenth century this form of idealism had a long history and had taken a variety of forms, beginning in the West with Plato and in America with Jonathan Edwards. It appeared again in American philosophy in the philosophy of Ralph Waldo Emerson and the transcendentalists, and in the latter part of the nineteenth century most prominently with Josiah Royce.[1]

In its metaphysical form, idealism is a philosophy that holds that the apparent self-sufficiency of nature is illusory and that whatever is ultimately real in the universe is of the stuff that ideas rather than stones and metals are composed. One reason idealism has persisted as a world view is found in its relationship with religion — sometimes lending support to religion, sometimes taking its place. Idealism's earliest forms in fact were in outgrowth of religion — in India, Brahmanism and the Vedanta philosophy, and in China, Lao-tze and Taoism. In early Greek philosophy Plato presented a view according to which the things of this world change and pass away while the forms which they exemplify remain forever unchanged; beautiful things reflect the true and changeless form of beauty itself. In fact, the word "idealism" comes from the Greek word "idea" (ιδέα) which means "something seen." Platonic forms were known not by sensation but by an intellectual vision. In medieval philosophy these forms were identified with ideas in the mind of God, patterns after which the universe was created.

Idealism took a somewhat different form in modern times and was associated with that period's interest in the problem of knowledge. Modern philosophy had begun with Descartes' (1596-1650) division of reality into two distinct forms — matter or extended substance, and mind or thinking substance. Once so differentiated a problem was clearly posed, it became difficult to conceive how mind could know a matter so unlike itself. Moreover, some modern philosophers supported the view that what we actually know are our own ideas of material things. The existence of things in themselves is an inference we make from the seeming passive character of knowledge. It was not difficult at all, then, for someone like the philosopher Berkeley (1685-1753) to dispense with something so useless, unknown, and unknowable as material substance. What we call rocks and trees, he held, are simply orderly groups or collections of sensations or ideas, caused to appear to us in an orderly fashion by God.

One of the problems of such a theory is its solipsism. If all we know are groups of sensations, how can we suppose that those "personal" shapes and colors belie a person, self, or other mind? The avoidance of such a subjective and solipsistic form of idealism was one of the aims of so-called objective idealists, among whom we may place Hegel in late-eighteenth- and early-nineteenth-century Germany and Josiah Royce in America. Objective idealism is the form of idealism that holds that we are not trapped inside our way of knowing and that there is a real (though ideal) existence independent of our finite selves which we can know.

This latter form of idealism was most prominent in late-nineteenth-century American philosophical circles. Nor is it surprising that this was so. The transcendentalists had access to and were influenced by German idealistic thought through Coleridge (see chapter 3). Moreover, by the middle of the nineteenth century it had become fashionable for American students to spend a year or two studying in Germany, thereby coming into contact with German philosophical idealism. After the revolution of 1848 in Germany, many German professors and well-educated laymen came to this country bringing with them a background in German idealistic philosophy.[2] Thus it was that a particular German immigrant, Henry Brokmeyer, in St. Louis, Missouri, the center of pre-Civil War struggles, attempted to make sense of the conflict through the philosophy of Hegel. Brokmeyer also believed that an idealistic philosophy could raise the cultural level in the Midwest.[3] Together with two educators, William Torry Harris and Denton J. Schneider, he formed a club dedicated to Kant, and the three set about to study and translate some of the works of Hegel. They provided an outlet for these translations and other sympathetic views in the first philosophy journal to be published in this country, *The Speculative Journal of Philosophy.*[4] On one occasion the transcendentalist Bronson Alcott visited a club session. Impressed with the Hegelianism he encountered there, he returned to New

England and sponsored what was called the Concord Summer School of Philosophy, two purposes of which were to promote such idealism in America and to attempt a synthesis of Platonism and Hegelianism.[5]

In addition to the idealists associated with these unofficial schools, there were a number of relatively important idealistic professors in academic positions, men who published significant works and gathered around themselves groups of followers.[6] Not quite a founding father of a school, but somewhat influential nonetheless, was George Holmes Howison (1834–1916). He began his career with the St. Louis group of Hegelians, then moved East to Boston and M.I.T., and finally ventured West where he taught at the University of California at Berkeley. It was at Berkeley that Royce studied as an undergraduate and also taught for a short period, thus coming under the influence of Howison. According to Howison, all that exists is minds and their experiences, matter being but the certain arrangement of these experiences. Howison's is a social idealism, one in which individuals are ultimate, and define themselves in relation to others. Their coexistence is what space and time are, the order of coexisting minds. God is simply the ideal toward which they individually and collectively strive; the striving itself accounts for evolution.

Addressing the problem of how to preserve a place for the finite individual in an idealistic philosophy was prominent in the philosophy of Bordon Parker Bowne (1847–1910). Bowne's type of idealism was strong at Boston University where he taught and where some of his followers continued his ideas after his death.[7] His form of idealism is called "personalism" because of the primacy it gives to persons. Persons are selves with personalities. A self is the name we give to a being that is active and has different states, while at the same time remains always identified with itself. When such a self has self-consciousness and memory, it is also a personality. Then it can create its own self-identity by contemplating its past and future. Such a being is the only real substance, in other words, something that retains permanence in the midst of change. The only permanent aspect of material things is the law of their change. Selves interact with one another. However, in order for interaction to occur, an individual must be able to be moved or affected by others as well as by himself. Bowne accounted for the interaction by supposing that the many are unified by their being created manifestations of one infinite, absolute, personal being. The being itself must be personal, according to Bowne, because of the intelligibility of the universe. The universe is a system of meanings, some of which we can know but the whole of which presupposes an absolute knower. As we will see, many of these ideas are similar to those of Josiah Royce.

JOSIAH ROYCE (1855–1916)

Josiah Royce was the most articulate and influential spokesman for the idealists in America in the later nineteenth and early twentieth centuries. His particular form of idealism was part of the mainstream of idealistic thought. However his formulation was also influenced by the voluntarist strain in pragmatic thought, and by William James in particular. One of the ironies of this period is the close relationship that existed between Royce and James in spite of the great differences in their philosophies. One would suppose that James, the New Englander, would be of an old world and traditional school of thought, while Royce, the westerner, brought up in the ruggedness of a California gold-mining town, would be more empirical, pluralistic, and practice oriented. And yet in their philosophies one finds just the opposite. James is the empiricist, pragmatist, and pluralist, while Royce is closer to the European idealistic tradition — metaphysical and rationalistic. Yet it is his own rugged native situation that may have posed for Royce one of the central problems of his philosophy — the problem of community. In his birth place, Grass Valley, California, a gold-mining town in the high Sierras where his parents had come in search of gold six years before Royce's birth (1855), he must have been struck by the diversity of individuals and by the rugged individualism of the place. At the same time he could sit on the hills surrounding the bay of San Francisco, where his family moved when he was eleven years old, and wonder whether there was not some larger perspective such as his own view from the hills gave him, some greater unity.[8]

Royce entered the University of California at Berkeley where he studied English; he studied some philosophy (chiefly Mill and Spencer) on his own. When he graduated in 1875, a group of San Francisco businessmen who were impressed by his talents, provided him funds for a year of study in Germany (1875–76). There he read Schopenhauer and Kant and came under the general influence of German idealism. Upon his return to the United States he began graduate work at Johns Hopkins, where he studied under the Hegelian George Morris (with whom Dewey also had studied), and graduated after having written a Ph.D. thesis entitled "On the Interdependence of Human Knowledge." He then returned to the University of California where he lectured on logic and rhetoric, since the institution had no philosophy department as such at the time. In 1882, when Royce was twenty-seven years old, he received an invitation from Harvard University for a one-year teaching position. While at Johns Hopkins Royce had met and was befriended by William James who had been lecturing there. When James took a sabbatical from Harvard, he recommended that Royce take his place for the year. Royce went to Harvard where he stayed until his death in 1916. He was an impressive person, and his students and colleagues found him to be a man of erudition and eloquence as well as one who would generously give his time to follow out any question or argument they would pose. He exemplified in his person the principled character of his philosophy. Thus, he refused to give the lucrative Lowell lectures when he discovered that a statement of his religious beliefs was required as a condition for giving the lectures. William James remained his friend and constant sparing partner, and Royce was open enough to attempt to revise his absolutism to take into account the insistent criticism by James of the "block universe" that absolutism seemed to imply.

In 1885 Royce published his first book, entitled *The Religious Aspect of Philosophy*,[9] in which he attempted to show that the objects of faith could be demonstrated. A religion, he wrote, involves a moral code, a set of rituals and myths that inspire enthusiasm for the code, and a doctrine about the nature of things. He was concerned about the code and the basis one might find for it in a metaphysics. Is there anything in the world, he asked, of intrinsic worth? A survey of the historical answers to this question might easily lead one to skepticism, because history presents only a warfare of different ideals, most of which rest on some form of "liking." But to point out what people *do* in fact like or desire is not yet to show what they *ought* to desire or seek. Royce himself found his basic moral principle by considering the diversity of wills among men and by supposing that the good must lie in some harmonizing of these wills, which could be achieved if individuals would consider their neighbor's life and desires as their own. He states this belief in the form of a moral principle: "In so far as in thee lies, act as if thou wert at once thy neighbor and thyself. Treat these two lives as one." [10] The ideal form of life would then be one in which the individual's goals were in harmony with those of the community, a point also to be developed in his later work in moral philosophy, *The Philosophy of Loyalty*.

If such a harmony were not possible, however, then such an imperative would be useless. Therefore, Royce next inquired as to what the underlying situation was in relation to the nature of things. His method was to analyze the conditions of error. We ordinarily make claims about the truth and falsity of judgments. What do these claims imply or presuppose? Since those judgments capable of truth or falsity refer to some object, a false or erroneous judgment would be one that failed to agree with its intended object. But how is such failure possible? There must, Royce argues, be some standard by which we can judge the failure. There must exist a higher thought or judgment that does fulfill that intention and judges that the erroneous thought does not do so. Peter's idea of Paul is erroneous if it fails to agree with the real truth, the true idea about Paul. Such a complete and true idea about Paul must exist and so must a total truth about everything else — the setting of this world in which Paul exists — since nothing exists or is true apart from the whole system of ideas of which it is a part. So also if our ideas about an expected future can even now be false or erroneous, this can be so, according to Royce, only because there exists already a truth about that future. Thus Royce holds that there exists an absolute truth, "an infinite unity of conscious thought to which is present all possible truth." [11]

Royce developed these and added other arguments concerning the existence of an Absolute Truth, Thought, or Consciousness. In *Our Conception of God* (1897) he argues that if, for example, we acknowledge that our thought is partial, we can do so only because we thereby acknowledge a whole against which this fragment is seen as fragmentary and partial.[12] Thus there exists a complete system of ideas in which we in our limited way share. Royce's thought about the Absolute was developed further in his two-volume series of lectures entitled *The World and the Individual* (1899, 1901).[13] Here he adds a voluntaristic element, an emphasis on will or intention. In these lectures Royce's approach is typical of idealistic philosophies in that the basic questions he asks are: What is an idea? How is it related to reality? He first surveys three historically posed answers to this question, those of realism, mysticism, and critical rationalism. Realism, the view according to which objects exist independent of the knower, does well to point out the resistance we meet in our attempts to know, but has the basic difficulty of being unable to explain how such independent objects can be known. Mysticism, which stresses the unity of being and the identity of knower and known, makes the finite illusory and our experience of passivity in knowing unintelligible. Critical rationalism, the view that to be real is to be valid or verified by future experience, ignores the fact that thoughts must conform to the real. Things are not real just because they conform to thought, whether that thought is Kant's categories or pragmatism's future experience.

Royce's own view is based on the distinction he makes between the internal and external meaning of an idea. Ideas do have an external meaning that consists in their conformity to or correspondence with outer facts. The internal meaning of ideas consists in their being the embodiment or expression of a purpose. This latter meaning is the one that is true and essential to an idea, since ideas have external reference only because of the purpose or intention we have to focus upon or "mean" them. If we could say exactly what we mean, we would have the complete expression of an idea. Thus when we come close to this exactitude, we utter such phrases as Now I've got it! or That's what I mean! As we come closer and closer to the adequate expression of the internal meaning of some idea, so we come closer and closer to truth and to reality. But we do not usually know precisely what we mean. As our ideas approach precision, they approach individuality and definiteness, and thus the real is also an individual. "What is, or what is real," Royce states, "is as such the complete embodiment, in individual form and in final fulfillment, of the internal meaning of finite ideas."[14] In the last analysis, therefore, the real is both something independent of us and at the same time defined in terms of meanings or ideas. The pragmatic or voluntaristic aspect of this form of objective idealism consists in the fact that according to Royce, ideas are true if they work, but only if they work to fulfill our finite purposes and ultimately the purpose of the Absolute. Royce, in fact, called his form of idealism "Absolute Pragmatism."

In 1908 Royce published *The Philosophy of Loyalty*.[15] As previously noted, one of the central problems of Royce's philosophy was that of understanding how many different and opposing wills could be harmonized without at the same time losing their individuality.[16] His philosophy of loyalty is his second attempt to answer that question, his first attempt being in *The Religious Aspect of Philosophy*. In its new form the supreme principle becomes: "Choose your cause and serve it so that, through your choice and your service, loyalty will be extended and increased among men."[17] Because the term "loyalty" is often misinterpreted, it is well to make clear exactly what Royce meant by it. Loyalty, he says, is "the willing and practical and thoroughgoing devotion of a person to a cause." [18] Loyalty, then, implies that a person freely chooses a cause — something external to him in which he personally believes — and gives himself to the pursuit of this cause in a practical and persevering manner. Of what good is such an effort? According to Royce, it unifies the self, in fact it is the source of self-identity or selfhood. Until one finds some goal or purpose toward which to aim and work, that person is but a bundle of separate and often conflicting interests. The question Who am I? is answered by stating one's hopes, ambitions, and goals. Or, as Royce writes, "a self is a life in so far as it is unified by a single purpose." [19] A self is thus not a static substance but a process, an achievement, something in the making. Moreover, one must be an individual self in order to serve a cause in such a way as not to be swallowed up by the group. While Royce's notion of loyalty is opposed to extreme individualism, it is also opposed both to mysticism in which the self is lost in the whole and to the blind sympathy of the mob. Roycean loyalty creates both selfhood and community among those who serve the same cause.

However, not all causes are good causes; some are even destructive and divisive. War is such a cause — a phenomenon in which the enemy's loyalty is attacked by one's own loyalty. Loyalty itself is not sufficient. One cause, however, to which we can be loyal in a unifying rather than a divisive way is loyalty itself. Thus Royce's new phrasing: Be loyal to loyalty. The goal is thus to increase the unity of the community itself. Where a conflict of loyalties exists, as between labor and management, for example, compromise is not the solution. Rather both sides must rise to a vision of the larger community that is involved and to do whatever will benefit this larger whole. Finally, a person is loyal only if he believes that the cause of unity is itself a real and not illusory good or goal. Loyalty must have a metaphysical basis. According to Royce this basis is again that unity of life and consciousness, the Absolute. In being loyal, the loyal person seeks to realize, exemplify, or manifest in his own finite way the absolute unity of consciousness.

The final form of Royce's philosophy is embodied in his book, *The Problem of Christianity*.[20] In this work Royce continued his examination of the nature and kinds of community, but in a somewhat new form that was due in great part to the influence of some of Charles Peirce's ideas about the nature and use of signs. In this development Royce presented a challenge to the understanding of his and succeeding generations. Basically, he develops the notion that a community is related to its parts, not as an organism to its components but as a community of interpreters. A community is a group of intercommunicating and mutually interpreting persons. Interpretation, in Royce's adaptation of Peirce, is the process by which things (or events) become endowed with meanings and thus function as signs (symbols invested with meaning by a community). Interpretation is triadic, involving (1) the sign, (2) the interpreter, and (3) the interpretee or one for whom the sign is interpreted by the interpreter. One may even interpret signs to oneself, and an interpretation may itself function as a sign to be reinterpreted by others. Signs are invested with meaning by the memories and hopes of a community, and thus form different communities — communities of memory (such as patriotic groups) and communities of hope (such as labor unions). The process of interpretation itself is ongoing within the community and is in fact the life of the community.

The ultimate object of interpretation, however, is the world as a whole. If we as a community of interpreters were totally successful in our interpretation and could arrive at a true interpretation of the world, we would have reached the real and would be but the spirit of the world itself, the Absolute. But we are rather more finite, and our interpretations are partial, always needing revision. We are the ways in which the Absolute interprets itself, the infinite variety of self-representations of the Absolute Spirit. Royce believed that such an infinite is not only possible but necessarily exists if there is to be any truth or knowledge at all. He makes use in his argumentation of some developments in modern mathematics, for example, the argument for the existence of a determinite infinite.[21] Such an infinite is one in which the whole can be placed in a one-to-one correspondence with itself. One example of such a self-representing infinite series is a bottle with a picture of itself on its label. It is infinitely represented in the picture. Royce believed that reality itself is such an ordered system of self-representation of the Absolute.

With this presentation of the rather abstruse notion of the absolute as a community of interpretation and an infinite system of self-representation, we conclude our summary of the philosophy of Josiah Royce and the second part of this book. Such an idealistic philosophy as that of Royce has a definite advantage in that it closely corresponds with humanity's own desire not to view itself as alien to a universe dead to idea and value. However, as James and others have been quick to point out, idealism has problems accounting for the reality of such things as evil, individuality, freedom, and time. Royce himself accepted this challenge and spent a great deal of effort explaining these concepts within his philosophy. To decide whether or not he succeeded would take an investigation of his writings beyond the limits of this introductory survey.

When Royce was writing, at the end of the nineteenth and beginning of the twentieth centuries, much of philosophical thought in America was moving more in the direction set by the pragmatists and empiricists than the idealists. Nevertheless, in the breadth of Royce's philosophy are many elements that can also be found in the discussions of twentieth-century philosophers. As one commentator suggests:

> Royce . . . represents a stage half way between the old and the new in contemporary western thought. His fundamental insights — the reality and self-transcendence of the concrete person, the fact that the whole is implicit in its parts, the notion of interpretation and of community — are as vivid and significant now as when he defended them. . . . That no isolated fact or individual is self-sufficient, that meanings

emerge only in a context of interpretation — all this is richly verified in experience and is affirmed furthermore in many living systems of thought today.[22]

It is to those twentieth-century systems that we next turn our attention.

Notes

[1] See chapter 1 for a discussion of Jonathan Edwards and chapter 3 for Ralph Waldo Emerson and transcendentalism. Idealism continued to appear in twentieth-century American philosophy, though it is certainly not the dominant philosophy of that period. See chapters 12 and 14 in particular and the discussion there of process philosophy and phenomenology. The persistence of idealism in America, at least until the twentieth century, may have been influenced, according to one commentator, by "the passionate search for wholeness and spiritual security mirrored [in] the struggle of disparate peoples to create, on this continent, order out of wilderness, [and] thereby to become one nation" (Otto F. Kraushaar in Fisch, *Classic American Philosopers,* p. 181).

[2] Noah Porter of Yale had attended lectures in Berlin and incorporated much German idealism into his philosophy of common sense; Laurens Perseus Hickok of Union College became an expositor of German idealism for a theological community there; George Herbert Palmer at Harvard taught a social ethics that combined puritanism and Hegelianism. Descriptions of these professors' influence and ideas can be found in Schneider, *History of American Philosophy,* pp. 375–88.

[3] Ibid.

[4] It is interesting to note that Brokmeyer later became lieutenant governor of Missouri and Harris U.S. commissioner of education. It is rare today that one finds persons of such philosophical interest involved in practical affairs as were these Hegelians. Cf. Schneider, *History of American Philosophy,* pp. 388–90.

[5] In chapter 4 we noted that John Fiske was one who delivered important lectures at this Concord gathering. For further description of this and other philosophical schools that developed around the country, ibid., pp. 390–400.

[6] Other contemporary leaders of schools of American idealism not mentioned here are James Edwin Creighton of Cornell University and George Sylvester Morris of Michigan University. Through the initiative of Creighton the American Philosophical Association was formed in 1902, the major philosophical organization in this country today. Sadly missing from our summary is William Ernest Hocking (1873–1966), and his impressive work *The Meaning of God in Human Experience* (New Haven: Yale University Press, 1912).

[7] Edgar Scheffield Brightman is one who most notably continued the philosophy of Bowne at Boston University.

[8] For sources of Royce's philosophy and life see Frank Oppenheim, *Royce's Voyage Down Under* (Lexington: University Press of Kentucky, 1980).

[9] Josiah Royce, *The Religious Aspect of Philosophy: A Critique of the Basis of Conduct and of Faith* (Boston: Houghton Mifflin, 1885).

[10] Ibid., p. 149.

[11] Ibid., pp. 430–35.

[12] Ibid.

[13] Josiah Royce, *The World and the Individual,* 2 vols. (New York: Macmillan, 1900–1901). First given as Gifford Lectures.

[14] Ibid., chapter 7, "The Internal and External Meaning of Ideas."

[15] Josiah Royce, *The Philosophy of Loyalty* (New York: Macmillan, 1908).

[16] This is one of the major emphases in the study of Royce in Smith's *Spirit of American Philosophy*, pp. 80–114.

[17] Royce, *Philosophy of Loyalty,* p. 121.

[18] Ibid., p. 16.

[19] Ibid., p. 171.

[20] Josiah Royce, *The Problem of Christianity,* 2 vols. (New York: Macmillan, 1913).

[21] See the supplementary essay appended to Royce, *The World and the Individual,* entitled "The One, the Many, and the Infinite."

[22] Otto F. Kraushaar in Fisch, *Classic American Philosophers,* p. 199.

JOSIAH ROYCE

THE POSSIBILITY OF ERROR*

What are the conditions that make doubt logically intelligible? These conditions really transcend the present moment. Plainly doubt implies that the statement doubted may be false. So here we have at least one supposed general truth, namely, "All but the immediate content of the present moment's judgment, being doubtful, we may be in error about it." But *what then is an error?* This becomes at once a problem of exciting interest. Attacking it, the author was led through the wilderness of the following argument.

. . . Common sense is willing to ask whether God exists, but unwilling to inquire how it is possible that there can exist an error about anything. But foreseeing that something is to follow from all this, we must beg common sense to be patient. We have not the shadow of doubt ourselves about the possibility of error. That is the steadfast rock on which we build. Our inquiry, ultra-skeptical as it may at moments seem, is into the question: *How* is the error possible? Or, in other words: *What is an error?* Now there can be little doubt that common sense is not ready with any general answer to such a question. Error is a word with many senses. By error we often mean just a statement that arouses our antipathy. Yet we all admit upon reflection, that our antipathy can neither make nor be

---

* Josiah Royce, "The Possibility of Error" *The Religious Aspect of Philosophy* (Boston: Houghton Mifflin, 1885), pp. 389–95, 408–10, 416–20.

used to define real error. Adam Smith declares, with common sense on his side, in his "Theory of the Moral Sentiments," that: "To approve or disapprove of the opinions of others is acknowledged, by everybody, to mean no more than to observe their agreement or disagreement with our own." Yet no one would accept as a definition of error the statement that: *Error is any opinion that I personally do not like.* Error has thus a very puzzling character. For common sense will readily admit that if a statement is erroneous, it must appear erroneous to every "right mind" that is in possession of the facts. Hence the personal taste of one man is not enough to define it. Else there might be as many sorts of error as there are minds. It is only the "right mind" whose personal taste shall decide what is an error in any particular case. But what then is a normal mind? Who is the right-minded judge? There seems to be danger that common sense shall run at this point into an infinite regress. I say: *That opinion is an error.* What do I mean? Do I mean that I do not like that opinion? Nay, I mean more. I mean that *I ought not to like or to accept it.* Why ought I not? *Because the ideally right-minded person would not,* seeing the given facts, hold that opinion about them. But who is the ideally right-minded person? Well, common sense may answer, *It is my ideal person, the right-minded man as I conceive him.* But why is my ideal the true ideal? *Because I like it?—Nay, because, to the ideal judge, that kind of mind would seem the ideal.* But who is the ideal judge? And so common sense is driven from point to point, unable to get to anything definite.

. . . We shall study our problem thus. We shall take either some accepted definition of error, or some special class of cases, and we shall ask: How is error in that case, or in accordance with that definition, possible? Since error plainly is possible in some way, we shall have only to inquire: *What are the logical conditions* that make it possible? We shall take up the ordinary suppositions that common sense seems to make about what here determines the possibility of error. We shall show that these suppositions are inadequate. Then the result will be that, on the ordinary suppositions, error would be impossible. But that result would be absurd, if these were the only possible suppositions. Hence the ordinary suppositions must somehow be supplemented. When, therefore, we seem to say in the following that error is impossible, we shall mean only, impossible under the ordinary suppositions of common sense. What supplement we need to these suppositions, our argument will show us. In sum we shall find the state of the case to be this: Common sense regards an assertion as true or as false apart from any other assertion or thought, and solely in reference to its own object. For common sense each judgment, as a separate creation, stands out alone, looking at its object, and trying to agree with it. If it succeeds, we have truth. If the judgment fails, we have error. But, as we shall find, this view of common sense is unintelligible. A judgment cannot have an object and fail to agree therewith, unless this judgment is part of an organism of thought. Alone, as separate fact, a judgment has no intelligible object beyond itself. And therefore the presuppositions of common sense must be supplemented or else abandoned. Either then there is no error, or else judgments are true or false only in reference to a higher inclusive thought, which they presuppose, and which must, in the last analysis, be assumed as Infinite and all-inclusive. This result we shall reach by no mystical insight, by no revelation, nor yet by any mere postulate such as we used in former discussions, but by a simple, dry analysis of the meaning of our own thought.

The most formidable opponent of our argument will be, after all, however, not common sense, but that thought mentioned in the last chapter,—the thought that may try to content itself with somewhat plausible jargon, and to say that: *"There is no real difference between truth and error at all, only a kind of opinion or consensus of men about a conventional distinction between what they choose to call truth and what they choose to call error."* This view, as the author has confessed, he once tried to hold. Still this meaningless doctrine of relativity is not the same as the view that contents itself with the postulates before discussed. That view might take, and for the author at one time did take, the possible and intelligible form thus expressible: *"Truth and error, though really distinguishable, are for us distinguished only through our postulates, in so far as relates to past and future time."* Such views, while not denying that there is real truth, despair of the attainability for us of more than momentary truth. But the doctrine of Total Relativity, this view above expressed, differs from genuine skepticism. It tries to put even skepticism to rest, by declaring the opinion, *that there is error,* to be itself an error. This is not merely a moderate expression of human limitations, but jargon, and therefore formidable, because jargon is always unanswerable. When the famous Cretan declared all statements made by Cretans to be in all cases lies, his declaration was hard to refute, because it was such honest-seeming nonsense. Even so with the statement that declares the very existence of error to be an erroneously believed fancy. No *consensus* of men can make an error erroneous. We can only find or commit an error, not create it. When we commit an error, we say what was an error already. If our skeptical view in previous chapters seemed to regard truth and error as mere objects of our postulates, that was only because, to our skepticism, the real truth, the real error, about any real past and future, seemed beyond our reach, so that we had to content ourselves with postulates. But that real error exists is absolutely indubitable.

. . . We must be more explicit. Let us take the now so familiar suggestion of our great humorist about the six people that take part in every conversation between two persons. If John and Thomas are talking together, then the real John and Thomas, their respective ideas of themselves, and their ideas of each other, are all parties to the conversation. Let us consider four of these persons, namely, the real John, the real Thomas, John as Thomas conceives him, and Thomas as John conceives him. When John judges, of whom does he think? Plainly of that which can be an object to his thoughts, namely, of *his* Thomas. About whom then can he err? About *his* Thomas? No, for he knows him too well. His conception of Thomas is his conception, and what he asserts it to be, that it is for him. About the real Thomas? No, for it should seem, according to common sense, that he has nothing to do with the real Thomas in his thought, since that Thomas never becomes any part of his thought at all. "But," says one, "there must be some fallacy here, since we are sure that John *can* err about the real Thomas." Indeed he can, say we; but ours is not this fallacy. Common sense has made it. Common sense has said: "Thomas never is in John's thought, and yet John can blunder about Thomas." How shall we unravel the knot?

One way suggests itself. Mayhap we have been too narrow in our defintion of *object*. Common sense surely insists that objects are outside of our thought. If, then, I have a judgment, and another being sees both my judgment and some outside object that was not in my thought, and sees how that thought is unlike the object in some critical respect, this being could say that my assertion was an error. So then with John and Thomas. *If Thomas could know John's thoughts about him,* then Thomas could possibly see John's error. That is what is meant by the error in John's thought.

But mere disagreement of a thought with any random object does not make the thought erroneous. The judgment must disagree with *its chosen* object. If John never has Thomas in thought at all, how *can* John choose the real Thomas as his object? If I judge about a penholder that is in this room, and if the next room is in all respects like this, save for a penholder in it, with which my assertion does not agree, who, looking at that penholder in that other room, can say that my judgment is false? For I meant not that penholder when I spoke, but this one. I knew perhaps nothing about that one, had it not in mind, and so could not err about it. Even so, suppose that outside of John there is a real Thomas, similar, as it happens, to John's ideal Thomas, but lacking some thought or affection that John attributes to his ideal Thomas. Does that make John's notion an error? No, for he spoke and could speak only of his ideal Thomas. The real Thomas was the other room, that he knew not of, the other side of the shield, that he never could conceive. His Thomas was his phantom Thomas. This phantom it is that he judges and thinks about, and his thoughts may have their own consistency or inconsistency. But with the real other person they have nothing to do. The real other is not his object, and how can he err about what is not object for him?

Absurd, indeed, some one will reply to us. John and Thomas have to deal with representative phantoms of each other, to be sure; but that only makes each more apt to err about the real other. And the test that they can err is a very simple one. Suppose a spectator, a third person, to whom John and Thomas were both somehow directly present, so that he as it were included both of them. Then John's judgment of his phantom Thomas would be by this spectator at once compared with the real Thomas, and even so would Thomas's judgment of John be treated. If now John's phantom Thomas agreed with the real Thomas, then John's ideas would be declared in so far truthful; otherwise they would be erroneous. And this explains what is meant by John's power to err about Thomas.

This result is foreign to our every-day thought, because this every-day thought really makes innocent use of two contradictory views of the relations of conscious beings. On the one hand we regard them as utterly remote from one another, as what Professor Clifford called ejects; and then we speak of them as if the thoughts of one could as such become thoughts of the other, or even as if one of them could as an independent being still become object in the thought of the other. No wonder that, with such contradictory assumptions as to the nature of our relations to our neighbors, we find it very easy to make absurd statements about the meaning of error. The contradiction of common sense has in fact just here much to do with the ethical illusion that we called the illusion of selfishness. To clear up this point will be useful to us, therefore, in more ways than one.

. . . That errors in matters of experience are common enough is indubitable, but equally evident becomes the difficulty of defining what they are and how they are possible. Take the case of error about an expected future. What do we mean by a future time? How do we identify a particular time? Both these questions plunge us into the sea of problems about the nature of time itself. When I say, *Thus and so will be at such and such a future moment,* I postulate certain realities not now given to my consciousness. And singular realities they are. For they have now no existence at all. Yet I postulate that I can err about them. Thus their non-existence is a peculiar kind of non-existence, and requires me to make just such and such affirmations about it. If I fail to correspond to the true nature of this non-existent reality, I make an error; and it is postulated not merely that my present statement will in that case hereafter turn out false or become false, but also that it is now false, is at this moment an error, even though the reality with which it is to agree is centuries off in the future. But this is not all the difficulty. I postulate also that an error in prediction can be discovered when the time comes by the failure of the prediction to verify itself. I postulate then that I can look back and say: Thus and thus I predicted about this moment, and thus and thus it has come to pass, and this event contradicts that expectation. But can I in fact ever accomplish this comparison at all? And is the comparison very easily intelligible? For when the event comes to pass, the expectation no longer exists. The two thoughts, namely, expectation and actual experience, are separate thoughts, far apart in time. How can I bring them together to compare them, so as to see if they have the same object? It will not do to appeal to memory for the purpose; for the same question would recur about the memory in its relation to the original thought. How can a past thought, being past, be compared to a present thought to see whether they stand related? The past thought lived in itself, had its own ideas of what it then called future, and its own interpretation thereof. How can you show, or intelligently affirm, that the conception which the past expectation had of its future moment is so identical with the conception which this present thought has of this present moment, as to make these two conceived moments one and the same? Here in short we have supposed two different ideas, one of an expected future, the other of an experienced present, and we have supposed the two ideas to be widely separated in time, and by hypothesis they are not together in one consciousness at all. Now how can one say that in fact they relate to the same moment at all? How is it intelligible to say that they do? How, in fine, can a not-given future be a real object of any thought; and how, when it is once the object thereof, can any subsequent moment be identified with this object?

A present thought and a past thought are in fact separate, even as were John and Thomas. Each one means the object that it thinks. How can they have a common object? Are they not once for all different thoughts, each with its own intent? But in order to render intelligible the existence of error about matters of fact, we must make the unintelligible assumption, so it would seem, that these two different thoughts have the same intent, and are but one. And such is the difficulty that we find in our second great class of cases.

. . . To explain how one could be in error about his neighbor's thoughts, we suggested the case where John and Thomas should be present to a third thinker whose thought should include them both. We objected to this suggestion that thus the natural presupposition that John and Thomas are separate self-existent beings would be contradicted. But on this natural presupposition neither of these two subjects could become object to the other at all, and error would here be impossible. Suppose then that we drop the natural presupposition, and say that John and Thomas are both actually present to and included in a third and higher thought. To explain the possibility of error about matters of fact seemed hard, because of the natural postulate that time is a pure succession of separate moments, so that the future is now as future non-existent, and so that judgments about the future lack real objects, capable of identification. Let us then drop this natural postulate, and declare time once for all present in all its moments to an universal all-inclusive thought. And to sum up, let us overcome all our difficulties by declaring that all the many Beyonds, which single significant judgments seem vaguely and separately to postulate, are present as fully realized intended objects to the unity of an all-inclusive, absolutely clear, universal, and conscious thought, of which all judgments, true or false, are but fragments, the whole being at once Absolute Truth and Absolute Knowledge. Then all our puzzles will disappear at a stroke, and error will be possible, because any one finite thought, viewed in relation to its own intent, may or may not be seen by this higher thought as successful and adequate in this intent.

. . . Even so we must conceive the relation of John's thought to the united total of thought that includes him and Thomas. Real John and his phantom Thomas, real Thomas and his phantom John, are all present as elements in the including consciousness, which completes the incomplete intentions of both the individuals, constitutes their true relations, and gives the thought of each about the other whatever of truth or of error it possesses. In short, error becomes possible as one moment or element in a higher truth, that is, in a consciousness that makes the error a part of itself, while recognizing it as error.

So far then we propose this as a possible solution for our puzzles. But now we may insist upon it as the only possible solution. *Either there is no such thing as error, which statement is a flat self-contradiction, or else there is an infinite unity of conscious thought to which is present all possible truth.*

What, then, is an error? An error, we reply, is an incomplete thought, that to a higher thought, which includes it and its intended object, is known as having failed in the purpose that it more or less clearly had, and that is fully realized in this higher thought. And without such higher inclusive thought, an assertion has no external object, and is no error.

THE PHILOSOPHY OF LOYALTY*

Our age, as I have said, is a good deal perplexed regarding its moral ideals and its standards of duty. It has doubts about what is really the best plan of human life. This perplexity is not wholly due to any peculiar waywardness of our time, or to any general lack of moral seriousness. It is just our moral leaders, our reformers, our prophets, who most perplex us. Whether these revolutionary moral teachers are right or wrong, they beset us, they give us no rest, they call in doubt our moral judgments, they undertake to "transmute values." And the result, for many of us, is a practical result. It tends to deprive us of that confidence which we all need in order to be ready to do good works. It threatens to paralyze the

---

* Josiah Royce, *The Philosophy of Loyalty* (New York: Macmillan, 1908), pp. 8–11, 13–20, 116–19, 121, 145–46, 168, 307–11, 356–57. Reprinted with permission of David Royce, 387 Main St., Westport, Conn. 06880.

effectiveness of many conscientious people. Hence any effort to reason calmly and constructively about the foundations of the moral life may serve, not merely to clarify our minds, but to give vigor to our deeds.

I indeed agree with the view that, in many ways, our traditional moral standards ought to be revised. We need a new heaven and a new earth. We do well to set out to seek for both, however hard or doubtful may be the quest. In so far as our restlessness about moral matters—our unsettlement—implies a sense of this need, it is a good thing. To use a comparison suggested by modern Biblical criticism—our conventional morality is indeed a sort of Pentateuch, made up of many ancient documents. It has often been edited afresh. It needs critical reëxamination. I am a student of philosophy. My principal business has always been criticism. I shall propose nothing in this course which I have not tried to submit to critical standards, and to revise repeatedly.

But, on the other hand, I do not believe that unsettlement is finality. Nor to my mind is the last word of human wisdom this: that the truth is inaccessible. Nor yet is the last word of wisdom this: that the truth is merely fluent and transient. I believe in the eternal. I am in quest of the eternal. As to moral standards, in particular, I do not like that mere homesickness and spiritual estrangement, and that confusion of mind about moral ideals, which is nowadays too common. I want to know the way that leads our human practical life homewards, even if that way prove to be infinitely long. I am discontented with mere discontent. I want, as well as I can, not merely to help you to revise some of your moral standards, but to help you to give to this revision some definitive form and tendency, some image and hint of finality.

The phrase, "Philosophy of Loyalty," is intended to indicate first, that we are here to consider loyalty as an ethical principle. For philosophy deals with first principles. And secondly, my title means to suggest that we are to view the matter critically and discriminatingly, as well as practically. For philosophy is essentially a criticism of life. Not everything, then, that calls itself loyalty, and not every form of loyalty, shall be put in our discussion on the same level with every other moral quality that uses or that deserves the ancient name in question. Moreover, the term "loyalty" comes to us as a good old popular word, without any exact definition. We are hereafter to define our term as precisely as possible, yet so as to preserve the spirit of the former usage. In estimating the place of loyalty in the moral life, we are, moreover, to follow neither traditional authority nor the voice of private prejudice. We are to use our reason as best we can; for philosophy is an effort to think out the reasons for our opinions.

But when all these efforts have been made towards a philosophical treatment of our topic, when certain discriminations between true and mistaken loyalty have been defined, when we have insisted upon the fitting objects of loyalty, and have throughout indicated our reasons, for our theses, there will then stand out one great practical lesson, which I shall try to illustrate from the start, and to bring to its fruition as our lectures close. And the lesson will be this: *In loyalty, when loyalty is properly defined, is the fulfilment of the whole moral law.*

Loyalty shall mean, according to this preliminary definition: *The willing and practical and thoroughgoing devotion of a person to a cause.* A man is loyal when, first, he has some *cause* to which he is loyal; when, secondly, he *willingly* and *thoroughly* devotes himself to this cause; and when, thirdly, he expresses his devotion in some *sustained and practical way,* by acting steadily in the service of his cause. Instances of loyalty are: The devotion of a patriot to his country, when this devotion leads him actually to live and perhaps die for his country; the devotion of a martyr to his religion; the devotion of a ship's captain to the requirements of his office when, after a disaster, he works steadily for his ship and for the saving of his ship's company until the last possible service is accomplished, so that he is the last man to leave the ship, and is ready if need be to go down with his ship.

Such cases of loyalty are typical. They involve, I have said, the willingness of the loyal man to do his service. The loyal man's cause is his cause by virtue of the assent over his own will. His devotion is his own. He chooses it, or, at all events, approves it. Moreover, his devotion is a practical one. He does something. This something serves his cause. Loyalty is never mere emotion. Adoration and affection may go with loyalty, but can never alone constitute loyalty. Furthermore, the devotion of the loyal man involves a sort of restraint or submission of his natural desires to his cause. Loyalty without self-control is impossible. The loyal man serves. That is, he does not merely follow his own impulses. He looks to his cause for guidance. This cause tells him what to do, and he does it. His devotion, furthermore, is entire. He is ready to live or to die as the cause directs.

And now for a further word about the hardest part of this preliminary definition of loyalty. A loyal man, I have said, has a cause. I do not yet say that he has a good cause. He might have a bad one. I do not say, as yet, what makes a cause a good one, and worthy of loyalty. All that is to be considered hereafter. But this I now premise: If one is loyal, he has a cause which he indeed personally values. Otherwise, how could he be devoted to it? He therefore takes interest in the cause, loves it, is well pleased with it. On the other hand, loyalty never means the mere emotion of love for your cause, and never means merely following your own pleasure, viewed *as* your private pleasure and interest. For if you are loyal, your cause is viewed by you as something outside of you. Or if, like your country, your cause includes yourself, it is still much larger than your private self. It has its own value, so you as a loyal person believe.

This essential value it would keep (so you believe) even if your private interest were left out of account. Your cause you take, then, to be something objective—something that is not your private self. It does not get its value merely from your being pleased with it. You believe, on the contrary, that you love it just because of its own value, which it has by itself, even if you die. That is just why one may be ready to die for his cause. In any case, when the loyal man serves his cause, he is not seeking his own private advantage.

Moreover, the cause to which a loyal man is devoted is never something *wholly* impersonal. It concerns other men. Loyalty is social. If one is a loyal servant of a cause, one has at least possible fellow-servants. On the other hand, since a cause, in general, tends to unite the many fellow-servants in one service, it consequently seems to the loyal man to have a sort of impersonal or superpersonal quality about it. You can love an individual. But you can be loyal only to a tie that binds you and others into some sort of unity, and loyal to individuals only through the tie. The cause to which loyalty devotes itself has always this union of the personal and the seemingly superindividual about it. It binds many individuals into one service. Loyal lovers, for instance, are loyal not merely to one another as separate individuals, but to their love, to their union, which is something more than either of them, or even than both of them viewed as distinct individuals.

. . . But if we have learned the moral law, or any part of it, and if we do not ask any longer how we first learned, or how we may still have to learn afresh our duty, but if, on the contrary, we rather ask: "What reason can I now give to myself why a given act is truly right? What reason can I give why my duty is my duty? "—then, indeed, we find that no external authority, viewed merely as external, can give one any reason why an act is truly right or wrong. Only a calm and reasonable view of what it is that I myself really will,—only this can decide such a question.

So far, then, we have a rather paradoxical situation before us. Yet it is the moral situation of every one of us. If I am to know my duty, I must consult my own reasonable will. I alone can show myself why I view this or this as my duty. But on the other hand, if I merely look within myself to find what it is that I will, my own private individual nature, apart fom due training, never gives me any answer to the question: What do I will? By nature I am a victim of my ancestry, a mass of world-old passions and impulses, desiring and suffering in constantly new ways as my circumstances change, and as one or another of my natural impulses comes to the front. By nature, then, apart from a specific training, I have no personal will of my own. One of the principal tasks of my life is to learn to have a will of my own. To learn your own will,—yes, to create your own will, is one of the largest of your human undertakings.

. . . Since no man can find a plan of life by merely looking within his own chaotic nature, he has to look without, to the world of social conventions, deeds, and causes. Now, a loyal man is one who has found, and who sees, neither mere individual fellow-men to be loved or hated, nor mere conventions, nor customs, nor laws to be obeyed, but some social cause, or some system of causes, so rich, so well knit, and, to him, so fascinating, and withal so kindly in its appeal to his natural self-will, that he says to his cause: "Thy will is mine and mine is thine. In thee I do not lose but find myself, living intensely in proportion as I live for thee." If one could find such a cause, and hold it for his lifetime before his mind, clearly observing it, passionately loving it, and yet calmly understanding it, and steadily and practically serving it, he would have one plan of life, and this plan of life would be his own plan, his own will set before him, expressing all that his self-will has ever sought. Yet this plan would also be a plan of obedience, because it would mean living for the cause.

Now, in all ages of civilized life there have been people who have won in some form a consciousness of loyalty, and who have held to such a consciousness through life. Such people may or may not have been right in their choice of a cause. But at least they have exemplified through their loyalty one feature of a rataional moral life. They have known what it was to have unity of purpose.

. . . In responding to the question, "Who are you? " a man may first mention his name. But his name is a mere tag. He then often goes on to tell where he lives, and where he comes from. His home and his birthplace, however, are already what one may call purposeful aspects of his personality. For dwelling-place, country, birthplace, and similar incidental facts about a man tend to throw light upon his personality mainly because they are of importance for a further knowledge of his social relations, and so of his social uses and activities.

But the answer to the question, "Who are you? " really begins in earnest when a man mentions his calling, and so actually sets out upon the definition of his purposes and of the way in which these purposes get expressed in his life. And when a man goes on to say, "I am the doer of these and these deeds, the friend of these friends, the enemy of these opposing purposes, the member of this family, the one whose ideals are such and such, and are so and so expressed in my life," the man expresses to you at length whatever is most expressible and worth knowing in answer to the question, "Who are you? "

To sum up, then, I should say that a person, an individual self, may be defined as a human life lived according to a plan. If a man could live with no plan at all, purposelessly and quite passively, he would in so far be an organism, and also, if you choose, he would be a psychological specimen, but he would be no personality. Wherever there is personality, there are purposes worked out in life. If, as often happens, there are many purposes connected with the life of this human creature, many plans in this life, but no discoverable unity and coherence of these plans, then in so far there are many glimpses of selfhood, many fragmentary selves present in connection with the life of some human organism. But there is so far no one self, no one person discoverable. You are one self just in so far as the life that goes on in connection with your organism has some one purpose running through it. By the terms "this person" and "this self," then, we mean this human life in so far as it expresses some one purpose. Yet, of course, this one purpose which is expressed in the life of a single self need not be one which is defined by this self in abstract terms. On the contrary, most of us are aware that our lives are unified, after a fashion, by the very effort that we more or less vaguely make to assert ourselves somehow as individuals in our world. Many of us have not yet found out how it would be best to assert ourselves. But we are trying to find out. This very effort to find out gives already a certain unity of purpose to our lives.

But in so far as we have indeed found out some cause, far larger than our individual selves, to which we are fully ready to be loyal, this very cause serves to give the required unity to our lives, and so to determine what manner of self each of us is, even though we chance to be unable to define in abstract terms what is the precise nature of this very cause.

If, then, we look over the field of human life to see where good and evil have most clustered, we see that the best in human life is its loyalty; while the worst is whatever has tended to make loyalty impossible, or to destroy it when present, or to rob it of its own while it still survives. And of all· things that thus have warred with loyalty, the bitterest woe of humanity has been that so often it is the loyal themselves who have thus blindly and eagerly gone about to wound and to slay the loyalty of their brethren. The spirit of loyalty has been misused to make men commit sin against this very spirit, holy as it is. For such a sin is precisely what any wanton conflict of loyalties means. Where such a conflict occurs, the best, namely, loyalty, is used as an instrument in order to compass the worst, namely, the destruction of loyalty.

It is true, then, that some causes are good, while some are evil. But the test of good and evil in the causes to which men are loyal is now definable in terms which we can greatly simplify in view of the foregoing considerations.

If, namely, I find a cause, and this cause fascinates me, and I give myself over to its service, I in so far attain what, for me, if my loyalty is complete, is a supreme good. But my cause, by our own definition, is a social cause, which binds many into the unity of one service. My cause, therefore, gives me, of necessity, fellow-servants, who with me share this loyalty, and to whom this loyalty, if complete, is also a supreme good.

So far, then, being loyal myself, I not only get but give good; for I help to sustain, in each of my fellow-servants, his own loyalty, and so I help him to secure his own supreme good. In so far, then, my loyalty to my cause is also a loyalty to my fellows' loyalty. But now suppose that my cause, like the family in a feud, or like the pirate ship, or like the aggressively warlike nation, lives by the destruction of the loyalty of other families, or of its own community, or of other communities. Then, indeed, I get a good for myself and for my fellow-servants by our common loyalty; but I war against this very spirit of loyalty as it appears in our opponent's loyalty to his own cause.

And so, a cause is good, not only for me, but for mankind, in so far as it is essentially a *loyalty to loyalty,* that is, is an aid and a furtherance of loyalty in my fellows. It is an evil cause in so far as, despite the loyalty that it arouses in me, it is destructive of loyalty in the world of my fellows. My cause is, indeed, always such as to involve some loyalty to loyalty, because, if I am loyal to any cause at all, I have fellow-servants whose loyalty mine supports. But in so far as my cause is a predatory cause, which lives by overthrowing the loyalties of others, it is an evil cause, because it involves disloyalty to the very cause of loyalty itself.

This principle is now obvious. I may state it thus: In so far as it lies in your power, so choose your cause and so serve it, that, by reason of your choice and of your service, there shall be more loyalty in the world rather than less. And, in fact, so choose and so serve your individual cause as to secure thereby the greatest possible increase of loyalty amongst men. More briefly: *In choosing and in serving the cause to which you are to be loyal, be, in any case, loyal to loyalty.*

Herewith we approach a thesis which is central in my whole philosophy of loyalty. I announced that thesis in other words in the opening lecture. My thesis is that *all those duties which we have learned to recognize as the fundamental duties of the civilized man, the duties that every man owes to every man, are to be rightly interpreted as special instances of loyalty to loyalty.* In other words, all the recognized virtues can be defined in terms of our concept of loyalty. And this is why I assert that, when rightly interpreted, loyalty is the whole duty of man.

For consider the best-known facts as to the indirect influence of certain forms of loyal conduct. When I speak the truth, my act is directly an act of loyalty to the personal tie which then and there binds me to the man to whom I consent to speak. My special cause is, in such a case, constituted by this tie. My fellow and I are linked in a certain unity,—the unity of some transaction which involves our speech one to another. To be ready to speak the truth to my fellow is to have, just then, no eye to see and no tongue to speak save as this willingly accepted tie demands. In so far, then, speaking the truth is a special instance of loyalty. But whoever speaks the truth, thereby does what he then can do to help everybody to speak the truth. For he acts so as to further the general confidence of man in man. How far such indirect influence may extend, no man can predict.

Benevolence, on the other hand, is that aspect of loyalty which directly concerns itself with your influence upon the inner life of human beings who enjoy, who suffer, and whose private good is to be affected by your deeds. Since no personal good that your fellow can possess is superior to his own loyalty, your own loyalty to loyalty is itself a supremely benevolent type of activity. And since your fellow-man is an instrument for the futherance of the cause of universal loyalty, his welfare also concerns you, in so far as, if you help him to a more efficient life, you make him better able to be loyal. Thus benevolence is an inevitable attendant of loyalty. And the spirit of loyalty to loyalty enables us to define wherein consists a wise benevolence. Benevolence without loyalty is a dangerous sentimentalism. Thus viewed, then, loyalty to universal loyalty is indeed the fulfilment of the whole law.

What must be true about the universe if even loyalty itself is a genuine good, and not a merely inevitable human illusion?

Well, loyalty is a service of causes. A cause, if it really is what our definition requires, links various human lives into the unity of one life. Therefore, if loyalty has any basis in truth, human lives can be linked in some genuine spiritual unity. Is such unity a fact, or is our belief in our causes a mere point of view, a pathetic fallacy? Surely, if any man, however loyal, discovers that his cause is a dream, and that men remain as a fact sundered beings, not really linked by genuine spiritual ties, how can that man remain loyal? Perhaps his supreme good indeed lies in the believing that such unities are real. But if this belief turns out to be an illusion, and if a man detects the illusion, can he any longer get the good out of loyalty?

How paradoxical a world, then, must the real world be, if the faith of the loyal is indeed well founded! A spiritual unity of life, which transcends the individual experience of any man, must be real. For loyalty, as we have seen, is a service of causes that, from the human point of view, appear superpersonal. Loyalty holds these unities to be good. If loyalty is right, the real goodness of these causes is never completely manifested to any one man, or to any mere collection of men. Such goodness, then, if completely experienced at all, must be experienced upon some higher level of consciousness than any one human being ever reaches. If loyalty is right, social causes, social organizations, friendships, families, countries, yes, humanity, as you see, must have the sort of unity of consciousness which individual human persons fragmentarily get, but must have this unity upon a higher level than that of our ordinary human individuality.

Some such view, I say, must be held if we are to regard loyalty as in the end anything more than a convenient illusion. Loyalty has its metaphysical aspect. It is an effort to conceive human life in an essentially superhuman way, to view our social organizations as actual personal unities of consciousness, unities wherein there exists an actual experience of that good which, in our loyalty, we only partially apprehend. If the loyalty of the lovers is indeed well founded in fact, then they, as separate individuals, do not constitute the whole truth. Their spiritual union also has a personal, a conscious existence, upon a higher than human level. An analogous unity of consciousness, an unity superhuman in grade, but intimately bound up with, and inclusive of, our apparently separate personalities, must exist, if loyalty is well founded, wherever a real cause wins the true devotion of ourselves. Grant such an hypothesis, and then loyalty becomes no pathetic serving of a myth. The good which our causes possess, then, also becomes a concrete fact for an experience of a higher than human level. That union of self-sacrifice with self-assertion which loyalty expresses becomes a consciousness of our genuine relations to a higher social unity of consciousness in which we all have our being. For from this point of view we are, and we have our worth, by virtue of our relation to a consciousness of a type superior to the human type.

We have called this realm of true life, and of genuine and united experience,—this realm which, if our argument at the last time was sound, includes our lives in that very whole which constitutes the real universe,— we have called this realm, I say, an eternal world,—eternal, simply because, according to our theory, it includes all temporal happenings and strivings in the conspectus of a single consciousness, and fulfils all our rational purposes together, and is all that we seek to be. For, as we argued, this realm of reality is conscious, is united, is self-possessed, and is perfected through the very wealth of the ideal sacrifices and of the loyal devotion which are united so as to constitute its fulness of being. In view of the philosophy that was thus sketched, I now propose a new definition of loyalty; and I say that this definition results from all of our previous study: *Loyalty is the will to manifest, so far as it is possible, the Eternal, that is, the conscious and superhuman unity of life, in the form of the acts of an individual Self.*

THE INTERNAL AND EXTERNAL MEANING OF IDEAS*

Experience and Thought are upon our hands; and together they determine for us the problems regarding Being. Realism offered to us the first solution

---

* Josiah Royce, "The Internal and External Meaning of Ideas," in *The World and the Individual,* 2 vols. (New York: Macmillan, 1899, 1901), vol. 1, pp. 265ff.

of this problem by attempting to define the Reality of the world as something wholly independent of our ideas. We rejected that solution on the ground that with an Independent Being our ideas could simply have nothing to do. Or, if you please so to interpret our discussion of Realism, we pointed out that our ideas, too, are realities; and that if Realism is true, they are therefore in their whole Being as independent of their supposed realistic objects as the latter are of the ideas. If, then, it makes no difference to the supposed external beings whether the ideas are or are not, it can make no difference to the ideas whether the independent external Beings are or are not. The supposed dependence of knowledge for its success upon its so-called independent object, proves, therefore, to be contradicted by the ontological independence inevitably possessed by the knowing idea, in case Realism is once accepted. For the realistic sort of independence is an essentially mutual relation. The idea can then say to the independent object, in a realistic world: "What care I for you? You are independent of me, but so am I of you. No purpose of mine would be unfulfilled if you simply vanished, so long as I then still remained what I am. And I could, by definition, remain in my whole Being unaltered by your disappearance. Accordingly, since my truth means merely the fulfilment of my own purpose, I should lose no truth if you vanished. In short, I not only do not need you, but observe, upon second thought, that I never meant you at all, never referred to you, never conceived you, and, in truth, am even now not addressing you. In short, you are Nothing."

With such reflections, we woke from the realistic dream, and knew that whatever Being is, it is not independent of the ideas that refer to it.

After our later experience with the fascinating paradoxes of Mysticism had equally shown us that Being cannot be defined as the ineffable immediate fact that quenches ideas, and that makes them all alike illusory, we passed, in the two foregoing lectures, to the realm of Validity, to the ontological conceptions of Critical Rationalism. What is, gives warrant to ideas, makes them true, and enables us to define determinate, or valid, possible experiences. That was the view that we illustrated as our Third Conception of Being. We dwelt upon it so lengthily because, if it is not the final truth, it is, unquestionably, as far as it goes, true.

What we found with regard to this definition of Reality may be summed up briefly thus: In the first place, the conception has an obvious foundation in the popular consciousness. Not only does the ontological vocabulary of ordinary speech illustrate this third conception in several ways; but, amongst the beings known to common sense, there are many that are regarded as real beings, but that are still explicitly defined only in terms of validity. Such beings are the prices and credits of the commercial world, the social standing of individuals, the constitutions of Empires, and the moral law.

In the second place, in science, mathematics deals exclusively with entities that are explicitly conceived by the science in question as of this third type, and of this type only. In the next place, as we found, the Being usually ascribed to the laws and to the objects of physical science, is capable, at least in very large part, of being interpreted in terms of this third conception. Such conceived entities as Energy are typical instances of beings of this sort. And, finally, all the entities of even a metaphysical Realism proved to be such that when one tries not to leave them unintelligibly independent, but to tell what they are, there is no means to define their character which does not first of all declare that their reality involves the validity of certain of our ideas, and the truth of the assertion that, under definable conditions, particular experiences would be possible. What else the Being of such entities would mean, remained for us so far undefinable.

On the other hand, as we concluded our former discussion, considerations crowded upon us, which forced us to observe that in some way this Third Conception of Being, despite all the foregoing, is inadequate.

Valid in its own measure it is,—to say that is to utter the deep commonplace of St. Augustine's form of the ontological proof of the existence of God. For it must indeed be true that there is a *Veritas.* Yet mere *Veritas,* mere validity, still remains to us a conception as unintelligible as it is insistently present to our thought. And our difficulty at the last time came thus to light: In mathematics, you define and prove valid assertions, and deal with entities, such as roots of equations, and properties of functions, whose Being seems to mean only their validity. But how do you prove these propositions about validity? How do you test the existence of your mathematical objects? Merely by experimenting upon your present ideas. What is there before you as you thus experiment? At each step of your procedure, one moment's narrow contents extend to the very horizon of your present finite mathematical experience. Yet if your procedure is, indeed, as it pretends to be, valid, the truth that you define embraces eternity, and predetermines the structure and the valid existence of an infinity of objects that you regard as external to the thought which defines them. Your world of objects then is here boundless; your human grasp of these objects is even pitiably limited. Validity thus implies, in the world of the mathematical entities, a twofold character. As presented, as seen by you, as here realized, the observed validity is apparently given in experience, indeed, but as a mere internal meaning,—the creature of the instant. But as objective, as genuine, the validity is a part of the endless realm of mathematical truth, a realm that is, to use Aristotle's term, the Unmoved Mover of all your finite struggle for insight in this region. How can the one form of Being be thus ambiguous, unless, in constitution, it is also much wealthier in nature than the mere abstraction expressed in our Third Conception makes it seem. Or, to put the case otherwise, the Third Conception of Being, in defining possibilities of experience, tells you only of mere abstract universals. But a mere universal is so far a bare *what*. One wants to make more explicit the *that,* to find something individual.

And, if you pass from mathematics to the physical instances of the third conception, and to the world of moral and social validity, it is of course true that every Being in heaven or in earth exists for you as determining a valid possibility of experience. But countless of these valid possibilities exist for you precisely as possibilities not yet tested by you, and therefore never to be tested. Herein lies the very essence of prudence, of generalizing science, and of moral choice, viz., in the fact that you recognize much experience as possible only to avoid it, and to refrain from verifying in your own person the valid possibility. But what is a mere possibility when not tested? Is it a mere internal meaning? Then where is its Truth? Is it external? Then what is its Being?

These were, in sum, our difficulties in regard to the Third Conception of Being. Their solution, logically speaking, lies now very near. But for us, the road must still prove long. Meanwhile, the formulation of all these difficulties may be condensed into the single question, the famous problem of Pontius Pilate, What is Truth? For the Third Conception of Being has reduced Being to Truth, or Validity. But now we need to make out what constitutes the very essence of Truth itself. It is this which at the last time we left still in obscurity. It is this which lies so near us, and which still, because of manifold misunderstandings, we must long seek as if it were far away.

It is customary to dwell upon the "crushing character," the "over-whelming power" of "stubborn empirical facts." The character in question is, of course, a valid one. Yet this crushing force of experience is never a barely immediate fact; it is something relative to the particular ideas in question. For, as I must repeat, our so-called external experience, that is, our experience taken as other than our meanings, and viewed as what confirms or refutes them here or there, never does more, in any question concerning the truth, than to decide our ideal issues, and to decide them in particular instances, whose character and meaning for us are determined solely by what ideas of our own are in question. Or, again, empirical judgments, as such, are always particular. Hence, they never by themselves absolutely confirm, or refute, *all* that our ideas mean. And what they confirm, or refute, depends upon what questions have been asked from the side of our internal meanings.

. . . Being is not an object that we men come *near at will* to finally observing, so that while we never get it wholly present in our internal meanings, we can come as near as we like to telling all that it is. But the Real, as our judgments and empirical investigations seek it, is that determinate object which all our ideas and experiences try to decide upon, and to bring within the range of our internal meanings; while, by the very nature of our fragmentary hypotheses and of our particular experiences, it always lies Beyond.

Yet *if we could* reach that limit of determination which is all the while our goal, if our universal judgments were confirmed by an adequate experience, not of *some* object (still indeterminate), but of *the individual* object, or of *all the individual objects,* so that no other empirical expression of our ideas remained possible, then, indeed, we should stand in the immediate presence of the Real. The Real, then, is, from this point of view, that which is *immediately beyond* the whole of our series of possible efforts to bring, by any process of finite experience and of merely general conception, our own internal meaning to a complete determination.

And so we conclude that the object does not, as a finished fact, predetermine the sort of likeness that the idea must possess in order to be true. It is the idea that so far decides its own meaning. And I may once more point out that in all this you may see afresh why, from the opening lecture of this course, I have laid such stress upon the essentially teleological inner structure of conscious ideas, and why I defined ideas as I did in our opening lecture, namely, as cases where conscious states more or less completely present the embodiment, the relative fulfilment of a present purpose. Whatever else our ideas are, and however much or little they may be, at any moment, expressed in rich, sensuous imagery, it is certain that they are ideas not because they are masses or series of images, but because they embody present conscious purposes. Every idea is as much a volitional process as it is an intellectual process. It may well or ill represent or correspond to something not itself, but it must, in any case, make more or less clearly articulate its own present purpose. The constructive character of all mathematical ideas, the sense of current control which accompanies all definite thinking processes, the momentary purposes more or less imperfectly fulfilled whenever we conceive anything,—these are evidences of what is essential to processes of ideation. Volition is as manifest in counting objects as in singing tunes, in conceiving physical laws as in directing the destinies of nations, in laboratory experiments as in artistic productions, in contemplating as in fighting. The embodied purpose, the internal meaning, of the instant's act, is thus a *conditio sine qua non* for all external meaning and for all truth. What we are now inquiring is simply how an internal meaning can be linked to an external meaning, how a volition can also possess truth, how the purpose of the instant can express the nature of an object other than the instant's purpose.

. . . In view of this apparent antinomy, how is the idea related to its object? How is error possible? What is truth? The answer to these questions,—the solution to all our previous difficulties, is in one respect so simple, that I almost fear, after this so elaborate preparation, to state it, lest by its very simplicity it may disappoint. Yet I must first state it,

abstractly, and perhaps unconvincingly, and then illustrate it as I close
the present discussion, leaving to a later lecture its fuller development.
The idea, I have said, *seeks its own. It can be judged by nothing but what
it intends.* Whether I think of God or of yesterday's events, of my own
death, or of the destiny of mankind, of mathematical truth, or of physical
facts, of affairs of business, or of Being itself, it is first of all what I mean,
and not what somebody merely external to myself might desire me to
mean, that both gives me an object, and determines for me the standard
of correspondence to the object whereby I must be judged. Moreover, my
idea is a cognitive process only in so far as it is, at the same time, a
voluntary process, an act, the partial fulfilment, so far as the idea consciously extends, of a purpose. The object meant by the idea is the object
because it is willed to be such, and the will in question is the will that
the idea embodies. And that is why Realism proved to be impossible;
that is why the Independent Beings were self-contradictory concepts; that
too, is why the resignation of all definite purpose which Mysticism required
of our ideas was impossible without a failure to define Being as any but
a mere Nothing. And every definition of truth or of Being must depend
upon a prior recognition of precisely this aspect of the nature of ideas.

. . . Whenever an idea of any grade aims at truth, it regards its object
as other than itself, and that the object shall be thus other than itself is
even a part of what the idea means and consciously intends. But as a
will seeking its own fulfillment, the idea so selects the object, that, if the
idea has a perfectly definite meaning and truth at all, this object is to be
a precisely determinate object, *such that no other object could take its
place as the object of this idea.* And in spite of the fact that the object
is such solely by the will of the idea, the idea undertakes submissively
to be either true or false when compared with that object.

Now the obvious way of stating the whole sense of these facts is to
point out that what the idea always aims to find in its objects is *nothing
whatever but the idea's own conscious purpose or will, embodied in some
more determinate form* than the idea by itself alone at this instant consciously possesses. When I have an idea of the world, my idea is a will,
*and the world of my idea is simply my own will itself determinately
embodied.*

And what this way of stating our problem implies may first be
illustrated by any case where, in doing what we often call "making up
our minds," we pass from a vague to a definite state of will and of
resolution. In such cases we begin with perhaps a very indefinite sort of
restlessness, which arouses the question, "What is it that I want? What
do I desire? What is my real purpose?" To answer this question may
take a long time and much care; and may involve many errors by the
way, errors, namely, in understanding our own purpose. Such search for
one's own will often occupies, in the practical life of youth, some very
anxious years. Idleness, defective modes of conduct, self-defeating struggles

without number, fickle loves that soon die out, may long accompany what the youth himself all the while regards as the search for his own will, for the very soul of his own inner and conscious purposes. In such cases one may surely err as to one's intent. The false or fickle love is a sort of transient dream of the coming true love itself. The transient choice is a shadow of the coming true choice. But how does one's own real intent, the object at such times of one's search, stand related to one's present and ill-defined vague restlessness, or imperfectly conscious longing. I answer, one's true will, one's genuine purpose, one's object here sought for, can be nothing whatever but one's present imperfect conscious will in some more determinate form. What one has, at such times, is the will of the passing moment,—an internal meaning, consciously present as far as it goes. And now it is this will and no other that one seeks to bring to clearer consciousness. But what other, what external meaning, what fact beyond, yes, what object, is the goal of this quest? I answer, nothing whatever in heaven or in earth but this present imperfect internal meaning rendered more determinate, less ambiguous in its form, less a general longing, more a precisely united and determinate life. And this, once rendered perfectly determinate, would be what the man in question calls "My life according to my conscious will."

Well, this case of the vague purpose that one seeks, not to abandon, but to get present to the moment's consciousness in another, that is a more explicit and precise, form, and if possible, in what would finally prove to be an absolutely determinate form,—this case, I insist, is typical of every case where an idea seeks its object. *In seeking its object, any idea whatever seeks absolutely nothing but its own explicit, and, in the end, complete, determination as this conscious purpose, embodied in this one way. The complete content of the idea's own purpose is the only object of which the idea can ever take note.*

Now this final embodiment is the ultimate object, and the only genuine object, that any present idea seeks as its Other. But if this be so, when is the idea true? It is true—this instant's idea—if, in its own measure, and on its own plan, it corresponds, even in its vagueness, to its own final and completely individual expression. Its expression would be the very life of fulfilment of purpose which this present idea already fragmentarily begins, as it were, to express. It is with a finite idea as it is with any form of will. Any of its transient expressions may be at any instant more or less abortive. But no finite idea is wholly out of correspondence to its object, as no will is wholly false to itself.

We have thus defined the object and the truth of an idea. But observe that thus we stand upon the threshold of a new definition of Being. Being, as our Third Conception declared, is what gives true ideas their truth; or in other words, to be real is to be the object of a true idea. We are ready, now that we have defined both object and truth, to assert, as our Fourth and final Conception of Being, this, that *What is, or what is real, is as such the complete embodiment, in individual form and in final fulfilment, of the internal meaning of finite ideas.*

COMMUNITY AND THE DOCTRINE OF SIGNS*

Just as each one of many present selves, despite the psychological or ethical barriers which now keep all of these selves sundered, may accept the same past fact or event as a part of himself, and say, "That belonged to my life," even so, each one of many present selves, despite these same barriers and sunderings, may accept the same future event, which all of them hope or expect, as part of his own personal future. Thus, during a war, all of the patriots of one of the contending nations may regard the termination of the war, and the desired victory of their country, so that each one says: "I shall rejoice in the expected surrender of that stronghold of the enemy. That surrender will be my triumph."

Now when many contemporary and distinct individual selves so interpret, each his own personal life, that each says of an individual past or of a determinate future event or deed: "That belongs to my life;" "That occured, or will occur, to me," then these many selves may be defined as hereby constituting, in a perfectly definite and objective, but also in a highly significant, sense, a community. They may be said to constitute a community *with reference* to that particular past or future event, or group of events, which each of them accepts or interprets as belonging to his own personal past or to his own individual future. A community constituted by the fact that each of its members accepts as part of his own individual life and self the same *past* events that each of his fellow-members accepts, may be called a *community of memory.* Such is any group of persons who individually either remember or commemorate the same dead,—each one finding, because of personal affection or of reverence for the dead, that those whom he commemorates form for him a part of his own past existence.

A community constituted by the fact that each of its members accepts, as part of his own individual life and self, the same expected *future* events that each of his fellows accepts, may be called a *community of expectation,* or upon occasion, a *community of hope.*

INTERPRETATION*

The Christian doctrine of life is dominated by the ideal of the Universal Community. Such was the thesis defended in the first part of this series

---

* Josiah Royce, "Community and the Doctrine of Signs," in *The Problem of Christianity,* 2 vols. (New York: Macmillan, 1913), vol. 2, lecture 8, pp. 49–50. Reprinted with the permission of David Royce.
* Ibid., lecture 14, pp. 322–25.

of lectures. The real world itself is, in its wholeness, a Community. This was the metaphysical result in which our study of the World of Interpretation, at the last time, culminated.

Herewith the two assertions to which our study of the Problem of Christianity leads, are before you. Our concluding lectures must make explicit the relations between these two assertions. Hereby each of them will be interpreted in the light of the other.

Metaphysical theory and religious experience are always contrasting realms of inquiry and of insight. Therefore the task of our three concluding lectures constitutes a typical exercise in the process of interpretation. We have to compare results which have been reached by widely different methods. We have to mediate between them. The method of interpretation is always the comparative method. To compare and to interpret are two names for the same fundamental cognitive process.

The fitting order for such an enterprise is determined by the subject-matter. Since the metaphysical thesis with which our last lecture closed is very general, it will prove to be, indeed, a worthless abstraction, unless we illustrate its application to various special problems of life as well as of philosophy. What I can hope, within the limits of our brief remaining time, to make clearer, is what I may call the ground plan of the World of Interpretation.

The universe, if my thesis is right, is a realm which is through and through dominated by social categories. Time, for instance, expresses a system of essentially social relations. The present interprets the past to the future. At each moment of time the results of the whole world's history up to that moment are, so to speak, summed up and passed over to the future for its new deeds of creation and of interpretation. I state this principle here in a simply dogmatic form, and merely as an example of what I have in mind when I say the system of metaphysics which is needed to define the constitution of this world of interpretation must be the generalized theory of an ideal society. Not the Self, not the Logos, not the One, and not the Many, but the Community will be the ruling category of such a philosophy.

I must attempt, then, within our brief remaining time, to make this general metaphysical theory less abstract and more articulate. I must contrast our theory with others. I must make more explicit its relation to the Christian ideas. And then I must, in conclusion, survey what we have won, and summarize the outcome.

Let me begin by a few purely technical formulations. Charles Peirce, in the discussions which we have now so freely used, introduced into logic the term "Sign." He used that term as the name for an object to which somebody gives or should give an interpretation. I have not here to deal, at any length, with Peirce's development of his theory of Signs. His doctrine was, as you will recall, not at first stated as the basis for a metaphysical system, but simply as a part of a logical theory of the categories. My own metaphysical use of Peirce's doctrine of signs, in my account of the World of Interpretation at the last time, is largely independent of Peirce's philosophy. For the moment it is enough to say that, according to Peirce, just as percepts have, for their appropriate objects, individually existent Things; and just as concepts possess, for their sole objects, Universals,—so interpretations have, as the objects which they interpret, Signs. In its most abstract definition, therefore, a Sign, according to Peirce, is something that determines an interpretation. A sign may also be called an expression of a mind; and, in our ordinary social intercourse, it actually is such an expression. Or again, one may say that a sign is, in its essence, either a mind or a quasi-mind,—an object that fulfills the functions of a mind.

Thus, a word, a clock-face, a weather-vane, or a gesture, is a sign. Our reason for calling it such is twofold. It expresses a mind, and it calls for an interpretation through some other mind, which shall act as mediator between the sign, or between the maker of the sign, and some one to whom the sign is to be read.

Since an interpretation of a sign is, in its turn, the expression of the interpreter's mind, it constitutes a new sign, which again calls for interpretation; and so on without end; unless the process is arbitrarily interrupted. So much can be asserted as a purely logical thesis, quite apart from metaphysics. A sign, then, is an object whose being consists in the fact that the sign calls for an interpretation.

The process of interpretation, as it occurs in our ordinary social life, sufficiently illustrates the meaning of Peirce's new term. Peirce insists that the signs, viewed simply from a logical point of view, constitute a new fundamentally important category. He sets this category as a "third,' side by side with the classic categories of the "universals" which form the "first" category, and the "individuals," which, in Peirce's logic, form the "second" category.

Peirce, as I have said, is not responsible for the metaphysical theory about the world of interpretation with which our last lecture closed. But his terminology enables us to summarize that theory by stating our own metaphysical thesis thus: "The universe consists of real Signs of their interpretation."

In the order of real time the events of the world are signs. They are followed by interpreters, or by acts of interpretation which our own experience constantly exemplifies. For we live, as selves, by interpreting the events and the meaning of our experience. History consists of such interpretations.

These acts of interpretation are, in their turn, expressed, in the order of time, by new signs. The sequence of these signs and interpretations constitutes the history of the universe. Whatever our experience exemplifies, our metaphysical doctrine of signs generalizes, and applies to the world at large.

The world's experience is, from this point of view, not merely a flux. For, as Bergson rightly asserts, the world of any present moment of time is a summary of the results of all past experience. This view of Bergson's, however, is no mere intuition, but is itself an interpretation. Our own metaphysical thesis states in terms of interpretation what Begson states as if it were a result of simple intuition.

Since any idea, and especially any antithesis or contrast of ideas, is, according to our metaphysical thesis, a sign which in the world finds it real interpretation, our metaphysical theory may be called a "doctrine of signs."

The title which I have given to this lecture serves to direct attention, through the use of a purely technical term, to the main issue. The issue is the one presented by the thesis that the very being of the universe consists in a process whereby the world is interpreted,—not indeed in its wholeness, at any one moment of time, but in and through an infinite series of acts of interpretation. This infinite series constitutes the temporal order of the world with all its complexities. The temporal order is an order of purposes and of deeds, simply because it is of the essence of every rational deed to be an effort to interpret a past life to a future life; while every act of interpretation aims to introduce unity into life, by mediating between mutually contrasting or estranged ideas, minds, and purposes. If we consider the temporal world in its wholeness, it constitutes in itself an infinitely complex Sign. This sign is, as a whole, interpreted to an experience which itself includes a synoptic survey of the whole of time. Such is a mere sketch of our doctrine of the world of interpretation.

. . . We have no ground whatever for believing that there is any real world except the ground furnished by our experience, and by the fact that, in addition to our perceptions and our conceptions, we have problems upon our hands which need interpretation. Our fundamental postulate is: *The world is the interpretation of the problems which it presents.* If you deny this principle, you do so only by presenting, as Bergson does, some other interpretation as the true one. But thus you simply reaffirm the principle that the world has an interpreter.

Using this principle, in your ordinary social life, you postulate your fellow-man as the interpreter of the ideas which he awakens in your mind, and which are not your own ideas. The same principle, applied to our social experience of the physical world, determines our ordinary interpretations of nature and guides our natural science. For, as we have seen, the physical world is an object known to the community, and through interpretation. The same principle, applied to our memories and to our expectations, gives us our view of the world of time, with all its infinite wealth of successive acts of interpretation.

In all these special instances, the application of this principle defines for us some form or grade of community, and teaches us wherein lies the true nature, the form, the real unity, and the essential life of this community.

Our Doctrine of Signs extends to the whole world the same fundamental principle. The World is the Community. The world contains its own interpreter. Its processes are infinite in their temporal varieties. But their interpreter, the spirit of this universal community,—never absorbing varieties or permitting them to blend,—compares and, through a real life, interprets them all.

The attitude of will which this principle expresses, is neither that of the affirmation nor that of the denial of what Schopenhauer meant by the will to live. It is the attitude which first expresses itself by saying "Alone I am lost, and am worse than nothing. I need a counsellor, I need my community. Interpret me. Let me join in this interpretation. Let there be the community. This alone is life. This alone is salvation. This alone is real." This is at once an attitude of the will and an assertion whose denial refutes itself. For if there is no interpreter, there is no interpretation. And if there is no interpretation, there is no world whatever.

In its daily form as the principle of our social common sense, this attitude of the will inspires whatever is reasonable about our worldly business and our scientific inquiry. For all such business and inquiry are in and for and of the community, or else are vanity.

In its highest form, this attitude of the will was the one which Paul knew as Charity, and as the life in and through the spirit of the Community.

Such, then, is the relation of the Christian will to the real world.

STUDY QUESTIONS

Review

1. What is idealism?
2. What is the difference between subjective and objective idealism? Between objective idealism and realism?
3. Summarize Royce's argument for the existence of the Absolute from the reality of error.
4. What is the difference according to Royce between the internal and external meaning of ides? How is the real defined in terms of the internal meaning of ideas?
5. According to Royce, what is loyalty? How does he see it contributing to the formation of self-identity?
6. What is his final moral imperative? In what way does it relate to the problem of the individual within a community?

For Further Thought

7. How can one respond to Berkeley when he argues that if what we know are our own ideas, and we never know such a thing as material substance but only suppose it to be the source of our ideas, we might as well dispense with such an unknowable substrate.

8. Do you think that error presupposes the existence of some truth by which to judge it an error? Do you think that what we now say about the future can be in error even before that future comes about? Does this imply that there is some truth about the future existing even now?

9. Do you think the only way there can be real community is through unity created by a cause to which all the members of the community are devoted? How would you descirbe the problem of individual and community? Is loyalty or loyalty to loyalty a solution?

10. What do we ordinarily mean by a "sign"? Is the interpretation of a sign triadic? What is involved in interpretation? What do you think it means to say that understanding involves a continuing (perhaps infinite) process of interpretation?

BIBLIOGRAPHY

Idealism

Blau, Joseph. "Varieties of Idealism." In chap. 6, *Men and Movements in American Philosophy.* Englewood Cliffs, N.J.: Prentice-Hall, 1952.

Cunningham, G. Watts. *The Idealistic Argument in Recent British and American Philosophy.* New York: The Century Co., 1933.

Edwards, Paul, ed. *Encyclopedia of Philosophy.* Vol. 4, pp. 110-18. New York: Macmillan, 1967.

Ewing, A. C. *The Idealist Tradition from Berkeley to Blanshard.* Glencoe, Ill.: The Free Press, 1957.

— — —. *Idealism: A Critical Survey.* London: Methuen and Co., Ltd., 1934.

Hocking, Wm. E. "Idealism." In *Types of Philosophy,* pp. 151-224. New York: Charles Scribner's, 1959.

Muirhead, J. H. *The Platonic Tradition in Anglo-Saxon Philosophy: Studies in the History of Idealism in England and America.* London: G. Allen and Unwin, Ltd., 1931.

Passmore, John. "Towards the Absolute." Chap. 3 in *A Hundred Years of Philosophy,* pp. 71-94. New York: Basic Books, 1957; rev. ed., 1966.

Royce, Josiah. *Lectures on Modern Idealism.* New Haven, Conn.: Yale University Press, 1919.

Schneider, Herbert W., "Idealism." Chap. 7, in *A History of American Philosophy,* pp. 374-430. 2d. ed. New York: Columbia University Press, 1963.

Smith, Norman Kemp. *Prolegomena to an Idealist Theory of Knowledge.* London, 1924.

Josiah Royce

Josiah Royce. *The Philosophy of Josiah Royce.* Ed. John K. Roth, New York: Thomas Y. Crowell Co., 1971.

— — —. *Royce's Logical Essays.* West Hanover, Mass.: Christopher Publishing House, 1971.

— — —. *The Basic Writings of Josiah Royce.* 2 vols. Ed. John J. McDermott. Chicago: University of Chicago Press, 1969.

— — —. *The Social Philosophy of Josiah Royce.* Ed. S. G. Brown. Syracuse: Syracuse University Press, 1950.

— — —. *Fugitive Essays.* Introduction by J. Lowenberg. Cambridge: Harvard University Press, 1925.

— — —. *Lectures on Modern Idealism.* New Haven: Yale University Press, 1919.

— — —. *War and Insurance.* New York: Macmillan, 1914.

— — —. *The Problem of Christianity.* 2 vols. New York: Macmillan, 1913. Reprint. Chicago: University of Chicago Press, 1968. Reprint includes an introduction by John E. Smith.

— — —. *The Sources of Religious Insight.* New York: Charles Scribner's, 1912.

— — —. *The Philosophy of Loyalty.* New York: Macmillan, 1908.

— — —. *Outlines of Psychology.* New York: Macmillan, 1903.

— — —. *The World and the Individual.* 2 vols. New York: Macmillan, 1899, 1901. Reprint. New York: Dover, 1959. First given as the Gifford Lectures.

— — —. *The Conception of Immortality.* Boston: Houghton Mifflin, 1900.

— — —. *Studies of Good and Evil.* New York: D. Appleton, 1898.

— — —. *The Conception of God: A Philosophical Discussion Concerning the Nature of the Divine Idea as a Demonstrable Reality.* New York: Macmillan, 1897.

— — —. *The Spirit of Modern Philosophy.* Boston: Houghton Mifflin, 1892.

— — —. *The Religious Aspect of Philosophy: A Critique of the Basis of Conduct and of Faith.* Boston: Houghton Mifflin, 1885.

Barrett, Clifford, ed. *Contemporary Idealism in America.* 1932. Reprint. New York: Atheneum, 1964.

Buranelli, Vincent. *Josiah Royce.* New York: Twayne Publishing, 1964.

Cotton, James Harry. *Royce on the Human Self.* Cambridge: Harvard University Press, 1954.

Creighton, J. E., ed. *Papers in Honor of Josiah Royce on His Sixtieth Birthday.* New York: Longmans, Green, 1916.

Fuss, Peter. *The Moral Philosophy of Josiah Royce.* Cambridge: Harvard University Press, 1965.

Hocking, Wm. E., "On Royce's Empiricism." *Journal of Philosophy* 53 (1956): pp. 57–63.

Kraushaar, Otto F. "Josiah Royce." In *Classic American Philosophers.* ed. Max H. Fisch, pp. 181–99. New York: Appleton-Century-Crofts, 1951.

Leidecker, K. F. *Josiah Royce and Indian Thought.* New York: Kailas Press, 1931.

Loewenberg, J. *Royce's Synoptic Vision.* Department of Philosophy, John Hopkins University, 1955.

Marcel, Gabriel. *Royce's Metaphysics.* Trans. V. Ringer. Chicago: Henry Regnery Co., 1956.

Montague, W. P. "Professor Royce's Refutation of Realism." *Philosophical* Review 11 (1902): pp. 43–55.

Oppenheim, Frank M. *Royce's Voyage Down Under: A Journey of the Mind.* Lexington: University Press of Kentucky, 1980.

Perry, Ralph Bargon. "Two American Philosophers: William James and Josiah Royce." In *The Spirit of William James.* New Haven: Yale University Press, 1938.

— — —. "Professor Royce's Refutation of Realism and Pluralism." *The Monist* 12 (1902): pp. 446–58.

Robinson, Daniel S. *Royce and Hocking: American Idealists.* West Hanover, Mass.: Christopher Publishing House, 1968.

Santayana, George. "Josiah Royce." In *Character and Opinion in the United States.* New York: Charles Scribners, 1920.

Singh, Bhagwan B. *The Self and the World in the Philosophy of Josiah Royce.* Springfield, Ill.: C. C. Thomas Press, 1973.

Smith, John E. "Josiah Royce: The Eternal, the Practical, and the Beloved Community." Chap. 3, in *The Spirit of American Philosopphy*, pp. 80–114. New York: Oxford University Press, 1966.

— — —. *Royce's Social Infinite: The Community of Interpretation.* New York: Liberal Arts Press, 1950.

Straton, George D. *Theistic Faith for Our Time: An Introduction to the Process Philosophies of Royce and Whitehead.* Lanham, Md.: University Press of America, 1978.

Thompson, Samuel M. "Idealism and Voluntarism in Royce." *Review of Metaphysics* 9 (1956): pp. 433–40.

White, Howard B. "Royce's Philosophy of Loyalty." *Journal of Philosophy* 53 (1956): pp. 99–103.

Part 3

Twentieth-Century Philosophy in America

Chapter 10

Early-Twentieth-Century Realism and Naturalism

Any summary of twentieth-century philosophy is bound to meet with a number of difficulties, as will any summary of twentieth-century philosophy in America. In the first place, from our perspective in the 1980s we may not yet be sufficiently distant from the first three-quarters of the century to be able to notice trends and evaluate the relative importance of the various philosophies and philosophers. Secondly, there are so many different types of philosophies that it is difficult to do more than simply catalogue them. Thirdly, the differences between types of philosophies often blur. For example, some naturalists are positivistically inclined and others are metaphysicians, language is also a focus of some phenomenologists, and it is difficult to classify philosophers such as Santayana, Lewis and Wilfrid Sellars. Our own classifications and selections are thus inevitably open to criticism both because of the types of philosophy we treat and the philosophers of these types that receive more emphasis. Part 3 is also more liable to the criticism that it includes too much rather than too little. However, it seemed better to give readers more rather than less of a choice. Since the chapters treat types of philosophies, the philosophers included are not always presented in a strictly historical order.

We have chosen to group together in this present chapter early American realism and naturalism. Some might suggest that we treat Marxism as a special case. Granted that in America there has been some interest in this type of philosophy, but the interest occurs later and is not of sufficient amount in our judgment to give more than this mention. The reader may follow his or her own interests and supplement our selections from suggestions in the bibliography.

We begin with a summary of the debate between the realists and idealists and between the different schools of realists. Next we summarize some of the so-called naturalist philosophies. Since John Dewey, a major example of this type of philosophy who was still active during this and later periods, has been discussed in a previous chapter, and since naturalistic ethics including those of Dewey will be dealt with in a separate later chapter, our treatment of naturalism here will be brief. We will conclude with a summary of the life and writings of George Santayana — a philosopher who may be classified as a naturalist but who also was associated with the self-described "critical realists."

REALISM

At the end of the nineteenth century in America, idealism "was everywhere rampant," as Wm. P. Montague describes it.[1] It was going strong in St. Louis with the Hegelian school, at the University of California at Berkeley with George Howison, and at Harvard with Royce. There was at that time little interest in realism. The Scottish school of common sense (see chapter 1) had had its day. Neo-Thomists presented a defense of realism but one that was too closely connected with Catholicism to be universally influential (see the separate treatment of Thomism in chapter 11). It was idealism that was the philosophy to be reckoned with. In England an attack on idealism was spearheaded by G. E. Moore. In this country too pragmatism had moved against idealism, especially its tendencies towards rationalism and monism, but the pragmatists' critique seemed not to lead to realism as much as to more scientific and empiricist philosophies (see chapter 15). While some interpretations of Peirce's theory of knowledge stress his realism, there are also interpretations that attempt to show its underlying idealism. Truth, for Peirce, is still thought of in terms of what we will come to know, and matter is but habit-bound mind. James's theory of truth also could be taken to support idealism. For example, a realist would hold, contrary to James, that the truth of a proposition antedates its verification or that it is true before we discover this fact. Some of the realists we will discuss in this chapter found that the pragmatic theory of truth, which identifies truth with the process of verification, is but another form of idealism.[2]

In 1901 two articles that might be said to mark the beginning of a twenty-year debate over realism appeared in philosophy journals. Both articles had been provoked by Josiah Royce's critique of realism in the first chapter of his work, *The World and the Individual* (1901). They contained the realist's response to "Professor Royce's Refutation of Realism." [3] The problem for realists was this: Kant said our knowledge is of how things appear to us, and that we can never know things as they are in themselves. The object of our knowledge, then, is always informed or changed by our particular mode of knowing. Royce had supposed that a realism must show the independence of the object of knowledge from consciousness. But if it were so independent then it could never come to be related to consciousness by being known. However, according to the realists, there are two ways things can be related to one another — internally or externally. An internal relation, they said, is one in which the terms of the relation are dependent on the relation for their character or existence, for example mother and daughter. Things could also be related externally and not have such a dependence; this was the kind of relation realists supposed knowledge to be. Objects could be related to consciousness by being known without being changed by this relatiion.

Ralph Barton Perry (professor of philosophy at Harvard) and Wm. Pepperal Montague (Columbia University) joined with Perry's colleague Edwin B. Holt and Montague's colleague Walter Pitkin, together with Edward G. Spaulding (Princeton) and Walter T. Marvin (Rutgers), to present a united front against criticisms of realism such as Royce's. In 1910 they jointly published "A Program and Platform of Six Realists." [4] That they published a joint statement was significant, for they believed that philosophy should follow the example of science and be a co-operative enterprise. Philosophers, they thought, should develop their theories, write their essays, and then expose them to the criticism of other philosophers in order to see how much common ground there was on which they could agree. Philosophy, they argued, should follow the lead of science, taking its problems one at a time. The new realists, as these men were called, thus thought they could tackle the problem of knowledge apart from any metaphysical consideration of the nature of either the knowing subject or the known object. (In fact some realists did do work in this area and differed in their conclusions.)

Of what, then, did realistic platform consist? Basically it asserted three things:

1. There are some particulars that exist when no one is conscious of them. In other words, the existence of particular things is independent of our knowledge of them. Ralph Barton Perry had written concerning what he believed to be a fallacy of idealism, namely that while knowledge is necesary for knowing an object, this does not prove that being known is essential to the object's existence. To assert this notion is to be in an "egocentric predicament." [5] The problem is that we cannot observe an object before we observe it to see whether the observing of it has changed the object. Nor can we do this in other cases, for example, as challenging astrologers by removing the stars to see whether or not they influence human behavior. Rather, the realists held, we should decide by inference from observed behavior, noting whether there is a presence or absence of causally significant correlations between the object and consciousness.[6]

2. A second thesis of the group was that some universals or essences subsist when we are not conscious of them. An example would be numbers or colors. They are what they are regardless of our conscious thoughts about them. However, which of them we think about is due to our conscious decision or attention.

3. Finally, the realists asserted that some of the things that exist independent of and external to us are grasped directly by the mind rather than indirectly through mental copies of them. While the perception of an object requires stimulation of the perceiving organism, this is simply the means by which the object is perceived. It is not the means that is perceived, but the object. And since things perceived appear to be external to us, the burden of proof is on those who would show the opposite.

Differences of opinion on these matters, however, appeared soon after the publication of the "Platform." For example, Perry and Holt were more behavioristically inclined and held that the awareness of the object was but the organism's response to the object. How could an awareness be identified with a motion, asked Montague, who with others of the group opposed such a mechanistic interpretation of knowledge. In 1912 the same group published *The New Realism,* a volume of "cooperative studies in philosophy." [7] Some of the disparities among members of this group are evident as they worked out in more detail in these essays their own individual views. Among the points of disagreement was one concerning the existential status of objects of error and illusion. Holt and Perry said such objects must exist in order to cause erroneous knowledge. Montague and others, however, thought of them as subsisting in some way (not quite existing), but unable to exert causal force.

This discussion of error and the view that we can know objects directly aroused the criticism of another group of philosophers (this time seven in all) who labeled their position on these matters "critical realism." They too produced a book entitled *Essays in Critical Realism* (1920).[8] In these essays they hoped to solve some of these philosophical problems in a more critical or less naïve fashion. Members of this group included Durant Drake of Vassar, Arthur O. Lovejoy of Johns Hopkins, Roy Wood Sellars of the University of Michigan, and for some time George Santayana from Harvard.[9] How, they asked of the new realists, was error possible if we were directly in contact with the object of our knowledge? And how could we be in direct contact with, for example, a distant star that has already gone out of existence by the time its light reaches us and we see it? And why do things then appear different to different people, and even to the same person from different perspectives?

Such things are explicable only if knowledge is more indirect and is mediated, the critical realists argued. We should distinguish between the object that is known and our states of consciousness by which we know the object. This much the new realists also admitted. However, the critical realists contended further that what we know is not this state of mind by which we infer the nature and character of the object, but another "given" or "datum." This given or datum is an essence, is objective, and, while more mental than physical, it is in some way external to the knower. The existential status of this given remained not entirely clear. Roy Wood Sellars attempted to explain it this way: knowledge is "an interpretative comprehension of the characters of things by means of, and in terms of, characters within consciousness." [10] These characters are not copies of, but are nevertheless caused by, external objects. The likeness that does exist is between the relations among the characters and the relations among the objects. We directly entertain these data and only indirectly know the things they are caused by and intend. We not only intend these objects and believe in them, but also we take various attitudes toward them. Moreover, we interpret the world by means of these characters within consciousness, and our interpretations can be more or less adequate. Those interpretations that are most adequate enable us to deal with the world successfully. [11]

NATURALISM

During this same period a number of the critical realists and others were working out and reworking ideas about the nature of knowledge that could be characterized as naturalistic. They believed, for example, that man or the human organism is an integral part of nature or the natural scheme of things. John Dewey continued to stress the belief that knowledge was not an unnatural event but a natural function of a natural organism — a function that was developed to meet the organism's needs.

In addition to epistemological problems, Roy Wood Sellars was interested in the larger metaphysical or cosmological questions. He characterized his own views as an "evolutionary naturalism." [12] The primary existing entity he referred to by the traditional term "substance," meaning something capable of enduring in itself. Substance could also be called matter in that it is spatial and can be molded. It is not passive, however, but can in some sense direct itself. While there is basically one kind of being, there are levels of its existence and different forms of organization that can emerge. Each existing whole is not simply the sum of parts that compose it and from which it emerged; each whole has novel or emergent properties as well. Life and mind are such emergent forms of matter. Sellars took evolution seriously and believed that a theory such as his was necessary to explain it. [13]

George Santayana was for some time a member of the critical realist group and, like Sellars, considered himself a materialist. As we shall see, however, Santayana's materialism is quite different from that of Sellars.

GEORGE SANTAYANA

Although George Santayana belonged to that group of realists called critical realists, he is known more for his own writings than for his membership in that group. [14] Santayana was neither born nor died in the United States, however, he lived here from age nine (1870) until age fifty (1912). His philosophy which was developed here had a significant influence on American philosophers at the time. Born in Madrid of Spanish parents in 1863, George was nine years old when he moved to Boston to join his mother and her children by her first marriage, his father remaining in Madrid. His mother had promised her first husband before he died that she would educate their children in America. George attended Boston Latin School for eight years and then went on to Harvard in 1882. While at Harvard he and some of his friends started the student humor magazine, the *Harvard Lampoon,* a paper that continues today. William James and Josiah Royce were among Santayana's teachers at Harvard, although he had little sympathy for the philosophy of either.

Santayana was never wealthy, and it was only from money provided by a fellowship that as a graduate student at Harvard he was able to study for two years in Berlin. William James then persuaded Harvard President Eliot to take on Santayana as a professor after his degree was attained; Santayana then taught at Harvard until he left America in 1912, to the surprise and hurt of many of his academic colleagues. From that time on Santayana lived in hotels or with friends, first in England during World War I, and in Rome beginning in 1920, where he remained for most of the rest of his life. He died in 1952 at a convent nursing home in Rome where he had spent the last thirteen years of his life, still more a naturalist than a religious believer, or rather one who believed that religion has a symbolic value. It is significant, however, that his later years showed a spirit of detachment from the world's interests and problems (including World War II which raged around him in Italy), a spirit celebrated by his later philosophy as the source of the highest of human pleasures and accomplishments.

His writings are many and varied. One of his first publications was a collection of poems, *Sonnets and Other Verse* (1894). He also authored a novel, *The Last Puritan* (1936).[15] These works as well as his more philosophical writings show a beauty of style unusual among philosophers. However, Santayana's writings also embody an elaborate philosophical system that deserves to be taken seriously on its own account. Santayana held that the goal of philosophy was a synthetic vision with aesthetic as well as intellectually valuable qualities. In fact it was *The Sense of Beauty* (1896), a treatise on aesthetics, that first gained him respect among philosophers. Here, as in his treatment of ethical values, a certain relativism is evident. Beauty is said to reside not in any characteristics of aesthetic objects but the feelings of pleasure we get in contemplating them.[16]

Santayana's ethics is for the most part contained in his five-volume publication, *The Life of Reason* (1905–6).[17] In this work Santayana describes the development of reason in human history as well as in the lives of individual human beings. He does not mean to suggest that there is some kind of inevitable progress built into the universe, some force at work within it, but rather that as a matter of fact, now and then the human race has made some progress towards a rational way of life, a life that is orderly and coherent. The various volumes detail this development: volume 1, *Reason in Common Sense;* volume 2, *Reason in Society;* volume 3, *Reason in Religion;* volume 4, *Reason in Art;* and volume 5, *Reason in Science.* Common sense and the perceptual and animal life of man in nature, according to Santayana, is the ground out of which we emerge and develop. The first society is a natural one; from this we develop other kinds of ideal or symbolic societies, for example patriotic organizations. Religion and art also have their function in the life of man and history. Religion is a symbolic rendering of the meaning and value of human existence, of moral ideals and their grounding in nature. Art shows us various harmonies and can help us increase harmony in other areas of life. Science is common sense refined and produces systems of interpretation that are also symbolic and thus not entirely different from those produced by art, religion, and poetry. There is also a pattern of growth towards rationality in the ethical life of men. The first ethics is prerational and primarily ruled by impulse and habit, while in the more mature stage one's ideals are consciously reflected on and made to govern one's life. However, the highest stage is postrational, one in which, through the free play of imagination or spirit, poetic and symbolic ideals give meaning and pleasure to one's life.

Santayana's theory of knowledge and reality is found first and most concisely in *Skepticism and Animal Faith* (1923) and later are more fully developed in his four-volume work, *Realms of Being* (1927–40).[18] Ordinary common sense makes one believe many things, he points out, but philosophers in the Cartesian mode have sought to determine which things one has good grounds for believing. Santayana comes to the conclusion that nothing is beyond doubt and that complete skepticism is possible. For example, there is nothing in my experience, he argues, to assure me of the existence of the material world. That of which we are certain is only what is given to us in our immediate experience. This is a complex scene. We do not experience any relation between our experience and something else that it represents. We do not directly experience existence. "I am using the word existence," he states, "to designate such being as is in flux, determined by external relations, and jostled by irrelevant events."[19] Things that exist stand in external relation to one another, but all we find in our immediate experience are interrelated essences. Further reflection on this experience reveals only what is part of the scene itself. It is essences, then, that are present to and intuited by consciousness, not the existence of things. Furthermore, if we are able to doubt the existence of things, we can also doubt the existence of a self with memory and experiences, for these depend on the natural world for a reference, according to Santayana. Nor can we rely on experience of a passing stream of events in temporal sequence from which an enduring self can be distinguished, for we have no immediate experience of the past or future and thus no experience of time. We are left with what Santayana calls the "solipsism of the present moment," a mental stance in which there is but a passing show with no past or future.[20]

If knowing means either intuiting the existence or having any kind of indubitable knowledge of things, then according to Santayana we cannot be said to know anything, and skepticism is the only possible position. On the other hand, if knowledge is reinterpreted as a kind of belief or faith, then we can be said to know certain things. It is with a kind of quasi-instinctive faith that we assume a past, future, self, and natural world. This faith is an irrational persuasion or a prompting of practical life; we believe certain things because we are inclined to do so by the way we live as biological beings. Thus we cannot reject a belief simply because it is open to doubt, because all beliefs are in that condition. Rather we must decide what beliefs we do have and see if they cannot be organized in some coherent way. Truth is more a matter of having a coherent set of beliefs than of seeing how our beliefs conform to reality. Furthermore, according to Santayana, naturalism or materialism is a more coherent account as a philosophy than is idealism because naturalism or materialism is more consistent with the notion of animal faith itself, namely a belief originating in the life seeking and death avoidance of the animal organism in a threatening environment.

Such is Santayana's solution to the dilemma posed by the critical realist's contention that we cannot know things directly. A thoroughgoing skepticism, rather than undermining a realist belief, makes room for it on a different basis, namely the basis of animal faith. The details of this philosophy are spelled out further in the four volumes of *Realms of Being*. Each volume is concerned with a different realm: essence, matter, truth, and spirit. Essences are immutable types — forms or universals that we intuit and take as symbols of what exists. All existence is dependent on matter which is the realm of action and power, while mind is viewed by Santayana as a kind of epiphenomenon of matter. Truth depicts existence but is determined by coherence of beliefs rather than by any direct perception of existence. Finally, the realm of spirit is the realm of consciousness. Santayana is never fully clear in his description of the manner in which consciousness is dependent on matter, its physical basis. However, there is some dependence, and in fact spirit cannot accomplish anything in the physical world; in this sense it is powerless. Its worth lies elsewhere. Spirit is the realm of fancy and freedom, of aesthetic forms and religious or moral ideals. It is what gives significance to life, even life in an otherwise irrational world (Santayana lived at close range through two world wars). The contemplation of forms of good and beauty produces a spontaneous delight, and since philosophy as well as poetry exhibits such forms, they are the most satisfying and among the highest of human achievements. The range of Santayana's philosophical interest is wide, and his particular conclusions are of interest to those looking not for proven and technically detailed treatments, but for a systematic ordering of a number of important philosophical problems and concepts.

Notes

[1] William Pepperell Montague, "The Story of American Realism," *Philosophy* 12, no. 46 (April 1937): p. 140.

[2] Ibid., pp. 147ff.

[3] William Pepperell Montague, "Professor Royce's Refutation of Realism," *Philosophical Review*, March 1901; Ralph Barton Perry, "Professor Royce's Refutation of Realism and Pluralism," *The Monist*, October 1901. Also see Josiah Royce, "The Independent Beings: A Critical Examination of Realism," in *The World and the Individual*, vol. 1 (New York: Macmillan, 1899; New York: Dover, 1959.)

[4] The Program and First Platform of Six Realists," *Journal of Philosophy, Psychology, and Scientific Methods* 7, no. 15 (21 July 1910): pp. 393–401; reprinted with additional essays by the various members of the group in *The New Realism* (New York: Macmillan, 1912).

[5] Ralph Barton Perry, "The Ego-centric Predicament," *Journal of Philosophy* 7, no. 1 (1910): pp. 5–14.

[6] Of course this reasoning may well be circular.

[7] E. B. Holt et al., *The New Realism* (New York: Macmillan, 1912).

[8] Durant Drake et al., *Essays in Critical Realism* (London: Macmillan, Ltd., 1920).

[9] Also in the group were J. B. Pratt of Williams College, Arthur K. Rogers of Yale University, and C. A. Strong who had formerly taught psychology at Columbia and was a friend of Santayana.

[10] Roy Wood Sellars, *The Principles and Problems of Philosophy* (New York: Macmillan, 1926), p. 125.

[11] Ibid. One might also note the pragmatic perspective evident in these views.

[12] Roy Wood Sellars, *Evolutionary Naturalism* (Chicago: Open Court Publishing, 1922). See also C. F. Delaney, *Mind and Nature: A Study of the Naturalistic Philosophy of Cohen, Woodbridge, and Sellars* (Notre Dame, Ind.: University of Notre Dame Press, 1969).

[13] There were a number of other philosophers of some importance writing during and just after this period whom we will not be able to treat in this book. Among those of some importance are William Ernest Hocking, Brand Blanshard, W. M. Urban and C. J. Ducasse. See the treatment of these philosophers in Charles Hartshorne, *Creativity in American Philosophy* (Albany: State University of New York Press, 1984).

[14] Santayana wrote a number of autobiographical essays, among which is "A General Confession," in *The Philosophy of George Santayana*, ed. Paul Arthur Schilpp (New York: Tudor Publishing, 1940), pp. 3–30.

[15] George Santayana, *Sonnets and Other Verses* (Cambridge and Chicago: G. S. Stone and Kimball, 1894); idem, *The Last Puritan: A Memoir in the Form of a Novel* (New York: Charles Scribner's, 1936).

[16] George Santayana, *The Sense of Beauty: Being the Outline of Aesthetic Theory* (New York: Charles Scribner's, 1896). In addition to his discussion of the nature of beauty, Santayana also discusses other questions in aesthetics such as the universal validity of aesthetic judgments and the nature of aesthetic pleasure.

[17] George Santayana, *The Life of Reason*, 5 vols. (New York: Charles Scribner's, 1905–6; New York: Collier Books, 1962).

[18] George Santayana, *Scepticism and Animal Faith* (New York: Charles Scribner's, 1923); idem, *Realms of Being* (New York: Charles Scribner's, 1927–40).

[19] Santayana, *Scepticism and Animal Faith*, p. 42.

[20] Ibid., pp. 15–16.

THE NEW REALISM

THE PROGRAM AND FIRST PLATFORM OF SIX REALISTS*

Philosophy is famous for its disagreements, which have contributed not a little towards bringing it into disrepute as being unscientific, subjective, or temperamental. These disagreements are due in part, no doubt, to the subject matter of philosophy, but chiefly to the lack of precision and uniformity in the use of words and to the lack of deliberate coöperation in research. In having these failings philosophy still differs widely from such sciences as physics and chemistry. They tend to make it seem mere opinion; for through the appearance of many figurative or loose expressions in the writings of isolated theorists, the impression is given that philosophical problems and their solutions are essentially personal. This impression is strengthened by the fact that philosophy concerns itself with emotions, temperaments, and taste. A conspicuous result of this lack of coöperation, common terminology, and a working agreement as to fundamental presuppositions is that genuine philosophical problems have been obscured, and real philosophical progress has been seriously hindered.

It is therefore with the hope that by coöperation genuine problems will be revealed, philosophical thought will be clarified, and a way opened

* "The Program and First Platform of Six Realists," *Journal of Philosophy, Psychology, and Scientific Methods* 7, no. 15 (21 July 1910): pp. 393–97. Reprinted with permission of the Editors of the *Journal of Philosophy*.

for real progress, that the undersigned have come together, deliberated, and endeavored to reach an agreement. Such coöperation has three fairly distinct, though not necessarily successive stages: first, it seeks a statement of fundamental principles and doctrines; secondly, it aims at a program of constructive work following a method founded on these principles and doctrines; finally, it endeavors to obtain a system of axioms, methods, hypotheses, and facts, which have been so arrived at and formulated that at least those investigators who have coöperated can accept them as a whole.

After several conferences the undersigned have found that they hold certain doctrines in common. Some of these doctrines, which constitute a realistic platform, they herewith publish in the hope of carrying out further the program stated above. Each list has a different author, but has been discussed at length, revised, and agreed to by the other conferees. The six lists, therefore, though differently formulated, are held to represent the same doctrines.

By conferring on other topics, by interchange of ideas, and by systematic criticism of one another's phraseology, methods, and hypotheses, we hope to develop a common technique, a common terminology, and so finally a common doctrine which will enjoy some measure of that authority which the natural sciences possess. We shall have accomplished one of our purposes if our publications tempt other philosophers to form small coöperative groups with similar aims.

EDWIN B. HOLT, *Harvard University.*
WALTER T. MARVIN, *Rutgers College.*
W. P. MONTAGUE, *Columbia University.*
RALPH BARTON PERRY, *Harvard University.*
WALTER B. PITKIN, *Columbia University.*
E. G. SPAULDING, *Princeton University.*

I

1. The entities (objects, facts, etc.) under study in logic, mathematics, and the physical sciences are not mental in any usual or proper meaning of the word 'mental.'

2. The being and nature of these entities are in no sense conditioned by their being known.

3. The degree of unity, consistency, or connection subsisting among entities is a matter to be empirically ascertained.

4. In the present stage of our knowledge there is a presumption in favor of pluralism.

5. An entity subsisting in certain relations to other entities enters into new relations without necessarily negating or altering its already subsisting relations.

6. No self-consistent or satisfactory logic (or system of logic) so far invented countenances the 'organic' theory of knowledge or the 'internal' view of relations.

7. Those who assert this (anti-realistic) view, use in their exposition a logic which is inconsistent with their doctrine.

EDWIN B. HOLT

II

1. Epistemology is not logically fundamental.[1]

2. There are many existential, as well as non-existential, propositions which are logically prior to epistemology.[2]

3. There are certain principles of logic which are logically prior to all scientific and metaphysical systems.

One of these is that which is usually called the external view of relations.

4. This view may be stated thus: In the proposition, "the term a is in the relation R to the term b," aR in no degree constitutes b, nor does Rb constitute a, nor does R constitute either a or b.

5. It is possible to add new propositions to some bodies of information without thereby requiring any modification of those bodies of information.

6. There are no propositions which are (accurately speaking) partly true and partly false, for all such instances can be logically analyzed into at least two propositions one of which is true and the other false. Thus as knowledge advances only two modifications of any proposition of the

---

[1] Some of the principles of logic are logically prior to any proposition that is deduced from other propositions. The theories of the nature of knowledge and of the relation of knowledge to its object are for this reason logically subsequent to the principles of logic. In short, logic is logically prior to any epistemological theory. Again, as theories of reality are deduced and are made to conform to the laws of logic they too are logically subsequent to logic; and in so far as logic is logically present in them it is itself a theory or part of a theory of reality.

[2] The terms 'knowledge,' 'consciousness,' and 'experience' found in common sense and in psychology are not logically fundamental, but are logically subsequent to parts at least of a theory of reality that asserts the existence of terms and relations which are not consciousness or experience. *E.g.* the psychical is distinguished from the physical and the physiological.

Now idealism has not shown that the terms 'knowledge,' 'consciousness,' and 'experience' of its epistemology or of its theory of reality are logically fundamental or indefinable, nor has it succeeded in defining them without logically prior terms that are elsewhere explicitly excluded from its theory of reality. In short, idealistic epistemologists have borrowed the terms 'knowledge,' 'consciousness,' and 'experience' from psychology, but have ignored or denied the propositions in psychology that are logically prior. In other words, epistemology has not thus far made itself logically independent of psychology nor has it freed itself logically from the common-sense dualism of psychology. On the contrary, epistemology from Locke until to-day has been and has remained, in part at least, a branch of psychology.

older knowledge are logically possible; it can be rejected as false or it can be analyzed into at least two propositions one of which is rejected.

As corollaries of the foregoing:

7. The nature of reality cannot be inferred merely from the nature of knowledge.

8. The entities under study in logic, mathematics, physics, and many other sciences are not mental in any proper or usual meaning of the word 'mental.'

9. The proposition, "This or that object is known," does not imply that such object is conditioned by the knowing. In other words, it does not force us to infer that such object is spiritual, that it exists only as the experiential content of some mind, or that it may not be ultimately real just as known.

WALTER T. MARVIN

III

I. *The Meaning of Realism.*

1. Realism holds that things known may continue to exist unaltered when they are not known, or that things may pass in and out of the cognitive relation without prejudice to their reality, or that the existence of a thing is not correlated with or dependent upon the fact that anybody experiences it, perceives it, conceives it, or is in any way aware of it.

2. Realism is opposed to subjectivism or epistemological idealism which denies that things can exist apart from an experience of them, or independently of the cognitive relation.

3. The point at issue between realism and idealism should not be confused with the points at issue between materialism and spiritualism, automatism and interactionism, empiricism and rationalism, or pluralism and absolutism.

II. *The Opposition to Realism.* Among the various classic refutations of realism the following fallacious assumptions and inferences are prominent:

1. The Psychological Argument: The mind can have for its direct object only its own ideas or states, and external objects, if they exist at all, can only be known indirectly by a process of inference, of questionable validity and doubtful utility. This principle is fallacious because a knowing process is never its own object, but is rather the means by which some other object is known. The object thus known or referred to may be another mental state, a physical thing, or a merely logical entity.

2. The Intuitional Argument: This argument stands out most prominently in the philosophy of Berkeley. It has two forms. The first consists of a confused identification of a truism and an absurdity. The truism: *We can only know that objects exist, when they are known.* The absurdity:

We know that objects can only exist when they are known. The second form of the arguments derives its force from a play upon the word 'idea,' as follows: *Every 'idea' (meaning a mental process or state) is incapable of existing apart from a mind; every known entity is an 'idea' (meaning an object of thought);* therefore, *every known entity is incapable of existing apart from a mind.* It is to the failure to perceive these fallacies that idealism owes its supposedly axiomatic character.

3. The Physiological Argument: Because the sensations we receive determine what objects we shall know, therefore the objects known are constructs or products of our perceptual experience. The fallacy here consists in arguing from the true premise that sensations are the *ratio cognoscendi* of the external world, to the false conclusion that they are therefore its *ratio fiendi* or *essendi.*

III. *The Implications of Realism.*

1. Cognition is a peculiar type of relation which may subsist between a living being and any entity.

2. Cognition belongs to the same world as that of its objects. It has its place in the order of nature. There is nothing transcendental or supernatural about it.

3. The extent to which consciousness pervades nature, and the conditions under which it may arise and persist, are questions which can be solved, if at all, only by the methods of empiricism and naturalism.

W. P. MONTAGUE

THE NEW REALISM AND THE OLD*

The problems of philosophy fall naturally into four groups:

(1) Problems of knowing; (2) problems of being; (3) problems of acting; (4) problems of feeling. The subjects with which these problems deal comprise, respectively, epistemology, metaphysics, ethics, and esthetics. Epistemology is itself concerned with two fairly distinct types of problems: (1) the functional problem of the criteria of truth and the way of attaining it; (2) the structural problem of the nature of knowledge and the relation of the knower to the known. Discussion of the functional problem of epistemology has given us such doctrines and attitudes as mysticism, rationalism, empiricism, and pragmatism, which are so many theories as to how we should get our knowledge and how we should test its truth. Discussion of the second or structural problem of epistemology has given us the doctrines of naïve realism, of dualistic realism, and of subjectivism, which are so many theories as to the nature of the relation of a knower

* W. P. Montague, "The New Realism and the Old," *Journal of Philosophy* 9, no. 2 (18 January 1922): pp. 39–46. Reprinted with the permission of the editors of the *Journal of Philosophy.*

to the objects known. These three epistemological theories, or rather types of theory (for there are, as we shall see, several variations of each), may be discussed pretty much on their own merits and in relative independence not only of metaphysical, ethical, and esthetical issues, but even of the epistemological problems of the methodological or functional kind. In this paper I shall undertake to define the theories of naïve realism, dualism, and subjectivism, as they appear to me, and to show how the difficulties inherent in the first theory have led to the adoption of the second, and how that has been given up for the third, the futility of which, in its turn, has led to a revival of the first.

The theory of naïve realism is the most primitive of the theories under discussion. It conceives of objects as directly presented to consciousness and being precisely what they appear to be. Nothing intervenes between the knower and the world external to him. Objects are not represented in consciousness by ideas; they are themselves directly presented. This theory makes no distinction between seeming and being; things *are* just what they *seem*. Consciousness is thought of as analogous to a light which shines out through the sense organs, illuminating the world outside the knower. There is in this naïve view a complete disregard of the personal equation and of the elaborate mechanism underlying sense perception. In a world in which there was no such thing as error, this theory of the knowledge relation would remain unchallenged; but with the discovery of error and illusion comes perplexity. Dreams are probably the earliest phenomena of error to arouse the primitive mind from its dogmatic realism. How can a man lie asleep in his bed and at the same time travel to distant places and converse with those who are dead? How can the events of the dream be reconciled with the events of waking experience? The first method of dealing with this type of error is to divide the real world into two realms, equally objective and equally external, but the one visible, tangible, and regular, the other more or less invisible, mysterious, and capricious. The soul after death, and sometimes during sleep, can enter the second of these realms. The objectified dreamland of the child and the ghostland of the savage are the outcome of the first effort of natural realism to cope with the problem of error. It is easy to see, however, that this doubling up of the world of existing objects will only explain a very limited number of dream experiences, while to the errors of waking experience it is obviously inapplicable. Whenever, for example, the dream is concerned with the same events as those already experienced in waking life, there can be no question of appealing to a shadow world. Unreal events that are in conflict with the experience of one's fellows, and even with one's own more inclusive experience, must be banished completely from the external world. Where, then, shall they be located? What is more reasonable than to locate them inside the person who experiences them? for it is only upon him that the unreal object produces any effect. The objects of our dreams and our fancies, and of illusions generally, are held to exist only "in the mind." They are like feelings and desires in being directly experienced only by a single mind. Thus the soul, already held to be the mysterious principle of life, and endowed with peculiar properties, transcending ordinary physical things, is further enriched by being made the habitat of the multitudinous hosts of non-existent objects. Still further reflection on the phenomena of error leads to the discovery of the element of relativity in all knowledge, and finally to the realization that no external happening can be perceived until after it has ceased to exist. The events we perceive as present are always past, for in order that anything may be perceived it must send energy of some kind to our sense organs, and by the time the energy reaches us the phase of existence which gave rise to it has passed away. To this universal and necessary temporal aberration of perceived objects is added an almost equally universal spatial aberration. For all objects that move relatively to the observer are perceived not where they are when perceived, but, at best, where they were when the stimulus issued from them. Not only may some of the stars which we see shining each night have ceased to shine years before we were born, but even the sun which we see at a certain place in the sky is there no longer. The present sun, the only sun that now exists, we never see. It fills the space that to us appears empty. Its distance from what we see as the sun is measured by the distance through which the earth has turned on its axis in the eight minutes which it has taken the sun's light to reach our eye. And in addition to these spatial and temporal aberrations of perception we know that what we perceive will depend not only upon the nature of the object but on the nature of the medium through which its energies have passed on their way to our organism; and also upon the condition of our sense organs and brain. Finally, we have every reason to believe that whenever the brain is stimulated in the same way in which it is normally stimulated by an object, we shall experience that object even though it is in no sense existentially present. These many undeniable facts prove that error is no trivial and exceptional phenomenon, but the normal, necessary, and universal taint from which every perceptual experience must suffer.

It is such considerations as these that have led to the abandonment of naïve realism in favor of the second theory of the nature of knowledge. According to this second theory, which is exemplified in the philosophies of Descartes and Locke, the mind never perceives anything external to itself. It can perceive only its own ideas or states. But as it seems impossible to account for the order in which these ideas occur by appealing to the mind in which they occur, it is held to be permissible and even necessary to infer a world of external objects resembling to a greater or less extent the effects, or ideas, which they produce in us. What we perceive is now held to be only a picture of what really exists. Consciousness is no longer thought of as analogous to a light which directly illumines the extra-organic world, but rather as a painter's canvas or a photographic plate on which objects in themselves imperceptible are represented. The great advantage of the second or picture theory is that it fully accounts for error and illusion; the disadvantage of it is that it appears to account for nothing else. The only external world is one that we can never experience, the only world that we can have any experience of is the internal world of ideas. When we attempt to justify the situation by appealing to inference as the guarantee of this unexperienceable externality, we are met by the difficulty that the world we infer can only be made of the matter of experience, *i.e.,* can only be made up of mental pictures in new combinations. An inferred object is always a perceptible object, one that could be in some sense experienced, and, as we have seen, the only things that according to this view can be experienced are our mental states. Moreover, the world in which all our interests are centered is the world of experienced objects. Even if, *per impossible,* we could justify the belief in a world beyond that which we could experience, it would be but a barren achievement, for such a world would contain none of the things that we see and feel. Such a so-called real world would be more alien to us and more thoroughly queer than were the ghostland or dreamland which, as we remember, the primitive realist sought to use as a home for certain of the unrealities of life.

It seems very natural at such a juncture to try the experiment of leaving out this world of extra-mental objects, and contenting ourselves with a world in which there exist only minds and their states. This is the third theory, the theory of subjectivism. According to it, there can be no object without a subject, no existence without a consciousness of it. To be, is to be perceived. The world of objects capable of existing independently of a knower (the belief in which united the natural realist and the dualistic realist) is now rejected. This third theory agrees with the first theory in being epistemologically monistic, *i.e.,* in holding to the presentative rather than to the representative theory of perception, for, according to the first theory, whatever is perceived must exist, and according to the present theory whatever exists must be perceived. Naïve realism subsumed the perceived as a species under the genus existent. Subjectivism subsumes the existent as a species under the genus perceived. But while the third theory has these affiliations with the first theory, it agrees with the second theory in regarding all perceived objects as mental states—ideas inhering in the mind that knows them and as inseparable from that mind as any accident is from the substance that owns it.

Subjectivism has many forms, or rather, many degrees. It occurs in its first and most conservative form in the philosophy of Berkeley. Descartes and Locke, and other upholders of the dualistic epistemology, had already gone beyond the requirements of the picture theory in respect to the secondary qualities of objects. Not content with the doctrine that these qualities as they existed in objects could only be inferred, they had denied them even the inferential status which they accorded to primary qualities. The secondary qualities that we perceive are not even copies of what exists externally. They are the cloudy effects produced in the mind by combinations of primary qualities, and they resemble unreal objects in that they are *merely* subjective. The chief ground for this element of subjectivism in the systems of dualistic realism immediately preceding Berkeley, was the belief that relativity to the percipient implied subjectivity. As the secondary qualities showed this relativity, they were condemned as subjective. Now it was the easiest thing in the world for Berkeley to show that an equal or even greater relativity pertained to the primary qualities. The perceived form, size, and solidity of an object depend quite as much upon the relation of the percipient to the object as do its color and temperature. If it be axiomatic that whatever is relative to the perceiver exists only as an idea, why, then, the primary qualities which were all that remained of the physical world could be reduced to mere ideas. But just here Berkeley brought his reasoning to an abrupt stop. He refused to recognize that (1) the *relations between* ideas or the order in which they are given to us, and (2) the *other minds* that are known, are quite as relative to the knower as are the primary and secondary qualities of the physical world. I can know other minds only in so far as I have experience of them, and to infer their independent existence involves just as much and just as little of the process of objectifying and hypostatizing my own ideas as to infer the independent existence of physical objects. Berkeley avoided this obvious result of his own logic by using the word "notion" to describe the knowledge of those things that did not depend for their existence on the fact that they were known. If you had an *idea* of a thing—say of your neighbor's body—then that thing existed only as a mental state. But if you had a *notion* of a thing—say of your neighbor's mind—then that thing was quite capable of existing independently of your knowing it. Considering the vigorous eloquence with which Berkeley inveighed against the tendency of philosophers to substitute words for thoughts, it is pathetic that he should himself have furnished such a striking example of that very fallacy. In later times Clifford and Pearson did not hesitate to avail themselves of a quite similar linquistic device for escaping the solipsistic conclusion of a consistent subjectivism. The distinction between the physical *objects* which as "constructs" exist only in the consciousness of the knower and *other minds* which as "ejects" can be known without being in any way dependent on the knower, is essentially the same both in its meaning and in its futility as the Berkeleian distinction of idea and notion. For the issue between realism and subjectivism does not arise from a psycho-centric predicament—a difficulty of conceiving of objects apart from any consciousness—but rather from the much more radical "ego-centric predicament"—the difficulty of conceiving known things to exist independently of my knowing them. And the poignancy of the predicament is quite independent of the nature of the object itself, whether that be a physical thing like my neighbor's body, or a psychical thing like my neighbor's mind.

Some part of this difficulty Hume saw and endeavored to meet in his proof that the spiritual substances of Berkeley were themselves mere ideas; but Hume's position is itself subject to two criticisms: First, it does not escape the ego-centric predicament—for it is as difficult to explain how one "bundle of perceptions" can have any knowledge of the other equally real "bundle of perceptions" as to explain how one "spirit" can have knowledge of other "spirits." Second, the Humean doctrine suffers from an additional difficulty peculiar to itself, in that by destroying the conception of the mind as a "substance," it made meaningless the quite correlative conception of perceived objects as mental "states." If there is no substance there can not be any states or accidents, and there ceases to be any sense in regarding the things that are known as dependent upon or inseparable from a knower.[1]

Passing on to that form of subjectivism developed by Kant, we may note three points: (1) A step back toward dualism, in that he dallies with, even if he does not actually embrace, the dualistic notion of a *ding-an-sich,* a reality outside and beyond the realm of experienced objects which serves as their cause or ground. (2) A step in advance of the subjectivism of Berkeley and Hume, in that Kant reduces to the subjective status not merely the *facts* of nature but also her *laws,* so far, at least, as they are based upon the forms of space and time and upon the categories. (3) There appears in the Kantian system a wholly new feature which is destined to figure prominently in later-systems. I mean the dualistic conception of the knower, as himself a twofold being, transcendental and empirical. It is the transcendental or noumenal self that gives laws to nature, and that owns the experienced objects as its states. The empirical or phenomenal self, on the other hand, is simply one ojbect among others, and enjoys no special primacy in its relation to the world of which it is a part.[2]

The post-Kantian philosophies deal with the three points just mentioned in the following ways: (1) The retrograde feature of Kant's doctrine—the belief in the *ding-an-sich*—is abandoned. (2) The step in advance—the legislative power conferred by Kant upon the self as knower—is accepted and enlarged to the point of viewing consciousness as the source not only of the *a priori* forms of relation, but of all relations whatsoever. (3) The doctrine of the dual self is extended to the point of identifying in one absolute self the plurality of transcendental selves held to by Kant, with the result that our various empirical selves and the objects of their experience are all regarded as the manifestations or

---

[1] For elaboration and proof of this, see the article by the author entitled "A Neglected Point in Hume's Philosophy," *Philosophical Review,* January 1905.

[2] *Cf.* what Kant called his refutation of (Berkeleian) idealism.

fragments of a single perfect, all-inclusive, and eternal self. But it is not hard to see that this new dualism of the finite and the absolute self involves the same difficulties as those which we found in the Cartesian dualism of conscious state and physical object. For either the experience of the fragment embraces the experiences of the absolute or it does not. If the former, then the absolute becomes knowable, to be sure, but only at the cost of losing its absoluteness and being reduced to a mere "state" of the alleged fragment. The existence of the absolute will then depend upon the fact that it is known by its own fragments, and each fragmentary self will have to assume that its own experience constitutes the entire universe—which is solipsism. If the other horn of the dilemma be chosen and the independent reality of the absolute is insisted upon, then it is at the cost of making the absolute unknowable, of reducing it to the status of the unexperienceable external world of the dualistic realist. The dilemma itself is the inevitable consequence of making knowledge an internal relation and hence constitutive of its objects. Indeed a large part of the philosophical discussion of recent years has been concerned with the endeavor of the absolutists to defend their doctrine from the attacks of empiricists of the Berkeleian and Humean tradition in such a way as to avoid equally the Scylla of epistemological dualism and the Charybdis of solipsism. But, as we have seen, the more empirical subjectivists of the older and strictly British school are open to the same criticism as that which they urge upon the absolutists, for it is as difficult for the Berkeleian to justify his belief in the existence of other spirits, or the phenomenalistic follower of Hume his belief in bundles or streams of experience other than his own, as for the absolutist to justify those features of the absolute experience which lie beyond the experience of the finite fragments.

And now enter upon this troubled scene the new realists, offering to absolutists and phenomenalists impartially their new theory of the relation of knower to known. On this point all subjectivists look alike to them, and they make no apology for lumping together for purposes of epistemological discussion such ontologically diverse theories as those of Fichte and Berkeley, of Mr. Bradley and Professor Karl Pearson. Indeed, it can not be too emphatically stated that the theory in question is concerned primarily with this single problem of the relation of knower to known. As such, it has no direct bearing on other philosophical issues, such as those of monism and pluralism, eternalism and temporalism, materialism and spiritualism, or even pragmatism and intellectualism. Of course this does not mean that those individuals who defend the new realism are without convictions on these matters, but only that as a basis for their clearer discussion it is first of all essential to get rid of subjectivism.

Like most new things this new theory is in essential very old. To understand its meaning it is necessary to go back beyond Kant, beyond Berkeley, beyond even Locke and Descartes—far back to that primordial common sense which believes in a world that exists independently of the knowing of it, but believes also that that same independent world can be directly presented in consciousness and not merely represented or copied by "ideas." In short, the new realism is almost identical with that naïve or natural realism which was the first of our three typic theories of the knowledge relation; and as such, it should be sharply distinguished from the dualistic or inferential realism of the Cartesians.

Now the cause of the abandonment of naïve realism in favor of the dualistic or picture theory was the apparently hopeless disagreement of the world as presented in immediate experience with the true or corrected system of objects in whose reality we believe. It follows that the first and greatest problem for the new realists is to amend the realism of common sense in such wise as to make it compatible with the universal phenomenon of error and with the mechanism of perception upon which that phenomenon is based and in terms of which it must be interpreted.

W. P. MONTAGUE

REALISM AS A POLEMIC AND
PROGRAM OF REFORM*

The Fallacy of Argument from the Ego-centric Predicament.[1]—The "ego-centric predicament" consists in the impossibility of finding anything that is not known. This is a predicament rather than a discovery, because it refers to a difficulty of procedure, rather than to a character of things. It is impossible to eliminate the knower without interrupting observation; hence the peculiar difficulty of discovering what characters, if any, things possess when not known. When this situation is formulated as a proposition concerning things, the result is either the redundant inference that all known things are known, or the false inference that all things are known. The former is, on account of its redundancy, not a proposition at all; and its use results only in confusing it with the second proposition, which involves a *petitio principii*. The falsity of the inference, in the case of the latter proposition, lies in its being a use of the method of agreement unsupported by the method of difference. It is impossible to argue from the fact that everything one finds is known, to the conclusion that knowing is a universal condition of being, because it is impossible to find non-things which are not known. The use of the method of agreement without negative cases is a fallacy. It should be added that at best the method of agreement is a preliminary aid to exact thought, and can throw no light whatsoever on what can be meant by saying that knowing is a condition of being. And yet this method, misapplied, is the main proof, perhaps

---

* R. B. Perry, "Realism as a Polemic and Program of Reform," *Journal of Philosophy* 7, no. 13 (23 June 1910): p. 339. Reprinted with permission of the editors of the *Journal of Philosophy*.
[1] I have discussed this error more fully in this JOURNAL, Vol. 7, no. 1.

the only proof, that has been offered of the cardinal principle of idealistic philosophies—the definition of being in terms of consciousness. It is difficult, on account of the very lack of logical form which I have noted to obtain pure cases of philosophical fallacies. And this particular fallacy has so far become a commonplace as to be regarded as a self-evident truth.[2]

RALPH BARTON PERRY

---

[2] There is doubtless a dim recognition of the invalidity of the argument in the plea which many idealistic writers make for its acceptance as self-evident. " 'The world is my idea,' " says Schopenhauer, "is a proposition which every one must recognize as true as soon as he understands it." ("World as Will and Idea," Haldane and Kemp's translation, vol. 2, p. 164.) "To what purpose," says Berkeley, "is it to dilate on that which may be demonstrated with the utmost evidence in a line or two? " ("Principles of Human Knowledge," Fraser's edition, p. 269). Cf. also Bradley, "Appearance and Reality," p. 144. This self-evident or easily demonstrated principle never receives, however, at the hands either of these writers or of any other, an axiomatic formulation or a rigid demonstration. There is an implied hope that the reader will accept it without further ado, and allow the idealist to proceed with his idealism.

THE APPROACH TO CRITICAL REALISM*

THE JUSTIFICATION OF REALISM

There are two familiar starting-points for knowledge, the objective and the subjective. The objectively-minded philosophers suppose that the data of perception are the very physical existents which we all practically believe to be surrounding and threatening our bodies. These physical objects themselves somehow get within experience, are directly apprehended; their surfaces constitute our visual and tactile data. The subjectively-minded philosophers suppose, on the contrary, that the data of perception are psychological existents, so many pulses or throbs of a stream of psychic life. At best they are merely copies or representatives of the outer objects. In so far, both approaches are realistic; but the subjectively-minded realist is, in a sense, shut in, according to his theory, to "ideas," *i.e.* to mental substitutes for outer objects, whereas the objectively-minded, or naïve, realist (for this seems to be the view of the plain man) believes that his experience extends beyond his body, and includes, in some of their aspects, those outer subjects. Whatever arguments are then adduced for "realistic epistemological monism" and "re-

---

* Durant Drake et al., "The Approach to Critical Realism," in *Essays in Critical Realism* (Hampshire, England: Macmillan, 1920), pp. 3–4, 5–6, 191, 194–95. Reprinted with the permission of the editors of Macmillan Press.

alistic epistemological dualism" respectively do little to shake the faith thus based upon an initial definition. An *impasse* exists here, and will exist until it is seen that *neither* starting-point, objective nor subjective, correctly describes what we have to start with, what is "given" (—what appears, what is apprehended) in immediate experience. It is the object of this paper, then, to expose the error in each of these views, and to point out a third view—we call it Critical Realism—which combines the insights of both these historic positions while free from the objections which can properly be raised to each.†

Before proceeding, however, to consider these two historic types of realism, it will be well to deal with the spectre of pure subjectivism, which is a likely, though not a logically necessary, deduction from the psychological starting-point. If we are shut in to our mental states, we can never know positively that anything exists beyond them. Perhaps, then, our experience (psychologically taken) = existence. It is doubtful, indeed, if any one practically believes this; for the content of our experience is very narrow, and we all really believe that many things exist, have existed, and will exist, that we, individually, and, for that matter, collectively, have never so much as thought of, and never will think of or know anything about. Moreover, those objects which we do think of, or

---

† In the above paragraph I have, for convenience, given the names *epistemological monism* and *epistemological dualism* to the two historic positions which we believe to be transcended by our analysis. There is, I should add, some doubt among us as to whether our position should be called a *dualism*.

On the one hand, in certain contexts it is desirable to emphasize the duality which we believe to exist between the cognitive state which is the vehicle of knowledge and the object known. By contrast with neo-realists, idealists, and believers in "pure experience," we are dualists.

On the other hand, the term "dualism" implies to most readers, probably, the notion that what we *know* is a mental state (or "idea"), an existent from which we have to infer the existence and character of the physical object. This notion, however, we repudiate. What we perceive, conceive, remember, think of, is the outer object itself (or, on occasion, the mental state introspected, remembered, or conceived), which is independent of the knowledge-process, and beyond which there is nothing else.

Further, if the analysis is accepted (made in this essay, and, at greater length, in the concluding essay) which discriminates the "datum" in cases of knowledge from the mental state which is the vehicle of its givenness, we cannot say that the datum (what is "given" to the knower, what we start with in our epistemological inquiry) is an existent, representing the object. On the contrary, it is (in so far as knowledge is accurate) simply the essence or character (the *what*) of the object known. Professors Sellars, Lovejoy, and Pratt, however, maintain that although what is *given* is a mere character-complex, it is in reality *in toto* the character of the mental state of the moment, and so *is* an existent, in spite of the fact that its existence is not given (see on this point the footnote on p. 20); they may perhaps therefore be called dualistic by somewhat better right than the rest of us, although we all agree as to what the existential situation in knowledge is, and as to the fact that what we *know* is the independent object itself. Critics of our view are asked, therefore, not to label us simply as "dualists," but to recognize precisely what sort of duality we do and do not admit.

perceive, are irresistibly believed to have an existence of their own, far more extensive, both as to nature and in time, than that of our evanescent and shallow experience. All who thus believe that existence is far wider than experience—that objects exist in or for themselves, apart from our experiencing them—are properly to be called realists. And we are now first to consider whether realism—any sort of realism—is philosophically indicated (as physicians say) as well as practically inevitable.

Now, as has been said above, it is the conviction of the authors of this volume that the psychological starting-point is as erroneous as the objective or physical. Our data—the character-complexes "given" in conscious experience—are simply character-complexes, essences, logical entities, which are irresistibly taken to be the characters of the existents perceived, or otherwise known. If this is true, it becomes necessary to ask what reason we have for believing in the existence of our mental states, as well as to ask what reason we have for believing in the existence of physical objects. For the present, however, we will postpone the former question, and confine ourselves to asking what right we have to believe in the existence of physical objects. The answer, in a word, is that our instinctive (and practically inevitable) belief in the existence of the physical world about us is pragmatically justifiable. We cannot, indeed, *deduce* from the character-complexes that follow one another in that stream that is the little private "movie" of each of us any proof of existence. This little realm of Appearance (*i.e.* what appears, what is "given") might conceivably be merely the visions of a mind in an empty world. But we instinctively feel these appearances to be the characters of real objects. We react to them as if they had an existence of their own even when we are asleep or forgetting them. We find that this belief, those reactions, *work*—in the strictest scientific sense. Realism works just as the Copernican theory works, but with overwhelmingly greater evidence. The alternative possibilities are far less plausible. We can, indeed, refuse to make any hypothesis, and content ourselves with a world consisting merely of appearance. A philosopher who refuses to consider anything beyond appearance can fully *describe* what appears to him. But he cannot *explain* its peculiarities. Why should our sense-data appear and disappear and change just as they do in this abrupt fashion? The particular nature and sequence of our data remain unintelligible to the subjectivist, surds in his doctrine. Whereas, if there is a whole world of existents, the characteristics and relations of our data become marvellously intelligible. The argument could be strengthened in many ways, some of which Professor Santayana's essay suggests; but this is surely enough for most of us. Everything is *as if* realism were true; and the *as if* is so strong that we may consider our instinctive and actually unescapable belief justified.

DURANT DRAKE

KNOWLEDGE AND ITS CATEGORIES*

THE NATURE OF KNOWLEDGE

The very existence of epistemology as a reflective science proves that the nature and the conditions of knowledge have become problems. For good and sufficient reasons the unsystematic and relatively uncritical outlook of common sense has ceased completely to satisfy, while the various special sciences have very naturally ignored all general queries which could not be allotted to their fields of investigation and be met by their methods. . . .

We have tried to make the knowledge-claim explicit and to distinguish between knowledge and the presence of contents. We have pointed out that the presence of contents is simply a necessary factor in knowledge. Because they have not sufficiently analysed the act of knowledge as reflection makes it explicit, the neo-realists dismiss what they call dualism in the following manner: "The only external world is one that we can never experience, the only world that we can have any experience of is the internal world of ideas. When we attempt to justify the situation by appealing to inference as the guarantee of this unexperienceable externality, we are met by the difficulty that the world we *infer* can only be made up of mental pictures in new combinations." † Now I think that it is clear that these thinkers assume that the assertion of the physical world as the object of knowledge must be based on an inference if you are not a naïve realist. The critical realist denies this assumption. The reasons for a belief in the physical world can be given to back up our instinctive assertion of it, but the critical realist is primarily only developing the act of knowledge. The distinction between the self and the external world has a genetic foundation. In the second place, the neo-realist does not distinguish between intuition and knowledge. The much-abused and ambiguous term "experience" is employed as a blanket to cover every type of what may indiscriminately be called knowledge. Suppose that we introduce more exact terms as follows: "The physical realm is one that we can never intuit, as common sense tends to suppose; the only realm we can intuit is the realm of data." But because we cannot intuit the physical realm it does not follow either that we cannot know it or that we must infer it.

If reflection convinces us that we cannot intuit the physical thing but that what is given is a character-complex, it is nonsense to continue to try to intuit the physical world. We should try to analyse our experience more fully, to see whether knowledge is necessarily the same as intuition or the awareness of content. Now the critical realist holds that we must

---

* Ibid., "Knowledge and Its Categories," pp. 191, 194–95, 197.
† *The New Realism*, p. 5.

distinguish between the givenness of content and knowledge of the physical thing, and that we do not *infer* a realm of existents co-real with ourselves but, instead, *affirm* it through the very pressure and suggestion of our experience. A genetic approach is quite essential to philosophy. Instead, then, of saying that "the world we *infer* can only be made up of mental pictures in new combinations," we should say that "the world we *affirm* can only be known in terms of the characters given in experience." In short, contents are given or intuited, while objects are known.

It has often been the tendency in epistemology to regard the contrast between perception and conception as basic. We now see that the contrast between intuition and a non-intuitional interpretation of knowledge is profounder. What kind of knowledge does man actually possess? I am at present concerned with knowledge of the physical world through external sense-perception. We shall consider knowledge of other kinds of reality (other at least as ordinarily interpreted) afterwards.

The factors of knowledge are now apparent: (1) the affirmation of an object or ideatum; (2) the idea or content given to the knowing self; and (3) the interpretation of the first in terms of the second. To these three on the subjective side, there must correspond the affirmed existent with its determinate nature on the objective side. The interpretation of the object may be of the almost automatic sort characteristic of perception, or it may be of the more conscious sort found in science.

Thus, when the knowledge-situation is made explicit, we realize that the object must be known in terms of the content which is given to the knowing self. In the act of knowledge, the content has a different status from the object, and yet is in some sense *assigned* to it. We are *compelled to think** the object as it is presented to us in the content. Of course, we can be as critical as we please in our construction of the idea which seems to us satisfactorily to give the object; but, after due selection and supplementation, the judged idea is *accepted* as revealing the object.

ROY WOOD SELLARS

---

* Emphasis added by the editor.

GEORGE SANTAYANA

SKEPTICISM AND ANIMAL FAITH*

I have now reached the culminating point of my survey of evidence, and the entanglements I have left behind me and the habitable regions I am looking for lie spread out before me like opposite valleys. On the one hand I see now a sweeping reason for scepticism, over and above all particular contradictions or fancifulness of dogma. Nothing is ever present to me except some essence; so that nothing that I possess in intuition, or actually see, is ever *there;* it can never exist bodily, nor lie in that place or exert that power which belongs to the objects encountered in action. Therefore, if I regard my intuitions as knowledge of facts, all my experience is illusion, and life is a dream. At the same time I am now able to give a clearer meaning to this old adage; for life would not be a dream, and all experience would not be illusion, if I abstained from believing in them. The evidence of data is only obviousness; they give no evidence of anything else; they are not witnesses. If I am content to recognise them for pure essences, they cannot deceive me; they will be like works of literary fiction, more or less coherent, but without any claim to exist on their own account. If I hypostatise an essence into a fact, instinctively placing it in relations which are not given within it, I am putting my trust in animal faith, not in any evidence or implication of

* George Santayana, *Skepticism and Animal Faith* (New York: Scribner's 1923; New York: Dover, 1958), pp. 99–103. Reprinted with permission of Scribner Book Companies.

my actual experience. I turn to an assumed world about me, because I have organs for turning, just as I expect a future to reel itself out without interruption because I am wound up to go on myself. To such ulterior things no manifest essence can bear any testimony. They must justify themselves. If the ulterior fact is some intuition elsewhere, its existence, if it happens to exist, will justify that belief; but the fulfilment of my prophecy, in taking my present dream for testimony to that ulterior experience, will be found only in the realm of truth—a realm which is itself an object of belief, never by any possibility of intuition, human or divine. So too when the supposed fact is thought of as a substance, its existence, if it is found in the realm of nature, will justify that supposition; but the realm of nature is of course only another object of belief, more remote if possible from intuition than even the realm of truth. Intuition of essence, to which positive experience and certitude are confined, is therefore always illusion, if we allow our hypostatising impulse to take it for evidence of anything else.

In adopting this conclusion of so many great philosophers, that all is illusion, I do so, however, with two qualifications. One is emotional and moral only, in that I do not mourn over this fatality, but on the contrary rather prefer speculation in the realm of essence—if it can be indulged without practical inconvenience—to alleged information about hard facts. It does not seem to me ignominious to be a poet, if nature has made one a poet unexpectedly. Unexpectedly nature lent us existence, and if she has made it a condition that we should be poets, she has not forbidden us to enjoy that art, or even to be proud of it. The other qualification is more austere: it consists in not allowing exceptions. I cannot admit that some particular essence—water, fire, being, atoms, or Brahma—is the intrinsic essence of all things, so that if I narrow my imagination to that one intuition I shall have intuited the heart and the whole of existence. Of course I do not deny that there is water and that there is being, the former in most things on earth, and the latter in everything anywhere; but these images or words of mine are not the things they designate, but only names for them. Desultory and partial propriety these names may have, but no metaphysical privilege. No more has the expedient of some modern critics who would take illusion as a whole and call it the universe; for in the first place they are probably reverting to belief in discourse, as conventionally conceived, so that their scepticism is halting; and in the second place, even if human experience could be admitted as known and vouched for, there would be an incredible arrogance in positing it as the whole of being, or as itself confined to the forms and limits which the critic assigns to it. The life of reason as I conceive it is a mere romance, and the life of nature a mere fable; such pictures have no metaphysical value, even if as sympathetic fictions they had some psychological truth.

The doctrine of essence thus renders my scepticism invincible and complete, while reconciling me with it emotionally.

If now I turn my face in the other direction and consider the prospect open to animal faith, I see that all this insecurity and inadequacy of alleged knowledge are almost irrelevant to the natural effort of the mind to describe natural things. The discouragement we may feel in science does not come from failure; it comes from a false conception of what would be success. Our worst difficulties arise from the assumption that knowledge of existences ought to be literal, whereas knowledge of existences has no need, no propensity, and no fitness to be literal. It is symbolic initially, when a sound, a smell, an indescribable feeling are signals to the animal of his dangers or chances; and it fulfils its function perfectly— I mean its moral function of enlightening us about our natural good—if it remains symbolic to the end. Can anything be more evident than that religion, language, patriotism, love, science itself speak in symbols? Given essences unify for intuition, in entirely adventitious human terms, the diffuse processes of nature; the aesthetic image—the sound, the colour, the expanse of space, the scent, taste, and sweet or cruel pressure of bodies—wears an aspect altogether unlike the mechanisms it stands for. Sensation and thought (between which there is no essential difference) work in a conventional medium, as do literature and music. The experience of essence is direct; the expression of natural facts through that medium is indirect. But this indirection is not obstacle to expression, rather its condition; and this vehicular manifestation of things may be knowledge of them, which intuition of essence is not. The theatre, for all its artifices, depicts life in a sense more truly than history, because the medium has a kindred movement to that of real life, though an artificial setting and form; and much in the same way the human medium of knowledge can perform its pertinent synthesis and make its pertinent report all the better when it frankly abandons the plane of its object and expresses in symbols what we need to know of it. The arts of expression would be impossible if they were not extensions of normal human perception. The Greeks recognised that astronomy and history were presided over by Muses, sisters of those of tragic and comic poetry; had they been as psychological as modern reflection has become, they might have had Muses of sight, hearing, and speech. I think they honoured, if they did not express, this complementary fact also, that all the Muses, even the most playful, are witnesses to the nature of things. The arts are evidences of wisdom, and sources of it; they include science. No Muse would be a humane influence, nor worthy of honour, if she did not studiously express the truth of nature with the liberty and grace appropriate to her special genius.

Philosophers would not have overlooked the fact that knowledge is, and ought to be, symbolical, if intuition did not exist also, giving them a taste of something which perhaps they think higher and more satisfying. Intuition, when it is placid and masterful enough to stand alone, free from anxiety or delusion about matters of fact, is a delightful exercise, like play; it employs our imaginative faculty without warping it, and lets us live without responsibility. The playful and godlike mind of philosophers has always been fascinated by intuition; philosophers—I mean the great ones—are the infant prodigies of reflection. They often take intuition of essence for their single ideal, and wish to impose it on the workaday thoughts of men; they make a play-world for themselves which it is glorious to dominate, much as other men of genius, prolonging the masterfulness of childhood, continue to play at this or at that in their politics and their religion. But knowledge of existence has an entirely different method and an entirely different ideal. It is playful too, because its terms are intuitive and its grammar or logic often very subjective. Perception, theory, hypothesis are rapid, pregnant, often humorous; they seize a fact by its skirts from some unexpected quarter, and give it a nickname which it might be surprised to hear, such as the rainbow or the Great Bear. Yet in the investigation of facts all this play of mind is merely instrumental and indicative: the intent is practical, the watchfulness earnest, the spirit humble.

STUDY QUESTIONS

Review

1. Explain the basic tenets of the "new realists" regarding knowledge.
2. Compare their views with those of the critical realists.
3. What is Santayana's position concerning the relation of matter and mind or spirit?
4. What is Santayana's "animal faith"? How does he believe it answers the skeptic?

For Further Thought

5. Do you think that we directly or immediately experience an independently existing physical world as it is? If so, how is this possible? If not, what does knowledge amount to?
6. Do you see any problems in asserting, as naturalists generally do, that mind or thought is an ability that evolved as man evolved?
7. Is complete skepticism possible? Do we know or only believe that things outside ourselves exist?
8. Is science symbolic in the same way that poetry is or religion might be (according to Santayana)?

BIBLIOGRAPHY

Realism and Naturalism

Bowman, Lars. *Criticism and Construction in the Philosophy of the American New Realism.* Stockholm: Almquest and Wiksell, 1955.

Delaney, C. F. *Mind and Nature: A Study of the Naturalistic Philosophy of Cohen, Woodbridge, and Sellars.* Notre Dame, Ind.: University of Notre Dame Press, 1969.

Drake, Durant, et al. *Essays in Critical Realism.* 1920. Reprint. New York: Gordian Press, 1968.

Harlow, V. E. *A Bibliography and Genetic Study of American Realism.* Oklahoma City: Harlow Publishing, 1931.

Holt, E. B., et al. *The New Realism.* New York: Macmillan, 1912.

Krikorian, Yervant, ed. *Naturalism and the Human Spirit.* New York: Columbia University Press, 1944.

Lovejoy, Arthur O. *The Revolt Against Dualism.* New York: Open Court Publishing, 1930.

Marcuse, Herbert. *One Dimensional Man.* Boston: Beacon Press, 1964.

— — —. *Soviet Marxism: A Critical Analysis.* New York: Columbia University Press, 1958.

Montague, William P. "The Story of American Realism." *Philosophy* 12 (1937): pp. 140–50, 155–61. Also published in *The Way of Things: A Philosophy of Knowledge, Nature, and Value.* New York: Prentice-Hall, 1940.

— — —. "The New Realism and the Old." *Journal of Philosophy* 8 (1911): pp. 589–99.

Moore, G. E. "The Refutation of Idealism." In *Philosophical Studies.* London: K. Paul, Trench and Co., Ltd., 1922.

Perry, Ralph Barton. "W. P. Montague and the New Realists." *Journal of Philosophy,* 51, 21 (Oct., 1954), pp. 604–608.

— — —. "The Ego-centric Predicament." *Journal of Philosophy* 7, no. 1 (1910): pp. 5–14.

Schneider, H. W. *Sources of Contemporary Philosophical Realism in America.* Indianapolis: Bobbs-Merrill, 1964.

Sellars, Roy Wood. *Evolutionary Naturalism.* Chicago: Open Court Publishing, 1922.

— — —. *Critical Realism.* New York: Russell and Russell, 1916.

— — —. "Critical Realism and Modern Materialism." In *Philosophical Thought in France and the United States,* ed. M. Farber, pp. 463–81. Buffalo: Buffalo University Publications, 1950.

— — —. "Realism, Naturalism, and Humanism." In *Contemporary American Philosophy,* ed. G. P. Adams and W. P. Montague. Vol. 2, pp. 261–85. New York: Macmillan, 1930.

Stace, Walter T. "The Refutation of Realism." *Mind* 43, no. 170 (1934): pp. 145–55.

Wild, John. *Introduction to Realistic Philosophy.* New York: Harper, 1948.

George Santayana

Santayana, George. *Critical Edition of the Complete Works of George Santayana.* Co-eds. Herman Saatkamp and William G. Holzberger. Cambridge, Mass.: MIT Press, 1984–. 20 volumes projected. Vol. 1, *Persons and Places,* Intro. by Richard C. Lyon, 1984; Vol. 2, *The Sense of Beauty,* Intro. by Arthur C. Danto, 1986; Vol. 3, *Interpretations of Poetry and Religion,* Intro. by Joel Porte, 1987.

— — —. *Letters.* Ed. Daniel Cory. New York: Scribner's, 1955.

— — —. *The Last Puritan.* New York: Scribner's, 1936.

— — —. *Philosophy of Santayana: Selections from the Works of George Santayana.* Ed. Irwin Edman. New York: Scribner's, 1936.

— — —. *Realms of Being.* 4 vols. New York: Scribner's, 1927–42.

— — —. *Scepticism and Animal Faith.* New York: Scribner's, 1923.

— — —. *Character and Opinion in the United States.* New York: Scribner's, 1920.

— — —. *Winds of Doctrine.* New York: Scribner's, 1913.

— — —. *The Life of Reason.* 5 vols. New York: Scribner's, 1905–6. Reprint. New York: Collier Books, 1962; Dover, 1980–83.

— — —. *Interpretations of Poetry and Religion.* New York: Scribner's, 1900.

— — —. *The Sense of Beauty.* New York: Scribner's, 1896.

Arnett, W. E. *Santayana and the Sense of Beauty.* Bloomington: Indiana University Press, 1955.

Butler, Richard. *Mind of Santayana.* 1955. Reprint. Westport, Conn.: Greenwood Press, 1968.

Cardiff, Ira, ed. *Wisdom of George Santayana.* New York: Philosophical Library, 1964.

Howgate, G. W. *George Santayana.* New York: Russell, 1938. Reprint. Westwood, Conn.: Greenwood, 1973.

Munitz, Milton K. *The Moral Philosophy of George Santayana.* New York: Columbia University Press, 1939.

Munson, T. N. *The Essential Wisdom of Santayana.* New York: Columbia University Press, 1962.

Saatkamp, Herman J., Jr., and John Jones. *George Santayana: A Bibliographical Checklist, 1880–1980.* Bowling Green: Philosophy Documentation Center, 1982.

Schilpp, Paul Arthur, ed. *The Philosophy of Santayana.* LaSalle, Ill.: Open Court Publishing, 1951. Includes bibliography and autobiographical sketch.

Singer, Beth J. *The Rational Society: A Critical Reading of Santayana's Social Thought.* Cleveland: Press of Case Western Reserve University, 1970.

Singer, Irving. *Santayana's Aesthetics: A Critical Introduction.* Cambridge: Harvard University Press, 1957. Reprint. Westport, Conn.: Greenwood, 1973.

Sprigg, Timothy L. S. *Santayana: An Examination of His Philosophy.* London: Routledge and Kegan Paul, 1974.

Stallknecht, Newton P. *George Santayana.* Minneapolis: University of Minnesota Press, 1971.

The Journal of Philosophy 61 (1964): pp. 5–69. Special issue for centenary of Santayana's birth.

The Southern Journal of Philosophy (1972). Special Santayana edition.

Chapter 11

Thomism

" "T"homism" is the name given to the philosophy of St. Thomas Aquinas and its various interpretations. St. Thomas was one of the most significant philosophers of medieval times. Much of the philosophizing carried on in America has been influenced by European philosophy, in particular European modern philosophy, and in some cases ancient Greek philosophy. However, it has been estimated that perhaps one-fifth of all teachers of philosophy in the United States in 1967 were teaching a philosophy that was Thomistic.[1] Any adequate survey of philosophy in America during the twentieth century, must, then, give an account of these ideas.

Lack of adequate historical treatment of the medieval period has given many the impression that nothing of lasting and independent value in philosophy was done during the Middle Ages. Recent studies have shown this notion to be erroneous. During the period a new availability of the works of Aristotle provided a basis for restudying ancient themes and problems. Much of the rethinking occurred within new university settings and was conducted mostly by friars whose religious beliefs obviously influenced what they found to be of interest in these ancient philosophies. Nevertheless, without such religious institutional support much ancient Greek philosophy as well as that of Arabic and Jewish commentators would not have been preserved for later generations. While Thomas Aquinas himself was primarily a theologian, one can still speak of a Thomistic philosophy as "that part of Thomas' theology which he considered rationally demonstrable and which has been taken out of its theological context."[2] Since much of the philosophizing that has taken place within the Thomistic tradition has consisted of explication and development of the philosophy of Thomas Aquinas, we will first give a brief summary of that philosophy.

Thomas Aquinas was born at the end of 1224 or early in 1225 at Roccasecca not far from Monte Cassino, Italy. He was educated at the Abbey of Monte Cassino from ages five to fourteen, studied briefly at the University of Naples, and then entered the Order of Preachers founded by St. Dominic (now the Dominican Order) where he was a student for some time of Albert the Great. After theological studies he taught on the Dominican faculty in Paris, at the papal court during the 1260s, in Paris again, and then at Naples. He died on the way to a church council in 1274 at the age of forty-nine. In a relatively short lifetime he produced an all-inclusive system that was a remarkable synthesis of theology, philosophy, and the science of his day. His best known work is the *Summa Theologiae* but he authored numerous teatises, including works on truth and evil, and commentaries on Aristotle's *Physics, Metaphysics, Nicomachean Ethics, De Anima,* and *Politics.*

Aristotle was, for Thomas Aquinas, "the Philosopher". Although there are significant ways in which his philosophy differed from that of Aristotle, and although there are also Platonic or neo-Platonic elements in his writings, Aquinas's philosophy is primarily Aristotelian in certain basic themes. As in Aristotle, one starts with a study of corporeal beings and the fact that they change and then argues to the existence of a basic hylomorphic composition within them, that is, a composition of matter and form. However, according to Thomas Aquinas, not all finite creatures are so composed. There exists a realm of creatures called angels who are immaterial substances and thus have no material element, and yet they are nevertheless finite and thus limited. Since, they do not of necessity exist, there must be another kind of composition in them, he argued, that of essence and existence. Angels are particular kinds of beings because they have specific essences. Existence is not a further characteristic of the essence, but the act by which what is exists. Material creatures also are composed of essence and existence. In introducing this distinction between essence and existence Thomas Aquinas differs from Aristotle who emphasized not existence but form.

Aquinas's philosophy also includes five "proofs" for the existence of God. The existence of such a being is not proved *a priori* from a consideration of the idea of such a thing and what this idea necessarily includes, but *a posteriori* from experience. The first proof, "from motion," argues from the fact that things change, eg. are heated, caused to change from one temperature to another or "moved" from being potentially hot (in potency)to being actually hot (in act). This change requires the existence of something which itself has the quality or form "hot" and thus can cause this form to be "actualized" in the being changed. If the cause of the change also needs an explanation of its possession of the quality or form, then it too must have a cause of the quality in it. This series cannot proceed to infinity or the present change or "motion" will remain unexplained. There must be some being which is pure act without any potency.

This is God. It is not a temporal series but one explaining dependency that is at issue. This is likewise true of the second proof "from contingency." That beings of our experience do not necessarily exist means that their very existence requires a causal explanation by a being that necessarily exists. This being, Aquinas believed, is that which we call God, the God also of theological revelation.

As with other corporeal beings, man, according to Aquinas, is a unified being, one composed of matter (body) and form (soul; which in Aquinas as well as Aristotle is simply the form of a living thing). Man is not his soul (as Plato had thought), but one composite being. However, since existence comes to man primarily through his form, his soul, immortality is made possible, though not without some complications since some relation to the body must be retained if it is the person and not the soul alone that is immortal. Since man is one being, he could not have three forms: vegetative, sensitive, and intellectual. When a man feels or thinks it is the whole unit that does so. Nevertheless, he possesses a hierarchy of powers, the highest being his rational powers to know and choose. When we know we proceed from sense experience through imagination and understanding, and finally to a judgment that what we know is so. The understanding has both a passive element and an active or illuminating element. The active function belongs to the individual person and is not, as Aristotle and some others may have postulated, a separate intelligence that is one for all. Choice is explained also in an Aristotelian fashion with revisions based on his notions of an ultimate good. Aquinas's system contains a moral and social philosophy as well. His theory of natural law remains one major moral theory still today.

While the breadth and power of the system of Thomas Aquinas was well recognized in his day, there were those who feared its innovations and reliance on the pagan Aristotle. Because of a general reaction against Thomas's type of Aristotelianism and the condemnation of some doctrines he shared with the followers of the philosopher Averroes, and because of the rise of such competing schools of thought as Scotism (Duns Scotus) and nominalism (William of Ockham), Thomism did not become the dominant intellectual influence of the late Middle Ages except within the Dominican order. Over a period of time creative speculative philosophical thinking gave way to the development of scholastic manuals with these presented in schematic form. The rationalistic ideal of deduction from certain truths replaced the Aristotelian idea of beginning by investigating natural phenomena, seeking a causal account, and forming inductive generalizations. The distinctively Thomistic stress on the act of existence as the ultimate integrating factor in any being was lost in an ontology that analyzed concepts proper to actual or possible beings.

In 1878 Pope Leo XIII established Thomism as the official Catholic philosophy. He thought of Thomism as the one philosophical system capable of incorporating contemporary advances in knowledge and giving them an adequate interpretation in terms of ultimate truths. Thus, in making Thomism normative, he thought of himself as an opening Catholicism to the modern world. What was taught, however, was often not the writings of St. Thomas but scholastic manuals. Only with historians such as Etienne Gilson in the 1930s and neo-Thomists such as Jacques Maritain were efforts again made to interpret the writings of Thomas Aquinas by returning to a study of these texts and their twentieth-century implications. Other scholarly and interpretative works followed both in the United States and Canada, especially in the more independent Catholic university centers such as Toronto and St. Louis. In 1926 the American Catholic Philosophical Association was founded and continues to function today. Journals such as *The Thomist, The Modern Schoolman,* and *New Scholasticism* provided a forum in which people could debate the issues important to the tradition (although today other topics are included in the journals).

Although Thomists in this country have been principally concerned to understand and explain the writings of their mentor, Thomas Aquinas, some philosophers have also sought to interpret Thomism in the light of developments in modern science and modern philosophy. Bernard Lonergan is one example of the latter type of Thomist. A neo-Thomist and a theologian with neo-Kantian leanings, his work *Insight: A Study of Human Understanding* is primarily a philosophical work. It is a study of that particular kind of understanding that is "not any recondite intuition but that familiar event that occurs easily and frequently in the moderately intelligent." [3] According to Lonergan, this type of knowing is so central as to give to the entire field of study of human inquiry an amazing unity. In any investigation, there are successively acts of seeking, accumulating, classifying, and finally insight. In the selection we have included in this chapter, Lonergan explains further the structure of human knowing as a combination of experiencing, understanding, and judging. He further attempts to elucidate what he calls "knowing knowing" in which one not only is conscious of knowing but is self-conscious as well. And finally, Lonergan attempts to show that knowledge is objective, i.e., of reality. In this he exemplifies some of the basic philosophical positions of Thomas Aquinas, but also with a certain originality of his own.

In the other selection in this chapter, Anton Pegis, former director of the Pontifical Institute of Medieval Studies, Toronto, comments not only on the phenomenon of Thomism as a philosophy in the United States, but also on one of the central problems faced by this philosophy. To what extent is it an independent philosophy and to what extent is it dependent on theological or religious beliefs? It has been described as a Christian philosophy; is it then indeed philosophy? With respect to possible difficulties for a Christian philosophy presented by the Aristotelian elements within Thomism, Pegis points out some ways in which he believes Thomism to be more consistent with certain biblical doctrines than a philosophy such as Augustinianism which is founded upon Platonic elements.

Notes

[1] Ernan McMullin, "Presidential Address: Who Are We? " *Proceedings of the American Catholic Philosophical Association* 61 (1967): p. 2.

[2] Armand Maurer, *Medieval Philosophy* (New York: Random House, 1962), p. 165.

[3] Bernard Lonergan, *Insight: A Study of Human Understanding* (London: Longmans, Green, 1957), p. ix.

BERNARD LONERGAN

COGNITIONAL STRUCTURE*

I have chosen cognitional structure as my topic, partly because I regard it as basic, partly because greater clarity may be hoped for from an exposition that does not attempt to describe the ingredients that enter into the structure, and partly because I have been told that my view of human knowing as a dynamic structure has been pronounced excessively obscure.

A whole, then, has parts. The whole is related to each of the parts, and each of the parts is related to the other parts and to the whole.

Not every whole is a structure. When one thinks of a whole, there may come to mind some conventional quantity or arbitrary collection whose parts are determined by an equally conventional or arbitrary division. In such a case, for example a gallon of milk, the closed set of relations between whole and parts will be a no less arbitrary jumble of arithmetic ratios. But it may also happen that the whole one thinks of is some highly organized product of nature or art. Then the set of internal relations is of the greatest significance. Each part is what it is in virtue of its functional relations to other parts; there is no part that is not determined by the exigences of other parts; and the whole possesses a

---

* Bernard Lonergan, S.J. "Cognitional Structure," *Continuum* 2 (Fall 1964): pp. 530–38. Also published in *Spirit as Inquiry: Studies in Honor of Bernard Lonergan* (Chicago: Xavier College, 1964). Reprinted with the permission of the editors of *Continuum* and the author.

certain inevitability in its unity, so that the removal of any part would destroy the whole, and the addition of any further part would be ludicrous. Such a whole is a structure.

The parts of a whole may be things, bricks, timbers, glass, rubber, chrome. But the parts may also be activites, as in a song, a dance, a chorus, a symphony, a drama. Such a whole is dynamic materially. But dynamism may not be restricted to the parts. The whole itself may be self-assembling, self-constituting; then it is formally dynamic. It is a dynamic structure.

Now, human knowing involves many distinct and irreducible activities: seeing, hearing, smelling, touching, tasting, inquiring, imagining, understanding, conceiving, reflecting, weighing the evidence, judging.

No one of these activities, alone and by itself, may be named human knowing. An act of ocular vision may be perfect as ocular vision; yet if it occurs without any accompanying glimmer of understanding, it is mere gaping; and mere gaping, so far from being the beau ideal of human knowing, is just stupidity. As merely seeing is not human knowing, so for the same reason merely hearing, merely smelling, merely touching, merely tasting may be parts, potential components, of human knowing, but they are not human knowing itself.

What is true of sense, is no less true of understanding. Without the prior presentations of sense, there is nothing for a man to understand; and when there is nothing to be understood, there is no occurrence of understanding. Moreover, the combination of the operations of sense and of understanding does not suffice for human knowing. There must be added judging. To omit judgment is quite literally silly: it is only by judgment that there emerges a distinction between fact and fiction, logic and sophistry, philosophy and myth, history and legend, astronomy and astrology, chemistry and alchemy.

Nor can one place human knowing in judging to the exclusion of experience and understanding. To pass judgment on what one does not understand is, not human knowing, but human arrogance. To pass judgment independently of all experience is to set fact aside.

Human knowing, then, is not experience alone, not understanding alone, not judgment alone; it is not a combination of only experience and understanding, or of only experience and judgment, or of only understanding and judgment; finally, it is not something totally apart from experience, understanding, and judgment. Inevitably, one has to regard an instance of human knowing, not as this or that operation, but as a whole whose parts are operations. It is a structure and, indeed, a materially dynamic structure.

But human knowing is also formally dynamic. It is self-assembling, self-constituting. It puts itself together, one part summoning forth the next, till the whole is reached. And this occurs, not with the blindness of natural process, but consciously, intelligently, rationally. Experience stimulates inquiry, and inquiry is intelligence bringing itself to act; it leads from experience through imagination to insight, and from insight to the concepts that combine in single objects both what has been grasped by insight and what in experience or imagination is relevant to the insight. In turn, concepts stimulate reflection, and reflection is the conscious exigence of rationality; it marshals the evidence and weighs it either to judge or else to doubt and so renew inquiry.

Such in briefest outline is what is meant by saying that human knowing is a dynamic structure. Let us briefly note its implications.

First, on the verbal level, it implies a distinction between *knowing* in a loose or generic sense and *knowing* in a strict and specific sense. Loosely, any cognitional activity may be named knowing; so one may speak of seeing, inquiring, understanding, thinking, weighing the evidence, judging, as each an instance of knowing. Strictly, one will distinguish animal, human, angelic, and divine knowing, and one will investigate what in each case is necessary and sufficient for an instance of knowing.

Secondly, the view that human knowing is a dynamic structure implies that human knowing is not some single operation or activity but, on the contrary, a whole whose parts are cognitional activities.

Thirdly, the parts of a structure are related to one another, not by similarity, but functionally. As in a motor-car the engine is not like the tires and the muffler is not like the differential, so too in human knowing, conceived as a dynamic structure, there is no reason to expect the several cognitional activities to resemble one another. It follows that a study of human knowing cannot safely follow the broad and downhill path of analogy. It will not do, for instance, to scrutinize ocular vision and then assume that other cognitional activities must be the same sort of thing. They may turn out to be quite different and so, if one is to proceed scientifically, each cognitional activity must be examined in and for itself and, no less, in its functional relations to other cognitional activities. This third conclusion brings us to the question of consciousness and self-knowledge, which calls for another section.

Where knowing is a structure, knowing knowing must be a reduplication of the structure. Thus, if knowing is just looking, then knowing knowing will be looking at looking.* But if knowing is a conjunction of experience, understanding, and judging, then knowing knowing has to be a conjunction of (1) experiencing experience, understanding and judging, (2) understanding one's experience of experience, understanding, and judging, and (3) judging one's understanding of experience, understanding, and judging to be correct.

On the latter view there follows at once a distinction between consciousness and self-knowledge. Self-knowledge is the reduplicated structure: it is experience, understanding, and judging with respect to experience,

---

* This is a corrected version of a sentence in the original publication—Ed.

understanding, and judging. Consciousness, on the other hand, is not knowing knowing but merely experience of knowing, experience, that is, of experiencing, of understanding, and of judging.

Secondly, it follows that all cognitional activities may be conscious yet none or only some may be known. So it is, in fact, that both acts of seeing and acts of understanding occur consciously, yet most people know what seeing is and most are mystified when asked what understanding is.

Thirdly, it follows that different cognitional activities are not equally accessible. Experience is of the given. Experience of seeing is to be had only when one actually is seeing. Experience of insight is to be had only when one actually is having an insight. But one has only to open one's eyes and one will see; one has only to open and close one's eyes a number of times to alternate the experience of seeing and of not seeing. Insights, on the other hand, cannot be turned on and off in that fashion. To have an insight, one has to be in the process of learning or, at least, one has to re-enact in oneself previous processes of learning. While that is not peculiarly difficult, it does require (1) the authenticity that is ready to get down to the elements of a subject, (2) close attention to instances of one's own understanding and, equally, one's failing to understand, and (3) the repeated use of personal experiments in which, at first, one is genuinely puzzled and then catches on.

Fourthly, because human knowing is a structure of different activities, experience of human knowing is qualitatively differentiated. When one is reflecting, weighing the evidence, judging, one is experiencing one's own rationality. When one is inquiring, understanding, conceiving, thinking, one is experiencing one's own intelligence. When one is seeing or hearing, touching or tasting, one is experiencing one's own sensitivity. Just as rationality is quite different from intelligence, so the experience of one's rationality is quite different from the experience of one's intelligence; and just as intelligence is quite different from sensitivity, so the experience of one's intelligence is quite different from the experience of one's sensitivity. Indeed, since consciousness is of the acting subject *qua* acting, the experience of one's rationality is identical with one's rationality bringing itself to act; the experience of one's intelligence is identical with one's bringing one's intelligence to act; and the experiencing of one's sensitivity is identical with one's sensitivity coming to act.

Fifthly, then, experience commonly is divided into external and internal. External experience is of sights and sounds, of odors and tastes, of the hot and cold, hard and soft, rough and smooth, wet and dry. Internal experience is of oneself and one's apprehensive and appetitive activities. Still, if the meaning of the distinction is clear, the usage of the adjectives, internal and external, calls for explanation. Strictly, only spatial objects are internal or external and, while external experiences may be of spatial objects, it itself is not a spatial object and, still less, is internal experience. Accordingly, we must ask what is the original datum that has been expressed by a spatial metaphor; and to that end we draw attention to different modes of presence.

There is material presence, in which no knowing is involved, and such is the presence of the statue in the courtyard. There is intentional presence, in which knowing is involved, and it is of two quite distinct kinds. There is the presence of the object to the subject, of the spectacle to the spectator; there is also the presence of the subject to himself, and this is not the presence of another object dividing his attention, of another spectacle distracting the spectator; it is presence in, as it were, another dimension, presence concomitant and correlative and opposite to the presence of the object. Objects are present by being attended to; but subjects are present as subjects, not by being attended to, but by attending. As the parade of objects marches by, spectators do not have to slip into the parade to become present to themselves; they have to be present to themselves for anything to be present to them; and they are present to themselves by the same watching that, as it were, at its other pole makes the parade present to them.

I have been attempting to describe the subject's presence to himself. But the reader, if he tries to find himself as subject, to reach back and, as it were, uncover his subjectivity, cannot succeed. Any such effort is introspecting, attending to the subject; and what is found is, not the subject as subject, but only the subject as object; it is the subject as subject that does the finding. To heighten one's presence to oneself, one does not introspect; one raises the level of one's activity. If one sleeps and dreams, one is present to oneself as the frightened dreamer. If one wakes, one becomes present to oneself, not as moved but as moving, not as felt but as feeling, not as seen but as seeing. If one is puzzled and wonders and inquires, the empirical subject becomes an intellectual subject as well. If one reflects and considers the evidence, the empirical and intellectual subject becomes a rational subject, an incarnate reasonableness. If one deliberates and chooses, one has moved to the level of the rationally conscious, free, responsible subject that by his choices makes himself what he is to be and his world what it is to be.

Sixthly, does this many-leveled subject exist? Each man has to answer that question for himself. But I do not think that the answers are in doubt. Not even behaviorists claim that they are unaware whether or not they see or hear, taste or touch. Not even positivists preface their lectures and their books with the frank avowal that never in their lives did they have the experience of understanding anything whatever. Not even relativists claim that never in their lives did they have the experience of making a rational judgment. Not even determinists claim that never in their lives did they have the experience of making a responsible choice. There exist subjects that are empirically, intellectually, rationally, morally conscious. Not all know themselves as such, for consciousness is not human knowing but only a potential component in the structured whole that is human knowing. But all can know themselves as such, for they have only to attend to what they are already conscious of, and understand what they attend to, and pass judgment on the correctness of their understanding.

At this point one may ask why knowing should result from the performance of such immanent activities as experiencing, understanding, and judging. This brings us to the epistemological theorem, namely, that knowledge in the proper sense is knowledge of reality or, more fully, that knowledge is intrinsically objective, that objectivity is the intrinsic relation of knowing to being, and that being and reality are identical.

The intrinsic objectivity of human cognitional activity is its intentionality. Nor need this intentionality be inferred, for it is the dominant content of the dynamic structure that assembles and unites several activities into a single knowing of a single object. Human intelligence actively greets every content of experience with the perplexity, the wonder, the drive, the intention, that may be thematized by (but does not consist in) such questions as, What is it? Why is it so? Inquiry through insight issues forth in thought that, when scrutinized, becomes formulated in definitions, postulates, suppositions, hypotheses, theories. Thought in turn is actively greeted by human rationality with a reflective exigence that, when thematized, is expressed in such questions as, Is that so? Are you certain? All marshaling and weighing of evidence, all judging and doubting, are efforts to say of what is that it is and of what is not that it is not. Accordingly, the dynamic structure of human knowing intends being. That intention if unrestricted, for there is nothing that we cannot at least question. The same intention is comprehensive, for questioning probes every aspect of everything; its ultimate goal is the universe in its full concreteness. Being in that sense is identical with reality: as apart from being there is nothing, so apart from reality there is nothing; as being embraces the concrete totality of everything, so too does reality.

This intrinsic relation of the dynamic structure of human knowing to being and so to reality primarily is not *pensée pensée* but *pensée pensante,* not *intentio intenta* but *intentio intendens,* not *noêma* but *noêsis.* It is the originating drive of human knowing. Consciously, intelligently, rationally it goes beyond: beyond data to intelligibility; beyond intelligibility to truth and through truth to being; and beyond known truth and being to the truth and being still to be known. But though it goes beyond, it does not leave behind. It goes beyond to add, and, when it has added, it unites. It is the active principle that calls forth in turn our several cognitional activities and, as it assembles them into single instances of knowing, so it assembles their many partial objects into single total objects. By inquiry it moves us from sensing to understanding only to combine the sensed and understood into an object of thought. By reflection it moves us from objects of thought through rationally compelling evidence to judgments about reality. From the partial knowledge we have reached it sends us back to fuller experiencing, fuller understanding, broader and deeper judgments, for what it intends includes far more than we succeed in knowing. It is all-inclusive, but the knowing we achieve is always limited.

As answers stand to questions, so cognitional activities stand to the intention of being. But an answer is *to* a question, because it and the question have the same object. So it is that the intrinsic relation of the dynamic structure of human knowing passes from the side of the subject to the side of the object, that the *intentio intendens* of being becomes the *intentio intenta* of this or that being. So the question, What's this?, promotes the datum of sense to a "this" that has a "what-ness" and "is." The promotion settles no issues, but it does raise issues. It is neither knowledge nor ignorance of essence and existence, but it is the intention of both. What the essence is and whether that essence exists are, not answers, but questions. Still the questions have been raised and the very fact of raising them settles what the answers will have to be about. The *intentio intendens* of the subject summons forth and unites cognitional activities to objectify itself in an *intentio intenta* that unites and is determined by the partial objects of the partial activities. As the *intentio intendens* of the dynamic structure, so the corresponding *intentio intenta* of the structured cognitional activities is intrinsically related to being and reality.

It remains that the two relations are not identical. The *intentio intendens* is not knowing but merely intending: it is objectivity in potency. But the *intentio intenta* resides not in mere intending but in structured activities of knowing: it is objectivity in act. Moreover, objectivity in act, because it resides not in a single operation but in a structured manifold of operations, is not some single property of human knowing but a compound of quite different properties. Empiricists have tried to find the ground of objectivity in experience, rationalists have tried to place it in necessity, idealists have had recourse to coherence. All are partly right and partly wrong, right in their affirmation, but mistaken in their exclusion. For the objectivity of human knowing is a triple cord; there is an experiential component that resides in the givenness of relevant data; there is a normative component that resides in the exigences of intelligence and rationality guiding the process of knowing from data to judging; there finally is an absolute component that is reached when reflective understanding combines the normative and the experiential elements into a virtually unconditioned, i.e., a conditioned whose conditions are fulfilled.

The objectivity of human knowing, then, rests upon an unrestricted intention and an unconditioned result. Because the intention is unrestricted, it is not restricted to the immanent content of knowing, to *Bewusstseinsinhalte;* at least, we can ask whether there is anything beyond that, and the mere fact that the question can be asked reveals that the intention, which the question manifests, is not limited by any principle of immanence. But answers are *to* questions, so that if questions are transcendent, so also must be the meaning of corresponding answers. If I am asked whether mice and men really exist, I am not answering the question when I talk about images of mice and men, concepts of mice and men, or the words, mice and men; I answer the question only if I affirm or deny the real existence of mice and men. Further, true answers express an unconditioned. Mice and men are contingent and so their existence has its conditions. My knowing mice and men is contingent and so my knowing of their existence has its conditions. But the conditions of the conditioned may be fulfilled and then the conditioned is virtually an unconditioned; it has the properties of an unconditioned, not absolutely, but *de facto*. Because human knowing reaches such an unconditioned, it transcends itself. For the unconditioned *qua* unconditioned cannot be restricted, qualified, limited; and so we all distinguish sharply between what is and, on the other hand, what appears, what seems to be, what is imagined or thought or might possibly or probably be affirmed; in the latter cases the object is still tied down by relativity to the subject; in the former the self-transcendence of human knowing has come to its term; when we say that something is, we mean that its reality does not depend upon our cognitional activity.

The possibility of human knowing, then, is an unrestricted intention that intends the transcendent, and a process of self-transcendence that reaches it. The unrestricted intention directs the process to being; the attainment of the unconditioned reveals that at some point being has been reached. So, quite manifestly, a grasp of dynamic structure is essential to a grasp of the objectivity of our knowing. Without the dynamism one may speak of concepts of being, affirmations of being, even the idea of being; but unfailingly one overlooks the overarching intention of being which is neither concept nor affirmation nor idea.* Again, without the structure there is no place for three quite different elements of objectivity and no thought of a third resulting from a reflective understanding of the other two; yet the empiricists are right in their insistence on data, for in the givenness of data resides the experiential component of objectivity; there is something to the idealist insistence on coherence, for in the directive exigences of intelligence and rationality there resides the normative component of objectivity; and there is something to the rationalist insistence on necessity, for a conditioned whose conditions are fulfilled is virtually an unconditioned, and reflective understanding grasps

---

* By an "idea" is meant the content of an act of understanding; hence the idea of being is the content of the act that understands being; as being is unrestricted, so the act must be unrestricted. The idea of being, then, is the divine essence *qua species intelligibilis* of divine understanding.

such a virtually unconditioned whenever it finds the fulfilment of conditions in the data of sense or consciousness and, at the same time, derives from normative objectivity the link that binds conditions with conditioned.

ANTON PEGIS

THOMISM AS A PHILOSOPHY*

In the following lecture I propose to discuss Thomism as a Christian philosophy. So far as this is possible, I shall do so in the light of that very special historical moment when St. Thomas found himself face to face with the great intellectual challenge of his age, namely, the entry of Aristotelian philosophy into the Latin Christian world. There are several reasons for examining this question at the present time and even for examining it under these specific conditions.

When I began teaching philosophy some thirty years ago there was considerable excitement about Thomism. It seemed then to be a popular philosophy and its intellectual vigor was proclaimed in many quarters; moreover, the circumstances that St. Thomas was a theologian merely proved to a considerable number of people that he knew how to keep his philosophy properly separated from his theology. But things have changed in the meantime. Today Thomism is not the popular philosophy it used to be in the twenties and thirties, and the main reason for this turn of events is the extraordinary fact about Thomism that concerns me in the present lecture. According to the Angelic Doctor himself, though philosophy is in its nature distinct from theology, it is nevertheless open to all the influences of divine truth that the Christian revelation has

---

* Anton Pegis, *The McAuley Lectures* (West Hartford, Conn.; St. Joseph College, 1960), pp. 15–30. Reprinted with the permission of the president of St. Joseph College.

brought with it. Distinct from theology, philosophy as St. Thomas taught it and practiced it is a Christian reality—a philosophy born and nourished in a Christian soil. As such it seems to have become a source of embarrassment to those Thomists who want to qualify as genuine philosophers in the eyes of their non-Catholic colleagues. Nothing, surely, is more natural than this desire, not to say anxiety, especially when the modern American Thomist is being told by the unbelieving among his colleagues that "Neo-Thomism is a philosophy of the *defeat* of humanism in a revived supernaturalism";[1] or when a very perceptive and sympathetic Protestant student of Christian philosophy can argue that St. Thomas undertook the impossible when he tried to reconcile Aristotle and the Bible and as a result found himself "uncomfortably suspended between the Aristotelian thinker-God and the Biblical Creator".[2] Yes, Thomism seems to have come upon difficult days. To the creedless philosopher, it is not philosophy but "special pleading".[3] To the non-Catholic Christian historian it appears to be an unsuccessful and unstable attempt to Christianize Aristotle; indeed, far from succeeding it rather paganized the texture of Christian teaching and led to the Reformation and the destruction of the medieval synthesis.[4]

In the face of these and similar embarrassments, research has been changing our perspective on medieval philosophy in a remarkable way. The men whom we used to call medieval philosophers were in reality theologians; they were at their creative best as thinkers when they employed philosophy in the service of their several theologies; and St. Thomas in particular was a theologian who created remarkably new ideas precisely in those parts of philosophy that were of special interest to the Christian revelation and its mission.[5] Hence, although St. Thomas knew perfectly well how to distinguish philosophy from theology and even used this distinction to define their respective domains, he also maintained that philosophy had acquired an improved and purer expresion of its own nature by living in a Christian environment. Should this Thomistic view of the benefits received by philosophy from its Christian climate be true, then our embarrassment is complete. Not only must we say with the historians that the philosophy used by St. Thomas in his theology was a Christian one but we must also hold that, according to St. Thomas' own view of the matter, the faith of the Christian believer illumines his intellect and benefits his philosophy in a way that is as authentically philosophical in its results as it is specifically religious in its origin.

We are now in the presence of the problem of Thomism as a philosophy in the United States today. What exactly is the status of Thomism as a philosophy if, by being Christian, it renders its own rationality suspect to those who are unbelievers? On the other hand, if St. Thomas never saw any need to separate his philosophy from his theology as the price of maintaining its rational autonomy, what precisely is going on in the minds of those modern Thomists who, contrary to St. Thomas' own practice, have established a "separated" Thomistic philosophy in the name of the autonomy of philosophy? Admittedly, a philosophy that is (or claims to be) both philosophy and Christian is an astonishing reality, and the strategem of removing the adjective is an understandable device used by Christians in philosophical conversation with non-Christians. The only question is whether a philosophy that feels obliged to forget or ignore its Christian origin in the name of its rationality can claim to be, in any recognizable historical sense, Thomistic.

Let us begin our discussion with a commonplace historical fact, namely, that St. Thomas learned his philosophy from Aristotle. To be sure, the encounter between St. Thomas and Aristotle is for most of us a faraway event. The passage of time has buried it deeply in history and recreated it inextricably in myth and prejudice. We have been told often enough that St. Thomas learned the nature and principles of philosophy from Aristotle and thereafter reported what he learned as though Aristotle was philosophy personified. In point of fact, did not St Thomas repeatedly say: "*secundum veritatem et Aristotelem:* according to truth and Aristotle" ? Moreover, since philosophy is on everyone's admission the native work of man's intellect, it would seem perfectly natural to suppose that the philosophy of St. Thomas used in his theology *was* Aristotelianism, which is to say, the work of the intellect belonging to an ancient pagan philosopher. Aristotelianism was philosophy pure and simple and St. Thomas so understood it; it was the purely natural and humanly discoverable world of truth that the Christian revelation had come to save, to correct and to complete.

Seen in this way, St. Thomas' reading of Aristotle was a fairly simple event. A Christian theologian became acquainted with the newly-Latinized writings of a pagan philosopher and learned from them exactly what that philosopher had to teach, namely, the nature of philosophy itself. Thereafter this Christian theologian became an Aristotelian in philosophy. That, being a theologian, St. Thomas used philosophy to develop notions of special interest to Christian religious teaching was scarcely cause for surprise. In the work of the theologian philosophy appears, not under its own banner, but as an instrument of theological reflection. But whatever his purpose as a theologian, the philosophy St. Thomas used was in itself the perfectly natural product of human intelligence, pre-Christian and Aristotelian in origin.

The distinctive feature in St. Thomas' attitude toward Aristotle was that he neither condemned Aristotelianism nor capitulated before it. Far from taking up arms against a pagan enemy, St. Thomas was at pains to lead that very enemy, with all his arsenal of truths, from the darkness of the errors that beset him to the liberating light of the Christian revelation. This, at least, was St. Thomas' guiding ambition. As he saw it, the truths of Aristotle and his teacher Plato far outweighed their errors, and their vision of the world and of man, of philosophy and its human purpose, was a permanent acquisition of Western civilization. In St. Thomas' hands, the philosophy of Aristotle did more than lose its pagan errors; it gained a profounder appreciation of its own meaning and ambition, much as though the same St. Thomas who was learning philosophy from Aristotle was teaching his teacher a deeper understanding of his own pagan words and a deeper desire at work beneath the surface of his philosophy.

When we make an effort to see it with St. Thomas' eyes, the philosophy of Aristotle was indeed a great human monument. It was even an enduring tribute to the nobility and the power of the human intellect living by its own light and without the guidance of a divine revelation. Think, in fact, how much Aristotle had achieved in philosophy, pagan though he had been. Following his teacher Plato, he had said that philosophy was the study of the highest realities and causes of the universe; it was a passionate search to find the order and the origin of things and thereby to understand the world, its nature and its destiny. Nor was this search impersonal, since the beatitude of man himself was its animating substance. To find divinity as the source of the universe was the highest aim of the Aristotelian metaphysics, and there was a divine urge in man's desire to reach this divine peak of reality. Whatever mistakes Aristotle made, and pagan though he was, it remains that the supreme goal of his philosophy was to become a theology, that is to say, the study of divine being. What is more, Aristotle conceived this study both as the noblest fulfillment of philosophy and as the perfection of man himself in the highest part of his nature, namely, his intellect. To become a philosopher thus meant ultimately to become a theologian, a student and disciple of divine truth; and to become a theologian was nothing less than to become a perfect— that is to say, a perfected—human being.

When St. Thomas came across such ideas in the *Metaphysics* and *Ethics* of Aristotle, how could he help but admire this ancient pagan thinker? True enough, Aristotle had made serious mistakes on the nature of divine being, since he seems to have believed in several gods, and he had made no less serious mistakes on the nature of human beatitude, since he did not know how to endow man with a personal intellectual soul or a personal beatitude beyond the present life. But these grave errors merely served to put into sharper focus some astonishing Aristotelian truths. St. Thomas the Christian theologian showed the measure of his own genius by giving to Aristotle's ideas a foundation that Aristotle had not known and by transforming the Aristotelian world at the very moment of verifying its deepest aspirations.

In itself, the extraordinary and far-reaching revolution accomplished by St. Thomas Aquinas was a simple one. It consisted in taking Aristotle seriously as a philosopher and in giving a central place to the two great notions he had contributed to the ancient Greek view of the world. One was the notion of form, while the other was the doctrine of the eternity of the world. Aristotle transformed the philosophies of his predecessors, and especially that of Plato, by means of his own conception of form and he gave to the Greek belief in the everlastingness of the world its final expression in his own doctrine of the eternity of motion and therefore of the world itself. The Aristotelian world of eternal forms, necessary and dynamic even in the realm of matter and motion, was in the thirteenth century a massive intellectual challenge to the Christian view of the contingency of time and the mortality of creation. The boldness of St. Thomas as a Christian theologian can be measured by the fact that he did not find it necessary to accept or to reject the eternal world of Aristotle; he did something bolder and more imaginative: he assimilated it. And just as at the origin of the Aristotelian view of the world there was a certain notion of form, so at the origin of St. Thomas' assimilation of the Aristotelian metaphysics of form we can see the decisive role played by the notion of act.

As understood by Aristotle, form contains two fundamentally different elements derived from two distinct historical sources. From Plato Aristotle learned that the world was intelligible but that its intelligibility lay in a realm of pure essences separated from the ceaseless change and instability that marked the domain of material things. But as a biologist Aristotle knew something else about reality, which came to him almost entirely from the observation of living things. All things, and especially living things, had a dynamic structural organization or form. Here begin the great differences between Plato and Aristotle on the nature of being as a whole. For Plato, being possessed intelligibility because it was constituted of pure essences; but Platonic being had to remain changeless in order to retain the permanence and the identity of the essences composing it. For Aristotle, the very intelligibility of being was a dynamic one; the essence of any given being was more like a living organism than a static geometric pattern. Whether Aristotle went too far in the direction of looking at all reality with the eyes of a biologist is not in question. Historians have told us often enough that Aristotle tended to classify even in those areas of human knowledge where he should have measured; as a result, it is a fact that the sciences of measurement (astronomy, physics and chemistry) were not established until after the sixteenth-century revolt against the scientific sterility of medieval Aristotelianism. But the triumph of Galileo in mechanics should not obscure what we owe to Aristotle the biologist and metaphysician.[6]

It is admittedly astonishing to see how far Aristotle went in thinking of all reality, including physical nature, in biological terms. Nature was for Aristotle a sort of soul, "an inborn force of change," while motion was "a sort of life belonging to naturally constituted things".[7] To Aristotle the *natural* was thus primarily the *living;* so that *nature* and *soul,* considered as internal principles of physical movement and of living operations, could be expressed in one and the same language—the language of the biologist describing the organization and activity of living things. But, even so, by thus looking at things qualitatively Aristotle did not miss (as Plato had missed) the dynamism of physical change itself; nor did he fail to see in the *natural* an internal order of finality born in a nature seeking through its power to accomplish a certain work and thereby to reach its end. It was a *felix culpa* that led Aristotle to endow the notion of form with so many of the characteristics of living things; for this mistake led to a metaphysics in which all immaterial beings were living intellectual substances. Where Plato's highest reality was an intelligible form as pure as it was abstract and non-living, Aristotle taught the Western world that all pure intelligible forms were intelligences, that is, forms whose intelligibility was rooted in the life exercised by an intellectual substance. And though Christian theologians did not need the lesson, it was Aristotle (and not Plato) who told them in his *Metaphysics* that the highest being in all reality was a living intelligence whose perfection of life and existence consisted in is identity with the object of its understanding.[8]

The same St. Thomas who was aware of Aristotle's errors in astronomy and mechanics looked beyond them to the Aristotelian notion of form in all the richness of its many metaphysical contributions. Form was the permanent and striving core of every being in the Aristotelian world. Form gave to each being its unity, its nature, its drive to fulfillment, its share in divinity and, lastly, its urge to exist eternally. The world of Aristotle had about it the air of being indestructible. Through form it was either divine or divinely centered; it was as little as possible a perishable world, being eternally necessary in its internal stability. This notion of form, which in Aristotle himself led to the ideal of an everlasting world order, was caused by St. Thomas to transform in a remarkable way an old Christian doctrine, the doctrine of creation. Here is the ultimate ground in the meeting between Athens and Jerusalem as seen by St. Thomas himself.

The Thomistic doctrine of creation was in its metaphysical spirit and meaning something genuinely original in the history of Christian thought. This is bound to sound rather strange if only because the idea of creation is as old as the first chapter of *Genesis.* But St. Thomas' Christian predecessors regularly identified "creation" with "a beginning in time"; and while as a Christian theologian St. Thomas believed that God created the world in time, he also held that in its essence creation meant, not a beginning in time, but an absolute beginning in the order of existence. In other words, whether endowed with an eternal or a non-eternal duration, a creature is a creature for the sole but radical reason that God is the unique, total and immediate cause of its existence. Thus defined by a total and unique dependence on God for its being, a creature is marked by its status as a beginner in the order of being. It endures because it exists, and though it exists in its own right it always exists because it is always being created. Creation is therefore measured by the nothingness of the creature taken absolutely in itself. To be sure, when a creature exists it does so with its own act of existence; even so, the creature is exercising an act of existence that never ceases to be a pure and simple gift from God—a gift of being, with which the creature is all that it is and without which it is absolutely nothing.[9]

Perhaps we can see at this point how St. Thomas has used Aristotle to express a deeply Christian truth. Where Aristotle had said that the nature of a thing is the source and the measure of its activity, St. Thomas has added that, since God is the creative cause of that nature, whatever a creature does begins and ends in God. Moreover, since whatever God does begins and ends with His love, he may well ask St. Thomas why God created a universe at all. Creation began, not in any desire on the part of God to have things in the sense of having possession, but the generous desire to give Himself and to share His life and beatitude. From this point of view, creation involves directly and primarily the existence of intellectual creatures. Among these intellectual creatures there is man, composed of soul and body, of spirit and matter. To St. Thomas it was perfectly evident that the reason why God created the material world was because He created man, and God created the intellectual creature man in order to give him the gift of beatitude.[10] Thus, as St. Thomas saw it, the creation of the physical universe reached its culmination and its full meaning in man. As an intellectual creature, man united the visible creation because he continued within himself the ultimate purpose of its existence. It is a fact that Aristotle did not know of man's destiny; but if he could not see the divine beatitude to which intellectual creatures were called, he yet located the indestructible aim and substance of the universe in divinity and in the imitation of divinity. Aristotle gave to St. Thomas a notion of *nature* that could serve as a vehicle for a metaphysics of creation. In St. Thomas' hands, Aristotelian natures expressed in their organization and movement the effort of creaturely beings to reach repose and completion in a return to their source.

Even at this point, when we can begin to see how completely St. Thomas centered the order of the physical universe in its meaning as the home of man himself, we have not yet reached the most distinctive aspect of his doctrine of creation. St. Thomas describes man's slow journey to God by means of the Aristotelian language of form. Man is a being made to endure, a being whose change and growth are an expansion of his internal drive to become in deed and in act the reality outlined in the intelligible structure of his nature. Man is a being, therefore, for whom the process of time is a road to fulfillment, that is, to self-discovery and realization, to permanence and even to an eternal endurance. Here, at this mysterious juncture, lies the lasting crisis posed by Aristotle for the

Christian theology of St. Thomas. Here Christianity came face to face with one of the deepest ambitions of pagan Athens, the ambition to give to the city of man—and to man himself—an eternal existence in an imperishable world.

This ambition, without any doubt, was the cornerstone of the very Aristotelianism that St. Thomas used so confidently to explain the permanence and finality of creatures. But how was this possible? How could a philosophy describing an uncreated and self-contained world, whose movement and development were the expression of its indestructible necessity, be used by a theologian to characterize a world of mutable and perishable creatures? To St. Augustine the change and mortality of creatures had meant that, but for God's saving hand, they would fall into the nothingness from which they had been drawn and to which they were constantly tending. St. Thomas did not see things in this way. In spite of St. Augustine, he did not think that creatures were perishable because they were creatures, and he did not agree that change was a normal creaturely tendency toward nothingness.[11]

It was a source of grievance and perplexity to many Augustinians that St. Thomas thought as he did. In his hands the scarcely substantial world of St. Augustine, which revealed God by all the ways it needed—and had—His support, was replaced by a world of enduring substances, which revealed the greatness of God by the enduringness written in His creatures. If St. Augustine had an acute awareness of the instability of creatures, St. Thomas had an even deeper sense of their tendency to exist rather than to perish. And though it is true that the physics of Aritotle stood between St. Thomas and St. Augustine, it is even more true that only a genuine theological optimism could have thought of using Aristotelian teaching as St. Thomas did. The theology of St. Thomas, rooted in the Christian vision of a world created by God to endure even to eternity, surely preceded and guided the astonishing use St. Thomas made of the Aristotelian doctrine of change; just as the same theology was not afraid to find necessity in God's creatures provided God Himself was its author or to learn about the nature of that necessity from Aristotle and Avicenna.

How could it be otherwise? St. Thomas had learned from Aristotle a doctrine that separated him both from Plato and from Christian Platonists. Where Plato and his followers had thought that *becoming* was an imitation of *being,* forever striving and forever failing, Aristotle had argued that of its very nature becoming was a road to being, a movement of the potential-but-perfectible toward its full actuality and perfection. Becoming was therefore a way *into* existence, not out of existence. For Aristotle, things changed, not because they were inferior or second-class beings, but because thereby they could become themselves as completely and as permanently as possible. To St. Thomas the follower of such a doctrine change was ultimately bound to be, not the way to corruption and death even when it remained true that some things were corrupted and died; nor was the world of time a world of the dying, and death itself was not primarily a mark of the world's basic mortality; no, change could not be such a constant victory for nothingness. If it was true to say with Aristotle that change was a movement toward actuality and completion, then the old Augustinian sense of the mortality of things, though genuine in its religious appreciation of the transitoriness of the world of time and the moral fragility of human nature, was in part grounded in a Platonic illusion. Only being changes, and it changes to become—that is, *to come to be*—itself in a more final and lasting way. In spite of St. Augustine, he did not think that creatures were perishable because endure, however much it had to change in order to reach its destiny. As a creature, each thing aims *to be,* and though God can at any moment annihilate His creatures, according to St. Thomas there is no inborn tendency in any creature toward non-existence. In other words, to be created is literally to be made *to be.* As much as possible there is in the creature a tendency toward existence and even toward necessity in existence, as though the same God Who created things intended to build them for all eternity.

The Thomistic world of creatures is a truly remarkable reality. In changing, it is striving to become more adequately what God meant in creating it; its mortality is therefore the vehicle of its eternal destiny. If the Thomistic world is not eternal in the sense of being without origin in existence, the world of Aristotle can still be recognized within it, even including its ambition to be everlasting. For St. Thomas believes with Aristotle that of its very nature the business of being is to be, and the purpose of becoming is to lead beings that are incompletely actual to the fullness of their actuality. In St. Thomas' teaching you can also see, if not the intellectual world of St. Augustine, at least its Christian feeling that time is building its very mortality toward eternity. As theologians, St. Augustine and St. Thomas both believe that eternity is the secret leaven of temporality. But in St. Augustine eternity saves the mortality of the world of time from the constant threat of dispersion and death; in St. Thomas, who is as serene as St. Augustine is troubled, eternity completes an edifice whose everlastingness God already prepared in creating it.

Perhaps we can now see why, in spite of its first flush of success and popularity immediately after the First World War, Thomism should have forced upon American thinkers, both Catholic and non-Catholic, the sort of decisions that of their very nature constitute a parting of the ways. In its spirit and temper as a philosophy Thomism is a daring experiment. It is the natural philosophy of the Christian man, being a complete vision of his nature, his world and their common destiny. It is not afraid to explore reality under the religious inspiration of revelation and with the philosophical tools of Aristotle. When St. Thomas philosophizes it is about the creatures that God has made; and when he examines creation with the technical notions of Aristotle the results are nothing less than astonishing. Never did the Christian world look more Greek than St. Thomas' effort to remove from creatures the Platonic impermanence that many theologians had taken to be an essential mark of creaturehood; never did the Aristotelian world of eternal forms and endless change find a bolder Christian expression than in the Thomistic dream of an enduring creation; never did a philosophy better serve the Christian destiny of the world than the Thomistic doctrine of being. In St. Thomas' hands creation tells a continuous story. Metaphysics studies this story in the dynamic intelligibility and movement of things, and this study is but the beginning of the history of the return of creatures to God.

Rationalists will necessarily find in St. Thomas a disconcerting teacher—disconcerting to their unbelief, their glorification of the physical sciences, their skepticism, their readiness to let man live and perish within the world of time. On the other hand, those religious thinkers for whom creation is mortal and corrupt, having the perishable value and meaning of a world of passing illusions that man must remove from the permanent direction of his life—such religious thinkers will find in Thomism a challenging optimism. The enduring substantiality of things shines forth in their very being. Here is a Christian theologian who knows the passing ways of the world but who constantly opposed all efforts. Christian, Jewish and Arabic, to weaken the strength and glory with which God had endowed His creatures in their very being. If things change, this is not to die but to grow; change is primarily the vehicle of perfection and not destruction. In a world in which creaturely natures are defined as Aristotelian essences, whole, stable, dynamic and internally directed toward the end that is their completion, time and change are truly the meeting point between metaphysics and history. Under the governance of a creating God, to Whom creatures are turned in the very structure and movement of their beings, the destiny of nature in God is nothing less than the fulfillment of the impulse it received in its creation.

In this way, the main and even unique issue posed by Thomism in the United States becomes remarkably clear. Thomism is no longer merely a popular or promising philosophy because we are beginning to recognize its distinctive Christian message. As a Christian philosophy, committed to the engagement of the natural in the supernatural and of human intelligence in the world of revealed truth, Thomism cannot but be disconcerting to rationalists, just as the very notion of Christian philosophy must remain foreign to those Thomists who dream of Thomism as a pure philosophy. As a philosophy Thomism reflects the whole world of nature as Catholic Christianity conceives it to be—glorious even in its all, infinitely more glorious in its redemption, at home within the world of revelation because the light of revelation is the first beginning and the last end of the existence and work of philosophy.

This conclusion is the key point in the present situation of Thomism in the United States. Thomism does not practice rationalism in philosophy or in theology. It does not think to close philosophy against any influence of revelation on the pretext that such an influence is against the nature of philosophy, nor does it hesitate to place philosophy in the service of revelation, realizing that in such a service the handmaid has been admitted to the household of her mistress. Seen in this way, Thomism is the philosophy of a theologian who always thought that the rationality of philosophy could not but be purified in its specific character by the help of revelation. Reason and faith, philosophy and theology, the natural and the supernatural are so related to one another that they constitute one world of truth; and nature and reason have only one goal, the supernatural destiny to which God has invited man.

NOTES

[1]. Joseph L. Blan, "Recent Philosophical Importations" in S. W. Baron, E. Nagel and K. S. Pimson (editors), *Freedom and Reason*, (Glencoe, Ill.: The Free Press, 1951), p. 94 (author's italics).

[2]. Richard Kroner, *Speculation and Revelation in the Age of Christian Philosophy* (Philadelphia: The Westminster Press, 1959), p. 204. Looking at St. Thomas' personality, Professor Kroner finds it lacking in religious passion and zeal and concludes: "If a saint is a man who resembles Jesus Christ, this man certainly was not a saint". (*op. cit.,* p. 211). A remarkable statement, surely.

[3]. Bertrand Russell, *A History of Western Philosophy.* (New York: Simon & Schuster, 1945), p. 463.

[4]. R. Kroner, *op. cit.,* p. 212.

[5]. Etienne Gilson, "Historical Research and the Future of Scholasticism" in A. C. Pegis (editor), *A Gilson Reader,* (Garden City, N.Y.: Hanover House, 1957), pp. 156-167.

[6]. See J.-M. Le Blond, S. J., *Aristote philosophe de la vie. Le livre premier du traité sur les Parties des Animaux* (Paris: Aubier, 1945), pp. 1-51; E. Gilson, "The Distinctiveness of the Philosophic Order" in A. C. Pegis (editor), *A Gilson Reader,* pp. 49-65.

[7]. Aristotle, *Physics,* II, 1.192 b18; VII, 1.250 b14.

[8]. Aristotle, *Metaphysics,* XII, 7,1072 b26-30.

[9]. Of the two requirements of the idea of creation, according to St. Thomas, the second is described by him as follows. "Secundum est, ut in re quae creari dicitur, prius sit non esse quam esse: non quidem prioritate temporis vel durationis, ut prius non fuerit et postmodum sit, sed prioritate naturae, ita quod res creata, si sibi relinquatur, consequatur non esse, cum esse non habeat nisi ex influentia causae superiris. Prius enim unicuique inest naturaliter quod non ex alio habet quam ab alio habet." (*In II Sent.,* d.1, q. prima, a.2; ed P. Mandonnet, p. 18). — Note also: "et ita non esse quod ex se habet [res creata] naturaliter est prius quam esse quod habet ab alio, etsi non duratione" (Ibid., a.5, ad 2 in contrarium; ed. cit., p. 38.

[10]. St. Thomas Aquinas, *Summa Contra Gentiles,* III, chapter 22; cf. also A. C. Pegis, "Creation and Beatitude in the *Summa Contra Gentiles* of St. Thomas Aquinas" in *Proceedings of the American Catholic Philosophical Association,* XXIX, 1955, pp. 52-62.

[11]. St. Thomas Aquinas, *In I Sent.,* d.8 q.prima, a.2 (ed. P. Mandonnet) pp. 213-214; *Summa Contra Gentiles,* I, chapter 30, no. 3; *Summa Theologiac,* I, q.9, a.2 — For a contrary view, see St. Bonaventure, *In I Sent.,* d.8, p.1, a.2, ad 7-8 (ed. minor, Quaracchi, 1934), p.126.

STUDY QUESTIONS

Review

1. Give two examples of the empirical orientation of the philosophy of Thomas Aquinas, i.e., two areas in which his arguments are based on matters knowable from sense experience.
2. In what ways is the philosophy of Thomas Aquinas like that of Aristotle, and in what ways different?
3. In what way is the existence of incorporeal limited beings (the angels) a key to understanding the metaphysics of Thomas Aquinas?
4. According to Aquinas, what makes immortality possible, and why does his philosophy of man or his metaphysics still pose problems for a theory of immortality?
5. Summarize the points that Lonergan makes concerning the nature of the process of understanding or knowing.
6. How does Lonergan argue that knowledge is of the real, i.e., is objective?
7. Summarize the points made by Pegis concerning whether the philosophy of Thomas Aquinas is influenced by and related to his theological beliefs.

For Further Thought

8. Do you think that any of the Thomistic arguments for the existence of God prove the existence of such a being?
9. What problems do you think are posed for a person with religious beliefs who attempts to reason philosophically?
10. Do you think it is possible to hold both the corporeal nature of human existence (i.e., that human beings are not just souls or spirits stuck in bodies), and that immortality is possible for such beings?
11. Do you think that philosophical knowledge should have its source in sense experience? Explain.
12. Respond to Lonergan's arguments concerning the objectivity of human knowledge.

BIBLIOGRAPHY

Aquinas, Thomas. *The Pocket Aquinas: Selected from the Writings of St. Thomas.* Ed. V. J. Bourke. New York: Washington Square Press, 1960.

— — —. *Basic Writings of Saint Thomas Aquinas.* Ed. A. C. Pegis. 2 vols. New York: Random House, 1948.

— — —. *Opera Omnia.* 25 vols. Parma, 1862–1870. Reprint. New York: Masurgia Press, 1948–50.

St. Thomas Aquinas, 1274–1974: Commemorative Studies. Foreward by Etienne Gilson. Toronto: Pontifical Institute of Medieval Studies, 1974.

Adler, Mortimer J. *Problems for Thomists; The Problem of Species.* New York: Sheed and Ward, 1940.

Armstrong, Rose A. *Primary and Secondary Precepts in Thomistic Natural Law Teaching.* The Hague: Martinus Nijhoff, 1966.

Bourke, Vernon J. *Aquinas' Search for Wisdom*. Milwaukee: Bruce Publishing, 1965.

— — —. *St. Thomas and the Greek Moralists*. Milwaukee: Marquette University Press, 1947.

— — —. "Thomistic Bibliography, 1920–1940." *The Modern Schoolman*. supp. to vol. 21 (1945).

Chenu, M. D. *Towards Understanding Saint Thomas*. Trans. with authorized corrections and bibliographical additions by A. M. Landry and D. Hughes, Chicago: Henry Regnery, 1964.

Chesterton, G. K. *St. Thomas Aquinas (The Dumb Ox)*. Ed. A. C. Pegis. New York: Doubleday, Image Books, 1955.

Collins, James D. *The Thomistic Philosophy of the Angels*. Baltimore: Catholic University of America Press, 1947.

Copleston, F. C. *Aquinas*. London, Penguin Books, 1955.

Eschmann, I. T. "A Catalogue of St. Thomas's Works." In E. Gilson, *The Christian Philosophy of St. Thomas Aquinas*. New York: Random House, 1956.

Gilson, Etienne. *The Christian Philosophy of St. Thomas Aquinas*. Trans. L. Shook. New York: Random House, 1956.

— — —. *History of Christian Philosophy in the Middle Ages*. London and New York, 1955.

— — —. *Wisdom and Love in St. Thomas Aquinas*. Milwaukee: Marquette University Press, 1951.

Hartley, Thomas J. *Thomistic Revival and the Modernist Era*. Toronto: Institute of Christian Thought, University of Toronto, St. Michael's College, 1971.

Kainz, Howard P. *Active and Passive Potency in Thomistic Angelology*. The Hague: Martinus Nijhoff, 1972.

Klubertanz, George. *The Discursive Power: Sources and Doctrine of the Vis Cogitative According to St. Thomas Aquinas*. St. Louis: Modern Schoolman, 1952.

Lamb, Matthew L. *Creativity and Method: Essays in Honor of Bernard Lonergan. S.J.* Rev. ed. Milwaukee; Marquette University Press, 1982.

Lonergan, Bernard J. F., S. J. *The Subject*. Milwaukee: Marquette University Press, 1970.

— — —. *Collection: Papers by Bernard Lonergan, S. J.* Edited F. E. Crowe, S. J. New York: Herder and Herder, 1967.

— — —. *Insight: A Study of Human Understanding*. London: Longmans, Green, 1957.

McInerny, Ralph. *Ethica Thomistica: The Moral Philosophy of Thomas Aquinas*. Baltimore: Catholic University of America Press, 1982.

— — —. *Rhyme and Reason: St. Thomas and Modes of Discourse*. Milwaukee: Marquette University Press, 1981.

— — —. *St. Thomas Aquinas*. Boston: Twayne Publishers, 1977.

McMullin, Ernan. "Presidential Address: Who Are We? " *Proceedings of the American Catholic Philosophical Association* 61 (1967): pp. 1–6.

Maritain, Jacques. *The Degress of Knowledge*. Trans. G. B. Phelan. New York: Charles Scribner's, 1959.

— — —. *Saint Thomas and the Problem of Evil*. Milwaukee: Marquette University Press, 1942.

— — —. *St. Thomas Aquinas: Angel of the Schools*. Trans. J. F. Scanlan. London: Sheed and Ward, 1933.

Mauer, Armand A. *St. Thomas and Historicity*. Milwaukee: Marquette University Press, 1979.

— — —. *Medieval Philosophy*. New York: Random House, 1962.

O'Connor, Daniel John. *Aquinas and Natural Law.* London: Macmillan, 1967.

Owens, Joseph. *St. Thomas Aquinas on the Existence of God: Collected Papers of Joseph Owens.* Ed. John R. Cates. Albany: State University of New York Press, 1980.

Pegis, Anton C. *St. Thomas and the Problem of the Soul in the Thirteenth Century.* Toronto: Pontifical Institute of Medieval Studies, 1976.

– – –. *At the Origin of the Thomistic Notion of Man.* New York: Macmillan, 1963.

– – –. "Saint Thomas Aquinas and Philosophy." In *The McAuley Lectures.* West Hartford, Conn.: Saint Joseph College, 1960. Reprint. Milwaukee: Marquette University Press, 1964.

Sertillanges, A. D. *The Foundations of Thomistic Philosophy.* Trans. G. Anstruther. St. Louis: B. Herder, 1931.

Smith, Vincent E. *St. Thomas on the Object of Geometry.* Milwaukee: Marquette University Press, 1954.

Steenberghen, Fernand van. *Thomas Aquinas and Radical Aristotelianism.* Baltimore: Catholic University of America Press, 1980.

Stockhammer, Morris, ed. *Thomas Aquinas Dictionary.* New York: Philosophical Library, 1965.

Weisheipl, Joseph A. *Friar Thomas D'Aquino: His Life, Thought, and work.* Garden City, N.Y.: Doubleday, 1974.

Chapter 12

Process Philosophy

The label "process philosophy" has been given to those philosophies that emphasize change or becoming over permanence or being. They address a problem that has been central to metaphysics since the ancient Greeks. Parmenides, for example, held that there is only being and no becoming. Heraclitus asserted to the contrary that no one can step into the same river twice. (More radical and perhaps tongue-in-cheek versions of this saying have it that one cannot even step into the same river once, for there is no such thing as the same identical river.) For the most part, however, philosophers have denied neither elements of change nor of permanence, and their positions have emphasized one or the other or have differed as to what changed or was permanent. In modern times, Henri Bergson, the French philosopher (1859–1941), is considered a process philosopher. He held that all attempts to characterize reality were doomed to failure in so far as all language necessarily categorized reality in such a way as to miss the flux of things, the *élan vital,* the vital life force, the underlying becoming that was the true reality. In American philosophy, William James has sometimes been called a process philosopher, especially in his process-like assertions that the self is not a substance but merely a process of experience or experiencing. However, the best-known American process philosopher is Alfred North Whitehead. In this chapter we will briefly summarize the main ideas of his philosophy as well as those of Charles Hartshorne, an American philosopher who was heavily influenced by Whitehead.

ALFRED NORTH WHITEHEAD

It may seem strange to count as an American philosopher one who came to the United States at the age of sixty-three. Yet the philosopher in question, Alfred North Whitehead, is generally considered an American philosopher because most of his philosophy was developed and written in this country and his influence has been strongest here. According to some, "his is the only philosophical synthesis ever produced in this country that compares with Europe's greatest." [1]

Whitehead was born at Ramsgate, a village on the east coast of Kent, England on 15 February 1861. [2] For generations his family had been concerned with education, religion, and local administration. The young Whitehead often accompanied his clergyman-educator father on his daily visits to his parish schools; there Whitehead acquired an interest in education and religion that never seems to have left him. Another early influence was his acquaintance with the archeological remains and historical remembrances with which he was surrounded in that part of England. From these he possibly gained his immense respect for history and time, two key concepts in his philosophical system.

When he was fourteen he left home to attend school at Sherborne where he received a classical education in Latin and Greek, with some mathematics. At this time he also began to develop on his own an interest in poetry, especially the work of Wordsworth and Shelley, and his independent study and reading in this area and others continued throughout his lifetime. In 1880 he attended Trinity College of Cambridge University, the college of Isaac Newton. Whitehead's entire undergraduate period there consisted of lectures in mathematics. "I never went inside another lecture room," he said. [3] However, this was not his only education at Cambridge. He often met with friends who had various interests, to dine and discuss politics, religion, philosophy, and literature. Later he joined the rather famous discussion group, the "apostles," a group established by Tennyson in the 1820s. In 1885 Whitehead began a twenty-five-year period of teaching mathematics at Cambridge and then at London, where he became especially involved in the problem of how to educate people for life in a modern industrial world. Just prior to moving to London he met and married his wife, whose vivid life, he said, taught him so much about moral and aesthetic beauty that he came to view it as "the aim of existence." [4] In 1924 he accepted an invitation to join the philosophy faculty at Harvard University, where he taught until he retired in 1937. He died in an apartment near Harvard at the age of eighty-seven in 1948.

Why would someone without any formal training in philosophy and with seemingly no philosophical publications have been invited to teach philosophy at Harvard, especially when he was nearing retirement age? In 1898, twenty-six years earlier, Whitehead had published *A Treatise on Universal Algebra*. [5] The book is entirely mathematical, and yet it is like philosophy in its aim at generality. In this book Whitehead attempts to describe the common elements in various algebras and geometries. Philosophy also has as one of its aims, according to many including Whitehead, the detection of underlying unities among the diversities of appearances. In 1910 Whitehead published with Bertrand Russell their groundbreaking *Principia Mathematica*.[6] In this work mathematics was held to be less a science of quantity than a deduction from formal logic. This book has contributed greatly to the enlargement of the meaning of mathematics that has occurred in the last one hundred years.

Between 1919 and 1922, Whitehead turned his attention to the application of mathematics and to certain philosophical and mathematical concepts such as space, time, and motion. His reflections on these matters were published in three books: *An Enquiry Concerning the Principles of Natural Knowledge, The Concept of Nature,* and *The Principle of Relativity*.[7] While Whitehead was critical of many of the elements of classical physics, he also found the Einsteinian formulations wanting, especially in the narrow empirical base on which they seemed to rely. (However, Whitehead's own theory of relativity was not taken up by physicists, partially because of his refusal to take into consideration the means by which we measure spatio-temporal relations.) His particular views on space and time and what he called "the extensive continuum" will not be pursued here, but are suggested for those interested in this problem.

This work in physics in turn prepared the way for Whitehead's more philosophical reflections about science in his first work published in America, *Science and the Modern World* (1925).[8] In this work Whitehead criticized the mechanistic view of reality that he thought stemmed from a particle analysis of matter together with an impact-transmission theory of sensation. Newtonian physics pictured a lifeless nature composed of hard massy particles, atoms, that could be moved locally by other particles but that were otherwise "unmoved." The real world consisted of matter in motion, while qualities, values, and feelings were thought to be subjective. Whitehead suggested that this view of the world presented a "bifurcation of nature." Nature was split into two realms, one real but lacking in life and values and the other, which included the living and qualitative elements, strictly speaking unreal. This dichotomy also relied for its support on another fallacy, according to Whitehead, the "fallacy of misplaced concreteness." Experience is rich and many faceted, yet we may focus on certain aspects of it abstracted from the rest, as for example on the size of a box and not its color, contents, or purpose. This is quite valid. What is fallacious, however, is to take the part or abstraction for the whole or the concretely real. And this is what the particle analysis of matter implies, according to Whitehead.

On the other hand, if we take our experience as it is, we arrive at a quite different picture of reality. What we experience is a life full of enjoyment and a world filled with change and interest. Even classical physics had need of such a recognition, for motion and acceleration could not truly be accounted for by speaking of particles at durationless instants of time. Whitehead's own views on the nature of reality are presented more technically and fully in the work published in 1929, *Process and Reality*.[9] More easily readable are his *Adventures of Ideas, Symbolism,* and *Modes of Thought*.[10]

According to Whitehead, philosophy is "an endeavor to frame a coherent, logical, necessary system of general ideas in terms of which every element of our experience can be interpreted." [11] These general ideas are tentative generalizations that give us the character of things and their interrelations, whether of the actual world as it is or of any possible world. Whitehead calls his own scheme the "philosophy of organism" because it depicts nature as a complex of ongoing and interconnected events. The detailing of this scheme required a new set of categories or terms, terms such as "actual entity," "occasion," or "event" for the basic facts, "prehension" for the grasping of past data by a present "concrescing" or growing actual entity, and "eternal object" for the forms of definiteness that actual entities exemplify or the possibilities yet to be embodied. These categories together with some other principles are detailed in chapter 2 of *Process and Reality*.

If we take our experience as it is, and the data from immediate experience is to be trusted as revelatory of reality, we get a picture of reality that, as has been noted, is quite different from that of classical Newtonian atomism. We experience, when we do, something coming to us from without whose causality we feel through our body. "Causal efficacy" is real and we experience it as such. (Contrast this view with that of Hume who asserted that we only experience conjunction and succession in what we call causation.) How we take this world — as pleasant, to be avoided, changed, etc. — or whether or not we take this or that part of it into ourselves — is dependent on our own coloration of that experience and our own choice of what and how we will experience something. This "subjective form" of our own individual experience makes it like no other, gives it a certain unique affective tone. Moreover, the character of the experience is also given direction by an "aim" to be achieved by the experience. This aim is partially influenced by another type of "prehension," a conceptual prehension, which is an idea of something that is possible for realization. The experience builds, is enjoyed, lived, and then added to our ongoing experiences. Each experience is a novel integration, in fact a self-creation. Each has aesthetic characteristics and a value of its own. These qualities are not to be taken as subjective but as constituting the very concrete essence of every experience.[12]

Could reality itself be so composed? Whitehead's thought experiment indicates that it is. Such a view would not necessarily imply that stones or atoms are conscious, but only that they are causally influenced in their very nature by their environment, that they have a unique way of being so influenced, and that their basic being is a becoming, a process. Individual actual entities, events, or occasions are the real facts. They consist of processes of becoming, "concrescences," which arise thorough the impingement of those aspects of their past world that they "prehend" according to their own "subjective form" until they reach a peak of "satisfaction," an aesthetic unity. At this point they "perish" and become data for the next successive moment or pulse of experience in which they become, through their formal characteristics, objectively (rather than subjectively) immortal. Things as we know them consist of "nexus" or societies, strands or series of pulses of experience. Their identity through time is due not to an enduring, unchanging, underlying substance but to a similarity of form or pattern inherent in the series. Just as a person's identity would thus consist of the enduring characteristics, bodily and psychological, so also would that of any microscopic bit of reality. A rock, however, is an aggregate of many strands of existence. Which items of our experience are to be considered actual entities is not clearly specified by Whitehead.

One of the questions raised concerning this view of the becoming of actual entities is their apparent self-creation. It would seem as though they were creating themselves, pulling themselves up by their own bootstraps. It is true that actual entities do not exist first in some substantial way and then come to have experiences. They are created in the process of becoming, which is a process of experiencing. In Whitehead's solution to this problem, we are also introduced to his theological views about God and His nature and relation to the world. If these processes or actual entities were not strictly determined by the influence of the past, if novelty were actually to exist, and if there were not to be pure chance, then something else had to exist as the source of the direction that any process takes, what Whitehead calls its "subjective aim." According to Whitehead, the source of this aim is some "unconditional actuality of conceptual feeling at the base of things," which Whitehead calls "God" in His "primordial nature." In this nature God is an actual entity that provides and orders the possibilities from which actual entities may choose and suggests initially which possibilities shall be chosen. In this nature, God functions not as a creator but as a "lure" or final cause.[13]

However, another nature or function of God exists, according to Whitehead. Not only does God act on the world by providing an ordered realm of possibilities for actualization by actual entities, but the world acts upon God. God has a derivative nature that is due to His comprehension and objectification of the world in Himself. This Whitehead calls his "consequent nature." It corresponds to the religious urge that nothing worthwhile can be permanently lost, in fact, to the desire for immortality. However, Whitehead's God is neither self-sufficient nor omnipotent, and other actual entities are as real as He. While Whitehead's view of God is in significant ways different from traditional Western accounts, it has had a significant influence on contemporary religious or philosophico-religious interpretations.

One further concept in Whitehead's metaphysics bears some comment in this summary — the notion of "creativity." It is the underlying drive toward production of new syntheses. However, creativity does not exist in itself. All that exists are actual entities in the process of self-creation. Creativity is "that ultimate notion of the highest generality at the base of actuality."[14] One can interpret the notion as referring to the creativity common to all actual entities. Thus interpreted, however, it would seem to have no power to unify the world.

Whitehead's metaphysical views are also present in his theory of man and the nature of knowledge, as well as in his writings on art, religion, and education. For example further details about the modes of knowledge called "causal efficacy" and "presentational immediacy" are found in *Process and Reality* and elsewhere. On the one hand this philosophy can be thought of as a type of epistemological realism. There is a real world independent of the knower which is experienced. Our most certain knowledge, however, is a felt knowledge, somewhat similar, perhaps, to what Santayana had called "animal faith." We interpret our immediate experience and symbolize it in language which thus has a "symbolic" reference. Nevertheless, Whitehead's philosophy is also considered idealistic, for the basic items of reality are described as pulses of experience and possibly as psychic in some sense. Thus his philosophy has also been labeled "panpsychism." Education, he says, requires the learning of skills and reflection on the lessons of the past. But if these skills and appreciations are not used with imagination and for creative change, they they are dead and deadening. In cultural and political life as well, what is needed is not simply order and stability, but "order entering upon novelty; so that the massiveness of order does not degenerate into mere repetition." [15] The type of process that Whitehead envisioned as constituting the structure of the basic facts of nature, he also saw as the ideal for all human development.

CHARLES HARTSHORNE

Charles Hartshorne is perhaps the best-known process philosopher after Whitehead. He was born in Kittanning, Pennsylvania, 5 June 1897.[16] Charles's father was rector of the local Episcopalian church, though his family before had been Quakers. After early training at a school near home, he was sent to New York for seminary training. Then, after some time studying at Haverford College, World War I broke out and Hartshorne went to work as a hospital orderly in France. When he returned to school it was to Harvard, where he also received an M.A. and Ph.D. in philosophy. During his early school years he had read Arnold, Emerson, and Royce. At Harvard he studied under Hocking and Lewis and wrote a dissertation entitled "The Unity of Being." After travel and study in Europe, Hartshorne returned to Harvard in 1925 as an instructor, where he also began editing the Peirce papers. Later he was joined in this project by Paul Weiss, and the papers were published in eight volumes from 1931 to 1958. Hartshorne's first publication of his own views was *The Philosophy and Psychology of Sensation* (1934), followed by (among others) *Man's Vision of God and the Logic of Theism* (1941), *The Divine Relativity: A Social Conception of God* (1948), *Reality as Social Process: Studies in Metaphysics and Religion* (1953), *The Logic of Perfection* (1962), and *Creative Synthesis and Philosophic Method* (1970). One can surmise his philosophic interests from the titles of the publications listed here.

Hartshorne is a metaphysician with a special interest in philosophical issues relative to time, freedom, and God. Freedom and chance are real. We freely and creatively decide how and what of the world we will experience. We can experience the feelings of others, but this is only possible if there is an all-inclusive feeling, a God who is also in process of becoming with the world.

One of the best ways to understand the process philosophy of Hartshorne, is to compare it with Whitehead's philosophy.[17] As in Whitehead, God has two natures — an abstract essence (Whitehead's primordial nature of God) and concrete states (Whitehead's consequent nature). However, while for Whitehead God is a single actual entity, for Hartshorne God is like other persons in being a society of occasions. Many have wondered whether Whitehead's description of God was consistent with biblical descriptions; for example, they questioned the nature of the Whiteheadean God's knowledge of the world. If it is true that God knows the world as other actual entities do only after the living beings in it have perished, this view is at odds with God's relation to the world as depicted by traditional biblical interpretations. However, Hartshorne holds that it is only the limitations of finite knowers that prevent them from experiencing the subjective feelings of other actual entities. This might not be true of God. Nevertheless, Hartshorne also seems to believe that there is a sense in which one can validly speak of God and the world as well as the world in God. Hartshorne also construes God's abstract essence as including not only conceptual feelings but also perceptual and volitional ones. This notion seemed to him more consistent with the personal deity of the Bible.

Another point of difference between Hartshorne and Whitehead concerned the nature of "eternal objects." For Whitehead, these are fairly definite traits or characteristics that are eternal, as their name indicates. While Hartshorne believes that some very general traits of existence might be eternal as possibilities, the particular characteristics that get embodied in actualities are not as much like the Platonic ideas as Whitehead's objects were. Here Hartshorne is much more sympathetic to Peirce and thinks of this realm of possibilities as a continuum of indefinite potentialities. No color, for example is so definite that it doesn't shade into others. And possibly no two actual colors are the same. It is not just that God cannot know in advance which potentialities will be realized (though He can suggest some initially), but Hartshorne further insists that God cannot even know which potentialities are there for realization. Hartshorne suggests that Whitehead's eternal objects threaten the process nature of reality, for they seem to instantiate the eternal Platonic-like world of possibilities.

Another interesting topic in Hartshorne's writings is his reformulation of the traditional "ontological argument" for God's existence. In *The Logic of Perfection* and *Anselm's Discovery* Hartshorne attempted to show that his views concerning the nature of God and of possibility and necessity would require that a "perfect being" necessarily exist.

This view as well as others of Hartshorne and Whitehead continue to be debated among process philosophers, and in particular among process theologians. Did this view of God leave too much in process, a God with too little power in the world? How could any divine persuasion (or supply of initial aim) be possible if there were no definite eternal objects or possibilities from which to choose? Is God's existence compatible with free choice? Some examples of the literature in which this debate continues can be found in the bibliography at the end of this chapter.

Notes

[1] Fisch, *Classic American Philosophers,* p. 395.

[2] See "Autobiographical Notes," in *The Philosophy of Alfred North Whitehead,* ed. Paul A. Schilpp (LaSalle, Ill.: Open Court Publishing, 1941).

[3] Ibid., p. 12.

[4] Ibid., p. 8.

[5] Alfred North Whitehead, *A Treatise on Universal Algebra* (Cambridge: Cambridge University Press, 1898).

[6] Alfred North Whitehead and Bertrand Russell, *Principia Mathematica,* 3 vols. (Cambridge: Cambridge University Press, 1910–13).

[7] Alfred North Whitehead, *An Enquiry Concerning the Principles of Natural Knowledge* (Cambridge: Cambridge University Press, 1920); idem, *The Concept of Nature* (Cambridge: Cambridge University Press, 1920); idem, *The Principle of Relativity* (Cambridge: Cambridge University Press, 1922).

[8] Alfred North Whitehead, *Science and the Modern World* (New York: Macmillan, 1925).

[9] Alfred North Whitehead, *Process and Reality: An Essay in Cosmology* (New York: Macmillan, 1929).

[10] Alfred North Whitehead, *Adventures of Ideas* (New York: Macmillan, 1933); idem, *Symbolism: Its Meaning and Effect* (New York: Macmillan, 1927); idem, *Modes of Thought* (New York: Macmillan, 1938).

[11] Whitehead, *Process and Reality,* p. 4.

[12] Ibid., pp. 334–38, 358.

[13] Ibid., pp. 46–47.

[14] Ibid., p. 47.

[15] Ibid., p. 515.

[16] A summary of the life of Charles Hartshorne can be found in Eugene Peters, *Hartshorne and Neoclassical Metaphysics* (Lincoln: University of Nebraska Press, 1970), pp. 1–15.

[17] An excellent comparison between Whitehead and Hartshorne is found in *Two Process Philosophers: Hartshorne's Encounter with Whitehead,* ed. Lewis S. Ford AAR Studies in Religion, no. 5 (American Academy of Religion, 1973), in particular "Hartshorne's Differences from Whitehead" by David R. Griffin and "Whitehead's Differences from Hartshorne" by Lewis Ford.

ALFRED NORTH WHITEHEAD

NATURE LIFELESS*

Philosophy is the product of wonder. The effort after the general characterization of the world around us is the romance of human thought. The correct statement seems so easy, so obvious, and yet it is always eluding us. We inherit the traditional doctrine: we can detect the oversights, the superstitions, the rash generalizations of the past ages. We know so well what we mean and yet we remain so curiously uncertain about the formulation of any detail of our knowledge. This word *detail* lies at the heart of the whole difficulty. You cannot talk vaguely about "Nature" in general. We must fix upon details within nature and discuss their essences and their types of inter-connection. The world around is complex, composed of details. We have to settle upon the primary types of detail in terms of which we endeavour to express our understanding of nature. We have to analyse and to abstract, and to understand the natural status of our abstractions. At first sight there are sharp-cut classes within which we can sort the various types of things and characters of things which we find in nature. Every age manages to find modes of classification which seem fundamental starting points for the researches of the special sciences. Each succeeding age discovers that the primary classifications of its pre-

* Alfred North Whitehead, "Nature Lifeless," in *Modes of Thought* (New York: Macmillan, 1938; New York: Free Press, 1966), pp. 127–29, 138–40, 144–45. Reprinted with permission of Macmillan Publishing Company. Copyright 1938 by Macmillan Publishing Company, renewed 1966 by T. North Whitehead.

decessors will not work. In this way a doubt is thrown upon all formulations of laws of nature which assume these classifications as firm starting points. A problem arises. Philosophy is the search for the solution.

Our first step must be to define the term *nature* as here used. Nature, in these chapters, means the world as interpreted by reliance on clear and distinct sensory experiences, visual, auditory, and tactile. Obviously, such an interpretation is of the highest importance for human understanding. These final chapters are concerned with the question,—How far does it take us?

For example, we can conceive nature as composed of permanent things, namely bits of matter, moving about in space which otherwise is empty. This way of thinking about nature has an obvious consonance with commonsense observation. There are chairs, tables, bits of rock, oceans, animal bodies, vegetable bodies, planets, and suns. The enduring self-identity of a house, of a farm, of an animal body, is a presupposition of social intercourse. It is assumed in legal theory. It lies at the base of all literature. A bit of matter is thus conceived as a passive fact, an individual reality which is the same at an instant, or throughout a second, an hour, or a year. Such a material, individual reality supports its various qualifications such as shape, locomotion, colour, or smell, etc. The occurrences of nature consist in the changes in these qualifications, and more particularly in the changes of motion. The connection between such bits of matter consists purely of spatial relations. Thus the importance of motion arises from its change of the sole mode of interconnection of material things. Mankind then proceeds to discuss these spatial relations and discovers geometry. The geometrical character of space is conceived as the one way in which nature imposes determinate relations upon all bits of matter which are the sole occupants of space. In itself, space is conceived as unchanging from eternity to eternity, and as homogeneous from infinity to infinity. Thus we compose a straight-forward characterization of nature, which is consonant to common sense, and can be verified at each moment of our existence. We sit for hours in the same chair, in the same house, with the same animal body. The dimensions of the room are defined by its spatial relations. There are colours, sounds, scents, partly abiding and partly changing. Also the major facts of change are defined by locomotion of the animal bodies and of the inorganic furniture. . . . [However,] the modern point of view is expressed in terms of energy, activity, and the vibratory differentiations of space-time. Any local agitation shakes the whole universe. The distant effects are minute, but they are there. The concept of matter presupposed simple location. Each bit of matter was self-contained, localized in a region with a passive, static network of spatial relations, entwined in a uniform relational system from infinity to infinity and from eternity to eternity. But in the modern concept the group of agitations which we term matter is fused into its environment. There is no possibility of a detached, self-contained local existence. The environment enters into the nature of each thing. Some elements in the nature of a complete set of agitations may remain stable as those agitations are propelled through a changing environment. But such stability is only the case in a general, average way. This average fact is the reason why we find the same chair, the same rock, and the same planet, enduring for days, or for centuries, or for millions of years. In this average fact, then, time-factor takes the aspect of endurance, and change is a detail. The fundamental fact, according to the physics of the present day, is that the environment with its peculiarities seeps into the group-agitation which we term matter, and the group-agitations extend their character to the environment. In truth, the notion of the self-contained particle of matter, self-sufficient within its local habitation, is an abstraction. Now an abstraction is nothing else than the omission of part of the truth. The abstraction is well-founded when the conclusions drawn from it are not vitiated by the omitted truth.

This general deduction from the modern doctrine of physics vitiates many conclusions drawn from the applications of physics to other sciences, such as physiology, or even such as physics itself. For example, when geneticists conceive genes as the determinants of heredity. The analogy of the old concept of matter sometimes leads them to ignore the influence of the particular animal body in which they are functioning. They pre-suppose that a pellet of matter remains in all respects self-identical whatever be its changes of environment. So far as modern physics is concerned, any characteristics may, or may not, effect changes in the genes, changes which are as important in certain respects, though not in others. Thus no *a priori* argument as to the inheritance of characters can be drawn from the mere doctrine of genes. In fact recently physiologists have found that genes are modified in some respects by their environment. The presuppositions of the old common sense view survive, even when the view itself has been abandoned as a fundamental description.

This survival of fragments of older doctrines is also exemplified in the modern use of the term *space-time.* The notion of space with its geometry is strictly coördinated to the notion of material bodies with simple location in space. A bit of matter is then conceived as self-sufficient with the simple location of the region which it occupies. It is just there, in that region where it is; and it can be described without reference to the goings on in any other region of space. . . .

The new view is entirely different. The fundamental concepts are activity and process. Nature is divisible and thus extensive. But any division, including some activities and excluding others, also severs the patterns of process which extend beyond all boundaries. The mathematical formulae indicate a logical completeness about such patterns, a complete-ness which boundaries destroy. For example, half a wave tells only half the story. The notion of self-sufficient isolation is not exemplified in modern physics. There are no essentially self-contained activities within limited regions. These passive geometrical relationships between substrata passively occupying regions have passed out of the picture. Nature is a theatre for the interrelations of activities. All things change, the activities and their interrelations. To this new concept, the notion of space with its passive, systematic, geometric relationship is entirely inappropriate. The fashionable notion that the new physics has reduced all physical laws to the statement of geometrical relations is quite ridiculous. It has done the opposite. In the place of the Aristotelian notion of the procession of forms, it has substituted the notion of the forms of process. It has thus swept away space and matter, and has substituted the study of the internal relations within a complex state of activity.

Finally, we are left with a fundamental question as yet undiscussed. What are those primary types of things in terms of which the process of the universe is to be understood? Suppose we agree that nature discloses to the scientific scrutiny merely activities and process. What does this mean? These activities fade into each other. They arise and then pass away. What is being enacted? What is effected? It cannot be that these are merely the formulae of the multiplication table—in the words of a great philosopher, merely a bloodless dance of categories. Nature is full-blooded. Real facts are happening. Physical nature, as studied in science, is to be looked upon as a complex of the more stable interrelations between the real facts of the real universe.

This lecture has been confined to nature under an abstraction in which all reference to life was suppressed. The effect of this abstraction has been that dynamics, physics, and chemistry were the sciences which guided our gradual transition from the full common-sense notions of the sixteenth century to the concept of nature suggested by the speculative physics of the present day.

This change of view, occupying four centuries, may be characterized as the transition from space and matter, as the fundamental notions to process conceived, as a complex of activity with internal relations between its various factors.

NATURE ALIVE*

The doctrine that I am maintaining is that neither physical nature nor life can be understood unless we fuse them together as essential factors in the composition of "really real" things whose interconnections and individual characters constitute the universe.

The first step in the argument must be to form some concept of what life can mean. Also we require that the deficiencies in our concept of

---

* Ibid., "Nature Alive," pp. 150–52.

physical nature should be supplied by its fusion with life. And we require that, on the other hand, the notion of life should involve the notion of physical nature.

Now as a first approximation the notion of life implies a certain absoluteness of self-enjoyment. This must mean a certain immediate individuality, which is a complex process of appropriating into a unity of existence the many data presented as relevant by the physical processes of nature. Life implies the absolute, individual self-enjoyment arising out of this process of appropriation. I have, in my recent writings, used the word *prehension* to express this process of appropriation. Also I have termed each individual act of immediate self-enjoyment an *occasion of experience*. I hold that these unities of existence, these occasions of experience, are the really real things which in their collective unity compose the evolving universe, ever plunging into the creative advance.

But these are forward references to the issue of the argument. As a first approximation we have conceived life as implying absolute, individual self-enjoyment of a process of appropriation. The data appropriated are provided by the antecedent functioning of the universe. Thus the occasion of experience is absolute in respect to its immediate self-enjoyment. How it deals with its data is to be understood without reference to any other concurrent occasions. Thus the occasion, in reference to its internal process, requires no contemporary process in order to exist. In fact this mutual independence in the internal process of self-adjustment is the definition of contemporaneousness.

This concept of self-enjoyment does not exhaust that aspect of process here termed *life*. Process for its intelligibility involves the notion of a creative activity belonging to the very essence of each occasion. It is the process of eliciting into actual being factors in the universe which antecedently to that process exist only in the mode of unrealized potentialities. The process of self-creation is the transformation of the potential into the actual, and the fact of such transformation includes the immediacy of self-enjoyment.

Thus in conceiving the function of life in an occasion of experience, we must discriminate the actualized data presented by the antecedent world, the non-actualized potentialities which lie ready to promote their fusion into a new unity of experience, and the immediacy of self-enjoyment which belongs to the creative fusion of those data with those potentialities. This is the doctrine of the creative advance whereby it belongs to the essence of the universe, that it passes into a future. It is nonsense to conceive of nature as a static fact, even for an instant devoid of duration. There is no nature apart from transition, and there is no transition apart from temporal duration. This is the reason why the notion of an instant of time, conceived as a primary simple fact, is nonsense.

But even yet we have not exhausted the notion of creation which is essential to the understanding of nature. We must add yet another character to our description of life. This missing characteristic is "aim." By this term *aim* is meant the exclusion of the boundless wealth of alternative potentiality, and the inclusion of that definite factor of novelty which constitutes the selected way of entertaining those data in that process of unification. The aim is at that complex of feeling which is the enjoyment of those data in what way. "That way of enjoyment" is selected from the boundless wealth of alternatives. It has been aimed at for actualization in that process.

Thus the characteristics of life are absolute self-enjoyment, creative activity, aim. Here aim evidently involves the entertainment of the purely ideal so as to be directive of the creative process. Also the enjoyment belongs to the process and is not a characteristic of any static result. The aim is at the enjoyment belonging to the process.

GOD*

We conceive actuality as in essential relation to an unfathomable possibility. Eternal objects inform actual occasions with hierarchic patterns, included and excluded in every variety of discrimination. Another view of the same truth is that every actual occasion is a limitation imposed on possibility, and that by virtue of this limitation the particular value of that shaped togetherness of things emerges. In this way we express how a single occasion is to be viewed in terms of possibility, and how possibility is to be viewed in terms of a single actual occasion. But there are no single occasions, in the sense of isolated occasions. Actuality is through and through togetherness—togetherness of otherwise isolated eternal objects, and togetherness of all actual occasions. It is my task in this chapter to describe the unity of actual occasions. The previous chapter centered its interest in the abstract: the present chapter deals with the concrete, *i.e.,* that which has grown together.

Consider an occasion *a:*—we have to enumerate how other actual occasions are in *a,* in the sense that their relationships with *a* are constitutive of the essence of *a.* What *a* is in itself, is that it is a unit of realised experience; accordingly we ask how other occasions are in the experience which is *a.* Also for the present I am excluding cognitive experience. The complete answer to this question is, that the relationships among actual occasions are as unfathomable in their variety of type as are those among eternal objects in the realm of abstraction. But there are fundamental types of such relationships in terms of which the whole complex variety can find its description.

---

* Alfred North Whitehead, "God," in *Science and the Modern World* (New York: Macmillan, 1925; New York: Free Press, 1967), pp. 174–79. Reprinted with permission of Macmillan Publishing Company from the 1967 Free Press edition.

A preliminary for the understanding of these types of entry (of one occasion into the essence of another) is to note that they are involved in the modes of realisation of abstractive hierarchies, discussed in the previous chapter. The spatio-temporal relationships, involved in those hierarchies as realised in *a*, have all a definition in terms of *a* and of the occasions entrant in *a*. Thus the entrant occasions lend their aspects to the hierarchies, and thereby convert spatio-temporal modalities into categorical determinations; and the hierarchies lend their forms to the occasions and thereby limit the entrant occasions to being entrant only under those forms. Thus in the same way (as seen in the previous chapter) that every occasion is a synthesis of all eternal objects under the limitation of gradations of actuality, so every occasion is a synthesis of all occasions under the limitation of gradations of types of entry. Each occasion synthesises the totality of content under its own limitations of mode.

In respect to these types of internal relationship between *a* and other occasions, these other occasions (as constitutive of *a*) can be classified in many alternative ways. These are all concerned with different definitions of past, present, and future. It has been usual in philosophy to assume that these various definitions must necessarily be equivalent. The present state of opinion in physical science conclusively shows that this assumption is without metaphysical justification, even although any such discrimination may be found to be unnecessary for physical science. This question has already been dealt with in the chapter on Relativity. But the physical theory of relativity touches only the fringe of the various theories which are metaphysically tenable. It is important for my argument to insist upon the unbounded freedom within which the actual is a unique categorical determination.

Every actual occasion exhibits itself as a process: it is a becomingness. In so disclosing itself, it places itself as one among a multiplicity of other occasions, without which it could not be itself. It also defines itself as a particular individual achievement, focussing in its limited way an unbounded realm of eternal objects.

Any one occasion *a* issues from other occasions which collectively form its *past*. It displays for itself other occasions which collectively form its *present*. It is in respect to its associated hierarchy, as displayed in this immediate present, that an occasion finds its own originality. It is that display which is its own contribution to the output of actuality. It may be conditioned, and even completely determined by the past from which it issues. But its display in the present under those conditions is what directly emerges from its prehensive activity. The occasion *a* also holds within itself an indetermination in the form of a future, which has partial determination by reason of its inclusion in *a* and also has determinate spatio-temporal relatedness to *a* and to actual occasions of the past from *a* and of the present for *a*.

This future is a synthesis in *a* of eternal objects as not-being and as requiring the passage from *a* to other individualisations (with determinate spatio-temporal relations to *a*) in which not-being becomes being.

There is also in *a* what, in the previous chapter, I have termed the 'abrupt' realisation of finite eternal objects. This abrupt realisation requires *either* a reference of the basic objects of the finite hierarchy to determinate occasions other than *a* (as their situations, in past, present, future); *or* requires a realisation of these eternal objects in determinate relationships, but under the aspect of exemption from inclusion in the spatio-temporal scheme of relatedness between actual occasions. This abrupt synthesis of eternal objects in each occasion is the inclusion in actuality of the analytical character of the realm of eternality. This inclusion has those limited gradations of actuality which characterise every occasion by reason of its essential limitation. It is this realised extension of eternal relatedness beyond the mutual relatedness of the actual occasions, which prehends into each occasion the full sweep of eternal relatedness. I term this abrupt realisation the 'graded envisagement' which each occasion prehends into its synthesis. This graded envisagement is how the actual includes what (in one sense) is not-being as a positive factor in its own achievement. It is the source of error, of truth, of art, of ethics, and of religion. By it, fact is confronted with alternatives.

This general concept, of an event as a process whose outcome is a unit of experience, points to the analysis of an event into (i) substantial activity, (ii) conditioned potentialities which are there for synthesis, and (iii) the achieved outcome of the synthesis. The unity of all actual occasions forbids the analysis of substantial activities into independent entities. Each individual activity is nothing but the mode in which the general activity is individualised by the imposed conditions. The envisagement which enters into the synthesis is also a character which conditions the synthesising activity. The general activity is not an entity in the sense in which occasions or eternal objects are entities. It is a general metaphysical character which underlies all occasions, in a particular mode for each occasion. There is nothing with which to compare it: it is Spinoza's one infinite substance. Its attributes are its character of individualisation into a multiplicity of modes, and the realm of eternal objects which are variously synthesised in these modes. Thus eternal possibility and modal differentiation into individual multiplicity are the attributes of the one substance. In fact each general element of the metaphysical situation is an attribute of the substantial activity.

Yet another element in the metaphysical situation is disclosed by the consideration that the general attribute of modality is limited. This element must rank as an attribute of the substantial activity. In its nature each mode is limited, so as not to be other modes. But, beyond these limitations of particulars, the general modal individualisation is limited in two ways: In the first place it is an actual course of events, which might be otherwise so far as concerns eternal possibility, but *is* that course. This limitation takes three forms, (i) the special logical relations which all events must conform to, (ii) the selection of relationships to which the events do conform, and (iii) the particularity which infects the course even within those general relationships of logic and causation. Thus this first limitation is a limitation of antecedent selection. So far as the general metaphysical situation is concerned, there might have been an indiscriminate modal pluralism apart from logical or other limitation. But there could not then have been these modes, for each mode represents a synthesis of actualities which are limited to conform to a standard. We here come to the second way of limitation. Restriction is the price of value. There cannot be value without antecedent standards of value, to discriminate the acceptance or rejection of what is before the envisaging mode of activity. Thus there is an antecedent limitation among values, introducing contraries, grades, and oppositions.

According to this argument the fact that there is a process of actual occasions, and the fact that the occasions are the emergence of values which require such limitation, both require that the course of events should have developed amid an antecedent limitation composed of conditions, particularisation, and standards of value.

Thus as a further element in the metaphysical situation, there is required a principle of limitation. Some particular *how* is necessary, and some particularisation in the *what* of matter of fact is necessary. The only alternative to this admission, is to deny the reality of actual occasions. Their apparent irrational limitation must be taken as a proof of illusion and we must look for reality behind the scene. If we reject this alternative behind the scene, we must provide a ground for limitation which stands among the attributes of the substantial activity. This attribute provides the limitation for which no reason can be given: for all reason flows from it. God is the ultimate limitation, and His existence is the ultimate irrationality. For no reason can be given for just that limitation which it stands in His nature to impose. God is not concrete, but He is the ground for concrete actuality. No reason can be given for the nature of God, because that nature is the ground of rationality.

In this argument the point to notice is, that what is metaphysically indeterminate has nevertheless to be categorically determinate. We have come to the limit of rationality. For there is a categorical limitation which does not spring from any metaphysical reason. There is a metaphysical need for a principle of determination, but there can be no metaphysical reason for what is determined. If there were such a reason, there would be no need for any further principle: for metaphysics would already have provided the determination. The general principle of empiricism depends upon the doctrine that there is a principle of concretion which is not discoverable by abstract reason. What further can be known about God must be sought in the region of particular experiences, and therefore rests on an empirical basis. In respect to the interpretation of these experiences, mankind have differed profoundly. He has been named respectively, Jehovah, Allah, Brahma, Father in Heaven, Order of Heaven, First Cause, Supreme Being, Chance. Each name corresponds to a system of thought derived from the experiences of those who have used it.

Among medieval and modern philosophers, anxious to establish the religious significance of God, an unfortunate habit has prevailed of paying to Him metaphysical compliments. He has been conceived as the foundation of the metaphysical situation with its ultimate activity. If this conception be adhered to, there can be no alternative except to discern in Him the origin of all evil as well as of all good. He is then the supreme author of the play, and to Him must therefore be ascribed its shortcomings as well as its success. If He be conceived as the supreme ground for limitation, it stands in His very nature to divide the Good from the Evil, and to establish Reason 'within her dominions supreme.'

REMARKS: ANALYSIS OF MEANING*

Your choice of my philosophic outlook as a topic for discussion is an honor for which I am deeply grateful. Your action is characteristic of the generous warmth of your countrymen. A group of American philosophers provides the best instrument for that sincere, critical discussion which is one essential feature in philosophic advance.

Philosophy in its advance must involve obscurity of expression, and novel phrases. The permanent, essential factors governing the nature of things lie in the dim background of our conscious experience—whether it be perceptual or conceptual experience. The variable factors first catch our attention, and we survive by reason of our fortunate adjustment of them. Language has been evolved to express 'clearly and distinctly' the accidental aspect of accidental factors. But no factor is wholly accidental. Everything which in any sense is something thereby expresses its dependence on those ultimate principles whereby there are a variety of existences and of types of existences in the connected universe.

Thus the task of philosophy is to penetrate beyond the more obvious accidents to those principles of existence which are presupposed in dim consciousness, as involved in the total meaning of seeming clarity. Philosophy asks the simple question, What is it all about?

In human experience, the philosophic question can receive no final answer. Human knowledge is a process of approximation. In the focus of experience there is comparative clarity. But the discrimination of this

---

* Alfred North Whitehead, "Remarks: Analysis of Meaning," *The Philosophical Review* 46, no. 2 (March 1937): pp. 178–86. Reprinted with the permission of the editors of *The Philosophical Review*.

clarity leads into the penumbral background. There are always questions left over. The problem is to discriminate exactly, what we know vaguely.

The endeavor to make our utmost approximation to analysis of meaning is human philosophy. For a being with complete knowledge, philosophy would take another aspect. He might say, 'Knowing everything, I will fix attention on this detail'. He will then enjoy the detail in its relation to the discriminated totality.

We enjoy the detail as a weapon for the further discrimination of the penumbral totality. In our experience there is always the dim background from which we derive and to which we return. We are not enjoying a limited dolls' house of clear and distinct things, secluded from all ambiguity. In the darkness beyond there ever looms the vague mass which is the universe begetting us.

The besetting sin of philosophers is that, being merely men, they endeavor to survey the universe from the standpoint of gods. There is a pretense at adequate clarity of fundamental ideas. We can never disengage our measure of clarity from a pragmatic sufficiency within occasions of ill-defined limitations. Clarity always means 'clear enough'.

With this preamble, we now turn to the papers read this afternoon. It is out of place to discuss them in detail at the close of this session. They will remain in my mind as a landmark for future thought. Also, where they indicate difficulties, I am in general agreement as to the need of clarification or revision in my written works. Of course you will not expect an adequate exposition of philosophy in thirty minutes.

John Dewey* asks me to decide between the 'genetic-functional' interpretation of first principles and the 'mathematical-formal' interpretation. There is no one from whom one more dislikes to differ, than from Dewey. William James and John Dewey will stand out as having infused philosophy with new life, and with a new relevance to the modern world. But I must decline to make this decision. They beauty of philosophy is its many facets. Our present problem is the fusion of the two interpretations. The historic process of the world, which requires the genetic-functional interpretation, also requires for its understanding some insight into those ultimate principles of existence which express the necessary connections within the flux.

For example, there are meaningful relations between these ten fingers, and the billions of stars, and the innumerable billions of atoms. The interrelations of the specific multiplicities of groups of individual things constitute the clearest example of metaphysical necessity issuing in meaningful relations amid the accidents of history. No explosion of any star can generate the multiplication-table by any genetic-functioning. But such functioning does exemplify interrelations of number. It is necessary that

---

* This paper was partly in response to another by John Dewey presented at this same meeting—ED.

the meaning of the explosion is partly expressed by arithmetic. This necessity underlies the accidents of the explosion.

By a queer chance in this epoch of the universe arithmetical patterns constitute some of the clearest insights of human intelligence. There are limits to this clarity. But such as it is, we teach it to infants. Metaphysical knowledge enters while we still remember the rocking cradle. The notion of 'many things' carries with it the necessity that there be numbers. And yet there is no necessity that any special relationship of numbers be in any one instance exemplified. In this way we can observe the curious interweaving of accident and necessity.

The notion of 'many things' is a slippery one. There are these ten fingers and there are the ten commandments. In what sense do these fingers and the ten commandments together constitute twenty things? We are here brought up against the difficulty of the subtle change of meaning in familiar notions according to the context in which they occur.

The vagueness of our insight prevents our exact understanding of the metaphysical basis of particular exemplification. For this reason our metaphysical notions are an approximation. They represent such disengagement of necessity from accident as we are able to attain. One illustration of this approximate character of metaphysical knowledge is that such knowledge is always haunted by alternatives which we reject. Now necessity permits no alternatives. A century ago, arithmetic as then understood seemed to exclude alternatives. Today, the enunciation of ultimate arithmetic principles is beset with perplexities, and is the favorite occupation of opposing groups of dogmatists. We have not yet arrived at that understanding of arithmetical principles which exhibits them as devoid of alternatives.

Plato's ultimate forms, which are for him the basis of all reality, can be construed as referring to the metaphysical necessity which underlies historic accident. In the case of his immediate successors, the superior lucidity of arithmetic insight triumphed. The result was that the Academy after his death tended to identify the forms with arithmetic notions. Indeed the Academy and subsequent European philosophers went further. They saw in Euclidean Geometry another example of necessity. We now know that they were wrong. The continual breakdown of pretensions to the achievement of final metaphysical truth is pathetic. But, on the other side, the persistent presupposition of final principles cannot be neglected by any philosopher who counts himself as a 'radical empiricist'. For example, to take John Dewey's language in his paper which is spread before me, the compound word 'genetic-functional' means an ultimate metaphysical principle from which there is no escape. I am here in complete agreement with Dewey. The idea is vague, and adumbrates something beyond exact definition. This vagueness arises because Plato and Dewey are men with the limitations of human insight.

This notion of human limitations requires guarding. There is an implicit philosophic tradition that there are set limitations for human experience, to be discovered in a blue-print preserved in some Institute of Technology. In the long ancestry of humans, from oysters to apes, and from apes to modern man, we can discern no trace of such set limitation. Nor can I discern any reason, apart from dogmatic assumption, why any factor in the universe should not be manifest in some flash of human consciousness. If the experience be unusual, verbalization may be for us impossible. We are then deprived of our chief instrument of recall, comparison, and communication. Nevertheless, we have no ground to limit our capacity for experience by our existing technology of expression.

Thus to say that human experience is limited is not to assert a standard limitation for all occasions of all humans. There are usual limitations depending on that dominant social order of our epoch, which we term the Laws of Nature and the habits of humanity.

This vagueness is not due to a morbid craving for metaphysics. It haunts our most familiar experiences. Consider the following set of notions:—The weight of that man: The height of that man: The intelligence of that man: The kindness of that man: The happiness of that man: The identity of that man with his previous self yesterday.

In the first place, the exact meaning of 'that man'—body and soul— would puzzle the wisest to express. Yet each phrase is sufficiently clear for inexact common sense. Secondly, the small inconspicuous words in various phrases seem to alter their meaning from phrase to phrase. In the above examples, consider the little word 'of'. There is nothing about it alarmingly metaphysical. My small dictionary gives as its first meaning "Associated or connected with". I suggest to you that 'weight', and 'height', and 'intelligence', and 'kindness', and 'happiness', and 'self-identity with a previous existence', are each of them 'associated or connected with' a man in its own peculiar way. Thus in each phrase the word 'of' has changed its meaning from its use in the other phrases. Yet, after all, there is a fundamental identity underlying all these changes; and the pompous phrase 'associated or connected with' is the best that the dictionary can do in the way of reminding us of that fact.

This conclusion has an important bearing on Logic. Consider the phrase 'S is P'. This proposition is a way of drawing your attention to 'the P-ness of S', either for the sake of belief, or for some other purpose. If we neglect the irrelevant psychological accompaniments in the production of this phrase, we see that the word 'is' in 'S is P' reproduces the meaning of the word 'of' in 'the P-ness of S'. Thus the meaning of 'is' varies with changes in S or in P.

But an argument consists in a preliminary grouping of propositions, together with a deduction of other propositions. Thus in addition to the criticism of the original propositions as to truth or falsehood, we require a criticism as to whether the undoubted changes of meaning, in the same word appearing in different propositions, are relevant to the argument. Also as new propositions are deduced the same criticism is required. Thus the simple-minded notion of logical premisses vanishes. The little words 'is', 'and', 'or', 'together', are traps of ambiguity.

Of course gross common sense can usually settle the matter. But experience has shown that as soon as you leave the beaten track of vague clarity, and trust to exactness, you will meet difficulties. I remember when Bertrand Russell discovered his well-known paradox. He sent it by letter to Frege who was then alive. Frege's answering letter began with the sentence, 'Alas, arithmetic totters'.

One source of vagueness is deficiency of language. We can see the variations of meaning; although we cannot verbalize them in any decisive, handy manner. Thus we cannot weave into a train of thought what we can apprehend in flashes. We are left with the deceptive identity of the repeated word. Philosophy is largely the effort to lift such insights into verbal expression. For this reason, conventional English is the twin sister to barren thought. Plato had recourse to myth.

The method of algebra embodies the greatest discovery for the partial remedy of defective language. The procedure of the method is to select a few notions of the simplest interconnections of things; such connections for example as are expressed by the words 'is', 'of', 'and', 'or', 'plus', 'minus', 'more than', 'less than', 'equivalent to', and so on indefinitely. A small group of such terms is selected, on the principle that expressions containing them are again capable of interconnection by these same notions.

The fundamental assumption is that these basic connectives retain an invariable meaning throughout the algebraic development of patterns, and of patterns of patterns. The legitimacy of this assumption is guarded by the device of the 'real variable', as it is termed. Symbols, such as the single letters, p, q, r, x, y, z, u, v, w, are used under the assumption that each symbol indicates one and the same individual thing in its repetitions throughout the complex pattern. Also it is assumed that the things represented yield meaningful patterns as thus connected. Also it is assumed that the inevitable variation of meaning infused into these basic symbols of interconnection by the diversity of the variables, is not such as to affect that meaning which the pattern contains for the observers in question.

There are thus four fundamental assumptions, namely: (1) The invariableness of the basic terms of interconnection (the connectives), (2) The invariableness of the unspecified entities indicated by the symbols for 'real variables', (3) The meanfulness of the patterns of real variables, thus connected, (4) The irrelevance to the argument of the completion of meaning infused into the basic connectives by the unspecified real variables thus connected. Namely, the meaning as in assumption (1) is not in fact invariable, but the variation is irrelevant.

These principles of algebraic symbolism express the concurrence of mathematical formal principles with accidental factors. This concurrence is inevitable for the production of meaningful composition. And apart from composition there is no meaning, that is to say, there is nothing. The clarity is deceptive, as the clash of the first and fourth assumptions shows. Finally we are forced back to the pragmatic justification—It works. And yet it 'totters', unless care be taken.

The basic connectives are the relevant mathematical-formal principles. The real variables are the unspecified accidental factors. But the connection of the accidents is not a mere mathematical-formal principle. It is the concrete accidental fact of those accidents as thus connected. This suffusion of the connective by the things connected is the most general expression of the genetic-functional character of the universe. It also explains the vagueness which shrouds our metaphysical insight. We are unable to complete the approximation of disengaging the principles from the accidents of their exemplifications.

Necessity requires accident and accident requires necessity. Thus the algebraic method is our best approach to the expression of necessity, by reason of its reduction of accident to the ghostlike character of the real variable.

It follows from this explanation of the algebraic method, that our mathematics and our symbolic logic, as hitherto developed, represent only a minute fragment of its possibilities. In making this statement I shelter myself behind a quotation (*Sophist* 253 CD):

Stranger. Now since we have agreed that the classes or genera also commingle with one another, or do not commingle, in the same way, must not he possess some science and proceed by the processes of reason [he] who is to show correctly which of the classes harmonize with which, and which reject one another, and also if he is to show whether there are *some elements extending through all and holding them together so that they can mingle, and again, when they separate, whether there are other universal causes of separation.*

Theaetetus. Certainly he needs science, and perhaps the greatest of sciences.

Also to Plato we can add the authority of Leibniz. And now having invoked such support, I can cease the defence of the attempt to bring together the genetic-functional and the mathematical-formal methods in one philosophic outlook.

Philosophic thought has to start from some limited section of our experience—from epistemology, or from natural science, or from theology, or from mathematics. Also the investigation always retains the taint of its starting point. Every starting point has its merits, and its selection must depend upon the individual philosopher.

My own belief is that at present the most fruitful, because the most neglected, starting point is that section of value-theory which we term aesthetics. Our enjoyment of the values of human art, or of natural beauty, our horror at the obvious vulgarities and defacements which force themselves upon us—all these modes of experience are sufficiently abstracted to be relatively obvious. And yet evidently they disclose the very meaning of things.

Habits of thought and sociological habits survive because in some broad sense they promote aesthetic enjoyment. There is an ultimate satisfaction to be derived from them. Thus when the pragmatist asks whether 'it works', he is asking whether it issues in aesthetic satisfaction. The judge of the Supreme Court is giving his decision on the basis of the aesthetic satisfaction of the harmonization of the American Constitution with the activities of modern America.

Now there are two sides to aesthetic experience. In the first place, it involves a subjective sense of individuality. It is *my* enjoyment. I may forget myself; but all the same the enjoyment is mine, the pleasure is mine, and the pain is mine. Aesthetic enjoyment demands an individualized universe.

In the second place, there is the aesthetic object which is identified in experience as the source of subjective feeling. In so far as such abstraction can be made, so that there is a definite object correlated to a definite subjective reaction, there is a singular exclusive unity in this aesthetic object. There is a peculiar unity in a good pattern.

Consider a good picture. It expresses a unity of mutual relevance. It resents the suggestion of addition. No extra patch of scarlet can be placed in it without wrecking its unity.

The point is that the subjective unity of feeling and the objective unity of mutual relevance express respectively a relation of exclusion to the world beyond. There is a completion which rejects alternatives. Mere omission is characteristic of confusion. Rejection belongs to intelligible pattern.

This doctrine extends, or distorts, the meaning of another saying of Plato, when he says that not-being is a form of being. Here I am saying that rejection is a form of prehension. But I fully agree with Dr. Ushenko that this doctrine requires examination, and probably should be recast. However, I adhere to the position that it is an approximation to an important truth.

We must end with my first love—Symbolic Logic. When in the distant future the subject has expanded, so as to examine patterns depending on connections other than those of space, number, and quantity—when this expansion has occurred, I suggest that Symbolic Logic, that is to say, the symbolic examination of pattern with the use of real variables, will become the foundation of aesthetics. From that stage it will proceed to conquer ethics and theology. The circle will then have made its full turn, and we shall be back to the logical attitude of the epoch of St. Thomas Aquinas.

It was from St. Thomas that the seventeenth century revolted by the production of its mathematical method, which is the re-birth of logic.

The result of our human outlook is the interweaving of apparent order with apparent accident. The order appears as necessity suffused with accident, the accident appears as accident suffused with necessity. The necessity is, in a sense, static; but it is the static form of functional process. The process is what it is by reason of its form, and the form exists as the essence of process.

To hold necessity apart from accident, and to hold form apart from process, is an ideal of the understanding. The approximation to this ideal is the romantic history of the development of human intelligence.

My relation to Hegel's philosophy has, I hope, been made plain by this paper. He is a great thinker who claims respect. My criticism of his procedure is that when in his discussion he arrives at a contradiction, he construes it as a crisis in the universe. I am not so hopeful of our status in the nature of things. Hegel's philosophic attitude is that of a god. But I must leave Hegel to those who have studied him at first hand.

CHARLES HARTSHORNE

A PHILOSOPHY OF
SHARED CREATIVE EXPERIENCE*

Various ideas have been taken by philosophers as fundamental. Substance, matter, form, being, are examples. Prior to the twentieth century, scarcely any philosopher (at least in the West) saw in the idea of creativity a fundamental principle, a category applicable to all reality. True, theologians had talked much about the divine 'creation' of the world, and also about human artistic creation. But they generally supposed that there were simply uncreative sub-human creatures. Also divine creation was generally thought to be entirely different from ours, since it is creation out of nothing, and ours, out of something already there. Finally if creativity is a first principle, not only must every being be capable of creating, but every being must actually create. However, God was said by most theologians to have faced the option of creating or not creating. Suppose he had not created: then creativity would have had no illustration whatever; there would have been no such thing. This shows that creativity was not, in such doctrines, treated as an ultimate principle. At most its possibility was so treated. Yet it is arguable that possibility presupposes creativity as already, though inexhaustively, exercised.

* Charles Hartshorne, "A Philosophy of Shared Creative Experience," in *Creative Synthesis and Philosophic Method* (LaSalle, Ill.: Open Court Publishing, 1970), pp. 1–13. Reprinted by permission of The Open Court Publishing Company, LaSalle, Illinois.

In our century there have been philosophers who take creativity as ultimate, for instance Bergson, Berdyaev, and Whitehead, most explicitly the last. They think that there is a sense in which every individual creates and could not fail to do so while existing at all. *To be is to create.* According to this view, when we praise certain individuals as 'creative', we can properly mean only that what they create is important or extensive, while what others create is trivial or slight. But what they create cannot be zero, so long as the individuals exist.

Why would anyone hold such a view? And what is it to create? Let us consult experience.

In every moment each of us accomplishes a remarkable creative act. What do we create? Our own experience at that moment. But, you may say, this experience is not of our own making, since it is produced in us by various causes. But, please note, they are many causes, not one. This is enough to show that the causes alone cannot fully determine the result. For the experience is one, not many. What causal law could prescribe in advance just how the many factors are to fuse together into a new single entity, an experience? There is no psychology textbook which seriously attempts such a thing, or sensibly could attempt it. By no logic can many entities, through law, exhaustively define a single new entity which is to result from them all.

A person experiences, at a given moment, many things at once, objects perceived, past experiences remembered. That he perceives certain objects and remembers certain things, we can more or less explain; the objects are there, the experiences are recent and connected by associations with the objects, and so on. But an experience is not fully described in its total unitary quality merely by specifying what it perceives and remembers. There is the question of how, with just what accent, in just what perspective of relative vividness and emotional colouring, the perceiving and remembering are done. And no matter how we deduce requirements for these aspects from the causes, we still have omitted the *unity* of all the factors and aspects. There is the togetherness of them all, in a unity of feeling which gives each perception and each memory its unique place and value in *this* experience, such as it could have in no other. Causal explanation is incurably pluralistic: on the basis of many past events, it has to explain a single present event or experience. It is, then, simple logic that something is missed by the causal account. Not because of our ignorance of causes: if we knew them all, the multiplicity of causal factors would only be the more obvious, and so would the jump from the many to the new unity. From *a, b, c, d* . . . one is to derive the *experience* of *a, b, c, d* . . ., and not just *an* experience of them, but precisely *this* experience of them. There can be no logic for such a derivation. The step is not logical, but a free creation. Each experience is thus a free act, in its final unity a 'self-created' actuality, enriching the sum of actualities by one new member.

Here is the ultimate meaning of creation—in the freedom or self-determination of any experience of a new 'one', arising out of a previous many, in terms of which it cannot, by any causal relationship, be fully described. Bergson and Peirce, I think independently, first came close to the point here. Whitehead, however, puts it even more plainly.

Once it is seen that each experience is a new unitary entity, deterministic arguments lose their cogency. For instance, the argument that action must be determined by character or by the strongest motive. A character or motive received from the past cannot be more than *one* of the factors entering into the experience; it cannot dictate the unity of itself with the other factors. Besides, if 'motive' means a purpose or plan of action, a goal set up in advance, it has to be something relatively vague, an outline, not a description of the new experience in its full unitary quality, but rather of some important aspect or aspects of the experience. The total unique feeling of the experience is still to be decided. And if the motive or character is *not* received from the past, it must be a *creation* of the present.

Experiential synthesis is the solution of the problem of 'the one and the many'. Experience puts together its data; these remain several, but the the experience in and by which they are put together is one. Each synthesis is a single reality, not reducible to interrelated parts. It is a 'whole of parts', yet it is more than that phrase clearly states: the safest language is to call it a synthesis, or an inclusive reality. But the including reality is as much a unitary entity as is any one of the included items. Concrete unity in this view is always a unification, an integration, and what is unified is always a many. Unity and plurality thus complement, and do not exclude, one another.

'Creative' means, as in Bergson's 'Creative Evolution', unpredictable, incompletely determined in advance by causal conditions and laws. Accordingly, it means *additions to the definiteness of reality*. Every effect is in some degree, however slight, an 'emergent whole'. Emergence is no special case, but the general principle of process, although it may have privileged instances in which the extent of novelty (not determined by the conditions) is unusually pronounced. As Bergson and Peirce insist, prediction is limited, not alone by ignorance, but by the very meaning of the future as a sphere of decisions yet unmade, issues not yet settled even by the totality of causes already operating. Reality is predictable just in so far as it is not creative, but rather mechanical, automatic, compulsive, habit-ridden. Much of life is thus uncreative and hence predictable. Science has enough to do if it seeks to trace out the mechanisms which underlie and limit creativity. The creative as such is perhaps outside the sphere of science; yet the denial of the creative (such as we find in the works of some psychologists, for instance) is also, and much more surely, outside its proper sphere. If anything is unscientific, it is the denial of aspects of existence because they seem inconvenient for our methods.

Of course you might argue that, though the experience is not entirely derivable causally, the physical behaviour is so. You would then be in some danger of claiming a higher degree of predictability than most physicists think is attainable, even in some inorganic systems. You would also be asserting that experience is without influence upon behaviour; for if experience does influence behaviour and is itself not entirely determined causally, then one of the conditions of behaviour escapes complete causal derivability and so does behaviour itself.

The most respectable deterministic argument is methodological, the contention that science should not set limits in advance to its success in the search for causal explanations. But a methodological rule is not *ipso facto* convertible into an established or even a probable truth about the universe. That we should, perhaps, as scientists, avoid setting limits in advance to our finding of causal derivations affords no evidence that such limits are lacking in the nature of things. This is an independent question. And the evidence is the other way. There must, as we have seen, be limits to causal derivability. Moreover, what we should, as scientists, avoid doing may be the very thing that, as philosophers, or as human beings, we ought to do. Science is specialization, abstraction; philosophy and religion exist to restore the total perspective, taking all legitimate interests of man into account. Among these interests, or supreme over them, is the interest in creating. We are not merely inquirers predicting, we are also agents deciding, the future. And decision has to be made step by step. We cannot get everything decided, then sit back and merely predict. We should be dead, since to live is to decide, and decide anew, each moment. Think of the psychological or sociological predicter, calmly foreseeing his own actions, the future decisions of statesmen, the future compositions of musicians, the poems of poets, the future discoveries of his own science of psychology or some other science, the jokes his friends will make with him during the coming day!

People have looked for freedom in action, and of course freedom must somehow show up in action. But the first stage of free action is the way in which one interprets or experiences the world. Only you or I can determine our own way of feeling and thinking our environment. The utmost slave has some freedom here which none can wholly suppress in him while he is alive. No matter how others coerce or persuade him, he finally must make his own unique and only relatively or partially predictable response to the stimuli others bring to bear upon him. It is vain to talk about psychological prediction as an absolute; for even after an experience has taken place, not all the words in all languages could precisely describe that experience. And what cannot be said even afterwards certainly cannot be said in advance. A man grows angry; suppose we have predicted this. There are as many forms and qualities of angry experience as there are cases, and only more or less rough and crude descriptions are possible of the various respects in which they may differ. However, the mere indescribability of an experience is not the whole story.

Let me restate the basic argument: the stimuli moulding an experience are many: the five or more senses are operating, memory is relating us, at least unconsciously, to thousands of incidents of the past: but all this multiplicity of influences is to produce a single unitary experience, yours or mine right now, let us say. The effect is one; the causes, however, are many, literally hundreds of thousands, billions even, considering the cells in our brains, for example. This vast multitude of factors must flow together to produce a single new entity, the experience of the moment. The many stimuli are given, and certainly they tell us much about the response. But it is a logical impossibility that they should tell us all. An emergent synthesis is needed, to decide just how each item is to blend in a single complex sensory-emotional-intellectual whole, the experience. Any 'motive' determining this whole is either but an item going into the synthesis, or else is the synthesis, and you are arguing in a circle. To experience must be a free act, or nothing intelligible.

Why is this not more generally realized? In part, because we have our minds chiefly upon the more important and exceptional modes of creativity, and so we overlook the humbler ones which are always there, like the man in Molière who did not realize that he had been talking 'prose' all his life. Freedom is always there, but the unusual kinds and degrees of freedom are not always there. It is important to distinguish between the higher and lower forms of freedom; yet we shall never understand life and the world until we see that the zero of freedom can only be the zero of experiencing, and even of reality. (For, apart from experience, the idea of reality is empty, as some though not all philosophers admit.) Accordingly, Whitehead, Varisco, and others have proposed that we generalize, and take the free act of experiencing as the universal principle of reality. Not that human experience is the principle of reality, far from it. But human experience is only one form; there are the other vertebrate animals and their modes of experiencing; the lower animals and theirs—and where shall we stop? From man to molecules and atoms we have a series of modes of organization; at no point can one say, below this there could be no experience. If atoms respond to stimuli (and they do), how else could they show that they sense or feel? And if you say, they have no sense organs, the reply is: neither do one-celled animals, yet they seem to perceive their environments.

For the sake of the argument at least, then, let us imagine the universe as a vast system of experiencing individuals on innumerable levels. Each such individual is in some measure free; for experiencing is a partly free act. Thus creativity, emergent novelty, is universal. In this way we perhaps understand why the physicists have had to reformulate the laws of nature as statistical, rather than absolute uniformities.

If life is thus creative, why are there uncreative aspects which make scientific and also commonsense predictions of the future possible? The need for these is plain: to live is indeed to decide, and to decide anew each moment; yet to live is also to foresee, to deal with the future to some extent as though it were already settled fact. How is this possible? We must here introduce the 'sharing' of creativity. The most obvious aspect of this is in memory. In memory one takes account of one's own previous decisions as relevant to the present decision. One participates or shares in past experiences, with their creative decisions. One also remembers past perceptions of how others thought and felt, and what they decided. Or one perceives now what they in the approximate present think, feel, and decide. One takes all this into account in one's own present decision. Thus the freedom of present creativity is not absolute, or in a vacuum. It accepts limits. But these limits are set by other acts of freedom, those that are known from memory or perception. Freedom is thus sharply limited, but by freedom itself, as embodied in other acts, either of oneself or one's acquaintances, enemies, friends, fellow animals, fellow creatures.

Why should one take free acts of the past into account? Why not ignore them? Because the very meaning of freedom is the transition from the experienced antecedent many to the new unit experience of that many, the many being the previous acts of freedom. We experience, in a free unique synthesis, the various experiences already actualized which we remember, or perceive in others. We cannot simply experience our present free experience—of what? There must be some content. In memory and social experience, and (some of us believe) in all experience, we find this content furnished by other experiences, each with its own freedom, belonging to other times or other individuals. Experience must have stimuli; there must be objects of experience, data which are already there, ready to be experienced. (Even in dreams, it is so.) Yet in this philosophy there is nothing in the world but creative experience. What, then, are the objects which are there to be experienced? Simply, previous cases of experience! Some of these are one's own earlier experiences as one now remembers them. The rest are of other types. For instance, the cells of one's body are, as various writers have suggested, constantly furnishing their little experiences or feelings which, being pooled in our more comprehensive experience, constitute what we call our sensations. And the cells, in their fashion, respond to or experience our experiences, as is shown by the influence which our thoughts and feelings have upon our bodily changes. Again, when two of us talk, each response of one becomes a stimulus to the other. Always there is a degree of freedom; and the inclusive limit upon the present act of freedom is the sum of past acts to which it is a reaction. Experience as emergent synthesis feeds on its own previous products, and on nothing else whatever! This is the 'ultimacy' of creativity.

Sharing of creativity is the social character of experience, its aspect of sympathy, participation, identification with others. Moreover, even one's own past self is, strictly speaking, 'another'—as hundreds of thousands of Buddhists have, for over a score of centuries, been trying to tell the world. I hold that in this they have simply been accurate. One can regard one's past self with love, but also with antipathy, much as one can the selves of other persons. Sheer identity or sheer non-identity cannot be the correct account of this matter. Our Western philosophies have, with rare exceptions, been excessively individualistic, but also insufficiently pluralistic. They have taken a perilous first step toward the mystic monism, the night of mere abstract identity in which 'all cows are black'.

It may seem that the entire content of a creative act cannot come from other cases of creativity. For what of the sensory material coming into our experiences? Let us grant that the stone we see is not a creative agent; also that our sense organs themselves are not literally such agents. However, atoms, molecules, and still more nerve cells, seem to exhibit signs of spontaneous activity not to be found in whole rocks or eye-balls. With reason many scientists hold that we can set no limits to the pervasiveness either of spontaneity or of feeling in nature. That there are statistical laws with very great exactitude and wide scope can be reconciled with this—as is widely admitted. This gives us a tremendous new speculative possibility, a great alternative to the Newtonian 'world-machine', and to the dualism of free mind and blindly obedient matter.

To exploit this new possibility we must overcome the prejudice that minds, or experiences, are 'inextended'. James, Peirce, Whitehead, and many others (and indeed modern physics itself, with its view of space as merely a pattern of causal inheritance among events, which may perfectly well be experiences) have shown that the denial of extension to experience is unfounded. With the abandonment of the definition of the psychical as inextended and with the admission of universal creativity, dualism loses its necessity. And only necessity will ever induce science or philosophy, with their drive toward conceptual unification, to accept an ultimate dualism. Yet the sole remaining alternative to psychical monism is a materialistic one whose implicit dualism is never successfully disguised. Experiences are facts; the only question is, what else is fact? If nothing else, then, and only then, is dualism avoided.

We have said that the limitation of freedom by past free acts is what makes a certain measure of prediction possible. The full explication of this would require us to consider not only human and subhuman types of freedom but also Supreme Freedom, the divine choice of certain patterns of order or laws for this world, this divine choice being taken into account—not consciously, as a rule, but nevertheless effectively—by all other forms of freedom. Freedom is limited only by acts of freedom already performed; but divine acts of cosmic relevance and influence must be included, to account for cosmic order. This brings us back to the theological problem of creation which was mentioned at the beginning of the chapter.

Let us consider again the traditional view of this matter. God was said to 'create' a world, something quite distinct from himself. The world was creature, God creator; the one wholly uncreative, the other wholly uncreated. This doctrine is neat and definitive, but there are reasons for thinking that the truth must be less simple. . . .

First, the act of creating was thought of as voluntary, a decision from which the creator might have refrained. Suppose he had refrained: the world would then not have existed; however, something else would also not have existed, the decision itself. There would instead have been the decision not to create, or to create some world other than ours. This shows us that a free agent must create something *in himself,* even if he decides not to create anything else; for the decision, if free, is itself a creation. The world resulted, we are told, from a free *fiat,* 'Let there be a world!' But this *fiat,* like the world, need not have been. Like the world, then, it exists contingently, and is brought into being by the creator, but within himself. In short, *freedom is self-creation,* whatever else it may be. The will which freely determines another, or freely refrains from doing so, in any case determines itself. But this means that it is untrue that the creator is in no sense or aspect created; rather he is, in some aspect, a creature, a product—at least of his own making. This is an old view, found in Egypt, India, and Central America.

Second, let us consider the view that the creature is *merely* creature, in no way creator. Take man: we are told that he is made; he does not make himself. Yet we also say, in good English, that a person 'makes' a resolution or decision; hence, since an adult person is, in substantial degree, composed of the sum of his past decisions, if he has made these, has he not to that extent made himself? And if it be denied that a man has made his decisions, why call them his? Are they God's decisions, and not the man's? Or are they both? Can exactly the same decision be that of two agents? This difficulty is childishly simple; but I am persuaded that it is genuine. I find no clarification in the classical discussions of the problem, such as that by Thomas Aquinas. Of course, it may be held that these divine mysteries are too high for us. However, as Berdyaev shrewdly hints, the mystery seems all too plainly man made. It is human beings who invented such neat little phrases as 'creator and creature' or 'creatio ex nihilo'. Nor is the doctrine we are attacking, in its bare simplicity and starkness, to be found in the Bible. Rather, it is a stylized version of biblical thought, a version invented by philosophical theology. The invention need not be taken as sacred, whatever be thought of the Bible. The stylization may have squeezed out some truth, and introduced some error.

It is often said that since God, or nature and society, 'made' my original character and environment, he or they thereby determined what my decisions would be. But the word 'character' is merely a label for the pervasive quality of a person's past actions. Hence to explain actions by character is word-juggling. You may indeed substitute 'inherited genes' for the word 'character'. However, if actions do strictly follow either from the genes and the surrounding cosmic situation, or from a timeless divine decree, in what sense is a man now creative at all? And if he is not creative, how does he know what he means when he attributes creativity to God?

You may say that creative or free action is simply voluntary action, doing as one wishes. But is this all that is meant when God is said to be free? For, please observe, when it is said that God is free to create or not to create this world, it is thereby denied that in *his* case actions follow necessarily from character. So theological determinism attributed to deity the supreme or perfect form of causally transcendent freedom, but to man the total absence of freedom in this sense! Thus the difference was not to be between the infinite and the finite, or perfect and imperfect, but between the infinite and zero. How, I ask, starting from zero, is there a path to the concept of the supreme case? One must start from something, not nothing, to derive the idea of the maximum or the unsurpassable.

The logical view of the situation is rather that God, being both self-creative and creative of others, produces creatures which likewise, though in radically inferior ways, are self-determining, and also productive of effects beyond themselves. In this fashion the theological view, with its inconsistencies removed, becomes a philosophy of universal creativity. We must not, however, stop with God and man, as self-creative creators; we must go on to conceive the lower animals, and even atoms, as in some slight or trivial way self-determining and creative of others. For if supreme creativity is the divine nature, and an inferior creativity is man's nature, then the lower animals must be still lower levels of creativity. The effect must in some way express the nature of its cause. How can an infinitely creative being produce an *absolutely* non-creative being? That which is absolutely devoid of what God supremely possesses—what can it be but the zero of actual existence?

A third difficulty with the supposedly absolute contrast between creative God and created world is the following. A free agent determines not only himself, in some aspect, but also all those who know him. If I 'make' the decision to perform such and such an act, and you are aware of my decision, then I will in effect have decided that you are to be the knower of my decision. Had I not made it, you certainly could not have known me as making it: and if you are a sufficiently close observer of me, I will by making the decision have established at least the probability that you should acquire knowledge of it.

This consideration applies also to our relation to God; indeed, it applies to that relation more strictly and absolutely than elsewhere. For no matter how well and closely you may have observed me, you might somehow fail to note my decision. But God cannot fail to know that I decide such and such—granted that I do so decide. This 'inability' not to know a thing if there is such a thing is his infallibility. Accordingly, all we have to do to determine something in God is to determine something in ourselves, as known to God, and if we cannot do this, we have no freedom whatever. Either we determine the divine knowing, in some degree, or we determine nothing at all. Jules Lequier, a hundred years ago, argued this out very carefully; he has not been refuted. He has, however, been widely ignored.

According to the old view, as set forth by most theologians and philosophers, God influences all things, nothing influences God. For him there are no 'stimuli'; hence when he influences or stimulates the world, it is in a wholly different way from the ordinary way. For normally, a stimulus or cause is but a previous effect, or response to some still earlier stimulus; yet God, it was thought, does not respond. He just—creates, 'out of nothing'. I think this was a mischievously unclear way of talking. We know creativity only as a responding to prior stimuli, and if we refuse to allow an analogy between such ordinary creative action and the divine 'creating' of the cosmos, we are using a word whose meaning we cannot provide. Our new philosophical doctrine is that even God's creativity is his higher form of emergent experiential synthesis, or response to stimuli. He influences us supremely because he is supremely open to our influence. He responds delicately to all things, as we respond more or less delicately to changes in our nerve cells. Of course, his delicacy is infinitely greater. He contributes to our lives in superior fashion because, in equally superior fashion, he receives contributions from us. Like the sensitive parent or ruler, he enjoys observing our feelings and thoughts, and responds to these with a perfection of appreciation to which no parent or ruler can attain. Because only God can appreciate us, or our neighbours, in our or their full worth, we unconsciously respond to this appreciation as we do to no other. And so the order of the world is possible, in spite of the assumption that only freedom exists to limit freedom.

Consider now some advantages of this way of viewing God. First, unlike the notion of divine creation as a purely one-way action proceeding from God, our view does not threaten to deny the freedom or creativity of the creatures. Of course a worshipful God must have the supreme, cosmic, or perfect form of creative power. But if to create is essentially to experience, and if this is to form an emergent synthesis of data coming from previous experiences, which must, in their way, also have been free, to say that in God is the perfect or infinite form of creative response is still to imply that he has the freedom of others to respond to.

Does such a view 'limit' the power of God? This way of putting the question prejudices the answer and is to be rejected. We must first ask, what is it to exert power? On our view it is to respond to the responses of others in such a way that the new response becomes in its turn a new stimulus. In this philosophy the word 'power' has no other meaning which could be used to describe God. So we do not have to limit God's power to make room for the freedom of the creatures (or to explain evil); we only have to take care that when we speak of divine or perfect 'power' we have a meaning for the word. This meaning will take care of creaturely freedom automatically. No special 'limits' are required.

So far we have argued that creative becoming is a reality, at least in human experiences, and that it is not obviously impossible that it should be universally real, present in all things from atoms to deity, and constitutive of reality as such. There is, however, a tradition that becoming is a secondary mode of reality, inferior to and less real than being. Our view affirms the contrary, that 'becoming is reality itself' (Bergson), and being only an aspect of this reality.

STUDY QUESTIONS

For Review

1. What is generally meant by "process philosophy" and what basic philosophical question does it address?
2. How did Whitehead's work in mathematics and physics help him prepare for his more strictly philosophical work?
3. What theories did Whitehead intend to criticize by his use of the phrase "the bifurcation of nature" and the "fallacy of misplaced concreteness" ?
4. Describe the nature of the real fact or beings in Whitehead's philosophy.
5. Describe the two natures of God and how God is related to the world in each.
6. Contrast Hartshorne and Whitehead on the nature of God and eternal objects.

For Further Thought

7. Do you think that nature or the things within it can best be understood as composed of substances that change in various ways or as at base a process of change or becoming?
8. Do you believe that new things come into existence, i.e., that there is novelty in the world? If so, how do you explain its existence or where it comes from?
9. Do you think there are any inert or lifeless beings? What do you make of the theory that every being is in some sense alive?
10. If you believe that there is a God, do you believe that God changes? Do you think that such a God can have the traditional characteristic of "perfect" ? Is God a "person" ?
11. Do possibilities exist? In what sense yes or no?
12. Do you think that God's existence is compatible with freedom of choice?

BIBLIOGRAPHY

Process Philosophy

Brown, Delwin, Ralph E. James, and Gene Reeves. *Process Philosophy and Christian Thought.* Indianapolis: Bobbs-Merrill, 1971.

Cobb, John B. *A Christian Natural Theology.* Philadelphia: Westminster Press, 1965.

Gilkey, Langdon. *Naming the Whirlwind.* Indianapolis: Bobbs-Merrill, 1969.

Hall, David. *Eros and Irony.* Albany: State University of New York Press, 1982.

Hamilton, Peter. *The Living God and the Modern World.* London: Hodder and Stoughton, 1967.

Lucas, George R., Jr. *The Genesis of Modern Process Thought.* Metuchen, N.J.: Scarecrow Press, 1983.

Neville, Robert. *Creativity and God.* New York: Seabury Press, 1980.

– – –. *The Cosmology of Freedom.* New Haven: Yale University Press, 1974.

Ogden, Schubert M. *The Reality of God and Other Essays.* New York: Harper and Row, 1966.

Peters, E. H. *The Creative Advance.* St. Louis: Bethany, 1966.

Pittenger, Norman. *Process Thought and Christian Faith.* New York: Macmillan, 1968.

Reese, William, and Eugene Freeman, eds. *Process and Divinity: Philosophical Essays Presented to Charles Hartshorne.* LaSalle, Ill.: Open Court, 1964.

Weiman, H. N. *The Sources of Human Good.* Chicago: University of Chicago Press, 1946.

Williams, D. D. *The Spirit and Forms of Love.* New York: Harper and Row, 1968.

Alfred North Whitehead

Whitehead, Alfred North. *Alfred North Whitehead: An Anthology.* Ed. F. S. C. Northrop and Mason W. Gross. New York: Macmillan, 1953.

– – –. *Essays in Science and Philosophy.* New York: Philosophical Library, 1947.

– – –. *Modes of Thought.* New York: Macmillan, 1938.

– – –. *Adventures of Ideas.* New York: Macmillan, 1933.

– – –. *The Aims of Education and Other Essays.* New York: Macmillan, 1929.

– – –. *Process and Reality.* New York: Macmillan, 1929. Corrected edition, ed. David Ray Griffin and Donald W. Sherburne. New York: Macmillan, Free Press, 1978.

– – –. *Symbolism: Its Meaning and Effect.* New York: Macmillan, 1927.

– – –. *Religion in the Making.* New York: Macmillan, 1926.

– – –. *Science and the Modern World.* New York: Macmillan, 1925.

– – –. *The Principle of Relativity.* Cambridge: Cambridge University Press, 1922.

– – –. *The Concept of Nature.* Cambridge: Cambridge University Press, 1920.

– – –. *An Enquiry Concerning the Principles of Natural Knowledge.* Cambridge: Cambridge University Press, 1919.

– – –. *A Treatise on Universal Algebra.* Cambridge: Cambridge University Press, 1898.

Whitehead, Alfred North, and Bertrand Russell. *Principia Mathematica.* 3 vols. Cambridge: Cambridge University Press, 1898.

Brumbaugh, Robert S. *Whitehead: Process Philosophy and Education.* Albany: State University of New York Press, 1982.

Cappon, Alexander P. *About Wordsworth and Whitehead*. New York: Philosophical Library, 1982.

Christian, William A. *An Interpretation of Whitehead's Metaphysics*. New Haven: Yale University Press, 1959.

Eisendrath, Craig R. *Unifying Moment: The Psychological Philosophy of William James and Alfred North Whitehead*. Cambridge: Harvard University Press, 1971.

Emmet, Dorothy M. *Whitehead's Philosophy of Organism*. London: Macmillan, 1932.

Fitzgerald, Janet A. *Alfred North Whitehead's Early Philosophy of Space and Time*. Washington, D.C.: University Press of America, 1979.

Ford, Lewis S. *Whitehead's Early Philosophy*. Albany: State University of New York Press, forthcoming.

– – –, ed. *Two Process Philosophers: Hartshorne's Encounter with Whitehead*. Chico, Calif.: Scholars Press, 1973.

Hall, David L. *The Civilization of Experience: A Whiteheadean Theory of Culture*. New York: Fordham University Press, 1973.

Johnson, A. H. *Whitehead and His Philosophy*. Washington, D.C.: University Press of America, 1983.

– – –. *Whitehead's Philosophy of Civilization*. Boston: Beacon Press, 1958.

– – –. *Whitehead's Theory of Reality*. Boston: Beacon Press, 1952.

Kline, George L., ed. *Alfred North Whitehead: Essays on His Philosophy*. 1963.

Kline, George L., and Lewis S. Ford, eds. *Explorations in Whitehead's Philosophy*. New York: Fordham University Press, 1983.

Lango, John. *Whitehead's Ontology*. Albany: State University of New York Press, 1972.

Lawrence, Nathaniel. *Whitehead's Philosophical Development*. Westport, Conn.: Greenwood Press, 1968.

Leclerc, Ivor, ed. *The Relevance of Whitehead*. London: Allen and Unwin, 1961.

Lowe, Victor. *Understanding Whitehead*. Baltimore: Johns Hopkins University Press, 1962.

Lucas, George R. *Two View of Freedom in Process Thought*. Chico, Calif.: Scholars Press, 1979.

Mays, W. *Whitehead's Philosophy of Science and Metaphysics*. The Hague: Martinus Nijhoff, 1977.

Palter, Robt. M. *Whitehead's Philosophy of Science*. Chicago: University of Chicago Press, 1960.

Philippson, Sten M. *A Metaphysics for Theology: A Study of Some Problems in the Later Philosophy of Alfred North Whitehead*. Atlantic Highlands, N.J.: Humanities Press, 1982.

Philosophical Essays for Alfred North Whitehead. New York: Longsmans, Green, 1936.

Pols, Edward. *Whitehead's Metaphysics: A Critical Examination of Process and Reality*. Edwardsville: Southern Illinois University Press, 1967.

Price, Lucien. *Dialogues of Alfred North Whitehead*. Boston: Little, Brown, 1954.

Ross, Stephen D. *Perspective in Whitehead's Metaphysics*. Albany: State University of New York Press, 1983.

Schilpp, Paul Arthur, ed. *The Philosophy of Alfred North Whitehead*. Evanston, Ill.: Northwestern University Press, 1941.

Sherburne, Donald W. *A Key to Whitehead's "Process and Reality."* Chicago: University of Chicago Press, 1981.

Wallack, F. Bradford. *The Epochal Nature of Process in Whitehead's Metaphysics*. Albany: State University of New York Press, 1980.

Wilmont, Laurence. *Whitehead and God: Prolegomena to Theological Reconstruction.* Atlantic Highlands, N.J.: Humanities Press, 1979.

Charles Hartshorne

Hartshorne, Charles. *Creativity in American Philosophy.* Albany: State University of New York Press, 1984.

— — —. *Insights and Oversights of Great Thinkers.* Albany: State University of New York Press, 1983.

— — —. *Omnipotence and Other Theological Mistakes.* Albany: State University of New York Press, 1983.

— — —. *Aquinas to Whitehead: Seven Centuries of Metaphysics of Religion.* Milwaukee: Marquette University Press, 1977.

— — —. *Whitehead's Philosophy: Selected Essays, 1935–70.* Lincoln: University of Nebraska Press, 1972.

— — —. *Creative Synthesis and Philosophic Method.* LaSalle, Ill.: Open Court Publishing, 1970.

— — —. *A Natural Theology for Our Time.* LaSalle, Ill.: Open Court Publishing, 1967.

— — —. *The Logic of Perfection, and Other Essays in Neoclassical Metaphysics.* LaSalle, Ill.: Open Court Publishing, 1962.

— — —. *Reality as Social Process: Studies in Metaphysics and Religion.* Boston: Beacon Press, 1953.

— — —. *The Divine Relativity: A Social Conception of God.* New Haven: Yale University Press, 1948.

— — —. *Man's Vision of God and the Logic of Theism.* Chicago: Willett, Clark and Co., 1941.

— — —. *Beyond Humanism: Essays in the New Philosophy of Nature.* Chicago: Willet, Clark and Co., 1937.

— — —. *The Philosophy and Psychology of Sensation.* Chicago: University of Chicago Press, 1934.

Hartshorne, Charles, and Creighton Peden. *Whitehead's View of Reality.* New York: Pilgrim Press, 1981.

Hartshorne, Charles, and William L. Reese. *Philosophers Speak of God.* Chicago: University of Chicago Press, 1953.

Goodwin, George L. *The Ontological Argument of Charles Hartshorne.* Chico, Calif.: Scholars Press, 1978.

Gunton, Colin E. *Becoming and Being: The Doctrine of God in Charles Hartshorne and Karl Barth.* New York: Oxford University Press, 1978.

Peters, Eugene H. *Hartshorne and Neoclassical Metaphysics: An Interpretation.* Lincoln: University of Nebraska Press, 1970.

Chapter 13

Systematic Metaphysics

Throughout the history of philosophy one of the most significant preoccupations of philosophers has been with what has come to be called metaphysics.[1] The history of philosophy in America is no exception. Jonathan Edwards and Josiah Royce as well as Charles Sanders Peirce were interested in the "real nature of things" and other metaphysical issues. In twentieth-century American philosophy both process philosophers and Thomists have given metaphysical issues and questions a central place in their philosophizing (see chapters 11 and 12). Other philosophers who are not so easily classified have done significant work in this area as well; this chapter contains examples of some of their writings. By way of introduction a brief indication of the nature and problems of metaphysics will be given, and then a few things will be noted about the writers and selections included in this chapter.

To the ordinary person the term "metaphysics" may conjure up notions of abstruse conversations and debates or even things related to the paranormal, supernatural, or occult. Such is implied on the shingle of the little Berkeley shop which reads "Astrology, Metaphysics, and Tarot." To the extent that metaphysics is primarily concerned with determining the "real nature of things," its investigations must necessarily be somewhat abstruse. However, as the selections themselves show, metaphysics is a demanding rational discipline. Among the questions metaphysicians have raised are the following: Do numbers or qualities or relations exist? Do they exist in the same sense in which tables and chairs exist? Are the molecules or atoms that physicists tell us compose tables and chairs more real than the chairs themselves? Are persons or minds of a different kind of reality than other things? Are there a certain number of basic kinds of real things?

The term "metaphysics" itself was the name first given to a group of Aristotle's writings. He had originally called it "First Philosophy" or "Theology." [2] However, since it dealt with matters that were beyond *(meta)* those dealt with in his other work, the "Physics," it came to be known as the "Metaphysics." Other early Greek philosophers were concerned with what are now considered cosmological rather than strictly speaking metaphysical questions, for example, the proposal that there were but four basic realities: earth, air, fire, and water. Aristotle gave a different account of things. Everything that exists, he wrote, is primarily a substance composed of a formal and a material element, i.e., an element that gives the essential and qualitative aspects of the thing and another than provides the basis for its remaining the same thing through its various changes. Any being that did not change would thus be pure form. Some philosophers like Plato held that reality itself consists primarily of eternally existing forms. The things of this world are patterned after and "participate in" these forms. Thus two-ness is more real than any group of two things, and the essence of beauty or humanness more real than beautiful things or human beings. Since the time of Immanuel Kant, however, metaphysicians have had to address other issues. Kant held that while we will always seek to know the answers to metaphysical questions (questions according to Kant about matters that lie beyond our experience — whether, for example, God, an immortal soul, and/or freedom exist), such knowledge is not humanly attainable. We may only in an extended sense be said to "know" the existence of such realities, as the necessary postulates of a moral life that demands their existence. [3]

In spite of the questions raised by Kant and others about the nature and possibility of metaphysics, philosophers have continued to be concerned with notions of existence, being, and reality or actuality. At times the real has been distinguished from the apparent or what appears as real. Both materialistic and idealistic metaphysics have had their supporters. The basic categories or kinds of being that philosophers have conceived, however, are more varied: nature, substance, ideas, life force, spirit, form, event, and many others have been proposed. Other concerns have also occupied metaphysicians. Is reality one or many, and in what sense or senses? What constitutes the individuality of any individual? How are beings related to one another? In what way is causality or time and space to be conceived? When their answers to such questions have been worked into a scheme of things, we have what may be called "systematic metaphysics."

Questions may be raised concerning the distinctiveness of metaphysics from other disciplines (such as those sciences that also in some sense claim to determine how things are), as well as its reliability, validity, or truthfulness. As to the first, metaphysics claims to be both more comprehensive and fundamental than any of the various sciences. Whereas they deal with particular branches of reality (physical reality, living beings, the human psyche, or human groups or societies), metaphysics proposes to inquire into the nature of any reality in so far as it exists. In regard to its claim to truthfulness, in some sense it does and in some sense it does not appeal to empirical fact. In Aristotle's work, for example, the fact that things change is the basic empirical observation grounding his physical scheme and ultimately his metaphysics. However, in another sense it matters not to the metaphysician what particular things exist. A metaphysics is concerned with determining what anything would be like if it did exist. Thus metaphysics aims to make sense of the data of experience without relying for its specific contents on that data. Nevertheless, metaphysics aims to propose a valid interpretation, not just a possible or likely account. Whether its criterion of validity or truth is the coherence of the scheme or some way in which the scheme fits the data of our experience remains a matter of debate among interpreters of metaphysics.

Excerpts from the writings of four philosophers have been included in this chapter. They have been chosen because they represent serious attempts to deal with metaphysical issues, and also because they present a variety of approaches. Justus Buchler (1914–) is considered an heir of Dewey's naturalism whose philosophizing includes a metaphysics and a theory of the self and of judgment.[4] Paul Weiss (1901–) is founder of the Peirce Society and the Metaphysical Society of America, as well as the *Review of Metaphysics* which he edited from its inception in 1947 until 1964. He also edited with Charles Hartshorne the standard collection of the works of Charles Sanders Peirce and is responsible for numerous publications on a wide range of topics from logic to metaphysics. Lately he has turned his attention to philosophical applications of his philosophy in such concrete fields as ethics, politics, law, art, history, education, and sport.[5] Robert Neville (1939–) has been influenced by the process philosophies of Whitehead and Hartshorne and, like Weiss, opposes reductionism. His primary concern is to demonstrate the cognitive and metaphysical nature of value.[6] In some ways Wilfrid Sellars (1912–) continues his father's (Roy Wood Sellars) naturalism, though he calls himself a "scientific realist"; he has been labeled by one interpreter "a neo-Kantian with some very novel twists."[7] Sellars makes use of techniques of language analysis and has many concerns in common with those who might best be placed in the chapter on the new empiricists. However here his treatment of certain metaphysical issues is singled out. Each of these metaphysicians exemplifies some of the primary concerns of this branch of philosophy, though, as the reader will see, each also has his own distinctive approach.

The selection by Justus Buchler is from his *Metaphysics of Natural Complexes*. The basic metaphysical category proposed here is that of "natural complex." Everything that is — physical bodies as well as relations between or among them, individuals and societies, ideas and feelings — is a natural complex. Although they are of different kinds, they are alike in so far as they can be (at least in principle) discriminated (i.e., imagined, sensed, apprehended, or made). Each can be differentiated from every other by discriminable qualities or traits. Each is complex and thus capable of being an object of continuous query and understanding. Nature itself is a natural complex and the source, though not providently, of all traits. There are no non-natural or super-natural complexes, according to Buchler, so the concept of God must also be placed within such a naturalistic framework.

Buchler believes that his terminology serves the goals of philosophy in its aim at general explanations and its ability to generate a conceptual scheme. It does so in a way that avoids some of the problems with other terms often used to denote the ultimate such as "being," "existence," and "reality." For example, one is thus able to speak of "a natural complex" in cases where it would not make sense to speak of "a being" or "an entity." In the case of the Buchler selection, as of the others presented in this chapter, an adequate understanding of the author's metaphysics takes one beyond the selection included here. Nevertheless, one can glimpse from the selection something of its essence.

Any systematic metaphysics must provide an adequate explanation of the person, human knowledge, and action. The selection from Paul Weiss's *Privacy* represents an approach to these problems of one contemporary American philosopher. "Privacy," according to Weiss, is that inner source of a person's activities that may or may not become public by being given a bodily expression or by making a difference to the body's functioning, to others, and to the world beyond.[8] A person's privacy has many expressions or epitomizations, including "sensitivity, desire, and other ways in which men express themselves in and through their bodies."[9] The problem that Weiss faces is how to argue this notion in the face of the many forms of reductionism that seem to deny the unique character of the human personality and anything private in his sense of that term. Physical reductionism explains everything in terms of physical or chemical simples. According to technological reductionism man's thought is as mechanical as the workings of a computer. Biological reductionism sees only a difference of degree between man and animals. Psychological reductionism reduces human action to controllable, observable behaviors. And linguistic reductionism conceives man's thought processes as essentially nothing but language manipulation. Weiss argues that all of these forms of reductionism assume or rely on what we already know about human privacy and thus actually support a belief in its existence. His more general metaphysical account explains the world as a mix of equally real, underlying and conditioning "finalities" and limited and conditioned "actualities" (earlier called "realities"). To explain these, however, would take us beyond the limits of this brief summary.

According to Robert Neville in *Reconstruction of Thinking,* a new account of the nature of human thinking is long overdue. While other philosophers have attempted to combine a qualitative mode of thought — the inheritance of the Greeks — with the more quantitative mode of modern science, these attempts have been unable to do justice in particular to the concept of value. Neville's own account, on the other hand, attempts to show "that thinking is founded in valuation."[10] Not only are our images a product of harmoniously combining focus and field, i.e., a product of valuing, but so also are our processes of interpretation, theorizing, and the development of moral ideals. Underlying this account of thought, however, is a metaphysics according to which to be is to be a harmony. For anything to be a determinate thing, it must be complex, possessing factors or characters by which it is both like other things (for influenced and conditioned by them) and elements by which it is different from them, unique, having its own essential characteristics. Together these characters are harmonized in the individual. To be so is to be of value, and the more rightly or ideally harmonized the more positively valuable. The nature of harmony is specified as a proper combination of unity and complexity, perhaps in an aesthetic sense, with not too much unity without sufficient diversity nor too much diversity without sufficient unity. For a being to be a determinate thing, it must have a certain de facto harmony (otherwise it could not be thought of as one thing). However a thing is also known to be what it is by reference to some ideal norm of harmony for that type of thing and as being a selection by the knower according to his or her own particular interests.

While the neophyte who surveys the myriad and complex writings of Wilfrid Sellars may come away with the impression that there is no unity or systematization there, according to Sellars the surveyor has missed what Sellars himself believes to be there. He has written that he has continually been aware of how each problem and treatment fits into some "scheme of things entire." [11] Sellars's primary interests are ontology, semantics, and philosophy of mind. One of the best introductions to his thought is the essay from which this selection included here is drawn. [12]

In this essay, Sellars draws a picture of two competing images or ways of regarding man-in-the-world — the "manifest" and the "scientific" images. While these images are seemingly incompatible, Sellars's aim is to show how in some sense they may form a coherent picture. The "manifest image" is not necessarily nonscientific, but it is built on an original commonsense image, or the way in which man-in-the-world encounters himself. Originally this image pictured the primary components of the world as personal, but gradually it came to distinguish persons from things. The so-called perennial philosophy built on this image, as did much of modern science which is concerned primarily with finding regularities among the objects of our experience as they are experienced.

The "scientific image" on the other hand involves the postulation of imperceptible entities in order to explain the entities of our experience. These are not pragmatic fictions. Nor are objects simply collections of these imperceptible entities. What the entities are of which Sellars speaks is not yet known; they are whatever the Peircean community of investigators in the long run will agree on. However, Sellars assumes that this would be some "complex physical system." [13]

To specify the manner in which Sellars believes these two images may be reconciled is difficult. The physical world of imperceptible realities is ontologically more basic, i.e., more real than the things of our experience. And yet Sellars is not a simple reductionist who believes that the world of our experience and the "manifest image" is reducible to the physical world or the "scientific image." His manner of relating these two images lies in his understanding of the nature of thought and its intentionality, the semantic category of "meaning," the concept of "person," and the correlative concepts of community, rights, and duties.[14] For example he believes that a neurophysiological framework should supply counterpart concepts for "person" talk. Such complications, however, take us beyond the scope of this introduction. The Sellars selection, however, again provides us with an example of one of the ways in which metaphysical issues have been addressed by philosophers in America in the mid to latter twentieth century. How, or the extent to which, such metaphysical issues will continue to be addressed by philosophers in America remains to be seen.

Notes

[1] An excellent survey article by W. H. Walsh on the nature and problems of metaphysics and another by Roger Hancock on the history of metaphysics can be found in *The Encyclopedia of Philosophy,* ed. Paul Edwards (New York: Macmillan, 1967), vol. 5, pp. 300–307, 289–300.

[2] Aristotle, *Metaphysics,* trans. Richard Hope (Ann Arbor: University of Michigan Press, 1960). See also Robert Brumbaugh, "Aristotle's Outline of the Problems of First Philosophy," *Review of Metaphysics* 7, no. 3 (1953); Joseph Owens, *The Doctrine of Being in the Aristotelian Metaphysics* (Toronto: University of Toronto Press, 1951).

[3] Immanuel Kant, *Prolegomena to Any Future Metaphysics,* ed. Lewis White Beck (New York: Bobbs-Merrill, 1950); idem, *Critique of Pure Reason,* 2d ed., trans N. K. Smith (New York: 1933).

[4] See Buchler's *Toward a General Theory of Human Judgment* (1951), *Nature and Judgment* (1955), *The Concept of Method* (1961), and the work from which our selection is taken, *Metaphysics of Natural Complexes* (1966).

[5] Weiss's metaphysics can be found in his *Modes of Being* (1958), *Beyond All Appearances* (1974), and *First Considerations* (1977). Some of his works that deal with the concrete applications of his philosophy are *Our Public Life* (1959), *Nine Basic Arts* (1961), *History: Written and Lived* (1962), *The God We Seek* (1964), and *Sport: A Philosophical Inquiry* (1969).

[6] See Neville's *God the Creator* (1968), *The Cosmology of Freedom* (1974), *Soldier, Sage, Saint* (1978), *Creativity and God* (1980), and the work from which our selection is taken, *Reconstruction of Thinking* (1981).

[7] For Sellars's own comments see his introduction to *Naturalism and Ontology* (1979), and for the label "neo-Kantian" see Richard Bernstein's "Sellars Vision of Man-in-the-Universe," *Review of Metaphysics* 20 (1966): pp. 115–43, 290–316; and the special edition of *The Monist* on Sellars's philosophy: vol. 65, no. 3 (July 1982).

[8] Paul Weiss, *Privacy* (Carbondale: Southern Illinois University Press, 1983), p. xi.

[9] Ibid., p. 13.

[10] Robert Neville, *Reconstruction of Thinking* (Albany: State University of New York Press, 1981), p. 9.

[11] Wilfrid Sellars, *Naturalism and Ontology* (Reseda, Calif.: Ridgeview Publishing, 1979), p. vii.

[12] Wilfrid Sellars, "Philosophy and the Scientific Image of Man," in *Science, Perception, and Reality* (New York: Humanities Press, 1963).

[13] Ibid., p. 25.

[14] See Bernstein's interpretation in the previously noted article in the *Review of Metaphysics*.

JUSTUS BUCHLER

THE RUDIMENTARY
CONSIDERATIONS*

I

Whatever is, in whatever way, is a natural complex. The entire sequel, in a sense, amplifies this statement. Relations, structures, processes, societies, human individuals, human products, physical bodies, words and bodies of discourse, ideas, qualities, contradictions, meanings, possibilities, myths, laws, duties, feelings, illusions, reasonings, dreams—all are natural complexes. All of these terms bespeak discriminations of some kind, and whatever is discriminated in any respect or in any degree is a natural complex (for short, "complex"). Precisely what kind of complex anything discriminated turns out to be; in what way its status, its location, its connections are to be interpreted; what traits it may or should be said to have after investigation or any other form of experience; is a distinct type of issue. Anything identified or discovered or imagined or discerned or inferred or sensed or posited or encountered or apprehended or made or acted upon—no matter whether deliberately or not—is here said to be "discriminated." There are initial and advanced phases of discrimi-

* Justus Buchler, "The Rudimentary Considerations," in *Metaphysics of Natural Complexes* (New York: Columbia University Press, 1966), pp. 1–11. Reprinted with permission of Columbia University Press and Justus Buchler, 3 Homestead Avenue, Garden City, New York 11530.

nation. The stress here is on the initial or minimal phase—on that which was not and now is present for us to take account of, to deal with. In this basic meaning, whatever is for us, plays a role for us, is discriminated— grasped or marked out as having traits, and contrasted with what is other than it.

Although whatever is in any way discriminated is a natural complex, it does not follow that all natural complexes are discriminated. Whether all natural complexes are humanly discriminable, we do not know. In view of the fact that so much of what has surrounded men has been found out by them in distant retrospect or through the provocations of accident, it is fair to believe that there are complexes influencing them and influenced by them which are never found out. And in general, it is hard to avoid the conviction that, notwithstanding the power known as method, innumerable complexes of nature elude the range of finite creatures.

The concept of natural complex permits the identification of all discriminanda generically, without prejudicing the pursuit and the analysis of differences, of further similarities within the differences, of further differences within these similarities. Should we speak of nature as a "complex of complexes" ? If this phrase can be justified at all, it cannot be justified all at once. Among other considerations, and in the light of the position to be developed, any complex is a complex of complexes. Although the phrase as applied to nature is not immediately felicitous, it is better than phrases like "infinite totality" and "system of systems." For it does not suggest a finished collectivity or an absolutely determinate whole, nor indeed a collectivity or whole of any kind; nor does it suggest immensity, as the terms "universe," "world," and "cosmos" do. The idea of nature, in so far as it means not merely the common factor of all "natures" but the source of all that is, implies the perennial conceivability of complexes more inclusive than any that is dealt with. Nature in the barest sense is the presence and availability of complexes. It is the provision and determination of traits—providingness, if we must strengthen the emphasis, but not providence, not providentness. It provides man, for instance, with the possibilities, the circumstances, and the substance of judgment.

The concept of natural complex not only permits satisfactory generic identification; it permits various distinctions and categorizations. It encourages striving after the functions of generalizing precisely and portraying uniquely.[1] Precise generalization is twin to precise differentiation. Neither is possible alone for very long, even on the least philosophic and most highly restricted plane of investigation. But the essential philosophic direction, if not the immediate commitment of philosophic strategy, is from differentiation toward generalization; so that every triumph in the making of distinctions and the clarification of meanings becomes the greater philosophically in so far as it fortifies a conceptual structure which grounds and locates it.

So far as sheer generic breadth is concerned, "being" remains the inevitable term. So far as philosophic value is concerned, "being" and other traditional terms of generic identification, mainly "reality" and "existence," are required in certain types of context and are useful when treated with circumspection. But they suffer from many disadvantages and perplexities. Their dubious status is indicated by the ways in which they have functioned. Thus philosophers for whom "being" is central have felt constrained to inquire into its relations with "non-being" or "nothing," or into "the being belonging to nothingness." Other philosophers have allowed the presence of discriminanda to which, not the term "reality" but actually the term "unreality" is applied. They have supported the notion that there are "degrees" of being and "degrees" of reality. Sometimes they have made "existence" synonymous with "being" or with "reality," and sometimes they have given it narrower scope, identifying it with that which is spatio-temporal or that which is temporal. For the most part, philosophers have not known how they should use "existence" *or* "being" *or* "reality" when confronted by problems concerning, for example, the relation between possibility and actuality. Many philosophers weaken the force of their ideas by this helplessness. A striking instance is G. H. Mead's allusion to "reality" as "existing": "reality exists in a present." The colloquial charity that is apparently expected or taken for granted does not condone the careless poverty of the usage. Nor is the usage without equally bad offspring. The present is said to be the "locus of reality," its "seat." [2]

The difficulties besetting the traditional terms of generic identification are the more evident when these terms are employed for instantial discriminations, singular or plural. No matter what it may be that is discriminated, we shall always find it expedient and desirable to call it "a" natural complex. But if we had to rely upon historical as well as twentieth-century ontological usage, we should surely hesitate to say that any one of the expressions "*a* being," "*an* entity," "*a* reality," "*an* existence" is applicable to every conceivable discriminandum. There is even a peculiar disparity in traditional habits of formulation, consisting on the one hand in a willingness to say that whatever is discriminable "has some kind of being," and on the other hand in an unwillingness to say that whatever is discriminable is "a being." There is also considerable awkwardness in the use of the plural terms "beings," "realities," "existences." The metaphysical applicability of all three is severely hindered by moral associations; that is, by associations which interfere with the desirable level of generality. Difficulties also beset the more colloquial terms that are widely used by philosophers for generic allusions—terms such as "things" and "objects." These are poor and clumsy when applied, say, to relations or laws.

One of the principal advantages of "natural complex" is an implication inherent in the uses of the term, namely, that every discriminandum whatever offers a prospect for query.[3] Some philosophers, whether enamored of ready-made standards or devoted to the ideal of calling a spade a spade, seem to distrust the very idea of complexity. But in the most fundamental sense, complexity implies the likelihood of access, and this means continuing experience and query. A further implication of the idea of complexity will here be defended with concepts deemed best for this defense, the implication that the traits of any complex can never be regarded as fully and finally ascertained or completely circumscribed. A complex, if it is accessible at all, is analyzable and interpretable without end; or to speak in a more generic way, is manipulatable in an indefinite number of orders.

II

The term "natural complex" is not set up to be contrasted with "non-natural" or "supernatural" complex. The latter terms are made possible, as terms, by the procedures of logic and the properties of grammar; but they represent nothing discriminable that is not continuous with all other discriminanda and all other processes of discrimination. When the term "complex of nature" is used instead of "natural complex," the impulse to ask whether there are complexes of an opposite kind is perhaps less likely to arise. Linguistic habits do not favor "Are there complexes of non-nature? " If the concept of God is thought of as viable metaphysically, and not blankly endured as a stimulus to animism, it must signify a natural complex. Nothing jeopardizes the strong uniqueness of this complex. Historically and persistently, there attaches to it a customary formal scheme of traits. This scheme, adhered to in its essentials by widely differing philosophers, serves to maintain a level of gravity and primacy for the idea of God. It predetermines the complex to be interpreted, however different the interpretations otherwise may be. It provides the "rules" with which all versions are to accord. Thus men have recognized in effect that to God belongs great pervasiveness, inexhaustible value as a paradigm, symbolic richness, "supremacy." Such traits prescribe the sphere of relevance, the formula as it were, for ceaseless translation of the idea. Translation presupposes an "original"; so that when a philosopher wishes to use and adapt the concept of God, but fails to grasp the sense of the schematic requirement and fails to grasp the compulsion behind it, he achieves not the metaphysical or poetic perception he might have sought, but a somewhat hollow categorial freedom.

Even as echoed by men without the power of translation, the guiding scheme of traits is too constant, too substantial, to permit for the conception of God any specific or dominant role, its metaphysical character forever warring with the confusions of classic anthropomorphism. It threatens always to expose the insidiously comic aspects of that which is cast as father, judge, chief, even "creator." The persistence of the scheme mirrors a difficult, unresolved union of natural (though not universal) discriminations: of that which is always present yet always dark; of unaccountable imbalance, dissonance, and hunger; of perfection, remoteness, inevitability, mystery. That God should have been delineated, historically, in terms of vulgar finite analogies is in itself a kind of natural irony, though not an absurdity, seeing that analogies of one kind and another are native to the texture of speculation.

If God were understood in part as that complex of nature which preserves overwhelming contrast with the finite, then to God might be ascribed perpetual consummations of a related kind—delimiting all other complexes, opening human ways beyond prevailing limits, and constantly renewing in the experiential orders of the world (in the perspectives of man) that sensitivity to the similar and the different which lies at the base of query. The expression "God willing" is a recognition that the traits, the boundaries, that prevail or arise, govern the life of man. Limitation and situation give birth to the conative forces of overcoming, aspiring. The principle that there always are questions beyond the questions that have been asked, and complexes beyond and within the complexes that are known, besides being defensible as such, preserves the momentum of life and query. At least for man, absolute delimitation—perfect boundaries, incorrigible knowledge, total freedom from indecision (which is freedom from decision)—would be death.

The question whether God "exists" or does not is a symptom of deficiency in the categorial equipment of a metaphysics. The use of "exist" in such a context tacitly shapes a crude conception of the subject-matter under debate. In the metaphysics of natural complexes it could be said that God prevails, not for this reason or that, but because God is a complex discriminated, and every complex prevails, each in its own way, whether as myth, historical event, symbol, or force; whether as actuality or possibility. The critical question must be, not whether God exists, nor whether there is an "entity" which satisfies the scheme of traits by which the concept of God is perpetuated, but in what way a natural complex thus discriminated is to be understood, analyzed, and experientially encompassed; or, in what way it is to be further discriminated and found related.

By the same standard, to describe metaphysics as inquiry into "generic traits of existence" is unacceptable. "Existence" itself is too problematical, and not generic enough to be taken as the base.[4] Seldom is it realized or even observed that one function of an adequate category is to provide a just basis for distinctions, and not to blanket or transcend them. It is when deliberately wrought categories are eschewed, and terms like "exist" are applied indifferently, for instance to relations, concepts, possibilities, or physical bodies, that the distinctions among these complexes are ignored and suppressed. Nor will it do for a philosopher to say that he simply is not interested in a single concept applicable to all that is discerned. What happens in such a disavowal is that a term serving this function *is* actually used—say "entity," "existence," "thing"—but used informally, and without a rationale; and when several terms are used instead of one, there is the same lack of interest in their basic differentiae as there is in their possible subsumption under a term that is comprehensive.

Whatever the traits of God, then, God is a complex which various philosophers methodically discriminate and to which they variously assign a scope. To reject this way of approaching the issue is, of course, to render "natural complex" ineligible as the term for universal identification. The historic lack of a single and sufficiently versatile term has helped to encourage the suspicion of radical discontinuity in nature and has even seemed to vindicate periodic appeal to "the inexplicable." Far more commonly than the history of philosophic thought reveals or concedes, miracle implicitly functions as a basic category or as an extra-systemic bulwark. By many philosophers nature is regarded as the realm of the regular and even of the rightful, sometimes tarnished by the devilish and the "unnatural," too poor to contain deity and mystery, but pointing to these heights, and sporadically illuminated and mended in a way that passes understanding.

The "unnatural" that has been bequeathed by philosophic tradition to everyday discourse is not the non-natural, whatever that would be, but a natural complex which is *(a)* irregular in the sense that it does not obtain "for the most part," and *(b)* uncongenial to common standards of morality or taste. It is thus the irregular in both a statistical and a cultural sense.

"Natural complex" and "human complex," though they stand to each other as genus and species, are so immeasurably different in scope, that they oppose each other in a stubborn kind of way. Nothing is more customary philosophically than the phrases "nature and man" and "nature and art." These contrasts usually do not suggest a gulf that requires belief in absolute discontinuity and inexplicability. They aim to distinguish two orders, even if one is included in the other, and they suggest corollary distinctions bearing on the human process. Most doctrines of inexplicability betray theoretical fatigue. Man, like God, is interpretable through the most fundamental categories that philosophy can devise. Neither owns an ontological domicile. Of course, nobody feels obliged to prove "the existence of man." But both complexes are primal discriminations. They spread wonder, and not of the philosophic kind alone. When their ramifications are pursued they are found, as all complexes are, to harbor both actuality and possibility. Actuality and possibility alike feed wonder, which manifests itself variously, for instance in horror or elation.

Notes

[1] Conceptual portrayal is part of the exhibitive function of philosophy, as distinguished from the assertive function. Philosophic method is discussed in each of the three predecessors of the present book, *The Concept of Method* (1961), *Nature and Judgment* (1955), *Toward a General Theory of Human Judgment* (1951).

[2] G. H. Mead, *The Philosophy of the Present,* ed. A. E. Murphy (LaSalle, Ill.: Open Court, 1932), p. 1.

[3] Methodic activity is the purposive ramification of judgment in any of its modes — assertive, active, exhibitive. When methodic activity is informed by the interrogative spirit, by invention and probing, it constitutes *query.* Query is the genus of which inquiry or science is one species — the species concerned with the ramification and validation of assertive judgment. See *The Concept of Method,* passim; *Nature and Judgment,* chapter 2; and *Toward a General Theory of Human Judgment,* passim.

[4] Quite apart from the definition of metaphysics, there are champions of the term "existence" who consider it adequate and versatile enough. W. V. Quine, for example, derides "those philosophers who have united in ruining the good old word 'exist.'" See his *From a Logical Point of View,* rev. ed. (Cambridge: Harvard University Press, 1961), p. 3.

PAUL WEISS

PRIVACY*

I

Considerable emphasis in the intellectual world today is placed on attempts to understand what is familiar, experienced, or complex in terms of simpler, more precisely characterized units. When these are treated as alone real, as the necessary predecessors or sources of the complexes, or are supposed to provide exhaustive explanations for whatever else occurs, an attitude, which can ground brilliantly successful investigations of great daring, becomes rigidified. The result is a reductionism in which the originally acknowledged items no longer have any role. Five forms are current.

   a. *Physical.* Physical reductionism is perhaps the oldest and the most widely accepted of all. It is to be found in pre-Socratic Greece and at the center of modern science, from its Galilean beginnings until today. More resolutely and precisely than other reductionisms do, it reduces its rivals as well as the objects of daily life. Accepting as correct the reduction of man and other living beings to biological units, and the reduction of these to chemical units, it goes on to hold that these are nothing more

---

* Paul Weiss, *Privacy* (Carbondale: Southern Illinois University Press, 1983), pp. 1–16. Reprinted by permission of Southern Illinois University Press.

than combinations of physical entities—particles, waves, or combinations of these. . . .

b. *Technological.* The most popular of reductionisms today is the technological, the attempt to understand all gross and some subtler occurrences in terms of the activities of machines. Today, the machine to which reference is usually made is the computer, an agency by which open and shut circuits follow one another in rapid order, and whose outcomes can be expressed in conventional numbers and eventually in conventional language. At a speed previously unknown, a computer can carry out a very complicated and sophisticated program and do it accurately.

If one supposes that a mind is a brain and that a brain is a computer, one is ready to speak as though whatever was known or knowable was the work of a computer. . . .

c. *Biological.* Biological reductionists resist the trend to speak of men and other living beings as though they were sums of ultimate units, or were kinds of machines. They are neo-Darwinians, convinced that mankind had an animal origin, and that man differs from all other living beings only in degree. That difference in degree, it is allowed, may be enough to make possible the production of tools and eventually of complicated machines, and the creation of language, society, the arts, and sciences. It might be conceded that some of these have natures, careers, and consequences which cannot be given a biological meaning—but only if one also abandons the idea that the living body is the only source and offers a complete explanation of what is and of what is done.

Men, in this reductionistic view, are held to be nothing other than living bodies whose differences in degree do not stand in the way of understanding them fully as subject to laws governing bodies, and as having constituents like those possessed by other living beings. . . .

d. *Psychological.* The history of psychology has been characterized as one in which it first lost its soul, then its mind, and subsequently its consciousness. Later it became irritable. Now it is reactionary. The last is the status enjoyed by a dominant school, behaviorism. Eschewing all attempts to speak of what goes on in a 'black box' or a supposed mind, it attends solely to reinforcements of activities by rewarding those that the experimenter endorses, and by punishing or refraining from rewarding those that he wants not to recur. The view seeks to state in as precise and predictable a manner as possible just how reinforcements are to be administered in order to achieve desired results most efficiently. It has proved to be an effective device for training stupid animals and birds; these have been made to engage in odd behaviors, quite different from anything they might otherwise do, solely by having their accidental moves reinforced again and again. . . .

e. *Linguistic.* There is a large segment of the Anglo-Saxon philosophical community which has taken its stand with linguistic reductionism, the attempt to understand everything in terms of language. For some, the language is that of logic, mathematics, or science; for others, it is the language of a society; for still others, it is an idealized language constructed to accord with the needs of a theory of knowledge, observation, or commonsense. Starting with the idea that all that is left of a distinction between men and animals is the possession of a mind by the former (Descartes' thesis), they accept the reduction of that mind to the status of a feeling of pain or pleasure, and then the reduction of this to a viable report that a pain or pleasure is being undergone. As a consequence, these thinkers find themselves left with nothing but words or sentences which they interchange. Or, starting with the idea that what is well-expressed in mathematical or logical terms or which is in accord with the most recent theories of science alone is intelligible or reliable, they find themselves unable to justify the claim that there is something to which the expressions refer. All are therefore left facing 'the problem of reference', the problem of how they could make contact with something to which some expressions in language supposedly lead us. . . .

Reductionisms are parasitical on the data, observations, and confirmations of what they had presumably replaced. They presuppose that there are men who use their bodies as agencies for the realization of prospects which may have no bodily value. Each is offered as a truth for others to accept as a truth. All exist only so far as they at least tacitly cling to what was supposedly reduced, if only to provide the reductionists with a world in which they too can live and where their reduction can have a heuristic role.

References to reductionism will crop up again and again throughout this work. It will be faced with the fact that we already know more than any reductionism allows. Without this more no reductionism would be possible. One of the things we know is that men live their bodies to realize prospects not within the purview, and outside the reach of physics, technology, biology, psychology, or language.

II

A well-entrenched, non-reductionist method for learning about men begins with the supposition that each man has a sure knowledge of himself, acquired through observation or introspection, or by supplementing and correcting the one by the other. When the result is taken by one man to apply to all the rest with only the changes that are needed to accommodate differences in opportunity, genesis, experience, and habit, a touch of arrogance and condescension will usually taint the conclusions. Left unexamined will be what is unimportant for that individual, though perhaps of considerable importance to others.

To avoid just supposing that others are like what one takes oneself to be, it is desirable to attend to what other men—and therefore oneself as well—publicly show themselves to be. If it is possible to then extricate evidence of the existence of powers present in any man, it will be possible to learn about the nature of human privacy. Different kinds of evidence will enable one to remark on the main divisions of that privacy, and to expose the differences they make to the body and the world. Evidences are continuous with their sources. To be acquainted with the one is already to be in contact with the other, and in a position to make an intensive, convergent, insistent further move into the sources as not yet expressed.

Our enterprise will go astray if it fails to take account of the fact that there are a number of living and non-living actualities, quite different in nature and activity from man, existing alongside, affecting, and being used by him. Though distinctive in nature, power, promise, and achievement, man is still but one kind of being among many.

There is a single public world occupied by men and other actualities because their expressions are countered by and united with universal conditions, themselves expressions of ubiquitous realities—'finalities,' I call them. The expressions of the actualities, and the conditions expressing the finalities, together constitute a single world of objective appearances. It is these which we daily face, but never as entirely separated from the actualities and the finalities. The constituents of appearances are actualities and finalities in attenuated forms, limiting and interplaying with one another.

One cannot, I think, avoid the acknowledgement of these two types of reality, one actual, limited, individual, and governed, the other final and persistent. The actualities resist one another and express themselves in opposition to conditions, themselves expressing and empowered by the finalities. I was not always aware of the fact. In my first book, *Reality,* I made a strenuous effort to present a naturalistic metaphysics which acknowledged only actualities. But the more I reflected on the view, the more evident it became that it could not be maintained. It did not and could not provide a warrant for its admission that actualities are together in a common space and time, able to act on one another. It was unable to explain how complex entities could arise, have distinctive natures, and function as single units. Nor did it or could it account for the future and the role this played in the present, and therefore for the difference that prospects, objectives, goals, and ends make to what is directed toward and occupied with realizing these. A view which affirms that there are actualities must sooner or later also affirm that there are finalities, different in range and kind, effectively conditioning those actualities and their expressions.

Were final realities all-powerful, or were they alone ultimately and irreducibly real, actualities would at best be offshoots, faint copies, or subdivisions of them. Were actualities all-powerful, or were they alone ultimate, there would be no power able to condition them. Laws, space, and time would then have to be treated as abstractions from the actualities, or as illusory. But were they abstractions, they would not make it possible for anything to be with anything else. And if they were illusions, actualities would not be governed by a common rationale, and would not be spatially distant from one another. Nor would any really come to be earlier or later than others.

Both finalities and actualities must be acknowledged. Nothing less than a knowledge of how they interplay through their expressions will account for the world we daily know and in which we daily live—the 'mixed' Plato called it—unless that world is necessarily without explanation, does not exist at all, or alone is real. The presence of evidence defeats the first of these suggestions; the claim itself defeats the second; while our decisions, the resistance our efforts encounter when we act, and common conditions, such as laws, space, and time, which encompass all actualities, defeat the third. The daily world is the product of the interplay of diverse realities distinct from it.

To remain with the mixed is to remain with what is confused, somewhat unintelligible, and overrun with contingency. The situation can be dealt with in at least four ways. With some phenomenologists, we may be content to describe it. With the 'soft sciences,' sociology particularly, we can try to reorganize it with the help of statistics. With the 'hard sciences,' particularly theoretical physics, we can look for highly general structures which all items instance. Or, with metaphysicians, we can try to get to the ultimate sources of the constituents of the mixed. The last is what I ventured in other places. The outcome provides a background for the present attempt to focus on the actuality, man, with a special emphasis on what he is privately. Though one need not attend to that background in order to understand man, it is surely presupposed in this as well as in any other effort that might be made to provide a justifiable, systematic characterization of him or any other actuality.

Because a resolute philosophic study seeks to know what is presupposed by every occurrence in the daily world and in the cosmos; what accounts for appearances, both those that mislead and those that do not; what the final conditioning realities are like and how they act; what actualities are, what they can do, and how the main kinds differ from one another; what human beings are, severally and together; because it takes seriously the existence of ultimate units, complexities of all sorts, inanimate and animate; and because it seeks to understand man both in his individual privacy and as a being together with others in a common world, it can to no less than acknowledge that the two distinct kinds of irreducible reality, actualities and finalities, are exhibited in a number of independent ways.

Like the hard sciences, philosophy is not content to describe, to classify, or to reorganize. What it seeks are the sources of those factors that constitute and explain what is daily encountered. With the soft sciences, it refuses to treat compounds, thoughts, responsibilities, and societies as non-existents, or as being beyond all knowing or understanding. It sees that these, though not ultimately real in the sense in which actualities and finalities are, have their own integrities and careers and that a view, which has no place for them and their properties and functions, has no place for what men are and do, and for the ways they in fact live together.

Hypotheses, formulae, and limited, local conditions apply to a number of actualities. None tells whether or not, apart from it, actualities are together, or how. Nor can we learn from a study of the way in which actualities are together how they originate or what kinds of groups they form.

We can learn about the nature of the finalities which empower conditions that relate all actualities, about the nature of actualities, and about the outcome of the meshing of the expressions of actualities with the expressions of finalities. We can also learn about the nature of privacy and its epitomizations, both those which do and those which do not achieve a bodily guise and, of course, that portion of them which, though not manifested, is continuous with what is being manifested. The knowledge we seek becomes available once we separate out the contributions that men and other actualities make to what appears, and use the result as the beginning of a move into their sources.

We seem unable to use evidences to get far into inanimate beings. Occasionally, it is possible to make sympathetic contact with some of the higher animals and to then understand the nature of their privacies by discovering what could have made the evidences available. We can do better with men. Not only is it possible for us to sympathize with humans more deeply than we can with animals, but it is possible to begin with evidences available in what men publicly are and do, and to proceed intellectually with considerable surety toward what sympathy had impinged upon. The intellectual adventure follows the same route that sympathy traverses, but moves more cautiously, arriving only at what might be a source in animals, and what is close to a source in men.

The privacy of animals, though never without a bodily form, is too indeterminate to enable one to make it intelligible without introducing illegitimate additions, but the privacy of a man is available to a thinking which proceeds convergently and intensively toward the source of what he exhibits. At both times, it is necessary to distinguish a publicly presented content from what sustains this; to extricate the distinguished item; to recognize the relation that the evidence has to its origin; to have one's thoughts follow the course of the relation; and, finally, to attend to what is not manifested bodily.

Supplementing an earlier study of the finalities as lying beyond and grounding what conditions actualities, the present work places its stress on the private origins of what men bodily express. Occupied initially with the distinguishing of the required evidences, it then makes use of them to promote the understanding of the nature and activity of human privacy and of its epitomizations. Man, it makes apparent, has a distinctive privacy specialized in a person and a self, able to function apart from the body, and epitomized in multiple ways. That privacy and its epitomizations lie behind and make possible sensitivity, desire, and other ways in which men express themselves in and through their bodies.

The private control man exercises stands athwart attempts to understand him solely in terms of genes, brains, behavior, or language—or other efforts to treat him as though he were wholly public. Such endeavors are self-annihilating, presupposing as they do the presence and activity of complex unified men who privately formulate the theories, cling to them, and urge their acceptance by others who are also exercising their privacies in acts of thinking and deciding.

Privately produced claims sustain the affirmations that public occurrences are or are not present. The theory that the occurrences are the counterparts, accompaniments, duplicates, causes, or criteria of what is private, refers to such occurrences from a private position. Replacements of what is private by what is public, denials that there is anything private, and claims that what is private is unintelligible or unavailable, are all privately produced and sustained.

What is observed could not warrantedly serve as a substitute for what was supposedly being privately undergone if it was not in fact relevant to the pains, fears, hopes, and thoughts which were to be replaced. If these were absent, we could not find out whether or not the chosen public occurrence was a proper substitute. No one knows whether or not this or that bodily occurrence in another is the right replacement or counterpart of what is privately undergone by him, except by engaging in a private act and looking to that other for confirmation that one has made the correct identification. What we can know of others is rooted in what is publicly available, but this is not yet to say that it was not made available by a privacy, or that it could be separated from this.

Conceivably, every one of a man's thoughts, beliefs, memories, fears, hopes, and fantasies might have a public form, enabling one to read off what had been privately entertained. Although there does not seem to be a good warrant for holding that this supposition answers to the facts, let it be granted. One could then suppose that a man expresses his privacy in an otherwise neutral body. His *lived* body—the body he privately possesses, governs, and acts on and through—could then be said to be produced by his imposing that privacy on what is understandable in terms applicable to all bodies. On the hypothesis, the result could not tell us what had been uniquely and privately begun and, therefore, what was transformed in the course of expressing it and giving it a publicly observable form. To understand men, we must be able to refer to what is not duplicated, and that requires us to move intensively and convergently toward the singular private origins of whatever was bodily manifested by them.

A man's body makes a difference to what he uniquely intrudes on it from his privacy. Sometimes his body overwhelms or obscures what intrudes on it, but it never converts the intruded into just a public occurrence. That is why it is possible to extricate evidence of an act that was privately begun and carried out. The setting in which a private expression is imbedded can be understood in universal objective terms, appropriate to any public occurrence, but that setting is quickened and enriched by an unduplicable insistence which originates in and remains continuous with what is unduplicable and unitary, not yet in any setting.

There are publicly available evidences that a man has a privacy and that this is specialized in a number of distinguishable ways. But the discovery of the evidences, the separating of them out of the mixed and from their public, bodily settings, the use of them, and the grasp of what they terminate in, is so difficult that one is readily tempted to slip over the fact that the evidences can be found and used, and to be content to acknowledge only what can be publicly observed. This would not justify the claim that all one can or need know—or only the reputable, intelligible, or verifiable—is what is common and expressible in either formal or public terms. It is not wise to privately think and decide that all that is or can be known is entirely public.

Beings are and do what they are then able to be and do. They have careers because they can still be and do what they then are not able to be and do. And, so far as there is a possibly more developed stage which they can attain, they are inseparable from the promise of this, making them quite different in kind from any other being which lacks such a promise. Even if there were nothing that an infant could do that was not duplicable by an animal, it still would not be possible to equate the two, for the infant, but not the animal, has a promise to be a child. An infant, consequently, is always more than just an infant. Able to be a child, it has a promise to be one, and is so far more than what it actually is. It is not then able to be a mature man. Only a youth has that promise, and then only because he realized a promise possessed by himself as a child and, in that act, acquired the promise to become a mature man. The promises are all partial determinations of a single constant privacy.

Because there is only one privacy from the beginning to the end of life, a mature man is necessarily the same being who was once an embryo. Over the course of his life, though his privacy remains self-same, the area of its indeterminacy is narrowed. As he develops, part of his indeterminate privacy is specialized in the form of person and self and their epitomizations, each with it own distinctive promise. His maturity is measured by a realization of a succession of instituted and realized promises, each originating with and sustained by a realized, preceding promise.

An infant's epitomizations use only a very limited portion of its privacy. It makes a part of the rest of its privacy partially determinate in the form of a promise whose realization brings it to the stage of childhood. The realization of its promise is not sudden; there is no jumping from one stage to the next. But once a promise is realized, there is an epitomization of privacy that had not been and could not have been present before. The new epitomization makes a difference to the epitomizations that had been realized earlier and are now exercised together with what is newly produced, affecting it and thereby making it be and act as it could not before.

Because a realized promise makes a difference to what had been realized earlier, the presence of those earlier epitomizations in a more developed being are not equatable with what they were at an earlier stage. A child's sensitivity is different from the sensitivity of an infant, for the child has made determinate what was only promissory in the infant, thereby making a difference to the functioning of the sensitivity that had been present in the infant. The infant's pain, consequently, is not only different from the pain undergone by anything non-human, but is not equatable with the pain of a child. Related observations apply to a youth and adult, and finally to a mature man, able to become a full member of a civilized world.

ROBERT C. NEVILLE

A METAPHYSICS OF VALUE*

Whereas cosmology deals with the generic traits of this world, metaphysics has been described as the study of the traits that would be exemplified in any possible world.[1] A preferable characterization is that metaphysics is the study of determinateness: any world would have to have some identity, and identity is being determinately one character rather than something else. The features that accrue to determinateness can be called transcendental in keeping with Western medieval usage; they must be exhibited in any determination. Vagueness is an attribute of cosmology and of metaphysics as well; in fact, cosmology is a specification of metaphysics to the traits of *this* world. Although some contemporary philosophers use the word *ontology* to mean study of the basic kinds of existence, here that study is covered by the terms *metaphysics* and *cosmology*. Thus, *ontology* can be reserved for its older meaning—the study of why anything determinate exists. The question of value, as conceived of here, is metaphysical because it is a transcendental property of anything determinate.

This use of "transcendental" differs from that common in contemporary philosophy, which derives from Immanuel Kant. For Kant, the

* Robert C. Neville, "A Metaphysics of Value," in *Reconstruction of Thinking* (Albany: State University of New York Press, 1981), pp. 79–85. Reprinted by permission of the State University of New York Press and the author.

chief problem of knowledge was whether the thinking of a subject could include necessary knowledge of external objects. If the object is external in the sense that it transcends experience, then knowledge of it is "transcendent," and Kant said we have no such knowledge. However, if the object conforms to the conditions for entering experience, and if we know those conditions, we can know the object as appearance through those conditions. Kant used the word "transcendental" (not "transcendent") to describe the conditions for an object's appearing in experience. The study of those conditions is transcendental philosophy.[2] There is no necessity, however, to share Kant's assumption about the privacy of thinking and the consequent transcendent character of external objects.[3] Rather, objects are external and objective but naturally available to enter the experience of knowers. Metaphysics proceeds through dialectical reflection on how things must be in order to have determinate character (this is not to suggest that determinate things are determinate in all respects).

As a preliminary consideration it may be observed that any determinate thing must be complex. It must contain some conditional features by virtue of which it is related to and different from other things; it must also contain essential features by which it has its own perspective in terms of which it can be different. Without conditional features the thing could never be "this" rather than "that"; part of being determinate is having some kind of otherness as a constituent part of the determinate character. Without essential features it would be impossible for the thing to have the self-standing by which it could be *other*.[4] Since metaphysical claims should be specifiable in any possible world, they may be made plausible by specification to an Aristotelian cosmology as well as to the axiological cosmology. In Aristotle, the essence in the formal cause of a substance constitutes its essential features, whereas the material, efficient, and final causes are the conditional features. Only because the material, final, and efficient causes connect the substance with other substances does its formal cause have to be expressed in a way that relates to other substances. By contrast, in the axiological cosmology, feelings of past occasions are the conditional features, and the contributions of the feeling occasion to the integration of what it feels are its essential features.

The complex of conditional and essential features is a harmony, whether it be the substantial harmony of an Aristotelian substance or the physical objectification of a processive occasion. The harmony integrates not only the conditional and the essential features, but also the conditional features with each other and the essential features with each other. A harmony is an *achievement* of having things together which would be separate without the harmony, or which would be together in a different way with another harmony. This achievement is a value. If the harmony is achieved without loss of the achievements of otherwise separate components, it is a net gain. (For reasons to be discussed, it is a matter of indifference here whether the net gain is a gain in reality or a gain in value.)

Is not a harmony a value, however, in a stronger sense than merely achieving additional togetherness? Is it not part of our common aesthetic sense that a harmony is *good,* all else being equal? Furthermore, do we not say that an arrangement of things is better if it is more harmonious? The greater the harmony, the greater the value. The argument here is an appeal to our common experience of responding to perceived harmonies. It makes sense to think "the greater the harmony, the better" only when one can imagine an alternate way by which a comparable set of components might be harmonized with greater or lesser harmony. Perhaps few things have alternate ways in which they can be harmonized, and probably we fail to imagine most that can be. However, the value that is appreciable in a harmony about which we can think of greater or lesser alternative harmonies, is also appreciable in a harmony without alternatives. In that case, appreciation is not *e*valuative in the sense of being compared with imagined alternatives; it is valuative. We may neglect noting that our response is valuative, because that noting is a further interpretation beyond the direct appreciation.

What are the factors in harmony determining why some ways of harmonizing components are more harmonious than others? [5] There are two principal factors in the structure of a harmony—complexity and simplicity. Complexity is the diversity of kinds of things included within the harmony; it is subject to degrees, and the minimal degree is homogeneity. Simplicity is the character of organization within the harmony whereby the togetherness of components constitutes a new reality within which the components are harmonized. Observed from the standpoint of the new reality, simplicity is the character by which the highest integrating principle contains or generates the multitude of components. There may be many levels in a harmony, each creating new realities that enter as components in yet higher realities. Simplicity, too, is subject to degrees, and the minimal degree is conjunction. A harmony is more harmonious to the degree that both its complexity and its simplicity are increased. A high degree of complexity and a low degree of simplicity would yield a low-level harmony of diverse things integrated merely by conjunction, with little difference being made to the components by virtue of their togetherness. A high degree of simplicity with a low degree of complexity would yield great self-reflection or self-reference but dull homogeneity. The structure of any harmony exhibits a certain degree of complexity and a certain degree of simplicity. Is it true that when we imagine better and worse ways of harmonizing the components of a harmony, we do so by imagining alterations in either complexity—removing or adding certain kinds of components—or simplicity—altering the ordering principles so that components are removed from relation to or brought into new relations with each other?

This discussion employs a distinction between the de facto harmony of a thing, imagined alternate harmonies, and ideal harmonies. The de facto harmony is the nature of the complex as it is. The imagined alternatives are ideas about alternate harmonies, although as products of the imagination they are highly abstract. An imagined harmony is an alternative only to certain abstract features of a concrete thing, unless the de facto harmony in question is itself abstract—as, for instance, a theory is. An ideal harmony is a maximal way of harmonizing the components. Whether or not the ideal harmony is imagined depends on the cleverness of the imagination. Presumably most ideal harmonies are glimpsed abstractly and at a confusing distance. That there are maximal ways of harmonizing components is presupposed by the fact that there are degrees of harmony. There need not be only one maximal harmony, however, since there may be many variations in complexity and simplicity that are merely trade-offs with the intensity of harmony. Thus, many equally good ideals may exist for a given set of components.

We must be careful to distinguish between a real ideal harmony and a conception of that ideal. In common speech, frequently we mean the *conception* when we speak of ideals. To prevent this confusion, a more technical term may be introduced for the real ideal harmony. As Plato did in the *Statesman,* we may call real ideal harmonies "normative measures." This phrase points out that the ideal is a normative way of measuring the components of a harmony. In Plato's discussion, normative measures are not so much objects of thought as "knacks" that good statesmen have for harmonizing the components of the state.

A normative measure takes its form from the manifold it is to measure, from the set of components it harmonizes maximally. Without components to harmonize, the normative measure would not be constrained to have one structure rather than another. A normative measure, therefore, presupposes the plurality of an actual world to which it is relevant. Whitehead hypothesized a realm of universal forms apart from occasions; these forms are "eternal objects" and constitute the possibilities for structuring the actual occasions. However, his theory of eternal objects is inconsistent with axiological cosmology, not only in failing to emphasize the normative character of the objects (except insofar as they are subjectively aimed at), but also in attributing to them prior reality independent of the actual world. Whitehead said that the eternal objects are, in themselves, indeterminate; this suggests that they are nothing. Whitehead also said they achieve determinateness by being graded in the divine mind. Yet what would God have to grade if they were intrinsically indeterminate? If all determinateness comes from God, why not say God creates the determinate eternal objects? [6] Even this would suppose that the eternal objects gain their determinateness solely with reference to each other. Although this might be a possible world, from our cosmological perspective it seems simpler to say that eternal objects are merely normative measures which take their form from measuring the actual components presented, and from the natures that each of the other eternal objects has by its own measuring of actual data.

Plato and Whitehead were both correct in noting that normative measures are, in a sense, eternal. The intrinsic relationship normative measures bear to the passing flow of actual things is to be normative—that is, ideal—for them. Whether a normative measure is, in fact, actualized depends on various cosmological causal factors and does not affect the "eternal" fact that it is ideal or normative for the things to which it is relevant. Whether a normative measure is *relevant* to the world is a temporal factor, because relevance depends on the existence of those things for which it is the measure. But it is eternally true that for certain components, this measure is a normative harmony.

Conceiving of normative measures in relation to the changing world is an extraordinarily complex problem. Alternate harmonies are discussed above for a *given* set of components. Yet what determines the membership of a given set? In certain moral situations some definite set of components may be specified as given. But in trying to imagine what the normative measure for a situation might be, it must be remembered that one way to vary a harmony is to vary its complexity; this means that harmonies differ by what they include or leave out. A major question in deliberating about normative measures, therefore, is how to group components so that this or that normative measure is relevant. Because of the eternality of the normativeness of these measures, however, the problem is an objective one. That is, if there are highly diverse ways of grouping the potential components for a variety of normative measures, there may be a grouping that maximizes the harmonies of all. A *concept* is a way of mentally grouping various components whose combination is valuable because of a normative measure. The "real" identity of things comes from the normative measure of which their de facto harmony is an approximation.

The metaphysical question of identity can thus be stated with respect to the notions of value involved. A thing's de facto identity is its de facto harmony. Its identity, therefore, has a de facto value, a value that is appreciated when the thing is felt. The de facto identity is intelligible only as an approximation of the structuring of the thing's components according to its normative measure. The nature of the approximation is determined by the various cosmological causes that go into its actualization; this approximation can be understood, in part, by grasping the cosmological causes. The approximation's integral nature as a harmony, however, is fully intelligible only by the reference to its normative measure. As the next section demonstrates, a description of a thing is a function not only of the values directing inquiry but also of recognizing the achieved de facto value in the thing. The difficulty in describing the actual thing lies in discerning the natural joints of what to describe—where to speak of electrons and where of tables and chairs, where to talk about historical movements within civilizations. The "where" questions are seen to depend on discerning the objective normative measures for the historical process relative to the interests of inquiry. If the world were fully rational, the normative measures of all things would be coherent in their juxtaposition, overlapping, and mutual determination; it is doubtful, however, that the world is rational.

From this highly abstract, metaphysical perspective, the falseness of a distinction between facts and values is apparent. The factual character of something is its de facto harmony, its way of embodying the normative measure in its components. The value of something is its de facto harmony considered as a harmony. The degree of its value is a function of how closely it approximates its normative measure. The degree to which its value is appreciated in an evaluative way depends on how successfully one imagines its normative measure as an ideal for comparison.

Value or goodness can be seen as a transcendental property of everything determinate. Every determinate thing has a de facto value *as* a de facto harmony. Each thing also has a real, ideal value as its normative measure; this may or may not be distinct from its de facto value. Each thing is subject to being conceived of with a value description, which relates the thing's components to its normative measure through the interests guiding inquiry. Finally, the normative measure of each thing can be described, albeit lamely, by developing an ideal construct. The ideal construct picks out from a welter of elements in process those things which are important for making certain normative measures relevant. Thinking, for instance, can be described—as it is in the next chapter—through ideal constructs in such a way that its various components are presented in relation to their normative measures. The normative measure can then be described as a norm. Each dimension of thinking—imagination, interpretation, theory, and responsibility—has different, though related, norms because they present different components as being important.

NOTES

[1] This characterization of metaphysics has been developed most fully in our time by Charles Hartshorne in his various writings. See esp. his *Creative Synthesis and Philosophic Method* (La Salle: Open Court Publishing, 1970), chap. 2.

[2] For Kant's distinction between "transcendent" and "transcendental," see *The Critique of Pure Reason*, B352f.

[3] Chapter 5 presents arguments to this effect.

[4] These highly abstract considerations are defended at length in my *God the Creator* (Chicago: University of Chicago Press, 1968), chap. 2 and Appendix.

[5] I examine this in detail in *the Cosmology of Freedom* (New Haven: Yale University Press, 1974), chap. 3. I present the thesis here only as a suggestion; later chapters develop it in an application to the concepts of thinking.

[6] See the debate between Lewis Ford and myself on this point in the *Southern Journal of Philosophy* 10, no. 1 (Spring 1972): pp. 79-86.

WILFRID SELLARS

PHILOSOPHY AND THE SCIENTIFIC IMAGE OF MAN*

I. THE PHILOSOPHICAL QUEST

The aim of philosophy, abstractly formulated, is to understand how things in the broadest possible sense of the term hang together in the broadest possible sense of the term. Under 'things in the broadest possible sense' I include such radically different items as not only 'cabbages and kings', but numbers and duties, possibilities and finger snaps, aesthetic experience and death. To achieve success in philosophy would be, to use a contemporary turn of phrase, to 'know one's way around' with respect to all these things, not in that unreflective way in which the centipede of the story knew its way around before it faced the question, 'how do I walk?', but in that reflective way which means that no intellectual holds are barred. . . .

. . . The philosopher is confronted not by one complex many-dimensional picture, the unity of which, such as it is, he must come to appreciate; but by *two* pictures of essentially the same order of complexity,

* Wilfrid Sellars, "Philosophy and the Scientific Image of Man," in *Science, Perception, and Reality* (New York: Humanities Press, 1963), pp. 1, 4–10, 18–20, 25–29, 31–34. Originally given as lectures at the University of Pittsburgh, December 1960, and published in *Frontiers of Science and Philosophy,* ed. Robert Colodny (Pittsburgh: University of Pittsburgh Press, 1962). Reprinted by permission of the University of Pittsburgh Press.

each of which purports to be a complete picture of man-in-the-world, and which, after separate scrutiny, he must fuse into one vision. Let me refer to these two perspectives, respectively, as the *manifest* and the *scientific* images of man-in-the-world. And let me explain my terms. First, by calling them images I do not mean to deny to either or both of them the status of 'reality'. I am, to use Husserl's term, 'bracketing' them, transforming them from ways of experiencing the world into objects of philosophical reflection and evaluation. The term 'image' is usefully ambiguous. On the one hand it suggests the contrast between an object, e.g. a tree, and a projection of the object on a plane, or its shadow on a wall. In this sense, an image is as much an existent as the object imaged, though, of course, it has a dependent status.

In the other sense, an 'image' is something imagined, and that which is imagined may well not exist, although the imagining of it does—in which case we can speak of the image as *merely* imaginary or unreal. But the imagined *can* exist; as when one imagines that someone is dancing in the next room, and someone is. This ambiguity enables me to imply that the philosopher is confronted by two projections of man-in-the-world on the human understanding. One of these projections I will call the manifest image, the other the scientific image. These images exist and are as much a part and parcel of the world as this platform or the Constitution of the United States. But in addition to being confronted by these images as existents, he is confronted by them as images in the sense of 'things imagined'—or, as I had better say at once, *conceived;* for I am using 'image' in this sense as a metaphor for conception, and it is a familiar fact that not everything that can be conceived can, in the ordinary sense, be imagined. The philosopher, then, is confronted by two conceptions, equally public, equally non-arbitrary, of man-in-the-world and he cannot shirk the attempt to see how they fall together in one stereoscopic view. . . .

II. THE MANIFEST IMAGE

The 'manifest' image of man-in-the-world can be characterized in two ways, which are supplementary rather than alternative. It is, first, the framework in terms of which man came to be aware of himself as man-in-the-world. It is the framework in terms of which, to use an existentialist turn of phrase, man first encountered himself—which is, of course, when he came to be man. For it is no merely incidental feature of man that he has a conception of himself as man-in-the-world, just as it is obvious, on reflection, that 'if man had a radically different conception of himself he would be a radically different kind of man'.

Now the manifest image is important for our purpose, because it defines one of the poles to which philosophical reflection has been drawn.

It is not only the great speculative systems of ancient and medieval philosophy which are built around the manifest image, but also many systems and quasi-systems in recent and contemporary thought, some of which seem at first sight to have little if anything in common with the great classical systems. That I include the major schools of contemporary Continental thought might be expected. That I lump in with these the trends of contemporary British and American philosophy which emphasize the analysis of 'common sense' and 'ordinary usage', may be somewhat more surprising. Yet this kinship is becoming increasingly apparent in recent years and I believe that the distinctions that I am drawing in this chapter will make possible an understanding and interpretation of this kinship. For all these philosophies can, I believe, be fruitfully construed as more or less adequate accounts of the manifest image of man-in-the-world, which accounts are then taken to be an adequate and full description in general terms of what man and the world really are. . . .

A fundamental question with respect to any conceptual framework is 'of what sort are the basic objects of the framework?' This question involves, on the one hand, the contrast between an object and what can be true of it in the way of properties, relations, and activities; and, on the other, a contrast between the basic objects of the framework and the various kinds of groups they can compose. The basic objects of a framework need not be things in the restricted sense of perceptible physical objects. Thus, the basic objects of current theoretical physics are notoriously imperceptible and unimaginable. Their basic-ness consists in the fact that they are not properties or groupings of anything more basic (at least until further notice). The questions, 'are the basic objects of the framework of physical theory *thing-like?* and if so, to what extent?' are meaningful ones.

Now to ask, 'what are the basic objects of a (given) framework?' is to ask not for a *list,* but a *classification.* And the classification will be more or less 'abstract' depending on what the purpose of the inquiry is. The philosopher is interested in a classification which is abstract enough to provide a synoptic view of the contents of the framework but which falls short of simply referring to them as objects or entities. Thus we are approaching an answer to the question, 'what are the basic objects of the manifest image?' when we say that it includes persons, animals, lower forms of life and 'merely material' things, like rivers and stones. The list is not intended to be complete, although it is intended to echo the lower stages of the 'great chain of being' of the Platonic tradition.

The first point I wish to make is that there is an important sense in which the primary objects of the manifest image are *persons.* And to understand how this is so, is to understand central and, indeed, crucial themes in the history of philosophy. Perhaps the best way to make the point is to refer back to the construct which we called the 'original' image of man-in-the-world, and characterize it as a framework in which *all* the 'objects' are persons. From this point of view, the refinement of the 'original' image into the manifest image, is the gradual 'de-personalization' of objects other than persons. That something like this has occurred with the advance of civilization is a familiar fact. Even persons, it is said (mistakenly, I believe), are being 'depersonalized' by the advance of the scientific point of view. . . .

My primary concern in this essay is with the question, 'in what sense, and to what extent, does the manifest image of man-in-the-world survive the attempt to unite this image in one field of intellectual vision with man as conceived in terms of the postulated objects of scientific theory?' The bite to this question lies, we have seen, in the fact that man is that being which conceives of itself in terms of the manifest image. To the extent that the manifest does not survive in the synoptic view, to that extent man himself would not survive.

IV. THE SCIENTIFIC IMAGE

My present purpose is to add to the account I have given of the manifest image, a comparable sketch of what I have called the scientific image, and to conclude this essay with some comments on the respective contributions of these two to the unified vision of man-in-the-world which is the aim of philosophy.

The scientific image of man-in-the-world is, of course, as much an idealization as the manifest image—even more so, as it is still in the process of coming to be. It will be remembered that the contrast I have in mind is not that between an *unscientific* conception of man-in-the-world and a *scientific* one, but between that conception which limits itself to what correlational techniques can tell us about perceptible and introspectible events and that which postulates imperceptible objects and events for the purpose of explaining correlations among perceptibles. It was granted, of course, that in point of historical fact many of the latter correlations were suggested by theories introduced to explain previously established correlations, so that there has been a dialectical interplay between correlational and postulational procedures. (Thus we might not have noticed that litmus paper turns red in acid, until this hypothesis had been suggested by a complex theory relating the absorption and emission of electromagnetic radiation by objects to their chemical composition; yet in principle this familiar correlation could have been, and, indeed, was, discovered before any such theory was developed.) Our contrast then, is between two ideal constructs: *(a)* the correlational and categorial refinement of the 'original image', which refinement I am calling the manifest image; *(b)* the image derived from the fruits of postulational theory construction which I am calling the scientific image.

It may be objected at this point that there is no such thing as *the* image of man built from postulated entities and processes, but rather as many images as there are sciences which touch on aspects of human behaviour. And, of course, in a sense this is true. There *are* as many scientific images of man as there are sciences which have something to say about man. Thus, there is man as he appears to the theoretical physicist—a swirl of physical particles, forces, and fields. There is man as he appears to the biochemist, to the physiologist, to the behaviourist, to the social scientist; and all of these images are to be contrasted with man as he appears to himself in sophisticated common sense, the manifest image which even today contains most of what he knows about himself at the properly human level. Thus the conception of *the* scientific or postulational image is an idealization in the sense that it is a conception of an integration of a manifold of images, each of which is the application to man of a framework of concepts which have a certain autonomy. For each scientific theory is, from the standpoint of methodology, a structure which is built at a different 'place' and by different procedures within the intersubjectively accessible world of perceptible things. Thus 'the' scientific image is a construct from a number of images, each of which is *supported by* the manifest world.

The fact that each theoretical image is a construction on a foundation provided by the manifest image, and *in this methodological sense* presupposes the manifest image, makes it tempting to suppose that the manifest image is prior in a *substantive* sense; that the categories of a theoretical science are logically dependent on categories pertaining to its methodological foundation in the manifest world of sophisticated common sense in such a way that there would be an absurdity in the notion of a world which illustrated its theoretical principles *without also illustrating the categories and principles of the manifest world.* Yet, when we turn our attention to 'the' scientific image which emerges from the several images proper to the several sciences, we note that although the image is *methodologically* dependent on the world of sophisticated common sense, and in this sense does not stand on its own feet, yet it purports to be a *complete* image, i.e. to define a framework which could be the *whole truth* about that which belongs to the image. Thus although methodologically a development *within* the manifest image, the scientific image presents itself as a *rival* image. From its point of view the manifest image on which it rests is an 'inadequate' but pragmatically useful likeness of a reality which first finds its adequate (in principle) likeness in the scientific image. . . .

But before attempting to throw some light on the conflicting claims of these two world perspectives, more must be said about the constitution of *the* scientific image from the several scientific images of which it is the supposed integration. There is relatively little difficulty about telescoping *some* of the 'partial' images into one image. Thus, with due precaution, we can unify the biochemical and the physical images; for to do this requires only an appreciation of the sense in which the objects of biochemical discourse can be equated with complex patterns of the objects of theoretical physics. To make this equation, of course, is not to equate the sciences, for as sciences they have different procedures and connect their theoretical entities via different instruments to intersubjectively accessible features of the manifest world. But diversity of this kind is compatible with intrinsic 'identity' of the theoretical entities themselves, that is, with saying that biochemical compounds are 'identical' with patterns of sub-atomic particles. For to make this 'identification' is simply to say that the *two* theoretical structures, each with its own connection to the perceptible world, could be replaced by *one* theoretical framework connected *at two levels of complexity* via different instruments and procedures to the world as perceived.

V. THE CLASH OF THE IMAGES

How, then, are we to evaluate the conflicting claims of the manifest image and the scientific image thus provisionally interpreted to constitute *the* true and, in principle, *complete* account of man-in-the-world?

. . . Three lines of thought seemed to be open: (1) Manifest objects are identical with systems of imperceptible particles in that simple sense in which a forest is identical with a number of trees. (2) Manifest objects are what really exist; systems of imperceptible particles being 'abstract' or 'symbolic' ways of representing them. (3) Manifest objects are 'appearances' to human minds of a reality which is constituted by systems of imperceptible particles. Although (2) merits serious consideration, and has been defended by able philosophers, it is (1) and (3), particularly the latter, which I shall be primarily concerned to explore.

First, some brief remarks about (1). There is nothing immediately paradoxical about the view that an object can be both a perceptible object with perceptible qualities *and* a system of imperceptible objects, none of which has perceptible qualities. Cannot systems have properites which their parts do not have? Now the answer to this question is 'yes', if it is taken in a sense of which a paradigm example would be the fact that a system of pieces of wood can be a ladder, although none of its parts is a ladder. Here one might say that for the system as a whole to be a ladder is for its parts to be of such and such shapes and sizes and to be related to one another in certain ways. Thus there is no trouble about systems having properties which its parts do not have *if these properties are a matter of the parts having such and such qualities and being related in such and such ways.* But the case of a pink ice cube, it would seem clear, cannot be treated in this way. It does not seem plausible to say that for a system of particles to be a pink ice cube is for them to have such and such imperceptible qualities, and to be so related to one another as to make up an approximate cube. *Pink* does not seem to be made up of imperceptible qualities in the way in which being a ladder is made up of being cylindrical (the rungs), rectangular (the frame), wooden, etc. The manifest ice cube presents itself to us as something which is pink through and through, as a pink continuum, all the regions of which, however small, are pink. It presents itself to us as *ultimately homogeneous;* and an ice cube variegated in colour is, though not homogeneous in its specific colour, 'ultimately homogeneous', in the sense to which I am calling attention, with respect to the generic trait of being coloured.

Now reflection on this example suggests a principle which can be formulated approximately as follows:

If an object is *in a strict sense* a system of objects, then every property of the object must consist in the fact that its constituents have such and such qualities and stand in such and such relations or, roughly, every property of a system of objects consists of properties of, and relations between, its constituents.

With something like this principle in mind, it was argued that if a physical object is *in a strict sense* a system of imperceptible particles, then it cannot as a whole have the perceptible qualities characteristic of physical objects in the manifest image. It was concluded that manifest physical objects are 'appearances' *to human perceivers* of systems of imperceptible particles which is alternative (3) above.

This alternative, (3), however, is open to an objection which is ordinarily directed not against the alternative itself, but against an imperceptive formulation of it as the thesis that the perceptible things around us 'really have no colour'. Against *this* formulation the objection has the merit of calling attention to the fact that in the manifest framework it is as absurd to say that a visible object has no colour, as it is to say of a triangle that it has no shape. However, against the above formulation of alternative (3), namely, that *the very objects themselves* are appearances to perceivers of systems of imperceptible particles, the objection turns out on examination to have no weight. The objection for which the British 'common sense' philosopher G. E. Moore is directly or indirectly responsible, runs:

Chairs, tables, etc., as we ordinarily think them to be, can't be 'appearances' of systems of particles lacking perceptible qualities, because we *know* that there are chairs, tables, etc., and it is a framework feature of chairs, tables, etc., that they have perceptible qualities.

It simply *disappears* once it is recognized that, properly understood, the claim that physical objects do not really have perceptible qualities is not analogous to the claim that something generally believed to be true about a certain kind of thing is actually false. It is not the denial of a belief *within a framework,* but a challenge to the framework. It is the claim that although the framework of perceptible objects, the manifest framework of everyday life, is adequate for the everyday purposes of life, it is ultimately inadequate and should not be accepted as an account of what there is *all things considered.* Once we see this, we see that the argument from 'knowledge' cuts no ice, for the reasoning:

We know that there are chairs, pink ice cubes, etc. (physical objects). Chairs, pink ice cubes are coloured, are perceptible objects with perceptible qualities. Therefore, perceptible physical objects with perceptible qualities exist operates *within* the framework of the manifest image and cannot *support* it. It fails to provide a point of view outside the manifest image from which the latter can be evaluated.

A more sophisticated argument would be to the effect that we successfully find our way around in life by using the conceptual framework of coloured physical objects in space and time, therefore, this framework represents things as they really are. This argument has force, but is vulnerable to the reply that the success of living, thinking, and acting in terms of the manifest framework can be accounted for by the framework which proposes to replace it, by showing that there are sufficient structural similarities between manifest objects and their scientific counterparts to account for this success.*

The same considerations which led philosophers to deny the reality of perceptible things led them to a dualistic theory of man. For if the human body is a system of particles, the body cannot be the subject of thinking and feeling, *unless thinking and feeling are capable of interpretation as complex interactions of physical particles;* unless, that is to say, the manifest framework of man as *one* being, a *person* capable of doing radically different kinds of things can be replaced without loss of descriptive and explanatory power by a postulational image in which he is a complex of physical particles, and all his activities a matter of the particles changing in state and relationship.

Dualism, of course, denied that either sensation or feeling or conceptual thinking could in this sense be construed as complex interactions of physical particles, or man as a complex physical system. They were prepared to say that a *chair* is really a system of imperceptible particles which 'appears' in the manifest framework as a 'colour solid' (cf. our example of the ice cube), but they were not prepared to say that man himself was a complex physical system which 'appears' to itself to be the sort of thing man is in the manifest image.

Now in the light of recent developments in neurophysiology, philosophers have come to see that there is no reason to suppose there can't be neurophysiological processes which stand to conceptual thinking as

---

* It might seem that the manifest framework accounts for the success of the scientific framework, so that the situation is symmetrical. But I believe that a more penetrating account of theoretical explanation than I have been able to sketch in this chapter would show that this claim is illusory. I discuss this topic at some length in chapter 4.

sensory states of the brain stand to conscious sensations. And, indeed, there have not been wanting philosophers (of whom Hobbes was, perhaps, the first) who have argued that the analogy should be viewed philosophically as an *identity,* i.e. that a world picture which includes *both* thoughts *and* the neurophysiological counterparts of thoughts would contain a redundancy; just as a world picture which included *both* the physical objects of the manifest image *and* complex patterns of physical particles would contain a redundancy. But to this proposal the obvious objection occurs, that just as the claim that 'physical objects are complexes of imperceptible particles' left us with the problem of accounting for the status of the perceptible qualities of manifest objects, so the claim that 'thoughts, etc., are complex neurophysiological processes' leaves us with the problems of accounting for the status of the *introspectable qualities* of thoughts. And it would seem obvious that there is a vicious regress in the claim that these qualities exist in introspective awareness of the thoughts which seem to have them, but not in the thoughts themselves. For, the argument would run, surely introspection is itself a form of thinking. Thus one thought (Peter) would be robbed of its quality only to pay it to another (Paul).

We can, therefore, understand the temptation to say that even if there are cerebral processes which are strikingly analogous to conceptual thinking, they are processes which *run parallel* to conceptual thinking (and cannot be identified with it) as the sensory states of the brain *run parallel* to conscious sensation. And we can, therefore, understand the temptation to say that all these puzzles arise from taking seriously the claim of *any* part of the scientific image to be *what really is,* and to retreat into the position that reality is the world of the manifest image, and that all the postulated entities of the scientific image are 'symbolic tools' which function (something like the distance-measuring devices which are rolled around on maps) to help us find our way around in the world, but do not themselves describe actual objects and processes. On this view, the theoretical counterparts of *all* features of the manifest image would be *equally* unreal, and that philosophical conception of man-of-the-world would be correct which endorsed the manifest image and located the scientific image within it as a conceptual tool used by manifest man in his capacity as a scientist.

VI. THE PRIMACY OF THE SCIENTIFIC IMAGE: A PROLEGOMENON

Is this the truth of the matter? Is the manifest image, subject, of course, to continual emperical and categorial refinements, the measure of what there really is? I do not think so. I have already indicated that of the three alternatives we are considering with respect to the comparative claims of the manifest and scientific images, the first, which, like a child, says 'both', is ruled out by a principle which I am not defending in this chapter, although it does stand in need of defence. The second alternative is the one I have just reformulated and rejected. I propose, therefore, to re-examine the case against the third alternative, the primacy of the scientific image. My strategy will be to argue that the difficulty, raised above, which seems to stand in the way of the identification of thought with cerebral processes, arises from the mistake of supposing that in self-awareness conceptual thinking presents itself to us in a qualitative guise. Sensations and images *do,* we shall see, present themselves to us in a qualitative character, a fact which accounts for the fact that they are stumbling blocks in the attempt to accept the scientific image as real. *But* one scarcely needs to point out these days that however intimately conceptual thinking is related to sensations and images, it cannot be equated with them, nor with complexes consisting of them.

It is no accident that when a novelist wishes to represent what is going on in the mind of a person, he does so by 'quoting' the person's thoughts as he might quote what a person says. For thoughts not only are the sort of things that find overt expression in language, we conceive of them as analogous to overt discourse. Thus, *thoughts* in the manifest image are conceived not in terms of their 'quality', but rather as inner 'goings-on' which are analogous to speech, and find their overt expression in speech—though they can go on, of course, in the absence of this overt expression. It is no accident that one learns to think in the very process of learning to speak.

From this point of view one can appreciate the danger of misunderstanding which is contained in the term 'introspection'. For while there is, indeed, an analogy between the direct knowledge we have of our own thoughts and the perceptual knowledge we have of what is going on in the world around us, the analogy holds only in as much as both self-awareness and perceptual observation are basic forms of non-inferential knowledge. They differ, however, in that whereas in perceptual observation we know objects as being of a certain quality, in the direct knowledge we have of what we are thinking (e.g. I am thinking that it is cold outside) what we know non-inferentially is that *something analogous to and properly expressed by the sentence, 'It is cold outside', is going on in me.*

The point is an important one, for if the concept of a thought is the concept of an inner state analogous to speech, this leaves open the possibility that the inner state conceived in terms of this analogy is *in its qualitative character* a neurophysiological process. To draw a parallel: if I begin by thinking of the cause of a disease as a substance (to be called 'germs') which is analogous to a colony of rabbits, in that it is able to reproduce itself in geometrical proportion, but, unlike rabbits, imperceptible and, when present in sufficient number in the human body, able to cause the symptoms of disease, and to cause epidemics by spreading from person to person, there is no logical barrier to a subsequent identification of 'germs' thus conceived with the *bacilli* which microscopic investigation subsequently discovers.

But to point to the analogy between conceptual thinking and overt speech is only part of the story, for of equally decisive importance is the analogy between speech and what sophisticated computers can do, and finally, between computer circuits and conceivable patterns of neurophysiological organization. All of this is more or less speculative, less so now than even a few years ago. What interests the philosopher is the matter of principle; and here the first stage is decisive—the recognition that the concept of a thought is a concept by analogy. Over and above this all we need is to recognize the force of Spinoza's statement: 'No one has thus far determined what the body can do nor no one has yet been taught by experience what the body can do merely by the laws of nature insofar as nature is considered merely as corporeal and extended' (*Ethics,* part 3, prop. II, note).

Another analogy which may be even more helpful is the following: suppose we are watching the telegraphic report of a chess game in a foreign country

White	*Black*
P—K3	P—QB3

And suppose that we are sophisticated enough to know that chess pieces can be made of all shapes and sizes, that chess boards can be horizontal or vertical, indeed, distorted in all kinds of ways provided that they preserve certain topological features of the familiar board. Then it is clear that while we will think of the players in the foreign country as moving kings, pawns, etc., castling and check-mating, our concepts of the pieces they are moving and the moving of them will be simply the concept of items and changes which play a role analogous to the pieces and moves which take place when *we* play chess. We know that the items must have some intrinsic quality (shape, size, etc.), but we think of these qualities as 'those which make possible a sequence of changes which are structurally similar to the changes which take place on our own chess boards'.

Thus our concept of 'what thoughts are' might, like our concept of what a castling is in chess, be abstract in the sense that it does not concern itself with the *instrinsic* character of thoughts, *save as items which can occur in patterns of relationships which are analogous to the way in which sentences are related to one another and* to the contexts in which they are used.

Now if thoughts are items which are conceived in terms of the roles they play, then there is no barrier *in principle* to the identification of conceptual thinking with neurophysiological process. There would be no 'qualitative' remainder to be accounted for. The identification, curiously enough, would be even more straightforward than the identification of the physical things in the manifest image with complex systems of physical particles. And in this key, if not decisive, respect, the respect in which both images are concerned with conceptual thinking (which is the distinctive trait of man), *the manifest and scientific images could merge without clash in the synoptic view.*

STUDY QUESTIONS

Review

1. What is the source and meaning of the term "metaphysics"?
2. Explain some of the basic problems or issues of metaphysics.
3. What does Buchler mean by his term "natural complex"?
4. What are the five types of reductionism described by Weiss? How do these differ from his own theory?
5. What does Neville mean when he says that to be a distinct determinate thing is to be a harmony or a value?
6. Distinguish the "manifest" and "scientific" images as these are defined by Sellars.

For Further Thought

7. What do you think about the possibility of saying what basic kinds of things exist as a metaphysician rather than as a scientist?
8. What do you think that the ultimate nature of reality is? Explain your basis for this view.
9. Is Buchler's term "natural complex" better as a basic metaphysical category than "being" or "existent" or "entity" or "thing"? Why or why not?
10. How do we know (if we know) that public human expressions or behavior come from a "private" source in Weiss's sense of that term?
11. What do you think distinguishes one thing from another and makes it a unique determinate thing? Compare your view with Neville's.
12. Do you agree with Sellars that the "scientific" image of man-in-the-world is more real than the "manifest" image? If so, what status would you give the "manifest" image? If not, what sense do you make of the "scientific" image?

BIBLIOGRAPHY

Justus Buchler

Buchler, Justus. *Metaphysics of Natural Complexes.* New York: Columbia University Press, 1966.
— — —. *The Concept of Method.* New York: Columbia University Press, 1961.
— — —. *Nature and Judgment.* New York: Columbia University Press, 1955.
— — —. *Toward a General Theory of Human Judgment.* New York: Columbia University Press, 1951. Reprint. New York: Dover, 1980.
— — —, ed. *The Philosophy of Peirce: Selected Writings.* New York: Harcourt, Brace, 1940.

— — —. *Charles Peirce's Empiricism*. New York: Harcourt, Brace, 1939.
Singer, Beth. *Ordinal Naturalism, An Introduction to the Philosophy of Justus Buchler*. Lewisburg, Pa.: Bucknell University Press, 1983.

Robert C. Neville

Neville, Robert C. *The Tao and the Daimon: Segments of a Religious Inquiry*. Albany: State University of New York Press, 1982.
— — —. *Reconstruction of Thinking*. Albany: State University of New York Press, 1981.
— — —. *Creativity and God*. New York: Seabury Press, 1980.
— — —. *Soldier, Sage, Saint*. New York: Fordham University Press, 1978.
— — —. *Cosmology of Freedom*. New Haven: Yale University Press, 1974.
— — —. *God the Creator*. Chciago: University of Chicago Press, 1968.

Wilfred Sellars

Wilfred Sellars. *Naturalism and Ontology*. Reseda, Calif.: Ridgeview Publishing, 1980.
— — —. *Pure Pragmatics and Possible Worlds: The Early Essays of Wilfrid Sellars*. Ed. Jeffrey Sicha. Reseda, Calif.: Ridgeview Publishing, 1980.
— — —. *Philosophical Perspectives*. Springfield, Ill.: C. C. Thomas, 1967. Part 1 is reprinted as *Philosophical Perspectives: History of Philosophy*, part 2 as *Philosophical Perspectives: Metaphysics and Epistemology*. Reseda, Calif.: Ridgeview Publishing, 1979.
— — —. *Action, Knowledge, and Reality: Critical Studies in Honor of Wilfrid Sellars*. Ed. Hector-Neri Castaneda. Indianapolis: Bobbs-Merill, 1975.
— — —. *Essays in Philosophy and Its History*. Dordrecht, Holland: D. Reidel Publishing, 1974.
— — —. *Form and Content in Ethical Theory*. Lawrence: University of Kansas, 1967. Lindley Lecture, 1967.
— — —. *Science, Perception, and Reality*. New York: Humanities Press, 1963.
Sellars, Wilfrid, Herbert Feigl, and Keith Lehrer, eds. *New Readings in Philosophical Analysis*. New York: Appleton-Century-Crofts, 1972.
Sellars, Wilfrid, and John Hospers, eds. *Readings in Ethical Theory*. New York: Appleton-Century-Crofts, 1970.
"The Philosophy of Wilfrid Sellars." *The Monist* 65, no. 3 (July 1982).

Paul Weiss

Weiss, Paul. *Privacy*. Carbondale: Southern Illinois University Press, 1983.
— — —. *You, I, and the Others*. Carbondale: Southern Illinois University Press, 1980.
— — —. *First Considerations: An Examination of Philosophical Evidence*. Carbondale: Southern Illinois University Press, 1977.
— — —. *Cinematics*. Carbondale: Southern Illinois University Press, 1975.
— — —. *Beyond All Appearances*. Carbondale: Southern Illinois University Press, 1974.
— — —. *Sport: A Philosophic Inquiry*. Carbondale: Southern Illinois University Press, 1969.
— — —. *The Making of Men*. Carbondale: Southern Illinois University Press, 1967.
— — —. *Philosophy in Process*. Vol. 1, *1955–60;* vol. 2, *1960–64;* vol. 3, *1964;* vol. 4, *1964–65;* vol. 5, *1965–68;* vol. 6, *1968–74;* vol. 7, *1975–76*. Carbondale: Southern Illinois University Press, 1966–78.

― ― ―. *The God We Seek*. Carbondale: Southern Illinois University Press, 1964.

― ― ―. *Religion and Art*. Milwaukee: Marquette University Press, 1963.

― ― ―. *History: Written and Lived*. Carbondale: Southern Illinois University Press, 1962.

― ― ―. *Modes of Being*. Carbondale: Southern Illinois University Press, 1961.

― ― ―. *Nine Basic Arts*. Carbondale: Southern Illinois University Press, 1961.

― ― ―. *The World of Art*. Carbondale: Southern Illinois University Press, 1961.

― ― ―. *Our Public Life*. Bloomington: Indiana University Press, 1959.

― ― ―. *Man's Freedom*. New Haven: Yale University Press, 1950.

― ― ―. *Reality*. Princeton: Princeton University Press, 1938. Reprint. New York: Peter Smith, 1949.

― ― ―. *Nature and Man*. New York: Henry Holt, 1947.

― ― ―. *The Nature of Systems*. La Salle, Ill.: Open Court Publishing, 1929.

Weiss, Paul, and Charles Hartshorne, eds. *The Collected Papers of Charles Sanders Peirce*. Vols. 1-5. Cambridge: Harvard University Press, 1931-35.

Weiss, Paul, and Jonathan Weiss. *Right and Wrong: A Philosophical Dialogue between Father and Son*. Carbondale: Southern Illinois University Press, 1967.

Chapter 14

Phenomenology

The term "Phenomenology" refers to that type of philosophy that stresses the importance of careful study *(logos)* of phenomena or of the world as it appears to us in our direct experience. Immanuel Kant had used the term "phenomenal" to refer to the world of our experience which is to be distinguished from the noumenal world, the world as it might exist in itself or apart from our experience. Hegel's work, *The Phenomenology of Spirit* (1807), described the development of consciousness in all its variety of forms or appearances. However the term "phenomenology" now usually refers to the philosophy developed by Edmund Husserl (1859–1938), or as Paul Ricoeur has noted, phenomenology is "the sum of the variations of Husserl's work and the heresies which have sprung from Husserl." [1] Among the other noted European phenomenologists are Max Scheler and Maurice Merleau-Ponty. The phenomenological method has also been used extensively by philosophers who have been usually classified as existentialists, for example the German Martin Heidegger and the Frenchman Jean-Paul Sartre.

Marvin Farber (1901–80) is said to have been responsible for introducing phenomenology into the United States with his 1928 dissertation entitled "Phenomenology as a Method and as a Philosophical Discipline." [2] In 1939 Farber organized the International Phenomenological Society which was mainly operative in the United States. The society published the journal *Philosophy and Phenomenological Research,* at first primarily an organ for phenomenologists and writings on this method, but today more broadly oriented. The society itself became inactive in 1947. A number of philosophers, even if not willing to call themselves phenomenologists, have had sufficiently similar interests to participate in meetings such as those of the Society for Phenomenology and Existential Philosophy and to publish their reflections in volumes labeled phenomenology.[3] Centers of phenomenology have existed at the New School for Social Research in New York where many of the European emigré phenomenologists first located in the 1930s, at Northwestern University outside of Chicago which became a center for Husserlian studies and translations, and at some private colleges and universities such as Duquesne.[4] Among the more noteworthy older American phenomenologists are Dorian Cairns (1901–1973), Aaron Gurwitsch (1901–1973), Alfred Schuetz (1899–1959), Felix Kaufmann (1895–1949), and Fritz Kaufmann (1891–1958), though there have been many other writers in this tradition as indicated by the bibliography at the end of this chapter.

Our introduction here will comment briefly on the life and writings of Husserl and then summarize in more detail the essential elements of phenomenology as a philosophy and a method of philosophizing. While there are different versions of phenomenology espoused by the variety of phenomenologists, it seems nevertheless that a common core is shared by them all, so that one may still speak or write of its essential elements. More recently some of those whose background training has been in the phenomenological tradition have come to be associated with two other movements — hermeneutics and structuralism.[5] Thus a brief summary of those types of philosophy will also be included in this chapter's introduction.

EDMUND HUSSERL

Edmund Husserl was born in 1859 in Czechoslovakia in Moravia. He studied mathematics, physics, and astromony at the University of Leipzig, and then more mathematics at Berlin and the University of Vienna from which he graduated in 1881. Although as an undergraduate he had attended few lectures in philosophy, he studied for some time under the philosopher Franz Brentano and then under the psychologist Carl Stumpf at Vienna. These associations and Husserl's mathematical and scientific studies prepared him for and stimulated his later interest and writings in the foundations of logic and mathematics and the methods of science and philosophy. Husserl taught briefly at the University of Halle, and then at Göttingen and Freiburg. He died in 1938.

Some commentators distinguish three different periods in Husserl's philosophizing: an early interest in the foundations of mathematics and philosophy, a period of concentration on philosophical method in particular, and finally writings on epistemological problems. The titles of some of his most significant works give some indication of the particular philosophical issues he addressed: *Philosophy of Arithmetic* (1891), *Prolegomena to Pure Logic* (1900), *Logical Investigations,* 2 vols. (1900–1901), *Lectures on Phemonenology* (1904–5), *Lectures on Phenomenology of Inner Time Consciousness* (1905–10), *The Idea of Phenomenology* (1906–7), *Philosophy as Rigorous Science* (1911), *Ideas* (1913), *Formal and Transcendental Logic* (1928), *Cartesian Meditations* (1931), and *Crisis of European Sciences and Transcendental Philosophy* (1970).

PHENOMENOLOGY

Husserl's phenomenology may be understood as a critical response to positivism, nominalism, and psychologism. Positivism holds that only what is given to us through the "positive" sciences is meaningful knowledge, and thus narrows the range of what is to count as legitimate experience. The directive not to multiply beings beyond necessity ("Ockham's razor") may have had a noble aim— namely, not to suppose to exist what cannot be experienced or is not necessary to account for our experience—but instead of simply banishing unnecessary explanations for sense phenomena, it also had the effect of rejecting much of our immediate experience as we experience it.[6] This effect was partly due to a certain sense-organ bias that led to prejudgments about what could be experienced—namely, only that that came to us specifically by way of particular senses. That experience that couldn't be so simply traced or explained was rejected. The aim of phenomenology was to widen the range of our experience, or rather to take experience as it is given without such prejudgments. It also advised the acceptance of experience as given, without judgments about its existential status, i.e., whether or not what we experience exists as it is experienced. Husserl called this acceptance the "bracketing" of existence or existential questions, and its purpose was to have us concentrate first on the immediate data of experience.

Phenomenology also provides a critique of nominalism, the theory that holds that our general terms are merely classificatory and do not refer to essences or common properties. For example, the terms "red" or "triangle" or "humanness," according to the nominalist, refer neither to any essential characteristics that exist independently in some sense, nor to any common characteristic that is in those things that are red or triangles or humans. Rather the terms are only names we give to groups of things for specific purposes such as classification. Phenomenology on the contrary stresses the attention to and analysis of essences without, however, taking a stand on the particular nature of their existence. What, it asks, is the essence of the experience of sound, or music, or red, or friendship. We often move too soon to explain or classify our experiences, before giving them an adequate chance to show what they are like. This supposed mistake phenomenologists attempt to remedy.

Phenomenology, especially the phenomenology of Husserl, can likewise stand as a critique of psychologism. Psychologism is the supposed fallacy of identifying what is known with the act of knowing. More commonly, it is the attempt to replace an examination of the contents of knowing or the truth of a particular theory with an examination of how the person believing it came to believe it. It asks what particular facts about his or her psychology must have led to such a belief. Phenomenology again directs us to concentrate on what is known without questioning how it came to be known.

However, there are other key concepts that have come to be identified with phenomenology, basically because they were significant concerns of Husserl as well as of some later followers. Husserl believed that philosophy could be an exact science, more exact than nonphilosophical sciences. Natural science relied on presuppositions about what was knowable and what methods would best yield the kind of knowledge that was valuable and valid. Philosophy, on the other hand, could examine presuppositions and could attempt to return to a primary experience of things that did not rely on any such narrowing assumptions. Experience is to be taken as given in an intuition or vision that is immediate. Husserl directed us to go back "to the things themselves" *(zu dem Sachen selbst).*

Moreover, it is essences of things that we are directed to examine. Our primary consciousness or intuition *(Schau)* is of essences *(Wesen),* and can thus be called a *"Wesensschau"*. Husserl directs philosophers to analyze these contents of consciousness. We are to concentrate on the invariant idea *(eidos)* exemplified in the objects we are examining. This he called an "eidetic reduction." There are certain "natural groupings" of phenomena, certain characteristics that belong together, and others that are peripheral or nonessential. It is the former that the method seeks to examine. Again, however, this examination is to be done without questioning whether or in what way the essence exists outside of consciousness. Philosophers varied, however, in the extent and manner in which they carried out this direction. In the selection in this chapter by Aron Gurwitsch, we find an example of a phenomenological analysis of the object of experience that differs somewhat from that of Husserl in its attempt to explain the relation between the object of consciousness and its referent.

Husserl, nevertheless, was interested in the relation between subject and object in knowledge, the knower and the known. His discussions of the notion of "intentionality" provide a clear example of this interest. The nature of the problem and something of his understanding of how it was to be interpreted he derived from Franz Brentano, and thus indirectly from the medieval scholasticism that influenced Brentano. Our knowledge has the essential quality that it intends objects. "All consciousness is consciousness-of-something." [7] However, it is not the external existing object that is meant, but the object as known by consciousness. In further analyses, Husserl came to think of the subject of experience as a nonempirical absolute ego that would exist as such even if it had no objects to experience. Because of such doctrines, the later writings of Husserl are sometimes said to contain idealist overtones. In his latest works, however, he turned in his analysis to that immediate experience of the object by the subject, to the world of lived experience, "the life world" *(Lebenswelt).* A consideration of whether these doctrines were effectively reconciled with each other, however, is beyond the scope of this brief introduction.

At the heart of phenomenology is its concern to take experience as it is given, without prejudices and assumptions about what experience should be like. As one writer puts it: "it constitutes a determined attempt to enrich the world of our experience by bringing out hitherto neglected aspects of this experience. . . . It might be called reverence for the phenomena." [8] Essentially phenomenology advises us against too quickly attempting to explain experience before we have taken adequate time to look at it.

More recently, when American philosophers trained in the phenomenological tradition turned their attention to the phenomena of language, they found already in existence certain Continental traditions that had been grappling with problems of language, hermeneutics, and structuralism. As far back as 1912, the Frenchman Ferdinande de Saussure had stressed the systematic character of language and its arbitrariness or conventionality.[9] Claude Lévi-Strauss had criticized the importance given to history in the later writings of the existentialist Jean-Paul Sartre, and suggested that language be analyzed in terms of its structure.[10] Structuralism is basically a method of analysis according to which structure, i.e., the combination and relation of formal elements within a whole, is stressed. Thus languages could be studied in terms of the way their elements were put together into a whole.[11] Rather than study the origins of language, structural linguistics emphasized its structure. Moreover, structuralists also tended to stress that users of a language necessarily view their world in a particular way dictated by their language. Structuralism was also applied to anthropological studies, to the study of particular literary and artistic forms, and to the analysis of the structures of the mind, eg., structures of the unconscious.[12]

Hermeneutics, according to the German philosopher with whom the name itself is most associated, Hans Gadamer, can be seen as the conjoining of three traditions: the descriptive phenomenology of Husserl, the emphasis on history of Dilthey, and the philosophy of Heidegger.[13] However, hermeneutics may also draw on the Hegelian notions that any culture or age has a wholistic character and that there is no point of view outside history. According to writers in the hermeneutic tradition, we always approach any object of study, be it history or a text or culture, with certain anticipations or prejudices. However, if we remain open and allow the object to speak for itself, we will be able to rid ourselves of distorting prejudices. This is the essence of the hermeneutic circle. We always interpret from some standpoint, but interpretation also consists in this dialectical relation between standpoint and object. Perception is necessarily socially and situationally conditioned. Objectivity, especially in the human sciences, is thus illusory. However, this is seen as the source of our ability to grasp or understand, since it gives us something in common with the age or culture or text that we may wish to understand. Those interested in the development of American philosophy might do well to follow the further developments of phenomenology in relation to its hermeneutical- and structuralist-oriented philosophizing.

In the selections collected in this chapter Richard Schmitt gives some further explanation of the type of concentration and analysis required by the phenomenological method. Aron Gurwitsch's essay presents an example of use of the method to examine the object of experience, but, as noted, in a manner that does not completely bracket existential concerns. The selection from the writings of Don Ihde is a good example of use of the phenomenological method to examine one particular type of phenomena, namely auditory phenomena. The final section of the bibliography for this chapter may be used as a source for writings in the structuralist and hermeneutic traditions.

Notes

[1] Herbert Spiegelberg, *The Phenomenological Movement,* 2d. ed. (The Hague: Martinus Nijhoff, 1965), vol. 2, p. 564.

[2] Spiegelberg, *Phenomenological Movement,* p. 627.

[3] James Edie, *Phenomenology in America* (Chicago: Quadrangle Books, 1967), pp. 7–10.

[4] Two examples of the research and translation activity that has come from such centers are: Northwestern University Studies in Phenomenology and Existential Philosophy, ed. John Wild and James Edie (since 1976 from Indiana University Press); Duquesne University Studies Philosophy Series and their journal *Research in Phenomenology.* SUNY Press has also begun a series of publications on phenomenology. See the bibliography for titles.

[5] While the major writers in these traditions have been Continental, there is sufficient interest in them in the United States to mention here; in particular there seems to be increasing interest in hermeneutics, which may justify some brief discussion in this chapter. However, in so far as this area places a heavy emphasis on language, an argument may also be made for placing such discussion in our later chapter on language.

[6] Spiegelberg, *Phenomenological Movement,* p. 658.

[7] Jos. Kockelmans, ed., *Phenomenology* (New York: Doubleday, 1967), pp. 32ff.

[8] Spiegelberg, *Phenomenological Movement,* p. 700.

[9] Ferdinand de Saussure, *Cours de linguistique generale* (Paris, 1915). Published in English as *Introduction to General Linguistics,* trans. Wade Baskin (New York: Philosophical Library, 1959).

[10] Claude Lévi-Strauss, *The Savage Mind* (Chicago: University of Chicago Press, 1966).

[11] See Zellig Harris, *Structural Linguistics* (Chicago: University of Chicago Press, 1951). Also see "Structuralism and Linguistics," pp. 5–19, and "The Linguistic Basis of Structuralism," pp. 20–36, in *Structuralism: An Introduction,* ed. D. Robey (Oxford: Clarendon Press, 1973).

[12] Claude Lévi-Strauss, *Structural Anthropology,* trans. C. Jacobson and B. G. Schoepf (New York: Basic Books, 1963). Also see Peter Berger and T. Luckmann, *The Social Construction of Reality* (London: Allen Lane, 1967); Patrick Gardiner, *The Nature of Historical Explanation* (London: Oxford University Press, 1961); Janet Wolff, *Hermeneutic Philosophy and the Sociology of Art* (London: Routledge and Kegan Paul, 1975); Edmund Leach, "Structuralism in Social Anthropology," in Robey, *Structuralism,* pp. 38–56.

[13] H.-G. Gadamer, *Wahrheit und Methode* (Tubingen: J. C. B. Mohr, 1965), p. xxix.

RICHARD SCHMITT

HUSSERL'S TRANSCENDENTAL-PHENOMENOLOGICAL REDUCTION*

Philosophers before, as well as since, Husserl have spoken of a philosophic discipline called "phenomenology" which describes its objects instead of constructing explanations. Husserl's phenomenology differs from all the others in the conditions which any inquiry must fulfill in order to deserve being called "phenomenological." Phenomenology, according to him, can begin only after the "transcendental-phenomenological reduction" has been performed by the beginning phenomenologist. Descriptions not preceded by this "reduction" are not phenomenological. Anyone who wants to understand the claims made by Husserl for his "Transcendental Phenomenology" and, even more, anyone who wants to employ the phenomenological method must first understand and practice the transcendental-phenomenological reduction. But such understanding is difficult to achieve; Husserl's own descriptions are quite perplexing and the commentators differ widely in their interpretations of these descriptions. I shall try to clarify this initial phase of phenomenology by showing that Husserl's characterizations of the transcendental-phenomenological reduction are, in fact, suggestions for a phenomenological description of reflection as

* Richard Schmitt, "Husserl's Transcendental-Phenomenological Reduction," *Philosophy and Phenomenological Research,* 20 (1959–60): pp. 238–45. Reprinted with permission of the author and the editors.

opposed to straightforward, nonreflective thinking. This will provide only a partial explication of the transcendental-phenomenological reduction. How phenomenological reflection differs from other kinds, as (for instance) scientific reflection, must be treated in a separate paper.

We must begin by rehearsing, once again, Husserl's descriptions of the transcendental-phenomenological reduction. There are a number of different ways of approaching the reduction. One may follow Descartes on his road of total doubt. Alternatively one may examine one of the traditional philosophic disciplines, e.g., logic, in an attempt to uncover the aims implicit in its development.[1] By either way one is led to question what had previously seemed self-evident. On the Cartesian road we are led to question all presuppositions of human experience; in logic the presuppositions of judging, of validity and truth become questionable. We begin, then, by questioning what we had previously taken for granted, or by wondering at what seems most familiar.[2] This involves a change of attitude *(Einstellung);*[3] we must look at the world with "new eyes." What exactly is this new attitude which I adopt as I perform the transcendental-phenomenological reduction? Here Husserl provides a variety of phrases designed to exhibit this new attitude to the reader: I no longer attach any validity to the "natural belief in the existence of what I experience";[4] I "invalidate," "inhibit," "disqualify," all commitments *(Stellungnahmen)* with reference to experienced objects; I "bracket the objective world."[5] This last is one of the best-known phrases used in this connection. Husserl draws his metaphor from mathematics where we place an expression in brackets and put a + or − sign in front of it. By thus bracketing the objective world we "give it a different value."[6] In performing the reduction, the phenomenologist establishes himself as "disinterested spectator"[7] and changes his practical aims.[8] The result of this change of attitude is a change in my experience. Previously experienced reality now becomes "mere phenomenon." This Kantian term is here used in a new sense; any object of experience becomes "phenomenon" for the observer who recognizes the object's claim to reality, but reserves decision on the

---

[1] *Formale und Transcendentale Logik,* Halle, 1929, pp. 6ff. This work will be referred to as *Formale.*

[2] *Die Krisis der Europäischen Wissenschaften und die Transcendentale Phänomenologie,* ed. Walter Biemel, Husserliana vol. 6, The Hague, 1954, p. 80. This work will be referred to as *Krisis.*

[3] *Ideen zu einer reinen Phänomenologie und phänomenologischen Philosophie,* ed. Walter Biemel, Husserliana vol. 3, The Hague, 1950, p. 61. This work will be referred to as *Ideen I.*

[4] *Cartesianische Meditationen,* ed. S. Strasser, Husserliana vol. 1, The Hague, 1950, p. 59. This work will be referred to as *Cart.*

[5] *Op. cit.,* p. 60.

[6] *Ideen I,* p. 174.

[7] *Cart.,* p. 73.

[8] *Krisis,* p. 399.

validity of that claim. In the "natural," preanalytic and prephenom-
enological attitude—sometimes Husserl also calls it the "naive" attitude,
but not in any pejorative sense—we generally believe that objects perceived
are real; we believe that we live in a real world. This belief is "put out
of action," suspended, we make no use of it.[9] We are left with a world-
as-phenomenon, a world which claims to be; but we refuse, for the time
being, to pass on the validity of these claims.[10]

A further result of this movement is the discovery of the transcendental
ego. I suddenly recognize that it is I who must decide whether the claims
to reality of the objects of experience in particular, and of the world as
a whole in general, are valid claims. I discover that whatever has sense
and validity, has sense and validity for me.[11] I thus discover the "absolute
being of the transcendental ego." [12] "Absolute being *(Seiendes)* is in the
form of an intentional life which, whatever else it may be aware of in
itself, is at the same time awareness of itself." [13] The "I" which transforms
the world into mere phenomenon is, in so doing, aware of itself as
transforming the world and cannot be subjected to the same transformation. But apart from its "modes of relatedness" and its "modes of
behavior," this "I" is completely devoid of any content which could be
studied or explicated. It is completely indescribable, being no more than
a pure ego.[14]

Husserl insists that the transcendental-phenomenological reduction in
no way limits experience. The phenomenologist does not turn away either
from the whole of experienced reality and actuality or from certain areas
of it; he only suspends judgment concerning the reality or validity of
what is experienced. The world before the transcendental-phenomenological reduction and the world which I have transformed into "mere phenomenon" do not differ in content, but in the way in which I am related
to each of them.[15]

We are now in a position to understand Husserl's choice of terminology
better. The transcendental-phenomenological reduction is called "transcendental" because it uncovers the ego for which everything has meaning
and existence. It is called "phenomenological" because it transforms the
world into mere phenomenon. It is called "reduction" because it leads
us back (Lat. *reducere*) to the source of the meaning and existence of the
experienced world, in so far as it is experienced,[16] by uncovering intentionality. Husserl also uses the term "epoché." At first it appears as a

---

[9] *Ideen I*, p. 65.
[10] *Cart.*, pp. 58–61.
[11] *Op. cit.*, p. 65.
[12] *Ideen I*, p. 72.
[13] *Formale*, p. 241.
[14] *Ideen I*, p. 195, and *Cart.* p. 99.
[15] *Cart.*, pp. 59–60.
[16] *Cart.*, p. 65.

synonym for "reduction." In his last writings he differentiates between the two terms: the change of attitude, i.e., the suspension of all natural belief in the objects of experience is called the "epoché"; it, in turn, is the precondition for reducing the natural world to a world of phenomena.[17] The term "transcendental-phenomenological reduction" covers both the *epoché* and the reduction in the narrower sense of Husserl's last writings.

Throughout his writings of the middle and late period Husserl insisted that phenomenology is a reflective enterprise.[18] It seems reasonable therefore to interpret the transcendental-phenomenological reduction as a phenomenological description of the transition from a nonreflective to a reflective attitude, albeit a reflective attitude of a particular kind. If phenomenology is a reflective enterprise, it does not follow that all reflection is, therefore, phenomenological. But, before we can distinguish phenomenological from other kinds of reflection, we must first turn to the more general question: what distinguishes reflection from nonreflective thinking? (henceforth to be referred to merely as "thinking").

Traditionally the distinction between thinking and reflection rested on the distinction between what was inside the mind and what was outside of it. According to John Locke, "the mind . . . when it turns its view inward upon itself and observes its own actions about the ideas it has, takes from hence other ideas," [19] and these ideas are ideas of reflection. Hume draws the distinction in a very similar way.[20] The traditional distinction is intimately tied up with the doctrine that the mind has an "inside" and since this view is no longer popular, the difference between thinking and reflection bears re-examination.

A more serious objection against this concept of reflection as "the mind thinking about itself" is, that there is much thinking about oneself which is anything but reflective, but is, on the contrary, often only a means to escape the necessity for reflection. This kind of nonreflective and evasive thinking about oneself is found in brooding about one's own feelings and emotions, self-pity, nursing feelings of resentment or a sense of injury and, in extreme cases, a hysterical exaggeration of emotions.[21] Take a child who has been punished for disobedience. He will retreat to his room in anger, turning over and over in his mind how he has been wronged, and how unjustly he has been dealt with. This child thinks, and he thinks about his own "mind" and the "ideas therein," about his own loneliness and unhappiness, and how no one loves him. But, so far, he does not reflect. He does not ask himself whether his punishment may

---

[17] *Krisis*, p. 155.
[18] Cf. *Ideen I*, p. 177; *Cart.*, p. 59; *Krisis*, p. 457.
[19] John Locke, *An Essay Concerning Human Understanding*, bk. 2, chap. 4, part 1.
[20] David Hume, *A Treatise on Human Nature*, part 1, bk. 1, sect. 2.
[21] Cf. Max Scheler, "Die Idole der Selbsterkenntnis" in *Vom Umsturz der Werte*, vol. 2, Leipzig, 1923, p. 61.

not, perhaps, be partially justified, whether it is really true that he is being punished merely out of sheer malice and ill will on his parents' part. Caught up in his own anger and misery the child has not been able to "stand back" and survey the situation calmly and with some detachment. In his anger he loses his "sense of proportion" and his "proper perspective." Reflection, on the other hand, involves just this critical detachment. Once the child begins to reflect, after the first violent emotion is spent, he will, to be sure, still think about himself but not merely about himself, his own suffering, and the sins of others against him. He will, instead, think about himself in relation to the other persons involved. He will review the events, try to see them from his parents' point of view, how his behavior may have embarrassed or hurt them. Thus taking "the other's point of view" will, at the same time, lead the child to think about himself in a different light. He will no longer merely interest himself in his own unhappiness—that is put aside for the moment—but will think about what he actually did do. Thus the scope of reflection about oneself is considerably wider than that of thinking about oneself, since it includes facts about one's relations to others and about oneself which had before remained unnoticed or had appeared irrelevant.

This difference between thinking and reflection does not only hold where one's person is the object; it also applies "outside" the mind. A political reformer (for instance) is firmly committed to his view of the world: he sees and experiences society rent by class dissensions. Yet he is not content to mouth tired political catch phrases. He thinks about this world in which he finds himself, and everywhere he discovers new evidence for his diagnoses of society's ills. Much thought also goes into the application of his proposed remedies. To be a successful revolutionary a man must think but he need not, and perhaps should not, reflect. If the reformer were to reflect he would have to temper his revolutionary zeal, detach himself from his aims and his habitual attitude toward the world, and question what had seemed self-evident before. He would have to raise the question whether the world which he had taken to be immediately experienced is not at least in part the embodiment of his own wishes and the product of his imagination. Here again reflection requires detachment and widens the scope of inquiry.

These examples show that the difference between thinking and reflection does not lie in the respective objects of these activities since any object can be the object of thinking as well as of reflection. The examples have also provided us with material for showing where the difference between thought and reflection does lie. Besides, we shall find that Husserl's description of the transcendental-phenomenological reduction provides us with all the terms and distinctions needed for the analysis of these two examples.

(a.) The person who thinks is "interested" in the objects of his thought; they attract him.[22] We saw this very clearly in our two examples: the child was overwhelmed by his anger and sense of injury; the reformer was "caught up" in his world which was waiting to be reformed. (b.) To be interested or to be attracted by an object brings with it that the object which is attracting me is accepted as it presents itself; it "imposes" itself on the observer.[23] For the child his anger and hurt are indubitably real. He would reject emphatically any suggestion that "things are really not so bad." The man who is, in this sense, attracted by or interested in the world or in himself accepts the world and himself "at face value." This attitude Husserl calls *"natuerlicher Seinsglaube"* [24] the unquestioning acceptance of the existence of what is experienced. (c.) In order to begin to reflect one must perform the *epoché,* i.e., one must suspend this interest, become disinterested.[25] Thus, the child begins to reflect only after his commitment to the existing experience is weakened, if he stands back and takes up a "neutral attitude." [26] This involves cancelling or suspending the earlier acceptance of experience, placing oneself, as Husserl puts it sometimes, "above" the natural world, where by "natural" he means "prereflective." [27]

(d.) The *epoché* thus renders questionable what previously had been taken as certain and self-evident. This does not mean that experience as a whole is rejected. To question something is not to deny it. The child does not suddenly say, "Oh, I'm not really angry"; the reformer does not deny that the world is riddled with injustices, but experience ceases to be unambiguous and the door is opened to questions. The certainty once possessed by experience now becomes a mere claim. World as well as psychological self become, in Husserl's language, "mere phenomenon." We are beginning to take up a properly reflective attitude, one of detachment and questioning. Here the *epoché* ends and we are entering the phase which Husserl calls the reduction.

For this new attitude, what was once a clear datum becomes a complex experience in need of clarification; what seemed actual becomes mere possibility,[28] and this transformation has several important implications:

(e.) What had, at one time, seemed to be a fact of immediate experience now looks as if it might have been merely an interpretation and, possibly, a false one. Maybe his father's severity was not a manifestation of ill will or sheer arbitrariness. Perhaps the poverty of the workers is

---

[22] *Erfahrung und Urteil,* ed. by Ludwig Landgrebe, Hamburg, 1949, p. 80. This work will be referred to as *Erfahrung.*

[23] Ibid.

[24] *Cart.,* p. 59.

[25] *Op. cit.,* p. 73.

[26] *Ideen I,* pp. 264ff.

[27] *Krisis,* p. 395.

[28] *Cart.,* p. 66.

not merely a result of exploitation and the greed of employers. Only in the reflective attitude do we begin to separate what is really given in experience, what close and attentive scrutiny reveals to be "really there" from what was merely added to this experience by the observer, as interpretation or anticipation. We distinguish here, Husserl says, between what is "self-given" *(selbstgegeben),*[29] what is given "in the flesh" *(leibhaft),*[30] and what is merely associated opinion *(Mitmeinung).*[31] It is here, in reflection, that the distinction between true belief and knowledge is first drawn.

(f.) On the other hand, interested thought is selective. As long as I accept the world of natural experience unquestioningly, certain facts of the situation are either not noticed at all or are put aside as unimportant. But now, in reflection, the facts which had previously seemed self-evident have become questionable, and thus facts which they had overshadowed before or which, in relation to them, had seemed insignificant now come to light and must be examined carefully. The scope of relevant subject matter is widened considerably as soon as we make the transition from thinking to reflection. The angry child goes beyond his own anger and reflects about this anger in relation to his own conduct and that of his parents. The reformer considers facts previously ignored or unnoticed; he must, among other things, face up to his own preconceptions. These new facts had previously been "anonymous"; now they lose this anonymity.[32] Concepts or feelings which had been merely "at the back of my mind," as well as objects which I had seen or heard without noticing them are now brought out into the open.

(g.) Reflection must describe these new facts rather than explain them.[33] Explanations are in order where we know what the world or my present condition is like, and we want to find out why they are in this state. But as we turn from thinking to reflection we relinquish former certainties. Accordingly, there is nothing definite that would require or even be capable of an explanation. Instead, there are facts, only causally observed before or perhaps not observed at all, which need to be examined or re-examined in order to separate what is evidently given in our experience from what is merely associated opinion or outright fiction. Once the revolutionary questions his former world-view the facts lose the ready-made significance which his previous theories had given them. The once intelligible world is replaced by disjointed experiences which refuse to fit into any kind of pattern, and his first task is to pay close attention to actual observation to find what his society is really like, what in his

---

[29] *Formale,* p. 251.
[30] *Ideen I,* p. 52.
[31] *Cart.,* p. 82.
[32] *Cart.,* p. 84.
[33] *Ideen I,* pp. 171–174.

former experience was genuine fact, and what merely supposition and interpretation.

(h.) Throughout the unfolding of these two transformations, the *epoché* and the reduction, repeated reference was made to the reflecting self. These must now be rendered more explicit. As the subject takes up a more detached attitude, his experience takes on a different complexion, and this is true whether the object is myself or the world. Thus, it appears, that the content of experience is dependent on myself as subject; experience presents to me its claim to validity: I must certify this claim. I can withdraw my confidence or belief from the object, thereby transforming it from a valid experience into a mere phenomenon. In this sense I, as a subject, am the source of the validity of experience,[34] but this, at the same time, transforms the meaning of the experience. Once the validity of present experience is put in question, one looks at the world with "new eyes" and the world looks different to one. In this sense the subject is not only the source of validity of experience, but also of its significance *(Sinn)*.[35]

(i.) As the scope of awareness widens, the self as subject falls under notice: the reformer begins to ask how much his own wishes, desires, needs, prejudices shaped his experience of the world. The child wonders whether his actions have merited the punishment inflicted. Reflection, thus, is always expanding in two directions: The world is examined in relation to myself when I try to distinguish those aspects of experience which are genuinely evident from those which I merely assume or suppose to be the case. The subject is examined in relation to the world when I inquire into the beliefs, feelings, desires, etc., which shaped the experiences about which I am now reflecting. Husserl distinguishes these two directions of reflection as the "noetic" and the "noematic" aspects of the intentional relation; the former refers to the subject-in-relation-to-the-object, the latter to the object-in-relation-to-the-subject.[36] These two aspects of the intentional relation are strictly correlative;[37] they determine each other and each can only be understood in the light of the other. There is no object unless it is object for some subject,[38] and no subject unless it has a world as its object.[39]

(j.) Noetic analysis only reveals the ego in so far as it has become the object of a reflective act; the ego which reflects here, as in all reflection, remains irrevocably anonymous. We are aware of its presence but it has no content, it cannot be described.[40] Reflection, then, takes a subjective

---

[34] *Cart.*, p. 65.
[35] Ibid.
[36] *Ideen I*, p. 218ff., and *Cart.*, p. 74.
[37] *Formale*, p. 231.
[38] *Ideen I*, pp. 110ff.
[39] *Cart.*, p. 99.
[40] *Ideen I*, p. 195.

turn in three different ways: The object of thinking is revealed as object-for-a-subject, as object whose validity and significance flows from this subject. The subject is seen as being the subject-of-this-object, the subject which, in Husserl's language, "constitutes" the object. At the same time the ego which reflects but eludes all descriptive grasp makes itself felt.

We have now shown that the transcendental-phenomenological reduction shows all the common features of the transition from thinking to reflection. It remains for another paper to show the distinguishing marks of phenomenological reflection which sets it apart from reflection in everyday life or in the sciences.

ARON GURWITSCH

ON THE OBJECT OF THOUGHT*

Contrasting with the objectivistic trend which, to a large extent, prevails in contemporary philosophy and psychology, phenomenology has insisted upon the orientation toward subjectivity, i.e., consciousness. It is to the defense and, if possible, the elaboration of this orientation that the present paper is devoted. We propose to discuss a concept which is of central importance in this respect, namely the concept of what may be called the "subjective object." Provisionally and roughly defined, it is the concept of the object not as it really is, but as it appears to the experiencing subject's mind through a given act of consciousness. What is meant hereby is called noema in Husserl's terminology.

Since, as far as I can see, William James was the first to lay down the concept of the "subjective object," it seems appropriate to begin by expounding some pertinent ideas of James'. His term for the concept in question is "object of thought" as distinguished from "topic"; it is this term with the sense James gives to it that I borrow as title of the present paper. It must be remarked that in dealing with theories of James, we are concerned only with James the psychologist, that is with ideas which James advanced in his *Principles of Psychology;* we shall have to disregard his later philosophical development. In the second part of my argument,

* Aron Gurwitsch, "On the Object of Thought," *Philosophy and Phenomenological Research* 7, no. 3 (March 1947): pp. 347–52. Reprinted with the permission of the editor.

I shall attempt to radicalize James' methodological reflections so as to open an avenue of approach towards constitutive phenomenology.

According to James, a most essential character of mental states or thoughts consists in their cognitive function or knowing reference to extramental facts. Such a fact is known to the mental state through which it presents itself and it is also known to the psychologist who studies the mental state in question, no matter whether the latter is his own experience or that of another person. The psychologist's knowledge of the extramental fact is assumed to be "true"; to be, at least, as true and as complete, but, as a rule, more true and more complete than that of the mental state under examination. We shall see presently that the knowledge of the psychologist extends in any case further than that of the mental state studied, since the former includes elements which are altogether absent from the thought in question, even when the latter happens to be one of the psychologist's own experiences. In this case, the knowledge which the psychologist has as a psychologist is obviously not conveyed to him by his mental state which he is just studying, but is derived from other sources, as, for instance, previous experiences concerning the extramental fact in question. In the case of introspective analysis, the psychologist has a double knowledge of the extramental fact concerned: (1) the knowledge he owes to his mental state which he is actually experiencing and goes on to analyse in introspection; (2) the knowledge which he has insofar as he is a psychologist and which James terms the "psychologist's reality."

The "psychologist's reality" comprises first of all the extramental fact which in the case of perception stimulates a certain section of the nervous system and provokes nerve- and brain-processes to which there corresponds the mental state to be studied. We must keep in mind that this mental state is not only aroused by, but also bears knowing reference to that extramental fact. As to this fact, the psychologist accepts the commonsense belief. This belief is supplemented by what the psychologist learns from the physical sciences. Thus when he has to discuss the perception of a black body, the psychologist will take account of the fact that no light is reflected from the surface of that body. The "psychologist's reality" furthermore includes the organic conditions of the stimulation and finally comprises a knowledge properly to be called psychological: the knowledge, namely, of what mental state other than the actual one would be given rise to, if the same extramental fact would stimulate the nervous system, but under conditions different, in this or that respect, from the present ones.

The "thought's object" is the specific knowledge which the thought studied has of the extramental fact or, as James likewise calls it, of the "topic" to which it bears cognitive reference. Accordingly, James defines the "object of thought" as the thought's "entire content or deliverance neither more nor less." Surveying the various examples James cites to illustrate his concept and the manifold applications he makes of it, one may say as follows: Whenever a mental state occurs, something appears to the experiencing subject's mind. This something may be a sense-datum as well as the meaning of a comparatively complicated sentence. It might be given directly, as in sense-perception, or in a rather symbolic manner. The something in question appears in a certain light, under a certain aspect, surrounded by a halo, escorted by fringes, swimming in a network of relations, and so on. What thus stands to the mind or to the thought studied, such—but exactly and only such—as it actually does, that is the "thoughts' object." This object *is* what it is experienced and known *as* through the particular mental state considered.

The preceding description may well be taken as a provisional characterisation of Husserl's concept of noema. As James distinguishes between "topic" and "object" of thought, so does Husserl between the "object which is intended" and the "object as it is intended." The latter, to borrow from Prof. Farber's paraphrase of Husserl's description, is to be taken just as it is intended, just as it is determined in the way in which it presents itself, in just the manner in which it is meant through the act of consciousness under consideration. To give one example, the distinction is between the meaning or sense of a proposition, that which is formulated and stated by the proposition, on the one hand, and, on the other hand, that about which the statement is made, the "objectivity" ("Gegenständlichkeit")—in Husserl's terminology—about which something is asserted and to which the proposition refers by means of its meaning. I refer to this example because some ideas which James has developed on this subject come rather close to certain aspects of Husserl's elaborate theory of meaning. Lack of time forbidding, I must refrain from pursuing the line along which there is agreement between James and Husserl as to the mentioned problem and I must also forsake surveying the elaboration of concepts analogous to that of the "object of thought" in contemporary psychological sciences. I have in view the abandonment of the constancy hypothesis in Gestalt-theory, the studies of late Gelb and Prof. Goldstein on the psychical effects of brain injuries, the late Lévy-Bruhl's account of mental functions in primitive societies, the views of the phonological school in linguistics, Max Weber's "verstehende Soziologie" and especially his distinction between "objektiver" and "subjektiver Sinn."

Turning to the second part of my argument, the radicalization of James' methodological reflections and the transition to constitutive phenomenology, I must, to begin with, characterize James' general position in which he established the concept of "object of thought."

This position is that of the psychologist, psychology being considered as a natural science, all philosophical questions put aside deliberately. Within the real world there are two domains: the domain of things known or to be known and the domain of mental states knowing, neither domain being reducible to the other. The cognitive function of mental states is simply posited and every inquiry as to its possibility or general nature is explicitly excluded. Thus a dualism and even a kind of preestablished harmony between things and thoughts is assumed. It is this dualism which gives rise to the specific philosophical questions. The line along which we are going to formulate these problems is, however, entirely different from that which James followed in his philosophical development subsequent to the *Principles of Psychology.*

The radicalization of the methodological reflections consists in enlarging the scope of the psychological point of view so as to apply this point of view also to that which falls within the "psychologist's reality." In a universal reflection, the psychologist makes himself aware of the fact that whatever he knows as a psychologist about the "topic" and about other items which pertain to the "psychologist's reality" is due to certain experiences. Just because he adopts the point of view of natural science, the psychologist does not consider the topic and other elements of the psychologist's reality" as metaphysical entities, but takes them as a matter of experience. For the point of view of empirical science, a thing is what it is known as, to refer to Hodgson's fortunate formulation of the sound principles of British empiricism. There is then a relation between any element of the "psychologist's reality" and experiences, both actual and possible, through which that element is known as that which it is, displays its qualities, properties and determinations, appears in its real existence, and exhibits the meaning of its existence. For the sake of simplicity, let us suppose that the psychologist is studying a mental state of his own. He is then confronted with a "thought's object," i.e., with the topic such— exactly and only such—as it stands to his mind through the mental state he is studying. But the psychologist does not lose sight of the topic as it really is. In the radicalization in question, the topic is considered in its relations to experiences, not only to the mental state which the psychologist is studying, at least not to this mental state alone, but also to experiences made in the past and which, under certain circumstances, the psychologist is free to repeat. Between these experiences, there is accordance, convergence and conformance, by virtue of which all of them present themselves as experiences of the topic in question. The same holds correspondingly for the other elements of the "psychologist's reality," e.g., for the organic conditions of the stimulation. Here too, there is reference to experiences, though not to mere perceptions, but to the latter as embodied in scientific interpretation and elaboration. The experiences which are here in question exhibit some complexity and a rather complex stratification.

Proceeding in this way, the psychologist becomes a psychologist throughout with regard to whatever exists and is valid for him; or, for that matter, he becomes a philosopher. By the same token, an *incipient* phenomenological reduction is performed, incipient, because it is not yet the phenomenological reduction in the developed and elaborated form in which Husserl has formulated it in the *Ideen* and, later, in the *Méditations Cartésiennes.* But the essential principle, the consideration of every object with reference to experience and to groups of experiences, is already laid down.

To exemplify the reference of a real existent to the experiences through which the existent appears and is known as that which it is, let us take a glance at perception. When we perceive a thing, we do so from a certain standpoint and at a certain distance. The thing is near to, or far remote from, us; it offers itself from this side or from that; it is seen under a certain aspect; situated in a perceptual field, the thing appears under the perspective of these or those other things belonging to that field. As we change our standpoint, come nearer to, go farther away, or go around the thing, the latter presents itself from different sides and appears under varying aspects and perspectives. We are here confronted with the phenomena which Husserl has brought out in his theory of perceptual adumbration (Wahrnehmungsabschattung). Allowance must furthermore be made for the experiences of the causal properties of the thing. If we go beyond the perceptual level, account must be taken also of the idealizing processes through which the causal properties receive mathematical formulation and find expression in the concepts of physics like mass, conductivity of heat, index of refraction, electrical conductance. Thus we are in the presense of a plurality of mental states, all different from each other, and yet all referring to the same real existent. James has laid down the "principle of constancy in the mind's meanings" to the effect that "the same matters can be thought of in successive portions of the mental stream, and some of these portions can know that they mean the same matters which the other portions meant." Adopting the point of view of psychology as a natural science, James could content himself with simply asserting this principle and with ascertaining its dominance in consciousness. If through the radicalization of the psychological point of view, we pass to the phenomenological level, the mentioned principle proves a title for far and deep reaching investigations. In fact, the identity of the object in the face of the multiple experiences referring to the former is the fundamental problem of constitutive phenomenology whose aim is to account for the object or existent in terms of the pertinent experiences.

Let us finally consider the form in which the dualism between the "thought's object" and the topic appears on the phenomenological level. Considered in its reference to the multiple pertinent experiences, the topic proves itself an "object of thought," related, to be sure, not to this or that particular experience, but to the totality of experiences through which it becomes or may become known as that real existent which it is. In this sense, the topic turns out to be an "object of thought" of an higher order. To put it in Husserl's terminology, through each of the experiences in question, the topic presents itself in a certain mode of appearance; to each of these experiences there corresponds a noema, viz., the topic as appearing under a certain aspect and perspective. To the totality of experiences there corresponds, ideally, the topic under the totality of its possible aspects and perspectives. In other words, the topic is a noematic entity itself, more precisely it proves the systematic concatenation of noemata. Now, the particular experience under consideration belongs to the group of experiences through which the topic discloses and unfolds itself in its properties, qualities and determinations. Accordingly, the noema which corresponds to this experience, belongs itself to the mentioned noematic system. Hence the relation between the "object of thought" and the "topic" is that between a member of a system and the system itself; there is the corresponding relation between a particular experience and the coherent group of experiences to which the former belongs. The problems which arise in this connection concern (1) the phenomenal features through which the reference and pertinence of this particular noema to the noematic system is given and (2) the nature of the coherence of the noematic system and of the group of corresponding experiences. The latter question refers, so to speak, to the dynamics of conscious life. Earlier we mentioned the accordance, conformance and convergence between experiences which are experiences of one and the same object. These terms refer to the internal structure of the system and group in question. Problems of this type arise with regard to all domains, perceptual and other, with which constitutive phenomenology is dealing.

I am too well aware of the little sympathy or, shall I better say, lack of sympathy which James, especially the older James would have had for this trend of ideas to present them as a continuation and development, let alone interpretation, of James' intentions. If notwithstanding the intention of the historical James, I started from his methodological reflections, it is because James has brought out the foundation problems of psychology with such clarity and rigour, that motives become apparent which lead towards the phenomenological position. In the present phase of phenomenology, it seems to me important to insist upon the possibility of disengaging such motives from the foundation problems of the sciences. I am very glad to find myself in full agreement with Prof. Farber's stand that phenomenology is not detached from the sciences, not separated from them by an unbridged gulf, but is accessible from the sciences. Accessibility means continuity by motivation. This holds not only for psychology, but applies also to the foundation problems of the other sciences, the mathematical and physical sciences as well as the historical and social sciences. As to the latter I refer to the work done by Dr. Schuetz. If phenomenology keeps in contact with the sciences and if, on the other hand, the foundation problems of the sciences are set forth in a radical way as to their philosophical implications, much clarification and advancement may be expected for the foundation problems along these convergent lines of research.

DON IHDE

SOME AUDITORY PHENOMENA*

The task of this paper is to point up certain phenomena which I believe have been neglected in philosophical investigation, i.e., *auditory phenomena.* In their most explicit relation to the history of philosophic discussion auditory phenomena would probably be considered within the larger problematic of the relation of perception to understanding or of sense and reason. It is my implicit contention that it may be wise to undertake a more complete examination of the phenomena of auditory perception—and of imagination—prior to arguing general implications for epistemological theory.

I should indicate from the very beginning that my investigations take place within a general philosophic commitment to phenomenological procedures. I hold to that tradition which contends that prior to tracing implications and relations one must examine the phenomena of experience. What I say about auditory phenomena is guided by the idea of phenomenological reporting at this point largely within the limits of what Husserl would have called *phenomenological psychology.* I should also indicate that when I use the terms "perception" and "imagination" I refer to descriptions of immediate experience and not to theories about perception

* Don Ihde, "Some Auditory Phenomena," *Philosophy Today* 10 (Winter 1966): pp. 227–35. Reprinted with the permission of the author.

and imagination which attempt to account for or to explain our experiences.

My explicit strategy is to begin with observations upon what I claim to be a narrowness in the traditions of philosophical discussion of both perception and imagination. (a) I first indicate that the mainstream of philosophic discussion of perception and imagination has often centered in visual models, metaphors, and understandings of the world. (b) Secondly, I seek to display what I take to be frequently ignored or hidden aspects of perception and imagination in terms of auditory phenomena. In this case I employ a descriptive and suggestive contrast between visual and auditory modes of perception. (c) Finally, by uncovering certain unique characteristics of auditory phenomena, I move to a brief description of auditory imagination which leads to the uncovery of a dual primacy of language and perception.

Thesis 1: *In questions of both perception and imagination philosophical discussion has largely resorted to visual models and metaphors.*

Early in our philosophic tradition Aristotle announces that:

> Above all, we value sight; disregarding its practical uses, we prefer it, I believe, to every other sense, even when we have no material end in view. Why? Because sight is the principal source of knowledge and reveals many differences between one object and another.[1]

One might even return to philosophy prior to Aristotle and find a similar affirmation concerning visual perception. Heraclitus claims, "Eyes are more accurate witnesses than ears."[2] In both cases it is the accuracy for distinctions which stands out. I suspect that even the later tradition of "clear and distinct ideas" in Cartesianism is also a visual metaphor. When one adds the notions of "insight," "intuition," "models," not to mention the many common expressions for understanding such as, "I see what you mean," the great emphasis upon the visual in both literal and metaphorical senses begins to emerge.

The importance of visual metaphor for thought in even its most abstract and theoretical uses is sometimes noticeable. One could almost endlessly suggest possibilities from the history of philosophy. For example: when Berkeley claims that we do not have any general ideas present to the mind because only specific ideas are so present, does he mean that we cannot imagine in a visual sense anything other than a specific triangle or a series of successive triangles? Or, when certain commentators upon current scientific theory remark that we have replaced picturable models with sheer mathematical ones does this mean we have finally moved out of the range of visual modelling and metaphor? Finally, note the great

---

[1] Aristotle, *Metaphysics,* trans. John Warrington (London: J. M. Dent and Sons, Ltd., 1956), p. 51.
[2] Wheelwright, ed., *The Presocratics* (New York: Odyssey Press, 1966), p. 70.

importance of visualizable graphs, such as the existential graphs of Peirce, for the teaching and understanding of logic.

The emphasis upon the visual is not less absent in phenomenology and existentialism. Indeed, one might well say that with Husserl's consistent use of *Anschauung, Wesenschau, Sicht, Eidos,* etc., the emphasis upon "seeing" and visual metaphor becomes more and not less pronounced. Sartre, in his discussion of other persons, again places the problem in terms of "the look."

To this point I have merely isolated a few examples which illustrate some ways in which visual models and metaphors have been frequently used in philosophical discussion—just as the same point could be made for visual metaphor on common speech. But if philosophy does rely upon such a visual emphasis the result is not inconsequential. A preoccupation with the visual has, in my opinion, at least two more important consequences: (a) In the first place the constant emphasis upon the visual in both perceptual and imaginative areas has the effect that a similarly extended investigation into auditory phenomena is frequently ignored. The reasons for this may be several, but I suspect that philosophers may often accept an "aristotelean" visual tradition as the most obvious place to discuss sense and perhaps go on to assume that whatever problems emerge there would apply equally well in the domains of the other senses. (b) But ignoring a certain area of phenomena may also have the effect of *hiding* what may be important and unique data for further consideration. It may be that hidden or ignored phenomena such as those of the audible may hold implications for a more general understanding of philosophical modelling processes.

We might begin by asking: Do all senses have the same characteristics? In what way is each sense unique? And what implications does each area of sense have for philosophical thought? For not all perception nor all imagination is visual in character. We are creatures of auditory perception and auditory imagination as well. Here we might do well to listen to the advice of Empedocles as well as to see the wisdom of Aristotle:

> Come now, with all your powers discern how each thing manifests itself, *trusting no more to sight than to hearing,* and no more to the echoing ear than to the tongue's taste: rejecting none of the body's parts that might be a means to knowledge, but attending to each particular manifestation. [italics mine] [3]

For while it is not necessarily the case that Aristotle and Heraclitus were wrong about the distinction and accuracy of the visual witness—in relation to the appearances of enduring objects—it might be that an examination of auditory phenomena would yield quite different insights.

---

[3] Ibid., p. 127.

Recently I found a sympathetic ear in the person of F. Joseph Smith of Emory, who incidentally is trained in both music and philosophy. Smith independently arrived at some of the same notions I had developed in a paper on Perceiving Persons.[4] In his paper, "Insights Leading to a Phenomenology of Sound," he notes:

> And yet it is necessary to do more than look into the situation. And perhaps it is precisely here that our great teachers fail us, in that they still make use of visual metaphor and the language of sight. In seeking the full phenomenological spectrum we may have to do more than just look into things . . . [he goes on to question Aristotle's assertion and adds] musicians of that time, whose ear was attuned to far more subtle tonal nuances than ours, and who had no such reliance on written music as we do . . . would not have been able to agree with Aristotle. . . . For most musicians feel that the sense of hearing is far more perceptive and profound than that of sight, since sound reaches to the very center of our being.[5]

Smith goes so far as to call for an examination of *akoumena* rather than the visually suggestive *phenomena* of the dominant tradition.

Thesis 2: *While there are certain common structural characteristics to every mode of perception each sense has its own distinctive mode of being.*

To get at the distinct characteristics of auditory phenomena as over against visual phenomena one needs a technique of reduction to purified phenomena. It is here that phenomenological reporting and reduction are important. The aim is to successively explore the region of auditory phenomena paying strict attention to the presentation of the phenomena.

Unfortunately this is not so simple as it might seem an ordinary introspection or casual noticing will not do. (a) In the first place the objects within our experience and our experiencing of them is global. We find ourselves thinking, seeing, hearing, being in a certain mood, having a certain bodily feeling, and so on. This is in no way to say that our experience is a buzzing, blooming confusion, because it isn't. It takes no apparent effort to experience in this globally primary way at all. One might add that it is our analysis which characterizes experience as multi-dimensioned. (b) But we can also focus or concentrate upon a given dimension of our experience. And here the problem is to focus upon the way in which auditory phenomena present themselves. (c) But even this is not completely sufficient because our listening, both perceptually and imaginatively, is imbedded in habits and beliefs and theoretical considerations which may further confuse the issue. Our language, for example, displays visual imagery in relation to auditory phenomena quite frequently:

---

[4] This paper was presented at the Society for Phenomenology and Existential Philosophy, 20 October 1966.

[5] F. Joseph Smith, "Heidegger and Insights Leading to a Phenomenology of Sound," unpublished paper, pp. 2–3.

"That was a brilliant sound." "A very bright little piece of music." "Oh, what a clear voice." These habitual and theoretical considerations hinder our getting at a reduced or purified auditory world. Phenomenologists have as a first rule the "bracketing" of such consideration in order that concentration upon the phenomena may be more complete.

Now while I presuppose a phenomenological reduction as a technique one can "short-cut" the method for purposes here if one is willing to resort to suggestive and often metaphorical language to point up the phenomena we wish to isolate. The ultimate appeal in the process is to a careful examination of your own experience. Finally, I employ one other "short-cut" by supplying a guiding clue as a heuristic device.

My suggestion is this: visual phenomena *tend* to be *spatially oriented:* auditory phenomena *tend* to be *temporally oriented.* This clue is probable open to a number of modifications if we pursue the matter to its ultimate extreme—but if we follow this clue at first certain notions emerge.

(1) To play up the contrast let us first concentrate upon the "spatiality" of sound—how does sound present itself to us? Case #1: We are in a room in which a stereo set is playing a Beethoven symphony; the sound is turned up enough to cover all background sounds. In this case if one were to ask about the "spatiality" of sound he might be tempted to describe it as either too poor or too rich. If we were asked to locate sound as we might locate a material object then phenomenal sound is too poor in a spatial sense. To be sure, we might be able to locate a certain general direction as the origin of the sound—especially if we use our eyes as a guide (we see the speakers). But if we reduce our experience to consideration of pure sound then the direction of sound becomes less precise (hide the speakers or blindfold the listener. Note, too, the interesting phenomena of seeing a person talk in an auditorium and hearing him "as if" the sound were coming from his mouth despite the fact that the speakers are located at the sides of the room). Even here we might be said to be able in a very general sense to locate the direction of sound due to sound clues such as relative loudness near the speakers, etc. But in spite of all this the precise location of sound is too poor to count as a basis for identifying particular spatial position.

Thus we might turn to the other temptation and say that sound is too rich in its spatiality. We might say that sound surrounds us; we are absorbed in the music; sound is fullness; or, for my own preference, sound is in "parmenidean fashion" a complete and well rounded whole. In either case, spatial poverty or spatial wealth, the spatiality of sound is not the same as that of sight.

With visual phenomena the case is normally otherwise. We are able to locate objects within a field with describable precision. The chair is on the right of the table; the blackboard is behind the desk; the book is on top of the shelf—and if these descriptions are not accurate enough you may add measurements down to millimeters.

Finally, if one attempts to apply visual spatial relations in a strict sense to auditory phenomena the contrast becomes sharp: It would be odd to say, in listening to the Beethoven symphony, that the sound of the oboe is to the right of the bass viol or that the sound of the trombone was in front of the sound of the cornet.

(2) This does not mean that sound lacks its own distinctions and precision. For there are other dimensions to auditory phenomena. The symphony is presented as a totality—but within that totality further variations can occur. Case #2: In a given passage the strong section plays *forte* but the other instruments "recede" to *pianissimo.* That is, within the totality of sound certain sounds "stand out." Note that even in this description the metaphors of visual space may well intrude themselves— yet strictly speaking we ought to say the sound of the strings is stronger, auditorily more penetrating, than that of the other instruments. The relations are not spatial ones at base at all.

We might be able, with effort, to elicit a language which does not revert to visual and spatial imagery if we wish to make more precise the mode of sound presence. The "standing out against the background" of sound against sound is auditory and not visual or spatial. One might better say that there is a "sounding out above sound." But we must admit that our words are ordinarily too poor to entice exactly the sense of sound presence.

Case #3: Another dimension of auditory phenomena similar to the piercing presentation of one sound in relation to the other is the ability we have to select from a field of sound certain given sounds. Again, as the symphony presents itself as a totality, I can within limits select out certain instruments. I can focus my auditory attention upon the flute rather than upon the violin or, for that matter, upon the symphony as a whole. I can make this sound "stand out" against the background— within limits. That is, within the sound world I can isolate dimensions of sounds almost as if they were individuals.

(3) But here I must be careful, for my speech opens itself to a spatializing and thus visualizing of sounds. I have broken up Sound into sounds; I have made the totality a series of parts. But is it necessary that this occur? I suspect that one reason sound appears "poor" is that we demand that it be of the same structure as visual phenomena.

Now I grant that the use of visual metaphor is so strong that even blind persons talk about "seeing" though it should be noted that their seeing is a hearing and a feeling. Their learning to use the terms correctly cannot have been from visual experience.

Since, for the present, we seem doomed to visual metaphor, I should like to suggest that rather than a model of discrete spatial individuals for the auditory world, we ought to employ a fluid-dynamic model. Sound, if we speak of spatiality at all, is like a fluid which surrounds us but it is a fluid which contains dimensions of varying shades and viscosities—

nor is this imaginative model out of keeping if physics holds any truth. We claim, after all, that that gaseous totality, air, carries sound to us.

(4) The global encompassing of sound is a pervasive sounding which seems, as Smith remarks, to penetrate to the center of our being. My control of sound is less complete and less spontaneous than my reaction and control of vision. A flash of bright light can make me blink my eyes; I have but to easily shut them if I wish to close off the obvious world; or I can turn my head to avoid seeing a painful spectacle. None of these escapes or controls is so easy with sound. When the children are fighting in the next room they can "get to me" in a hurry for I cannot avoid them except by removing my presence; by placing my fingers in my ears; or by insulating and soundproofing my study. Turning my head may help me to hear a barely audible sound—but it will not shut off a loud one. Sound pervades my world and it invades my being.

Thus I would note that sound is "spatially poor" in respect to discrete individuals; but it is "spatially rich" in its fluid ability to flood and intrude itself upon my consciousness—perhaps it is this one characteristic which turns the metaphorical table upon sight when we talk about "loud colors." But let us now turn the coin around and examine temporality, following our clue that sight is temporally poor when compared to auditory phenomena.

(1) In the history of philosophic thought enduring, stable, and usually fixed objects have frequently provided a norm for discussion. Much ink has been used to discuss doors, tables, and chairs (or when we think about unchanging substances) they seem to be permanent fixtures of the world. This is the case whether or not something "underlies" them. Such statics of metaphysical discussion often never rise to the question of temporality.

Yet the puzzles of time are among the most difficult and complex for philosophical investigation. I suggest that part of this difficulty may well lie at the door of the quasi-visual norms we have allowed to dominate philosophical literature.

Even within the visual domain one can find an approximation to the difficulty of time. While most discussion seems to be directed to enduring and seemingly almost timeless or changeless entities, the more difficult discussion has been had over how to deal with motion. For even within the visual domain motion entices a sense of time. Time is inseparable from motion whereas stable objects may be said to allow time to "float over them."

But now turn to auditory phenomena. The ever-changing presence of sound is time-ful. Sound is in normal situation never static. Its coming into being and its passing from being is continual in its variation. The world of sound is one of fury save in ideal situations or in exceptional isolation in a desert. I suspect it is not without reason that Husserl turns to musical experience when he describes the protentive and retentive characteristics of internal time consciousness.

The constant temporality of sound presence is almost total, and, despite those who would maintain that nature is mute, the presentation of varied sound occurs there as well. At my summer home in the mountains of Vermont the world is surrounded with sound. It may appear to be quiet—by contrast to the Honda culture of Carbondale—but it is not silent. From bubbling stream to babbling bird to breathful wind the mountains are full of sound.

By contrast the two situations which would be the most shattering and eerie would probably be complete silence or the presence of a single, unending note of sound. In either case the timeful variance of sound would suddenly become de-timed and one might well be disoriented. In the rare cases when there is an absence of sound many persons comment that time becomes unreal or stands still.

(2) Now to this point concerning time and sound I would like to add a higher level speculation which I find extremely enticing but have yet to fully work out. Scholars have long remarked that one of the distinctive elements in our cultural past was the development of a philosophy, or better a theology of history among the Hebrews. A sense of history and historical consciousness was acutely present with this Semitic tribe in comparison to their surrounding neighbors. Note that among other aspects of their cultural outlook was a unique theology of the Word. Word, for the Old Testament thinkers, was not a stable structure in the later Greek sense of *Logos,* but was rather the expression of a "willful" power through breath.

Word, for the Hebrews, was living or timeful word. In addition, the Hebrews held an absolute prohibition against *images* or representations of God. God could not be visually represented. Visual representation was idolatry and the prophets mocked idols because of their static lifelessness. But curiously enough, there were no prohibitions against God manifesting himself in Word. Indeed, it was through Word that God did manifest Himself. Could it be that the strong sense of temporality and history has its basis in a theology of the word in more than a metaphorical sense?

Again, independently, F. J. Smith has made a similar point:

> Speech is a thing of sound, not a phenomenon, but an akoumenon. . . . Nothing I am saying is appearing to you in the full sense of what I aim to be at this time. My words, as alive, as "acoustical phenomena" are what bring meaning. . . . [Just as in] prophetism the sense of hearing is foremost, for the prophet must listen to the God and then in turn must speak for the God to the people. It is the dialectic of listening and speaking that is at the basis of a phenomenology of prophetism.[6]

---

[6] Ibid., p. 3.

This last speculation, however, opens still another area for investigation of auditory phenomena. Certainly spoken and heard language is to be found within the larger spectrum of acoustical phenomena. Here I turn to a more specific examination of the experience of the audible in relation to language.

Thesis 3: *The auditory presence of language is an almost total constant of experience.*

This statement may at first seem odd. Yet I think it can be supported by an examination of our on-going experience. In the first place allow me to underline what should have been obvious, but which is frequently unnoticed, i.e., that all the language of vision, the metaphorical and imagistic language, may be *said* and not *seen.* The auditory phenomena of my speaking may be the basis for visual imagery. Spoken and heard language is the enticer of visual imagery and not the other way around. While visual models may be basic for our understanding ultimately I would argue that language is more basic and that language is first thought, spoken and listened to within the domain of auditory phenomena.

Now when I claim that the auditory presence of language is an almost total constant of experience, I do not nor could I maintain that one constantly hears audible speech in a perceptual mode. Thank goodness for the fact that outside universities people are not constantly talking! I perceive language only when it is spoken or when I say something out loud myself.

However, I do, so long as I am conscious, "think." And here I have immediately entered deep water—but allow me to foolishly tread this angelic domain of fancy. My sub-thesis is that a very explicit form of thinking is an *inner speech* which I would like to call an *auditory imagination.* Now I am open to a rather vast series of misunderstandings which might occur because "thinking" as we employ it covers so many types of conscious activity. I would not wish to deny that the phenomena of thinking are much more varied than inner speech in a strict sense. For that matter *auditory imagination* is also broader than *inner speech* since one can imaginatively "hear" music, another person's voice, etc. But what I am after for the limited purpose of this paper is the linguistic thinking which I suspect is the on-going ordinary accompaniment of our experience.

Ordinarily we are so absorbed by our interests and our projects that we may fail to notice the linguistic structure of our thought. Spoken language "hides itself" in order to reveal that which it refers to. This can be shown by asking ourselves if we can hear our native tongue as "mere noise." I suspect it would be hard to attain this in experience—but it is not quite so hard to attain when listening to a strange tongue. But thinking, inner speech, auditory imagination, is so ultimate in our experience that it is even more hidden as language. Inner speech as an auditory imagination which is linguistic in structure is further hidden by its time structure. My thinking in this form is "faster," for example than my speaking—just as my speaking is much faster than my writing or typing. I suspect this accounts for both confusions over the relation of thought and language and for our frequent failure to notice the linguistic structure of our thinking.

One can begin to approximate directness even in this case when we employ the imaginative variations suggested by Husserl. For example, my thinking as an auditory imagination in language can be found to be English. This becomes apparent if I try to think in French or German—neither of which I do spontaneously—though I hope some day to be able to do so. Recently I asked a quadralingual person what language she used for thinking. Her answer that she alternatively thought in one of the four languages and added that this was in some ways a disability since she felt that even though she had four forms for thinking she was master of none.

This auditory imagination in the form of language displays certain characteristics which are common to other forms of imagination. For example, as with visual imagination I can vary the object of my thinking freely. Visually I can imagine a purple butterfly or a green cow; auditorily I can think about Plato's ideas or the voice of my wife. Moreover, no matter how brilliant my visual imaginations may be they are present as "irreal" for the object of imagination is distinct from the object of perception. In a similar way my inner speech or auditory imagination has the "irreal" presence which is distinct from the language I hear from another through a hearing perception. My auditory imagination is the unsounded correlate of my perceived or spoken language.

But just as visual and auditory perception differ, so are visual and auditory imaginations different. For example, I can turn my visual imaginations off and on at will just as perceptually as I can close and open my eyes. Visual images are not constant. This is clearly not so easily the case with auditory imagination. My "thinking" in this linguistic form accompanies my various activities. I suggest you try to "turn off" this thinking altogether.

To be sure, auditory imagination may from time to time "recede" just as sounds recede. I may be so engrossed with a given project that I fail to notice in any explicit fashion the presence of auditory imagination. But if I but ask after it and its presence it appears as immediately there. Thus just as I find it hard to isolate myself from the pervading presence of sound I find I cannot escape my auditory imagination or thinking.

Its presence varies with my attention; if I am concentrating on a philosophical problem it fills my consciousness; if I am cutting a tree down to add to my cabin it is present only on the fringes. But it is rarely absent and the only time it appears to be so in anything approximating a total way is when I change to the imagination of music rather than thinking. (One might note that in the German version of the arts music was classified as one of the *redente Künste.* Music would constitute a special problem for a phenomenology of the auditory.)

Further, this auditory language is often totally imageless. It may be accompanied by visual imagery, but it need not be. Ordinarily I "hear" myself think (note that in the presence of distracting noise we might well say: "quiet down, I can't hear myself think"). One could say in an almost Wittgensteinian sense that there is linguistic thinking were it not that I had a fairly high degree of control over this activity or that the presence of such thinking raises again the question of a transcendental age.

Further auditory imagination, just as perceived sound, displays the already discussed temporalistic structures. It is timeful, on-going, constant. Indeed, if described in detail it sounds very like the structure of consciousness described by Husserl. This pervasive presence of auditory imagination, "thinking," may well be a more primary mode of self-awareness than any other. I would only note that a visual image of myself is quite rare if not impossible. But my auditory self-awareness is usual and it is in a nonimagistic mode that I project my possibilities toward the world. But here I am getting off the track.

As auditory imagination in the form of thought language I find an imaginative accompaniment to my perceiving. Thus at least in this single case I must modify the perceptualist emphasis of phenomenology to say that *both* language and the perceived world are co-present. With Merleau-Ponty I would maintain that a complete reduction to a pure perception is impossible—but I would add that what is discovered at the limit of the reduction is the juncture of perception and language (as thought) in the co-presence of auditory imagination and the life-world of perception.

STUDY QUESTIONS

Review

1. What is the meaning and significance of the term "phenomenology" for the philosophy of this name?
2. How are its criticisms of positivism, nominalism, and psychologism related or relatable?
3. Explain the characteristic terms: "Wesensschau," "eidetic reduction," "phenomenological reduction," "bracketing," and the direction to go "to the things themselves."
4. Summarize the points made in any of the selections in this chapter.

For Further Thought

5. Is it possible to have a presuppositionless science or knowledge?
6. What is the difference between describing and explaining the content of one's immediate experience? Can one describe without explaining?

7. Does science illegitimately narrow the field of what is admitted as objective knowledge?
8. Is human knowing intentional in Husserl's sense? How is the difference between our knowledge of existing and nonexisting things different if it is?

BIBLIOGRAPHY

Edmund Husserl

Husserl, Edmund. *Husserl: Shorter Works*. Ed. P. McCormick and F. A. Elliston. Notre Dame, Ind.: University of Notre Dame Press, 1981.
― ― ―. *Experience and Judgment: Investigations in a Genealogy of Logic*. Rev. and ed. Ludwig Landgrebe. Trans. James S. Churchill and Karl Ameriks. Introduction by James S. Churchill. Afterword by Lothar Eley. Evanston, Ill.: Northwestern University Press, 1973.
― ― ―. *The Crisis of European Sciences and Transcendental Phenomenology*. Trans. with introduction, David Carr. Evanston, Ill.: Northwestern University Press, 1970.
― ― ―. *Phenomenology and the Crisis of Philosophy*. Trans. with notes and introduction, Quentin Lauer. New York: Harper and Row, 1965.
― ― ―. *The Idea of Phenomenology*. Trans. W. P. Alston and G. Nakhnikian. The Hague: Martinus Nijhoff, 1964.
― ― ―. *Cartesian Meditations*. Trans. Dorion Cairns. The Hague: Martinus Nijhoff, 1960.
― ― ―. *Ideas*. Trans. W. R. Boyce Gibson. New York: Macmillan, 1931.

Phenomenology

Bruzina, Ronald, and Bruce Wilshire, eds. *Phenomenology: Dialogues and Bridges*. Albany: State University of New York Press, 1982.
Carr, David. *Phenomenology and the Problem of History: A Study of Husserl's Transcendental Phenomenology*. Northwestern University Studies in Phenomenology and Existential Philosophy. Evanston, Ill.: Northwestern University, 1974.
Casey, Edward S. *Imagining: A Phenomenological Study*. Bloomington: Indiana University Press, 1976.
Earle, William. *The Autobiographical Consciousness*. Chicago: Quadrangle Books, 1972.
Edie, James. *Speaking and Meaning: The Phenomenology of Language*. Bloomington: Indiana University Press, 1976.
― ― ―, ed. *New Essays in Phenomenology*. Chicago: Quadrangle Books, 1969.
― ― ―. *Phenomenology in America*. Chicago: Quadrangle Books, 1967.
Farber, Marvin, ed. *Philosophical Essays in Memory of Edmund Husserl*. New York: Greenwood Press, 1968.
― ― ―. *Phenomenology and Existence: Toward a Philosophy within Nature*. New York: Harper and Row, 1967.
― ― ―. *Naturalism and Subjectivism*. Springfield, Ill.: C. C. Thomas, 1959.
― ― ―. *The Foundation of Phenomenology: Edmund Husserl and the Quest for a Rigorous Science of Philosophy*. Albany: State University of New York Press, 1943.

Gier, N. *Wittgenstein and Phenomenology*. Albany: State University of New York Press, 1981.

Gurwitsch, Aron. *The Field of Consciousness*. Pittsburgh: Duquesne University Press, 1964.

— — —. *Human Encounters in the Social World*. Ed. A. Metraux. Trans. F. Kersten. Pittsburgh: Duquesne University Press, 1979.

Heelan, Patrick. *Space-Perception and the Philosophy of Science*. Berkeley: University of California Press, 1983.

Ihde, Don. *Listening and Voice: A Phenomenology of Sound*. Athens: Ohio University Press, 1976.

— — —. *Sense and Significance*. New York: Humanities Press for Duquesne University Press, 1973.

Ihde, Don, and Richard Zaner. *Philosophy and Existence*. New York: Putnam's, 1973.

Kockelmans, Joseph J., ed. *Phenomenology*. New York: Doubleday, 1967.

— — —. *Phenomenology and Physical Science*. New York: Humanities Press for Duquesne University Press, 1966.

Lauer, Quentin. *Phenomenology: Its Genesis and Prospect*. New York: Harper and Row, 1965.

Luijpen, H., O.S.A. *Existential Phenomenology*. Pittsburgh: Duquesne University Press, 1963.

McBride, William, and Calvin Schrag, eds. *Phenomenology in a Pluralistic Context*. Albany: State University of New York Press, 1983.

Mohanty, J.N. *Edmund Husserl's Theory of Meaning*. The Hague: Martinus Nijhoff, 1964.

Natanson, Maurice. *Phenomenology and the Social Sciences*. Northwestern University Studies in Phenomenology and Existential Philosophy. Evanston, Ill.: Northwestern University Press, 1973.

— — —. *Edmund Husserl: Philosopher of Infinite Tasks*. Northwestern University Studies in Phenomenology and Existential Psychology. Evanston, Ill.: Northwestern University Press, 1973.

Richardson, W. J. "Heidegger's Critique of Science." *New Scholasticism* 42: pp. 511–36.

Ricoeur, Paul. *Husserl: An Analysis of his Phenomenology*. Trans. Edward G. Ballard and Lester E. Embree. Northwestern University Studies in Phenomenology and Existential Psychology. Evanston, Ill.: Northwestern University Press, 1967.

Sallis, John, ed. *Research in Phenomenology*. New York: Humanities Press for Duquesne University Press. Published annually.

— — —. *Phenomenology and the Return to Beginnings*. Pittsburgh: Duquesne University Press, 1973.

— — —. *Husserl and Contemporary Thought*. Atlantic Highlands, N.J.: Humanities Press, 1983.

Schutz, Alfred. *On Phenomenology and Social Relations*. Ed. Helmut R. Wagner. Chicago: University of Chicago Press, 1970.

— — —. *The Phenomenology of the Social World*. Trans. G. Walsh and F. Lehnert. Northwestern University Studies in Phenomenology and Existential Philosophy. Evanston, Ill.: Northwestern University Press, 1967.

Schutz, Alfred, and Thomas Luckmann. *The Structures of the Life-World*. Trans. Richard M. Zaner and H. Tristram Englehardt, Jr. Evanston, Ill.: Northwestern University Press, 1973.

Sokolowski, Robert. *Presence and Absence.* Bloomington: Indiana University Press, 1978.

Spiegelberg, Herbert. *The Phenomenological Movement.* 2 vols. The Hague: Martinus Nijhoff, 1960.

Strasser, Stephan. *Phenomenology and the Human Sciences.* Pittsburgh: Duquesne University Press, 1963.

Thevenaz, Pierre. *What Is Phenomenology?* Chicago: Quadrangle Books, 1962.

Structuralism and Hermeneutics

Bauman, Zygmunt. *Hermeneutics and Social Science.* New York: Columbia University Press, 1978.

Berger, Peter, and T. Luckmann. *The Social Construction of Reality.* London: Allen Lane, 1967.

Bernstein, Richard J. *Objectivism and Relativism: Science, Hermeneutics, and Praxis.* Philadelphia: University of Pennsylvania Press, 1983.

Culler, Jonathan. *On Deconstruction: Theory and Criticism after Structuralism.* Ithaca, N.Y.: Cornell University Press, 1982.

DeGeorge, Richard T., and Fernande M. DeGeorge, eds. *The Structuralists: From Marx to Lévi-Strauss.* Garden City, N.Y.: Doubleday, 1972.

Gadamer, Hans-Georg. *Philosophical Hermeneutics.* Trans. and ed. David E. Linge. Berkeley: University of California Press, 1976; paperback, 1977.

Gardner, Patrick. *The Nature of Historical Explanation.* London: Oxford University Press, 1961.

Habermas, J. *Knowledge and Human Interests.* London: Heinemann, 1972.

Ihde, Don. *Hermeneutic Phenomenology: The Philosophy of Paul Ricoeur.* Evanston, Ill.: Northwestern University Press, 1971.

Klems, David E. *Hermeneutical Theory of Paul Ricoeur: A Constructive Analysis.* Bucknell, Pa.: Bucknell University Press, 1983.

Lane, Michael. *Structuralism: A Reader.* New York: Basic Books, 1970.

Leiber, Justin. *Structuralism: Skepticism and Mind in the Psychological Sciences.* Boston: Twayne Publishers, 1978.

Palmer, Richard E. *Hermeneutics: Interpretation Theory in Schleiermacher, Dilthey, Heidegger, and Gadamer.* Northwestern University Studies in Phenomenology and Existential Psychology. Evanston, Ill.: Northwestern University Press, 1969.

Piaget, J. *Structuralism.* 1968. Reprint. London: Routledge and Kegan Paul, 1971.

Ricoeur, Paul. *Hermeneutics and the Human Sciences: Essays on Language, Action, and Interpretation.* Ed. and trans. John B. Thompson. Cambridge: Cambridge University Press, 1981.

— — —. *The Rule of Metaphor: Multidisciplinary Studies of the Creation of Meaning in Language.* Trans. Robt. Czerny with Kathleen McLaughlin and John Costello, S. J. Toronto: University of Toronto Press, 1977.

— — —. *The Conflict of Interpretations: Essays on Hermeneutics.* Ed. Don Ihde. Evanston, Ill.: Northwestern University Press, 1974.

— — —. *Freedom and Nature: The Voluntary and the Non-Voluntary.* Trans. with introduction, Erazim U. Kohak. Northwestern University Studies in Phenomenology and Existential Psychology. Evanston, Ill.: Northwestern University Press, 1966.

Robey, David, ed. *Structuralism: An Introduction.* Oxford: Clarendon Press, 1973.

Seung, T. K. *Structuralism and Hermeneutics.* New York: Columbia University Press, 1982.

Wolff, Janet. *Hermeneutic Philosophy and the Sociology of Art.* London: Routledge and Kegan Paul, 1975.

Chapter 15

The New Empiricism

Empiricism is the name given to the general tendency to take experience rather than intuition, reason, or revelation as the fundamental source of knowledge. This tendency has assumed a variety of philosophical forms from Greek through modern times and into the twentieth century. We will use the term "new empiricism" to designate one special form found in twentieth-century philosophy chiefly in the United States and other English-speaking countries. Like their counterparts in the modern period in philosophy (for example, David Hume), these new empiricists have put forth as one of their main theses the distinction between formal or necessary truths (as found in logic and mathematics) and empirical truths (knowledge from experience). More explicitly than the earlier empiricists, however, the new empiricists also held some form of a doctrine of verification. Let us take a brief look at these two empiricist doctrines before examining particular twentieth-century empiricist philosophies in America.

Some sentences are either true or false by virtue of their logical form. "Either it is raining or it is not raining." This statement is inevitably true regardless of the weather. Similarly, "It is raining and it is not raining" is, under normal interpretation, necessarily false. Adopting Kant's terminology, such sentences were called "analytic" and were contrasted with empirical or synthetic sentences. Thus, "It is raining" may be either true or false, depending on what the weather is. Such synthetic sentences are either particular sentences, "The cat is on the mat," whose truth can be determined, at least in principle, by observation, or they are generalizations such as "All men are mortal." Since one cannot determine the truth of such generalizations by observing all actual and possible cases, some other method must be found. The method that seems to work in science is that of hypothetical-deductive reasoning. One treats a generalization as a general statement from which particular conclusions may be deduced. These conclusions, if true, support the statement in question; if false they contradict it. Various forms of this method of verification were developed by the new empiricists (as well as others), and we shall examine some of these forms in the following sections. Generally, those who held this strict distinction between analytic and synthetic sentences or propositions also held that there were no sentences that were, in Kant's terminology, both synthetic (i.e., not just a matter of analysis of the meaning of its terms) and a priori (necessary and known independently of experience). For these empiricists, there seemed to be no way in which we could have strict certainty in our knowledge of matters of fact, and thus there seemed to be some problem in speaking of verification (truth making). Some adjustments, at the least, would have to be made in the theory.[1]

Difficulties notwithstanding, empiricists came to rely on the theory of verification for interpreting empirical knowledge. Verification and the scientific method as a way of knowing were not new to American philosophy. John Dewey had stressed the scientific way of knowing, while C. S. Peirce had spoken of the truth of a statement in terms of verification (albeit in the long run and by the scientific community). In fact, according to Peirce, the very meaning of a statement was connected with practical results — the meaning of a term is the practical expectations one has concerning it, future sensible experience included. In the early twentieth century stronger versions of the theory of verification were developed, including the operationalism of the American Percy Bridgman (1882–1962).[2] Basing himself on what he took to be scientific method, especially as practiced by Einstein, Bridgman came to insist that the meaning of a scientific term like "simultaneity" is determined by the practical operations through which it is tested or measured. This theory encountered basic difficulties because different methods of measurement of the same thing should give distinctly different meanings. Thus "temperature," whose meaning is set by noting the rise of a mercury column in a cylinder, is a different concept from "temperature" that is measured by radiated energy. We shall see that not all of the new empiricists adopted this particular view of meaning and verification. Nevertheless it did become a central issue for them, especially in its implication that terms and propositions that had no such empirical or practical meaning were in fact meaningless.

LOGICAL POSITIVISM

To a great extent contemporary empiricist treatments of the problem of knowledge have taken the form of an analysis of the way we speak about things, our language (sentences, propositions, arguments). Thus this form of twentieth-century empiricism has often been called language or linguistic analysis. There are basically two trends in contemporary language analysis — one that concentrates on formal or artificial languages (such as those of logic and mathematics) and one that devotes itself to the analysis of ordinary everyday language. In this chapter we shall be concerned with the former group and in the next chapter the latter.

The origin of logical positivism (also variously called logical empiricism and scientific empiricism) dates back to the formation in the late 1920s in Vienna, Austria of what has been called the Vienna or Viennese Circle. In 1922 a physicist at the University of Vienna, Moritz Schlick, was appointed professor of philosophy of the inductive sciences (the chair formerly held by the physicist-philosopher Ernst Mach). Within a few years Schlick had gathered around him a group of mathematicians and scientists who met regularly to discuss philosophical questions. The stated aim of the group was (1) to provide a secure foundation for the sciences, and (2) to demonstrate the meaninglessness of all metaphysics.[3] The method used to achieve this aim was the logical analysis of language. The group sought, for example, to show how concepts or propositions in the sciences were connected and to demonstrate that the statements of metaphysics are actually pseudostatements because they violate the rules of our language. Thus the group held that metaphysical statements such as "Time is unreal," or "The Nothing nothings" (Heidegger), while they may seem profound, are really nonsense statements because they misuse words or grammar.[4]

The group had been influenced by the empiricism of Hume, Mill, and Mach; the views on scientific method of Poincaré, Duhem, and Einstein; and the mathematical theories of Peano, Hilbert, Frege, Russell, and Whitehead.[5] However, one of the most significant influences on the members of the Vienna Circle, the logical empiricists, was the *Tractatus Logico Philosophicus* (1921) of Ludwig Wittgenstein, the Austrian who became a British philosopher.[6] More will be said of this unique philosopher in the next chapter. However, it might be noted here that one aspect of this book that influenced the thinking of the logical positivists was Wittgenstein's teaching that the task of philosophy is the clarification of thought. Philosophers were not to write or speak about the world but to analyze our language or thought about the world, thus clarifying much of the confusion that reigns there.

Some technical developments in logic and mathematics at the turn of the century also had a strong influence on this philosophy. Here we can only sketch enough of a background to show why philosophers, at least in some schools, suddenly manifested an intense interest in issues that previously were considered either secondary or peripheral to philosophy. We will begin with a brief consideration of some developments in logic. Logic traditionally was defined as a study of the science or art of valid inference or argument. Though logic was still taught in philosophy departments, it was generally considered a completed science. No significant advances in the science of logic occurred from the death of Leibniz (1646–1716) until the nineteenth-century advances associated with the mathematicians G. Boole, A. deMorgan, E. Schroeder, and G. Frege.[7] By introducing a logic that stressed the relation of classes, Boole tried to make logic a subordinate part of algebra and developed the Boolean algebra that is still basic to modern computers. Frege, the greatest systematizer of modern logic, suggested that Boole's ordering should be reversed, and thus was developed the so-called logistic thesis.

THE LOGISTIC THESIS AND ITS DIFFICULTIES

The logistic thesis, which was developed independently by Frege and Bertrand Russell, claims that all of mathematics can be derived from logic alone. Though the development of this thesis involves many technical issues, the central idea can be presented rather informally. What is a number? Instead of attempting to answer this question in terms of some theory of numbers or their ontological status, one can begin with the way one actually experiences numbers as numbers — by learning to count. Thus one learns that 5 is the number of fingers on a right hand; it is also the number of anything else that can be counted on these five fingers. What is five apart from five fingers or five toes? It is a concept that applies to any set that can be put into one-to-one correspondence (matched) with the fingers of one's right hand. More abstractly, the number five is the class of all classes that have five members. The new logic treats classes. Numbers can be defined in terms of classes (or sets) of classes. To see how this notion might suffice to give a foundation for mathematics we need a brief digression on some then-current developments in mathematics.

From antiquity it was generally felt that the counting numbers were, in some sense, given by reality, by the fact that things could be put in categories and counted and that the process could go on indefinitely. In 1889 the Italian mathematician, Guiseppe Peano, showed how the counting numbers could be "constructed" by using the methods of set theory (or the theory of classes) and some primitive undefined concepts: "set," "natural number," "successor," and "belongs to." Granted the counting numbers, or the integers, one could proceed in a step-by-step way to construct fractions, negative numbers, real numbers, and functions over numbers.[8]

The implementation of this program might seem straightforward. Using the tools of logic (or set theory — the technical differences between the two are still matters of dispute) one could derive Peano's postulates for mathematics and then, through a step-by-step process, all of mathematics. The straightforward program, however, soon encountered difficulties. Here we will only consider the most basic. If a deductive system leads to inconsistencies, then there must be something radically wrong in the foundations. The logistic program encountered paradoxes or apparent inconsistencies. Consider, for example, the liar paradox. Let p stand for: *The only italicized sentence on this page is false.* Suppose p is true; then what it says is true. But p says that it is false. Therefore, if p is true, it is false. Suppose p is false; then its contradiction must be true. But to contradict p is to assert that its assertion of falsity is false. Or, if p is false, then p is true.

This paradox of the liar was known from antiquity. It is in fact sometimes attributed to St. Paul.[9] However, a more pivotal role was played by the paradox that Bertrand Russell found to be implicit in Frege's axioms of his logic and his reliance on the notion of classes of classes. Some classes are members of themselves. The term "polysyllabic" is a member of the class of polysyllabic terms; some are not. Consider, for example, "monosyllabic." It is not a monosyllabic word and would not be a member of the class of monosyllabic words. We could make a class of all classes that are not members of themselves and call this class *C*. Is *C* a member of itself? As with the liar paradox: if it is, it isn't; if it is not, then it is.

Bertrand Russell sent this paradox to Frege when Frege was completing a treatise on the foundations of mathematics. Frege thought, as has many a logician since, that Russell's paradox, and the other paradoxes that were soon discovered, shook the foundations of mathematics, for they seemed to suggest that the key criterion of a logical system, namely consistency, was impossible to attain in such systems. Russell himself tried to circumvent the paradoxes in his monumental attempt to supply a foundation for mathematics on a logistic basis, the *Principia Mathematica* (written with A. N. Whitehead, in three volumes, from 1910–13).[10] A little reflection shows that the difficulties in both the liar paradox and the Russell paradox stem from self-reference, from sentences that speak of themselves and classes that may be members of themselves. To treat these paradoxes one may invoke the old Roman slogan: divide and conquer. Separate questions of truth from questions of reference. Remove the apparent contradictions in the truth values of apparently ambiguous sentences (such as the liar paradox, and such statements as "the present King of France is bald" when there is no existing King of France) by rephrasing them in strict logical form (Russell's theory of definite descriptions). Handle difficulties of self-reference by refusing to allow classes to refer to themselves (the ramified theory of types). However, such solutions seemed inadequate and the question of truth (in logic and science) remained a problem for these philosophers we are considering.

Another important issue that arose in discussions concerning the foundations of logic and mathematics and the problems of truth, reference, and meaning was the distinction between an intensional concept of meaning and an extensional one. In standard set theory a class is determined exclusively by its members. Thus if all red objects are round and all round things are red, then the class of "red objects" and that of "round objects" would have the same extension; the terms would have the same extensional meaning since they denote the same items. However, the meaning or significance of red and round are still distinct in that they have a different intension or connotation. Now the purely extensional notion of a class supplies a foundation for mathematics, which in turn supplies a structure for empirical science. There was, accordingly, a programmatic necessity for some members of our group of philosophers to demonstrate that intensional concepts, e.g., predicates that refer to properties rather than classes, are either reducible to extensional concepts or have no significance for the ultimate synthesis.

This distinction and the strategy of reductionism just mentioned became a major point of debate among the new empiricists; other points of debate were the sharp distinction of all meaningful sentences into analytic and synthetic, the neat separation of truth and reference, the principle of verification, and the presupposition that ambiguities and paradoxes could only be avoided by submitting ordinary language usage to the rigors of formal logical analysis. We now turn to a discussion of the life and writings of three American philosophers of this period who have contributed significantly to the debate on these issues — Clarence Irving Lewis, Rudolf Carnap, and Willard Van Orman Quine.

CLARENCE IRVING LEWIS (1883–1964)

In an autobiographical note, Lewis wrote, "Both by inheritance and temperament, I am, I think, an upcountry New England Yankee." [11] Lewis was born in Stoneham, Massachusetts in 1882. His father, a shoemaker marked by a strong social conscience, was involved in the temperance movement, labor strikes, and Fabian (evolutionary) socialism. In contrast to his father, Lewis's philosophy was to become primarily devoted to theoretical issues, and only at the end of his life did he turn to the moral and practical issues that had so concerned his father. From his mother Lewis imbibed the New England belief that "there were high things to be won, and that, with courage, self-reliance and hard work, it would always be possible to attain whatever one put first." [12] With this inspiration Lewis set out to attain a college education with his own funding. His Haverhill, Massachusetts high-school college preparatory courses put him in good stead for the then-gruelling Harvard College entrance exams — twelve of them, three hours each. However, Lewis's interest in philosophy, which he studied at Harvard along with English and economics, had begun years earlier when at the age of thirteen he was already troubled by such puzzles as whether the universe had an end in time, whether anything endured in the flux of events, whether we know things as they really are, and whether there was any truth in orthodox religion. He also had read some history of Greek philosophy and Spencer's *First Principles,* along with Marx's *Capital* (at his father's direction). Such are the early makings of this philosopher.

The highlight of his study at Harvard, Lewis writes, was the yearlong seminar he attended in metaphysics — taught half of the year each by William James and Josiah Royce.

> It was immense. James, I thought, scored the most points, but Royce won on a technical knockout. James's quick thrusts and parries, his striking apercus, and his stubborn sense of mundane fact were not well matched against Royce's ponderous and indefatigable cogency. Royce became then, and remained thereafter, my ideal of a philosopher. [13]

Following graduation from Harvard in 1905, Lewis spent two years teaching English, first at Quincy [Massachusetts] High School and then at the University of Colorado. While in Boulder, he also taught some philosophy, and married and a son was born. In 1908 he returned to Harvard to continue his study of philosophy. There he studied Plato with Santayana and Kant with Perry and produced a thesis for his Ph.D. in 1910 entitled "The Place of Intuition in Knowledge." After graduation he assisted Royce for a while in his course on logic; then in 1911 Lewis accepted a position at the University of California where he continued his interest in logic and produced for use in his logic course his first book, *Survey of Symbolic Logic* (1918).[14] In 1920 he was invited to return to teach at Harvard where he remained until retirement in 1953. His other publications during this time continued his interest in certain problems concerning knowledge and later in moral values. Thus were published *Mind and the World Order* (1929) and *An Analysis of Knowledge and Valuation* (1946).[15] Lewis died in Menlo Park, California in 1964.

C. I. Lewis was one of the contributors to the growth of modern symbolic logic, that type of logic that uses symbols for terms and propositions, and that grounds much of modern mathematics. In two related areas Lewis seems to have made a significant contribution to this field — first, in his discussion of various ways in which terms (and propositions) can "mean" something, and secondly, in his proposal of what he called "strict implication." Terms, Lewis wrote, have four different modes or ways of meaning: (1) through *denotation* a term can mean or point to a certain class of actual things, (2) through its *comprehension* a term can mean or apply to a certain class of possible or consistently thinkable things, (3) a term may *signify* a certain property in those things to which it applies, and (4) a term's *intension* makes it identifiable with all those other terms that would correctly apply to whatever this term applies.[16] When asking for the meaning of a term, then, one must specify the sense of meaning that is meant.

For Lewis it is the latter sense, intensional meaning, that is most significant. It too, however, is of two kinds: first, a *linguistic* intensional meaning in which we refer to all the linguistic expressions that could be substituted for the term at hand. It is this that dictionary synonyms give us. However without the second kind, *sense* intensional meaning, we may not know how to apply these terms. The second kind gives us the criterion of application of the term — either to presented or imagined things or situations.[17] It will do this by giving us a scheme or rule to use in order to apply the term or expression. For instance, when one says "there is a piece of white paper before me," one means that if one looks in a certain direction, one will experience a sensation of whiteness. The term "kilogon" means that imagined operation of counting the sides of a certain plane figure, concluding with the number 1000. One can note here the similarity of this notion of meaning to that of both Peirce and Bridgman. However, for Lewis, it is simply one of several kinds of meaning that one can distinguish.

Lewis's emphasis on intensional meaning and its distinction from meaning by denotation (or extension) is important also for the second of his contributions to modern logic. Certain logical advances in the latter nineteenth and early twentieth centuries included the notion of what was called "material implication." Now implication is the relation expressed by the "if-then" language of, for example, "if today is Monday, then tomorrow is Tuesday," or "if I cut myself, then I will bleed." However, because the meaning of class terms had been limited to extensional meaning, to the items in the class denoted by the term, certain paradoxes arose. For example, if there are no centaurs, then all the centaurs that there are (namely none) will be Greeks, and this is true regardless of the intensional meaning or connotation of the terms "centaur" and "Greeks." It has nothing to say about whether centaurs would be Greeks if there were any.[18] Moreover, according to the theory of material implication, a false proposition "implies" anything. Consider the statement: "If today is Monday, then I'm a monkey's uncle." If today actually is not Monday, then the statement, the implication, is true. This is certainly a strange theory of implication and is inconsistent with the "if-then" phrase as used ordinarily. According to Lewis, only a theory based upon intensional (not extensional meaning) would throw light upon what would be implied if it were true that today were Monday, and only such a theory would fit ordinary usage and be applicable to the process of deduction or to describing causal relations. The intensional implication relation Lewis developed he called "strict." Some proposition, p, "strictly implies" another proposition, q, in the sense that it could not possibly be the case that p be true and q false.[19] This notion set the stage for debates about how to interpret the term "implies."

Questions about the meaning of our concepts are central to the theory of knowledge, and this was Lewis's primary interest. When he was a graduate student at Harvard absolute idealism (that of Royce in particular) was being challenged by both pragmatism and the new realisms. In one seminar he attended Perry (the realist) was in the chair, but Royce (the idealist) was next door; Lewis found himself unable to accept the idealist metaphysics but at the same time unconvinced by the realist arguments against it.[20] One mistake made by many, Lewis pointed out, was to "confuse validity with truth." One should distinguish, he believed, between the ideal of truth and "the validity of such knowledge of the real as is achievable by humans."[21]

How, then, did he believe we should distinguish what was achievable by humans? What was justified belief as distinguished from unjustified? While Lewis was greatly influenced by Kant, he nevertheless held that there were no "synthetic a priori" judgments, i.e., judgments that were not just a matter of spelling out in the predicate what was already contained in the subject, and yet were certain and necessary. Judgments (and the knowledge there given) were either analytic (and thus true by reference to the meaning of the terms in them) or synthetic and empirical. The truth of *analytic judgments* was to be found by analysis of the meaning of the concepts in them, and their truth was independent of the facts of experience. Nevertheless there was something about these judgments that showed them to be not just a matter of convention, i.e., the way we stipulate the linguistic meaning of our terms. In judgments such as "every square is a rectangle" there are meanings that are independent and in some way determine our language systems. Once we assign symbols to certain meanings, he contended, they take on relations that we are not free to change at will. Nevertheless, Lewis also contended that the fact that we adopt a certain language or mathematics or logical system is partly a matter of choice. Whatever system works best for the purposes we have in mind is the one that should be used. That certain logics, for instance the logic of strict implication, work better for physical inference shows something about the nature of things.[22] This belief contrasts with that of other philosophers we will discuss in this chapter.

Empirical knowledge, or *synthetic judgments,* on the other hand, is generally accepted as being knowledge directed to or of the world or nature or facts. According to Lewis, there is a certain "given" in our experience (seeing red, for example, or feeling hardness or pain) that is immediately experienced and is indubitable. Without such a basis, Lewis claimed, empirical knowledge would be impossible. However, there is no knowledge in the strict sense of the "given." Knowledge, strictly speaking, exists only where interpretation and judgment begin, for only there is error possible. Here Lewis distinguished terminating from nonterminating empirical judgments. The former are judgments of the following form: "S being given, if A then E." [23] Or "if in the presence of a certain sensum S, a certain act A seems to be performed, a certain sensum E will result." If E does occur under these conditions, then the judgment is so far verified. Again there is a certain similarity of thought here with that of Peirce for whom "hard" means that "if I scratch it, it will mar only with difficulty." For Lewis, however, the verifying experience is personal, and hence his theory of knowledge here seems to be more subjective than that of Peirce.

While these terminating judgments are more basic for closer to immediate experience, nonterminating judgments are more prevalent and important. These are all of the judgments we make about physical objects, such as "there is a piece of white paper before me," or "the universe is expanding." [24] These judgments, however, are reducible to terminating judgments or observations which nevertheless can never fully verify them. However, some nonterminating judgments are more firmly confirmed than others and even possess a kind of practical certitude, which is the best knowledge that we can have of the objective world.

While this summary of Lewis's philosophy has been concerned mainly with his logic and theory of knowledge, there is some evidence that for Lewis these investigations were but preliminary to that concerned with values.[25] Lewis's theory of value is a more integral part of his system than that of many other philosophers. In fact there are many parallels, he believes, between judgments of value and empirical judgments. Both are predictions. To speak of an object as having value is to attribute some sensible property to it such that we believe it will satisfy us. Our future experience will confirm this prediction and so verify our value judgment. Thus value judgments are objective in the same sense that empirical judgments are. For this reason, Lewis's philosophy of value is quite at odds with the moral philosophy of many of the logical empiricists whose philosophy became a dominant influence in the first half of the twentieth century.[26] Nevertheless value judgments retain some element of subjectivity for Lewis in that they are based on the notion of "satisfaction." How this term is to be defined or the experience recognized and whether or not the individual is to be judge of what is satisfying are questions that such a theory must answer. The details of Lewis's own answer cannot be spelled out here. However a later chapter is devoted to twentieth-century American ethical theories, and we shall return to such problems at that time.

RUDOLF CARNAP (1891-1969)

Rudolf Carnap was born in 1891 in Ronsdorf in northwestern Germany. His father was an industrious and respected weaver and his mother a casual writer. It was concerning his mother's biography of her father that Rudolf writes, "I was fascinated by the magical activity of putting thought on paper, and have loved it ever since." [27] And so it was the problem of the nature and character of human language that continued to interest the later philosopher. His first academic studying was done at home and then in a program of classical languages and mathematics at the local gymnasium. His father died when he was seven, and in 1909 he and his mother moved to Jena. Later he studied at the university there and then at Freiberg, concentrating first on mathematics and later on physics and philosophy. Of particular importance to him during this period were the lectures he attended by Gottlob Frege (1848-1925), lectures that touched issues on the borderline between philosophy and mathematics, namely symbolic logic and the foundations of mathematics.

Carnap first elected to do his doctoral work in physics, attempting a dissertation on the emission of electrons from a heated electrode in a vacuum. But he admits he was not a good experimenter, and the class came to an abrupt end with the outbreak in August 1914 of World War I and the death, in its first days, of his physics professor. While he was opposed to settling international conflicts by war, nevertheless at the outbreak of the war Carnap felt it his duty to serve, doing so first at the front and later as a physicist in a military institution. Even here he found time through reading to become acquainted with Einstein's relativity theory, and was later to continue his interest in its methodological problems. After the war, Carnap completed his doctoral work in philosophy with a dissertation on the different theories of the nature of space maintained by mathematicians, physicists, and philosophers. He spent some time in Berlin where he met and discussed philosophy with Hans Reichenbach (a physicist philosopher of logical positivist persuasion who later also came to the United States), and devoted some study to the symbolic mathematical logic of Russell and Whitehead's *Principia Mathematica*. It was from this work and from the study with Frege that Carnap came to believe that the rules of inference in logic can be formulated without any reference to meaning, i.e., in extensional rather than intensional terms. This belief was also the basis for his later work on logical syntax. Only after some time did he also come to appreciate the importance of intensional meaning and to do work in semantics.[28]

From 1922 to 1925 Carnap worked on material that contributed to his first major publication, *Der logische Aufbau der Welt (The Logical Building Up of the World)*, published in German in 1928.[29] Inspired by Russell, Carnap here attempted a rational reconstruction of certain concepts of ordinary language, i.e., a schematized description, logical not genetic, of how certain elements of experience could be formed from basic psychic states. By this method he attempted to show how one could build up the various sensory domains — from position in the visual field, to colors, temporal order, things, one's own body, the bodies of others, mental states, etc. The first version of the book was ready for publication when Carnap went to Vienna and began his association with the Vienna Circle positivists in 1926.

From 1926 until 1931 Carnap was an instructor of philosophy at the University of Vienna. Here, he writes that he experienced "one of the most stimulating, enjoyable, and fruitful periods of my life." [30] The other members of the Circle showed an interest in his work, and he also supported the goals and aims of the group. From 1931 to 1935 Carnap lived in Prague, Czechoslovakia where, without the discussions of the former period, he had more time to spend on his second book on logical syntax (later published as the *Logical Syntax of Language*).[31] With the beginning of the Hitler regime in Germany in 1933, the political atmosphere, even in Prague, became more intolerable as the Nazi ideology spread through the universities as well as through the general public. For this reason Carnap left Germany in 1935 and came to the United States where he was offered a position in philosophy at the University of Chicago, a position he held from 1936 to 1952. He recalls how gratified he was to find so many young philosophers in this country interested in the scientific method in philosophy and logic. And the logical positivist theories were not to be without ardent followers in this country. At Chicago he had as a colleague the student of pragmatism, Charles Morris; it might be noted that perhaps partially from this influence Carnap later incorporated some elements of pragmatism into his own philosophy.[32]

From 1952 to 1954 Carnap worked at the Institute for Advanced Study at Princeton, where, among other things, he had "some interesting talks with Einstein," who was also there at the time.[33] Together they questioned whether science can say all there is to be said; whether, for example, our experience of the "now" could be adequately conveyed by the scientific definition of it. Einstein at least doubted that it could. In 1954 Carnap occupied the chair in philosophy at UCLA, the chair that had recently been vacated by the sudden death of another German emigré, Hans Reichenbach. Carnap remained at UCLA until his retirement from active teaching in 1961 and his death in 1969. While many had accused the logical positivists of being narrow in their philosophy and without proper concern for morality (according to their theory of morality, moral judgments were a matter of emotive response rather than cognitive appraisal — see chapter 17), Carnap himself made significant changes in his philosophy through the years at the suggestion of some of his critics, and he himself had strong moral beliefs which he followed even when they involved danger to himself.[34]

Carnap's principle orientation is the result of his own logical studies and the influence of the Vienna Circle: the task of philosophy is to analyze the logic of the language that we use to talk about the world rather than to talk about the world itself. Because metaphysics claims to talk about the world and because of the manner in which it uses language to do so, it is nonsense; proper talk about the world should use the language of science, or more properly physics. Like most of the other logical positivists, Carnap did not have much knowledge of the history of philosophy. His training was more in science and mathematics, a fact that might help explain his particular interest and perspective, even if it does not make it immune from criticism.

One of the clearest explanations of Carnap's philosophy pictures his theory of knowledge as "an upstairs-downstairs world."[35] Upstairs live the masters, the scientists whose task it is to find out the facts of the world. Downstairs live the servants, the philosophers, "whose task it is to keep the house of knowledge clean and to set an occasional Upstairs novice straight on matters of taste and manners."[36] Within the upstairs lodgings there was also a division. Some buildings were devoted to physical experiment — their language reducible either to protocol sentences, i.e., statements reporting immediate sensations, such as "there is a triangular red patch here now" or to object statements such as "this book." Other buildings housed those who engaged in physical speculation and theory — the creators of scientific hypotheses whose meaning was given in terms of the protocols to which they were reducible and by which they were verified.

Carnap was skeptical that philosophers could talk about anything other than language. Thus the philosophers lived downstairs, and their object of study and observance was the talk of the upstairs people, the scientists. Moreover, just as there had been a variety of geometries from which one could pick what best served a particular interest or purpose, so, Carnap held, one could choose from a variety of languages by which to talk about the world — a realist language, an idealist language, or a language in which statements and hypotheses are reducible to sensations or object statements. It remained the upstairs people, however, who did the choosing, not the downstairs people, the philosophers. Philosophers were thus relieved even of the job of attempting to determine which language gave the correct picture of the world, a job that Carnap thought no one could really do. Nevertheless, he did seem to hold that the language of physics was somewhat preferable to others, because it was more consistent and perhaps more practical. Still what metaphysics it implied, if any, he was not willing to say.

In his early work, *The Logical Syntax of Language,* Carnap developed two languages or formal systems with different definitions, axioms, etc. His primary interest was in the syntax, the form or structure, of the languages. One point of particular interest in this work was his distinction between sentences in the formal mode and sentences in the material mode. When we speak about the language used by the physicists, that language is our object of discourse, and the language in which we speak about the object language is a metalanguage. When we do not distinguish these two we are speaking in what he called the material mode. The statement "smiles is the longest word because there is a mile between the first and last letters" presents such a confusion. In this statement we are talking both about real miles or smiles and a word with certain letters. Carnap held that we are in a similar way confused by certain metaphysical statements, such as "a number is not a thing." Clarity can be maintained, he suggested, by translation into the formal mode such that the statement becomes "a thing word is not a number word." When the statement's syntax has been analyzed and clarified, according to Carnap, it is seen to be a proposal about how a certain language is to be formed, not a factual assertion.[37]

Before 1930 Carnap had maintained that the sole business of philosophy was logical syntax—to analyze the form and structure of language without reference to the meaning of terms or their reference. A significant change in his conceptual framework followed upon his acceptance of the Polish logician Tarski's interpretation of "true" as a metalinguistic term, i.e., a term that is predicated of sentences rather than of things. This, as Carnap interpreted it, allowed for a formal, logical treatment of semantics, i.e. questions of truth and reference. This enrichment of syntactical analysis does not deny the division of labor. The philosopher does not determine which terms refer to which objects or which sentences are true; this remains the work of the scientist. But the philosopher can and should clarify the rules underlying such linguistic practices.

In the late thirties Carnap added to *syntactics* and *semantics* the further dimension *pragmatics,* which was concerned with use and acceptance. A simple example may clarify the significance of this new dimension. Given two competing theories, a philosopher may analyze the logical syntax and the roles of denoting terms in each system. But it is the scientific community, rather than the philosopher, that eventually decides which theory is to be accepted. There is little point in analyzing the truth value of sentences in rejected theories. Some critics thought that Carnap's enlarged system was leading him back along the primrose path to metaphysics. Thus his treatment of semantics in the extensional spirit inevitably involved rules that related terms in a language or scientific system and the things in the world such terms denoted. Thus, to accept atomic physics as an explanatory theory seemed to entail accepting "atom" as denoting a class of really existing objects, atoms. But Carnap attempted to obviate such criticisms by yet another influential distinction. *Internal* to this scientific system, the statement "There are atoms" must be accepted as true. Yet its truth is analytic, since axioms of the system are axioms about atoms. Suppose one attempts to go from the internal question, "Does atomic physics speak about atoms? " to the *external* and apparently metaphysical question, "Do atoms really exist? " Such a question, Carnap insists, is poorly phrased. The operative question is, "Should atomic physics be accepted? " This is pragmatics, rather than semantics; the question calls for a decision rather than a truth value.[38] This notion may not entirely relieve Carnap of the burden of metaphysics, however, for such a normative question (asking whether something should be done) may require reasons, and reasons why those are considered good reasons. But this far Carnap was not willing to go.

In developing this larger framework, nevertheless, Carnap gradually redeveloped and enlarged some of the narrower concepts characterizing the earlier stage of logical positivism. Thus in his influential article "Testability and Meaning" he abandoned the either-or notion of verification for the more flexible notion of confirmation which admits of degrees. As might be expected, Carnap developed his doctrine of confirmation through a technical logical innovation called reduction sentences. Along with the abandonment of the either-or notion of verification came the development by Carnap of contributions to the theory of probable inference. Where others such as Reichenbach developed theories about probabilities of events, e.g., the probability that a throw of the dice will yield a seven, Carnap, as always, made sentences his concern and developed a technical theory for the probability of hypotheses relative to supporting evidence. Moreover he distinguished such notions as "degree of confirmation" from "incidence," and various kinds of probable inference such as that directly from a population to a sample and prediction from one sample to another.[39]

Because of the highly technical nature of his writing, Carnap's style is not evident from the nontechnical excerpts included in this chapter. Perhaps the best measure of his influence is the fact that those who have gone beyond Carnap in the fields in which he worked have generally done so by using tools Carnap himself forged. Among those doing philosophy in Carnap's style but moving in a new direction was W. V. O. Quine.

WILLARD VAN ORMAN QUINE (1908–   )

A cursory glance through the indexes of philosophical journals in the English-speaking world reveals something of the enormous influence of W. V. O. Quine. Not only are there articles clarifying, commenting on, or disagreeing with his positions on various issues, but even more significantly, his work serves as the point of departure for many further studies. Quine was born in Akron, Ohio in 1908. He majored in mathematics at Oberlin College from which he graduated in 1930. He then went on to Harvard where he received an M.S. (1931) and a Ph.D. (1932) in philosophy, the latter with a dissertation on logic under the direction of Alred North Whitehead. Quine did further study in philosophy at Oxford in 1932–33 and then returned to begin a long teaching career at Harvard.

During this time he lectured widely and has published fourteen books and four times that many articles on philosophy and symbolic logic.[40]

In 1934 Quine visited in Austria with members of the Vienna Circle, studied some logic at Warsaw, and then followed Carnap to Prague. While in Prague he attended Carnap's lectures and describes them as "my first really considerable experience of being intellectually fired by a living teacher rather than by a dead book."[41] Quine returned to a teaching position at Harvard in 1939. That same year Carnap came to Harvard as a visiting professor, and Russell and the Polish logician Tarski were also there — "historic months," according to Quine. While Quine was very much influenced by Rudolf Carnap and the logical empiricist philosphy, he went on to develop from within that philosophy his own unique viewpoint. Some of his criticisms of logical empiricism, moreover, have had a significant influence on contemporary American philosophy.

Why this influence wielded by a logician whose philosophical point of departure was an effort to develop an improved logical foundation for mathematics, an abstract topic remote from the basic issues of philosophy? There are some obvious answers to this question. Quine has reinterpreted the significance of logic and the foundational role it has been assigned in science. His idea of the indeterminacy of translation of language has provoked a great amount of discussion. Undoubtedly part of Quine's influence is due to his sparkling style of writing, enlivening even the most abstruse issues with crisp prose and dry wit. Technical competence in logic, creative originality, and a lucid literary style — these factors certainly contribute to Quine's influence. Yet the basic cause of his influence must, it seems, be sought elsewhere. Quine's work marks a subtle but significant turn in a major stream of American philosophy, a turn back towards the basic metaphysical and epistemological issues that have traditionally been philosophy's paramount concern.

Yet Quine began not by opposing the positivist tradition but by making fundamental contributions to its intellectual core — the role of logic in the foundations of mathematics. The technical issues involved are not our concern here. More to the point is the fact that such logicians and logically oriented philosophers as Bertrand Russell, Rudolf Carnap, and Alfred Tarski accepted Quine as one of their own, an analyst's analyst. Quine's earliest efforts were directed towards a purification of the tradition of logical empiricism. The movement towards synthesis, toward developing another philosophical viewpoint, initially emerged as a by-product, from certain criticisms of logical empiricism.

"Two Dogmas of Empiricism" is a pivotal article in Quine's development and the point of departure for the movement towards a new synthesis.[42] The first so-called dogma, the analytic-synthetic distinction of the logical empiricist tradition, divided meaningful statements into logically disjointed sets. Synthetic statements are true, when they happen to be true, because of what the world is. Each one stands on its own. Even empirical generalizations are tested by individual verifiable consequences flowing from them. Analytic statements do cohere into systems, but into systems like logic and mathematics whose truth does not depend on the way the world is. The empirical sciences were seen as something of a hybrid of an analytic form and a synthetic content.

This neat distinction, Quine suggested, involved a fundamental ambiguity. Some statements are true merely by virtue of their logical form. The truth of "Every X is an X" does not hinge on what "X" is or denotes. However, the truth of "Every bachelor is an unmarried man" depends more on the meanings of the constitutive terms than on the sheer logical form. However, if "unmarried man" could be replaced by its synonym, "bachelor," then the statement would be reduced to the logical truth, "All bachelors are bachelors." Quine thus shifted the focus from analyticity to synonymy. But an account of analytic statements that depends on the notion of synonymy was, according to Quine, quite unsatisfactory. Synonymy cannot be explicated by definition since definitions are reports about our usage of terms, including synonymous terms. Nor does interchangeability of terms explain it for although "creature with a kidney" and "creature with a heart" are interchangeable, they are not synonymous. After several other attempts, Quine concludes that analyticity had not been yet defined, and thus the distinction of analytic from synthetic statements had not been drawn. The distinction could only be held by empiricists and others as an unproven or unexplained dogma.

This conclusion leads Quine to his discussion and critique of the second empiricist dogma, the theory of verification. In opposition to this tradition, Quine claims that individual statements and terms cannot be reduced to sense data for verification by direct sense report, for it is not individual statements or terms that are verified by experience, but whole systems of interrelated concepts and theories. Scientific statements face the tribunal of experience not one by one, but together.[43] Quine compares science to a field of force that has a periphery where experience is met and an interior that consists of theories and more basic logical principles. Adjustments are made because of experiential observations, adjustments often involving changes throughout the entire system or scientific theory. We are reluctant to do this to an established scientific system, especially where the change would involve adjustments in the basic theories or certain logical principles at its center. In these cases we may even disbelieve the observation, thinking it illusory, for example.[44] We are basically conservatives in this matter, wanting to make as few changes as possible in established theories.[45] However, we nevertheless do make those changes that help us to manage our experience better. In the final analysis, then, the criteria for acceptance of both analytic and synthetic statements is pragmatic. Which entities we accept as real and which theories as true is a matter of which work best for us for the purposes we have at hand.

Quine's major work, *Word and Object* (1960), is, according to one analyst of contemporary philosophy, "the most discussed American philosophical book of the post-1945 period."[46] In it Quine further developed his theory of meaning with a discussion of the difficulties that would be encountered in any attempt to translate the language of a hidden culture or tribe. His account is dependent on a behavioristic theory of how language is learned (something he held in common with his colleague at Harvard, B. F. Skinner). First we note the stimulus meaning of a sentence, that is, the class of stimuli to which the speaker of the sentence would give assent. Two statements are stimulus synonymous if there is sameness of stimulus for the speaker or for various speakers of the language. It would seem then that one entering a foreign culture would be able to note certain sentences that are uttered upon the presentation of certain stimuli, and then to determine what those same stimuli call forth in his own language. Thus, if the native utters "*gavagai*" upon seeing a rabbit, we might assume that the term or sentence means our "rabbit," or "there is a rabbit." However, we cannot be certain that *gavagi* does not mean, for example, "rabbit stage," or something else. To determine this would necessitate our seeing how this sentence fits the rest of the language and language stimuli of this culture. There are more than practical difficulties involved here, according to Quine. He contends that it would be possible in principle to develop different and incompatible manuals for translation for that language, each fitting the speech dispositions of competent native speakers; there would thus be no sense in asking which is the correct translation manual.[47] This idea is Quine's so-called principle of the indeterminacy of translation. It is also related to his discussion of the problem of synonymy and to his thesis that physical reality, as observed, underdetermines the meaning of even the most basic of observational terms.

These theses raised problems for metaphysics or ontology, as Quine himself noted. In contrast to Carnap who was content to speak of and analyze languages without questioning whether or not they fit reality or correctly described the world, Quine was not so content and opened the door, however slightly, to metaphysical questions. In so doing he also questioned the empiricist under-standing of the nature and task of philosophy. To appreciate the significance of this shift we should view it in a broad historical perspective. The gradual breakaway of first the physical and then the social and psychological sciences from the matrix of philosophy left philosophers, particularly those in the empirical tradition, with a fundamental uncertainty concerning the nature and functioning of philosophy. Carnap's internal-external distinction seemed to resolve such professional uncertainties. The scientist is concerned with the world; the philos-opher with language about the world. This distinction, as we have seen, supplied Carnap with a means of blocking ontological questions. "Do molecules exist? " Within the framework of molecular physics any statement concerning the real existence of molecules is, Carnap argued, an analytic statement, essentially a clarification of what is implicit in the axioms. If this statement is viewed as an external question then it must be considered a pragmatic question, one requiring a decision on whether or not the system in question should be accepted, rather than a question requiring a yes-or-no answer.

This dismissal of ontology hinges on the analytic-synthetic distinction. How does it fare when this distinction is denied? Here Quine argues that it is rationally inconsistent to accept a system as explanatory and irreducible and yet not accept the entities the system is about.[48] The primacy of pragmatics leads to the reintroduction of ontological questions. Once introduced, however, Quine endeavors to keep such questions to the absolute minimum, to the ontic commitments that prove indispensible in the systems accepted as explanatory and irreducible. The net result is something in between traditional ontology, concerned with theories of reality, and traditional analysis, concerned with explaining the way language functions. One begins with the way language functions and gets at ontology through this linguistic turn, by asking what ontic commitments are indispensible in the successful functioning of our language about the world.

With this discussion of the philosophy of W. V. O. Quine, we end our description of the formalist branch of language analysis. In the following chapter we shall outline developments in the tradition of language analysis which led in quite another direction.

Notes

[1] On the analytic-synthetic distinction see A. J. Ayer, chap. 4 in *Language, Truth, and Logic,* 2d ed. (London: V. Gollanez, ltd., 1946); Arthur Pap, *Semantics and Necessary Truth* (New Haven: Yale University Press, 1958); F. Waismann, "Analytic and Synthetic," *Analysis,* vols. 10, 11, and 13 (1949–52). On the principle of verifiability see A. J. Ayer, "The Principle of Verifiability," *Mind* 45 (1936); Hans Reichenbach, "The Verifiability Theory of Meaning," *Proceedings of the American Academy of Arts and Sciences* 80 (1951), reprinted in Feigl and Brodbeck, eds., *Readings in the Philosophy of Science* (New York, 1953); E. J. Nelson, "The Verification Theory of Meaning," *Philosophical Review* 43 (1954); D. J. O'Connor, *A Critical History of Western Philosophy* (Glencoe, Ill.: Free Press, 1964), pp. 495ff.

[2] See Percy Bridgman, *The Logic of Modern Physics* (New York: Macmillan, 1927; B. A. Cornelius, *Operationism* (Springfield, Ill.: Thomas, 1955).

[3] J. R. Weinberg, *An Examination of Logical Positivism* (Patterson, N.J.: Littlefield, Adams, 1960), p. 1.

[4] The objection to the use of the term "nothing" as a noun was because they believed the only intelligible use for the term was one that corresponded roughly to the negative existential quantifier in logic. Thus "We know the Nothing" should be translated as "It is not the case that there is an x such that we know x." Such terms not only have no empirical meaning, according to the logical positivists, but they are usually also used with an incorrect syntax.

[5] O'Connor, *Critical History,* p. 493.

[6] Ludwig Wittgenstein, *Tractatus Logico-Philosophicus* (London, 1922. New English translation by Pears and McGuinness, 1961.

[7] The best treatment of the history of modern logic may be found in William Kneale and Martha Kneale, *The Development of Modern Logic* (Oxford: Oxford University Press, 1962). There are also many textbook treatments among which is A. H. Basson and D. J. O'Connor, *Introduction to Symbolic Logic,* 3d. ed. (London: 1959; New York: 1960).

[8] The most disputed point here was the transition from rational numbers, or numbers that can be expressed as a ratio of two integers, to real numbers, not all of which can

be so expressed. Georg Cantor, the chief developer of set theory, accomplished this by introducing the idea of a succession of infinities. The counting numbers, and any set that can be put into one-to-one correspondence with them, constitutes the lowest-order infinity; the continuum, the number of points in a line of finite length, constitutes the next highest order of infinity. The details of this transition are more than can be presented here, but can be found in Kneale and op. cit. Kneale, *Development of Modern Logic.*

[9] See St. Paul, *Epistle to Titus,* 1: 12–13.

[10] Bertrand Russell and Alfred N. Whitehead, *Principia Mathematica.*

[11] Paul Arthur Schilpp, ed., *The Philosophy of C. I. Lewis* (LaSalle, Ill.: Open Court Publishing, 1968), p. 1.

[12] Ibid., p. 2.

[13] Ibid., p. 5.

[14] C. I. Lewis, *A Survey of Symbolic Logic* (Berkeley: University of California Press, 1918).

[15] C. I. Lewis, *Mind and the World Order: Outline of a Theory of Knowledge* (New York: Charles Scribner's, 1929); idem, *An Analysis of Knowledge and Valuation* (LaSalle, Ill.: Open Court Publishing, 1946).

[16] Lewis, *Analysis of Knowledge and Valuation,* p. 39.

[17] Ibid., pp. 132–34.

[18] C. I. Lewis, "Logic and Pragmatism," in *Contemporary American Philosophy,* ed. G. P. Adams and W. P. Montague (New York: Russell and Russell, 1962), vol. 2, p. 33.

[19] Ibid., p. 36.

[20] P. A. Schilpp, *The Philosophy of C. I. Lewis,* p. 10.

[21] Ibid., p. 11.

[22] C. I. Lewis, "A Pragmatic Conception of the *A Priori,*" *Journal of Philosophy* 20, no. 7 (1923): pp. 169–77.

[23] Lewis, *Analysis of Knowledge and Valuation,* pp. 184ff.

[24] Ibid.

[25] Note the title of his major work: *An Analysis of Knowledge and Valuation.* Book 3 is devoted exclusively to this topic.

[26] See chapter 17 for a discussion of twentieth-century American moral philosophies.

[27] P. A. Schilpp, ed., *The Philosophy of Rudolf Carnap* (LaSalle, Ill.: Open Court Publishing, 1963), p. 3.

[28] See the following discussion of syntactics, semantics, and pragmatics.

[29] Rudolf Carnap, *Der Logische Aufbau Der Welt* (Berlin-Schlachtensee: Weltkreis-Verlag, 1928).

[30] Schilpp, *Philosophy of Rudolf Carnap,* p. 20.

[31] Rudolf Carnap, *The Logical Syntax of Language,* trans. Amethe Smeaton, Countess von Zeppelin. International Library of Psychology, Philosophy and Scientific Method. (London: Kegan Paul Trench, Trubner & Co., 1937).

[32] See Charles Morris, "Pragmatism and Logical Empiricism," in Schilpp, *Philosophy of Rudolf Carnap,* pp. 87–98.

[33] Ibid., p. 37.

[34] He had, for example, traveled to Mexico to support a certain group of philosophers who were being politically persecuted.

[35] J. Alberto Coffa, "Carnap's Sprachanschauung Circa 1932," *Philosophy of Science Association,* vol. 2, 1976.

[36] Ibid.

[37] Carnap, *Logical Syntax of Language,* pp. 312–15.

[38] This idea is developed in Carnap's article, "Empiricism, Semantics, and Ontology," included in a slightly revised form as an appendix to his *Meaning and Necessity,* rev. ed. (Chicago: University of Chicago Press, 1956), pp. 205–21.

[39] Carnap's "Testability and Meaning," originally published in *Philosophy of Science* in 1936 and 1937, was reproduced, with some omissions in H. Feigl and W. Sellars, eds., *Readings in the Philosophy of Science* (New York: Appleton-Century-Crofts, 1953), pp. 47–92. His ideas on probabilistic reasoning are developed in his *Logical Foundations of Probability,* 2d rev. ed. (Chicago: University of Chicago Press, 1962).

[40] See the bibliography in *Words and Objections: Essays on the Work of W. V. Quine,* ed. Donald Davidson and Jaakko Hintikka (Dordrecht-Holland: D. Reidel Pub. Co., 1969), pp. 353–66.

[41] Willard V. O. Quine, "Homage to Rudolf Carnap," in *The Ways of Paradox and Other Essays,* rev. and enlarged ed. (Cambridge: Harvard University Press, 1976), p. 42. It was Quine also who helped make it possible for Carnap to come to the United States. See Schilpp, *Philosophy of Rudolf Carnap,* p. 34.

[42] Willard V. O. Quine, "Two Dogmas of Empiricism," *Philosophical Review* 60 (1951): pp. 20–43. Reprinted in *From a Logical Point of View,* 2d ed. rev. (New York: Harper and Row, Harper Torchbooks, 1961), pp. 20–46.

[43] "Our statements about external reality face the tribunal of sense experience not individually but as a corporate body." From Quine's *Introduction to Methods of Logic,* rev. ed. (New York: Holt, Rinehart, and Winston, 1959), p. xii.

[44] For a much-discussed and similar point of view on changes in scientific theories see Thomas Kuhn, *The Structure of Scientific Revolutions* (Chicago: University of Chicago Press, 1962).

[45] For a simplified discussion of Quine's views on this point see *The Web of Belief,* with J. S. Ullian, 2d ed. (1970; reprint, New York: Random House, 1978), pp. 66ff. Also note the similarity with some views of William James in chapter 7.

[46] Anthony Quinton, "Philosophy in America," *Times Literary Supplement,* 13 June 1975, pp. 664ff.

[47] These ideas are developed in chap. 2 of Quine's *Word and Object* (Cambridge: Massachusetts Institute of Technology Press, 1960), chap. 2, especially pp. 68–72.

[48] This pragmatic doctrine of ontic commitments was developed in various articles by Quine, especially "On What There Is," in *From a Logical point of View* (Cambridge: Harvard University Press, 1953), pp. 1–19. It was given a more definitive development in *Word and Object,* especially pp. 238–43 and 270–76.

C. I. LEWIS

A PRAGMATIC CONCEPTION OF THE *A PRIORI**

The conception of the *a priori* points two problems which are perennial in philosophy; the part played in knowledge by the mind itself, and the possibility of "necessary truth" or of knowledge "independent of experience." But traditional conceptions of the *a priori* have proved untenable. That the mind approaches the flux of immediacy with some godlike foreknowledge of principles which are legislative for experience, that there is any natural light or any innate ideas, it is no longer possible to believe.

Nor shall we find the clue to the *a priori* in any compulsion of the mind to incontrovertible truth or any peculiar kind of demonstration which establishes first principles. All truth lays upon the rational mind the same compulsion to belief; as Mr. Bosanquet has pointed out, this character belongs to all propositions or judgments once their truth is established.

The difficulties of the conception are due, I believe, to two mistakes: whatever is *a priori* is necessary, but we have misconstrued the relation of necessary truth to mind. And the *a priori* is independent of experience, but in so taking it, we have misunderstood its relation to empirical fact. What is *a priori* is necessary truth not because it compels the mind's acceptance, but precisely because it does not. It is given experience, brute

* C. I. Lewis, "A Pragmatic Conception of *A Priori*," *Journal of Philosophy* 20, no. 7 (29 March 1923): pp. 169–77. Reprinted by permission of the *Journal of Philosophy*.

fact, the *a posteriori* element in knowledge which the mind must accept willy-nilly. The *a priori* represents an attitude in some sense freely taken, a stipulation of the mind itself, and a stipulation which might be made in some other way if it suited our bent or need. Such truth is necessary as opposed to contingent, not as opposed to voluntary. And the *a priori* is independent of experience not because it prescribes a form which the data of sense must fit, or anticipates some preëstablished harmony of experience with the mind, but precisely because it prescribes nothing to experience. That is *a priori* which is true, *no matter what*. What it anticipates is not the given, but our attitude toward it: it concerns the uncompelled initiative of mind or, as Josiah Royce would say, our categorical ways of acting.

The traditional example of the *a priori* par excellence is the laws of logic. These can not be derived from experience since they must first be taken for granted in order to prove them. They make explicit our general modes of classification. And they impose upon experience no real limitation. Sometimes we are asked to tremble before the spectre of the "alogical," in order that we may thereafter rejoice that we are saved from this by the dependence of reality upon mind. But the "alogical" is pure bogey, a word without a meaning. What kind of experience could defy the principle that everything must either be or not be, that nothing can both be and not be, or that if x is y and y is z, then x is z? If anything imaginable or unimaginable could violate such laws, then the ever-present fact of change would do it every day. The laws of logic are purely formal; they forbid nothing but what concerns the use of terms and the corresponding modes of classification and analysis. The law of contradiction tells us that nothing can be both white and not-white, but it does not and can not tell us whether black is not-white, or soft or square is not-white. To discover *what contradicts what* we must always consult the character of experience. Similarly the law of the excluded middle formulates our decision that whatever is not designated by a certain term shall be designated by its negative. It declares our purpose to make, for every term, a complete dichotomy of experience, instead—as we might choose—of classifying on the basis of a tripartite division into opposites (as black and white) and the middle ground between the two. Our rejection of such tripartite division represents only our penchant for simplicity.

Further laws of logic are of similar significance. They are principles of procedure, the parliamentary rules of intelligent thought and speech. Such laws are independent of experience because they impose no limitations whatever upon it. They are legislative because they are addressed to ourselves—because definition, classification, and inference represent no operations of the objective world, but only our own categorical attitudes of mind.

And further, the ultimate criteria of the laws of logic are pragmatic. Those who suppose that there is, for example, *a* logic which everyone would agree to if he understood it and understood himself, are more optimistic than those versed in the history of logical discussion have a right to be. The fact is that there are several logics, markedly different, each self-consistent in its own terms and such that whoever, using it, avoids false premises, will never reach a false conclusion. Mr. Russell, for example, bases *his* logic on an implication relation such that if twenty sentences be cut from a newspaper and put in a hat, and then two of these be drawn at random, one of them will certainly imply the other, and it is an even bet that the implication will be mutual. Yet upon a foundation so remote from ordinary modes of inference the whole structure of *Principia Mathematica* is built. This logic—and there are others even more strange—is utterly consistent and the results of it entirely valid. Over and above all questions of consistency, there are issues of logic which can not be determined—nay, can not even be argued—except on pragmatic grounds of conformity to human bent and intellectual convenience. That we have been blind to this fact, itself reflects traditional errors in the conception of the *a priori.*

We may note in passing one less important illustration of the *a priori*—the proposition "true by definition." Definitions and their immediate consequences, analytic propositions generally, are necessarily true, true under all possible circumstances. Definition is legislative because it is in some sense arbitrary. Not only is the meaning assigned to words more or less a matter of choice—that consideration is relatively trivial—but the manner in which the precise classifications which definition embodies shall be effected, is something not dictated by experience. If experience were other than it is, the definition and its corresponding classification might be inconvenient, fantastic, or useless, but it could not be false. Mind makes classifications and determines meanings; in so doing it creates the *a priori* truth of analytic judgments. But that the manner of this creation responds to pragmatic considerations, is so obvious that it hardly needs pointing out.

If the illustrations so far given seem trivial or verbal, that impression may be corrected by turning to the place which the *a priori* has in mathematics and in natural science. Arithmetic, for example, depends *in toto* upon the operation of counting or correlating, a procedure which can be carried out at will in any world containing identifiable things— even identifiable ideas—regardless of the further characters of experience. Mill challenged this *a priori* character of arithmetic. He asked us to suppose a demon sufficiently powerful and maleficent so that every time two things were brought together with two other things, this demon should always introduce a fifth. The implication which he supposed to follow is that under such circumstances $2 + 2 = 5$ would be a universal law of arithmetic. But Mill was quite mistaken. In such a world we should be obliged to become a little clearer than is usual about the distinction between arithmetic and physics, that is all. If two black marbles were put in the same urn with two white ones, the demon could take his choice of colors, but it would be evident that there were more black marbles or more white ones than were put in. The same would be true of all objects in any wise identifiable. We should simply find ourselves in the presence of an extraordinary physical law, which we should recognize as universal in our world, that whenever two things were brought into proximity with two others, an additional and similar thing was always created by the process. Mill's world would be physically most extraordinary. The world's work would be enormously facilitated if hats or locomotives or tons of coal could be thus multiplied by anyone possessed originally of two pairs. But the laws of mathematics would remain unaltered. It is because this is true that arithmetic is *a priori.* Its laws prevent *nothing;* they are compatible with anything which happens or could conceivably happen in nature. They would be true in any possible world. Mathematical addition is not a physical transformation. Physical changes which result in an increase or decrease of the countable things involved are matters of everyday occurrence. Such physical processes present us with phenomena in which the purely mathematical has to be separated out by abstraction. Those laws and those laws only have necessary truth which we are prepared to maintain, no matter what. It is because we shall always separate out that part of the phenomenon not in conformity with arithmetic and designate it by some other category—physical change, chemical reaction, optical illusion—that arithmetic is *a priori.*

The *a priori* element in science and in natural law is greater than might be supposed. In the first place, all science is based upon definitive concepts. The formulation of these concepts is, indeed, a matter determined by the commerce between our intellectual or our pragmatic interests and the nature of experience. Definition is classification. The scientific search is for such classification as will make it possible to correlate appearance and behavior, to discover law, to penetrate to the "essential nature" of things in order that behavior may become predictable. In other words, if definition is unsuccessful, as early scientific definitions mostly have been, it is because the classification thus set up corresponds with no natural cleavage and does not correlate with any important uniformity of behavior. A name itself must represent *some* uniformity in experience or it names nothing. What does not repeat itself or recur in intelligible fashion is not a thing. Where the definitive uniformity is a clue to other uniformities, we have successful scientific definition. Other definitions can not be said to be false; they are merely useless. In scientific classification the search is, thus, for *things worth naming.* But the naming, classifying, defining activity is essentially prior to investigation. We can not interrogate experience in general. Until our meaning is definite and our classification correspondingly exact, experience can not conceivably answer our questions.

In the second place, the fundamental laws of any science—or those treated as fundamental—are *a priori* because they formulate just such definitive concepts or categorical tests by which alone investigation becomes possible. If the lightning strikes the railroad track at two places, *A* and *B,* how shall we tell whether these events are simultaneous? "We . . . require a definition of simultaneity such that this definition supplies us with the method by means of which . . . we can decide whether or not both the lightning strokes occurred simultaneously. As long as this requirement is not satisfied, I allow myself to be deceived as a physicist (and of course the same applies if I am not a physicist), when I imagine that I am able to attach a meaning to the statement of simultaneity. . . .

"After thinking the matter over for some time you then offer the following suggestion with which to test simultaneity. By measuring along the rails, the connecting line *AB* should be measured up and an observer placed at the mid-point *M* of the distance *AB.* This observer should be supplied with an arrangement (*e.g.,* two mirrors inclined at 90°) which allows him visually to observe both places *A* and *B* at the same time. If the observer perceives the two flashes at the same time, then they are simultaneous.

"I am very pleased with this suggestion, but for all that I can not regard the matter as quite settled, because I feel constrained to raise the following objection: 'Your definition would certainly be right, if I only knew that the light by means of which the observer at *M* perceives the lightning flashes travels along the length *A—M* with the same velocity as along the length *B—M.* But an examination of this supposition would only be possible if we already had at our disposal the means of measuring time. It would thus appear as though we were moving here in a logical circle.'

"After further consideration you cast a somewhat disdainful glance at me—and rightly so—and you declare: 'I maintain my previous definition nevertheless, because in reality it assumes absolutely nothing about light. There is only *one* demand to be made of the definition of simultaneity, namely, that in every real case it must supply us with an empirical decision as to whether or not the conception which has to be defined is fulfilled. That light requires the same time to traverse the path *A—M* as for the path *B—M* is in reality *neither a supposition nor a hypothesis* about the physical nature of light, but a *stipulation* which I can make of my own free-will in order to arrive at a definition of simultaneity.' . . . We are thus led also to a definition of 'time' in physics." *

As this example from the theory of relativity well illustrates, we can not even ask the questions which discovered law would answer until we have first by *a priori* stipulation formulated definitive criteria. Such concepts are not verbal definitions, nor classifications merely; they are

---

* Einstein, *Relativity,* pp. 26–28.

themselves laws which prescribe a certain uniformity of behavior to whatever is thus named. Such definitive laws are *a priori;* only so can we enter upon the investigation by which further laws are sought. Yet it should also be pointed out that such *a priori* laws are subject to abandonment if the structure which is built upon them does not succeed in simplifying our interpretation of phenomena. If, in the illustration given, the relation "simultaneous with," as defined, should not prove transitive— if event A should prove simultaneous with B, and B with C, but not A with C—this definition would certainly be rejected.

And thirdly, there is that *a priori* element in science—as in other human affairs—which constitutes the criteria of the real as opposed to the unreal in experience. An object itself is a uniformity. Failure to behave in certain categorical ways marks it as unreal. Uniformities of the type called "natural law" are the clues to reality and unreality. A mouse which disappears where no hole is, is no real mouse; a landscape which recedes as we approach is but illusion. As the queen remarked in the episode of the wishing-carpet: "If this were real, then it would be a miracle. But miracles do not happen. Therefore I shall wake presently." That the uniformities of natural law are the only reliable criteria of the real, is inescapable. But such a criterion is *ipso facto a priori.* No conceivable experience could dictate the alteration of a law so long as failure to obey that law marked the content of experience as unreal.

This is one of the puzzles of empiricism. We deal with experience: what any reality may be which underlies experience, we have to learn. What we desire to discover is natural law, the formulation of those uniformities which obtain amongst the real. But experience as it comes to us contains not only the real but all the content of illusion, dream, hallucination, and mistake. The *given* contains both real and unreal, confusingly intermingled. If we ask for uniformities of this unsorted experience, we shall not find them. Laws which characterize all experience, of real and unreal both, are nonexistent and would in any case be worthless. What we seek are the uniformities of the *real;* but *until we have such laws, we can not sift experience and segregate the real.*

The obvious solution is that the enrichment of experience, the separation of the real from the illusory or meaningless, and the formulation of natural law, all grow up together. If the criteria of the real are *a priori,* that is not to say that no conceivable character of experience would lead to alteration of them. For example, spirits can not be photographed. But if photographs of spiritistic phenomena, taken under properly guarded conditions, should become sufficiently frequent, this *a priori* dictum would be called in question. What we should do would be to redefine our terms. Whether "spook" was spirit or matter, whether the definition of "spirit" or of "matter" should be changed; all this would constitute one interrelated problem. We should reopen together the question of definition or classification, of criteria for this sort of real, and of natural law. And the solution of one of these would mean the solution of all. Nothing could *force* a redefinition of spirit or of matter. A sufficiently fundamental relation to human bent to human interests, would guarantee continuance unaltered even in the face of unintelligible and baffling experiences. In such problems, the mind finds itself uncompelled save by its own purposes and needs. I *may* categorize experience as I will; but *what* categorical distinctions will best serve my interests and objectify my own intelligence? What the mixed and troubled experience shall be—that is beyond me. But what I shall do with it—that is my own question, when the character of experience is sufficiently before me. I am coerced only by my own need to understand.

It would indeed be inappropriate to characterize as *a priori* a law which we are wholly prepared to alter in the light of further experience, even though in an isolated case we should discard as illusory any experience which failed to conform. But the crux of the situation lies in this; beyond such principles as those of logic, which we seem fully prepared to maintain no matter what, there must be further and more particular criteria of the real prior to any investigation of nature whatever. We can not even interrogate experience without a network of categories and definitive concepts. And we must further be prepared to say what experimental findings will answer what questions, and how. Without tests which represent anterior principle, there is no question which experience could answer at all. Thus the most fundamental laws in any category—or those which we regard as most fundamental—are *a priori,* even though continued failure to render experience intelligible in such terms might result eventually in the abandonment of that category altogether. Matters so comparatively small as the behavior of Mercury and of starlight passing the sun's limb may, if there be persistent failure to bring them within the field of previously accepted modes of explanation, result in the abandonment of the independent categories of space and time. But without the definitions, fundamental principles, and tests, of the type which constitute such categories, no experience whatever could prove or disprove anything. And to that mind which should find independent space and time absolutely necessary conceptions, no possible experiment could prove the principles of relativity. "There must be some error in the experimental findings, or some law not yet discovered," represents an attitude which can never be rendered impossible. And the only sense in which it could be proved unreasonable would be the pragmatic one of comparison with another method of categorical analysis which more successfully reduced all such experience to order and law.

At the bottom of all science and all knowledge are categories and definitive concepts which represent fundamental habits of thought and deep-lying attitudes which the human mind has taken in the light of its total experience. But a new and wider experience may bring about some alteration of these attitudes, even though by themselves they dictate nothing as to the content of experience, and no experience can conceivably prove them invalid.

Perhaps some will object to this conception on the ground that only such principles should be designated *a priori* as the human mind *must* maintain, no matter what; that if, for example, it is shown possible to arrive at a consistent doctrine of physics in terms of relativity, even by the most arduous reconstruction of our fundamental notions, then the present conceptions are by that fact shown not to be *a priori*. Such objection is especially likely from those who would conceive the *a priori* in terms of an absolute mind or an absolutely universal human nature. We should readily agree that a decision by popular approval or a congress of scientists or anything short of such a test as would bring to bear the full weight of human capacity and interest, would be ill-considered as having to do with the *a priori*. But we wish to emphasize two facts: first, that in the field of those conceptions and principles which have altered in human history, there are those which could neither be proved nor disproved by any experience, but represent the uncompelled initiative of human thought—that without this uncompelled initiative no growth of science, nor any science at all, would be conceivable. And second, that the difference between such conceptions as are, for example, concerned in the decision of relativity versus absolute space and time, and those more permanent attitudes such as are vested in the laws of logic, there is only a difference of degree. The dividing line between the *a priori* and the *a posteriori* is that between principles and definitive concepts which *can* be maintained in the face of all experience and those genuinely empirical generalizations which *might* be proven flatly false. The thought which both rationalism and empiricism have missed is that there are principles, representing the initiative of mind, which impose upon experience no limitations whatever, but that such conceptions are still subject to alteration on pragmatic grounds when the expanding boundaries of experience reveal their infelicity as intellectual instruments.

Neither human experience nor the human mind has a character which is universal, fixed, and absolute. "The human mind" does not exist at all save in the sense that all humans are very much alike in fundamental respects, and that the language habit and the enormously important exchange of ideas has greatly increased our likeness in those respects which are here in question. Our categories and definitions are peculiarly social products, reached in the light of experiences which have much in common, and beaten out, like other pathways, by the coincidence of human purposes and the exigencies of human coöperation. Concerning the *a priori* there need be neither universal agreement nor complete historical continuity. Conceptions, such as those of logic, which are least likely to be affected by the opening of new ranges of experience, represent the most stable of our categories; but none of them is beyond the possibility of alteration.

Mind contributes to experience the element of order, of classification, categories, and definition. Without such, experience would be unintelligible. Our knowledge of the validity of these is simply consciousness of our own fundamental ways of acting and our own intellectual intent. Without this element, knowledge is impossible, and it is here that whatever truths are necessary and independent of experience must be found. But the commerce between our categorical ways of acting, our pragmatic interests, and the particular character of experience, is closer than we have realized. No explanation of any one of these can be complete without consideration of the other two.

Pragmatism has sometimes been charged with oscillating between two contrary notions; the one, that experience is "through and through malleable to our purpose," the other, that facts are "hard" and uncreated by the mind. We here offer a mediating conception: through all our knowledge runs the element of the *a priori,* which is indeed malleable to our purpose and responsive to our need. But throughout, there is also that other element of experience which is "hard," "independent," and unalterable to our will.

AN ANALYSIS OF KNOWLEDGE AND VALUATION*

LINGUISTIC MEANING AND SENSE MEANING

1. The original determinations of analytic truth, and the final court of appeal with respect to it, cannot lie in linguistic usage, because meanings are not the creatures of language but are antecedent, and the relations of meanings are not determined by our syntactic conventions but are determinative of the significance which our syntactic usages may have. Once we have penetrated the circle of independent meanings and made genuine contact with them by our modes of expression, the appeal to linguistic relationships can enormously facilitate and extend our grasp of analytic truth. But the first such determinations and the final tests must lie with meanings in that sense in which there would be meanings even if there were no linguistic expression of them, and in which the progress of successful thinking must conform to actual connections of such meanings even if this progress of thought should be unformulated.

When the subject of intension was first mentioned in chapter 3, we noted the possibility of more than one interpretation of intensional meaning, compatible with all that was there said of it. It is in fact possible to think of intension in either of two ways. First, it may be taken as constituted by the pattern of definitive and analytic relationships of the

* C. I. Lewis, "Linguistic Meaning and Sense Meaning." in *An Analysis of Knowledge and Valuation* (LaSalle, Ill.: Open Court Publishing), pp. 131–35, 171–75, 178–85. Reprinted by permission of Open Court Publishing Company, LaSalle, Illinois. Copyright © 1946.

word or expression in question to other words and other expressions.[1] Or second, it may be taken as the criterion in terms of sense by which the application of expressions is determined. The first of these, we shall call linguistic meaning; the second, sense meaning.

The linguistic meaning of an expression is the intension of it as that property which is common to all expressions which could be substituted for the one in question without altering the truth or falsity of any statement, or altering the signification of any other context in which this expression in question should be constituent. It is intensional meaning in the sense in which the intension of a term would be discursively exhibited by the totality of other terms which must be applicable to a thing if the term in question applies; and in which the intensional meaning of a statement would be discursively exhibited by the totality of other statements deducible from it. It is intensional meaning in the sense in which what a word means is other *words* and phrases; and what a statement means is other *statements*. One who tries to find out how otherwise he may express himself when those addressed fail to understand him, is concerned with linguistic meaning; as is also one who fails to understand an expression and seeks to remove his difficulty by the discovery of linguistic equivalents.

Or to take a more nearly adequate example: one who tried to learn the meaning of an Arabic word with only an Arabic dictionary at hand, might—if his acquaintance with Arabic be slight—be obliged to look up also words used in defining the one whose meaning he sought, and the further words defining these, and so on.[2] He might thus eventually determine an extended pattern of linguistic relations of the word in question to other Arabic expressions. If the process of this example could, by some miracle, be carried to its logical limit, a person might thus come to grasp completely and with complete accuracy the linguistic pattern relating the term in question to all other terms in Arabic with which it had any essential or analytic relationship. But—supposing the person in question to be also lacking in wit, so that he learned nothing through his investigation excepting that of which the dictionary informed him—he might still fail to understand, in a sense which will be obvious, what any one of these words *meant*. What he would grasp would be their linguistic meaning. And what he might still fail to grasp would be their sense meaning.

---

[1] Some would say 'syntactic' here instead of 'analytic'. But we are using 'syntax' and 'syntactic' in the narrower meaning previously indicated and nearer to the customary significations of these terms. A relationship of two expressions is analytic if the statement of it is an analytic statement.

[2] It would improve the illustration if we should suppose that while all words defined, and all which define them, are in Arabic, the *relations* between these are expressed in English; that is, that the 'syntactic language' is one already understood.

What we indicate by this phrase *sense meaning* is intension as a *criterion in mind,* by reference to which one is able to apply or refuse to apply the expression in question in the case of presented, or imagined, things or situations.[3] One who should be able to apply or refuse to apply an expression correctly under all imaginable circumstances, would grasp its sense meaning perfectly. But if, through faulty language sense or poor analytic powers, he could still not offer any correct definition, then he would fail to grasp (at least to grasp explicitly) its linguistic meaning.

Because many logicians have of late been somewhat preoccupied with language, intension as linguistic (or 'syntactic' meaning) has been over-emphasized, and sense meaning has been relatively neglected. These two aspects of intensional meaning are supplementary, not alternative; and separable by abstraction rather than separated. One would seldom, if ever, carry out any investigation of meaning in terms of either one of them exclusively. Traditionally, the notion of intension has been explained, now in the manner of linguistic meaning, now in that of sense meaning, and oftentimes in ways which speak of them both together. This failure, or refusal, to separate the two is fundamentally right-minded rather than mistaken. But there are motives of some importance for epistemology which lead to their distinction; and on the whole it is sense meaning which is the more important for investigation of knowledge, and should be emphasized. For example, those who demand theoretical verifiability or confirmability for significance in a statement, have in mind sense meaning as the prime requisite of meaningfulness in general. Likewise those who would set up the criterion of making some empirically deter-minable difference as the test of any genuine difference of meaning. And those who would demand operational significance in any precise and acceptable concept are insisting upon the requirement of sense meaning.

2. For sense meaning, imagery is obviously requisite. Only through the capacity called imagination could one have in mind, in advance, a workable criterion for applying or refusing to apply an expression under all circumstances of presentation. But for reasons made familiar by the long controversy betwen nominalists, conceptualists and realists in logic, sense meaning cannot be vested directly and simply in imagery. The nominalist denies the possibility of sense meaning on such grounds as the impossibility of imaging dog in general or triangle in general, or of

---

[3] As criterion in *mind,* sense meaning is intensional meaning rather than signification: it is that in mind which *refers* to signification. Signification comprises essential properties; and these properties have their being when and where they are instanced, regardless of the association of them with any term or expression. Animality, for example, is a certain property objectively incorporated in animals, which would be just what it is regardless of any linguistic usage associating it with the symbol "animal". It was in order to dispel the subtle ambiguity of the traditional usage of 'intension'—ambiguity as between a meaning in mind and an objective character meant—that it seemed necessary to add signification to the list of fundamental modes of meaning.

having in mind any representation of a chiliagon which should be adequate for distinguishing between a polygon of 1000 sides and one having 999. It is the persistence of such nominalism which, in large measure, is responsible for the current tendency to identify meaning with linguistic meaning exclusively.

The utter weakness of nominalism lies in the obvious fact that we *do* entertain general meanings, as we could not if the nominalist were right. But the nominalistic premises are likewise obvious facts; and it is the weakness of logical realism and of most conceptualist doctrines that they offer nothing better than verbal and unintelligible answers to these nominalist objections.

The valid answer was indicated by Kant. A sense meaning, when precise and explicit, is a schema; a rule or prescribed routine and an imagined result of it which will determine applicability of the expression in question. We cannot adequately imagine a chiliagon, but we easily imagine counting the sides of a polygon and getting 1000 as the result. We cannot imagine triangle in general, but we easily imagine following the periphery of a figure with the eye or a finger and discovering it to be a closed figure with three angles.

Many protagonists of operational significance forget to mention the imagined result, and would—according to what they *say*—identify the concept or meaning exclusively with the routine. Presumably this is merely an oversight: no procedure of laying meter sticks on things would determine length without some anticipatory imagery of a perceivable result which would, for example, corroborate statement that the thing is three meters long.[4] When the meter stick has been applied, it is some observed coincidence which gives the decision of length; else there is none. The operations are requisite only in the sense of setting up conditions under which an observation giving this decision will be possible. If the physicist find a meter stick already lying on the object to be measured, in the required fashion, he will not insist on taking it up and performing the operation of applying it before taking his reading.

But although the notion of what we here call sense meaning has been emphasized by pragmatists, operationists and holders of empiricistic theories in general, it would be claiming too much for these theories of knowledge to grant them any monopoly of the conception. Because attribution of meaning in this sense requires only two things; (1) that determination of applicability or non-applicability of a term, or truth or

---

[4] The concept of a length of three meters is general, since many things may have this property. The concept of *length* is *more* general, and does not contain what is peculiar to any one length. Nevertheless it contains something more than the general rule for the routine of length-measurement—we include with or in that rule a mode of determining *what* length the thing measured will be determined to have, or a mode of deciding for *any* given length, whether the thing measured has that length.

falsity of a statement, be possible by way of sense-presentable characters, and (2) that *what* such characters will, if presented, evidence applicability or truth should be fixed in advance of the particular experience, in the determination of the meaning in question.

THE BASE OF EMPIRICAL KNOWLEDGE

1. If the conclusions of the preceding discussion are to be accepted, then all knowledge has an eventual empirical significance in that all which is knowable or even significantly thinkable must have reference to meanings which are sense-representable.

2. Let us turn to the simplest kind of empirical cognition; knowledge by direct perception. And let us take two examples.

I am descending the steps of Emerson Hall, and using my eyes to guide my feet. This is a habitual and ordinarily automatic action. But for this occasion, and in order that it may clearly constitute an instance of perceptual cognition instead of unconsidered behavior, I put enough attention on the process to bring the major features of it to clear consciousness. There is a certain visual pattern presented to me, a feeling of pressure on the soles of my feet, and certain muscle-sensations and feelings of balance and motion. And these items mentioned are fused together with others in one moving whole of presentation, within which they can be genuinely elicited but in which they do not exist as separate. Much of this presented content, I should find it difficult to put in words. I should find it difficult because, for one reason, if I tried to express it precisely in objectively intelligible fashion, I should have to specify such items as particular muscles which are involved and the behavior of them, and other things of this kind; and I do not in fact know which muscles I am using and just how. But one does not have to study physiology in order to walk down stairs. I know by my feelings when I am walking erect—or I think I do. And you, by putting yourself in my place, know how I feel—or think you do. That is all that is necessary, because we are here speaking of direct experience. You will follow me through the example by using your imagination, and understand what I mean—or what *you* would mean by the same language—in terms of your own experience.

Let us take another and different example; different not in any important character of the situation involved, but different in the manner in which we shall consider it.

I believe there is a piece of white paper now before me. The reason that I believe this is that I see it: a certain visual presentation is given. But my belief includes the expectation that so long as I continue to look in the same direction, this presentation, with its qualitative character essentially unchanged, will persist; that if I move my eyes right, it will be displaced to the left in the visual field; that if I close them, it will disappear; and so on. If any of these predictions should, upon trial, be disproved, I should abandon my present belief in a real piece of paper before me, in favor of belief in some extraordinary after-image or some puzzling reflection or some disconcerting hallucination.

I do look in the same direction for a time; then turn my eyes; and after that try closing them: all with the expected results. My belief is so far corroborated. And these corroborations give me even greater assurance in any further predictions based upon it. But theoretically and ideally it is not completely verified, because the belief in a real piece of white paper now before me has further implications not yet tested; that what I see could be folded without cracking as a piece of celluloid could not; that it would tear easily, as architect's drawing-cloth would not; that this experience will not be followed by waking in quite different surroundings; and others too numerous to mention. If it is a real piece of paper before me now, then I shall expect to find it here tomorrow with the number I just put on the corner: its reality and the real character I attribute in my belief imply innumerable possible verifications, or partial verifications, tomorrow and later on.

4. Let us now give attention to our two examples, and especially to the different manner in which the two have been considered. Both represent cases of knowledge by perception. And in both, while the sensory cues to this knowledge are provided by the given presentation, the cognitive significance is seen to lie not in the mere givenness of these sensory cues but in prediction based upon them. In both cases, it is such prediction the verification of which would mark the judgment made as true or as false.

This use of language to formulate a directly presented or presentable content of experience, may be called its *expressive* use. This is in contrast to that more common intent of language, exemplified by, "I see (what in fact *is*) a flight of granite steps before me," which may be called its *objective* use. The distinctive character of expressive language, or the expressive use of language, is that such language signifies *appearances.* And in thus referring to appearances, or affirming what appears, such expressive language *neither asserts any objective reality of what appears nor denies any.* It is confined to description of the content of presentation itself.

In such expressive language, the cognitive judgment, "If I act in manner *A,* the empirical eventuality will include *E,*" is one which can be verified by putting it to the test—supposing I can in fact put it to the test; can act in manner *A*. When the hypothesis of this hypothetical judgment is made true by my volition, the consequent is found true or found false by what follows; and this verification is decisive and complete, because nothing beyond the content of this passage of experience was implied in the judgment.

In the second example, as we considered it, what was judged was an *objective fact:* "A piece of white paper is now before me." This judgment will be false if the presentation is illusory; it will be false if what I see is not really paper; false if it is not really white but only looks white. This objective judgment also is one capable of corroboration. As in the other example, so here too, any test of the judgment would pretty surely involve some way of acting—*making* the test, as by continuing to look, or turning my eyes, or grasping to tear, etc.—and would be determined by finding or failing to find some expected result in experience. But in this example, if the result of any single test is as expected, it constitutes a partial verification of the judgment only; never one which is absolutely decisive and theoretically complete. This is so because, while the judgment, so far as it is significant, contains nothing which could not be tested, still it has a significance which outruns what any single test, or any limited set of tests, could exhaust. No matter how fully I may have investigated this objective fact, there will remain some theoretical possibility of mistake; there will be further consequences which must be thus and so if the judgment is true, and not all of these will have been determined. The possibility that such further tests, if made, might have a negative result, cannot be altogether precluded; and this possibility marks the judgment as, at the time in question, not fully verified and less than absolutely certain. To quibble about such possible doubts will not, in most cases, be common sense. But we are not trying to weigh the degree of theoretical dubiety which commonsense practicality should take account of, but to arrive at an accurate analysis of knowledge. This character of being further testable and less than theoretically certain characterizes every judgment of objective fact at all times; every judgment that such and such a real thing exists or has a certain objectively factual property, or that a certain objective event actually occurs, or that any objective state of affairs actually is the case.

A judgment of the type of the first example—prediction of a particular passage of experience, describable in expressive language—may be called *terminating.* It admits of decisive and complete verification or falsification. One of the type of the second example—judgment of objective fact which is always further verifiable and never completely verified—may be called *non-terminating.*

However, if the suggested account should be correct, then the judgment of objective fact implies nothing which is not theoretically verifiable. And since any, even partial, verification could be made only by something disclosed in *some* passage of experience, such an objective and non-terminating judgment must be translatable into judgments of the terminating kind. Only so could confirmation of it in experience come about. If particular experiences should not serve as its corroborations, then it cannot be confirmed at all; experience in general would be irrelevant to its truth or falsity; and it must be either analytic or meaningless. Its non-terminating character reflects the fact, not that the statement implies anything which is not expressible in some terminating judgment or other, but that no limited set of such terminating judgments could be sufficient to exhaust its empirical significance.

To be sure, the sense of 'verifiable' which is appropriate to the principle that a statement of supposed objective fact which should not be verifiable would be meaningless, is one which will call for further consideration. 'Verifiable', like most 'able' words, is a highly ambiguous term, connoting conditions which are implied but unexpressed. For example, the sense in which it is verifiable that there are lines on the other side of this paper, is somewhat different from the sense in which it is verifiable that there are mountains on the other side of the moon. But such various senses in which 'verifiable' may be taken, concern the sense in which the verifying experience is 'possible'; not the character of the experience which would constitute verification. And in general we may safely say that for *any* sense in which statement of objective fact is 'meaningful', there is a coordinate and indicated sense in which it is 'verifiable'.

It may also be the case that, for some judgments at least—those called 'practically certain'—a degree of verification may be attained such that no later confirmation can render what is presently judged more certain than it is at the moment. That turns on considerations which are not yet ready to examine. But as will appear, these postponed considerations further corroborate, instead of casting doubt upon, the conclusion that no objective statement is theoretically and completely certain. For that conclusion—which is the present point—the grounds mentioned would seem to be sufficient.

5. The conception is, thus, that there are three classes of empirical statements. First, there are formulations of what is presently given in experience. Only infrequently are such statements of the given actually made: there is seldom need to formulate what is directly and indubitably presented.

Apprehensions of the given which such expressive statements formulate, are not judgments; and they are not here classed as knowledge, becuase they are not subject to any possible error. Statement of such apprehension is, however, true or false; there could be no doubt about the presented content of experience as such at the time when it is given, but it would be possible to tell lies about it.[5]

Second, there are terminating judgments, and statements of them. These represent some prediction of further possible experience. They find their cue in what is given: but what they state is something taken to be verifiable by some test which involves a way of acting. Thus terminating judgments are, in general, of the form, "If A then E," or "S being given, if A then E," where 'A' represents some mode of action taken to be possible, 'E' some expected consequent in experience, and 'S' the sensory cue. The hypothesis 'A' must here express something which, if made true by adopting action, will be *indubitably* true, and not, like a condition of my musculature in relation to the environment, an objective state of affairs only partially verified and not completely certain at the time. And the consequent 'E' represents an eventuality of *experience,* directly and certainly recognizable in case it accrues; not a resultant objective event, whose factuality could have, and would call for, further verification. Thus both antecedent and consequent of this judgment, "If A then E," require to be formulated in expressive language; though we shall not call it an expressive statement, reserving that phrase for formulations of the given. Also, unlike statements of the given, what such terminating judgments express is to be classed as knowledge: the prediction in question calls for verification, and is subject to possible error.

Third, there are non-terminating judgments which assert objective reality; some state of affairs as actual. These are so named because, while there is nothing in the import of such objective statements which is intrinsically unverifiable, and hence nothing included in them which is not expressible by some terminating judgment, nevertheless no limited set of particular predictions of empirical eventualities can completely exhaust the significance of such an objective statement. This is true of the simplest and most trivial, as much as of the most important. The statement that something is blue, for example, or is square—as contrasted with merely looking blue or appearing to be square—has, always, implications of further possible experience, beyond what should, at any par-

---

[5] It would be possible to take statements of the given as involving judgment of correspondence between the character of the given itself and a fixed (expressive) meaning of words. But a judgment, "What is given is what '___' expresses," is not expression of the given but of a relation between it and a certain form of words. There is such a 'judgment of formulation' in the case of *any* statable fact. Let 'P' be an empirical statement which says nothing about language. "This fact is correctly stated by 'P'" is then a different statement, stating a relation between the fact which 'P' asserts and the verbal formulation 'P.' Correlatively, it is always possible to make a mistake of formulation, even where there could be no possible error concerning what is formulated. (In Book I, where we were frequently concerned with matters of logic, we used small letters, p, q, etc., to represent statements, following the current logical usage. But from this point on it will make for easier reading if we represent statements by capital letters, P, Q, etc.

ticular time, have been found true. Theoretically complete and absolute verification of any objective judgment would be a never ending task: any actual verification of them is no more than partial; and our assurance of them is always theoretically, less than certain.

Non-terminating judgments represent an enormous class; they include, in fact, pretty much all the empirical statements we habitually make. They range in type from the simplest assertion of perceived fact—"There is a piece of white paper now before me"—to the most impressive of scientific generalizations—"The universe is expanding." In general, the more important an assertion of empirical objective fact, the more remote it is from its eventual grounds. The laws of science, for example, are arrived at by induction from inductions from inductions - - -. But objective judgments are all alike in being non-terminating, and in having no other eventual foundation than data of given experience.

6. The point of distinguishing expressive statements of given data of experience from predictive and verifiable statements of terminating judgments, and both of them from statements of objective fact, representing non-terminating judgments, is that without such distinctions it is almost impossible so to analyze empirical knowledge as to discover the grounds of it in experience, and the manner of its derivation from such grounds.

RUDOLF CARNAP

INTELLECTUAL AUTOBIOGRAPHY*

My own philosophical work began with the doctoral dissertation just mentioned. The men who had the strongest effect on my philosophical thinking were Frege and Russell. I was influenced by Frege first through his lectures and later, perhaps even to a greater extent, through his works, most of which I read only after the war. His main work, *Die Grundgesetze der Arithmetik* (2 vols., 1893 and 1903), I studied in 1920. From Frege I learned carefulness and clarity in the analysis of concepts and linguistic expressions, the distinction between expressions and what they stand for, and concerning the latter between what he called *"Bedeutung"* (denotation or *nominatum*) and what he called *"Sinn"* (sense or *significatum*). From his analysis I gained the conviction that knowledge in mathematics is analytic in the general sense that it has essentially the same nature as knowledge in logic. I shall later explain how this view became more radical and precise, chiefly through the influence of Wittgenstein. Furthermore the following conception, which derives essentially from Frege, seemed to me of paramount importance: It is the task of logic and of mathematics within the total system of knowledge to supply the forms of concepts, statements, and inferences, forms which are then applicable

* Rudolf Carnap, "Intellectual Autobiography," in *The Philosophy of Rudolf Carnap,* ed. Paul A. Schilpp (LaSalle, Ill.: Open Court Publishing), pp. 12–13, 16–19, 20–21, 24–25, 28–29, 45–46, 53–59. Reprinted by permission of Open Court Publishing Company, LaSalle, Illinois. Copyright © 1963.

everywhere, hence also to non-logical knowledge. It follows from these considerations that the nature of logic and mathematics can be clearly understood only if close attention is given to their application in non-logical fields, especially in empirical science. Although the greater part of my work belongs to the fields of pure logic and the logical foundations of mathematics, nevertheless great weight is given in my thinking to the application of logic to non-logical knowledge. This point of view is an important factor in the motivation for some of my philosophical positions, for example, for the choice of forms of languages, for my emphasis on the fundamental distinction between logical and non-logical knowledge. The latter position, which I share with many contemporary philosophers, differs from that of some logicians like Tarski and Quine, with whom I agree on many other basic questions. From Frege I learned the requirement to formulate the rules of inference of logic without any reference to meaning, but also the great significance of meaning analysis. I believe that here are the roots of my philosophical interest—on the one hand in logical syntax, and on the other hand in that part of semantics which may be regarded as a theory of meaning.

The largest part of my philosophical work from 1922 to 1925 was devoted to considerations out of which grew the book, *Der logische Aufbau der Welt* [1928–1].

Inspired by Russell's description of the aim and the method of future philosophy, I made numerous attempts at analyzing concepts of ordinary language relating to things in our environment and their observable properties and relations, and at constructing definitions of these concepts with the help of symbolic logic. Although I was guided in my procedure by the psychological facts concerning the formation of concepts of material things out of perceptions, my real aim was not the description of this genetic process, but rather its rational reconstruction—i.e., a schematized description of an imaginary procedure, consisting of rationally prescribed steps, which would lead to essentially the same results as the actual psychological process. Thus, for example, material things are usually immediately perceived as three-dimensional bodies; on the other hand, in the systematic procedure they are to be constructed out of a temporal sequence of continually changing forms in the two-dimensional visual field. At first I made the analysis in the customary way, proceeding from complexes to smaller and smaller components, e.g., first from material bodies to instantaneous visual fields, then to color patches, and finally to single positions in the visual field. Thus the analysis led to what Ernst Mach called the elements. My use of this method was probably influenced by Mach and phenomenalist philosophers. But it seemed to me that I was the first who took the doctrine of these philosophers seriously. I was not content with their customary general statements like "A material body is a complex of visual, tactile, and other sensations," but tried actually to construct these complexes in order to show their structure. For the description of the structure of any complex, the new logic of relations as in *Principia Mathematica* seemed to me just the required tool. While I worked on many special problems, I was aware that this ultimate aim could not possibly be reached by one individual, but I took it as my task to give at least an outline of the total construction and to show by partial solutions the nature of the method to be applied.

A change in the approach occurred when I recognized, under the influence of the Gestalt psychology of Wertheimer and Köhler that the customary method of analyzing material things into separate sense-data was inadequate—that an instantaneous visual field and perhaps even an instantaneous total experience is given as a unit, while the allegedly simple sense-data are the result of a process of abstraction. Therefore I took as elements total instantaneous experiences *(Elementarerlebnisse)* rather than single sense-data. I developed a method called "quasi-analysis," which leads, on the basis of the similarity-relation among experiences, to the logical construction of those entities which are usually conceived as components. On the basis of a certain primitive relation among experiences, the method of quasi-analysis leads step by step to the various sensory domains—first to the visual domain, then to the positions in the visual field, the colors and their similarity system, the temporal order, and the like. Later, perceived things in the three-dimensional perceptual space are constructed, among them that particular thing which is usually called my own body, and the bodies of other persons. Still later, the so-called other minds are constructed; that is to say, mental states are ascribed to other bodies in view of their behavior, in analogy to the experience of one's own mental states.

Leaving aside further details of the system, I shall try to characterize one general feature of it that seems to me important for the understanding of my basic attitude towards traditional philosophical ways of thinking. Since my student years, I have liked to talk with friends about general problems in science and in practical life, and these discussions often led to philosophical questions. My friends were philosophically interested, yet most of them were not professional philosophers, but worked either in the natural sciences or in the humanities. Only much later, when I was working on the *Logischer Aufbau,* did I become aware that in talks with my various friends I had used different philosophical languages, adapting myself to their ways of thinking and speaking. With one friend I might talk in a language that could be characterized as realistic or even as materialistic; here we looked at the world as consisting of bodies, bodies as consisting of atoms; sensations, thoughts, emotions, and the like were conceived as physiological processes in the nervous system and ultimately as physical processes. Not that the friend maintained or even considered the thesis of materialism; we just used a way of speaking which might be called materialistic. In a talk with another friend, I might adapt myself to his idealistic kind of language. We would consider the question of how things are to be constituted on the basis of the given. With some I talked a language which might be labelled nominalistic, with others again Frege's language of abstract entities of various types, like properties, relations, propositions, etc., a language which some contemporary authors call Platonic.

I was surprised to find that this variety in my way of speaking appeared to some as objectionable and even inconsistent. I had acquired insights valuable for my own thinking from philosophers and scientists of a great variety of philosophical creeds. When asked which philosophical positions I myself held, I was unable to answer. I could only say that in general my way of thinking was closer to that of physicists and of those philosophers who are in contact with scientific work. Only gradually, in the course of years, did I recognize clearly that my way of thinking was neutral with respect to the traditional controversies, e.g., realism vs. idealism, nominalism vs. Platonism (realism of universals), materialism vs. spiritualism, and so on. When I developed the system of the *Aufbau,* it actually did not matter to me which of the various forms of philosophical language I used, because to me they were merely modes of speech, and not formulations of positions. Indeed, in the book itself, in the description of the system of construction or constitution, I used in addition to the neutral language of symbolic logic three other languages, in order to facilitate the understanding for the reader; namely, first, a simple translation of the symbolic formula of definition into the word language; second, a corresponding formulation in the realistic language as it is customary in natural science; and third, a reformulation of the definition as a rule of operation for a constructive procedure, applicable by anybody, be it Kant's transcendental subject or a computing machine.

The system of concepts was constructed on a phenomenalistic basis; the basic elements were experiences, as mentioned before. However, I indicated also the possibility of constructing a total system of concepts on a physicalistic basis. The main motivation for my choice of a phenomenalistic basis was the intention to represent not only the logical relations among the concepts but also the equally important epistemological relations. The system was intended to give, though not a description, still a rational reconstruction of the actual process of the formation of concepts.

This neutral attitude toward the various philosophical forms of language, based on the principle that everyone is free to use the language most suited to his purpose, has remained the same throughout my life. It was formulated as "principle of tolerance" in *Logical Syntax* and I still hold it today, e.g., with respect to the contemporary controversy about a nominalist or Platonic language. On the other hand, regarding the criticism of traditional metaphysics, in the *Aufbau* I merely refrained from taking sides; I added that, if one proceeds from the discussion of language forms to that of the corresponding metaphysical theses about the reality or unreality of some kind of entities, he steps beyond the bounds of science.

THE VIENNA CIRCLE (1926–1935)

In the summer of 1924, through Reichenbach, I had become acquainted with Moritz Schlick. Schlick told me that he would be happy to have me as an instructor in Vienna. In 1925 I went for a short time to Vienna and gave some lectures in Schlick's Philosophical Circle. From the fall of 1926 to the summer of 1931 I was an instructor of philosophy at the University of Vienna.

For my philosophical work the period in Vienna was one of the most stimulating, enjoyable, and fruitful periods of my life. My interests and my basic philosophical views were more in accord with those of the Circle than with any group I ever found.

The task of fruitful collaboration, often so difficult among philosophers, was facilitated in our Circle by the fact that all members had a first-hand acquaintance with some field of science, either mathematics, physics or social science. This led to a higher standard in clarity and responsibility than is usually found in philosophical groups, particularly in Germany. Also, the members of the Circle were familiar with modern logic. This made it possible to represent the analysis of a concept or proposition under discussion symbolically and thereby make the arguments more precise. Furthermore, there was agreement among most of the members to reject traditional metaphysics. However, very little time was wasted in a polemic against metaphysics. The anti-metaphysical attitude showed itself chiefly in the choice of the language used in the discussion. We tried to avoid the terms of traditional philosophy and to use instead those of logic, mathematics, and empirical science, or of that part of the ordinary language which, though more vague, still is in principle translatable into a scientific language.

Characteristic for the Circle was the open and undogmatic attitude taken in the discussions. Everyone was willing constantly to subject his views to a re-examination by others or by himself. The common spirit was one of co-operation rather than competition. The common purpose was to work together in the struggle for clarification and insight.

Wittgenstein's book exerted a strong influence upon our Circle. But it is not correct to say that the philosophy of the Vienna Circle was just Wittgenstein's philosophy. We learned much by our discussions of the book, and accepted many views as far as we could assimilate them to our basic conceptions. The degree of influence varied, of course, for the different members.

For me personally, Wittgenstein was perhaps the philosopher who, besides Russell and Frege, had the greatest influence on my thinking. The most important insight I gained from his work was the conception that the truth of logical statements is based only on their logical structure and on the meaning of the terms. Logical statements are true under all conceivable circumstances; thus their truth is independent of the contingent facts of the world. On the other hand, it follows that these statements do not say anything about the world and thus have no factual content.

Another influential idea of Wittgenstein's was the insight that many philosophical sentences, especially in traditional metaphysics, are pseudo-sentences, devoid of cognitive content. I found Wittgenstein's view on this point close to the one I had previously developed under the influence of anti-metaphysical scientists and philosophers. I had recognized that many of these sentences and questions originate in a misuse of language and a violation of logic. Under the influence of Wittgenstein, this conception was strengthened and became more definite and more radical.

All of us in the Circle had a lively interest in science and mathematics. In contrast to this, Wittgenstein seemed to look upon these fields with an attitude of indifference and sometimes even with contempt. His indirect influence on some students in Vienna was so strong that they abandoned the study of mathematics. It seems that later in his teaching activities in England he had a similar influence on even wider circles there. This is probably at least a contributing factor to the divergence between the attitude represented by many recent publications in analytic philosophy in England and that of logical empiricism in the United States.

Closely related is Wittgenstein's view of the philosophical relevance of constructed language systems. Chiefly because of Frege's influence, I was always deeply convinced of the superiority of a carefully constructed language and of its usefulness and even indispensability for the analysis of statements and concepts, both in philosophy and in science. All members of the Vienna Circle had studied at least the elementary parts of *Principia Mathematica*. For students of mathematics Hahn gave a lecture course and a seminar on the foundations of mathematics, based on the *Principia*. When I came to Vienna I continued these courses for students both of mathematics and of philosophy. In the Circle discussions we often made use of symbolic logic for the representation of analyses or examples. When we found in Wittgenstein's book statements about "the language," we interpreted them as referring to an ideal language; and this meant for us a formalized symbolic language. Later Wittgenstein explicitly rejected this view. He had a skeptical and sometimes even a negative view of the importance of a symbolic language for the clarification and correction of the confusions in ordinary language and also in the customary language of philosophers which, as he had shown himself, were often the cause of philosophical puzzles and pseudo-problems. On this point, the majority of British analytic philosophers share Wittgenstein's view, in contrast to the Vienna Circle and to the majority of analytical philosophers in the United States.

Furthermore, there is a divergence on a more specific point which, however, was of great importance for our way of thinking in the Circle. We read in Wittgenstein's book that certain things show themselves but cannot be said; for example the logical structure of sentences and the relation between the language and the world. In opposition to this view, first tentatively, then more and more clearly, our conception developed that it is possible to talk meaningfully about language and about the relation between a sentence and the fact described. Neurath emphasized from the beginning that language phenomena are events *within* the world, not something that refers to the world from outside. Spoken language consists of sound waves; written language consists of marks of ink on paper. Neurath emphasized these facts in order to reject the view that there is something "higher," something mysterious, "spiritual," in language, a view which was prominent in German philosophy. I agreed with him, but pointed out that only the structural pattern, not the physical properties of the ink marks, were relevant for the function of language. Thus it is possible to construct a theory about language, namely the geometry of the written pattern. This idea led later to the theory which I called "logical syntax" of language.

The most decisive development in my view of metaphysics occurred later, in the Vienna period, chiefly under the influence of Wittgenstein. I came to hold the view that many theses of traditional metaphysics are not only useless, but even devoid of cognitive content. They are pseudo-sentences, that is to say, they seem to make assertions because they have the grammatical form of declarative sentences, and the words occurring in them have many strong and emotionally loaded associations, while in fact they do not make any assertions, do not express any propositions, and are therefore neither true nor false. Even the apparent questions to which these sentences allegedly give either an affirmative or a negative answer, e.g., the question "is the external world real? " are not genuine questions but pseudo-questions. The view that these sentences and questions are non-cognitive was based on Wittgenstein's principle of verifiability. This principle says first, that the meaning of a sentence is given by the conditions of its verification and, second, that a sentence is meaningful if and only if it is in principle verifiable, that is, if there are possible, not necessarily actual, circumstances which, if they did occur, would definitely establish the truth of the sentence. This principle of verifiability was later replaced by the more liberal principle of confirmability.

Unfortunately, following Wittgenstein, we formulated our view in the Vienna Circle in the oversimplified version of saying that certain metaphysical theses are "meaningless." This formulation caused much unnecessary opposition, even among some of those philosophers who basically agreed with us. Only later did we see that it is important to distinguish the various meaning components, and therefore said in a more precise way that such theses lack cognitive or theoretical meaning. They often have other meaning components, e.g., emotive or motivative ones, which, although not cognitive, may have strong psychological effects.

The general view that many sentences of traditional metaphysics ae pseudo-sentences was held by most members of the Vienna Circle and by many philosophers in other empiricist groups, such as Reichenbach's group in Berlin. In the discussions of the Vienna Circle I maintained from the beginning the view that a characterization as pseudo-sentences must also be applied to the thesis of realism concerning the reality of the external world, and to the countertheses, say, those of idealism, solipsism, and the like.

THE LOGICAL SYNTAX OF LANGUAGE

I mentioned earlier that the members of the Circle, in contrast to Wittgenstein, came to the conclusion that it is possible to speak about language and, in particular, about the structures of linguistic expressions. On the basis of this conception, I developed the idea of the logical syntax of a language as the purely analytic theory of the structure of its expressions. My way of thinking was influenced chiefly by the investigations of Hilbert and Tarski in metamathematics, which I mentioned previously. I often talked with Gödel about these problems. In August 1930 he explained to me his new method of correlating numbers with signs and expressions. Thus a theory of the forms of expressions could be formulated with the help of concepts of arithmetic. He told me that, with the help of this method of arithmetization, he had proved that any formal system of arithmetic is incomplete and incompletable. When he published this result in 1931, it marked a turning point in the development of the foundation of mathematics.

After thinking about these problems for several years, the whole theory of language structure and its possible applications in philosophy came to me like a vision during a sleepless night in January 1931, when I was ill. On the following day, still in bed with a fever, I wrote down my ideas on forty-four pages under the title "Attempt at a metalogic." These shorthand notes were the first version of my book *Logical Syntax of Language* [1934–6]. In the spring of 1931 I changed the form of language dealt with in this essay to that of a co-ordinate language of about the same form as that later called "language I" in my book. Thus arithmetic could be formulated in this language, and by use of Gödel's method, even the metalogic of the language could be arithmetized and formulated in the language itself. In June of 1931 I gave three lectures on metalogic in our Circle.

In the metalogic I emphasized the distinction between that language which is the object of the investigation, which I called the "object language," and the language in which the theory of the object language, in other words the metalogic, is formulated, which I called the "metalanguage." One of my aims was to make it the metalanguage more precise so that an exact conceptual system for metalogic could be constructed in it. Whereas Hilbert intended his metamathematics only for the special purpose of proving the consistency of a mathematical system formulated in the object language, I aimed at the construction of a general theory of linguistic forms.

At that time I defined the term "metalogic" as the theory of the forms of the expressions of a language. Later I used the term "syntax" instead of "metalogic," or, in distinction to syntax as part of linguistics, "logical syntax."

I thought of the logical syntax of language in the strictly limited sense of dealing exclusively with the forms of the expression of the language, the form of an expression being characterized by the specification of the signs occurring in it and of the order in which the signs occur. No reference to the meaning of the signs and expressions is made in logical syntax. Since only the logical structure of the expressions is involved, the syntax language, i.e., the metalanguage serving for the formulation of logical syntax, contains only logical constants.

My interest in the development of logical syntax was chiefly determined by the following points of view. First, I intended to show that the concepts of the theory of formal deductive logic, e.g., provability, derivability from given premises, logical independence, etc., are purely syntactical concepts, and that therefore their definitions can be formulated in logical syntax, since these concepts depend merely on the forms of the sentences, not on their meanings.

Second, it seemed important to me to show that many philosophical controversies actually concen the question whether a particular language form should be used, say, for the language of mathematics or of science. For example, in the controversy about the foundations of mathematics, the conception of intuitionism may be construed as a proposal to restrict the means of expression and the means of deduction of the language of mathematics in a certain way, while the classical conception leaves the language unrestricted. I intended to make available in syntax the conceptual means for an exact formulation of controversies of this kind. Furthermore, I wished to show that everyone is free to choose the rules of his language and thereby his logic in any way he wishes. This I called the "principle of tolerance"; it might perhaps be called more exactly the "principle of the conventionality of language forms." As a consequence, the discussion of controversies of the kind mentioned need only concern first, the syntactical properties of the various forms of language, and second, practical reasons for preferring one or the other form for given purposes. In this way, assertions that a particular language is the correct language or represents the correct logic such as often occurred in earlier discussions, are eliminated, and traditional ontological problems, in contradistinction to the logical or syntactical ones, for example, problems concerning "the essence of number," are entirely abolished. The various language forms which are to be investigated and compared and from which one or several are to be chosen for a given purpose comprise, of course, not only historically given language forms, like the natural word languages or the historically developed symbolic languages of mathematics, but also any new form that anyone may wish to construct. This possibility of constructing new languages was essential from our point of view.

The chief motivation for my development of the syntactical method, however, was the following. In our discussions in the Vienna Circle it had turned out that any attempt at formulating more precisely the philosophical problems in which we are interested ended up with problems of the logical analysis of language. Since in our view the issue in philosophical problems concerned the language, not the world, these problems should be formulated, not in the object language, but in the metalanguage. Therefore it seemed to me that the development of a suitable metalanguage would essentially contribute toward greater clarity in the formulation of philosophical problems and greater fruitfulness in their discussions.

During the thirties, while I was in Prague, I began a systematic investigation of the logical relations between scientific concepts and basic concepts, say, observable properties of material things. The results were published in the article "Testability and Meaning" [1936–10]. I shall now explain some of these considerations.

Hypotheses about unobserved events of the physical world can never be completely verified by observational evidence. Therefore I suggested that we should abandon the concept of verification and say instead that the hypothesis is more or less confirmed or disconfirmed by the evidence. At that time I left the question open whether it would be possible to define a quantitative measure of confirmation. Later I introduced the quantitative concept of degree of confirmation or logical probability. I proposed to speak of confirmability instead of verifiability. A sentence is regarded as confirmable if observation sentences can contribute either positively or negatively to its confirmation.

Furthermore, I investigated possible sentence forms and methods for the introduction of new predicates on the basis of given primitive predicates for observable properties of things. My aim was to choose the sentence forms and methods of concept formation in such a way that the confirmability of the resulting sentences was assured. If a concept is introduced by a method which fulfills this requirement on the basis of given primitive predicates, then I called it reducible to those primitive predicates.

In addition to the requirement of complete verifiability we must abandon the earlier view that the concepts of science are explicitly definable on the basis of observation concepts; more indirect methods of reduction must be used. For this purpose I proposed a particular form of reduction sentences. In the course of further investigations it became clear that a schema of this simple form cannot suffice to introduce concepts of theoretical science. Still, the proposed simple form of reduction sentences was useful because it exhibited clearly the open character of the scientific concepts, i.e., the fact that their meanings are not completely fixed.

I made a distinction between confirmability and a somewhat stronger concept for which I proposed the term "testability." A sentence which is confirmable by possible observable events is, moreover, testable if a method can be specified for producing such events at will; this method is then a test procedure for the sentence. I considered the question of whether we should take testability or only confirmability as an empiricist criterion of significance. I proposed to take the more liberal requirement of confirmability. The stronger requirement of testability corresponds approximately to Bridgman's principle of operationism.

The thesis of physicalism, as originally accepted in the Vienna Circle, says roughly: Every concept of the language of science can be explicitly defined in terms of observables; therefore every sentence of the language of science is translatable into a sentence concerning observable properties. I suggested that only reducibility to observation predicates need be required of scientific concepts, since this requirement is sufficient for the confirmability of sentences involving those concepts.

Furthermore, I showed that our earlier thesis of phenomenalistic positivism was in need of a more liberal reformulation in an analogous way, so that translatability was replaced by confirmability.

W. V. O. QUINE

TWO DOGMAS OF EMPIRICISM*

Modern empiricism has been conditioned in large part by two dogmas. One is a belief in some fundamental cleavage between truths which are *analytic,* or grounded in meanings independently of matters of fact, and truths which are *synthetic,* or grounded in fact. The other dogma is *reductionism:* the belief that each meaningful statement is equivalent to some logical construct upon terms which refer to immediate experience. Both dogmas, I shall argue, are ill-founded. One effect of abandoning them is, as we shall see, a blurring of the supposed boundary between speculative metaphysics and natural science. Another effect is a shift toward pragmatism.

1. BACKGROUND FOR ANALYTICITY

Kant's cleavage between analytic and synthetic truths was foreshadowed in Hume's distinction between relations of ideas and matters of fact, and

* W. V. O. Quine, "Two Dogmas of Empiricism," *Philosophical Review* 60, no. 1 (January 1951): pp. 20–43. Also published in *From a Logical Point of View: Nine Logico-Philosophical Essays,* 2d ed. (Cambridge: Harvard University Press, 1961), pp. 20–25, 27, 31, 36–37, 38–39, 41–46.

in Leibniz's distinction between truths of reason and truths of fact. Leibniz spoke of the truths of reason as true in all possible worlds. Picturesqueness aside, this is to say that the truths of reason are those which could not possibly be false. In the same vein we hear analytic statements defined as statements whose denials are self-contradictory. But this definition has small explanatory value; for the notion of self-contradictoriness, in the quite broad sense needed for this definition of analyticity, stands in exactly the same need of clarification as does the notion of analyticity itself. The two notions are the two sides of a single dubious coin.

Kant conceived of an analytic statement as one that attributes to its subject no more than is already conceptually contained in the subject. This formulation has two shortcomings: it limits itself to statements of subject-predicate form, and it appeals to a notion of containment which is left at a metaphorical level. But Kant's intent, evident more from the use he makes of the notion of analyticity than from his definition of it, can be restated thus: a statement is analytic when it is true by virtue of meanings and independently of fact. Pursuing this line, let us examine the concept of *meaning* which is presupposed.

Meaning, let us remember, is not to be identified with naming. Frege's example of 'Evening Star' and 'Morning Star', and Russell's of 'Scott' and 'the author of *Waverley*', illustrate that terms can name the same thing but differ in meaning. The distinction between meaning and naming is no less important at the level of abstract terms. The terms '9' and 'the number of the planets' name one and the same abstract entity but presumably must be regarded as unlike in meaning; for astronomical observation was needed, and not mere reflection on meanings, to determine the sameness of the entity in question.

The above examples consist of singular terms, concrete and abstract. With general terms, or predicates, the situation is somewhat different but parallel. Whereas a singular term purports to name an entity, abstract or concrete, a general term does not; but a general term is *true of* an entity, or of each of many, or of none. The class of all entities of which a general term is true is called the *extension* of the term. Now paralleling the contrast between the meaning of a singular term and the entity named, we must distinguish equally between the meaning of a general term and its extension. The general terms 'creature with a heart' and 'creature with kidneys', for example, are perhaps alike in extension but unlike in meaning.

Confusion of meaning with extension, in the case of general terms, is less common than confusion of meaning with naming in the case of singular terms. It is indeed a commonplace in philosophy to oppose intension (or meaning) to extension, or, in a variant vocabulary, connotation to denotation.

The Aristotelian notion of essence was the forerunner, no doubt, of the modern notion of intension or meaning. For Aristotle it was essential in men to be rational, accidental to be two-legged. But there is an important difference between this attitude and the doctrine of meaning. From the latter point of view it may indeed be conceded (if only for the sake of argument) that rationality is involved in the meaning of the word 'man' while two-leggedness is not; but two-leggedness may at the same time be viewed as involved in the meaning of 'biped' while rationality is not. Thus from the point of view of the doctrine of meaning it makes no sense to say of the actual individual, who is at once a man and a biped, that his rationality is essential and his two-leggedness accidental or vice versa. Things had essences, for Aristotle, but only linguistic forms have meanings. Meaning is what essence becomes when it is divorced from the object of reference and wedded to the word.

For the theory of meaning a conspicuous question is the nature of its objects: what sort of things are meanings? A felt need for meant entities may derive from an earlier failure to appreciate that meaning and reference are distinct. Once the theory of meaning is sharply separated from the theory of reference, it is a short step to recognizing as the primary business of the theory of meaning simply the synonymy of linguistic forms and the analyticity of statements; meanings themselves, as obscure intermediary entities, may well be abandoned.

The problem of analyticity then confronts us anew. Statements which are analytic by general philosophical acclaim are not, indeed, far to seek. They fall into two classes. Those of the first class, which may be called *logically true,* are typified by:

(1)   No unmarried man is married.

The relevant feature of this example is that it not merely is true as it stands, but remains true under any and all reinterpretations of 'man' and 'married'. If we suppose a prior inventory of *logical* particles, comprising 'no', 'un-', 'not', 'if', 'then', 'and', etc., then in general a logical truth is a statement which is true and remains true under all reinterpretations of its components other than the logical particles.

But there is also a second class of analytic statements, typified by:

(2)   No bachelor is married.

The characteristic of such a statement is that it can be turned into a logical truth by putting synonyms for synonyms; thus (2) can be turned into (1) by putting 'unmarried man' for its synonym 'bachelor'. We still lack a proper characterization of this second class of analytic statements, and therewith of analyticity generally, inasmuch as we have had in the above description to lean on a notion of "synonymy' which is no less in need of clarification than analyticity itself.

2. DEFINITION

There are those who find it soothing to say that the analytic statements of the second class reduce to those of the first class, the logical truths, by *definition;* 'bachelor', for example, is *defined* as 'unmarried man'. But how do we find that 'bachelor' is defined as 'unmarried man'? Who defined it thus, and when? Are we to appeal to the nearest dictionary, and accept the lexicographer's formulation as law? Clearly this would be to put the cart before the horse. The lexicographer is an empirical scientist, whose business is the recording of antecedent facts; and if he glosses 'bachelor' as 'unmarried man' it is because of his belief that there is a relation of synonymy between those forms, implicit in general or preferred usage prior to his own work. The notion of synonymy presupposed here has still to be clarified, presumably in terms relating to linguistic behavior. Certainly the "definition" which is the lexicographer's report of an observed synonymy cannot be taken as the ground of the synonymy.

Definition is not, indeed, an activity exclusively of philologists. Philosophers and scientists frequently have occasion to "define" a recondite term by paraphrasing it into terms of a more familiar vocabulary. But ordinarily such a definition, like the philologist's, is pure lexicography, affirming a relation of synonymy antecedent to the exposition in hand.

Just what it means to affirm synonymy, just what the interconnections may be which are necessary and sufficient in order that two linguistic forms be properly describable as synonymous, is far from clear; but, whatever these interconnections may be, ordinarily they are grounded in usage. Definitions reporting selected instances of synonymy come then as reports upon usage.

In formal and informal work alike, thus, we find that definition— except in the extreme case of the explicitly conventional introduction of new notations—hinges on prior relations of synonymy. Recognizing then that the notion of definition does not hold the key to synonymy and analyticity, let us look further into synonymy and say no more of definition.

3. INTERCHANGEABILITY

A natural suggestion, deserving close examination, is that the synonymy of two linguistic forms consists simply in their interchangeability in all contexts without change of truth value—interchangeability, in Leibniz's phrase, *salva veritate*. Note that synonyms so conceived need not even be free from vagueness, as long as the vaguenesses match.

In an extensional language, therefore, interchangeability *salva veritate* is no assurance of cognitive synonymy of the desired type. That 'bachelor' and 'unmarried man' are interchangeable *salva veritate* in an extensional language assures us of no more than that (3) is true. There is no assurance here that the extensional agreement of 'bachelor' and 'unmarried man' rests on meaning rather than merely on accidental matters of fact, as does the extensional agreement of 'creature with a heart' and 'creature with kidneys'.

For most purposes extensional agreement is the nearest approximation to synonymy we need care about. But the fact remains that extensional agreement falls far short of cognitive synonymy of the type required for explaining analyticity in the manner of §1. The type of cognitive synonymy required there is such as to equate the synonymy of 'bachelor' and 'unmarried man' with the analyticity of (3), not merely with the truth of (3).

So we must recognize that interchangeability *salva veritate,* if construed in relation to an extensional language, is not a sufficient condition of cognitive synonymy in the sense needed for deriving analyticity in the manner of §1. If a language contains an intensional adverb 'necessarily' in the sense lately noted, or other particles to the same effect, then interchangeability *salva veritate* in such a language does afford a sufficient condition of cognitive synonymy; but such a language is intelligible only in so far as the notion of analyticity is already understood in advance.

4. SEMANTICAL RULES

It is obvious that truth in general depends on both language and extralinguistic fact. The statement 'Brutus killed Caesar' would be false if the world had been different in certain ways, but it would also be false if the word 'killed' happened rather to have the sense of 'begat'. Thus one is tempted to suppose in general that the truth of a statement is somehow analyzable into a linguistic component and a factual component. Given this supposition, it next seems reasonable that in some statements the factual component should be null; and these are the analytic statements. But, for all its a priori reasonableness, a boundary between analytic and synthetic statements simply has not been drawn. That there is such a distinction to be drawn at all is an unempirical dogma of empiricists, a metaphysical article of faith.

THE VERIFICATION THEORY AND REDUCTIONISM

In the course of these somber reflections we have taken a dim view first of the notion of meaning, then of the notion of cognitive synonymy, and finally of the notion of analyticity. But what, it may be asked, of the verification theory of meaning? This phrase has established itself so firmly as a catchword of empiricism that we should be very unscientific indeed not to look beneath it for a possible key to the problem of meaning and the associated problems.

The verification theory of meaning, which has been conspicuous in the literature from Peirce onward, is that the meaning of a statement is the method of empirically confirming or infirming it. An analytic statement is that limiting case which is confirmed no matter what.

As urged in §1, we can as well pass over the question of meanings as entities and move straight to sameness of meaning, or synonymy. Then what the verification theory says is that statements are synonymous if and only if they are alike in point of method of empirical confirmation or infirmation.

. . . For a statement may be described as analytic simply when it is synonymous with a logically true statement.

So, if the verification theory can be accepted as an adequate account of statement synonymy, the notion of analyticity is saved after all. However, let us reflect. Statement synonymy is said to be likeness of method of empirical confirmation or infirmation. Just what are these methods which are to be compared for likeness? What, in other words, is the nature of the relation between a statement and the experiences which contribute to or detract from its confirmation?

The most naïve view of the relation is that it is one of direct report. This is *radical reductionism.* Every meaningful statement is held to be translatable into a statement (true or false) about immediate experience. Radical reductionism, in one form or another, well antedates the verification theory of meaning explicitly so called. Thus Locke and Hume held that every idea must either originate directly in sense experience or else be compounded of ideas thus originating; and taking a hint from Tooke we might rephrase this doctrine in semantical jargon by saying that a term, to be significant at all, must be either a name of a sense datum or a compound of such names or an abbreviation of such a compound. So stated, the doctrine remains ambiguous as between sense data as sensory events and sense data as sensory qualities; and it remains vague as to the admissible ways of compounding. Moreover, the doctrine is unnecessarily and intolerably restrictive in the term-by-term critique which it imposes. More reasonably, and without yet exceeding the limits of what I have called radical reductionism, we may take full statements as our significant units—thus demanding that our statements as wholes be translatable into sense-datum language, but not that they be translatable term by term.

But the dogma of reductionism has, in a subtler and more tenuous form, continued to influence the thought of empiricists. The notion lingers that to each statement, or each synthetic statement, there is associated a unique range of possible sensory events such that the occurrence of any of them would add to the likelihood of truth of the statement, and that there is associated also another unique range of possible sensory events whose occurrence would detract from that likelihood. This notion is of course implicit in the verification theory of meaning.

The dogma of reductionism survives in the supposition that each statement, taken in isolation from its fellows, can admit of confirmation or infirmation at all. My countersuggestion, issuing essentially from Carnap's doctrine of the physical world in the *Aufbau,* is that our statements about the external world face the tribunal of sense experience not individually but only as a corporate body.

6. EMPIRICISM WITHOUT THE DOGMAS

The totality of our so-called knowledge or beliefs, from the most casual matters of geography and history to the profoundest laws of atomic physics or even of pure mathematics and logic, is a man-made fabric which impinges on experience only along the edges. Or, to change the figure, total science is like a field of force whose boundary conditions are experience. A conflict with experience at the periphery occasions readjustments in the interior of the field. Truth values have to be redistributed over some of our statements. Reëvaluation of some statements entails reëvaluation of others, because of their logical interconnections—the logical laws being in turn simply certain further statements of the system, certain further elements of the field. Having reëvaluated one statement we must reëvaluate some others, which may be statements logically connected with the first or may be the statements of logical connections themselves. But the total field is so underdetermined by its boundary conditions, experience, that there is much latitude of choice as to what statements to reëvaluate in the light of any single contrary experience. No particular experiences are linked with any particular statements in the interior of the field, except indirectly through considerations of equilibrium affecting the field as a whole.

If this view is right, it is misleading to speak of the empirical content of an individual statement—especially if it is a statement at all remote from the experiential periphery of the field. Furthermore it becomes folly to seek a boundary between synthetic statements, which hold contingently on experience, and analytic statements, which hold come what may. Any statement can be held true come what may, if we make drastic enough adjustments elsewhere in the system. Even a statement very close to the periphery can be held true in the face of recalcitrant experience by pleading hallucination or by amending certain statements of the kind called logical laws. Conversely, by the same token, no statement is immune to revision. Revision even of the logical law of the excluded middle has been proposed as a means of simplifying quantum mechanics; and what difference is there in principle between such a shift and the shift whereby Kepler superseded Ptolemy, or Einstein Newton, or Darwin Aristotle?

For vividness I have been speaking in terms of varying distances from a sensory periphery. Let me try now to clarify this notion without metaphor. Certain statements, though *about* physical objects and not sense experience, seem peculiarly germane to sense experience—and in a selective way: some statements to some experiences, others to others. Such statements, especially germane to particular experiences, I picture as near the periphery. But in this relation of "germaneness" I envisage nothing more than a loose association reflecting the relative likelihood, in practice, of our choosing one statement rather than another for revision in the event of recalcitrant experience. For example, we can imagine recalcitrant experiences to which we would surely be inclined to accommodate our system by reëvaluating just the statement that there are brick houses on Elm Street, together with related statements on the same topic. We can imagine other recalcitrant experiences to which we would be inclined to accommodate our system by reëvaluating just the statement that there are no centaurs, along with kindred statements. A recalcitrant experience can, I have urged, be accommodated by any of various alternative reëvaluations in various alternative quarters of the total system; but, in the cases which we are now imagining, our natural tendency to disturb the total system as little as possible would lead us to focus our revisions upon these specific statements concerning brick houses or centaurs. These statements are felt, therefore, to have a sharper empirical reference than highly theoretical statements of physics or logic or ontology. The latter statements may be thought of as relatively centrally located within the total network, meaning merely that little preferential connection with any particular sense data obtrudes itself.

As an empiricist I continue to think of the conceptual scheme of science as a tool, ultimately, for predicting future experience in the light of past experience. Physical objects are conceptually imported into the situation as convenient intermediaries—not by definition in terms of experience, but simply as irreducible posits comparable, epistemologicallly, to the gods of Homer. For my part I do, qua lay physicist, believe in physical objects and not in Homer's gods; and I consider it a scientific error to believe otherwise. But in point of epistemological footing the physical objects and the gods differ only in degree and not in kind. Both sorts of entities enter our conception only as cultural posits. The myth of physical objects is epistemologically superior to most in that it has proved more efficacious than other myths as a device for working a manageable structure into the flux of experience.

Positing does not stop with macroscopic physical objects. Objects at the atomic level are posited to make the laws of macroscopic objects, and ultimately the laws of experience, simpler and more manageable; and we need not expect or demand full definition of atomic and subatomic entities in terms of macroscopic ones, any more than definition of macroscopic things in terms of sense data. Science is a continuation of common sense, and it continues the common-sense expedient of swelling ontology to simplify theory.

Physical objects, small and large, are not the only posits. Forces are another example; and indeed we are told nowadays that the boundary between energy and matter is obsolete. Moreover, the abstract entities which are the substance of mathematics—ultimately classes and classes of classes and so on up—are another posit in the same spirit. Epistemologically these are myths on the same footing with physical objects and gods, neither better nor worse except for differences in the degree to which they expedite our dealings with sense experiences.

The over-all algebra of rational and irrational numbers is underdetermined by the algebra of rational numbers, but is smoother and more convenient; and it includes the algebra of rational numbers as a jagged or gerrymandered part. Total science, mathematical and natural and human, is similarly but more extremely underdetermined by experience. The edge of the system must be kept squared with experience; the rest, with all its elaborate myths or fictions, has as its objective the simplicity of laws.

The issue over there being classes seems more a question of convenient conceptual scheme; the issue over there being centaurs, or brick houses on Elm Street, seems more a question of fact. But I have been urging that this difference is only one of degree, and that it turns upon our vaguely pragmatic inclination to adjust one strand of the fabric of science rather than another in accommodating some particular recalcitrant experience. Conservatism figures in such choices, and so does the quest for simplicity.

Carnap, Lewis, and others take a pragmatic stand on the question of choosing between language forms, scientific frameworks; but their pragmatism leaves off at the imagined boundary between the analytic and the synthetic. In repudiating such a boundary I espouse a more thorough pragmatism. Each man is given a scientific heritage plus a continuing barrage of sensory stimulation; and the considerations which guide him in warping his scientific heritage to fit his continuing sensory promptings are, where rational, pragmatic.

STUDY QUESTIONS

Review

1. What are the major characteristics of logical positivism or logical empiricism? What are some of the influences on the development of this philosophy?
2. What is the "analytic-synthetic" distinction? What is the "principle of verifiability"? What is the "logistic thesis"?
3. C. I. Lewis is sometimes described as a "conceptual pragmatist." Explain the pragmatic elements in his theory of the nature of sense-intensional meaning and his belief about why we adopt certain logical or mathematical systems.
4. In the interpretation of Carnap's philosophy that describes it as an "upstairs-downstairs world," what occurs on each of the two levels?
5. What are the two dogmas of empiricism of which Quine is critical? What are his own views on and criticism of these dogmas?

6. Contrast Carnap and Quine on the significance of metaphysics; i.e., what role if any does it have?

For Further Thought

7. Would you consider yourself an empiricist? Why? What does it say about the kinds and sources of knowledge? Do you agree?
8. Do you agree with the analytic-synthetic distinction? Why or why not? What about the principle of verification?
9. What do you believe is the role or task of philosophy? Metaphysics? How does it function differently from or in relation to science?
10. How do systems of thought come to be accepted? Is there some place they touch down in experience? Are they accepted part by part or only as a whole? Is it proper to describe them as "verified," "confirmed," "useful," "chosen for now," or more or less true or probable?

BIBLIOGRAPHY

Logical Positivism

Ayer, A. J. *Logical Positivism.* Glencoe, Ill.: The Free Press, 1959.
− − −. *Language, Truth, and Logic.* London: V. Gollanez, ltd., 1936. New York: Dover, 1950.
Bergmann, Gustav. *The Metaphysics of Logical Positivism.* London: Longmans, Green, 1954.
Bridgman, P. W. *The Logic of Modern Physics.* New York: Macmillan, 1927.
Feigl, H., and W. Sellars, eds. *Readings in Philosophical Analysis.* New York: Appleton, 1949.
Hanfling, Oswald, ed. *Essential Readings in Logical Positivism.* London: Basil Blackwell, 1981.
Hempel, C. G. *Fundamentals of Concept Formation in Empirical Science.* Chicago: University of Chicago Press, 1952.
Hill, Thomas E. "Analytic Theories." Part 5 in *Contemporary Theories of Knowledge.* New York: Ronald Press, 1961.
Hospers, John. *An Introduction to Philosophical Analysis.* New York: Prentice-Hall, 1953.
Joergensen, Joergen. *Development of Logical Empiricism: Foundations of the Unity of Science.* Vol. 2, no. 9. Chicago: University of Chicago Press, 1951. Reprinted in *International Encyclopedia of Unified Science,* vols. 1 and 2, 1970.
Morris, Charles W. *Logical Positivism: Pragmatism and Scientific Empiricism.* Paris: Hermann et cie., 1937.
Neurath, O., et al, eds. *International Encyclopedia of Unified Science.* Chicago: University of Chicago Press, 1938– .
Pap, Arthur. *Elements of Analytic Philosophy.* New York: Macmillan, 1949.
Passmore, John. "Logical Positivism." Chap. 16 in *A Hundred Years of Philosophy.* London: Duckworth, 1957.
Reichenbach, H. *The Rise of Scientific Philosophy.* Berkeley: University of California Press, 1951; paperback, 1958.

Stebbing, L. Susan. *Logical Positivism and Analysis.* Bowling Green Sta., N.Y.: Gordon Press, 1974.

Urmson, J. O. "Logical Positivism and the Downfall of Logical Atomism." Part 2 in *Philosophical Analysis.* Oxford: Oxford University Press, 1956.

Warnock, G. J. "Logical Positivism." Chap. 4 in *English Philosophy since 1900.* Oxford: Oxford University Press, 1958.

Wittgenstein, L. *Tractatus Logico-Philosophicus.* London: K. Paul, Trench, Trubner and co., ltd., 1922. New translation by Pears and McGuinness. New York: The Humanities Press, 1961.

Weinberg, J. *An Examination of Logical Positivism.* London: K. Paul, Trench, Trubner and co., ltd., 1963.

C. I. Lewis

Lewis, C. I. *Our Social Inheritance.* Bloomington: Indiana University Press, 1957.

— — —. *The Ground and Nature of the Right.* New York: Columbia University Press, 1955.

— — —. *An Analysis of Knowledge and Valuation.* La Salle, Ill.: Open Court Publishing, 1946.

— — —. *Mind and the World Order.* New York: Charles Scribner's, 1929.

— — —. *A Survey of Symbolic Logic.* Berkeley: University of California Press, 1918.

— — —. "Logic and Pragmatism." In *Contemporary American Philosophy: Personal Statements,* ed. G. P. Adams and W. P. Montague, vol. 2, pp. 31–54. New York: Russell and Russell, 1962.

Lewis, C. I., and H. Langford. *Symbolic Logic.* New York: Century Co., 1932.

Baylis, C. A. "C. I. Lewis, Mind and the World-order." *Journal of Philosophy* 27 (1930): pp. 320–27.

Boas, George. "Mr. Lewis's Theory of Meaning." *Journal of Philosophy* 28 (1931): pp. 314–25.

Ducasse, C. J. "C. I. Lewis' *Analysis of Knowledge and Valuation.*" *Philosophical Review* 57 (1948): pp. 260–80.

Firth, R., et al. "Commemorative Symposium on C. I. Lewis." *Journal of Philosophy* 61 (1964): pp. 545–70.

Harbert, David L. *Existence, Knowing, and Philosophical Systems.* Washington, D.C.: University Press of America, 1983.

Henle, Paul. "Lewis's *An Analysis of Knowledge and Valuation.*" *Journal of Philosophy* 45 (1948): pp. 524–32.

Luizzi, Vincent. *A Naturalistic Theory of Justice: Critical Commentary on and Selected Readings From C. I. Lewis' Ethics.* Washington, D.C.: University Press of America, 1981.

Pratt, J. B. "Logical Positivism and Professor Lewis." *Journal of Philosophy* 31 (1934): pp. 701–10.

Schilpp, P. A. *The Philosophy of C. I. Lewis.* Vol. 13, *Library of Living Philosophers.* La Salle, Ill.: Open Court Publishing, 1966.

Rudolf Carnap

Carnap, Rudolf. *Introduction to Symbolic Logic and Its Applications.* New York: Dover Press, 1958.

— — —. *Logical Foundations of Probability.* Chicago: University of Chicago Press, 1950; 2d ed., 1962.

— — —. *Meaning and Necessity: A Study in Semantics and Modal Logic.* Chicago: University of Chicago Press, 1947; enlarged ed., 1956.

— — —. *Formalization of Logic: Studies in Semantics.* Vol. 2. Cambridge: Harvard University Press, 1943.

— — —. *Introduction to Semantics.* Cambridge: Harvard University Press, 1942.

— — —. *The Foundations of Logic and Mathematics.* International Encyclopedia of Unified Science, I, 3. Chicago: University of Chicago Press, 1939.

— — —. *The Unity of Science.* London: Routledge and Kegan Paul, 1938.

— — —. *The Logical Syntax of Language.* New York: Harcourt, Brace, 1937.

— — —. *Philosophy and Logical Syntax.* London: Kegan Paul, 1935.

— — —. "Intellectual Autobiography." In *The Philosophy of Rudolf Carnap,* ed. P. A. Schilpp, pp. 3–84. LaSalle, Ill.: Open Court, 1963. Also in this volume see Carnap, "The Philosopher Replies," pp. 859–999, and articles on Carnap's philosophy by other writers.

— — —. "Testability and Meaning." *Philosophy of Science* 3 (1936): pp. 419–71; 4 (1937): pp. 1–40.

Black, Max. "Carnap on Logic and Semantics." In *Problems of Analysis.* Ithaca, New York: Cornell University Press, 1954.

Bulrich, Richard, Jr. *Carnap on Meaning and Analyticity.* Hawthorne, N.Y.: Mouton Publishers, 1970.

Coffa, J. Alberto. "Carnap's Sprachanschauung circa 1932." In *Philosophy of Science Association* 2 (1976).

Goodman, Nelson. *The Structure of Appearance.* Cambridge, Mass.: Harvard University Press, 1951. Contains a detailed analysis of *Der logische Aufbau.*

Kazemeir, B. H., and D. Vuysje, eds. *Logic and Language.* Dordrecht, Netherlands: D. Reidel, 1962. A collection of studies dedicated to Carnap on the occasion of his seventieth birthday.

W. V. O. Quine

Quine, W. V. O. *Theories and Things.* Cambridge: Harvard University Press, 1981.

— — —. *Ontological Relativity and Other Essays.* New York: Columbia University Press, 1969.

— — —. *Selected Logic Papers.* New York: Random House, 1966.

— — —. *The Ways of Paradox and Other Essays.* New York: Random House, 1966. Rev. and enlarged ed. Cambridge: Harvard University Press, 1976.

— — —. *Word and Object.* New York: John Wiley, 1960.

— — —. *From a Logical Point of View: Nine Logico-Philosophical Essays.* Cambridge: Harvard University Press, 1953.

— — —. *Methods of Logic.* New York: Henry Holt, 1950.

— — —. *Mathematical Logic.* New York: W. W. Norton, 1940; rev. ed., 1951.

— — —. *Elementary Logic.* New York: Ginn, 1941.

— — —. *A System of Logistic.* Cambridge: Harvard University Press, 1934.

Quine, W. V. O., and J. S. Ullian. *The Web of Belief.* New York: Random House, 1970.

Davidson, D., and J. Hintikka, eds. *Words and Objections: Essays on the Work of W. V. Quine.* Dordrecht-Holland: D. Reidel Pub. Co., 1969.

Grice, H. P., and P. F. Strawson. "In Defence of a Dogma." *Philosophical Review* 65 (1956): pp. 141–58.

Orenstein, Alex. *Willard van Orman Quine.* Twayne's World Leader Series, 65. Boston: G. K. Hall, 1977.

Presley, C. F. "Quine's Word and Object." *Australasian Journal Of Philosophy* 39 (1961): pp. 175–90.

Romanos, George D. *Quine and Analytic Philosophy: The Language of Language.* Cambridge: MIT Press, 1983.

Strawson, P. F. "Propositions, Concepts and Logical Truths." *Philosophical Quarterly* 7 (1957): pp. 15–25.

Warnock, G. J. "Metaphysics in Logic." In *Essays in Conceptual Analysis,* ed. A. G. N. Flew. London: Macmillan, 1956.

Chapter 16

Language
Philosophy

Philosophy is characterized by the constant examination of what is often taken for granted, by its probing of the foundations and presuppositions of what is or is established. Language is just such a common establishment, and philosophers of late have become peculiarly interested in its foundations and presuppositions, its adequacy and relation to nature and mind. Yet language and its presuppositions provide a peculiarly difficult area for analysis. It is hard to get at language objectively because it is impossible to get away from it. The presuppositions of language are unavoidably operative in the very attempt to insulate and analyze these presuppositions.

"By indirection," Polonius advised Laertes, "find directions out." Philosophers, sometimes inadvertantly, have been following such advice, approaching language by paths through and detours around selected fragments of linguistic experience. The differing directions philosophers have taken after making the "linguistic turn," this concentration on the way we talk about the world rather than the world itself, are reflected in such labels as "analytic philosophy," "linguistic analysis," "conceptual analysis," "philosophy of language," and "ordinary language analysis." The contribution of historical linguists, depth grammarians, and logical reconstructionists complicate an already complex scene. In this chapter we merely intend to indicate some common concerns and shared methods and sketch, in rough outline, some of the more influential developments in contemporary language philosophy, in particular in the United States.[1]

Like most philosophical revolutions, the linguistic turn brought the heady feeling that a new method would sweep away the recalcitrant problems of past philosophy. Thus, as Richard Rorty summarized it, many English and American philosophers shared "the view that philosophical problems are problems which may be solved (or dissolved) either by reforming language, or by understanding more about the language we presently use."[2] Some people accustomed to doing philosophy in the traditional manner were, and still are, baffled by the switch from talking about the world to talking about a suitable language. Among the many reasons for this change, one of the most fundamental was given by Quine. A "semantic ascent," a "shift from talk about objects to talk about words," provides philosophers with a basis for agreement.[3] They can, he contends, agree on the meaning of words more easily than on the nature of objects. Whether or not that is the case and whether this switch has been profitable for philosophy readers can surmise for themselves.

ARTIFICIAL VERSUS NATURAL LANGUAGES

In the last chapter we saw something of the manner in which certain twentieth-century American philosphers with positivist or empiricist backgrounds turned their attention to language and logic. Recent developments and puzzles in mathematics and mathematical logic as well as skepticism about the enterprise of metaphysics contributed to this shift of attention. They analyzed and constructed various formal systems, at first concentrating primarily on elements of *syntax* (the rules that underlay the formal structure of the systems). Later many became concerned with *semantics* (questions of meaning, connotation, or intension and questions of reference, denotation, or extension). While the additional area of *pragmatics* (the use of language) was also distinguished, little technical development occurred in this area.[4]

In addition to this interest in formal or artificial languages, philosophers more recently in this century have come to be concerned with the nature and relation to philosophical issues of the natural languages that we speak — English, French, etc. And here too a variety of reasons for the shift leads to a variety of types of philosophical endeavor. For example, there are those philosophers who are struck by the fact that many (if not all) philosophical problems arise because of our use or misuse of English ordinary language terms such as "know," "see," "free," etc. (See the selection from Norman Malcolm and his discussion of the term "know.") Studying formal and technical analogues of these language terms would not solve the problems they generate unless such study enables us somehow to return to clarify ordinary usage. They contended, moreover, that formalizing ordinary language concepts would distort such concepts rather than clarify or render them more precise and unambiguous.[5]

ORDINARY LANGUAGE ANALYSIS

Ordinary language philosophy or ordinary language analysis, as this type of philosophy is called, was influenced especially by the Austrian-born Cambridge (England) philosophy professor, Ludwig Wittgenstein.[6] In his earlier writings (see *Tractatus,* published in 1920, in English in 1921), Wittgenstein had contended that the purpose of language was to picture the facts, reality, the world.[7] The ideal language is composed of names that picture objects and stand in a similar relation to each other as the objects they picture. Later, from 1930 to 1947, and in his *Philosophical Investigations* (published in 1953, two years after his death), Wittgenstein abandoned the naming or picture theory of language meaning.[8] A significant consequence of this change was his distinction between the bearer of the name and the meaning of the term. To ask for the meaning of a term is to ask for its use, he contended. If one were to say ''I am here,'' in order to understand that statement's meaning one would have to ask about the particular circumstances in which a person might say it. The statement does not have a meaning apart from these circumstances or its use in them.

Moreover, Wittgenstein pointed out the philsophical difficulties inherent in a private language theory, — the theory that holds that to understand the meaning of a term one need only turn within one's own mind to contemplate some mental entity accessible there solely to oneself. Meaning is essentially public, the ordinary usage of a term is the way in which it is used in a shared public language. According to many analysts, philosphical problems are, for the most part, generated by misuse of language or a lack of understanding of ordinary usage. Philosophy, then, should function as therapy to restore us to ordinary usage and by so doing show us that the problems have ceased to exist. We are to be cured of our philosophizing! While ordinary language philosophy has been strongest in Great Britain, it has also had some followers in America. Examples of such philosophizing can be found in the writings of Norman Malcolm, Alice Ambrose, and M. Lazerowitz.[9]

In our selections here we have included two somewhat different types of ordinary language philosophy. The selection from John Searle's *Speech Acts* is a more general analysis of various uses to which words or sentences in our language can be put.[10] It follows a distinction made by the British philosopher, John L. Austin, who noticed that some utterances do not state facts but rather are performances.[11] Some examples are: ''I name this ship the Benjamin Franklin'' and ''I promise to pay back what I owe.'' Through further analysis of such performative verbs, Austin concluded that whenever we say anything we do a number of different and distinguishable things. There is the *phonetic* act of making certain noises and the *phatic* act of uttering certain words according to a certain grammar. In addition, when we say something we perform the *locutionary* act of using words with a definite sense and reference, for example, ''this house.'' Also contained in such usage is the *illocutionary* act of stating, suggesting, asking, etc., and the *perlocutionary* act of causing something to happen by my speech act, for example getting another to agree with or respond to one or to do something that one wants. In our selection, Searle uses this distinction to give an account of the meaning of utterances.

The second selection is from Norman Malcolm, who holds that many philosophical arguments are misconceived because they misuse ordinary language.[12] A classic example of this type of philosophizing is Malcolm's discussions of G. E. Moore's attempts to defend realistic knowledge claims. In our selection, "Defending Common Sense," Malcolm considers the claim of Moore that, contrary to epistemological skeptics' claims, Moore "knows" that he has a body, a hand, and that he is not now dreaming when he holds up his hand and says, "Here is a hand." According to Malcolm, Moore misuses the word "know" and the phrases in which it occurs in his argument. Malcolm shows, by many examples, when in ordinary language we say things like, "I know that is an X." Moore's use of the term does not follow this ordinary usage. However, the upshot of this analysis is that in his misuse of the term "know," Moore makes a bad argument against those skeptics who say that we only believe such things as that there is a world or I have a body, and that we do not *know* them.

PHILOSOPHY OF LANGUAGE, LINGUISTIC PHILOSOPHY, AND LINGUISTICS

Searle and Malcolm provide examples of what may be distinguished as "philosophy of language" (Searle) and "linguistic philosophy" (Malcolm). Searle himself makes the distinction as follows:

> Linguistic philosophy is the attempt to solve particular philosophical problems by attending to the ordinary use of particular words or other elements in a particular language. The philosophy of language is the attempt to give philosophically illuminating descriptions of certain general features of language, such as reference, truth, meaning, and necessity, and it is concerned only incidentally with particular elements in a particular language.[13]

Linguistic philosophy is primarily a method and can be used in the philosophy of language as well as in investigating epistemological, metaphysical, and ethical issues.

In addition to these two disciplines there is also the discipline called "linguistics," which, again according to Searle, "attempts to describe the actual structures — phonological, syntactical, and semantic — of natural human languages."[14] Linguistics, though an old topic for study, has become a new science.[15] Naturally, some areas of it are of more interest to philosophers than others. Thus the semantic and syntactical rather than the phonetic studies have been the basis of philosophical investigation. Similarly, philosophers have been more intrigued by the attempts to develop general theories of language than they have been by historical language studies. Here, in fact, it is sometimes most difficult to distinguish the so-called scientific study of linguistics from more philosophical approaches.

Thus Noam Chomsky, a linguist, has not only raised philosophical issues, but has proposed philosophical theories. The familiar grammar traditionally taught in grammar schools describes what has come to be called the "surface structure" of the language we use. In his highly influential and still controversial work, *Syntactic Structures,* published in 1957, Noam Chomsky argues that something more than surface structure, a depth analysis, is needed to explain linguistic competence.[16] According to Chomsky, one of the most striking features of a language use is the ease with which children learn their native language, in particular its structural regularities or grammatical rules. From the limited number of examples they hear from parents and others, children are soon able both to understand and to construct an indefinite number of grammatically correct and meaningful new sentences. Using a detailed mathematical analysis Chomsky argued that neither computer analogues nor behaviorist theories of learning can explain such a capacity.

Chomsky's positive contributions to linguistics involve two aspects that should be carefully distinguished. To explain our sentence-forming capacity Chomsky introduced the idea of depth grammar, a linguistic structure that lies beneath and explains why surface grammar or linguistic patterns are the way they are. This notion precipitated a conceptual revolution in the science of linguistics. Secondly, Chomsky, as philosopher, attempted to explain our innate capacity to handle depth grammar through a revival of the older rationalist doctrine of innate ideas.[17] Though this revival has won little philosophical support except at Chomsky's home base, M.I.T., it has certainly stimulated a renewed interest in the old problem of the relation between thought and language.

Between 1960 and 1980, however, philosophers in the linguistic tradition have tended to disagree about the relevance of work in linguistics to philosophy. While some (eg., Jerold Katz and Jerry Fodor) have continued to support this work, others (eg., Donald Davidson, Saul Kripke, Hilary Putnam, Michael Dummett, and others) have taken the tradition into other areas of concern.[18] There were still developments, for example, in the theory of meaning, and they still talked about language and the meaning of language (rather than of ideas or concepts),[19] but instead of focusing upon meaning as something distinct from words, these philosophers turned their attention elsewhere, to concerns about reference — about the relation of language to the world, for example. For others, however, the focus was still basically linguistic. How, they asked, could statements like "Snow is white" or "Schnee ist weiss" represent the fact that snow is white. The problem seemed to be at least partially a problem of translation.

The third selection in this chapter, "On the Very Idea of a Conceptual Scheme," is from Donald Davidson — a philosopher who represents some of the concerns just mentioned. According to Davidson and others, there is no uninterpreted reality. We always think in terms of or organize our experience according to some conceptual scheme. These schemes are embedded in our language. Different languages may thus organize our experience in different ways. Some have suggested that these schemes and languages are incommensurable. The question Davidson raises is whether we can say that people possess the same conceptual scheme only if their languages are translatable into each other.

While it has been argued persuasively that throughout its history much of the philosophy in America has not been original (excepting pragmatism), but has followed the lead of and been secondary to British and Continental schools, America now seems to have taken the lead in analytic philosophy. Commenting on the work of Quine, Chomsky, Davidson, and others, the British philosopher Anthony Quinton remarks:

> In what I have said about the most recent developments in American philosophy I have confined myself to those formalistic views which have attracted most interest among philosophers here, and on which the claim that America is now the philosophical centre of the English-speaking world must rest. . . . The recently secured primacy of American philosophy can be traced back, in in virtue of its particular style and methods, to the hospitable intellectual and institutional reception accorded in the late 1930's to the European positivists, whose work is being continued and innovatively developed.[20]

However, what is being innovatively developed is just that — something in the process of being developed. Moreover, we do not yet know how the various other types of twentieth-century American philosophy might progress, nor do we know what overlapping might occur. This is one reason why it is difficult to distinguish and relate the various movements and to record them as history. Which of these developments will be of enduring interest and significance, or where they will lead, remains to be seen.

Notes

[1] Our term "language philosophy" is meant to cover this variety of types of contemporary philosophy concerned with language and is not meant to denote a particular kind of contemporary philosophy itself.

[2] Richard Rorty, *The Linguistic Turn: Recent Essays in Philosophical Method* (Chicago: University of Chicago Press, 1967), p. 3. The phrase "the linguistic turn" Rorty borrowed from Gustav Bergmann as used in his *Logic and Reality* (Madison: University of Wisconsin Press, 1964), p. 177. See also the excellent bibliography in Rorty's book.

[3] Willard V. O. Quine, *Word and Object* (New York: John Wiley, 1960), pp. 271–72.

[4] While this distinction is found in the writings of Carnap, Quine, and others interested in the analysis of formal or artificial language systems, the different activities that they define are also found in those concerned with ordinary or natural languages and with linguistics. However, the treatment is significantly different. In syntactic studies, for example, those concerned with ordinary language concentrate on grammar while those concerned with formal language systems analyze logical structure.

[5] Among those most strongly critical of the formalist approach are Gilbert Ryle and P. F. Strawson, two British philosophers. Some of their key works in this area are noted in the bibliography in Rorty, *The Linguistic Turn*.

[6] One recent study of the life and writings of Wittgenstein is William W. Bartley III, *Wittgenstein* (New York: J. B. Lippincott, 1973).

[7] Ludwig Wittgenstein, *Tractatus Logico-Philosophicus*, trans. D. F. Pears and B. F. McGuinness (London: Routledge and Kegan Paul, 1961).

[8] Ludwig Wittgenstein, *Philosophical Investigations*, trans. G. E. Anscombe (New York: Macmillan, 1953; Oxford: Blackwell, 1953).

[9] See the bibliography for some of the writings of these philosophers.

[10] John Searle, *Speech Acts: An Essay in the Philosophy of Language* (Cambridge: Cambridge University Press, 1969).

[11] John L. Austin, *How To Do Things With Words* (Oxford: Oxford University Press, 1962).

[12] Norman Malcolm, "Defending Common Sense," *Philosophical Review* 58 (1949): pp. 201-20.

[13] Searle, *Speech Acts*, p. 4.

[14] Ibid.

[15] See Francis P. Dinneen, *An Introduction to General Linguistics* (New York: Holt, Rinehart, and Winston, 1967).

[16] Noam Chomsky, *Syntactic Structures* (The Hague: Mouton, 1957).

[17] Note, for example, the title of one of Chomsky's works: *Cartesian Linguistics: A Chapter in the History of Rationalist Thought* (New York: Harper and Row, 1966).

[18] See the bibliography to this chapter for some of the works of these authors. Another good source is the bibliography in Ian Hacking, *Why Does Language Matter to Philosophy?* (Cambridge: Cambridge University Press, 1975).

[19] This point is made by Hacking *(Why Does Language Matter)*: while there is some similarity in the concern for the relation between ideas and reality in traditional epistemology and the concern for the relation between language and reality, etc. in contemporary language philosophies, the traditional empiricisms, while concerned about ideas, were not really concerned about the *meaning* of ideas — that concern for meaning is a new concern.

[20] Anthony Quinton, "Philosophy in America," *Times Literary Supplement,* 13 June 1975, p. 664.

JOHN SEARLE

SPEECH ACTS*

The hypothesis of this work is that speaking a language is engaging in a rule-governed form of behavior. To put it more briskly, talking is performing acts according to rules. In order to substantiate that hypothesis and explicate speech, I shall state some of the rules according to which we talk. The procedure which I shall follow is to state a set of necessary and sufficient conditions for the performance of particular kinds of speech acts and then extract from those conditions sets of semantic rules for the use of the linguistic devices which mark the utterances as speech acts of those kinds. That is a rather bigger task than perhaps it sounds, and this chapter will be devoted to preparing the ground for it by introducing distinctions between *different kinds of speech acts,* and discussing the notions of *propositions, rules, meaning, and facts.*

EXPRESSIONS AND KINDS OF SPEECH ACTS

Let us begin this phase of our inquiry by making some distinctions which naturally suggest themselves to us as soon as we begin to reflect on simple speech situations. (The simplicity of the sentences in our examples will not detract from the generality of the distinctions we are trying to make.)

---

* John Searle, *Speech Acts* (Cambridge: Cambridge University Press, 1969), pp. 22–26, 42–47. Reprinted by permission of Cambridge University Press and the author.

Imagine a speaker and a hearer and suppose that in appropriate circumstances the speaker utters one of the following sentences:

1. Sam smokes habitually.
2. Does Sam smoke habitually?
3. Sam, smoke habitually!
4. Would that Sam smoked habitually.

Now let us ask how we might characterize or describe the speaker's utterance of one of these. What shall we say the speaker is doing when he utters one of these?

One thing is obvious: anyone who utters one of these can be said to have uttered a sentence formed of words in the English language. But clearly this is only the beginning of a description, for the speaker in uttering one of these is characteristically saying something and not merely mouthing words. In uttering 1 a speaker is making (what philosophers call) an assertion, in 2 asking a question, in 3 giving an order, and in 4 (a somewhat archaic form) expressing a wish or desire. And in the performance of each of these four different acts the speaker performs certain other acts which are common to all four: in uttering any of these the speaker *refers to* or mentions or designates a certain object Sam, and he predicates the expression "smokes habitually" (or one of its inflections) of the object referred to. Thus we shall say that in the utterance of all four the reference and predication are the same, though in each case the same reference and predication occur as part of a complete speech act which is different from any of the other three. We thus detach the notions of referring and predicating from the notions of such complete speech acts as asserting, questioning, commanding, etc., and the justification for this separation lies in the fact that the same reference and predication can occur in the performance of different complete speech acts. Austin baptized these complete speech acts with the name "illocutionary acts," and I shall henceforth employ this terminology.[1] Some of the English verbs denoting illocutionary acts are "state," "describe," "assert," "warn," "remark," "comment," "command," "order," "request," "criticize," "apologize," "censure," "approve," "welcome," "promise," "object," "demand," and "argue." Austin claimed there were over a thousand such expressions in English.[2]

The first upshot of our preliminary reflections, then, is that in the utterance of any of the four sentences in the example a speaker is characteristically performing at least three distinct kinds of acts. *(a)* The

---

[1] J. L. Austin, *How to Do Things with Words* (Oxford, 1962). I employ the expression, "illocutionary act," with some misgivings, since I do not accept Austin's distinction between *locutionary* and *illocutionary* acts. Cf. J. R. Searle, "Austin on Locutionary and Illocutionary Acts," *Philosophical Review,* Oct. 1968, pp. 405–24.

[2] Austin, *op cit.,* p. 149.

uttering of words (morphemes, sentences); *(b)* referring and predicating; *(c)* stating, questioning, commanding, promising, etc.

Let us assign names to these under the general heading of speech acts:

(a) Uttering words (morphemes, sentences) = performing *utterance acts.*

(b) Referring and predicating = performing *propositional acts.*

(c) Stating, questioning, commanding, promising, etc. = performing *illocutionary acts.*

I am not saying, of course, that these are separate things that speakers do, as it happens, simultaneously, as one might smoke, read and scratch one's head simultaneously, but rather that in performing an illocutionary act one characteristically performs propositional acts and utterance acts. Nor should it be thought from this that utterance acts and propositional acts stand to illocutionary acts in the way buying a ticket and getting on a train stand to taking a railroad trip. They are not means to ends; rather, utterance acts stand to propositional and illocutionary acts in the way in which, e.g., making an "X" on a ballot paper stands to voting.

The point of abstracting each of these kinds is that the 'identity criteria' are different in each case. We have already seen that the same propositional acts can be common to different illocutionary acts, and it is obvious that one can perform an utterance act without performing a propositional or illocutionary act at all. (One can utter words without saying anything.) And similarly, if we consider the utterance of a sentence such as:

5. Mr. Samuel Martin is a regular smoker of tobacco
we can see reasons for saying that in certain contexts a speaker in uttering it would be performing the same propositional act as in 1–4 (reference and predication would be the same), the same illocutionary act as 1 (same statement or assertion is made), but a different utterance act from any of the first four since a different sentence, containing none of the same words and only some of the same morphemes, is uttered. Thus, in performing different utterance acts, a speaker may perform the same propositional and illocutionary acts. Nor, of course, need the performance of the same utterance act by two different speakers, or by the same speaker on different occasions, be a performance of the same propositional and illocutionary acts: the same sentence may, e.g., be used to make two different statements. Utterance acts consist simply in uttering strings of words. Illocutionary and propositional acts consist characteristically in uttering words in sentences in certain contexts, under certain conditions and with certain intentions, as we shall see later on.

So far I make no claims for dividing things up this way, other than its being a permissible way to divide them—vague though this may be. In particular, I do not claim that it is the only way to divide things. For example, for certain purposes one might wish to break up what I have called utterance acts into phonetic acts, phonemic acts, morphemic acts, etc. And, of course, for most purposes, in the science of linguistics it is not necessary to speak of acts at all. One can just discuss phonemes, morphemes, sentences, etc.

To these three notions I now wish to add Austin's notion of the *perlocutionay act*. Correlated with the notion of illocutionary acts is the notion of the consequences or *effects* such acts have on the actions, thoughts, or beliefs, etc. of hearers. For example, by arguing I may *persuade* or *convince* someone, by warning him I may *scare* or *alarm* him, by making a request I may *get him to do something*, by informing him I may *convince him (enlighten, edify, inspire him, get him to realize)*. The italicized expressions above denote perlocutionary acts.

Correlative with the notion of propositional acts and illocutionary acts, respectively, are certain kinds of expressions uttered in their performance: the characteristic grammatical form of the illocutionary act is the complete sentence (it can be a one-word setence); and the characteristic grammatical form of the propositional acts as parts of sentences: grammatical predicates for the act of predication, and proper names, pronouns, and certain other sorts of noun phrases for reference. Propositional acts cannot occur alone; that is, one cannot *just* refer and predicate without making an assertion or asking a question or performing some other illocutionary act. The linguistic correlate of this point is that sentences, not words, are used to say things. This is also what Frege meant when he said that only in the context of a sentence do words have reference— "Nur im Zusammenhang eines Satzes bedeuten die Wörter etwas." [3] The same thing in my terminology: One only refers as part of the performance of an illocutionary act, and the grammatical clothing of an illocutionary act is the complete sentence. An utterance of a referring expression only counts as referring if one says something.

The parallel between kinds of expressions and propositional acts is not, of course, exact. If I say, e.g., "He left me in the lurch," I am not referring to a particular lurch in which I was left, though phrases of the form "the so-and-so" are characteristically referring expressions.

. . . Illocutionary acts are characteristically performed in the utterance of sounds or the making of marks. What is the difference between *just* uttering sounds or making marks and performing an illocutionary act? One difference is that the sounds or marks one makes in the performance of an illocutionary act are characteristically said to *have meaning*, and a second related difference is that one is characteristically said to *mean something* by the utterance of those sounds or marks. Characteristically, when one speaks one means something by what one says; and what one says, the string of sounds that one emits, is characteristically said to have a meaning. Here, incidentally, is another point at which our analogy

---

[3] G. Frege, *Die Grundlagen der Arithmetik* (Breslau, 1884), p. 73.

between performing speech acts and playing games breaks down. The pieces in a game like chess are not characteristically said to have a meaning, and furthermore, when one makes a move one is not characteristically said to mean anything by that move.

But what is it for one to mean something by what one says, and what is it for something to have a meaning? To answer the first of these questions, I propose to borrow and revise some ideas of Paul Grice. In an article entitled *Meaning,*[4] Grice gives the following analysis of the notion of "non-natural meaning." To say that a speaker *S* meant something by *X* is to say that *S* intended the utterance of *X* to produce some effect in a hearer *H* by means of the recognition of this intention. Though I do not think this an adequate account, for reasons to be made clear later, I think it is a very useful beginning of an account of meaning, first because it makes a connection between meaning and intention, and secondly because it captures the following essential feature of linguistic communication. In speaking I attempt to communicate certain things to my hearer by getting him to recognize my intention to communicate just those things. I achieve the intended effect on the hearer by getting him to recognize my intention to achieve that effect, and as soon as the hearer recognizes what it is my intention to achieve, it is in general achieved. He understands what I am saying as soon as he recognizes my intention in uttering what I utter as an intention to say that thing.

I shall illustrate this with a simple example. When I say "Hello," I intend to produce in a hearer the knowledge that he is being greeted. If he recognizes it as my intention to produce in him that knowledge, then he thereby acquires that knowledge.

However valuable this account of meaning is, it seems to me to be defective in at least two crucial respects. First, it fails to account for the extent to which meaning can be a matter of rules or conventions. This account of meaning does not show the connection between one's meaning something by what one says, and what that which one says actually means in the language. Secondly, by defining meaning in terms of intended effects it confuses illocutionary with perlocutionary acts. Put crudely, Grice in effect defines meaning in terms of intending to perform a perlocutionary act, but saying something and meaning it is a matter of intending to perform an illocutionary, not necessarily a perlocutionary, act. I shall now explain both these objections and attempt to amend Grice's account to deal with them.

In order to illustrate the first point, I shall present a counter-example to this analysis of meaning. The point of the counter-example will be to illustrate the connection between what a speaker means and what the words he utters mean.

---

[4] *Philosophical Review,* July 1957, pp. 377–88.

Suppose that I am an American soldier in the Second World War and that I am captured by Italian troops. And suppose also that I wish to get these troops to believe that I am a German soldier in order to get them to release me. What I would like to do is to tell them in German or Italian that I am a German soldier. But let us suppose I don't know enough German or Italian to do that. So I, as it were, attempt to put on a show of telling them that I am a German soldier by reciting those few bits of German I know, trusting that they don't know enough German to see through my plan. Let us suppose I know only one line of German which I remember from a poem I had to memorize in a high school German course. Therefore, I, a captured American, address my Italian captors with the following sentence: *Kennst du das Land wo die Zitronen blühen?*[5] Now, let us describe the situation in Gricean terms. I intend to produce a certain effect in them, namely, the effect of believing that I am a German soldier, and I intend to produce this effect by means of their recognition of my intention. I intend that they should think that what I am trying to tell them is that I am a German soldier. But does it follow from this account that when I say, *Kennst du das Land . . . etc.*, what I mean is, "I am a German soldier"? Not only does it not follow, but in this case I find myself disinclined to say that when I utter the German sentence what I mean is "I am a German soldier," or even "Ich bin ein deutscher Soldat," because what the words mean and what I remember that they mean is "Knowest thou the land where the lemon trees bloom?" Of course, I want my captors to be deceived into thinking that what I mean is: "I am a German soldier," but part of what is involved in that is getting them to think that that is what the words I utter mean in German. In the *Philosophical Investigations,*[6] Wittgenstein (discussing a different problem) writes "*Say* "it's cold here" and *mean* "it's warm here." " The reason we are unable to do this without further stage setting is that what we can mean is at least sometimes a function of what we are saying. Meaning is more than a matter of intention; it is also at least sometimes a matter of convention. One might say that on Grice's account it would seem that any sentence can be uttered with any meaning whatever, given that the circumstances make possible the appropriate intentions. But that has the consequence that the meaning of the sentence then becomes just another circumstance.

---

[5] If it seems implausible that one could intend to produce the desired effects with such an utterance in these circumstances, a few imaginative additions to the example should make the case more plausible, e.g., I know that my captors know there are German soldiers in the area wearing American uniforms. I know that they have been instructed to be on the lookout for these Germans and to release them as soon as they identify themselves. I know that they have lied to their commander by telling him that they can speak German when in fact they cannot, etc.

[6] Para. 510.

Grice's account can be amended to deal with counter-examples of this kind. We have here a case where I intend to produce a certain effect by means of getting the hearer's recognition of my intention to produce that effect, but the device I use to produce this effect is one which is conventionally, by the rules governing the use of that device, used as a means of producing quite different illocutionary effects, and the stage setting or conditions which would permit us to say one thing and mean something totally unrelated are not present. We must, therefore, reformulate the Gricean account of meaning in such a way as to make it clear that one's meaning something when one utters a sentence is more than just randomly related to what the sentence means in the language one is speaking. In our analysis of illocutionary acts, we must capture both the intentional and the conventional aspects and especially the relationship between them. In the performance of an illocutionary act in the literal utterance of a sentence, the speaker intends to produce a certain effect by means of getting the hearer to recognize his intention to produce that effect; and furthermore, if he is using words literally, he intends this recognition to be achieved in virtue of the fact that the rules for using the expressions he utters associate the expression with the production of that effect. It is this *combination* of elements which we shall need to express in our analysis of the illocutionary act.

I now turn to my second objection to Grice's account. In effect, the account says that saying something and meaning it is a matter of intending to perform a perlocutionary act. In the examples Grice gives, the effects cited are invariably perlocutionary. I wish to argue that saying something and meaning it is a matter of intending to perform an illocutionary act. First, it could not be the case that in general intended effects of meant utterances were perlocutionary because many kinds of sentences used to perform illocutionary acts have no perlocutionary effect associated with their meaning. For example, there is no associated perlocutionary effect of greeting. When I say, "Hello" and mean it, I do not necessarily intend to produce or elicit any state or action in my hearer other than the knowledge that he is being greeted. But that knowledge is simply his *understanding* what I said, it is not an additional response or effect. Furthermore, there is no perlocutionary effect of, for example, promising which will distinguish promises from firm statements of intention and emphatic predictions. All three tend to create expectations in the hearer about the future, but "I promise" does not mean "I predict" or "I intend." Any account of meaning must show that when I say "I promise" or "Hello" and mean it, I mean it in exactly the same sense of "mean" as when I say "Get out" and mean it. Yet Grice's account seems to suit only the last of these three sentences, since it is the only one whose meaning is such that in the ordinary cases the speaker who utters and means it intends to produce an 'effect' on the hearer of the kind Grice discusses. The meaning of the sentence "Get out" ties it to a particular intended perlocutionary effect, namely getting the hearer to leave. The meanings of "Hello" and "I promise" do not.

Secondly, even where there generally is a correlated perlocutionary effect, I may say something and mean it without in fact intending to produce that effect. Thus, for example, I may make a statement without caring whether my audience believes it or not but simply because I feel it my duty to make it.

Third, it is not in general the case that when one speaks to someone with the intent of, e.g., telling him some item of information, that one intends that his reason, or even one of his reasons, for believing what one tells him should be that one intends him to believe it. When I read, say, a book of philosophy there are all sorts of reasons for believing or disbelieving what the author says, but it is not one of my reasons for believing what the author says that I recognize that he intends me to believe it. Nor, unless he is an extraordinarily egocentric author, will it have been his intention that I should believe it because I recognize that he intends me to believe it. The Gricean reflexive intention does not work for perlocutionary effects.

Well, then, how does it work? Let us remind ourselves of a few of the facts we are seeking to explain. Human communication has some extraordinary properties, not shared by most other kinds of human behavior. One of the most extraordinary is this: If I am trying to tell someone something, then (assuming certain conditions are satisfied) as soon as he recognizes that I am trying to tell him something and exactly what it is I am trying to tell him, I have succeeded in telling it to him. Furthermore, unless he recognizes that I am trying to tell him something and what I am trying to tell him, I do not fully succeed in telling it to him. In the case of illocutionary acts we succeed in doing what we are trying to do by getting our audience to recognize what we are trying to do. But the 'effect' on the hearer is not a belief or response, it consists simply in the hearer understanding the utterance of the speaker. It is this effect that I have been calling the illocutionary effect.

NORMAN MALCOLM

DEFENDING COMMON SENSE*

In "A Defence of Common Sense" [1] G. E. Moore wrote down a list of propositions which he called "truisms." The following are some of the propositions in that list: "There exists at present a living human body, which is *my* body"; "The earth had existed for many years before my body was born"; "Ever since it was born it has been either in contact with or not far from the surface of the earth"; "I am a human being"; "I have often perceived both my own body and other things which formed part of its environment, including other human bodies." Moore said that every one of the propositions in his list "I *know,* with certainty, to be true." [2]

In his "Proof of an External World" [3] Moore gave what he considered to be "a perfectly rigorous proof" of the existence of "things outside of us." [4] He said that he could prove that two human hands exist. "How? By holding up my two hands, and saying, as I make a certain gesture with the right hand, 'Here is one hand,' and adding, as I make a certain

---

* Norman Malcolm, "Defending Common Sense," *Philosophical Review* 58 (1949): pp. 201–11, 215–16, 218–20. Reprinted by permission of Norman Malcolm and *Philosophical Review.*

[1] In J. H. Muirhead, ed., *Contemporary British Philosophy,* 2d ser.

[2] *Op. cit.,* p. 224.

[3] In *Proceedings of the British Academy,* 25, 1939.

[4] Ibid., p. 295.

gesture with the left, 'and here is another.' " [5] He said that this would not have been a proof unless (among other things) "the premiss which I adduced was something which I *knew* to be the case, and not merely something which I believed but which was by no means certain, or something which, though in fact true, I did not know to be so." But, he continued,

> I certainly did at the moment *know* that which I expressed by the combination of certain gestures with saying the words, 'there is one hand and here is another.' I *knew* that there was one hand in the place indicated by combining a certain gesture with my first utterance of 'here' and that there was another in the different place indicated by combining a certain gesture with my second utterance of 'here.' How absurd it would be to suggest that I did not know it, but only believed it, and that perhaps it was not the case! You might as well suggest that I do not know that I am now standing up and talking— that perhaps after all I'm not, and that it's not quite certain that I am! " [6]

Again: "I *do* know that I held up two hands above this desk not very long ago. As a matter of fact in this case you all know it too. There's no doubt whatever that I did." [7] Again: "I have, no doubt, conclusive evidence for asserting that I am not now dreaming; I have conclusive evidence that I am awake." [8]

I wish to put forward the contention that there is something wrong with Moore's assertions. What I have to say, however, will not be in support of the philosophers who have argued that it is not certain that the earth has existed for many years, or that Moore did not know for certain that he was a human being, or that it is not perfectly certain that he held up a hand during his lecture to the British Academy.

What then is it which, according to me, is wrong with Moore's assertions? I believe that, in the two essays from which I quoted, Moore *misused* the expressions "I know," "I know with certainty," "It is certain," "I have conclusive evidence." I wish to show that Moore's use of those expressions, as illustrated in those essays, is contrary to their ordinary and correct use.

Moore said that he *knew* that the statement "Here's a hand," which he uttered as he held up his hand before the audience at his British Academy lecture, was true. That assertion implies that it would have been correct for him to have said, at a time when he and his audience had a clear view of his hand, "I know that here's a hand." At this moment I am holding a pen, there is a desk before me, I am seated in a chair, and through the window I see a near-by tree. Let us imagine that there is another person in this room who has a clear view of me seated in this

---

[5] Ibid.
[6] Ibid., p. 296.
[7] Ibid., p. 298.
[8] Ibid., p. 300.

chair, before this desk, with this pen in my hand, and who has an unobstructed view of that near-by tree. Moore's assertion implies that it would be correct for me to say to that person "I know that I am holding a pen," "I know with certainty that I am sitting in a chair and before a desk," "It's perfectly certain that that [pointing at the tree] is a tree." I contend that I should misuse language if I were to make any of these statements.

Consider the sentence "It's perfectly certain that that is a tree." If we are walking on a meadow in a heavy fog and a tall, indistinct object looms ahead, and one of us wonders whether it is a tree or a telephone pole, it would be a natural thing for one of us to say, "It's perfectly certain that that is a tree, because if you look carefully you will see the faint outline of the branches on either side." That is one example of circumstances in which the sentence "It's perfectly certain that that is a tree" would be correctly used, although it might not be *true* that that object was a tree. Whether or not it was a tree could be determined by walking closer to it. Consider another example: We are seated in the audience at an open-air theatre, the stage of which is bordered by trees. The stage scenery is painted to represent a woodland, and the painting is so skillfully executed that we are in doubt as to whether that which we see on one side of the stage is a real tree or a painted tree. Finally one of us exclaims "I know that that is a real tree, because just now I saw the leaves move in the breeze." This would be a natural use of language. If a doubt remained as to whether it was a real tree the matter could be finally settled by approaching nearer to the stage. Consider still another example: We are examining an elder plant and the question arises as to whether it is properly called a "tree" or a "shrub." One of us says, "I know that that's a tree because I heard a botany professor say that elders are 'trees' and not 'shrubs.' " Whether or not it is proper to call it a "tree" could be determined by consulting an authoritative book on plants.

Three cases have been described in which it would be a correct use of language, although it might be false, to say, "I know that that's a tree"; and innumerable other cases could be given. Let us notice some features common to these three cases: (1) There is in each case a question at issue and a doubt to be removed. (2) In each case the person who asserts "I know that that's a tree" is able to give a reason for his assertion. (3) In each case there is an investigation which, if it were carried out, would settle the question at issue. I wish to show that all of these features are missing when Moore says in a philosophical context "I know that that's a tree."

(1) Consider the circumstances in which, according to Moore, he would have spoken correctly if he had said, during his British Academy lecture, "I know that here is a hand." He and his audience had a clear view of his hand. If his hand had been concealed in a bag it is unlikely

that he would have pointed at the bag and said to his audience "I know that here is a hand." Or if it had been rumored that Moore had an artificial hand which closely resembled a human hand, it is likely that he would have changed the example. Perhaps he would have pointed at his head and said, "It's certain that this is a head." The point is that he would have chosen to utter the sentence "I know that here is a hand" in circumstances where there was not even any *question* as to whether there was a hand where he pointed! This feature alone of his use of the sentence "I know that here is a hand" would mark it as not an ordinary use of that sentence. If Moore was having a discussion with someone who had produced an argument in favor of saying that it is never certain that any perceptual judgment is true, Moore would point at a tree which stood close by in plain view of both of them and declare "It's perfectly certain that that is a tree." He would not choose circumstances for uttering that sentence in which the outline of the tree was obscured by heavy fog; or in which there was any question as to whether the thing at which he pointed was a real tree and not a section of painted scenery, or a real tree and not a mirror image of a tree; or in which there was any question as to whether it was properly called a "tree" or a "shrub." He would pick circumstances for saying "It's perfectly certain that that's a tree" or "I *know* that that's a tree" in which there was no question at all as to whether the thing at which he pointed was a tree.

The first respect, therefore, in which Moore's usage of the expression "I know," in the philosophical contexts which we are considering, departs from ordinary usage is that Moore says "I know that so and so is true" in circumstances where no one doubts that so and so is true and where there is not even any question as to whether so and so is true. It will be objected: "His opponent has a philosophical doubt as to whether so and so is true, and there is a philosophical question as to whether so and so is true." That is indeed the case. What I am saying is that the philosophical doubt and the philosophical question are raised in circumstances in which there isn't any *doubt* and isn't any *question* as to whether so and so is true. Moore's opponent would not raise a philosophical question as to whether it is certain that an object before them is a tree if the object were largely obscured or too distant to be easily seen. If he said "I wish to argue that it isn't certain that that object is a tree" and Moore replied "I can't tell at this distance whether it is a tree or a bush," then Moore's opponent would *change the example*. He would not want to use as an example for his philosophical argument an object with regard to which there was some doubt as to whether it was a tree. The use of an object as an example for presenting his philosophical doubt is spoiled for him if there *is* any doubt as to what the object is. It must be the case that there is no doubt that the given object is a tree *before* he can even raise a philosophical question as to whether it is certain that it is a tree.

It will be objected, "Moore's opponent may truly doubt that the object is a tree in the respect that he may be in doubt as to whether he is dreaming." It is indeed the case that one of the most powerful arguments for the view that the truth of no perceptual judgment is ever certain is the argument used by Descartes for the purpose of proving that one can never know for certain that one is not dreaming. Suppose that we were watching Descartes through the window of his room while he wrote down that argument which produced in him an astonishment "such that it is almost capable of persuading me that I now dream." Suppose that we saw him facing the fire, sometimes placing a fresh log on it, sometimes placing a kettle to boil, as he formulated the considerations which aroused in him that "astonishment." Wouldn't it be unnatural to say in such a case that Descartes was "in doubt" as to whether there was a fire, even if we heard him exclaim, "Perhaps I dream and there is no fire here" ? Compare that situation with one in which we are watching through the window a man seated in a room whose view of the fire is cut off by a screen. Twice the fire has gone out and he has started it again, and frequently now he lays down his writing in order to peer over the screen. It would be natural to say in such a case that each time he rose to peer over the screen he was in doubt as to whether there was a fire. The sort of circumstances in which it would be unnatural to say of a man that he "doubts" that there is a fire are the very circumstances in which that man might express a philosophical doubt as to whether there is a fire!

Consider this case: A man awakes from sleep and sees a fire burning brightly in the grate. He is astonished because he has no recollection of having started a fire. He shakes his head as if to rouse himself, stares hard at the fire, says, "Perhaps I dream and there is no fire," dashes cold water in his face and looks at the fire again, walks to it with hand extended to feel its warmth, and, continuing to express astonishment, calls in his neighbor from the next apartment, to whom he addresses the question "Am I dreaming, or do I really see a fire? "

This man is in doubt as to whether he is dreaming or awake, in the ordinary sense of those words. His doubt is expressed in *actions* of doubting. When a man is entertaining a philosophical doubt as to whether he is dreaming or awake he does not perform actions of that sort. We must not understand this to mean merely that he does not, *in fact,* perform actions of that sort, although he *could* do so. The truth is that if he did perform actions of that sort then we should no longer say that he was entertaining a philosophical doubt. The very actions which would count in favor of saying that he was *in doubt* as to whether he was awake would count *against* saying that he was feeling a philosophical doubt.

It will be said that Moore's philosophical opponent may be in doubt as to whether he is seeing a real tree or is instead suffering from hallucination. Let us consider the sort of circumstances in which I (or any philosopher) should give utterance to a philosophical doubt as to whether

I was having a hallucination. I should fix my eyes upon some object in plain view at close range, such as the chair in that corner. I should say or think "How do I know that I see a chair? Perhaps I am having a hallucination. Perhaps I am really looking at a dog and because of my hallucination it seems to me that I see a chair." I should turn over in my mind one or more of the several philosophical arguments which have been offered to prove that it is never absolutely certain that one is not having a hallucination. If as I looked at that chair it should suddenly turn into a dog, or seem to, then I should be enormously startled. I should think "Is this a hallucination? Is it a dog I see? " I should be apprehensive of the thing in the corner. I should look about me with anxiety to see whether anything else in the room presented an unusual appearance. I should have ceased my philosophical reflection. I should have been jarred out of my philosophical doubt! I should be *in doubt,* in the ordinary sense of the words, as to whether I was having a hallucination. If I said "Do I really see a dog or is this hallucination? " I should *not* now be expressing a philosophical doubt. If the thing in the corner continued to look and behave and sound like a dog, and if everything else around me looked entirely normal, then I should begin to feel confident that it was really a dog I saw. And if my wife, when I called her in, should express astonishment at there being a dog there, then it would be a natural thing for me to say "I thought for a moment that perhaps I was having a hallucination or was dreaming. Now I know that I'm not. It really is a dog! " Once I was perfectly reassured that I was not having a hallucination, then I could resume my philosophical reflection—that is, I could proceed again to entertain a philosophical doubt as to whether I was having a hallucination.

Let us compare the natural use of the sentence "I know that I'm not dreaming or having a hallucination," which we have just described, with Moore's philosophical use of it. One feature of the circumstances of its natural use was that something *extraordinary* had occurred. Another feature was that my anxiety as to whether I was suffering from hallucination or had actually seen a chair turn into a dog, expressed itself in such actions as rising from my chair in alarm, glancing apprehensively about me, scrutinizing closely the thing in the corner, calling in my wife. Another feature was that as a result of performing those actions my anxiety and doubt were removed. Now consider the circumstances in which Moore, in his British Academy lecture, said "I have, no doubt, conclusive reasons for asserting that I am not now dreaming; I have conclusive evidence that I am awake." [9] Nothing extraordinary had occurred. Neither Moore nor anyone present had any reason to think that he was dreaming. Neither he nor anyone present had any doubt about it. There was not even any *question* as to whether he was dreaming. Yet in those circumstances Moore

---

[9] Ibid.

uttered the sentence "I have conclusive evidence that I am awake." Ordinarily a statement like that would be made only if there was some reason to think that he was dreaming, and only if he or someone else felt a doubt about it, and only if he had done something to remove the doubt. None of these things are true of the circumstances in which Moore made his statement. His use of the sentence "I have conclusive evidence that I am awake" was an enormous departure from ordinary usage.

With respect to the objection, therefore, that Moore's philosophical opponent does have a doubt as to whether he really sees a tree or is, instead, dreaming or having an hallucination, it should be answered: Moore's opponent has a *philosophical* doubt as to whether he is dreaming, but this does not imply that he is *in doubt* as to whether he is dreaming. To call a philosophical doubt a *doubt* is as misleading as to call a rhetorical question a *question*. We should not say that a man was feeling a philosophical doubt as to whether he was having an hallucination if he was, *in the ordinary sense of the words,* in doubt as to whether he was having an hallucination. Nor should we say that he was raising a philosophical question as to whether he might not be dreaming if the circumstances were such that there *was* some question as to whether he was dreaming.

(2) The second thing that we noticed about the natural use of the sentence "I know that that is a tree" is that the person who utters it is able to support his assertion with a *reason.* Suppose that we were on the top of a high hill and were curious as to whether something which we saw in the valley below was a tree or a shrub. If one of us said "I know that it is a tree," it would be natural to ask "How do you know?" This question is a request for a reason, for proof, for evidence. Many different reasons might be given, e.g., "I was down at that place yesterday and remember seeing a tree there"; or "If you will compare the height of it with that of the barn nearby you will see that it must be a tree." If the person answered our question with "I have no reason" or "I have a reason but I don't know what it is," we should think it rather queer. We should think that he should not have said, "I know that that is a tree" but should have said instead, "I am inclined to believe that that is a tree but I have no reason for it." We should feel that the use of the word "know," unaccompanied by a reason, was inappropriate.

Now a striking thing about Moore's utterance, in a philosophical context, of a statement like "I know that that is a tree," is that he cannot offer any reason in support of his statement. In his British Academy lecture he said: "How am I to prove now that 'Here's one hand, and here's another'? I do not believe I can do it. In order to do it, I should need to prove for one thing, as Descartes pointed out, that I am not now dreaming. But how can I prove that I am not? I have, no doubt, conclusive reasons for asserting that I am not now dreaming; I have conclusive evidence that I am awake: but that is a very different thing from being able to prove it. I could not tell you what all my evidence is; and I should require to do this at least, in order to give you a proof." [10] He insisted, however, that "I can know things, which I cannot prove." [11] In "A Defence of Common Sense" he said, "But do I really *know* all the propositions in (1) to be true? " [" (1) " is the list of propositions such as "there exists at present a living human body, which is *my* body," "the earth had existed for many years before my body was born," "I am a human being," etc.] "Isn't it possible that I merely believe them? or know them to be highly probable? In answer to this question, I think I have nothing better to say than that it seems to me that I do know them, with certainty. . . . We are all, I think, in this strange position that we do *know* many things, with regard to which we *know* further that we must have had evidence for them, and yet we do not know *how* we know, i.e., we do not know what the evidence was." [12]

Moore's remark, "I can know things which I cannot prove," possesses on the surface of it a certain plausibility. In ordinary life circumstances do occur in which we should say that someone knew that so and so was true although he could not prove it. I might know, for example, that Mr. R. entered the apartment house on the night of the crime. If the district attorney asked, "How do you know? " I might reply, "I saw him." If the district attorney asked, "How do you know that it was Mr. R. you saw? " I might reply, "Because I had a clear, close view of his face." If my testimony was doubted, I might prove that Mr. R. did enter the apartment house that night by producing several reliable witnesses to testify that they too saw him enter it. If, however, I was not able to produce those other witnesses, because they were all dead, I would not be able to prove it, although I knew it. In this case there was something which the district attorney would have called proof *if* I could have produced it.

The philosophical context in which Moore would say "I know that that is a tree" is very dissimilar. Although Moore's opponent asks "How do you know that that is a tree? " there is nothing which he would *call* a proof that it is a tree. There is not even anything which he would call a *reason* for saying that it is a tree. It would be pointless for Moore to say to him, "I know that it is a tree because I see that it is a tree"; or to say "I know that it is a tree because I have a clear, close view of it." In the philosophical context these remarks would be utterly irrelevant. If Moore were to say, "I know that I do see a tree and am not suffering from hallucination, because just now I saw my wife point at the place I am looking and heard her say 'I must trim that tree,' " the philosophical reply would be, "That is no reason, because it may be part of your hallucination that you saw and heard your wife." There is nothing at all which Moore could offer in defense of his statement "I know that that

---

[10] Ibid., pp. 299–300.
[11] Ibid., p. 300.
[12] "A Defence of Common Sense," p. 206.

is a tree." There is nothing which in that context would be called "proof" or "reason" or "evidence" for that statement. It follows from this that Moore's use of "know" in that context is a departure from its ordinary use. In ordinary discourse we are reluctant to say that someone *knows* that so and so is true if he cannot give some reason or some evidence for saying that so and so is true. If he can offer no reason or evidence at all then we are inclined to say that he should not have said that he *knew* that so and so is true. Moore's philosophical usage of "know" breaks this connection between the ordinary use of the word "know" and the being able to give a *reason*.

It also breaks the connection between the ordinary use of the word "know" and the being able to give a *proof.* Let me make this clearer. As was noted before, we do permit it to be said, in some circumstances, that a person knows something which he cannot prove. He *may* know that that thing at the base of the cliff is a tree, and not a bush, because he says that he was down there a month ago; but he cannot *prove* that it is a tree because the recent landslide prevents those who doubt his word from climbing to the bottom and seeing for themselves whether it is a tree. We all understand perfectly well, however, that there is something which we should call a proof. If by some extraordinary feat we *were* able to descend, then his assertion would be proved or disproved, because then we should have a close view of the thing. His claim would have been proved true or false, depending on the outcome.

In the philosophical context the difficulty in the way of proving that the thing at which we are looking is a tree is not that none of the procedures of proof appropriate to normal contexts of doubt can, in fact, be carried out. The difficulty is that there is no procedure whatever which, even if it *were* carried out, would be called a "proof" that the thing we see is a tree. In this context there is not, therefore, a *concept* of proof. In ordinary discourse the statement, "I know it, although I cannot prove it," is made in circumstances where there is a concept of proof, but where a proof cannot, *as a matter of fact,* be obtained. In the philosophical context anyone who says "I know it is a tree, although I cannot prove it" is trying to fit the concept of *knowledge* into a context in which there is no concept of *proof.* To try to divorce in this way the concept of knowledge from the concept of proof is a radical violation of the logic of ordinary language. . . .

I am contending that if Moore and I were sitting within a few feet of an apple tree which was in plain view of both of us, it would be a misuse of ordinary language for either of us to point at it and say, "I know that that's a tree." Someone might be inclined to reply, "It would be queer, undoubtedly, for either of you to utter that sentence in such a case; but what would make it queer is that *it is so obvious to both of you that it is a tree* that there is no need to say it! To utter that sentence in those circumstances would be an odd use but not a misuse."

This reply contains a mistake. The mistake lies in the assumption that in those circumstances it would be correct to say "It is obvious that it is a tree." Consider this example: We are looking at something a mile away on the side of a hill and because of the distance and angle of view we cannot make out whether it is a tree or a bush. As we approach it, it more and more distinctly assumes the shape of a tree, until, at a point several hundred yards from it, one of us says "It's perfectly obvious now that it is a tree." This is an ordinary use of those words. In the first place, a doubt existed. The use of those words was to remove the doubt. They were like saying, "You need not have that doubt any longer." In the second place, further investigation would not be unreasonable. If one of us had weak vision and still doubted that it was a tree he could walk closer. There would come a point, still at a considerable distance from the tree, at which he too would say, "Yes, it obviously is a tree."

Suppose now that we should walk right up to the tree and begin to pick apples from it. If one of us should then say, "It's obvious that this is a tree," that would be a *mis*use of those words and would raise a laugh. In the first place, no one has any doubt on the matter and the utterance of those words is not fulfilling its normal purpose, which is to remove doubt. In the second place, there is no further investigation which would "back up" those words. Should we pick more apples? Should we take photographs? Should we strip the bark? None of those things would be called "making certain" or "further verifying" or "trying to find out" whether it is a tree. There is nothing which, in those circumstances, we should call "trying to find out whether it is a tree." This means that, in those circumstances, we don't attach any sense to the question "Is it a tree? " We don't know what to *do* with it. In those circumstances the sentence "It's obvious that it's a tree" is a *misfit*. It doesn't *belong* there. It is a set of idle words. It has no function. It has a function only in those contexts where we attach sense to the question "Is it a tree? "

I am contending that Moore's philosophical assertions, such as "I know that here's a hand" or "I know that I am a human being," are made in circumstances where it is a misuse of words to say either "I know that here's a hand" or "I don't know that here's a hand," or to say either "I know that I'm a human being" or "I don't know that I'm a human being." To this the following objection will be made: "Either I know that I am a human being or I don't know it. One or the other *must* be the case."

If my contention sounds to you like an absurd paradox and this reply seems irrefutable, it is because you have before your mind the normal usage of "I know" and "I don't know." If I see something moving on the top of a distant hill it is true that either I know that it is a human being or I don't know it. In those circumstances we attach sense to the question "Is it a human being? " There is something which we should call "investigating" and "finding out" whether it is or it isn't. This is one of the contexts of the normal usage of "know" and "don't know." In these contexts "I know" is opposed to "I don't know." "Either I know or I don't know" is a rule which applies to these expressions when they occur in their normal contexts. But when these expressions occur in unnatural contexts this rule no longer applies. Consider the sentence, "My desk is good-natured." There is no paradox involved in saying that my desk neither is good-natured nor isn't good-natured. It would be fantastic to insist that either my desk is good-natured or it isn't and that it must be one or the other. We don't attach sense to the words, "Is it a good-natured desk? " There is nothing which we should recognize as an "investigation" into whether it is or it isn't.

Just as "good-natured" does not belong to certain contexts, so "I know" does not belong to certain contexts. If I should come up to you and ask with earnest countenance "Am I a human being? " you would be taken quite aback. It would not be clear to you what my words mean. You would not understand to what investigation they referred. You would not know what *sort* of thing an "answer" would be. You would be equally perplexed if I should solemnly declare to you, "I *know* that I'm a human being." My statement would seem to you as strange and outlandish as "My desk isn't good-natured."

There could be circumstances in which "Am I a human being? " would be a question with sense. Suppose that I have fallen from a height and have been knocked unconscious. Gradually I return to consciousness. I am dazed and confused. There is utter darkness, and I cannot feel my body. I dimly recall the fall and wonder if I am now "dead." Am I a spirit? Am I without a body? Or "Am I still a human being? " If I should then begin to feel my body and to sort out my limbs, I might exclaim, "I know that I am still a human being." Here is a usage of "Am I a human being? " and "I know that I am a human being" which has sense. The circumstances in which Moore said "I know that I am a human being" were quite unlike this. In his case there was no "question," no "doubt," and no "investigation." When I maintain that in the circumstances in which he uttered those words, neither "I know that I'm a human being" nor "I don't know that I'm a human being" was correct language, I do not contend against a law of logic.

I hold, therefore, that Moore was not defending "common sense" at all when he declared "I know with certainty" that "There exists at present a living human body which is *my* body," that "The earth had existed many years before this body was born," that "For many of these years large numbers of human bodies had, at every moment, been alive upon it," that "I am a human being." His assertions were made in circumstances where there was no question, and it wouldn't have made sense to raise a question, as to whether Moore had a body and was a human being, or as to whether the earth had existed before he was born, or as to whether there were other human beings living on it. Moore's assertions do not belong to "common sense," i.e., to ordinary language, at all. They involve a use of "know" which is a radical departure from ordinary usage.

Moore wished to attack all those philosophers who hold views from which it follows that no human being knows that he is a human being and that no human being knows any proposition like "Here's a hand" to be true. Moore, to his everlasting credit, saw that it would be a misuse of language for him to say (when writing in his study), "I don't know that I'm a human being," or to say (when holding up his hand in plain view before him), "I don't know that this is a hand."[13] Therefore, he stoutly affirmed, "I *know* that I'm a human being," "I *know* that this is a hand." He did not see that these statements too are a misuse of language.

---

[13] Let me warn, if it is necessary, that what Moore "saw" is a controversial matter. Moore might deny that he then saw or that he now sees any such thing.

DONALD DAVIDSON

ON THE VERY IDEA OF A CONCEPTUAL SCHEME*

Philosophers of many persuasions are prone to talk of conceptual schemes. Conceptual schemes, we are told, are ways of organizing experience; they are systems of categories that give form to the data of sensation; they are points of view from which individuals, cultures, or periods survey the passing scene. There may be no translating from one scheme to another, in which case the beliefs, desires, hopes and bits of knowledge that characterize one person have no true counterparts for the subscriber to another scheme. Reality itself is relative to a scheme: what counts as real in one system may not in another.

Even those thinkers who are certain there is only one conceptual scheme are in the sway of the scheme concept; even monotheists have religion. And when someone sets out to describe "our conceptual scheme," his homey task assumes, if we take him literally, that there might be rival systems.

Conceptual relativism is a heady and exotic doctrine, or would be if we could make good sense of it. The trouble is, as so often in philosophy, it is hard to improve intelligibility while retaining the excitement. At any rate that is what I shall argue.

* Donald Davidson, "On the Very Idea of a Conceptual Scheme," *Proceedings and Addresses of the American Philosophical Association* 47 (1973–74): pp. 5–7, 12–17. Reprinted by permission of the American Philosophical Association and the author.

We are encouraged to imagine we understand massive conceptual change or profound contrasts by legitimate examples of a familiar sort. Sometimes an idea, like that of simultaneity as defined in relativity theory, is so important that with its addition a whole department of science takes on a new look. Sometimes revisions in the list of sentences held true in a discipline are so central that we may feel that the terms involved have changed their meanings. Languages that have evolved in distant times or places may differ extensively in their resources for dealing with one or another range of phenomena. What comes easily in one language may come hard in another, and this difference may echo significant dissimilarities in style and value.

But examples like these, impressive as they occasionally are, are not so extreme but that the changes and the contrasts can be explained and described using the equipment of a single language. Whorf, wanting to demonstrate that Hopi incorporates a metaphysics so alien to ours that Hopi and English cannot, as he puts it, "be calibrated," uses English to convey the contents of sample Hopi sentences. Kuhn is brilliant at saying what things were like before the revolution using—what else?—our post-revolutionary idiom. Quine gives us a feel for the "pre-individuative phase in the evolution of our conceptual scheme," while Bergson tells us where we can go to get a view of a mountain undistorted by one or another provincial perspective.

The dominant metaphor of conceptual relativism, that of differing points of view, seems to betray an underlying paradox. Different points of view make sense, but only if there is a common coordinate system on which to plot them; yet the existence of a common system belies the claim of dramatic incomparability. What we need, it seems to me, is some idea of the considerations that set the limits to conceptual contrast. There are extreme suppositions that founder on paradox or contradiction; there are modest examples we have no trouble understanding. What determines where we cross from the merely strange or novel to the absurd?

We may accept the doctrine that associates having a language with having a conceptual scheme. The relation may be supposed to be this: if conceptual schemes differ, so do languages. But speakers of different languages may share a conceptual scheme provided there is a way of translating one language into the other. Studying the criteria of translation is therefore a way of focussing on criteria of identity for conceptual schemes. If conceptual schemes aren't associated with languages in this way, the original problem is needlessly doubled, for then we would have to imagine the mind, with its ordinary categories, operating with a language with *its* organizing structure. Under the circumstances we would certainly want to ask who is to be master.

Alternatively, there is the idea that *any* language distorts reality, which implies that it is only wordlessly if at all that the mind comes to grips with things as they really are. This is to conceive language as an inert (though necessarily distorting) medium independent of the human agencies that employ it: a view of language that surely cannot be maintained. Yet if the mind can grapple without distortion with the real, the mind itself must be without categories and concepts. This featureless self is familiar from theories in quite different parts of the philosophical landscape. There are, for example, theories that make freedom consist in decisions taken apart from all desires, habits and dispositions of the agent; and theories of knowledge that suggest that the mind can observe the totality of its own perceptions and ideas. In each case, the mind is divorced from the traits that constitute it; a familiar enough conclusion to certain lines of reasoning, as I said, but one that should always persuade us to reject the premises.

We may identify conceptual schemes with languages, then, or better, allowing for the possibility that more than one language may express the same scheme, sets of intertranslatable languages. Languages we will not think of as separable from souls; speaking a language is not a trait a man can lose while retaining the power of thought. So there is no chance that someone can take up a vantage point for comparing conceptual schemes by temporarily shedding his own. Can we then say that two people have different conceptual schemes if they speak languages that fail of inter-translatability?

. . . The failure of inter-translatability is a necessary condition for difference of conceptual schemes; the common relation to experience or the evidence is what is supposed to help us make sense of the claim that it is languages or schemes that are under consideration when translation fails. It is essential to this idea that there be something neutral and common that lies outside all schemes. This common something cannot, of course, be the *subject mattter* of contrasting languages, or translation would be possible. Thus Kuhn has recently written:

> Philosophers have now abandoned hope of finding a pure sense-datum language . . . but many of them continue to assume that theories can be compared by recourse to a basic vocabulary consisting entirely of words which are attached to nature in ways that are unproblematic and, to the extent necessary, independent of theory. . . . Feyerabend and I have argued at length that no such vocabulary is available. In the transition from one theory to the next words change their meanings or conditions of applicability in subtle ways. Though most of the same signs are used before and after a revolution, e.g., force, mass, element, compound, cell—the ways in which some of them attach to nature has somehow changed. Successive theories are thus, we say, incommensurable.[1]

---

[1] Thomas Kuhn, "Reflection on my Critics" in *Criticism and the Growth of Knowledge,* eds. I. Lakatos and A. Musgrave, Cambridge, 1970, pp. 266, 267.

"Incommensurable" is, of course, Kuhn and Feyerabend's word for "not intertranslatable." The neutral content waiting to be organized is supplied by nature.

Feyerabend himself suggests that we may compare contrasting schemes by "choosing a point of view outside the system or the language." He hopes we can do this because "there is still human experience as an actually existing process." [2] independent of all schemes.

The same, or similar, thoughts are expressed by Quine in many passages: "The totality of our so-called knowledge or beliefs . . . is a man-made fabric which impinges on experience only along the edges. . . . total science is like a field of force whose boundary conditions are experience" [3] "As an empiricist I . . . think of the conceptual scheme of science as a tool . . . for predicting future experience in the light of past experience." [4] And again:

> We persist in breaking reality down somehow into a multiplicity of identifiable and discriminable objects. . . . We talk so inveterately of objects that to say we do so seems almost to say nothing at all; for how else is there to talk? It is hard to say how else there is to talk, not because our objectifying pattern is an invariably trait of human nature, but because we are bound to adapt any alien pattern to our own in the very process of understanding or translating the alien sentences.[5]

The test of difference remains failure or difficulty of translation: "to speak of that remote medium as radically different from ours is to say no more than that the translations do not come smoothly." [6] Yet the roughness may be so great that the alien has an "as yet unimagined pattern beyond individuation." [7]

The idea is then that something is a language, and associated with a conceptual scheme, whether we can translate it or not, if it stands in a certain relation (predicting, organizing, facing or fitting) to experience (nature, reality, sensory promptings). The problem is to say what the relation is, and to be clearer about the entities related.

The images and metaphors fall into two main groups: conceptual schemes (languages) either *organize* something, or they *fit* it (as in "he warps his scientific heritage to fit his . . . sensory promptings" [8]). The first group contains also *systematize, divide up* (the stream of experience);

---

[2] Paul Feyerabend, "Problems of Empiricism," in *Beyond the Edge of Certainty*, ed. R.G. Colodny, Englewood Cliffs, New Jersey, 1965, p. 214.

[3] W.V.O. Quine, "Two Dogmas of Empiricism," reprinted in *From a Logical Point of View*, 2d edition, Cambridge, Mass., 1961, p. 42.

[4] Ibid., p. 44.

[5] W.V.O. Quine, "Speaking of Objects," reprinted in *Ontological Relativity and Other Essays*, New York, 1969, p. 1.

[6] Ibid., p. 25.

[7] Ibid., p. 24.

[8] "Two Dogmas of Empiricism," p. 46.

further examples of the second group are *predict, account for, face* (the tribunal of experience). As for the entities that get organized, or which the scheme must fit, I think again we may detect two main ideas: either it is reality (the universe, the world, nature), or it is experience (the passing show, surface irritations, sensory promptings, sense data, the given).

We cannot attach a clear meaning to the notion of organizing a single object (the world, nature etc.) unless that object is understood to contain or consist in other objects. Someone who sets out to organize a closet arranges the things in it. If you are told not to organize the shoes and shirts, but the closet itself, you would be bewildered. How would you organize the Pacific Ocean? Straighten out its shores, perhaps, or relocate its islands, or destroy its fish.

A language may contain simple predicates whose extensions are matched by no simple predicates, or even by any predicates at all, in some other language. What enables us to make this point in particular cases is an ontology common to the two languages, with concepts that individuate the same objects. We can be clear about breakdowns in translation when they are local enough, for a background of generally successful translation provides what is needed to make the failures intelligible. But we were after larger game: we wanted to make sense of there being a language we could not translate at all. Or, to put the point differently, we were looking for a criterion of languagehood that did not depend on, or entail, translatability into a familiar idiom. I suggest that the image of organizing the closet of nature will not supply such a criterion.

How about the other kind of object, experience? Can we think of a language organizing *it?* Much the same difficulties recur. The notion of organization applies only to pluralities. But whatever plurality we take experience to consist in—events like losing a button or stubbing a toe, having a sensation of warmth or hearing an oboe—we will have to individuate according to familiar principles. A language that organizes *such* entities must be a language very like our own.

Experience (and its classmates like surface irritations, sensations and sense data) also makes another and more obvious trouble for the organizing idea. For how could something count as a language that organized *only* experiences, sensations, surface irritations or sense data? Surely knives and forks, railroads and mountains, cabbages and kingdoms also need organizing.

This last remark will no doubt sound inappropriate as a response to the claim that a conceptual scheme is a way of coping with sensory experience; and I agree that it is. But what was under consideration was the idea of *organizing* experience, not the idea of *coping with* (or fitting or facing) experience. The reply was apropos of the former, not the latter, concept. So now let's see whether we can do better with the second idea.

When we turn from talk of organization to talk of fitting we turn our
attention from the referential apparatus of language—predicates, quanti-
fiers, variables and singular terms—to whole sentences. It is sentences
that predict (or are used to predict), sentences that cope or deal with
things, that fit our sensory promptings, that can be compared or confronted
with the evidence. It is sentences also that face the tribunal of experience,
though of course they must face it together.

The proposal is not that experiences, sense data, surface irritations
or sensory promptings are the sole subject matter of language. There is,
it is true, the theory that talk about brick houses on Elm Street is ultimately
to be construed as being about sense data or perceptions, but such
reductionistic views are only extreme, and implausible, versions of the
general position we are considering. The general position is that sensory
experience provides all the *evidence* for the acceptance of sentences (where
sentences may include whole theories). A sentence or theory fits our
sensory promptings, successfully faces the tribunal of experience, preducts
future experience, or copes with the pattern of our surface irritations,
provided it is borne out by the evidence.

In the common course of affairs, a theory may be borne out by the
available evidence and yet be false. But what is in view here is not just
actually available evidence; it is the totality of possible sensory evidence
past, present and future. We do not need to pause to contemplate what
this might mean. The point is that for a theory to fit or face up to the
totality of possible sensory evidence is for that theory to be true. If a
theory quantifies over physical objects, numbers or sets, what it says
about these entities is true provided the theory as a whole fits the sensory
evidence. One can see how, from this point of view, such entities might
be called posits. It is reasonable to call something a posit if it can be
contrasted with something that is not. Here the something that is not is
sensory experience—at least that is the idea.

The trouble is that the notion of fitting the totality of experience, like
the notions of fitting the facts, or being true to the facts, adds nothing
intelligible to the simple concept of being true. To speak of sensory
experience rather than the evidence, or just the facts, expresses a view
about the source or nature of evidence, but it does not add a new entity
to the universe against which to test conceptual schemes. The totality of
sensory evidence is what we want provided it is all the evidence there
is; and all the evidence there is is just what it takes to make our sentences
or theories true. Nothing, however, no *thing,* makes sentences and theories
true: not experience, not surface irritations, not the world, can make a
sentence true. *That* experience takes a certain course, that our skin is
warmed or punctured, that the universe is finite, these facts, if we like
to talk that way, make sentences and theories true. But this point is put
better without mention of facts. The sentence "My skin is warm" is true

if and only if my skin is warm. Here there is no reference to a fact, a world, an experience, or a piece of evidence.[9]

Our attempt to characterize languages or conceptual schemes in terms of the notion of fitting some entity has come down, then, to the simple thought that something is an acceptable conceptual scheme or theory if it is true. Perhaps we better say *largely* true in order to allow sharers of a scheme to differ on details. And the criterion of a conceptual scheme different from our own now becomes: largely true but not translatable. The question whether this is a useful criterion is just the question how well we understand the notion of truth, as applied to language, independent of the notion of translation. The answer is, I think, that we do not understand it independently at all.

We recognize sentences like " 'Snow is white' is true if and only if snow is white" to be trivially true. Yet the totality of such English sentences uniquely determines the extension of the concept of truth for English. Tarski generalized this observation and made it a test of theories of truth: according to Tarski's Convention T, a satisfactory theory of truth for a language L must entail. for every sentence *s* of L, a theorem of the form "*s* is true if and only if *p*" where "*s*" is replaced by a description of *s* and "*p*" by *s* itself if L is English, and by a translation of *s* into English if L is not English.[10] This isn't, of course, a definition of truth, and it doesn't hint that there is a single definition or theory that applies to languages generally. Nevertheless, Convention T suggests, though it cannot state, an important feature common to all the specialized concepts of truth. It succeeds in doing this by making essential use of the notion of translation into a language we know. Since Convention T embodies our best intuition as to how the concept of truth is used, there does not seem to be much hope for a test that a conceptual scheme is radically different from ours if that test depends on the assumption that we can divorce the notion of truth from that of translation.

Neither a fixed stock of meanings, nor a theory-neutral reality, can provide, then, a ground for comparison of conceptual schemes. It would be a mistake to look further for such a ground if by that we mean something conceived as common to incommensurable schemes. In abandoning this search, we abandon the attempt to make sense of the metaphor of a single space within which each scheme has a position and provides a point of view.

---

[9] These remarks are defended in my "True to the Facts," *The Journal of Philosophy,* vol. 66 (1969), pp. 748–64.

[10] Alfred Tarski, "The Concept of Truth in Formalized Languages," in *Logic, Semantics, Metamathematics,* Oxford, 1956.

STUDY QUESTIONS

Review

1. What is "the linguistic turn" in philosophy? How does it differ from more traditional types of philosophy? Why have some contemporary philosophers proposed it?
2. What is the difference between syntactics, semantics, and pragmatics? Explain as clearly as possible your understanding of each.
3. What is the difference between linguistic philosophy, philosophy of language, and linguistics? In what way or in what cases might they overlap?
4. What is the difference between formalist language analysis and ordinary language analysis?
5. How does the explanation of the development of language of Noam Chomsky differ from that of a behaviorist?
6. Why does Norman Malcolm think that Moore was misusing the term "know"?
7. According to Davidson, what is a "conceptual scheme"? How is his discussion of it related to the problem of truth?

For Further Thought

8. What do you think of the linguistic turn in philosophy? Do you think that all philosophical problems (as you know them) are a matter of incorrect use or misunderstanding of language? Explain why or why not.
9. Catalogue the different types of language philosophy discussed in this chapter. With which do you most sympathize? Which do you find most difficult to understand or accept?
10. What do you think of the relation between a conceptual scheme or language and the world? How do you believe that we could ever know (if we could) how adequate our schemes were?
11. Discuss what you understand by "grammar." Could there be a difference between a surface grammar of a language and a depth grammar which many or all languages might have in common? Speculate a bit or use what knowledge you have of linguistics to comment.

BIBLIOGRAPHY

Alston, William P. *Philosophy of Language.* Englewood Cliffs, N.J.: Prentice-Hall, 1964.
Ambrose, Alice. "Linguistic Approaches to Philosophical Problems," *Journal of Philosophy* 49 (1952): pp. 289–301.
Austin, John L. *How To Do Things With Words.* Oxford: Oxford University Press, 1962.
Bach, Kent, and Robt. M. Harmish. *Linguistic Communication and Speech Acts.* Cambridge: MIT Press, 1979.
Black, Max, ed. *Philosophical Analysis.* Ithaca, N.Y.: Cornell University Press, 1950.

Caton, C. E. *Philosophy and Ordinary Language.* Urbana: University of Illinois Press, 1963.

Chappell, V. C., ed. *Ordinary Language.* Englewood Cliffs, N.J.: Prentice-Hall, 1963.

Chomsky, Noam. *Rules and Representations.* New York: Columbia University Press, 1980.

— — —. *Reflections on Language.* New York: Random House, Pantheon Books, 1975.

— — —. *Language and Mind.* New York: Harcourt, Brace, and World, 1968.

— — —. *Cartesian Linguistics: A Chapter in the History of Rationalist Thought.* New York: Harper and Row, 1966.

— — —. *Current Issues in Linguistic Theory.* The Hague: Mouton, 1964.

— — —. *Syntactic Structures.* The Hague: Mouton, 1957.

Davidson, Donald. "Thought and Talk." In Guttenplan, *Mind and Language.* Oxford: Clarendon Press, 1975.

Davidson, Donald, and Gilbert Harman, eds. *Semantics of Natural Language.* 2d ed. Dordrecht-Holland: D. Reidel Publishing Co., 1972.

Dennett, Daniel. *Brainstorms: Philosophical Essays on Mind and Psychology.* Cambridge: MIT Press, 1981.

Dummett, Michael. *Truth and Other Enigmas.* Cambridge: Harvard University Press, 1978.

— — —. *Frege: Philosophy of Language.* London: Duckworth, 1973.

Elew, A.N., ed. *Essays in Conceptual Analysis.* London: Macmillan, 1960.

— — —, ed. *Logic and Language.* Oxford: Blackwell, 1951; 1953.

Fodor, Jerry A. *Modularity of Mind.* Cambridge: MIT Press, 1983.

— — —. *Representation: Philosophical Essays on the Foundations of Cognitive Science.* Cambridge: MIT Press, 1981.

Fodor, J., and J. Katz, eds. *The Structure of Language.* Englewood Cliffs, N.J.: Prentice-Hall, 1964.

Harman, Gilbert, ed. *On Noam Chomsky: Critical Essays.* 2d ed. Amherst: University of Massachusetts Press, 1982.

Gunderson, Keith, ed. *Language, Mind, and Knowledge.* Vol. 7 in *Minnesota Studies in the Philosophy of Science.* Minneapolis: University of Minnesota Press, 1975.

Guttenplan, Samuel. *Mind and Language.* Oxford: Clarendon Press, 1975.

Hacking, Ian. *Why Does Language Matter to Philosophy?* Cambridge: Cambridge University Press, 1975.

Harman, Gilbert. "Language, Thought and Communication." In *Language, Mind, and Knowledge,* pp. 270–98. See K. Gunderson, ed.

Kripke, Saul. *Naming and Necessity.* Cambridge: Harvard University Press, 1980.

Linsky, Leonard, ed. *Semantics and the Philosophy of Language.* Urbana: University of Illinois Press, 1952.

Lewis, David. "Languages and Language." In *Language, Mind, and Knowledge,* pp. 3–35. See K. Gunderson, ed.

Malcolm, Norman. *Memory and Mind.* Ithaca, N.Y.: Cornell University Press, 1977.

— — —. "Philosophy and Ordinary Language." *Philosophical Review* 60 (1951): pp. 530–59.

Rorty, Richard, ed. *The Linguistic Turn: Recent Essays in Philosophical Method.* Chicago: University of Chicago Press, 1968.

Ryle, Gibert. *The Concept of Mind.* London: Hutchinson, 1949.

Searle, John. *Intentionality.* New York: Cambridge University Press, 1983.

— — —. *Speech Acts: An Essay in the Philosophy of Language.* Cambridge: Cambridge University Press, 1969.

Sellars, Wilfrid. *Science, Perception, and Reality.* London: Routledge and Kegan Paul, 1963.

— — —. "Realism and the New Way of Words." *Philosophy and Phenomenological Research* 8 (1947–48): pp. 601–34.

Strawson, P. F. "On Referring," *Mind* 59 (1950): pp. 320–44.

Urmson, J. O. *Philosophical Analysis: Its Development Between the Two World Wars.* Oxford: Clarendon Press, 1960.

Vendler, Zeno. "Comments on the Relevance of Linguistics to Philosophy." *Journal of Philosophy* 62 (1965): pp. 602–5.

— — —. "Each and Every, Any and All." *Mind* 71 (April 1962): pp. 145–60.

Wittgenstein, Ludwig. *Philosophical Investigations.* Trans. G. E. Anscombe. Oxford: Blackwell, 1953.

— — —. *Tractatus Logico-Philosophicus.* London: K. Paul, Trench, Trubner and co., ltd., 1922. New trans. by Pears and McGuinness. New York: Humanities Press, 1961.

Chapter 17

Twentieth-Century American Moral Philosophy

Moral philosophy or ethics has its own unique concerns: What is the good life? What ought we to do? How should we decide what is good or bad, better or worse, right or wrong? Whether the particular approaches to these problems taken by American philosophers can be said to involve anything distinctively American remains an open question. There are ways in which the issues probed and the manner of probing by Americans are in line with those of other English-speaking twentieth-century moral philosophers and different from those of Continental philosophers. English-speaking philosophers are generally more empirical and naturalistic than their more metaphysically or theologically inclined Continental counterparts. Nevertheless, it may well be that the particular type of empiricism or naturalism of some American moral philosophers is distinctive.

While naturalistic and realistic moral philosophies predominated in American moral philosophy in the first quarter of this century, in the second quarter the problems inherent in naturalistic views together with the influence of positivism led to the development of more analytic types of moral philosophy and to an emotivist theory of moral judgments in particular. Other metaethical problems also occupied the interest of moral philosophers. One of these was the question of the relation of facts (and descriptions of them) and values (or evaluations). Were moral judgments or other kinds of evaluations based on facts or did a person's moral judgments only accidentally, if at all, bear on or derive from beliefs about empirical matters? Furthermore, moral philosophers began to analyze the nature of morality itself. What had it to do with self-interest, with reason giving, with moral rules? Did it require taking a distinctive point of view? What type of answer could be given to the question Why be moral?

While such metaethical issues had dominated ethical discussion in the third quarter of this century, more practical issues were never entirely lost sight of, and in the last quarter of the century they have come to be of as much interest as the more theoretical ones. The number and circulation of philosophy journals that include or specifically deal with such problems, for example, has increased dramatically.[1] Now it is philosophers, not just social scientists, who write books and publish anthologies on practical moral issues. There is a growing philosophical interest in such issues as environmental pollution, bio-medical practices, and the development and use of modern technologies.[2] After this sketchy overview of the main line of development and major concerns in contemporary American moral philosophy, we now turn to a more detailed analysis and summary of the issues, theories, and philosophers.

ETHICAL NATURALISM

We have already noted some of the characteristics and writers in the so-called naturalistic tradition in philosophy in the United States. Their belief that human existence and knowledge are natural phenomena also influenced their views in moral philosophy. Recall, for example, the views of John Fiske that human interrelations and sympathetic appreciation of the interests of others developed naturally from the lengthy period of human infancy. Recall the position of John Dewey that mind is but a new way in which a natural organism has come to be able to deal with its environment. Recall these and the stage will be set for understanding American ethical naturalism.

American ethical naturalism consistently identifies the good with natural human interests or desires. According to Ralph Barton Perry, for example, the good or what has value is "any object of interest." "A thing — any thing — has value, or is valuable, in the original and generic sense when it is the object of an interest — any interest. Or, whatever is the object of interest is ipso facto valuable."[3] Thus it is not things themselves that either do or do not have value. Rather, things are made valuable or given value by the interest placed in them by persons. Value is thus of a dependent or relative nature. The commonsense element in this point of view is that things and acts simply are what they are in themselves and might only be said to be good when seen in relation to persons. This can be taken either in the sense that it is the interest or welfare of persons that these things promote, or in the sense that persons happen to take an interest in them. Perry's view is the latter rather than the former.

If taken in this latter sense, then, Perry's theory can be considered a form of ethical relativism. Relativistic theories of ethics, in general, are those that hold in some form or other the relativity of values — that values are relative to a time, place, or group of persons, for example. Some forms of relativistic ethics seem to suggest that something is good just because a person believes it to be so, has a positive interest in it, or takes or finds pleasure in it. Thus something that may poison one or disrupt a society may be called "good" if someone wants, likes, or approves of it. Under such a theory, there is no possibility of being mistaken in judgment, for there is no standard by which to judge mistakes as mistakes.

However, perhaps Perry avoids this form of relativism, for he also introduces a more objective standard: the social good consists in the harmonious integration of the interests of the people of the society. Not just any interest proves overall to be morally good, only those that fit into or contribute to the overall integration of interests.[4] However, this position also leaves a number of questions unanswered, as is also the case with the ethical naturalism of John Dewey.

The moral philosophy of John Dewey flows from his views on the nature of knowledge and problem solving as well as from his understanding of nature generally.[5] Moral decisions are required when customary morality breaks down or when for some reason we cannot follow traditional or accustomed modes of behavior. We must then reflect on such things as whether we ought to do this or that, or which line of action is better or worse. The good, for Dewey, is identified with the "desirable." It is thus to be distinguished from what is in fact desired. What is valuable or desirable is that that is desired under appropriate conditions, or what will prove satisfactory for the fulfillmennt of some need, or in the long run. These are ends that we seek, and the means we choose are valuable in so far as they lead to these ends. However, there are no final ends, for these themselves are always means to something else. Moreover, the ends must not be judged apart from the means used to attain them. In fact, the cost of the means needed to attain some end may be so great as to lead us to change our ideas of the value of the end. Dewey wanted to break down the boundaries separating fact and value, means and ends, science and morality. He thought he had done so by asserting that what is desired or good is determined by the method of science. We must be empirical and consider what is actually desired, but we must also consider the causes and results of satisfying some desire and how it fits in with other desires. There is no other final test or standard than this one unless it be inferred from Dewey's statement that "growth is the only end."[6] The more harmonious interconnections that are established by an act (this is growth), the better the act. Other than this statement Dewey gives no hint as to how to distinguish the process of growth from that of decay, no goal by which to judge when one is progressing toward the better rather than the worse.

Dewey's views on education and democracy for which he is also noted flow from his views on the nature of the good and moral decision making.[7] His theory of education is very closely related to his views about what knowledge is and is not; education is not, for example, passively taking in facts already known. Learning is achieved by doing and exists for the purpose of doing. Children have a natural curiosity and naturally approach events as problems. However, Dewey does not suggest that the child should be left to decide his own plan of study or that the child does not need to be taught habits of intelligence and a critical mind. Nor did Dewey ignore the aesthetic and moral sides of the education of the child. Education had a social significance for Dewey; it was the best method for changing society. Gradual evolution was preferable to revolution and upheaval. Democracy, moreover, is the form of government that best provides the means for this change because democracy is grounded in a faith in the common man and in the necessity of retaining free inquiry in a society. It is self-correcting and shows a faith in the process of experience. Rather than seeking to establish a particular result, democracy exists for the purpose of broadening and humanizing the experience of men. Whether as a member of society or as an individual actor, man's good and the broadening and humanizing of experience is still a function of natural human desires and their interrelated fulfillment. As we shall see, this view that the good can be identified with such empirically determinable characteristics as these was already being challenged.

EMOTIVISM

In the mid-1930s American moral philosophy took a decisive, new turn due in part to criticisms of naturalistic positions and also influenced by the epistemological stance of logical positivism. Theories such as those of Perry and Dewey, according to which one decides what is good by attending to what satisfies desire under some conditions, seemed to identify "good" with "satisfying." The identification of "good" with any such describable, empirical, or natural property was, according to some, a fallacy. According to the British philosopher G. E. Moore, for example, who branded it "the naturalistic fallacy," such identification was a mistake because one could always ask (i.e., it was always an "open question") whether some particular satisfaction or pleasure-producing activity or thing was good. In other words, it was not contradictory to hold or one might find that a particular activity was both pleasant and not good. One could not do this, however, if "good" meant or was identifiable with "pleasant." [8]

Moore, however, believed that when one called anything good it was because of something that that thing, person, or action actually possessed, some property that one pointed to or alluded to in calling it good. Since the property could not be any natural describable empirical property, it must be "goodness" itself. Although many pleasant things may also possess goodness, goodness and pleasantness were separate properties or qualities. "Goodness," accordingly, was thought of as an objective property possessed by good things. Though it was not an empirical or observable property, it was nevertheless knowable through a kind of intuition.

As might be expected, many philosophers objected to a theory that posited unobservable properties and that relied on a special intuition. Such objections notwithstanding, many accepted Moore's basic contention that in calling anything good we are doing something different from and more than simply describing an empirical property such as pleasantness. The question of shared concern was: What could this "more" be?

Before we look at the answer given to this question by emotivists such as C. L. Stevenson, we should also backtrack a little and examine the role that logical positivism played in this debate. As you will recall, according to logical positivism there are only two kinds of meaningful statements or propositions — synthetic statements that are empirically verifiable and analytic statements that are logically true, i.e., statements whose truth is determined by the form of the statements themselves. Now ethical statements such as "This is good" seemed to fall into neither category. If such a statement were synthetic, then one could determine whether something is good by sensibly examining it. Yet, all one found through such observation were the empirical properties possessed, not something extra called "good" or "value." Nor, on the other hand, did such statements seem to be a matter of logical truth such that one could tell by analyzing the subject term whether or not the predicate "good" necessarily belonged to it. If ethical propositions were neither synthetic nor analytic, then they could not be meaningful statements. They were, positivists implied, like the nonsense statements of metaphysics. Such statements may have some purpose such as influencing other people, but they are not cognitively meaningful.[9]

Logical positivism became less extreme in the course of its development. So too did the ethical theory associated with it. Instead of labeling ethical statements as meaningless, attention was paid to the peculiar meaning that they might positively have. Charles Stevenson suggested that ethical statements are characterized by the *emotive meaning* that they have, by the fact that they are dynamic and affective, i.e., they express our pro or con attitudes towards their objects. Though others made similar suggestions. Stevenson was the first to give an extended and developed treatment of this position. In his book, *Ethics and Language* (1944), as well as in articles published previous to it, he outlined his particular "emotive theory of ethics."[10] What more did calling something "good" do than simply point to some property that a thing possessed? According to Stevenson, calling something good did two things. First, it expressed our attitudes toward that thing, be they positive or negative. Secondly, it attempted to exert a motive force or create an influence on others. Thus "This is good" could be translated into some such locution as "I approve of this . . . do so also."

In developing this theory, Stevenson drew attention to a distinction between beliefs and attitudes. With regard to a certain social policy, for example, we may hold beliefs about what it is and what its consequences will be. Yet whether we are also in favor of it or opposed to it, or whether we have a positive or negative attitude toward it, is quite another thing. While differences in attitudes may rest on differences in belief, it is possible that one's attitude does not rest on this. For example, two persons who agree on what a particular policy is and what its consequences are likely to be, still may disagree on whether or not it should be adopted. According to Stevenson, moral disagreements are just such disagreements in attitude rather than disagreements in belief. If the attitudes do rest on beliefs, they do so only accidentally. When we express our beliefs we may or may not intend to influence others to agree with us. But when we express our attitudes toward something, we do so intend. In fact, Stevenson sometimes hints, the major use of ethical judgments is to create such an influence, to move others. To summarize briefly: for Stevenson, moral terms or judgments have a dual function — they express attitudes or emotions, and they attempt to move others to have similar attitudes or emotions.

One can hardly disagree with the fact that ethical terms are dynamic. They have a motive or moving force and are not blandly and neutrally descriptive. Yet some of the implications of the emotive theory of ethics, as developed by Stevenson and others, were found to be less acceptable and more problematic. For example, according to this theory, no contradiction exists between one person's statement that a particular war is wrong and another's that it is right. Neither person could be mistaken or incorrect in their judgment. In no sense could the war be said to be really good or bad, justified or unjustified. Moreover, this theory seemed to make moral judgments and moral debate basically irrational, since one need not have reasons for approval or disapproval, let alone good reasons. Thirdly, some philosophers found the identification of emotion and attitude too simplistic. Whether or not a person can have feelings of abhorence or disgust at some action, he may still disapprove of it or have a negative attitude toward it. Moreover, he may seek to change someone's attitude quite apart from being interested in or being able to arouse the other's feelings.[11]

Emotivism, it might be argued, is unacceptable in that it makes moral judgment and moral argument into an exercise of power rather than of reason. However, if one is to avoid the naturalistic fallacy and the type of intuitionism espoused by Moore, what remains as a basis for an interpretation of moral judgment? The British moral philosopher Richard Hare's writings on this problem provided a position that was also discussed in the United States. In his work *Freedom and Reason* Hare suggested that emotivism is mistaken in claiming that reasons are not necessary for moral judgment.[12] If a person calls something good, there is something about that object of which he approves and on which he bases his judgment. In fact his approval is so tied to those characteristics, which are his reasons for moral judgment, that in order to be rational he must also call similar things good or recommend anything else like it in those respects. According to this view, his moral judgment is rational. However, it is also free in the sense that he is not required by anything inherent in moral judging to use these reasons rather than others, or these characteristics rather than different ones, as the basis for judgment. When the naturalists had said that there must be some definite connection between certain characteristics of objects and judgments of good or bad about them, later philosophers in Britain and America hesitated to interpret the connection as a tight or necessary connection. Something of emotivism, therefore, perdured, in the sense of a belief that moral judgments are something personal or free, if not necessarily tied to or an expression of emotion. Nevertheless, there remained some inclination to accept the view that moral judgments require reasons, and these reasons must relate in some sense to certain aspects of the thing or situation judged.

THE IS-OUGHT DEBATE

The debate over the relation of moral judgments to reasons and to characteristics of the thing or action judged was sometimes referred to as the "is-ought debate." [13] What was the relation, philosophers asked, between what *is* the case and what *ought* to be the case? That the cases are distinct is manifested by the commonly held belief that while certain social problems do exist, for example, we would not always say that they ought to exist or that it is good that they do. However, philosophers also wondered whether there was not some connection between the fact that something does exist or will happen (say that by making this choice I will produce much happiness) and what ought to be done or is good to produce. Some philosophers held that the connection is a direct one, either because of an identification of certain properties like happiness with "good" (that is, what "good" is or means), or because of some teleological explanation (that is, the direction nature herself has set, or the goal towards which things naturally tend). [14] Naturalism was not entirely dead. Neonaturalisms of various sorts survived. Other philosophers, however, continued to question these types of derivation of an "ought" from an "is." Why, for example, because a nature tends in a certain direction or because we naturally desire x, y, or z, ought a nature continue to so tend or we be given what we desire? There continued to be problems with attempts to derive an "ought" from an "is."

One rather unique and provocative attempt to do so was suggested by John Searle in his article of that name. [15] Searle followed Austin (see chapter 16) in emphasizing the kind of things that we *do* by our talk. There are certain forms of talk that describe events and things and other forms that evaluate them. "You stole that letter" is descriptive, and "you ought not to have done so" is evaluative. But it is from such examples, Searle points out, that an "ought" can be derived from an "is." The fact that one belongs to a society where the institution of private property exists serves as a basis for the conclusion that one ought not to steal (all other things being equal). Searle's noted example is that of promise keeping. From the *fact* that one makes a promise (or says "I promise . . .") one can reason to the evaluative conclusion that that person *ought* to do what he promised to do. Thus one can move from a description of certain facts or events, the act of making a promise, to an evaluative conclusion.

Certain institutional facts (the institution of promise keeping or private property) do exist and entail certain obligations.

However, Searle himself admits that this "ought" may not be a "moral ought" and the obligation undertaken by promising may not be a "moral" obligation. According to Searle, the gravity of the circumstances and what is promised must be taken into account, rather than the promise itself. What Searle's argument does, then, is to show us that we need to distinguish different kinds of oughts or obligations. Moreover, it directs us to look at the fact that we exist in a society that has certain rules and that we may have some obligation to follow the rules. Nevertheless, the rules may not be good rules. There are two separate questions here. One relates to what we must do if we have certain rules, and the other questions the rules themselves.[16]

There are two important metaethical questions that are raised here: (1) What is a *moral* "ought" as distinct from other "oughts"? (2) What is the place of moral rules in the scheme of morality? Both of these questions have been much debated in recent American moral philosophy, and we will next briefly outline some of the issues involved in them.

MORAL RULES AND UNIVERSALIZABILITY

For some individuals the following of moral rules is the epitomy of morality, while others believe that reliance on rules militates against individually committed moral choice. In recent American (and other English-speaking) moral philosophy the issue of the nature and value of moral rules has surfaced, among other ways, in the form of a debate between two types of utilitarianism — act utilitarianism and rule utilitarianism.[17] In deciding what is the morally right or good thing to do, some philosophers believe that one must pay attention only to the act under consideration and its individual consequences (act utilitarianism). Whether or not a person should keep a promise depends on what the likely consequences of doing so might be. The only reason someone may attend to the so-called rule of promise keeping is for advice about what the consequences are likely to be. If it seems that one's case will be an exception to historical experience as exemplified in the rule, then one should forget the rule.

Others (rule utilitarians) believe that one ought to consider not primarily the consequences of this particular action of keeping or breaking a promise (including its influence on others), but rather what the consequences would be if that action were to become a general rule of behavior, a general practice, or a particular rule were to be adopted. As a form of utilitarianism, it advises us to consider the consequences of the practice of promise keeping or promise beaking, what would be the consequences if it were adopted as a general rule of behavior. What if everybody did that? Another version asks us to compare various rules or sets of rules and the consequences of general adoption of one or the other.

What is given as the basis for judging in terms of the general rule or practice rather than the individual act has varied. Some philosophers emphasize that it is a matter of logical consistency, of making similar judgments about similar acts. For others, it is only fair that if I cannot say that others in similar situations should break their promise, then I should not break my promise. The golden rule ("Do unto others . . .") or its negative form ("Don't do to others . . .") exemplifies a similar form of reasoning. If a person would be willing for the action to be done not by himself but by some other when he is on the receiving end of the action, then his own doing of that action might be morally permissible. All of these forms of reasoning require some form of universalizing.[18] Either a person should consider his action as one of a kind or as done by all (or all in a certain position). The requirement that we take our moral judgments as universalizable has also been discussed from another point of view. Morality, it is said, requires that we take the moral point of view, and this in turn requires that we universalize our moral judgments. Just what the particular point of view is and what it involves has also been the topic of debate in recent American moral philosophy.[19]

THE MORAL POINT OF VIEW

We all know persons who act on principle, as we say. Whether or not we agree with their particular principles or actions, we tend to respect such persons and to consider them as notable examples of acting morally. They certainly are not amoral persons, persons who do not consider morality important. On the other hand persons who seem to operate for their own self-interest alone we often regard as either amoral or immoral. But why should it be considered a sign of immorality or amorality to act for one's own interest, egoistically, or with merely practical or pragmatic goals in mind? Some would say it is because taking the moral point of view involves judging from a broader or more universal perspective than that of self-interest. For others, it is simply a matter of requiring reasons for moral judgments. People who neither have nor seem willing to give reasons for their moral judgments may not even be judging morally. While we seem willing not to require reasons (at least justifying reasons) for our likes and dislikes or for our personal taste, we do think it appropriate to require reasons for moral judgments.[20]

Others suggest that the moral point of view is taking a point of view in which one recognizes that others are like oneself and thus equal as persons. Exceptions should not be made in one's own favor over others for no good reason, especially as regards matters that are more closely related to essential human needs and interests. This latter interpretation of the moral point of view is more substantive than that that simply requires one to be consistent or say similar things about similar cases. It includes beyond this latter formal requirement some notion or concept about the nature and value of persons as persons. For example, it might emphasize that while persons differ in many ways in character and circumstances, they are alike in that they can reason, speak a language, or choose goals or ends. It is from some such basis that the notion of rights arises.

Closely related to the issue of the nature and basis of the moral point of view is the further question: Why take the moral point of view? or Why be moral? [21] The question, of course, needs interpretation. In some respects it might seem self-answering. Morality tells us what we should do, that we should be moral. One might also respond that we must first decide whether to play the moral game, so to speak. Why be concerned about morality at all? One answer posed is that if no one played by moral rules, the situation would not be a happy one. Yet the question only asks why *I* should be moral, not why everyone should be. I might want to excuse myself, and only the moral point of view requires that I do not make such excuses — a point of view I may refuse to take. Others argue that an answer might be found by considering that only human beings can take this point of view; to ignore it is to miss something unique to humans and perhaps not to be fully human, or even fully happy. Whether or not this answer is sufficient or would convince an amoralist is an open question and one that continues to puzzle moral philosophers.

NORMATIVE ISSUES IN TWENTIETH-CENTURY AMERICAN MORAL PHILOSOPHY

As noted earlier, in recent times American moral philosophers have begun to return to and perhaps be more concerned with practical or normative (as opposed to metaethical) moral issues. One central and impressive example of this trend is the debate over the nature of justice as typified and spurred on by John Rawls's *A Theory of Justice* (1971).[22] This work is first of all a theoretical treatise on the nature of distributive justice; it attempts to secure a reasoned foundation for decisions about just and unjust arrangements or distributions of goods in a society. Rawls's basic argument can be summarized briefly as follows. "The fundamental idea in the concept of justice is fairness."[23] Now fairness obtains where institutional arrangements are such that no arbitrary distinctions are made in the distribution of goods in a society. It might be fair that Mary Jones possesses more wealth than John Smith (or rather that those societal institutions that allow this imbalance may be fair), but only if there is some nonarbitrary reason for the difference.

Rawls approaches the question by considering the manner in which institutions in a society (political, educational, etc.) function so as to contribute to long-range expectations of people in that society for positions and goods that they might possess. In evaluating these institutions (the expectations they set up and the arrangements of goods they allow), Rawls believes that certain principles must be used. These principles are derived in the following way.[24] Imagine persons who were to form a society coming together to plan for that society (call them the people in the "original position" as to the forming of that society, the POPS). These POPS join together in order to better secure the goods that they want. They are self-interested. Moreover, they are rational in the sense that they are able to choose the best means to reach their ends, and they are guided by their reason, rather than by, say, envy or jealousy. In order to guarantee that they will be fair and not seek their own interest above that of others, i.e., that they will be neutral and objective, we must also imagine that they do not know what particular talents they have or what socio-economic position they occupy in this society. Rawls calls this the "veil of ignorance." The POPS may be at the top, bottom, or middle. Thus they will be more inclined to watch out for all the positions equally.

Rawls believes that people so situated would agree that the following two principles should be used in evaluating the justness of their social institutions.

> First: each person is to have an equal right to the most extensive basic liberty compatible with a similar liberty for others.
> Second: social and economic inequalities are to be arranged so that they are both a) reasonably expected to be to everyone's advantage, and b) attached to positions and offices open to all.[25]

Thus Rawls believes that fairness entails equality where political liberties such as free speech, etc., are concerned. However, as regards other economically based goods, he believes that some inequality would be fair, provided the two conditions were met. There must be an equal opportunity provision whereby every person with a similar interest and talent would have equal access to the positions to which these goods are attached. Equal access would require that inequalities due to other factors such as poor beginnings, training, etc., must be eliminated. According to the other half of the second principle, inequalities would be allowed only if they are to the advantage of everyone, or, as he later adds, to the advantage in particular of those on the bottom of the socio-economic ladder, the least advantaged.

That persons in the initial fair situation described, the POPS, might allow this inequality with these provisions attached can be seen by considering the fact that they are self-interested, rational, and to a certain extent neutral. They would want to increase their goods, even if by so doing others had more or advanced more than they themselves. This choice is a risk-aversive type and differs from one in which such persons would be willing to risk getting less for the chance to "win big." Moreover, the theory seems to imply that it would be just for great inequalities to exist as long as those less well off are in fact just slightly better off because of the inequality. Criticisms of Rawls's theory have been made on these points as well as on many others.[26] Nevertheless, he sets forth a theory that differs dramatically from some utilitarian theories that in principle allow disadvantages to some if they are outweighed by advantages to others. Rawls's theory is also opposed to the notion that liberty may be restrained for the sake of greater goods to the community, for the first principle takes precedence over the second. Exception is made for stituations in which the economic conditions of a society are so bad that political freedom is thereby rendered meaningless. (If someone is starving, he is not much interested in voting.) But freedom may be curtailed only temporarily and then only for the sake of restoring freedom when it again becomes meaningful.

We cannot here follow the debates over the adequacy of Rawls's theory of justice, but the reader may do so from suggestions in the bibliography. While this work remains quite theoretical, there are applications to particular issues such as civil disobedience. Many other serious theoretical treatises are being produced by American moral philosophers which bridge the gap between the theoretical and the practical. We include here a selection from Ruth Macklin as a fine example of the manner in which American moral philosophers are now applying the results of theoretical analysis (of justice and rights in this case) to concrete ethical issues.

American moral philosophy in the second half of the twentieth century will most probably continue to develop both of its two present currents — one a theoretical discussion of issues surrounding the nature and basis of morality and the meaning of moral terms and propositions, and the other directed to applications of moral theory to particular practical moral issues, medical and other societal and personal moral problems. One of the difficulties in dealing philosophically with the latter type of issue is that adequate analysis involves not only philosophical and analytical expertise but also thorough acquaintance with the circumstances of the practice under consideration. For this reason we may see more cooperation between philosophers and social scientists and practitioners or more philosophers with dual backgrounds and expertise. Perhaps it is also in this area that the so-called American penchant for the practical and concrete will again have its day in philosophy.

Notes

[1] See, for example, *Philosophy and Public Affairs, Philosophy and Medicine, The Hastings Center Report, Social Theory and Practice,* and *Ethics.*

[2] See the selected bibliography on these topics.

[3] Ralph Barton Perry, *Realms of Value: A Critique of Human Civilization* (Cambridge: Harvard University Press, 1954), chap. 5.

[4] Ralph Barton Perry, *The Moral Economy* (New York: Charles Scribner's, 1909), p. 54.

[5] See the references to the moral philosophy writings of John Dewey in the bibliography. Also refer back to chapter 8. The selections from John Dewey included in this chapter are from *The Quest for Certainty* and *Reconstruction in Philosophy.*

[6] John Dewey, "Reconstruction in Moral Conceptions," chap. 7, in *Reconstruction in Philosophy,* (New York: Henry Holt, 1920).

[7] Among the works on education and democracy are: *Democracy and Education, Individualism, Old and New, Philosophy and Civilization, Liberalism and Social Action, Freedom and Culture,* and *The Public and Its Problems.*

[8] G. E. Moore, *Principia Ethica* (Cambridge: Cambridge University Press, 1903).

[9] See chapter 12.

[10] See the selection for Stevenson included in this chapter, "The Emotive Meaning of Ethical Terms," *Mind,* 1938.

[11] Many of these criticisms as well as an explanation of emotivist ethics can be found in J. O. Urmson, *The Emotive Theory of Ethics* (New York: Oxford University Press, 1968).

[12] Richard Hare, *Freedom and Reason* (New York: Oxford University Press, 1963); idem, *The Language of Morals* (New York: Oxford University Press, 1952).

[13] For a discussion of the is-ought debate see W. D. Hudson, *Modern Moral Philosophy* (Garden City, N.Y.: Doubleday, 1970), pp. 249ff.

[14] On ethical naturalism as it occurs in recent moral philosophy, see Hudson *Modern Moral Philosophy,* pp. 66ff., 294ff.

[15] John Searle, "How to Derive 'Ought' from 'Is'," *Philosophical Review* 73 (1964): pp. 43ff. Reprinted with commentaries in *Theories of Ethics,* ed. P. Foot (New York: Oxford University Press, 1967), pp. 101–14.

[16] See John Rawls, "Two Concepts of Rules," *Philosophical Review* 64 (January 1955).

[17] For explanation of the act and rule utilitarian positions see the books listed in the bibliography for this chapter.

[18] See the bibliographical items on universalizability.

[19] See the bibliographical items on the moral point of view.

[20] See F. Snare, "Wants and Reasons," *Personalist,* no. 53 (August 1972): pp. 395–407.

[21] See Kai Nielsen, "Why Should I Be Moral? " *Methodos* 15, nos. 59–60 (1963): pp. 275–306.

[22] John Rawls, "Justice as Fairness," *Philosophical Review* 67 (1958): pp. 164–75. Selections included in this chapter. This essay was reworked and published as *Theory of Justice.*

[23] Rawls, "Justice as Fairness," p. 164.

[24] It should be noted that there are some differences between the outline of his theory in the 1958 article and his published book. Among the differences is his introduction of the "veil of ignorance" and the "people in the original position." The latter form is more similar to various social-contract theories in which one is called upon to imagine some original (however imaginary) situation.

[25] John Rawls, *A Theory of Justice,* (Cambridge: Harvard University Press, 1971), p. 60.

[26] In particular see Robert Nozick, *Anarchy, State, and Utopia* (Basic Books, 1974): Brian Barry, *The Liberal Theory of Justice: A Critical Examination of the Principal Doctrines in "A Theory of Justice" by John Rawls* (Oxford: Oxford University Press, 1973).

JOHN DEWEY

THE CONSTRUCTION OF THE GOOD*

A psychological theory of desire and liking is supposed to cover the whole ground of the theory of values; in it, immediate feeling is the counterpart of immediate sensation.

I shall not object to this empirical theory as far as it connects the theory of values with concrete experiences of desire and satisfaction. The idea that there is such a connection is the only way known to me by which the pallid remoteness of the rationalistic theory, and the only too glaring presence of the institutional theory of transcendental values can be escaped. The objection is that the theory in question holds down value to objects *antecedently* enjoyed, apart from reference to the method by which they come into existence; it takes enjoyments which are casual because unregulated by intelligent operations to be values in and of themselves. Operational thinking needs to be applied to the judgment of values just as it has now finally been applied in conceptions of physical objects. Experimental empiricism in the field of ideas of good and bad is demanded to meet the conditions of the present situation.

The scientific revolution came about when material of direct and uncontrolled experience was taken as problematic; as supplying material

---

* John Dewey, "The Construction of the Good," in *The Quest for Certainty* (New York: G. P. Putnam's, 1929), pp. 258–63. Reprinted by permission of G. P. Putnam's Sons. Copyright 1929 by John Dewey; renewed © 1957.

to be transformed by reflective operations into known objects. The contrast between experienced and known objects was found to be a temporal one; namely, one between empirical subject-matters which were had or "given" prior to the acts of experimental variation and redisposition and those which succeeded these acts and issued from them. The notion of an act whether of sense or thought which supplied a valid measure of thought in immediate knowledge was discredited. Consequences of operations became the important thing. The suggestion almost imperatively follows that escape from the defects of transcendental absolutism is not to be had by setting up as values enjoyments that happen anyhow, but in defining value by enjoyments which are the consequences of intelligent action. Without the intervention of thought, enjoyments are not values but problematic goods, becoming values when they re-issue in a changed form from intelligent behavior. The fundamental trouble with the current empirical theory of values is that it merely formulates and justifies the socially prevailing habit of regarding enjoyments as they are actually experienced as values in and of themselves. It completely side-steps the question of regulation of these enjoyments. This issue involves nothing less than the problem of the directed reconstruction of economic, political and religious institutions.

There was seemingly a paradox involved in the notion that if we turned our backs upon the immediately perceived qualities of things, we should be enabled to form valid conceptions of objects, and that these conceptions could be used to bring about a more secure and more significant experience of them. But the method terminated in disclosing the connections or interactions upon which perceived objects, viewed as events, depend. Formal analogy suggests that we regard our direct and original experience of things liked and enjoyed as only *possibilities* of values to be achieved; that enjoyment becomes a value when we discover the relations upon which its presence depends. Such a causal and operational definition gives only a conception of a value, not a value itself. But the utilization of the conception in action results in an object having secure and significant value.

The formal statement may be given concrete content by pointing to the difference between the enjoyed and the enjoyable, the desired and the desirable, the satis*fying* and the satis*factory*. To say that something is enjoyed is to make a statement about a fact, something already in existence; it is not to judge the value of that fact. There is no difference between such a proposition and one which says that something is sweet or sour, red or black. It is just correct or incorrect and that is the end of the matter. But to call an object a value is to assert that it satisfies or fulfills certain conditions. Function and status in meeting conditions is a different matter from bare existence. The fact that something is desired only raises the *question* of its desirability; it does not settle it. Only a child in the degree of his immaturity thinks to settle the question of desirability by reiterated proclamation: "I want it, I want it, I want it." What is objected to in the current empirical theory of values is not connection of them with desire and enjoyment but failure to distinguish between enjoyments of radically different sorts. There are many common expressions in which the difference of the two kinds is clearly recognized. Take for example the difference between the ideas of "satisfying" and "satisfactory." To say that something satisfies is to report something as an isolated finality. To assert that it is satis*factory* is to define it in its connections and interactions. The fact that it pleases or is immediately congenial poses a problem to judgment. How shall the satisfaction be rated? Is it a value or is it not? Is it something to be prized and cherished, *to be* enjoyed? Not stern moralists alone but everyday experience informs us that finding satisfaction in a thing may be a warning, a summons to be on the lookout for consequences. To declare something satis*factory* is to assert that it meets specifiable conditions. It is, in effect, a judgment that the thing "will do." It involves a prediction; it contemplates a future in which the thing will continue to serve; it *will* do. It asserts a consequence the thing will actively institute; it will *do*. That it is satisfying is the content of a proposition of fact; that it is satisfactory is a judgment, an estimate, an appraisal. It denotes an attitude *to be* taken, that of striving to perpetuate and to make secure.

It is worth notice that besides the instances given, there are many other recognitions in ordinary speech of the distinction. The endings "able," "worthy" and "ful" are cases in point. Noted and notable, noteworthy; remarked and remarkable; advised and advisable; wondered at and wonderful; pleasing and beautiful; loved and lovable; blamed and blameable, blameworthy; objected to and objectionable; esteemed and estimable; admired and admirable; shamed and shameful; honored and honorable; approved and approvable, worthy of approbation, etc. The multiplication of words adds nothing to the force of the distinction. But it aids in conveying a sense of the fundamental character of the distinction; of the difference between mere report of an already existent fact and judgment as to the importance and need of bringing a fact into existence; or, if it is already there, of sustaining it in existence. The latter is a genuine practical judgment, and marks the only type of judgment that has to do with the direction of action. Whether or no we reserve the term "value" for the latter, (as seems to me proper) is a minor matter; that the distinction be acknowledged as the key to understanding the relation of values to the direction of conduct is the important thing.

This element of direction by an idea of value applies to science as well as anywhere else. For in every scientific undertaking, there is passed a constant succession of estimates; such as "it is worth treating these facts as data or evidence; it is advisable to try this experiment; to make that observation; to entertain such and such a hypothesis; to perform this calculation," etc.

The word "taste" has perhaps got too completely associated with arbitrary liking to express the nature of judgments of value. But if the word be used in the sense of an appreciation at once cultivated and active, one may say that the formation of taste is the chief matter wherever values enter in, whether intellectual, esthetic or moral. Relatively immediate judgments, which we call tact or to which we give the name of intuition, do not precede reflective inquiry, but are the funded products of much thoughtful experience. Expertness of taste is at once the result and the reward of constant exercise of thinking. Instead of there being no disputing about tastes, they are the one thing worth disputing about, if by "dispute" is signified discussion involving reflective inquiry. Taste, if we use the word in its best sense, is the outcome of experience brought cumulatively to bear on the intelligent appreciation of the real worth of likings and enjoyments. There is nothing in which a person so completely reveals himself as in the things which he judges enjoyable and desirable. Such judgments are the sole alternative to the domination of belief by impulse, chance, blind habit and self-interest. The formation of a cultivated and effectively operative good judgment or taste with respect to what is esthetically admirable, intellectually acceptable and morally approvable is the supreme task set to human beings by the incidents of experience.

Propositions about what is or has been liked are of instrumental value in reaching judgments of value, in as far as the conditions and consequences of the thing liked are thought about. In themselves they make no claims; they put forth no demand upon subsequent attitudes and acts; they profess no authority to direct. If one likes a thing he likes it; that *is* a point about which there can be no dispute:—although it is not so easy to state just *what* is liked as is frequently assumed. A judgment about what is to *be* desired and enjoyed is, on the other hand, a claim on future action; it possesses *de jure* and not merely *de facto* quality. It is a matter of frequent experience that likings and enjoyments are of all kinds, and that many are such as reflective judgments condemn. By way of self-justification and "rationalization," an enjoyment creates a tendency to assert that the thing enjoyed is a value. This assertion of validity adds authority to the fact. It is a decision that the object has a right to exist and hence a claim upon action to further its existence.

The analogy between the status of the theory of values and the theory of ideas about natural objects before the rise of experimental inquiry may be carried further. The sensationalistic theory of the origin and test of thought evoked, by way of reaction, the transcendental theory of *a priori* ideas. For it failed utterly to account for objective connection, order and regularity in objects observed. Similarly, any doctrine that identifies the mere fact of being liked with the value of the object liked so fails to give direction to conduct when direction is needed that it automatically calls forth the assertion that there are values eternally in Being that are the standards of all judgments and the obligatory ends of all action. Without the introduction of operational thinking, we oscillate between a theory that, in order to save the objectivity of judgments of values, isolates them from experience and nature, and a theory that, in order to save their concrete and human significance, reduces them to mere statements about our own feelings.

CHARLES STEVENSON

THE EMOTIVE MEANING
OF ETHICAL TERMS*

Traditional interest theories hold that ethical statements are *descriptive* of the existing state of interests—that they simply *give information* about interests. (More accurately, ethical judgments are said to describe what the state of interests is, was, or will be, or to indicate what the state of interests *would* be under specified circumstances.) It is this emphasis on description, on information, which leads to their incomplete relevance. Doubtless there is always *some* element of description in ethical judgments, but this is by no means all. Their major use is not to indicate facts, but to *create an influence.* Instead of merely describing people's interests, they *change* or *intensify* them. They *recommend* an interest in an object, rather than state that the interest already exists.†

For instance: When you tell a man that he oughtn't to steal, your object isn't merely to let him know that people disapprove of stealing. You are attempting, rather, to get *him* to disapprove of it. Your ethical judgment has a quasi-imperative force which, operating through suggestion, and intensified by your tone of voice, readily permits you to begin to *influence,* to *modify,* his interests. If in the end you do not succeed in

---

* Charles Stevenson, "The Emotive Meaning of Ethical Terms," *Mind* 46 (1937): pp. 18–20, 24–30. Reprinted by permission of the editors of *Mind.*
† See G. E. Moore's *Principia Ethica,* chap. 1. I am simply trying to preserve the spirit of Moore's objection, and not the exact form of it.

getting *him* to disapprove of stealing, you will feel that you've failed to convince him that stealing is wrong. You will continue to feel this, even though he fully acknowledges that you disapprove of it, and that almost everyone else does. When you point out to him the consequences of his actions—consequences which you suspect he already disapproves of— these *reasons* which support your ethical judgment are simply a means of facilitating your influence. If you think you can change his interests by making vivid to him how others will disapprove of him, you will do so; otherwise not. So the consideration about other people's interest is just an additional means you may employ, in order to move him, and is not a part of the ethical judgment itself. Your ethical judgment doesn't merely describe interests to him, it directs his very interests. The difference between the traditional interest theories and my view is like the difference between describing a desert and irrigating it.

Another example: A munition maker declares that war is a good thing. If he merely meant that he approved of it, he would not have to insist so strongly, nor grow so excited in his argument. People would be quite easily convinced that he approved of it. If he merely meant that most people approved of war, or that most people would approve of it if they knew the consequences, he would have to yield his point if it were proved that this wasn't so. But he wouldn't do this, nor does consistency require it. He is not *describing* the state of people's approval; he is trying to *change* it by his influence. If he found that few people approved of war, he might insist all the more strongly that it was good, for there would be more changing to be done.

This example illustrates how "good" may be used for what most of us would call bad purposes. Such cases are as pertinent as any others. I am not indicating the *good* way of using "good." I am not influencing people, but am describing the way this influence sometimes goes on. If the reader wishes to say that the munition maker's influence is bad— that is, if the reader wishes to awaken people's disapproval of the man, and to make him disapprove of his own actions—I should at another time be willing to join in this undertaking. But this is not the present concern. I am not using ethical terms, but am indicating how they *are* used. The munition maker, in his use of "good," illustrates the persuasive character of the word just as well as does the unselfish man who, eager to encourage in each of us a desire for the happiness of all, contends that the supreme good is peace.

Thus ethical terms are *instruments* used in the complicated interplay and readjustment of human interests. This can be seen plainly from more general observations. People from widely separated communities have different moral attitudes. Why? To a great extent because they have been subject to different social influences. Now clearly this influence doesn't operate through sticks and stones alone; words play a great part. People praise one another, to encourage certain inclinations, and blame one another, to discourage others. Those of forceful personalities issue commands which weaker people, for complicated instinctive reasons, find it difficult to disobey, quite apart from fears of consequences. Further influence is brought to bear by writers and orators. Thus social influence is exerted, to an enormous extent, by means that have nothing to do with physical force or material reward. The ethical terms facilitate such influence. Being suited for use in *suggestion,* they are a means by which men's attitudes may be led this way or that. The reason, then, that we find a greater similarity in the moral attitudes of one community than in those of different communities is largely this: ethical judgments propagate themselves. One man says "This is good"; this may influence the approval of another person, who then makes the same ethical judgment, which in turn influences another person, and so on. In the end, by a process of mutual influence, people take up more or less the same attitudes. Between people of widely separated communities, of course, the influence is less strong; hence different communities have different attitudes.

Let us now apply these remarks in defining "good." This word may be used morally or non-morally. I shall deal with the non-moral usage almost entirely, but only because it is simpler. The main points of the analysis will apply equally well to either usage.

As a preliminary definition, let us take an inaccurate approximation. It may be more misleading than helpful, but will do to begin with. Roughly, then, the sentence "X is good" means *We like X.* ("We" includes the hearer or hearers.)

At first glance this definition sounds absurd. If used, we should expect to find the following sort of conversation: A. "This is good." B. "But I *don't* like it. What led you to believe that I did? " The unnaturalness of B's reply, judged by ordinary word-usage, would seem to cast doubt on the relevance of my definition.

B's unnaturalness, however, lies simply in this: he is assuming that "We like it" (as would occur implicitly in the use of "good") is being used descriptively. This won't do. When "We like it" is to take the pace of "This is good," the former sentence must be used not purely descriptively, by dynamically. More specifically, it must be used to promote a very subtle (and for the non-moral sense in question, a very easily resisted) kind of *suggestion.* To the extent that "we" refers to the hearer, it must have the dynamic use, essential to suggestion, of leading the hearer to *make* true what is said, rather than merely to believe it. And to the extent that "we" refers to the speaker, the sentence must have not only the descriptive use of indicating belief about the speaker's interest, but the quasi-interjectory, dynamic function of giving direct expression to the interest. (This immediate expression of feelings assists in the process of suggestion. It is difficult to disapprove in the face of another's enthusiasm.)

For an example of a case where "We like this" is used in the dynamic way that "This is good" is used, consider the case of a mother who says to her several children, "One thing is certain, *we all like to be neat.*" If she really believed this, she wouldn't bother to say so. But she is not using the words descriptively. She is *encouraging* the children to like neatness. By telling them that they like neatness, she will lead them to *make* her statement true, so to speak. If, instead of saying "We all like to be neat" in this way, she had said "It's a good thing to be neat," the effect would have been approximately the same.

But these remarks are still misleading. Even when "We like it" is used for suggestion, it isn't quite like "This is good." The latter is more subtle. With such a sentence as "This is a good book," for example, it would be practically impossible to use instead "We like this book." When the latter is used, it must be accompanied by so exaggerated an intonation, to prevent its becoming confused with a descriptive statement, that the force of suggestion becomes stronger, and ludicrously more overt, than when "good" is used.

The definition is inadequate, further, in that the definiens has been restricted to dynamic usage. Having said that dynamic usage was different from meaning, I should not have to mention it in giving the *meaning* of "good."

It is in connection with this last point that we must return to emotive meaning. The word "good" has a pleasing emotive meaning which fits it especially for the dynamic use of suggesting favourable interest. But the sentence "We like it" has no such emotive meaning. Hence my definition has neglected emotive meaning entirely. Now to neglect emotive meaning is likely to lead to endless confusions, as we shall presently see; so I have sought to make up for the inadequacy of the definition by letting the restriction about dynamic usage take the place of emotive meaning. What I should do, of course, is to find a definiens whose emotive meaning, like that of "good," simply does *lead* to dynamic usage.

Why didn't I do this? I answer that it isn't possible, if the definition is to afford us increased clarity. No two words, in the first place, have quite the same emotive meaning. The most we can hope for is a rough approximation. But if we seek for such an approximation for "good," we shall find nothing more than synonyms, such as "desirable" or "valuable"; and these are profitless because they do not clear up the connection between "good" and favourable interest. If we reject such synonyms, in favour of non-ethical terms, we shall be highly misleading. For instance: "This is good" has something like the meaning of "I *do* like this; do so as well." But this is certainly not accurate. For the imperative makes an appeal to the conscious efforts of the hearer. Of course he can't like something just by trying. He must be led to like it through suggestion. Hence an ethical sentence differs from an imperative in that it enables one to make changes in a much more subtle, less fully conscious way.

Note that the ethical sentence centres the hearer's attention not on his interests, but on the object of interest, and thereby facilitates suggestion. Because of its subtlety, moreover, an ethical sentence readily permits counter-suggestion, and leads to the give and take situation which is so characteristic of arguments about values.

Strictly speaking, then, it is impossible to define "good" in terms of favourable interest if emotive meaning is not to be distorted. Yet it is possible to say that "This is good" is *about* the favourable interest of the speaker and the hearer or hearers, and that it has a pleasing emotive meaning which fits the words for use in suggestion. This is a rough description of meaning, not a definition. But it serves the same clarifying function that a definition ordinarily does; and that, after all, is enough.

A word must be added about the moral use of "good." This differs from the above in that it is about a different kind of interest. Instead of being about what the hearer and speaker *like,* it is about a stronger sort of approval. When a person *likes* something, he is pleased when it prospers, and disappointed when it doesn't. When a person *morally approves* of something, he experiences a rich feeling of security when it prospers, and is indignant, or "shocked" when it doesn't. These are rough and inaccurate examples of the many factors which one would have to mention in distinguishing the two kinds of interest. In the moral usage, as well as in the non-moral, "good" has an emotive meaning which adapts it to suggestion.

And now, are these considerations of any importance? Why do I stress emotive meanings in this fashion? Does the omission of them really lead people into errors? I think, indeed, that the errors resulting from such omissions are enormous. In order to see this, however, we must return to the restrictions, mentioned in section I, with which the "vital" sense of "good" has been expected to comply.

V

The first restriction, it will be remembered, had to do with disagreement. Now there is clearly some sense in which people disagree on ethical points; but we must not rashly assume that all disagreement is modelled after the sort that occurs in the natural sciences. We must distinguish between "disagreement in belief" (typical of the sciences) and "disagreement in interest." Disagreement in belief occurs when A believes *p* and B disbelieves it. Disagreement in interest occurs when A has a favourable interest in X, when B has an unfavourable one in it, and when neither is content to let the other's interest remain unchanged.

Let me give an example of disagreement in interest. A. "Let's go to a cinema to-night." B. "I don't want to do that. Let's go to the symphony." A continues to insist on the cinema; B on the symphony. This is disagreement in a perfectly conventional sense. They can't agree on where they want to go, and each is trying to redirect the other's interest. (Note that imperatives are used in the example.)

It is disagreement in *interest* which takes place in ethics. When C says "This is good," and D says "No, it's bad," we have a case of suggestion and counter-suggestion. Each man is trying to redirect the other's interest. There obviously need be no domineering, since each may be willing to give ear to the other's influence; but each is trying to move the other none the less. It is in this sense that they disagree. Those who argue that certain interest theories make no provision for disagreement have been misled, I believe, simply because the traditional theories, in leaving out emotive meaning, give the impression that ethical judgments are used descriptively only; and of course when judgments are used purely descriptively, the only disagreement that can arise is disagreement *in belief.* Such disagreement may be disagreement in belief *about* interests; but this is not the same as disagreement *in* interest. My definition doesn't provide for disagreement in belief about interests, any more than does Hobbes's; but that is no matter, for there is no reason to believe, at least on common-sense grounds, that this kind of disagreement exists. There is only disagreement *in* interest. (We shall see in a moment that disagreement in interest does not remove ethics from sober argument—that this kind of disagreement may often be resolved through empirical means.)

The second restriction, about "magnetism," or the connection between goodness and actions, requires only a word. This rules out *only* those interest theories which do *not* include the interest of the speaker, in defining "good." My account does include the speaker's interest; hence is immune.

The third restriction, about the empirical method, may be met in a way that springs naturally from the above account of disagreement. Let us put the question in this way: When two people disagree over an ethical matter, can they completely resolve the disagreement through empirical considerations, assuming that each applies the empirical method exhaustively, consistently, and without error?

I answer that sometimes they can, and sometimes they cannot; and that at any rate, even when they can, the relation between empirical knowledge and ethical judgments is quite different from the one which traditional interest theories seem to imply.

This can best be seen from an analogy. Let's return to the example where A and B couldn't agree on a cinema or a symphony. The example differed from an ethical argument in that imperatives were used, rather than ethical judgments; but was analogous to the extent that each person was endeavouring to modify the other's interest. Now how would these people argue the case, assuming that they were too intelligent just to shout at one another?

Clearly, they would give "reasons" to support their imperatives. A might say, "But you know, Garbo is at the Bijou." His hope is that B, who admires Garbo, will acquire a desire to go to the cinema when he knows what play will be there. B may counter, "But Toscanini is guest conductor to-night, in an all-Beethoven programme." And so on. Each supports his imperative ("*Let's* do so and so") by reasons which may be empirically established.

To generalize from this: Disagreement in interest may be rooted in disagreement in belief. That is to say, people who disagree in interest would often cease to do so if they knew the precise nature and consequences of the object of their interest. To this extent disagreement in interest may be resolved by securing agreement in belief, which in turn may be secured empirically.

This generalization holds for ethics. If A and B, instead of using imperatives, had said, respectively, "It would be *better* to go to the cinema," and "It would be better to go to the symphony," the reasons which they would advance would be roughly the same. They would each give a more thorough account of the object of interest, with the purpose of completing the redirection of interest which was begun by the suggestive force of the ethical sentence. On the whole, of course, the suggestive force of the ethical statement merely exerts enough pressure to start such trains of reasons, since the reasons are much more essential in resolving disagreement in interest than the persuasive effect of the ethical judgment itself.

Thus the empirical method is relevant to ethics simply because our knowledge of the world is a determining factor to our interests. But note that empirical facts are not inductive grounds from which the ethical judgment problematically follows. (This is what traditional interest theories imply.) If someone said "Close the door," and added the reason "We'll catch cold," the latter would scarcely be called an inductive ground of the former. Now imperatives are related to the reasons which support them in the same way that ethical judgments are related to reasons.

Is the empirical method *sufficient* for attaining ethical agreement? Clearly no. For empirical knowledge resolves disagreement in interest only to the extent that such disagreement is rooted in disagreement in belief. Not all disagreement in interest is of this sort. For instance: A is of a sympathetic nature, and B isn't. They are arguing about whether a public dole would be good. Suppose that they discovered all the consequences of the dole. Isn't it possible, even so, that A will say that it's good, and B that it's bad? The disagreement in interest may arise not from limited factual knowledge, but simply from A's sympathy and B's coldness. Or again, suppose, in the above argument, that A was poor and unemployed, and that B was rich. Here again the disagreement might not be due to different factual knowledge. It would be due to the different social positions of the men, together with their predominant self-interest.

When ethical disagreement is not rooted in disagreement in belief, is there *any* method by which it may be settled? If one means by "method" a *rational* method, then there is no method. But in any case there is a "way." Let's consider the above example, again, where disagreement was due to A's sympathy and B's coldness. Must they end by saying, "Well, it's just a matter of our having different temperaments" ? Not necessarily. A, for instance, may try to *change* the temperament of his opponent. He may pour out his enthusiasms in such a moving way—present the sufferings of the poor with such appeal—that he will lead his opponent to see life through different eyes. He may build up, by the contagion of his feelings, an influence which will modify B's temperament, and create in him a sympathy for the poor which didn't previously exist. This is often the only way to obtain ethical agreement, if there is any way at all. It is persuasive, not empirical or rational; but that is no reason for neglecting it. There is no reason to scorn it, either, for it is only by such means that our personalities are able to grow, through our contact with others.

The point I wish to stress, however, is simply that the empirical method is instrumental to ethical agreement only to the extent that disagreement in interest is rooted in disagreement in belief. There is little reason to believe that all disagreement is of this sort. Hence the empirical method is not sufficient for ethics. In any case, ethics is not psychology, since psychology doesn't endeavour to *direct* our interests; it discovers facts about the ways in which interests are or can be directed, but that's quite another matter.

To summarize this section: my analysis of ethical judgments meets the three requirements for the "vital" sense of "good" that were mentioned in section I. The traditional interest theories fail to meet these requirements simply because they neglect emotive meaning. This neglect leads them to neglect dynamic usage, and the sort of disagreement that results from such usage, together with the method of resolving the disagreement. I may add that my analysis answers Moore's objection about the open question. Whatever scientifically knowable properties a thing may have, it *is* always open to question whether a thing having these (enumerated) qualities is good. For to ask whether it is good is to ask for *influence*. And whatever I may know about an object, I can still ask, quite pertinently, to be influenced with regard to my interest in it.

KURT BAIER

THE SUPREMACY OF MORAL REASONS*

Are moral reasons really superior to reasons of self-interest as we all believe? Do we really have reason on our side when we follow moral reasons against self-interest? What reasons could there be for being moral? Can we really give an answer to "Why should we be moral? " It is obvious that all these questions come to the same thing. When we ask, "Should we be moral? " or "Why should we be moral? " or "Are moral reasons superior to all others? " we ask to be shown the reason for being moral. What is this reason?

Let us begin with a state of affairs in which reasons of self-interest are supreme. In such a state everyone keeps his impulses and inclinations in check when and only when they would lead him into behavior detrimental in his own interest. Everyone who follows reason will discipline himself to rise early, to do his exercises, to refrain from excessive drinking and smoking, to keep good company, to marry the right sort of girl, to work and study hard in order to get on, and so on. However, it will often happen that people's interests conflict. In such a case, they will have to resort to ruses or force to get their own way. As this becomes known, men will become suspicious, for they will regard one another as scheming

* Kurt Baier, "The Supremacy of Moral Reasons," in *The Moral Point of View: A Rational Basis of Ethics* (Ithaca, N.Y.: Cornell University Press, 1958), pp. 308–15. Copyright 1958 by Cornell University. Used by permission of the Cornell University Press and the author.

competitors for the good things in life. The universal supremacy of the
rules of self-interest must lead to what Hobbes called the state of nature.
At the same time, it will be clear to everyone that universal obedience
to certain rules overriding self-interest would produce a state of affairs
which serves everyone's interest much better than his unaided pursuit of
it in a state where everyone does the same. Moral rules are universal
rules designed to override those of self-interest when following the latter
is harmful to others. "Thou shalt not kill," "Thou shalt not lie," "Thou
shalt not steal" are rules which forbid the inflicting of harm on someone
else even when this might be in one's interest.

The very *raison d'être* of a morality is to yield reasons which overrule
the reasons of self-interest in those cases when everyone's following self-
interest would be harmful to everyone. Hence moral reasons are superior
to all others.

"But what does this mean? " it might be objected. "If it merely means
that we do so regard them, then you are of course right, but your contention
is useless, a mere point of usage. And how could it mean any more? If
it means that we not only do so regard them, but *ought* so to regard
them, then there must be *reasons* for saying this. But there could not be
any reasons for it. If you offer reasons of self-interest, you are arguing in
a circle. Moreover, it cannot be true that it is always in my interest to
treat moral reasons as superior to reasons of self-interest. If it were, self-
interest and morality could never conflict, but they notoriously do. It is
equally circular to argue that there are moral reasons for saying that one
ought to treat moral reasons as superior to reasons of self-interest. And
what other reasons are there? "

The answer is that we are now looking at the world from the point
of view of *anyone*. We are not examining particular alternative courses
of action before this or that person; we are examining two alternative
worlds, one in which moral reasons are always treated by everyone as
superior to reasons of self-interest and one in which the reverse is the
practice. And we can see that the first world is the better world, because
we can see that the second world would be the sort which Hobbes describes
as the state of nature.

This shows that I ought to be moral, for when I ask the question
"What ought I to do? " I am asking, "Which is the course of action
supported by the best reasons? " But since it has just been shown that
moral reasons are superior to reasons of self-interest, I have been given
a reason for being moral, for following moral reasons rather than any
other, namely, they are better reasons than any other.

But is this always so? Do we have a reason for being moral whatever
the conditions we find ourselves in? Could there not be situations in
which it is not true that we have reasons for being moral, that, on the
contrary, we have reasons for ignoring the demands of morality? Is not

Hobbes right in saying that in a state of nature the laws of nature, that is, the rules of morality, bind only *in foro interno?*

Hobbes argues as follows.

(i) To live in a state of nature is to live outside society. It is to live in conditions in which there are no common ways of life and, therefore, no reliable expectations about other people's behavior other than that they will follow their inclination or their interest.

(ii) In such a state reason will be the enemy of co-operation and mutual trust. For it is too risky to hope that other people will refrain from protecting their own interests by the preventive elimination of probable or even possible dangers to them. Hence reason will counsel everyone to avoid these risks by preventive action. But this leads to war.

(iii) It is obvious that everyone's following self-interest leads to a state of affairs which is desirable from no one's point of view. It is, on the contrary, desirable that everybody should follow rules overriding self-interest whenever that is to the detriment of others. In other words, it is desirable to bring about a state of affairs in which all obey the rules of morality.

(iv) However, Hobbes claims that in the state of nature it helps nobody if a single person or a small group of persons begins to follow the rules of morality, for this could only lead to the extinction of such individuals or groups. In such a state, it is therefore contrary to reason to be moral.

(v) The situation can change, reason can support morality, only when the presumption about other people's behavior is reversed. Hobbes thought that this could be achieved only by the creation of an absolute ruler with absolute power to enforce his laws. We have already seen that this is not true and that it is quite different if people live in a society, that is, if they have common ways of life, which are taught to all members and somehow enforced by the group. Its members have reason to expect their fellows generally to obey its rules, that is, its religion, morality, customs, and law, even when doing so is not, on certain occasions, in their interest. Hence they too have reason to follow these rules.

Is this argument sound? One might, of course, object to step (i) on the grounds that this is an empirical proposition for which there is little or no evidence. For how can we know whether it is true that people in a state of nature would follow only their inclinations or, at best, reasons of self-interest, when nobody now lives in that state or has ever lived in it?

However, there is some empirical evidence to support this claim. For in the family of nations, individual states are placed very much like individual persons in a state of nature. The doctrine of the sovereignty of nations and the absence of an effective international law and police force are a guarantee that nations live in a state of nature, without commonly accepted rules that are somehow enforced. Hence it must be granted that living in a state of nature leads to living in a state in which individuals act either on impulse or as they think their interest dictates. For states pay only lip service to morality. They attack their hated neighbors when the opportunity arises. They start preventive wars in order to destroy the enemy before he can deliver his knockout blow. Where interests conflict, the stronger party usually has his way, whether his claims are justified or not. And where the relative strength of the parties is not obvious, they usually resort to arms in order to determine "whose side God is on." Treaties are frequently concluded but, morally speaking, they are not worth the paper they are written on. Nor do the partners regard them as contracts binding in the ordinary way, but rather as public expressions of the belief of the governments concerned that for the time being their alliance is in the interest of the allies. It is well understood that such treaties may be canceled before they reach their predetermined end or simply broken when it suits one partner. In international affairs, there are very few examples of *Nibelungentreue,* although statesmen whose countries have profited from keeping their treaties usually make such high moral claims.

It is, moreover, difficult to justify morality in international affairs. For suppose a highly moral statesman were to demand that his country adhere to a treaty obligation even though this meant its ruin or possibly its extinction. Suppose he were to say that treaty obligations are sacred and must be kept whatever the consequences. How could he defend such a policy? Perhaps one might argue that someone has to make a start in order to create mutual confidence in international affairs. Or one might say that setting a good example is the best way of inducing others to follow suit. But such a defense would hardly be sound. The less skeptical one is about the genuineness of the cases in which nations have adhered to their treaties from a sense of moral obligation, the more skeptical one must be about the effectiveness of such examples of virtue in effecting a change of international practice. Power politics still govern in international affairs.

We must, therefore, grant Hobbes the first step in his argument and admit that in a state of nature people, as a matter of psychological fact, would not follow the dictates of morality. But we might object to the next step that knowing this psychological fact about other people's behavior constitutes a reason for behaving in the same way. Would it not still be immoral for anyone to ignore the demands of morality even though he knows that others are likely or certain to do so, too? Can we offer as a justification for morality the fact that no one is entitled to do wrong just because someone else is doing wrong? This argument begs the question whether it *is* wrong for anyone in this state to disregard the demands of morality. It cannot be wrong to break a treaty or make preventive war if we have no reason to obey the moral rules. For to say that it is wrong to do so is to say that we ought not to do so. But if we have no reason for obeying the moral rule, then we have no reason overruling self-interest, hence no reason for keeping the treaty when keeping it is not in our interest, hence it is not true that we have a reason for keeping it, hence not true that we ought to keep it, hence not true that it is wrong not to keep it.

I conclude that Hobbes's argument is sound. Moralities are systems of principles whose acceptance by everyone as overruling the dictates of self-interest is in the interest of everyone alike, though following the rules of a morality is not of course identical with following self-interest. If it were, there could be no conflict between a morality and self-interest and no point in having moral rules overriding self-interest. Hobbes is also right in saying that the application of this system of rules is in accordance with reason only in social conditions, that is, when there are well-established ways of behavior.

The answer to our question "Why should we be moral? " is therefore as follows. We should be moral because being moral is following rules designed to overrule self-interest whenever it is in the interest of everyone alike that everyone should set aside his interest. It is not self-contradictory to say this because it may be in one's interest *not* to follow one's interest at times. We have already seen that enlightened self-interest acknowledges this point. But while enlightened self-interest does not require any genuine sacrifice from anyone, morality does. In the interest of the possibility of the good life for everyone, voluntary sacrifices are sometimes required from everybody. Thus, a person might do better for himself by following enlightened self-interest rather than morality. It is not possible, however, that *everyone* should do better for himself by following enlightened self-interest rather than morality. The best possible life *for everyone* is possible only by everyone's following the rules of morality, that is, rules which quite frequently may require individuals to make genuine sacrifices.

It must be added to this, however, that such a system of rules has the support of reason only where people live in societies, that is, in conditions in which there are established common ways of behavior. Outside society, people have no reason for following such rules, that is, for being moral. In other words, outside society, the very distinction between right and wrong vanishes.

JOHN RAWLS

JUSTICE AS FAIRNESS[1]

1. It might seem at first sight that the concepts of justice and fairness
are the same, and that there is no reason to distinguish them, or to say
that one is more fundamental than the other. I think that this impression
is mistaken. In this paper I wish to show that the fundamental idea in
the concept of justice is fairness; and I wish to offer an analysis of the
concept of justice from this point of view. To bring out the force of this
claim, and the analysis based upon it, I shall then argue that it is this
aspect of justice for which utilitarianism, in its classical form, is unable
to account, but which is expressed, even if misleadingly, by the idea of
the social contract.

   To start with I shall develop a particular conception of justice by
stating and commenting upon two principles which specify it, and by
considering the circumstances and conditions under which they may be
thought to arise. The principles defining this conception, and the conception itself, are, of course, familiar. It may be possible, however, by
using the notion of fairness as a framework, to assemble and to look at

[1] John Rawls, "Justice as Fairness," *Philosophical Review* 67 (1958): pp. 164–75. Reprinted
by permission of the editors of *Philosophical Review* and the author. An abbreviated version
of this paper (less than one-half the length) was presented in a symposium with the same
title at the American Philosophical Association, Eastern Division, 28 December 1957, and
appeared in the *Journal of Philosophy,* 54, 653–662.

them in a new way. Before stating this conception, however, the following preliminary matters should be kept in mind.

Throughout I consider justice only as a virtue of social institutions, or what I shall call practices.[2] The principles of justice are regarded as formulating restrictions as to how practices may define positions and offices, and assign thereto powers and liabilities, rights and duties. Justice as a virtue of particular actions or of persons I do not take up at all. It is important to distinguish these various subjects of justice, since the meaning of the concept varies according to whether it is applied to practices, particular actions, or persons. These meanings are, indeed, connected, but they are not identical. I shall confine my discussion to the sense of justice as applied to practices, since this sense is the basic one. Once it is understood, the other senses should go quite easily.

Justice is to be understood in its customary sense as representing but *one* of the many virtues of social institutions, for these may be antiquated, inefficient, degrading, or any number of other things, without being unjust. Justice is not to be confused with an all-inclusive vision of a good society; it is only one part of any such conception. It is important, for example, to distinguish that sense of equality which is an aspect of the concept of justice from that sense of equality which belongs to a more comprehensive social ideal. There may well be inequalities which one concedes are just, or at least not unjust, but which, nevertheless, one wishes, on other grounds, to do away with. I shall focus attention, then, on the usual sense of justice in which it is essentially the elimination of arbitrary distinctions and the establishment, within the structure of a practice, of a proper balance between competing claims.

Finally, there is no need to consider the principles discussed below as *the* principles of justice. For the moment it is sufficient that they are typical of a family of principles normally associated with the concept of justice. The way in which the principles of this family resemble one another, as shown by the background against which they may be thought to arise, will be made clear by the whole of the subsequent argument.

2. The conception of justice which I want to develop may be stated in the form of two principles as follows: first, each person participating in a practice, or affected by it, has an equal right to the most extensive liberty compatible with a like liberty for all; and second, inequalities are arbitrary unless it is reasonable to expect that they will work out for everyone's advantage, and provided the positions and offices to which

---

[2] I use the word "practice" throughout as a sort of technical term meaning any form of activity specified by a system of rules which defines offices, roles, moves, penalties, defenses, and so on, and which gives the activity its structure. As examples one may think of games and rituals, trials and parliaments, markets and systems of property. I have attempted a partial analysis of the notion of a practice in a paper "Two Concepts of Rules," *Philosophical Review,* 64 (1955), 3–32.

they attach, or from which they may be gained, are open to all. These principles express justice as a complex of three ideas: liberty, equality, and reward for services contributing to the common good.[3]

The term "person" is to be construed variously depending on the circumstances. On some occasions it will mean human individuals, but in others it may refer to nations, provinces, business firms, churches, teams, and so on. The principles of justice apply in all these instances, although there is a certain logical priority to the case of human individuals. As I shall use the term "person," it will be ambiguous in the manner indicated.

The first principle holds, of course, only if other things are equal: that is, while there must always be a justification for departing from the initial position of equal liberty (which is defined by the pattern of rights and duties, powers and liabilities, established by a practice), and the burden of proof is placed on him who would depart from it, nevertheless, there can be, and often there is, a justification for doing so. Now, that similar particular cases, as defined by a practice, should be treated similarly as they arise, is part of the very concept of a practice; it is involved in the notion of an activity in accordance with rules.[4] The first principle expresses an analogous conception, but as applied to the structure of practices themselves. It holds, for example, that there is a presumption against the distinctions and classifications made by legal systems and other practices to the extent that they infringe on the original and equal liberty of the persons participating in them. The second principle defines how this presumption may be rebutted.

It might be argued at this point that justice requires only an equal liberty. If, however, a greater liberty were possible for all without loss or conflict, then it would be irrational to settle on a lesser liberty. There is no reason for circumscribing rights unless their exercise would be incompatible, or would render the practice defining them less effective. Therefore no serious distortion of the concept of justice is likely to follow from including within it the concept of the greatest equal liberty.

---

[3] These principles are, of course, well-known in one form or another and appear in many analyses of justice even where the writers differ widely on other matters. Thus if the principle of equal liberty is commonly associated with Kant (see *The Philosophy of Law,* tr. by W. Hastie, Edinburgh, 1887, pp. 56 f.), it may be claimed that it can also be found in J. S. Mill's *On Liberty* and elsewhere, and in many other liberal writers. Recently H. L. A. Hart has argued for something like it in his paper "Are There Any Natural Rights?," *Philosophical Review,* 64 (1955), 175–191. The injustice of inequalities which are not won in return for a contribution to the common advantage is, of course, widespread in political writings of all sorts. The conception of justice here discussed is distinctive, if at all, only in selecting these two principles in this form; but for another similar analysis, see the discussion by W. D. Lamont, *The Principles of Moral Judgment* (Oxford, 1946), ch. 5.

[4] This point was made by Sidgwick, *Methods of Ethics,* 6th ed. (London, 1901), bk. 3, chap. 5, sec. 1. It has recently been emphasized by Sir Isaiah Berlin in a symposium, "Equality," *Proceedings of the Aristotelian Society,* n.s. 56 (1955–56), 305 f.

The second principle defines what sorts of inequalities are permissible; it specifies how the presumption laid down by the first principle may be put aside. Now by inequalities it is best to understand not *any* differences between offices and positions, but differences in the benefits and burdens attached to them either directly or indirectly, such as prestige and wealth, or liability to taxation and compulsory services. Players in a game do not protest against there being different positions, such as batter, pitcher, catcher, and the like, nor to there being various privileges and powers as specified by the rules; nor do the citizens of a country object to there being the different offices of government such as president, senator, governor, judge, and so on, each with their special rights and duties. It is not differences of this kind that are normally thought of as inequalities, but differences in the resulting distribution established by a practice, or made possible by it, of the things men strive to attain or avoid. Thus they may complain about the pattern of honors and rewards set up by a practice (e.g., the privileges and salaries of government officials) or they may object to the distribution of power and wealth which results from the various ways in which men avail themselves of the opportunities allowed by it (e.g., the concentration of wealth which may develop in a free price system allowing large entrepreneurial or speculative gains).

It should be noted that the second principle holds that an inequality is allowed only if there is reason to believe that the practice with the inequality, or resulting in it, will work for the advantage of *every* party engaging in it. Here it is important to stress that *every* party must gain from the inequality. Since the principle applies to practices, it implies that the representative man in every office or position defined by a practice, when he views it as a going concern, must find it reasonable to prefer his condition and prospects with the inequality to what they would be under the practice without it. The principle excludes, therefore, the justification of inequalities on the grounds that the disadvantages of those in one position are outweighed by the greater advantages of those in another position. This rather simple restriction is the main modification I wish to make in the utilitarian principle as usually understood. When coupled with the notion of a practice, it is a restriction of consequence[5],

---

[5] In the paper referred to above, footnote 2, I have tried to show the importance of taking practices as the proper subject of the utilitarian principle. The criticisms of so-called "restricted utilitarianism" by J. J. C. Smart, "Extreme and Restricted Utilitarianism," *Philosophical Quarterly*, 6 (1956), 344–354, and by H. J. McCloskey, "An Examination of Restricted Utilitarianism," *Philosophical Review*, 66 (1957), 466–485, do not affect my argument. These papers are concerned with the very general proposition, which is attributed (with what justice I shall not consider) to S. E. Toulmin and P. H. Nowell-Smith (and in the case of the latter paper, also, apparently, to me); namely, the proposition that particular moral actions are justified by appealing to moral rules, and moral rules in turn by reference to utility. But clearly I meant to defend no such view. My discussion of the concept of rules as maxims is an explicit rejection of it. What I did argue was that, in the *logically special* case of

and one which some utilitarians, e.g., Hume and Mill, have used in their discussions of justice without realizing apparently its significance, or at least without calling attention to it.[6] Why it is a significant modification of principle, changing one's conception of justice entirely, the whole of my argument will show.

Further, it is also necessary that the various offices to which special benefits or burdens attach are open to all. It may be, for example, to the common advantage, as just defined, to attach special benefits to certain offices. Perhaps by doing so the requisite talent can be attracted to them and encouraged to give its best efforts. But any offices having special benefits must be won in a fair competition in which contestants are judged on their merits. If some offices were not open, those excluded would normally be justified in feeling unjustly treated, even if they benefited from the greater efforts of those who were allowed to compete for them. Now if one can assume that offices are open, it is necessary only to consider the design of practices themselves and how they jointly, as a system, work together. It will be a mistake to focus attention on the varying relative positions of particular persons, who may be known to us by their proper names, and to require that each such change, as a once for all transaction viewed in isolation, must be in itself just. It is the system of practices which is to be judged, and judged from a general point of view: unless one is prepared to criticize it from the standpoint of a representative man holding some particular office, one has no complaint against it.

3. Given these principles one might try to derive them from a priori principles of reason, or claim that they were known by intuition. These are familiar enough steps and, at least in the case of the first principle, might be made with some success. Usually, however, such arguments,

---

practices (although actually quite a common case) where the rules have special features and are not moral rules at all but legal rules or rules of games and the like (except, perhaps, in the case of promises), there is a peculiar force to the distinction between justifying particular actions and justifying the system of rules themselves. Even then I claimed only that restricting the utilitarian principle to practices as defined strengthened it. I did not argue for the position that this amendment alone is sufficient for a complete defense of utilitarianism as a general theory of morals. In this paper I take up the question as to how the utilitarian principle itself must be modified, but here, too, the subject of inquiry is not all of morality at once, but a limited topic, the concept of justice.

[6] It might seem as if J. S. Mill, in paragraph 36 of chapter 5 of *Utilitarianism,* expressed the utilitarian principle in this modified form, but in the remaining two paragraphs of the chapter, and elsewhere, he would appear not to grasp the significance of the change. Hume often emphasizes that *every* man must benefit. For example, in discussing the utility of general rules, he holds that they are requisite to the "well-being of every individual"; from a stable system of property "every individual person must find himself a gainer in balancing the account. . . . Every member of society is sensible of this interest; everyone expresses this sense to his fellows along with the resolution he has taken of squaring his actions by it, on the conditions that others will do the same." *A Treatise of Human Nature,* bk. 3, pt. 2, section 2, paragraph 22.

made at this point, are unconvincing. They are not likely to lead to an understanding of the basis of the principles of justice, not at least as principles of justice. I wish, therefore, to look at the principles in a different way.

Imagine a society of persons amongst whom a certain system of practices is *already* well established. Now suppose that by and large they are mutually self-interested; their allegiance to their established practices is normally founded on the prospect of self-advantage. One need not assume that, in all senses of the term "person," the persons in this society are mutually self-interested. If the characterization as mutually self-interested applies when the line of division is the family, it may still be true that members of families are bound by ties of sentiment and affection and willingly acknowledge duties in contradiction to self-interest. Mutual self-interestedness in the relations between families, nations, churches, and the like, is commonly associated with intense loyalty and devotion on the part of individual members. Therefore, one can form a more realistic conception of this society if one things of it as consisting of mutually self-interested families, or some other association. Further, it is not necessary to suppose that these persons are mutually self-interested under all circumstances, but only in the usual situations in which they participate in their common practices.

Now suppose also that these persons are rational: they know their own interests more or less accurately; they are capable of tracing out the likely consequences of adopting one practice rather than another; they are capable of adhering to a course of action once they have decided upon it; they can resist present temptations and the enticements of immediate gain; and the bare knowledge or perception of the difference between their condition and that of others is not, within certain limits and in itself, a source of great dissatisfaction. Only the last point adds anything to the usual definition of rationality. This definition should allow, I think, for the idea that a rational man would not be greatly downcast from knowing, or seeing, that others are in a better position than himself, unless he thought their being so was the result of injustice, or the consequence of letting chance work itself out for no useful common purpose, and so on. So if these persons strike us as unpleasantly egoistic, they are at least free in some degree from the fault of envy.[7]

Finally, assume that these persons have roughly similar needs and interests, or needs and interests in various ways complementary, so that

---

[7] It is not possible to discuss here this addition to the usual conception of rationality. If it seems peculiar, it may be worth remarking that it is analogous to the modification of the utilitarian principle which the argument as a whole is designed to explain and justify. In the same way that the satisfaction of interests, the representative claims of which violate the principles of justice, is not a reason for having a practice (see sec. 7), unfounded envy, within limits, need not to be taken into account.

fruitful cooperation amongst them is possible; and suppose that they are sufficiently equal in power and ability to guarantee that in normal circumstances none is able to dominate the others. This condition (as well as the others) may seem excessively vague; but in view of the conception of justice to which the argument leads, there seems no reason for making it more exact here.

Since these persons are conceived as engaging in their common practices, which are already established, there is no question of our supposing them to come together to deliberate as to how they will set these practices up for the first time. Yet we can imagine that from time to time they discuss with one another whether any of them has a legitimate complaint against their established institutions. Such discussions are perfectly natural in any normal society. Now suppose that they have settled on doing this in the following way. They first try to arrive at the principles by which complaints, and so practices themselves, are to be judged. Their procedure for this is to let each person propose the principles upon which he wishes his complaints to be tried with the understanding that, if acknowledged, the complaints of others will be similarly tried, and that no complaints will be heard at all until everyone is roughly of one mind as to how complaints are to be judged. They each understand further that the principles proposed and acknowledged on this occasion are binding on future occasions. Thus each will be wary of proposing a principle which would give him a peculiar advantage, in his present circumstances, supposing it to be accepted. Each person knows that he will be bound by it in future circumstances the peculiarities of which cannot be known, and which might well be such that the principle is then to his disadvantage. The idea is that everyone should be required to make *in advance* a firm commitment, which others also may reasonably be expected to make, and that no one be given the opportunity to tailor the canons of a legitimate complaint to fit his own special condition, and then to discard them when they no longer suit his purpose. Hence each person will propose principles of a general kind which will, to a large degree, gain their sense from the various applications to be made of them, the particular circumstances of which being as yet unknown. These principles will express the conditions in accordance with which each is the least unwilling to have his interests limited in the design of practices, given the competing interests of the others, on the supposition that the interests of others will be limited likewise. The restrictions which would so arise might be thought of as those a person would keep in mind if he were designing a practice in which his enemy were to assign him his place.

The two main parts of this conjectural account have a definite significance. The character and respective situations of the parties reflect the typical circumstances in which questions of justice arise. The procedure whereby principles are proposed and acknowledged represents constraints, analogous to those of having a morality, whereby rational and mutually self-interested persons are brought to act reasonably. Thus the first part reflects the fact that questions of justice arise when conflicting claims are made upon the design of a practice and where it is taken for granted that each person will insist, as far as possible, on what he considers his rights. It is typical of cases of justice to involve persons who are pressing on one another their claims, between which a fair balance or equilibrium must be found. On the other hand, as expressed by the second part, having a morality must at least imply the acknowledgment of principles as impartially applying to one's own conduct as well as to another's, and moreover principles which may constitute a constraint, or limitation, upon the pursuit of one's own interests. There are, of course, other aspects of having a morality: the acknowledgment of moral principles must show itself in accepting a reference to them as reasons for limiting one's claims, in acknowledging the burden of providing a sepcial explanation, or excuse, when one acts contrary to them, or else in showing shame and remorse and a desire to make amends, and so on. It is sufficient to remark here that having a morality is analogous to having made a firm commitment in advance; for one must acknowledge the principles of morality even when to one's disadvantage.[8] A man whose moral judgments always coincided with his interests could be suspected of having no morality at all.

Thus the two parts of the foregoing account are intended to mirror the kinds of circumstances in which questions of justice arise and the constraints which having a morality would impose upon persons so situated. In this way one can see how the acceptance of the principles of justice might come about, for given all these conditions as described, it would be natural if the two principles of justice were to be acknowledged. Since there is no way for anyone to win special advantages for himself, each might consider it reasonable to acknowledge equality as an initial principle. There is, however, no reason why they should regard this position as final; for if there are inequalities which satisfy the second principle, the immediate gain which equality would allow can be considered as intelligently invested in view of its future return. If, as is quite likely, these inequalities work as incentives to draw out better efforts, the members of this society may look upon them as concessions to human nature: they, like us, may think that people ideally should want to serve one another. But as they are mutually self-interested, their acceptance of these inequalities is merely the acceptance of the relations in which they actually

---

[8] The idea that accepting a principle as a moral principle implies that one generally acts on it, failing a special explanation, has been stressed by R. M. Hare, *The Language of Morals* (Oxford, 1952). His formulation of it needs to be modified, however, along the lines suggested by P. L. Gardiner, "On Assenting to a Moral Principle," *Proceedings of the Aristotelian Society,* n.s. 55 (1955), 23–44. See also C. K. Grant, "Akrasia and the Criteria of Assent to Practical Principles," *Mind,* 65 (1956), 400–407, where the complexity of the criteria for assent is discussed.

stand, and a recognition of the motives which lead them to engage in their common practices. *They* have no title to complain of one another. And so provided that the conditions of the principle are met, there is no reason why they should not allow such inequalities. Indeed, it would be short-sighted of them to do so, and could result, in most cases, only from their being dejected by the bare knowledge, or perception, that others are better situated. Each person will, however, insist on an advantage to himself, and so on a common advantage, for none is willing to sacrifice anything for the others.

These remarks are not offered as a proof that persons so conceived and circumstanced would settle on the two principles, but only to show that these principles could have such a background, and so can be viewed as those principles which mutually self-interested and rational persons, when similarly situated and required to make in advance a firm commitment, could acknowledge as restrictions governing the assignment of rights and duties in their common practices, and thereby accept as limiting their rights against one another. The principles of justice may, then, be regarded as those principles which arise when the constraints of having a morality are imposed upon parties in the typical circumstances of justice.

4. These ideas are, of course, connected with a familiar way of thinking about justice which goes back at least to the Greek Sophists, and which regards the acceptance of the principles of justice as a compromise between persons of roughly equal power who would enforce their will on each other if they could, but who, in view of the equality of forces amongst them and for the sake of their own peace and security, acknowledge certain forms of conduct insofar as prudence seems to require. Justice is thought of as a pact between rational egoists the stability of which is dependent on a balance of power and a similarity of circumstances.[9] While the previous account is connected with this tradition, and with its most

---

[9] Perhaps the best known statement of this conception is that given by Glaucon at the beginning of book 2 of Plato's *Republic*. Presumably it was, in various forms, a common view among the Sophists; but that Plato gives a fair representation of it is doubtful. See K. R. Popper, *The Open Society and Its Enemies,* rev. ed. (Princeton, 1950), pp. 112–118. Certainly Plato usually attributes to it a quality of manic egoism which one feels must be an exaggeration; on the other hand, see the Melian Debate in Thucydides, *The Peloponnesian War,* book 5, chap. 7, although it is impossible to say to what extent the views expressed there reveal any current philosophical opinion. Also in this tradition are the remarks of Epicurus on justice in *Principal Doctrines,* 31–38. In modern times elements of the conception appear in a more sophisticated form in Hobbes *The Leviathan* and in Hume *A Treatise of Human Nature,* book 3, pt. 2, as well as in the writings of the school of natural law such as Pufendorf's *De jure naturae et gentium.* Hobbes and Hume are especially instructive. For Hobbes's argument see Howard Warrender's *The Political Philosophy of Hobbes* (Oxford, 1957). W. J. Baumol's *Welfare Economics and the Theory of the State* (London, 1952), is valuable in showing the wide applicability of Hobbes's fundamental idea (interpreting his natural law as principles of prudence), although in this book it is traced back only to Hume's *Treatise.*

recent variant, the theory of games,[10] it differs from it in several important respects which, to forestall misinterpretations, I will set out here.

First, I wish to use the previous conjectural account of the background of justice as a way of analyzing the concept. I do not want, therefore, to be interpreted as assuming a general theory of human motivation: when I suppose that the parties are mutually self-interested, and are not willing to have their (substantial) interests sacrificed to others, I am referring to their conduct and motives as they are taken for granted in cases where questions of justice ordinarily arise. Justice is the virtue of practices where there are assumed to be competing interests and conflicting claims, and where it is supposed that persons will press their rights on each other. That persons are mutually self-interested in certain situations and for certain purposes is what gives rise to the question of justice in practices covering those circumstances. Amongst an association of saints, if such a community could really exist, the disputes about justice could hardly occur; for they would all work selflessly together for one end, the glory of God as defined by their common religion, and reference to this end would settle every question of right. The justice of practices does not come up until there are several different parties (whether we think of these as individuals, associations, or nations and so on, is irrelevant) who do press their claims on one another, and who do regard themselves as representatives of interests which deserve to be considered.

---

[10] See J. von Neumann and O. Morgenstern, *The Theory of Games and Economic Behavior,* 2d ed. (Princeton, 1947). For a comprehensive and not too technical discussion of the developments since, see R. Duncan Luce and Howard Raiffa, *Games and Decisions: Introduction and Critical Survey* (New York, 1957). Chaps. 6 and 14 discuss the developments most obviously related to the analysis of justice.

RUTH MACKLIN

MORAL CONCERNS AND APPEALS TO RIGHTS AND DUTIES*

A few years ago, in a Canadian city a dispute arose that ostensibly concerned a question of human rights. The issue was this: welfare recipients demanded an increase in their payments to allow them to buy food for their dogs and cats. They invoked "the right to own a pet" in support of their claims. Now there are those to whom this so-called right may appear self-evident—be they pet-lovers or moral intuitionists—but *appearances* of self-evidence do not guarantee the *truth* of the claims.

In earlier eras, masters believed that they had rights with respect to their legally owned slaves, and parents enjoyed absolute dominion over their children. But the alleged rights of slaveholders and the presumed absolute rights of parents regarding their children are no longer claimed to exist, much less held to be self-evident. With the abolition of slavery and the growing awareness that it was an inherently immoral institution, most people came to hold that no one had the right to own another person. Instead, the alleged rights of slave holders gave way to a different conception—the right of all persons to be free. And, while parents still exercise great power and authority over their children, these rights are

* Ruth Macklin, "Moral Concerns and Appeals to Rights and Duties," *Hastings Center Report* 6, no. 5 (October 1976): pp. 31–38. Reprinted with permission of the Hastings Center (Institute of Society, Ethics and The Life Sciences, 360 Broadway, Hastings on the Hudson, N.Y. 10706) and the author.

by no means absolute. The state may remove children from their parents in cases of child abuse or neglect, and courts have ruled that physicians may perform surgery on minors or give blood transfusions to children even where parents refuse to grant consent for such procedures.

Even greater problems exist when alleged rights come into conflict with one another, or when specific rights are claimed to exist by one group while their existence is denied by others. Some believe that non-human creatures, such as the animals we eat, and marginal persons, such as fetuses, possess rights. Some even hold that it is meaningful and proper to ascribe rights to nonexistent entities, like future generations. Most of us who are meat-eaters are prepared to deny that animals have rights at all, much less rights that can be pitted against the rights of human carnivores in a moral argument. Yet we may still argue strongly, on moral grounds, that animals should be treated decently and that curelty to beasts and wanton killing of living creatures is unethical. Similarly, proabortionists are prepared to deny that the fetus has any rights, while in arguing for the immorality of abortion antiabortionists invoke precisely those rights. If animals and fetuses have rights, questions of conflict of rights immediately arise. Because there are no easy or obvious solutions to these dilemmas, we are led to suspect that the concept of rights is by no means as clear or as unproblematic as the rights-claimers take it to be. We also begin to wonder why talk about human rights has reached its current pitch in a variety of contexts: the "right to clean air," a subset of which is nonsmokers' rights; the patient's "right to know" about matters connected with the nature and prognosis of his condition, especially in cases of teminal disease; rights of privacy, in the courtroom, and rights of confidentiality, in a wide range of cases.

CONFUSIONS IN THE NOTION OF RIGHTS

I should like to argue this: appeals to abstract notions of rights, in the absence of a moral theory in which appeals might be grounded, are bound to be arbitrary, *ad hoc,* or give rise to controversies that are impossible to settle, in principle. In addition, the attempt to *discover* the existence of human rights is an enterprise that is essentially misconceived. The existence and nature of human rights are matters for moral *decision,* not of empirical or a priori discovery. In arguing for this thesis, I shall sketch briefly the two major historical traditions from which talk about so-called "natural rights" has emerged. The inadequacy of these approaches suggests that if the concept of rights is to have any consistent, meanginful application, it must be a derivative notion rather than a primitive or fundamental concept. In other words, in the absence of a broader moral theory—in particular, a theory of justice—a well-grounded account of human rights will not be forthcoming. It is, then, within the framework of an overall theory of justice that we might expect to resolve at least some of the debates and uncertainties about questions of rights. Without such a generally accepted theory, claims about the existence and nature of specific rights cannot be adequately grounded or justified; yet they may still serve as expressions of moral outrage or as demands for social and legislative reform.

In recent decades there has been an acceleration in the pattern of recognizing and laying claim to a variety of rights of persons—a pattern that has emerged over a number of centuries. Sometimes this process has taken the form of asserting certain rights for all persons—rights that had not previously been claimed on behalf of any persons, such as the "right to health care," or the right to a free, public education. Other instances are more typical of a movement in the direction of social justice, marked by attempts to equalize the rights of persons, for example, granting the right to vote to nonproperty owners, then to women; instituting and protecting the rights of oppressed minorities or other groups who were granted only a second-class citizenship in society. Most recently, a trend toward claiming rights on behalf of all sorts of special classes of persons has emerged: the rights of patients, prisoners, the retarded, the mentally ill, the elderly, the dying—and even the rights of the fetus.

It is not so much the embodiment of these concerns in terms of the *rights* of persons that is morally significant; it is, rather, the heightened sensitivity to the needs and suffering of members of humanity outside one's own immediate circle (family, friends, or other associates) that seems to indicate a degree of moral progress in man's humane treatment of his fellow humans. Both conceptual and ethical issues in applied contexts seem to be confused rather than clarified by too much appeal to rights of all sorts and on behalf of biological entities in various forms, as well as nonexistent entities. Conceiving of these moral issues in terms of rights and duties is only one way of placing them in an ethical framework, as years of debate in ethical theory have shown. In thinking about the notion of rights in biomedical contexts, we should bear in mind that not all our obligations can be derived from the rights of some persons or group of persons.

Phrasing our moral concerns in terms of rights results in familiar sorts of questions. How ought persons who are functionally incapacitated in some way be viewed, in general, with respect to the presence or absence of their human rights? What sorts of attributes must a person have—or lack—in order to retain basic human rights, such as the right not to be interfered with or to be granted full-fledged freedom and autonomy? Who, if anyone, has the "right to decide" when to pull the plug in cases where severely defective newborns or terminally ill persons are kept biologically alive by the impressive skills of modern medicine? Who, if anyone, has the right to grant consent for medical or psychological experiments on persons who cannot grant such consent for themselves (for example, children, the retarded, the mentally ill)? Questions of this sort do not seem to be made clearer or easier to answer by formulating them in terms of rights. It would appear that the ethical waters are often muddied by a variety of claims about people's rights that are difficult to substantiate.

The range of problems associated with the notion of rights is a long-standing one in moral and political philosophy. Where do rights come from? How do we know when they exist or in whom they reside? How do we settle conflicts of rights or disagreements about their existence or nonexistence in particular cases? While many of these theoretical issues pertaining to human rights remain unresolved, there has, nevertheless, been substantial progress in bringing practical reforms to a variety of social and legal contexts. Although knotty philosophical problems have not been aided by all the talk about rights, still the *pragmatic* consequence of using a language of rights seems to have been a reduction in suffering and an enhancement of the dignity and self-esteem of many people through the official recognition of their presumed rights.

If this observation is sound, then there is surely a pragmatic value in conceptualizing moral issues in terms of the rights of persons. Phrasing our moral concerns in the language of rights and duties demonstrates the exhortative power of moral language. Its function is to get people to do something, to move them to action—not to report facts (moral or other-wise) or to describe things about the world that are open to empirical verification. Yet it remains true that when rights and duties are claimed by their proponents to exist, it is usually held that such claims *do* embody moral facts of some sort—facts that are discoverable or knowable in the way that the truths of science or mathematics can be discovered and justified. Let us look briefly at two traditional derivations of the presumed natural rights of humans.

NATURAL LAW TRADITIONS

According to one viewpoint prevalent since Roman times, natural rights are derived from natural law, where natural law is conceived "as an ideal or standard, not yet completely exemplified in any existing legal code, but as a standard fixed by nature to be discovered and gradually applied by men." [1] The natural law tradition is perhaps best known through its theological proponents, who claimed that natural law is God-given. This divine source is supposed to supply the answer to questions about the origin and authority of the natural law—a law that is held to apply impartially to all people in all circumstances, and is seen as the basis for moral obligation as well as for natural rights. Natural law is thus held to be perfect, stemming as it does from God (or from nature), and insures perfect justice. But the chief problem with the doctrine of natural law—whether or not the source is held to be divine—is how humans can come to know this law and to justify the claims about rights and duties that are supposed to be derived from it.

The solution to this problem is, unfortunately, far from satisfactory. Natural law theorists accord a special status to the possession of *reason* by man, claiming that the intrinsic or essential nature of man is the rationality. It is, therefore, by means of reason—the rational faculty peculiar to man—that natural laws and what flows from them are knowable. The Roman secular tradition maintained this view, as did the Christian doctrine of natural law. We thus find Cicero claiming, "There is, in fact, a true law—namely right reason—which is in accordance with nature, applies to all men and is unchangeable and eternal." [2] But unlike the laws of nature embodied in scientific theories, whose truth or acceptability is determined by the inductive method, the "natural law" cannot be arrived at by means of empirical inquiry. Instead, the *a priori* use of man's rational faculty is supposed to yield a universally applicable, immutable moral law. The epistemological problems associated with this methodology are similar to those found in appeals to self-evidence or to a special form of intuition as ways of obtaining moral knowledge. Why should such a questionable methodology be more acceptable in the domain of ethics than it is in the natural sciences?

There is no objective way of verifying or certifying one use of *a priori* reason over another, when they disagree. How, then, can the human attribute of *reason* provide an adequate basis for knowing the so-called natural law or for justifying the claims that follow from it? The purpose of natural law theory is to provide an objective source for human rights, which are supposed to be natural, universal, and inalienable. But if the only means by which these alleged natural rights can be known is by the exercise of human reason, there remains no way of settling disputes that arise when one exercise of reason conflicts with another. Unless each person's use of reason is self-certifying—surely an unsatisfactory epistemological viewpoint—the theory fails in what it purports to do.

The other traditional basis for natural rights is the Aristotelian doctrine that man has a nature or an essence. Here, again, the essence of man is rationality, but there is no explicit appeal to any natural *law* that is knowable by reason. Instead, man—the rational animal—is held to have a fixed nature or essence. Precisely what this nature is and what follows from it are by no means clear, but it is at least debatable whether the nature of man can properly be characterized as "rational" in the way required by such a theory. For one thing, determination of the nature or essence of man should be construed, in large part, as a scientific or empirical matter, with answers supplied by well-developed theories in psychology and psychiatry. It is instructive that one of the major approaches in this domain—psychoanalytic theory—views human nature as essentially irrational, claiming that we are largely governed by instinctual forces rather than by reason and common sense.

Moreover, some deny that there is anything like a fixed nature or essence of man. These include existentialists, among philosophers who address the issue, and behaviorists (strict learning theorists) among psychologists. Still others maintain that even if it is meaningful and correct to speak of the nature of man, the elements of human nature are so complex and variable that there are bound to be sigificant differences among all the individuals who comprise humanity.

So it is not clear how far we can get by an appeal to human nature, or the essence of man, in our attempt to derive natural rights from some such basis. Even if it is correct to hold, with Aristotelians, that man has a fixed nature, we are still no closer to knowing how to derive *moral* elements like rights and duties from a set of *facts* about human nature. Aristotle's own ethical theory focuses on the notion of *virtue,* where the moral and intellectual virtues are linked to man's essential characteristics. But it is yet another matter to ascertain what follows from man's nature regarding the assignment of rights and duties to persons—a task that requires a clear address to the problem of the relationship between facts (human nature) and values (rights and duties).

DECLARATION OF RIGHTS

It will be helpful at this point to take a brief look at the various declarations and documents that have made assertions about the rights of man. The Virginia Declaration of Rights, written over two hundred years ago, and the French Declaration of the Rights of Man and of Citizen of 1789 include the following diverse list of rights: the right to a speedy trial by an impartial jury of twelve men, and the right to liberty, property, security and resistance to oppression. The Universal Declaration of Human Rights, adopted almost thirty years ago by the United Nations, goes somewhat farther in proclaiming for each person the right to marry, to work, and to an adequate standard of living for the health and well-being of himself and of his family, including food, clothing, housing, and medical care and necessary social services.

It is evident that the natural rights of an enormous number of people are being violated, if these lists represent anything like an accurate account of what should be construed as human rights. But merely *asserting* these or other rights provides no justification for the claim that they exist. Such assertions must be backed up by a general moral theory, or else a sound methodology must be supplied that specifies how anyone—in principle— can discover the existence of such rights and know what to do when two or more legitimate rights conflict. But as we have seen, the two traditional approaches to natural rights—natural law theory and the Aristotelian view of the nature of man—both fail to supply an adequate epistemological basis for an acceptable doctrine of natural rights. If a clear and unambiguous account of human rights is not forthcoming from these sources, where else might we hope to find an objective grounding for claims about rights? If no such basis can be found that yields a complete and consistent set of rights and duties, then of what use are such concepts for the problematic moral contexts in which they are meant to apply? If there is no intersubjective agreement on how to settle disputes about whether or not rights ought to be ascribed to a fetus, or whether nonexistent entities like future generations can properly be said to have rights, or whether physicians' sole obligation is to their own patients, and not to society at large or to other present sufferers from disease, or even future sufferers—if there are no generally agreed upon principles or methods for settling these controversial questions, then how can an appeal to rights and duties aid us in confronting moral problems in the biomedical arena?

One answer to this question, as I mentioned at the outset, might be to *deny* an independent, objective status to rights and duties as "knowable" moral artifacts. Instead, it might be urged, the function of claims about human rights is to incite people to a certain type of action or to moral reform. The aim and impact of claims about rights lie in the area of social and political action, not in the assertion of moral truths. But this would be to hold that rights are not the sorts of things whose existence can be discovered and justified. Rather, they represent *decisions* of the moral community to treat persons or other creatures as having rights—decisions that require arguments in support of them, but which do not rest on appeals to presumed facts about man's nature or on the *a priori* use of reason. The problem with this answer, of course, is that it brings us no closer to settling disputes about conflicts of rights or to adjudicating opposing views about which kinds of entities can properly be said to possess rights. Let's take a brief look at the notion of duty to see if it fares any better in these respects.

DERIVING RIGHTS FROM DUTIES

It is generally held that rights and duties are correlative notions; this doctrine maintains that all duties entail other people's rights, and all rights entail other people's duties. Let us concentrate on the first part of this doctrine, since the second presupposes that we already have some legitimate way of knowing which rights exist.

The doctrine of the correlativity of rights and duties is not as simple as it may appear at first, and so in order to avoid oversimplification of the issues, we need to note an asymmetry that exists. It is customary to divide moral duties into two classes: duties of so-called "perfect obligation" and duties of "imperfect obligation." As described by the English utilitarian, John Stuart Mill, duties of imperfect obligation are "those in which, though the act is obligatory, the particular occasions of performing it are left to our choice, as in the case of charity or beneficence, which we are indeed bound to practice but not toward any definite person, nor at any prescribed time. . . . [D]uties, of perfect obligation are those duties in virtue of which a correlative *right* resides in some person or persons;

duties of imperfect obligation are those moral obligations which do not give birth to any right. . . . No one has a moral right to our generosity or beneficence because we are not morally bound to practice those virtues toward any given individual." [3]

If we accept this distinction between duties of perfect and imperfect obligation, it will turn out that only in cases or perfect obligation can we derive some assignable rights of persons from the motion of duty. But this, too, is bound to be unsatisfactory, since among the rights claimed for people in recent times are those noted earlier as expressed in the Universal Declaration of Human Rights, including "the right to a standard of living adequate to the health and well-being of [oneself] and [one's] family, including food, clothing, housing, medical care, and necessary social services." If this is indeed to be considered a right—rather than a privilege—of persons living in modern society, then to whom does the correlative duty belong? Surely no particular person has a duty to ensure that others enjoy a standard of living adequate to their health and well-being. It must, then, be the state or the government that has a duty or obligation to maintain such an adequate standard of living. But if we cannot gain agreement on whether or not persons have a *right* to health care or to welfare or other social services, how can it be any easier to answer the question by framing it in terms of the *duties* of government or other agencies?

It would seem, then, that an attempt to derive rights of persons from duties of perfect obligation is bound to be unhelpful. For it is precisely in the domain traditionally thought of as duties of *imperfect* obligation that many of the recent claims about rights have been advanced, as in the example of "the right to own a pet." We should normally expect that if claims about rights are justifiable, it is easy to pick out a correlative duty in virtue of which such rights may be guaranteed. But if we remain just as uncertain—if not more so—when it comes to certifying the existence of particular duties, such as the duty of the state to provide medical care, social services, or food for people's pets, then the logical correlativity of rights and duties does not bring us any nearer to a solution to the problems with which we began.

What are the ways in which duties can be known, and are the approaches to the notion of duty any clearer than those we have examined with respect to rights? Let us begin by considering deontological theories, which make the concept of duty central to the institution of morality. According to this view, morally right actions are those that conform to what duty prescribes, or are done for the sake of duty. It is not the good consequences of actions that gives them their moral worth; it is, rather, their conformity to duty that confers moral rightness on actions. Since the notion of duty is central to these sorts of ethical theories, we might reasonably expect some enlightenment from them on the question of what our duties are, how we may come to know them, and what to do in cases of conflict. We find, alas, that the notion of duty fares little better than the notion of rights in this regard.

Perhaps the most common position of deontological theorists concerning knowledge of our duties is *intuitionism.* Sometimes this alleged mode of knowledge is referred to directly as a form of intuition in the moral realm; at other times, deontologists make an appeal to the notion of *self-evidence,* akin to the self-evident truths of logic or mathematics. But in both cases the problems are the same. They are, once again, the epistemological problems we found earlier in connection with appeals to reason or to man's rational nature as ways of apprehending the natural law and, hence, the supposed natural rights of man. What do we do when two people's intuitions conflict, when each makes a claim about the existence or priority of some specified duties? Intuitionism as an epistemological method is inherently unsatisfactory, since it provides no way of settling disputes, or resolving conflicting claims about duties. The usual ploy of intuitionists is to retreat behind the reflections of the "best men in society," or to defer to the views of reflective, rational persons who have highly developed moral sentiments. But this solution is arbitrary, if not wholly circular, for we then need a criterion for selecting the "best men" to whose moral intuitions we must defer. A standard claim of the intuitionist is that anyone who fails properly to intuit his duties suffers from a form of "moral blindness," akin to color blindness. But one accused of such "moral blindness" in failing to apprehend duty can as easily reply to those who claim to intuit the duty in question, that the latter are "morally hallucinating"—they perceive duties that simply are not there. So long as intuition (or self-evidence) is invoked as an epistemic method, disputes about the existence or priority of duties cannot be resolved, and we are no closer to a solution in our quest for an adequate justificatory account of rights and duties.

It is important to remember that on a *consequentialist* approach to ethics—an approach usually contrasted with that of deontological theories, which stress duties and correlative rights—one ought to perform whichever action maximizes good consequences, among all those alternatives open to the agent. Here there is, presumably, a unique solution to cases of moral conflict. If only we can assess the probable consequences of our actions, *and* if we have a criterion for which results are the good ones (the ones that ought to be maximized), then we have a superior method to that offered by deontological theories for coming to know which actions we ought to perform. Deontologists commonly charge consequentialist theories with allowing us to default on our duties if some actions other than those prescribed by duty, such as the duty of keeping one's promises, can bring about better consequences, on the whole, than would adhering to duty. So while consequentialist theories are, in general, *epistemologically* superior to deontological theories in that they enable us to arrive at unique solutions to moral dilemmas about how we should act, many would argue that such theories are, nonetheless, *ethically* inferior to deontological ones since they fail to provide a jusification for why we should do our duty when duty conflicts with maximizing other desirable consequences of an action.

CONTEMPORARY APPROACHES TO RIGHTS

We have not advanced very far in our attempt to explicate the nature and justification of rights and duties. Before despairing utterly of finding a satisfactory approach to the subject, let's look briefly at a few contemporary accounts. The first is that offered by the British philosopher, H. L. A. Hart. In an article entitled, "Are There Any Natural Rights? " Hart begins by asserting that "if there are any moral rights at all, it follows that there is at least one natural right, the equal right of all men to be free." [4] Put in this hypothetical form, it is easy to agree with Hart's assertion. But as he himself notes, "my contention that there is this one natural right . . . is only the conditional assertion that *if* there are any moral rights then there must be this one natural right. . . . But it is still important to remember that there may be codes of conduct quite properly termed moral codes (though we can of course say they are "imperfect") which do not employ the notion of *a* right, and there is nothing contradictory or otherwise absurd in a code or morality consisting wholly of prescriptions or in a code which prescribed only what should be done for the realization of happiness or some ideal of personal perfection." [5] So Hart is prepared to acknowledge that the *idea* of having a morality does not rule out, in principle, a moral system devoid of the notion of rights. The notion Hart adopts in his account of the concept of a right is *too narrow* to cover the large range of cases in which claims about rights are in dispute, such as the right to health care or the right to a minimum standard of living; in addition, his notion remains unhelpful in disputes about the status of entities that can serve as the bearers of rights, such as fetuses, animals, or nonexistent entities. Now perhaps it is not a part of Hart's purpose to identify such bearers of rights, but it surely should be a requirement of a full theory of rights to address such issues.

But I do not want to criticize Hart's account on the grounds of its failure to deal with questions of what sorts of properties an entity should have for it properly to be a bearer of rights. Instead, I want to focus on the charge that his concept is too narrow to be applicable to a wide range of cases that have engendered current interest. Its narrowness stems directly from Hart's own characterization of the domain of rights. He says. "the concept of a right belongs to that branch of morality which is specifically concerned to determine when one person's freedom may be limited by another's. . . . [T]o have a right entails having a moral justification for limiting the freedom of another person and for determining how he should act." [6] While this characterization fits the sorts of cases in which conflicts of rights are at issue, it fails to apply to claims like "the right to health care." One might, of course, stretch the notion of "limiting the freedom of another person" to include such things as the government's increase in taxes to provide for the health care needs of society. But this does not seem to be a case of one person limiting another's freedom, as Hart's characterization of rights specifies. Cases like the right to health care or to social services seem to fall under the category of what the state owes to its members and, hence, what are their legitimate expectations, or "rights," vis-à-vis the government. Such cases of rights seem quite unlike individual property rights and the right not to be injured by other persons. If this is correct, then Hart's account of rights will be unhelpful for adjudicating claims about the right to own a pet, or the more important rights-claims of this general type.

Hart's analysis does, however, go part way toward resolving rights disputes about the other range of cases where limitations of people's freedom are at stake. It is useful to follow a distinction he makes between "special rights" and "general rights." Hart describes special rights as follows:

> When rights arise out of special transactions between individuals or out of some special relationship in which they stand to each other, both the persons who have the right and those who have the corresponding obligation are limited to the parties to the special transaction or relationship.[7]

The categories into which such *special* rights fall include the following: first, the obvious cases of promises; and second, rights that exist as a result of one "person consenting or authorizing another to interfere in matters which but for this consent or authorization he would be free to determine for himself";[8] this is what is usually meant when we speak of one person surrendering his rights to another. Another set of special rights and obligations are those in which the parties have a special *natural* relationship, as in the case of parent and child. Both the parental right to obedience from children, and the child's right to proper care, nutrition, and nurture seem to arise out of this special type of natural relationship.

If all the sorts of rights about which we are concerned could be packed into this category of *special* rights, then although we would still have some problems—notably in cases of conflict of rights—the difficulties of determining the existence and nature of rights would be made easier. But as Hart himself acknowledges, there is aother big category—that of *general* rights—and it is here that most of the problems I have been addressing appear to fall. Hart's notion of general rights closely follows his definition of the concept of rights as described earlier. Indeed, he explicitly states that "the assertion of general rights directly invokes the principle that all men equally have the right to be free." [9] But how far does his account go—on balance—in helping to answer our skeptical questions about rights?

I think it is fair to say that *given* an adequate account of what sorts of entities are proper bearers of rights, Hart's analysis can apply to debates about fetal rights and the rights of future generations. In addition, it may shed some light on questions relating to behavior control in schools or in prison, and the moral limitations of efforts to alter or control the behavior of persons in institutions. But Hart's account cannot be the whole story concerning rights, since otherwise the Universal Declaration of Human Rights would be speaking nonsense when it asserts that everyone has the "right to security in the event of unemployment, sickness, disability, widowhood, old age or other lack of livelihood in circumstances beyond his control." [10] It is claims made on behalf of these and other goods, which some people believe they are owed by society, that serve to characterize this notion of rights—a somewhat different notion from the one sketched by Hart in his analysis.

Another contemporary philosopher—noted for his contributions to the literature on rights and duties—is Joel Feinberg, who argues that we need to understand the notion of rights in connection with the activity of *claiming.* In an essay entitled "The Nature and Value of Rights," Feinberg alleges that a right is a kind of claim, and a claim is "an assertion of right"; he acknowledges the impossibility of giving what he calls a "formal definition" of the notion of a right. Feinberg asks us to accept the notion of a right as a "simple, undefinable, unanalysable primitive." [11] It is best elucidated, he thinks, by viewing it in conjunction with the rule-governed activity of claiming. Feinberg offers not so much a theory for enabling us to know when rights properly can be said to exist, or how to resolve conflicts among them; but rather, as the title of his article reveals, he wants to explicate *the nature and value of rights.* First, he invites us to imagine what a society would be like if it lacked the things we refer to as rights. He illustrates this by noting that in such a society, there would be no justified or valid claims about rights made by people. We can agree with Feinberg that such a world would be morally inferior to our own. But does Feinberg's account help us to gain insight into when claims about rights are legitimate and when they are not? Unfortunately, we do not move much closer to a resolution of the problem.

Feinberg asserts: "To have a right is to have a claim against someone whose recognition as valid is called for by some set of governing rules or moral principles. To have a *claim* in turn, is to have a case meriting consideration, that is, to have reasons or grounds that put one in a position to engage in . . . claiming." [12]

But what Feinberg's account lacks—and what is sorely needed in applied moral contexts—is a normative ethical position stating criteria for the *validity* of claims, or a *justification* for the governing rules or moral principles that are used to validate claims. What reasons or grounds are *good* ones for engaging in the activity of making claims about rights? Feinberg does not give us an account of what these normative considerations should be like or where we may seek guidance. He has given an essentially pragmatic justification for viewing rights as valid claims of a certain sort. But in the absence of some further guidelines, we shall be unable to assess whether claims about the rights of the fetus or the rights of future generations or the rights of schoolchildren against drug researchers are *valid* claims or not.

I suspect that part of the problem with Feinberg's account stems from his starting point in taking the notion of a right as an "unanalysable primitive." As I indicated at the outset, I think the notion of a right is properly to be understood as a derivative moral concept. Following John Stuart Mill, I contend that the things we call rights are intimately bound up with the theory of justice we adopt. If systematic judgments about the existence of rights and objective resolutions of conflicts of rights can be made at all, it will only be possible when mediated by a well-worked-out theory of justice, such as that set out by the contemporary moral philosopher John Rawls in his book, *A Theory of Justice*.[13] Indeed, I believe that treating the notion of rights as an "unanalysable primitive" is just what has led to the many and varied claims about rights that have been advanced in the past decade. If people disagree about the legitimacy of claims about rights, it is probably because they disagree about the basic precepts of social justice. And, it would seem, the reason such disagreements persist is that there *is* no generally accepted, fully worked-out theory of justice.

Our final question is: *can* there be such a theory of social justice to which all will subscribe? Is it possible to secure agreement among persons who hold moderately different—much less radically different—views about the nature and dictates of social justice? The theory urged by John Rawls is attractive and impressive. But it has its detractors and harsh critics, as well as its defenders. If I am correct in viewing the concept of rights as a derivative notion—to be derived from some sound, well-articulated theory of justice—there will be as many disputes about rights as there are different conceptions of distributive and retributive justice. The different rights-claimers subscribe—implicitly or explicitly—to different conceptions or dictates of justice; hence, their views about the nature and existence of rights are bound to differ.

There is, however, one final possibility: the position that there simply *is* no objective grounding for claims about rights; they are not claims that should properly be viewed as true or false. Instead, claims about rights are instances of the dynamic use of language, whose function is to promote change, to move people to action, in the form of social and legislative reform, but not to assert any objective truths about the moral order. Some rights-claims are more justifiable than others, according to this view, with their justifiability to be judged according to a set of pragmatic criteria. But whether we lean toward this latter view—that rights-claims represent people's attitudes toward what counts as a better social order—or toward the former view—that we can derive particular claims about rights from a larger theory of justice—in either case we need to recognize that rights are not the sorts of things that involve a *discovery* about some facts—moral, religious, or other. To accept a right as existent and as applicable to a social circumstance is to make a moral *decision* about the legitimate expectations of persons. As society has changed and will continue to change in a multitude of ways, so, too, will there be changes about which expectations that people have are legitimate ones, and which not. There are probably some legitimate expectations that are timeless and universal. If so, these would be the basic human rights, such as the right to be free. While identifying such expectations and justifying their legitimacy may be a difficult task, it nonetheless seems like an epistemologically superior method for arriving at basic human rights than the methods that rely on the use of reason or on the ability to discover man's essence. There are probably other legitimate expectations whose validity depends on time, place, and circumstance, such as the right to health care or to a minimum income. But which of these legitimate expectations are universal or timeless and which not, and what should be the criteria for legitimacy of expectations—these are hard topics, which must be reserved for another inquiry.

This article is based on a presentation at the Institute's General Meeting, held June 18-19, 1976, at Manhattanville College, Purchase, N.Y.

REFERENCES

¹ Margaret MacDonald, "Natural Rights," in A. I. Melden, editor, *Human Rights* (Belmont, California: Wadsworth Publishing Co., 1970), p. 43.

² Ibid., p. 45.

³ John Stuart Mill, *Utilitarianism* (Bobbs Merrill—Library of Liberal Arts, 1957), pp. 61–62.

⁴ H. L. A. Hart, "Are There Any Natural Rights?" in Melden, p. 61.

⁵ Ibid., p. 62.

⁶ Ibid., pp. 63, 68.

⁷ Ibid.

⁸ Ibid., p. 69.

⁹ Ibid., p. 73.

¹⁰ *Universal Declaration of Human Rights,* in Melden, p. 148.

¹¹ Joel Feinberg, "The Nature and Value of Rights," *The Journal of Value Inquiry,* 4 (1970), 250.

¹² Ibid., p. 257.

¹³ John Rawls. *A Theory of Justice* (Cambridge: Harvard University Press, 1971).

STUDY QUESTIONS

Review

1. Compare Dewey and Perry on the empirical character of ethical judgments. Discuss to what extent their theories may be relativistic.
2. What is the "naturalistic fallacy" according to G. E. Moore?
3. Explain the two senses in which moral terms are emotive, according to Stevenson. Explain one criticism of this theory and one point of value.
4. What is meant by the "is-ought" debate? How does John Searle attempt to derive an ought from an is? Does he derive a moral ought? Why or why not?
5. What is the difference between act and rule utilitarianism? Give some examples of how each would approach a particular moral problem. What other senses does universalizability have than that found in rule utilitarianism?
6. What is the ultimate moral question? What are some possible responses that can be given to it? What is Baier's answer?
7. Explain John Rawls's two principles of justice. How does he arrive at these two principles? What is their function?
8. What are the different positions on the sources of rights that Macklin discusses? What is her own position on this matter?

For Further Thought

9. What do you think is the proper way to understand the purpose of moral judgments? Do you believe they describe anything? Are they primarily expressions or emotion? Are they capable of being true or false, or more or less adequate? If so, what does this imply?
10. Do you think it makes sense to ask "What if everyone did that?" in order to determine if some action is morally permissible? Do you think that reasons are required for moral judgments?
11. Do you believe that persons choosing in the initial situation so described by Rawls would choose his two principles? Do you agree that these principles would correctly determine which distribution of goods allowed is just and which not?
12. Do you believe that there are natural or basic human rights that people can validly claim, regardless of whether or not the law recognizes them or they can otherwise effectively realize them? How would you support such a notion? Give one example.

BIBLIOGRAPHY

Early-Twentieth-Century Moral Philosophy

Dewey, John. *Theory of Valuation*. Vol. 2, *International Encyclopedia of Unified Science*, ed. O. Newrath. Foundations of the Unity of Science, no. 4. Chicago: University of Chicago Press, 1939.

— — —. "Reconstruction in Moral Concepts." Chap. 7 in *Reconstruction in Philosophy*. New York: Henry Holt, 1920.

— — —. *Human Nature and Conduct*. New York: Henry Holt, 1922.

Dewey, John, and J. H. Tufts. *Ethics*. Rev. ed. New York: Henry Holt, 1932. Part 2 reprinted as *Theory of the Moral Life,* with an introduction by A. Isenberg.

Gouinlock, James. *John Dewey's Philosophy of Value* (New York: Humanities Press, 1972.

Lewis, Clarence Irving. *The Ground and Nature of the Right*. New York: Columbia University Press, 1955.

— — —. *An Analysis of Knowledge and Valuation*. La Salle, Ill.: Open Court Publishing, 1946.

Munitz, Milton K. *The Moral Philosophy of Santayana*. New York: Humanities Press, 1958.

Perry, Ralph Barton. *Realms of Value: A Critique of Human Civilization*. Cambridge: Harvard University Press, 1954.

— — —. *General Theory of Value: Its Meaning and Basic Principles Construed in Terms of Interest*. New York: Longmans, Green and Co., 1926.

Santayana, George. *The Life of Reason: Reason in Science*. New York: Charles Scribner's, 1906.

— — —. *The Sense of Beauty*. New York: Charles Scribners' 1896.

Saydah, Roger J. *The Ethical Theory of C. I. Lewis*. Athens: Ohio University Press, 1969.

Stroh, Guy W. *American Ethical Thought*. Chicago: Nelson-Hall Publishers, 1977.

Emotivism

Ayer, A. J. *Language, Truth, and Logic*. London: Victor Gollancz, 1936.

Edwards, Paul. *The Logic of Moral Discourse*. Glencoe, Ill.: Free Press, 1955.

Kerner, G. C. *The Revolution in Ethical Theory*. Oxford: Clarendon Press, 1966.

Hancock, Roger N. *Twentieth Century Ethics*. New York: Columbia University Press, 1974.

Hudson, W. D. *Modern Moral Philosophy*. Garden City, N.Y.: Doubleday, 1970.

Sellars, W., and J. Hospers, eds. *Readings in Ethical Theory*. New York: Appleton-Century-Crofts, 1952.

Stevenson, Charles. *Facts and Values*. New Haven: Yale University Press, 1963.

— — —. *Ethics and Language*. New Haven: Yale University Press, 1944.

— — —. "Persuasive Definitions," *Mind,* 1938.

— — —. "The Emotive Meaning of Ethical Terms." *Mind,* 1937.

Urmson, J. O. *The Emotive Theory of Ethics*. New York: Oxford University Press, 1968.

Warnock, G. J. *Contemporary Moral Philosophy*. London: Macmillan, 1967.

Warnock, Mary. *Ethics Since 1900*. New York: Oxford University Press, 1960.

The Naturalistic Fallacy and the Is-Ought Debate

Adams, E. M. *Ethical Naturalism and the Modern World-view*. Chapel Hill: University of North Carolina Press, 1960.

Frankena, W. K. "The Naturalistic Fallacy." *Mind,* 1939. Reprinted in Sellars and Hospers, *Readings in Ethical Theory*.

Hare, Richard. *Freedom and Reason*. London: Oxford University Press, 1963.

Hudson, W. D. *Modern Moral Philosophy.* Garden City, N.Y.: Doubleday, 1970.
— — —, ed. *The Is/Ought Question.* London: Macmillan, 1969.
Moore, G. E. *Principia Ethica.* Cambridge: Cambridge University Press, 1903. The preface and chapter 2 are reprinted in Sellars and Hospers, *Readings in Ethical Theory.*
Searle, John. *Speech Acts.* Cambridge: Cambridge University Press, 1969.
— — —. "How to Derive 'Ought' from 'Is.'" *The Philosophical Review* 73 (January 1964). Reprinted in Sellars and Hospers, *Readings in Ethical Theory,* 1970 edition.
Thomson, James, and Judith Thomson. "How Not to Derive 'Ought' from 'Is.'" *The Philosophical Review* 73 (October 1964). Reprinted in Sellars and Hospers, *Readings in Ethical Theory,* 1970 edition.
Wellman, Carl. *Challenge and Response: Justification in Ethics.* Carbondale: Southern Illinois University Press, 1971.

Moral Rules, Universalizability, and the Moral Point of View

Baier, K. *The Moral Point of View.* Ithica, N.Y.: Cornell University Press, 1958.
Brandt, Richard. "Some Merits of One Form of Rule-Utilitarianism." *University of Colorado Studies, Series in Philosophy,* No. 3 (January 1967), pp. 41–55.
Dworkin, R. "Non-Neutral Principles." *Journal of Philosophy* 71, no. 14 (August 1974).
Gewirth, Alan. "The Non-Trivializability of Universalizability." *Australasian Journal of Philosophy,* no. 47 (August 1969): pp. 123–31.
Harrison, J. "Utilitarianism, Universalizability, and Our Duty to be Just." *Proceedings of the Aristotelian Society,* 1952–53.
Locke, Don. "The Trivialization of Universalizability." *Philosophical Review,* no. 78 (1968): pp. 25–44.
Lycan, W. G. "Hare, Singer, and Gewirth on Universalizability." *Philosophical Quarterly,* no. 19 (August 1969): pp. 135–44.
Lyons, D. *Forms and Limits of Utilitarianism.* Oxford: Clarendon Press, 1965.
Nielsen, Kai. "The 'Good Reasons Approach' and 'Ontological Justifications of Morality.'" *Philosophical Quarterly,* 1959.
— — —. "Is 'Why Should I Be Moral?' An Absurdity?" *Australasian Journal of Philosophy,* 1958.
Phillips, D. Z. "Does It Pay To Be Good?" *Proceedings of the Aristotelian Society,* 1964–65.
Singer, Marcus. *Generalization in Ethics.* New York: Knopf, 1961.
Smart, J. J. C. "Extreme and Restricted Utilitarianism." In *Theories of Ethics,* ed. P. Foot. New York: Oxford University Press, 1967.
Snare, F. "Wants and Reasons." *Personalist,* no. 53 (August 1972): pp. 395–407.
Stout, A. K. "But Suppose Everyone did the Same." *Australasian Journal of Philosophy,* 1954.
Toulmin, S. *The Place of Reason in Ethics.* Cambridge: Cambridge University Press, 1950.
Ullman-Margalit, Edna. "The Generalization Argument: Where Does the Obligation Lie?" *Journal of Philosophy,* 1976.

Justice and Other Contemporary Ethical Issues

Balbus, Issac. *Marxism and Domination.* Princeton: Princeton University Press, 1980.
Barry, Brian. *The Liberal Theory of Justice.* Oxford: Clarendon Press, 1973.

Bayles, Michael D. *Professional Ethics.* Belmont, Calif.: Wadsworth Pub. Co., 1981.

Bedau, Hugo Adam. *The Death Penalty in America.* 3d. ed. Oxford: Oxford University Press, 1982.

Blocker, H. Gene, and Elizabeth H. Smith, eds. *John Rawls' Theory of Social Justice: An Introduction.* Athens: Ohio University Press, 1980.

Bok, Sissela. *Lying: Moral Choice in Public and Private Life.* New York: Random House, 1978.

— — — . *Secrets, on the Ethics of Concealment and Revelation.* N.Y.: Pantheon Books, 1982.

Clark, Ian. *Limited Nuclear War.* Princeton: Princeton University Press, 1980.

Cohen, Marshall, et al. *Equality and Preferential Treatment.* Princeton: Princeton University Press, 1977.

Connolly, William E. *The Terms of Political Discourse.* Princeton: Princeton University Press, 1982.

Feinberg, Joel. *Rights, Justice, and the Bounds of Liberty.* Princeton: Princeton University Press, 1980.

Galston, William. *Justice and the Human Good.* Chicago: University of Chicago Press, 1980.

Goldman, Alan H. *Justice and Reverse Discrimination.* Princeton: Princeton University Press, 1981.

Gorovitz, Samuel, et al. *Moral Problems in Medicine.* Englewood Cliffs, N.J.: Prentice-Hall, 1976.

Hirschman, Albert O. *Shifting Involvements.* Princeton: Princeton University Press, 1979.

Laszlo, Ervin, and Donald Keys, eds. *Disarmament: The Human Factor.* Oxford: Pergamon Press, 1981.

MacIntyre, Alasdair. *After Virtue: A Study in Moral Theory.* Notre Dame, Ind.: University of Notre Dame Press, 1981.

Macklin, Ruth. *Man, Mind, and Morality: The Ethics of Behavior Control.* Englewood Cliffs, N.J.: Prentice-Hall, 1982.

Mason, David T., and J. H. Wellbanks. *John Rawls and His Critics.* New York: Garland Publishers, 1982.

Murphy, Jeffrie G. *Punishment and Rehabilitation.* Belmont, Calif.: Wadsworth Pub. Co., 1973.

Nozick, Robert. *Anarchy, State, and Utopia.* New York: Basic Books, 1974.

Parekh, Bhikhu. *Contemporary Political Thinkers.* Baltimore: Johns Hopkins University Press, 1983.

Partridge, Ernest. *Responsibilities to Future Gennerations.* New York: Prometheus Books, 1980.

Pellegrino, Edmund D., and David C. Thomasma. *A Philosophical Basis of Medical Practice.* New York: Oxford University Press, 1981.

Rawls, John. *A Theory of Justice.* Cambridge: Harvard University Press, 1971.

Regan, Tom. *All That Dwell Therein: Animal Rights and Environmental Ethics.* Berkeley: University of California Press, 1981.

Singer, Peter. *The Expanding Circle: Ethics and Sociobiology.* New York: Farrar, Straus and Giroux, 1981.

Walzer, Michael. *Just and Unjust Wars.* New York: Basic Books, 1977.

Wasserstrom, Richard A., ed. *Morality and the Law.* Belmont, Calif.: Wadsworth Pub. Co., 1971.

— — —, ed. *War and Morality.* Belmont, Calif.: Wadsworth Pub. Co., 1970.

Wolff, Robert P. *Understanding Rawls: A Reconstruction and Critique of a Theory of Justice.* Princeton: Princeton University Press, 1977.

Epilogue

Is There an
American Philosophy?

This epilogue is intended to give the reader an opportunity to consider whether the philosophizing that has been done in this country (some of which has been collected in this anthology) can be said to be typically American in some sense. One of the reasons why the question Is there an American philosophy? has been and is so difficult to answer is that it is not easy to be clear about just what is being asked. We are not asking here whether or not there is a specifically American character or temperament, nor if a set of political and social ideals exist that is peculiar to Americans. Cultural and intellectual historians and other social scientists have been puzzled by this question since the eighteenth-century French immigrant Crèvecoeur first asked about the so-called new American man. Crèvecoeur's idea was that this man was epitomized by the happy farmer.

Others have pointed to particular historical and environmental forces that they supposed had molded the American character. Free land, unlimited opportunity, and separation from socio-cultural roots elsewhere, they surmised, had contributed to the American practical inventiveness, restlessness, and freedom-loving individualism. In his 1893 paper, "The Significance of the Frontier in American History," Frederick Jackson Turner challenged the European-heritage thesis with his own stress on the importance of environmental influences.[1] According to this thesis the ever-moving frontier, by providing unlimited opportunity for self-advancement, helped forge the new American person. Alexis de Tocqueville's *Democracy in America* (1835) stressed the democratic element in the new American life, while David Riesman's *The Lonely Crowd* (1950) described the typically lonely American who seeks security in the crowd. Writers have variously characterized the American as capitalist and materialist, as the outgoing adventurer in a world of abundance and promise, and as the result of a peculiar mix of freedom and authority in the family.[2]

However, we want to inquire here about the writings of the philosophers. They have been as diverse as the different nationalities of people that populated this country. Nevertheless the task of deciding whether or not there is some common theme or themes exemplified in the diversity of philosophies may be less liable to free speculation and premature generalization than the effort of those who seek to characterize the American temperament. Still, this task may not be entirely different from the one of the intellectual historian. John Smith, for example, writes of a distinctive spirit characterizing American philosophy and explains what he means by this term in the following way.

> By the spirit of a philosophical development is meant something which is at once more and less than a set of doctrines. A spirit is something more because it means, in addition to formulated beliefs, a style, a stance toward life in the world, and strong convictions about the importance of reflective thought. A spirit is something less than a body of consciously formulated doctrines because it stands deeply rooted in the life of a people as a kind of unwritten philosophy.[3]

This way of interpreting the question is in some ways similar to that of the cultural historians, because it directs us to search for a spirit that is "rooted in the life" of the American people or that lies beneath "formulated beliefs." This broader approach to the question about a typically American philosophy, however, is not entirely immune to the criticism of Herbert Schneider who was concerned about the "general and generalizing works on American thought and culture." These works, he wrote, yielding

> to the temptation created by de Tocqueville and perhaps by the Garden of Eden, profess to understand the basic meaning and values of American existence and offer a certain amount of historical evidence for their insights. The philosophies of culture, like literary criticism, still belong to literary art rather than to historical science, and as such deserve thoughtful reading and skeptical reflection.[4]

The purpose of the question we are asking is to determine whether there is some particular theme or themes that have pervaded the writings of the majority of philosophers who have either plied their trade in this country or who have been part of some mainstream of American philosophy, or whether there is in some sense a unique manner in which philosophizing has been carried on here.

PHILOSOPHY AND ITS SETTING

Might we reasonably expect to find that the content or manner of philosophizing of a people is peculiar to their particular nation? Some ideas from Hegel are suggestive. In the introduction to his *Philosophy of Right,* for example, he writes that philosophy is "its own time apprehended in thought."

> As the thought of the world, it appears only when actuality is already there cut and dried, after its process of formation has been completed. . . . The Owl of Minerva spreads its wings only with the falling of dusk.[5]

And again he writes,

> It is just as absurd to fancy that a philosophy can transcend its contemporary world as it is to fancy that an individual can overleap his own age, jump over Rhodes. . . . Here is the rose, dance thou here.[6]

Obviously an entire philosophy of history lies behind these comments. Nevertheless it is not unreasonable to believe that the peculiar circumstances of life that a people hold in common may influence their philosophizing as well as their particular temperament or character. In this same vein some pertinent comments of George Santayana may be understood. Speaking to members of the Philosophical Union at the University of California at Berkeley in 1911, Santayana said that if certain philosophies exemplifying what he called the "genteel tradition" in America "had lived among your mountains, their systems would have been different from what they are."[7] The systems of philosophy, he surmised, would have been less "genteel," that is, less idealistic, religious, and optimistic, for then they would be taught by the strength of time and the fertility of matter, and their indifference and infinity, and the philosophies would have reflected this. The irony, of course, is that Josiah Royce was born and grew up among these mountains and nevertheless became part of that "genteel" tradition.

Nevertheless, the picture Santayana paints of the situation of the early settlers may be more to the point: "They have all been uprooted from their several soils and ancestries and plunged together into one vortex, whirling irresistably in a space otherwise quite empty.[8] Those first settlers who came to this country came to an unformed land that had more of a future than a past. Moreover, they came from a variety of origins, the beginning of the melting pot. Perry Miller has described the Puritan spirit and project, for example, as an "errand into the wilderness."[9] The Puritans came to a new land, but they came nevertheless with an errand. Thus they would not be entirely molded by the new land. Could it not be the case, then, that the philosophy developed in this country also had a dual source — their errand or purpose and the wilderness in which they would realize it.

Roy Wood Sellars in his *Reflections on American Philosophy from Within* (1969) seems to support a similar notion when writing about nineteenth-century American philosophy. For Sellars philosophy combines an internal momentum, dominated by theses with respect to its recognized problems, with the influence upon it of the cultural outlook. The United States was in the 19th century still in the climate of the religious view of the world. But this climate was altering, owing to both industrial and scientific developments. By itself, this alteration did not dictate to philosophy the handling of its problems but, rather, led it to reconsider accepted assumptions. Its influence was thus indirect and yet powerful.[10]

If, as Sellars suggests, philosophy has its own problems and its own history, it may nevertheless be powerfully, even if indirectly, influenced by the situation within which it develops.

Nevertheless the belief that philosophically America has been and still lives (at least until recently) on the fringes of European and British culture and philosophy perdures. In support of this position one can point to the Platonic and Calvinistic inheritance of the Puritans, the Lockean and deistic influences on the statesmen philosophers of the American Enlightenment, the Kantian influence through Coleridge and Schelling on transcendentalism, and the Hegelian, utilitarian, and Darwinian influences on the pragmatists. Did not William James give *Pragmatism* the subtitle "A New Name for Some Old Ways of Thinking"? Its dedication was to John Stuart Mill. A certain mixture of Mill's thesis about the good that comes from a free interplay of ideas, together with the Darwinian theory of survival of the fittest, might well issue in some such view of truth as ideas that are able to survive the struggle. Pertinent is Oliver W. Holmes Jr.'s dictum: "The best test of truth is the power of the thought to get itself accepted in the competition of the market."[11] The notion that the essence of belief is a readiness to act is said by the members of the Metaphysical Club to have had its origins in the writings of the Scotsman Alexander Bain.[12] And on the contemporary scene one can point to the transportation of logical empiricism or positivism into the United States from Vienna, and the import of ordinary language analysis from Britain and phenomenology from Continental sources.

That American philosophy has undoubtedly been influenced by philosophies from elsewhere, however, does not settle the question of whether or not they simply continue in their original forms. What one wants to know is whether what was received was, to quote a phrase, "received after the manner of the receiver."[13] Evidence for this view abounds. For example, the idealism of Josiah Royce is not simply another version of German idealism, for it has its own voluntaristic or pragmatic character. Furthermore, the empiricism of the pragmatists is not the passive type espoused by the British empiricists. For the pragmatists, experience is an activity, a seeking to make sense of, an interpreting for the sake of certain purposes, a solution to problems. Peirce was probably influenced by Hegel, but if so he was a Hegelian with a different twist. He states of himself: "The principles supported by Mr. Peirce bear a close affinity with those of Hegel: perhaps are what Hegel's might have been had be been educated in a physical laboratory instead of a theological seminary."[14]

Moreover, the positivism of Carnap, and certainly the empiricism of Quine, is much evolved from its European origins, and in fact in Quine has strong pragmatic overtones. Ernest Gellner writes of Quine whom he calls "the Last Pragmatist," that each of the following pragmatic themes are present in his writings:

> a joyful acceptance of change, trial and error, impermanence (as opposed to the old pursuit of absolute repose), and a view which considers human activities and cognition in a biological perspective.[15]

And he quotes from Quine:

> With Dewey I hold that knowledge, mind, and meaning are part of the same world, that they have to do with and that they are to be studied in the same empirical spirit that animates natural science.[16]

And:

> It is meaningless . . . to inquire into the absolute correctness of a conceptual scheme. . . . Our standard . . . must be . . . a pragmatic standard . . . the purpose of concepts and language is efficacy in communication and prediction. Such is the ultimate duty of language, science and philosophy, and it is in relation to that duty that a conceptual scheme has finally to be appraised.[17]

Who also cannot read in this last quotation some Puritan moral tone?

However, so far our response to the question is merely suggestive and based on selected examples. We have only speculated on the possibility that the philosophy of a particular country and people could be influenced by their situation. We have also given a few examples of philosophizing that, although coming from European sources, were significantly different in their American versions. What remains is to consider the further question of whether the new versions themselves have anything in common.

PRAGMATISM: THE AMERICAN PHILOSOPHY

One way to approach the question of American philosophy might be to take the philosophy that is most clearly original, pragmatism, and attempt to show its continuity with philosophizing that came both before and after it in the United States. For example, one can point to the practical orientation of the American Enlightenment thinkers, Franklin in particular. The philosophical society that he founded was not simply for shining light into the occurrences of nature but also for increasing the conveniences of men.[18] Emerson described the true scholar as one who must learn from experience and could know only so much truth as he had lived.[19] The above quotations from Quine could be supplemented by others from C. I. Lewis, for example. One could also describe certain cultural and historical influences that might have contributed to this type of philosophy being developed in America. However, this theory is not entirely satisfactory. On the one hand it does not adequately consider the other significant non-pragmatic philosophies before or after pragmatism. Moreover, it may be rightly accused of construing pragmatism so broadly as to include any philosophy that pays any attention to action. Other theories have also been proposed.

AMERICAN PHILOSOPHY: A CONFLICT OF SCIENCE WITH SENTIMENT

In his *Science and Sentiment in America* (1972), Morton White writes that we can best understand American philosophy if we consider "its response to the challenge of modern science and scientific method." [20] According to White, for the most part, and until the twentieth century, American philosophers

> subscribed to the idea that there are methods of establishing knowledge which are fundamentally different from that used by the sciences; and all of them appealed to some form of emotion, sentiment, or passion as centrally involved in the use of these non-scientific methods. [21]

Jonathan Edwards had held that a certain "sense of the heart" was required to appreciate the truth and beauty of reality; the American transcendentalists appealed to an intuitive type of knowledge, not unlike Edwards's version except that it was the property of every man and had not the specifically religious sense that Edwards's notion had. According to White, transcendentalism was a populist version of anti-intellectualism, for "they endowed infant saints and poetic farmers with power to see the truth with their hearts." [22] While Chauncey Wright had opened up the door for a more scientific-empiricist type of philosophizing, William James followed the lead of the earlier writers. According to James, one is sometimes justified in believing something on passional grounds. In fact most of our theorizing is governed by our need to make satisfactory sense of things and by our particular individual temperaments. [23]

According to White, this same anti-intellectualism showed itself in the more widespread social attitudes toward the "life of the mind" in America, especially the America of the 1970s when he was writing.

> We meet it in the quietistic form when we are urged to give up discourse for vision or television . . . or to take seriously the maxim that one flower speaks louder than a thousand words. And we meet in in an activistic form when we are urged to abandon all efforts at scientifically studying society as so much collaboration with the class enemy. . . . In the field of business, the importance of theory was minimized and the school of hard knocks took precedence over the school of Athens. In education the training of pupils in lifemanship was put way above training in arithmetic. [24]

Examples such as this can certainly be found. Morris Cohen writes of the very low prestige that the intellect wins in this country, pointing out that people don't read serious books; business executives do not retire early to engage in more intellectual or cultural pursuits, for they have never developed an interest in them; lawyers do not study jurisprudence or history; and the professor in

America is regarded as an advanced type of elementary school teacher imparting to the young what is already known.[25]

What the relation of these manifestations might be to certain characteristics of the writings of philosophers is another issue, however. White's case is a strong one, at least as to a central character of much pre-twentieth-century American philosophy. One wonders, however, whether his notion of the rational and intellectual may not be too narrow and whether what he labels anti-intellectual may simply suppose a different concept of reason. It is not clear why rationality must be identified with scientific reasoning. Furthermore, one can also point to examples in which the earlier periods showed an admirable respect for science. For instance, a few years after Newton's *Mathematical Principles of Natural Science* was published, the Newtonian system was being taught at Puritan Harvard.[26] Moreover, the interest of the American Enlightenment thinkers in science was not solely for the advantages that its knowledge could bring to men. Even Benjamin Franklin was interested in the theoretical explanation of electricity as well as in the practical implications of lightning rods. Moreover, the influence of Darwin on American philosophy was significant, particularly on the development of pragmatism. O. W. Holmes, Jr. noted that the influence of science was one of the chief differences between his own and his father's age — not just particular scientific ideas, but the fact of "the increasing frequency with which people in all occupations turned to science for answers to problems arising in the course of business and the conduct of life." [27] According to Roy Wood Sellars, American philosophy was distinguished from European philosophy on this very basis. "American philosophy as it developed in the 20th century as the universities got underway, had more intimate contact with science than did British philosophy or German philosophy. In those countries it had more or less culturally isolated itself." [28] White's thesis, as he conceives it, however, is to be applied primarily to pre-twentieth-century philosophy. Just how satisfactory a thesis it is may be judged by the reader after considering also another view.

AMERICAN PHILOSOPHY'S PRACTICO-MORAL BIAS

Another viewpoint can be found in the writings of John Smith. According to one analysis,

> There are three dominant or focal beliefs through which our philosophical spirit can be articulated. First, the belief that thinking is primarily an *activity* in response to a concrete situation and that this activity is aimed at solving problems. Second, the belief that ideas and theories must have a "cutting edge" or *make a difference* in the conduct of people who hold them and in situations in which they live. Third, the belief that the earth *can be civilized* and obstacles to progress overcome by the application of knowledge. Taken together these beliefs define a basically humanistic outlook — in the end, the spirit of philosophical thinking in America represents another outcropping of that ancient tradition established by the reflective genius of Socrates and Plato in which the Good is the dominant category.[29]

On this view, American philosophy has either an activist orientation or a moral one. Let us consider first that American philosophy might be distinguishable by having a distinctly moral bias. Puritan philosophy was certainly dominated by this interest. It stressed the importance of a "right will," a kind of moral sincerity or conscientiousness that was required not only for the attainment of salvation, but also of true knowledge. Furthermore, one of the major interests of the Enlightenment writers was explaining and defending certain natural human rights, in particular certain individual freedoms. They stressed the utilitarian value of traditional virtues as means to happiness and the good life. One also finds ample evidence to support this theory in transcendentalist thought. Think but of Emerson's counsel of self-reliance according to which every person had the right to believe in his or her own intuitions, and his counsel to be whole rather than part men. James was concerned about Royce's block universe and determinism because they seemed to make the moral life unreal. Regret, which seemed real (and which seeming his radical empiricism advised us to trust), would only make sense if there really were a good and bad, a right and wrong, and a freedom to choose one or the other. Royce was above all concerned with the moral community and loyalty by which we would participate in it. Peirce exhorted us not to block the road to inquiry, in a manner that suggested it was our moral duty to pursue the truth. Dewey viewed intelligence as an instrument designed to promote the ends of man, and criticized the notion that knowledge is contemplation of true and unchanging reality, calling it "irresponsible aestheticism." Whether this moral emphasis continues into the twentieth century and whether this concern for morality is uniquely stressed by American philosophers would have to be decided before the worth of the theory were determined. Nevertheless, this thesis has merit.

One may also interpret Smith's thesis as pointing out the pragmatic or activist orientation of American philosophy. Combined with the moral interpretation, this thesis has a certain appeal. One would nevertheless have to account for the more metaphysically oriented philosophies and also for the seemingly technical theoretical orientation of much of twentieth-century philosophizing. If one could show that even in these philosophies there was a moral or pragmatic aspect that distinguished them from the other types of metaphysics or logical or language philosophies, then this interpretation would have the support it would seem to need.

AMERICAN PHILOSOPHY'S CONCRETE NOTION OF EXPERIENCE

One more interesting and appealing theory that we want briefly to summarize here is a view of John McDermott's (and perhaps others) which takes as its key notion "experience" and points to the distinctive meaning the notion has taken on in American philosophy. In *The Culture of Experience: Philosophical Essays in the American Grain* (1976), McDermott both comments upon and exemplifies (according to John Smith in his forward in the book) the notion that thought must remain in touch with practice, with the culture (be it urban or wilderness) in which it occurs.[30] The early settlers had to tame nature to their purposes; thus they learned both the meaning and real power of their own action to make a temporal difference. According to McDermott, "Nineteenth-century pragmatism, so often regarded as the typically American philosophical product, is but a pale reflection of an ingrained attitude affirming the supremacy of experience over thought."[31] This attitude emphasized the primacy of experience over reflection. Our reasoning should not dictate in advance how the world or our understanding of it ought to be.

McDermott draws on both John Dewey and William James to exemplify some of the aspects of this more concrete notion of experience as it came to be interpreted by the philosophers. According to Dewey, experience was no passive reception of sense data but included all the interactions between ourselves and our environment, both natural and social, all that "men do and suffer, what they strive for, love, believe and endure, and also how men act and are acted upon, the ways in which they do and suffer, desire and enjoy, see, believe, imagine."[32] According to McDermott, if these are the sources of and constitute experience, then any philosophical analysis of experience that abstracts from them will necessarily be truncated. James too stressed the full-bodied character of experience. In particular he found in it relations and feelings, and real plurality. For James, time, growth, and development were also experienced and thus real. The idea that this notion of the richness of experience as it has been interpreted by American philosophers might provide a key to understanding what is unique about American philosophy has strong appeal. But what of twentieth-century philosophy in America?

TWENTIETH-CENTURY AMERICAN PHILOSOPHY — AN EXCEPTION?

Twentieth-century American philosophy seems often to be an exception to the above as well as to other interpretations of the distinctiveness of American philosophy. As philosophy became more analytic and language oriented, it turned to analyzing theoretical issues that had little direct bearing on practical or moral issues. Smith laments this fact. As philosophy retreated to academia and to an analysis of its own problems, the problems of men that it had formerly dealt with were left to the social scientists, politicians, and humanists, who suffered from lack of "training necessary for dealing in a clear and critical way with vague but important issues that are basically of great interest to large numbers of people."[33] There is now reason to believe that this trend may be changing, as was noted in our chapter on twentieth-century American moral philosophy.

Positivism in particular seems to present problems because of its logical orientation and its lack of concern with specifically "human" problems. In a 1982 article, "Philosophy in America Today," Richard Rorty describes the rise and fall of positivism in this country.[35] According to Rorty, logical positivists thought of themselves as doing scientific philosophy, as enumerating the problems to be solved, and by use of the proper method, hoping to solve each of them in turn. In actual fact, however, the hope was misplaced and never realized. Rorty writes, "I think that analytic philosophy culminates in Quine, the later Wittgenstein, Sellars, and Davidson — which is to say that it transcends and cancels itself." [36] These philosophers attacked the positivistic distinctions between analytic and synthetic statements, theory and observation, and scheme and content. Our theories and our language are but the means by which we manage our experience and our lives. Dewey's instrumentalism lives on. In fact, Rorty characterizes the history of positivism in this country as the "gradual 'pragmaticization' of the original tenets of logical positivism." [37] Today, instead of grand schemes for solving all the important philosophical problems, philosophy in America in the 1980s, according to Rorty, is now a matter of individual sharp-witted philosophers working out whatever problems happen to interest them. [38] And yet there remain some standards of what is to count as good analysis or argumentation. This characterization is obviously open to debate. One can think, for example, of the attempt of Wilfrid Sellars to develop a more systematic philosophy. If there are few philosophers in the United States today with philosophical world views, there are many who are working systematically in some general area of philosophy or on some problem with general application.

In this anthology one can see the variety of types of philosophizing that have been supported in this century in the United States. Nevertheless, some find reason to believe that "some features of the human spirit that are distinctively emphasized on the American scene and which may still be maintaining a pattern that is consonant with the American cultural traditions" may be found. [34] It may well be that the notion of temporality, its metaphysical and epistemological significance, might provide a way to understand what is distinctive about twentieth-century as well as previous American philosophy. It also might incorporate elements of some of the theories about what is distinctive about American philosophy which have been briefly summarized here. Moreover, it would have support in process philosophies and phenomenology as well as in some analytic philosophies.

ANOTHER VIEW

However, for those who may be skeptical about the success of finding any distinctive or distinguishing characteristics of American philosophy, I offer a more formal view. We have been wont to characterize America as a melting pot. We were originally a nation of immigrants and continue to be so. Such diversity creates problems for integration of all into the mainstream of political and social participation. Might the same thing be true of philosophy and philosophizing in this country? On the one hand one may seek to determine whether or not there are any common themes, or a common spirit, in the writings of philosophers throughout the history of philosophy in this country. On the other hand one may also notice that we have had a generous variety of philosophies. Consider the many different types of thinkers and thoughts represented in this anthology of American philosophy, many of which have migrated here from Great Britain and the Continent. There are idealisms and realisms, substance philosophies and process philosophies, positivism and antipositivistic phenomenologies. Moreover, there have not been in this country the kind of academic traditions and monopolies over academic positions by thinkers of particular persuasions as there have been on the Continent and Great Britain. While there have been times when some traditions are more represented than others in the major universities, that situation has not continued for very long. While to a certain extent it is true that dialogue between different groups has been rare, in other cases dialogue has provided the source for development and change.

Instead of concentrating on product, process may be stressed. Peirce, for example, did not so much tell us what was true, but how to reach it. Democracy itself may be understood as a belief in a process, and the freedoms of speech, press, and assembly may be understood to be not only for the sake of the individual but for the sake of the opportunity these provide for better ideas to surface. It is again a manifestation of the evolutionary idea that competition and a struggle for survival lead to survival of the fittest. Perhaps, as Peirce or Hegel might have suggested, something similar might obtain in philosophy. Competitive dialogue, an almost uniquely American experience, can lead to the overcoming of the inadequacies of partial views. Neither mind nor matter, neither analysis nor experience is by itself sufficient. The American tradition can be only partially captured by Emerson's "only so much do I know, as I have lived." [39] What is most characteristic about American philosophy may well be its openness and its eventual dissatisfaction with all one-sided or partial viewpoints.

Notes

[1] Frederick Jackson Turner, "The Significance of the Frontier in American History," in *The Frontier in American History* (New York, 1920); Alexis de Tocqueville, *Democracy and the American Spirit,* trans. G. Lawrence (1935; reprint, New York: Harper and Row, 1966); David Riesman, *The Lonely Crowd* (New Haven: Yale University Press, 1950).

[2] See *The Character of Americans: A Book of Readings,* ed. Michael McGiffert (Homewood, Ill.: Dorsy Press, 1964), especially the annotated bibliography of works of this topic, pp. 361–77.

[3] Smith, *Spirit of American Philosophy,* p. 187.

[4] Schneider, *History of American Philosophy,* p. xiv.

[5] G. W. F. Hegel, *Hegel's Philosophy of Right,* trans. T. M. Knox (Oxford: Clarendon Press), pp. 12–13. Minerva, it will be recalled, is the Roman goddess of wisdom. Hegel continues: "Whatever happens, every individual is a child of his time; so philosophy is its own time apprehended in thought."

[6] Ibid.

[7] George Santayana, "The Genteel Tradition in American Philosophy," *University of California Chronicle* 13, no. 4 (October 1911): pp. 357–80.

[8] George Santayana, *Character and Opinion in the United States, with Reminiscences of William James and Josiah Royce and Academic Life in America* (New York: Charles Scribner's, 1920), p. 168.

[9] Miller, "Errand into the Wilderness." The title is from a sermon by Rev. Samuel Danforth in 1670. Rather than Frederick Jackson Turner's thesis that democracy came out of the forest, Miller suggests that it was the form, the errand, that controlled the matter. The errand was the purpose to establish a biblical polity, a city upon the hill for all to see.

[10] Sellars, *Reflections on American Philosophy*, p. 26. Also see Andrew Reck, "Conceptions of the Role of Philosophy in American Civilization," *Southwestern Journal of Philosophy* 15 (Fall 1977); pp. 341-60.

[11] O. W. Holmes, Dissenting in 1919 in *Abrams v. United States,* 250 U.S. 616, 624 (Dissenting Opinions, 1929, 50); cf. idem, *Collected Legal Papers,* New York: Harcourt, Brace, 1920, pp. 310-16.

[12] Alexander Bain, *The Emotions and the Will* (London: John W. Parker and Son, 1859), pp. iv, 568, 573, 580, 585. As noted in Fisch, *Classic American Philosophers,* p. 13.

[13] This is a principle often used by Thomas Aquinas. See for example *Summa Theologiae,* I, 85, v, ad 3.

[14] C. S. Peirce, *Principles of Philosophy,* 1893; Peirce Papers, Harvard University Archives; as quoted in Fisch, *Classic American Philosophers,* p. 17.

[15] Gellner, "Philosophy of W. V. O. Quine," p. 848.

[16] Ibid.

[17] Ibid. Gellner's references are not specific, but, as he notes, come from Quine's *Methods of Logic* (1950), *From a Logical Point of View* (1953), *Word and Object* (1960), and *Ontological Relativity and Other Essays* (1969).

[18] See Benjamin Franklin's "Plan for the American Philosophical Association: A Proposal for Promoting Useful Knowledge among the British Plantations in America" (1743), in *The Writings of Benjamin Franklin,* ed. Albert H. Smyth (New York: Macmillan, 1905-7), vol. 2, pp. 228-30.

[19] Ralph Waldo Emerson, "The American Scholar" (1837), in *The Complete Works* (Boston: Houghton Mifflin, 1903-4), vol. 2, pp. 82-115.

[20] White, *Science and Sentiment in America,* p. 3.

[21] Ibid., p. 297.

[22] Ibid., p. 295.

[23] William James, "The Sentiment of Rationality," and "The Will to Believe," in *The Will to Believe and Other Essays in Popular Philosophy* (New York: Longmans, Green, 1896).

[24] White, *Science and Sentiment,* pp. 303, 308.

[25] Morris Cohen, *American Thought* (New York: Free Press, 1954).

[26] For more detail on the influence of science on early American philosophy see Flower and Murphey, *History of Philosophy in America,* vol. 1, chap. 2.

[27] A letter of Holmes to Morris Cohen as quoted in Fisch, *Classic American Philosophers,* p. 9.

[28] Sellars, *Reflections on American Philosophy,* p. 5.

[29] Smith, *Spirit of American Philosophy,* p. 188. See also his comments on this issue in *Themes in American Philosophy.*

[30] John J. McDermott, *The Culture of Experience: Philosophical Essays in the American Grain* (New York, New York University Press, 1976). Also see McDermott's "The American Angle of Vision," *Cross Currents* 15 (Winter 1965): pp. 69–93, 433–60.

[31] McDermott, *Culture of Experience,* p. 4.

[32] Ibid., p. 8; the quote from Dewey is from *Experience and Nature,* 2d ed. (LaSalle, Ill.: Open Court Publishing, 1929), p. 10.

[33] Smith, *Spirit of American Philosophy,* p. 220.

[34] Flower and Murphey, *History of Philosophy in America,* vol. 2, p. 963.

[35] Richard Rorty, *Consequences of Pragmatism* (Minneapolis: The University of Minnesota Press, 1982), p. xviii.

[36] Ibid.

[37] Rorty, *Philosophy and the Mirror of Nature* (Princeton: Princeton University Press, 1979).

[38] Ibid.

[39] Ralph Waldo Emerson, "The American Scholar."

Index

Absolute, the, 120, 121; Josiah Royce and, 292; William James and, 251
Absolute Truth: Josiah Royce and, 289, 301
action, 82; John Dewey and, 265
actuality, 440; Whitehead and, 402–6
aesthetic enjoyment: Whitehead and, 412
aesthetic experience: John Dewey and, 261
aesthetics: Santayana and, 332
agapism. *See* Peirce, Charles Sanders
Agassiz, Louis, 106, 108
Alcott, Bronson, 67
Allen, Ethan, 34
Ambrose, Alice, 572
American Enlightenment, 33–35; deism and, 34; European and, 35; God and, 34; reaction to, 38–39, 66; reason and, 33
American Philosophical Society, 51
American Revolution, 33
analysis: linguistic, 509, 570; ordinary language, 570
angels, 362
animal faith: Santayana and, 357
animals, 447
appearance, 352, 446
Aristotle, 429, 452, 494, 559; thomism and, 362, 378–85
Arminianism, 6–7

art: Santayana and, 333; Whitehead and, 412
Association: American Philosophical, 36
atomism: Whitehead and, 392
Austin, John L., 572
Averroes, 363

Baier, Kurt: The Moral Point of View, 633–37
Baldwin, Mark, 110
beauty, 76; Whitehead and, 412
being, 15, 312, 437; becoming and, 382; John Dewey and, 265; Josiah Royce and, 315–16
belief: C. S. Peirce and, 174, 186, 187, 188; John Dewey and, 273; Peirce and the fixation of, 166; pragmatism and, 165; Santayana and, 334; William James on moral, 230
beliefs: attitudes and, 611
benevolence, 308
Bergson, Henri, 319, 389; Charles Hartshorne and, 416
Berkeley, 286, 340, 345, 346, 347
body, 11, 12; Weiss and, 449
Bowne, Bordon Parker, 287
Bradley, 347, 349
Bridgman, Percy, 509